Discovering Eton

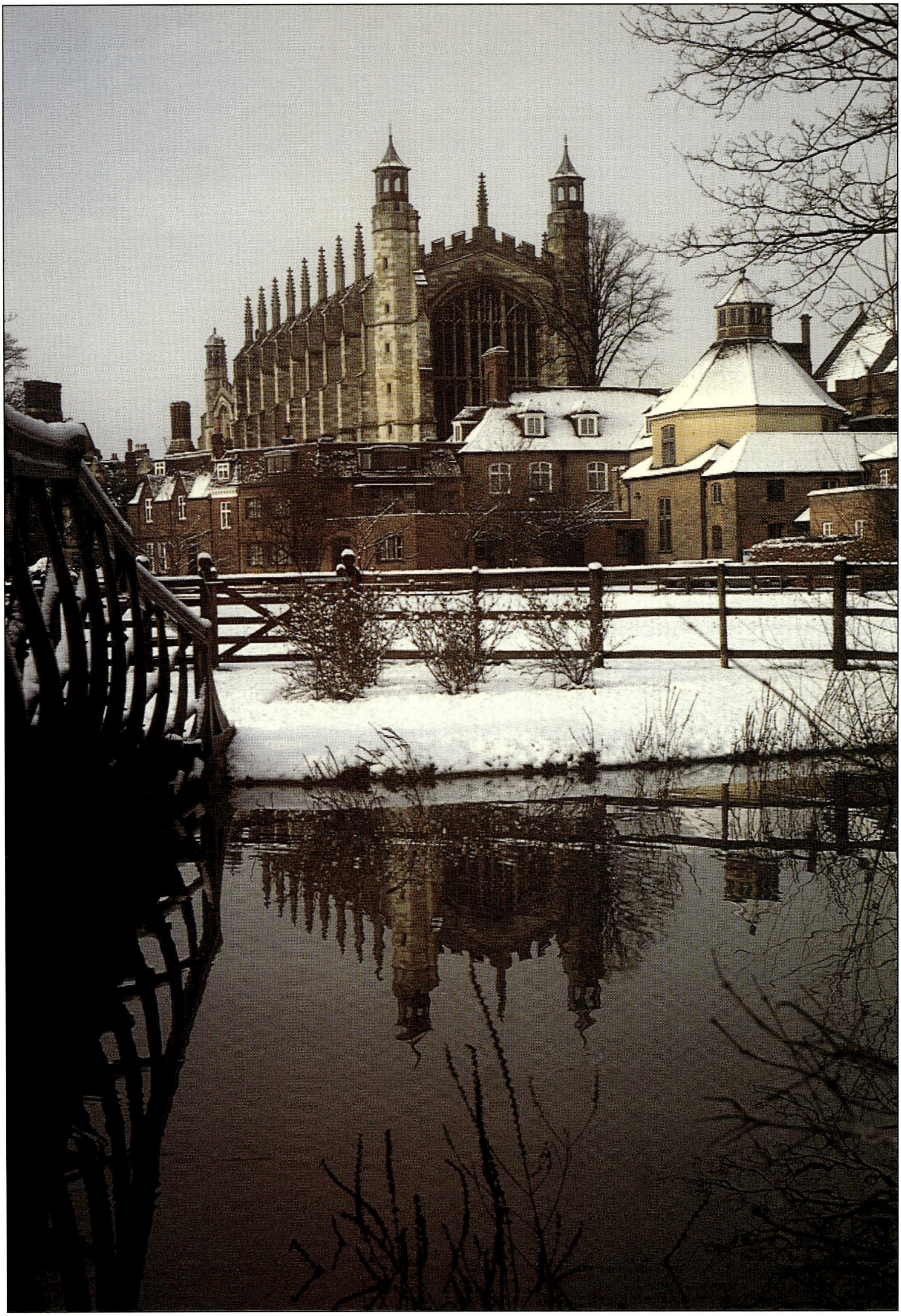

East end of College Chapel from Luxmoore's Garden.

Discovering Eton

Compiled by

Mark Phillips

Curator of the Eton College
Photographic Archive

Photographic Archive Eton College
Published in Association with Alden & Blackwell

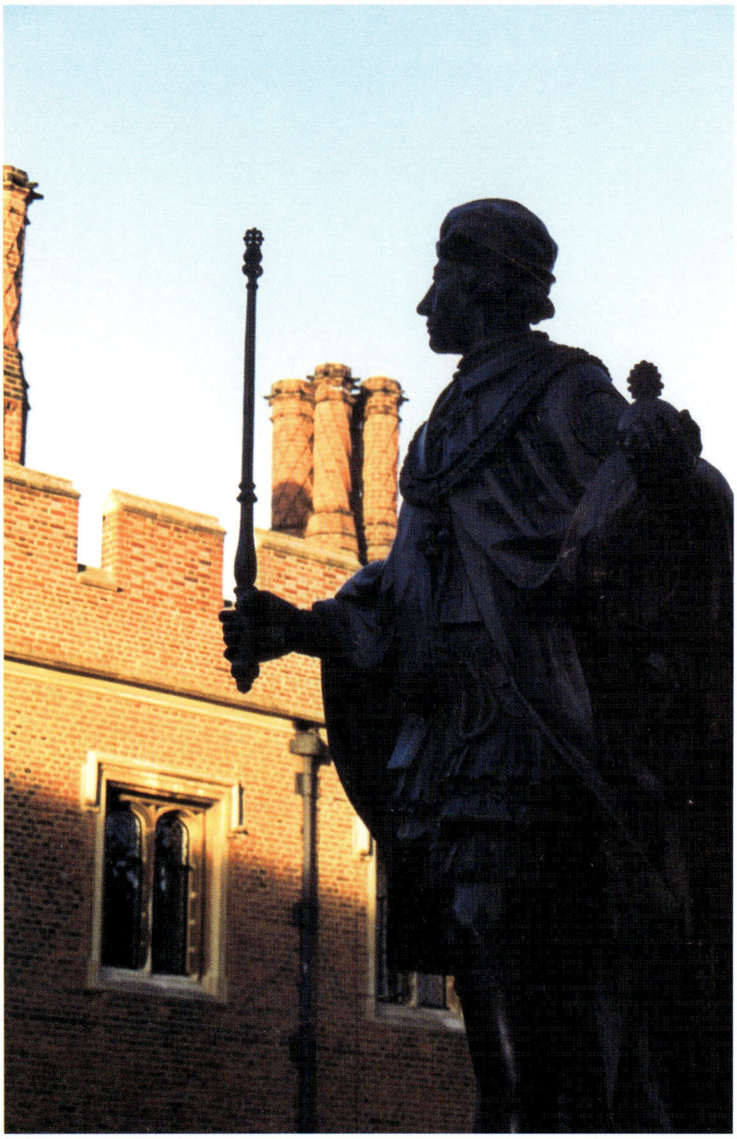

ISBN 0-630-20000-9

Typeset by Columns Design Ltd, Reading
Printed and bound in the UK at the University Press, Cambridge

Contents

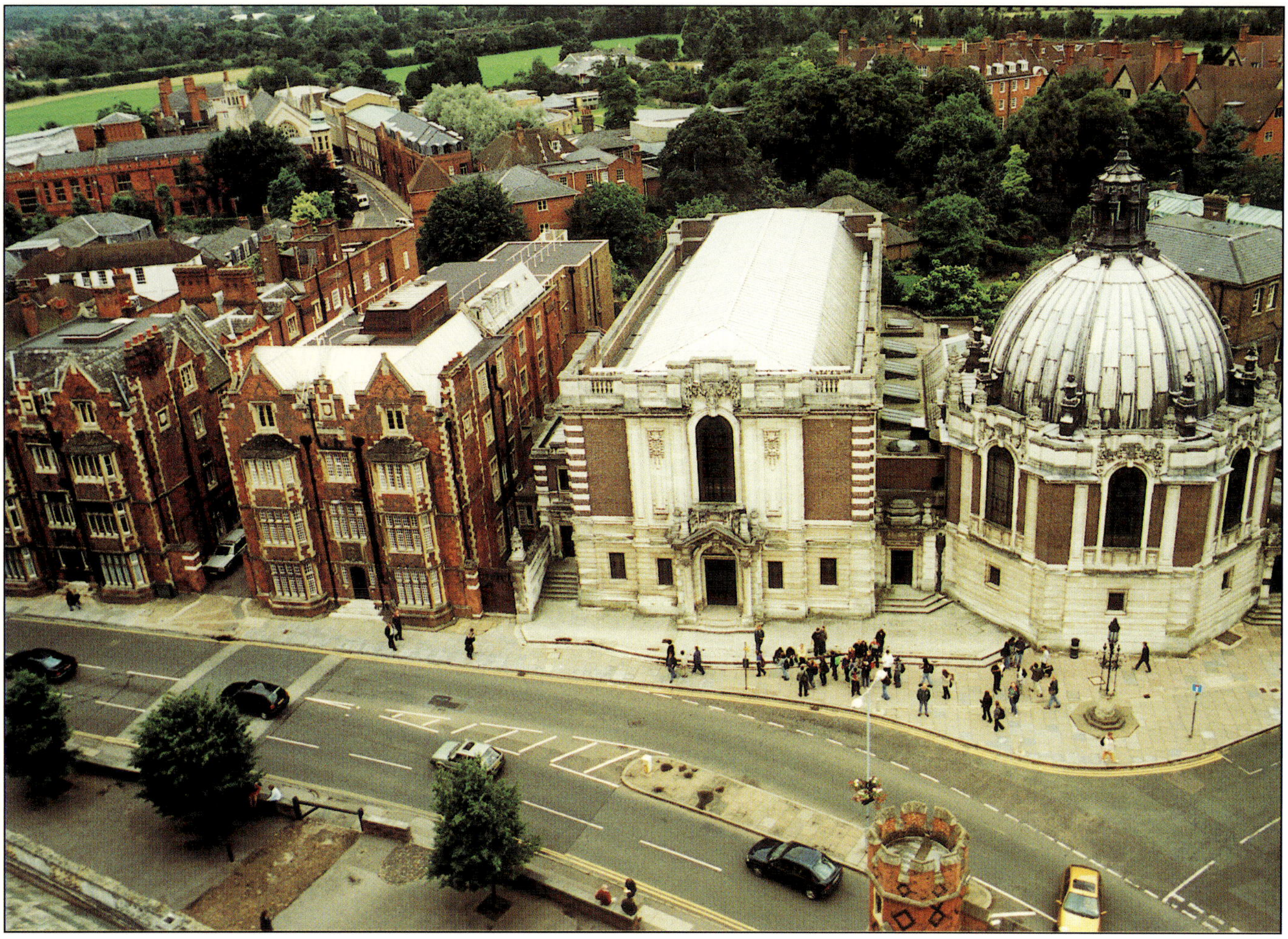

From left to right: Hawtrey House, Durnford House, School Hall and School Library

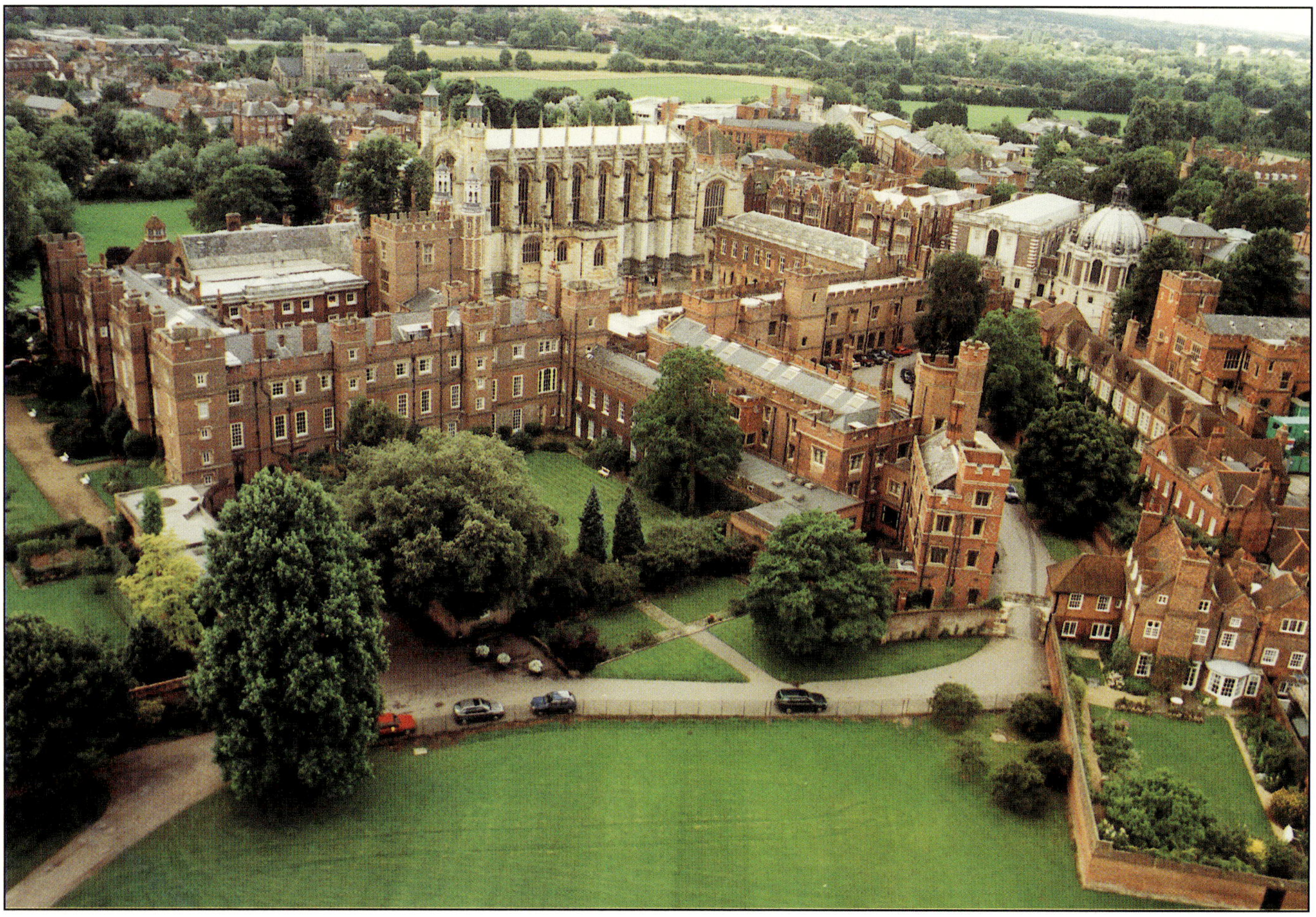

Eton from the north-east

Acknowledgements

In producing this book, I should like to thank those who have made important contributions:

The numerous people who appear in the photographs. Care has been taken to avoid embarrassment to any individual. Where there was doubt about suitability, permission has been sought to use the photograph.

Masters in charge of the various activities who provided valuable information about their areas of responsibility.
The Provost, Sir Eric Anderson, for his general support and for writing the Preface.
Sir Antony Acland, Provost (1991-2000), for his general support of the Archive.
John Lewis, Head Master (1994-2002), for his interest and encouragement.
Tony Little, Head Master (2002-), and Jenny Little for their considerable help and input.
Matthew Pinsent for laying down his oar and taking up his pen to write the Foreword.
Nigel Jaques for checking and proof-reading the text, for writing one section and for his general advice.
Michael Meredith and Howard Moseley for contributing one section each and for much valuable advice.
Matt Mowbray and Nick Baker for advice and support.
Nick Hitchock for professional advice.
Jonathan Palmer and Alden & Blackwell Limited.
Russell Polden and David Cooper for making their photographs available.
Sue Saunders, Lesley Stewart, Kate Lindsey, David Babb and Alan Cowen of Columns Design Limited for their patience, expertise and assistance.

Since the founding of the Photographic Archive in 1985 Christine Vickers has been its Secretary. Her knowledge of the collection is second to none, likewise her ability to search and find photographs of historic interest. In helping to piece together the disparate elements of this volume, she has worked with characteristic efficiency, calm and stamina. All those who take pleasure in this volume are in her debt.

Mark Phillips
(Curator)

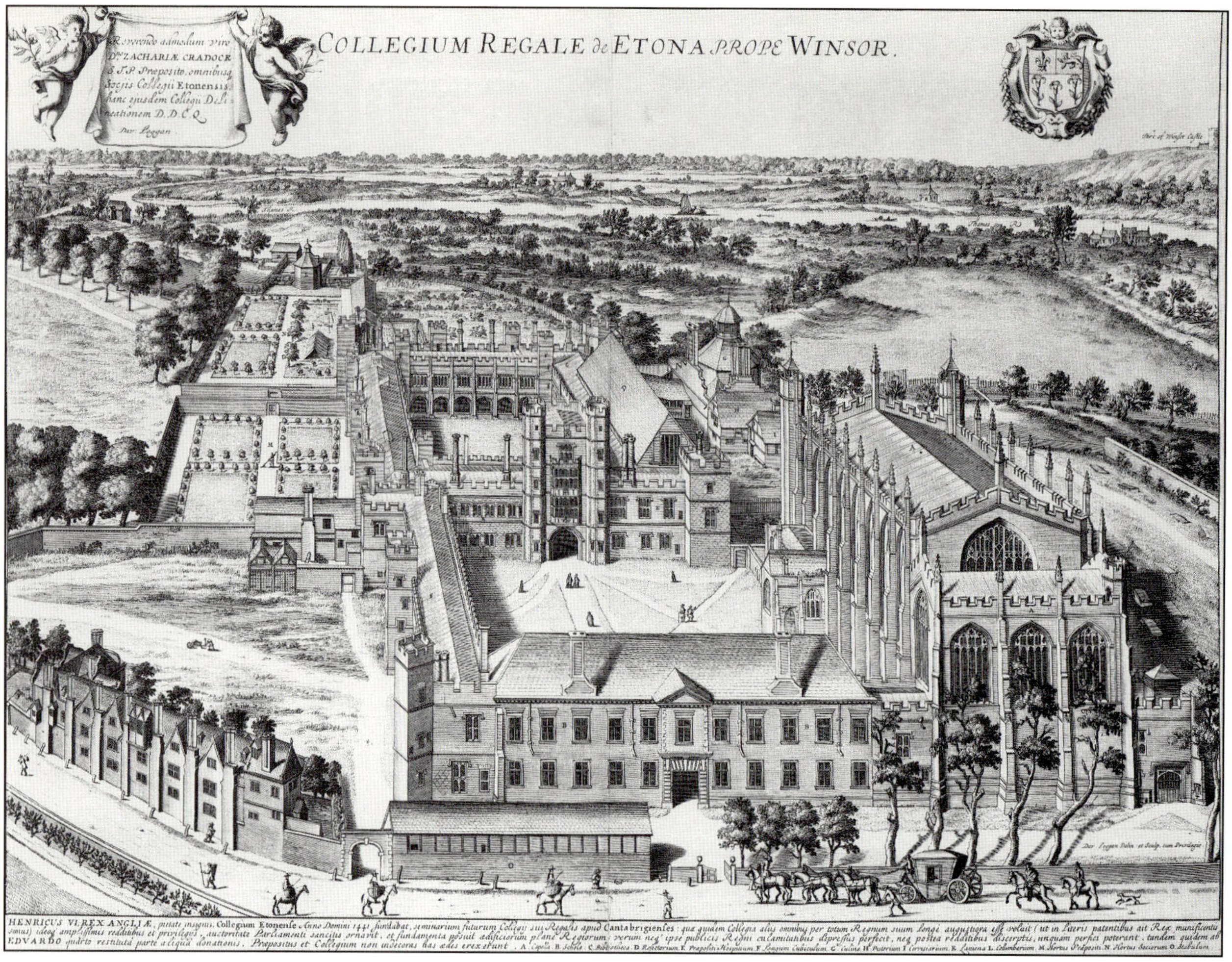

Collegium Regale de Etona prope Winsor, c1690, by David Loggan.
'The conscientious accuracy, as well as the artistic ability which characterises Loggan's views, can hardly be sufficiently praised. Every detail of the buildings, the courts and the gardens is carefully noted, so that they present not merely a record of the architecture, but of the life of the period.' Dictionary of National Biography.

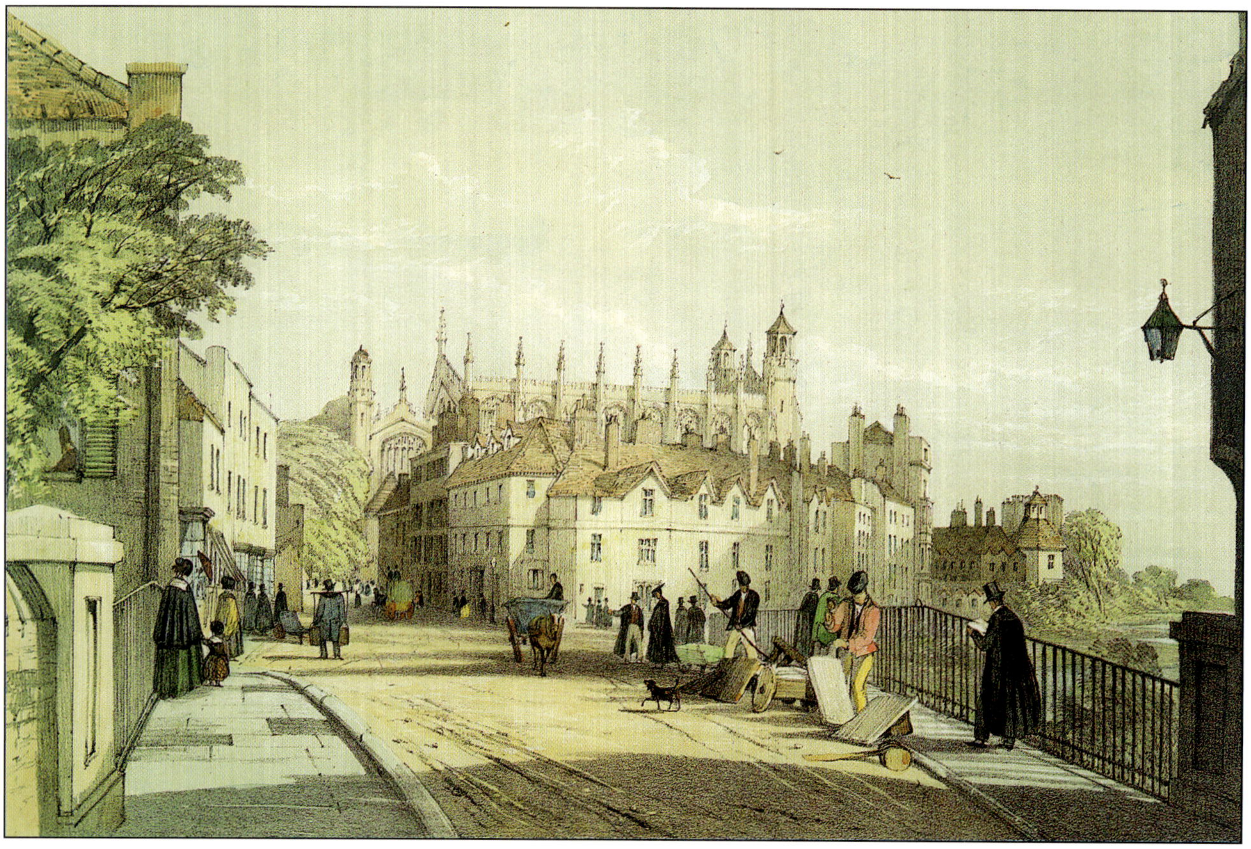

The Chapel as seen from Barnes Pool Bridge, 1844, by C.W. Radclyffe.

Introduction

"And so took the coach and away to Eton." No, this is not an excerpt from the diary of a twenty-first century tourist, but Samuel Pepys describing the events of 26th February, 1666. Pepys seems to have enjoyed his day-trip to Eton. "There (I) find all mighty fine and the school good," he says. He was amused to see that leaving boys had been carving their names into the wooden shutters (of Lower School, one imagines). He admired the boys' efforts at poetry, drank some college beer and watched the boys disporting themselves on the playing fields. It is a pity he does not describe the game being played. Perhaps it was an early form of football. His journey back to the City was free from modern delays and congestion charges: ". . . and so took coach, and finely, but sleepy, away home, and get thither about 8 at night, and after a little at my office, I to bed." We hope that those who dip into this volume concur with Pepys's positive judgement of the School, but perhaps gain a greater insight into Eton than he did in one day.

The Photographic Archive was officially established in 1985, thanks to the efforts of Peter Lawrence and the support of the then Provost, Martin Charteris. The basis for the Archive was Peter Lawrence's own photographic collection, accumulated over his many years as a Master at Eton. A key moment had been his letter to The Times of 1952 reproduced below in which he had appealed for suitable photographs of Eton. The response to this and other letters was very good, and additional gifts of albums and individual photographs over the years have improved our resources. Peter Lawrence produced two interesting volumes entitled *An Eton Camera 1859-1919* and *An Eton Camera 1920-59*, the photographs accompanied by detailed captions.

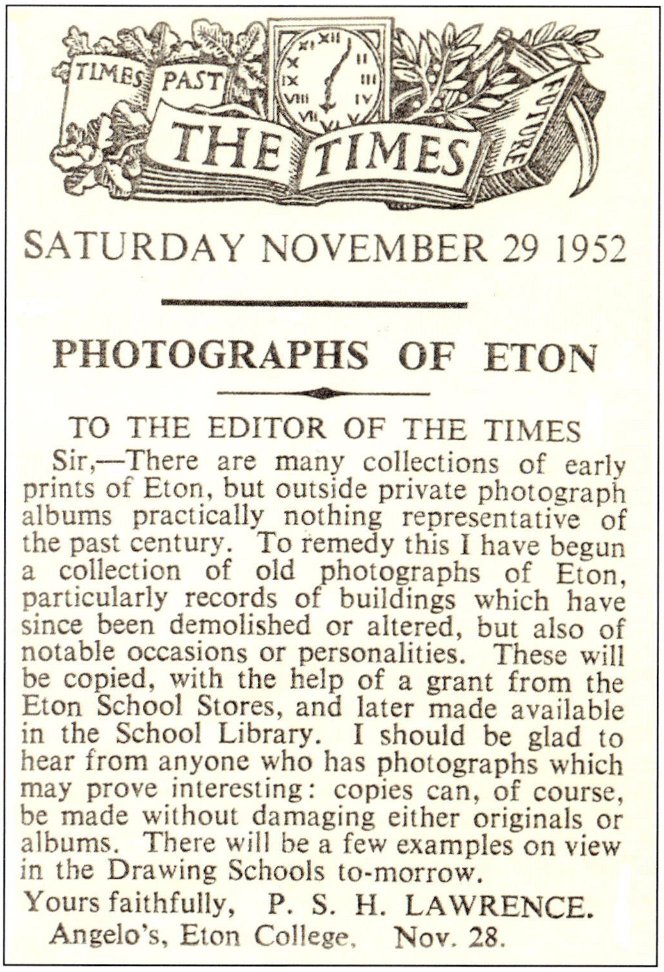
TIMES PAST THE TIMES FUTURE

SATURDAY NOVEMBER 29 1952

PHOTOGRAPHS OF ETON

TO THE EDITOR OF THE TIMES

Sir,—There are many collections of early prints of Eton, but outside private photograph albums practically nothing representative of the past century. To remedy this I have begun a collection of old photographs of Eton, particularly records of buildings which have since been demolished or altered, but also of notable occasions or personalities. These will be copied, with the help of a grant from the Eton School Stores, and later made available in the School Library. I should be glad to hear from anyone who has photographs which may prove interesting: copies can, of course, be made without damaging either originals or albums. There will be a few examples on view in the Drawing Schools to-morrow.

Yours faithfully, P. S. H. LAWRENCE.

Angelo's, Eton College, Nov. 28.

This volume focuses chiefly on the years 1990-2002. The early 1990s marked the end of an era with the retirement of Lord Charteris as Provost, and celebrations marking the 550th anniversary of the founding of the College, the highlight of which was the visit of HM The Queen. Since 1990 there have been changes aplenty. There have been curricular changes, examination reforms, alterations to the entry procedure, the communications revolution and much building. And yet "plus ça change, plus c'est la même chose". Eton retains its essential character and charm, unmistakable to those who have known it at any stage in their lives. And indeed, David Loggan's fine print of c1690, which shows the Eton that Samuel Pepys would have seen, is instantly recognisable in the year 2003.

Many of the photographs included in this book were exhibited in the exhibitions of 1999 and 2001 in the Brewhouse Gallery at Eton, and some have appeared on the extensive Eton web-site. Our aim has been to let formality and spontaneity exist side by side.

Mark Phillips
(Curator)

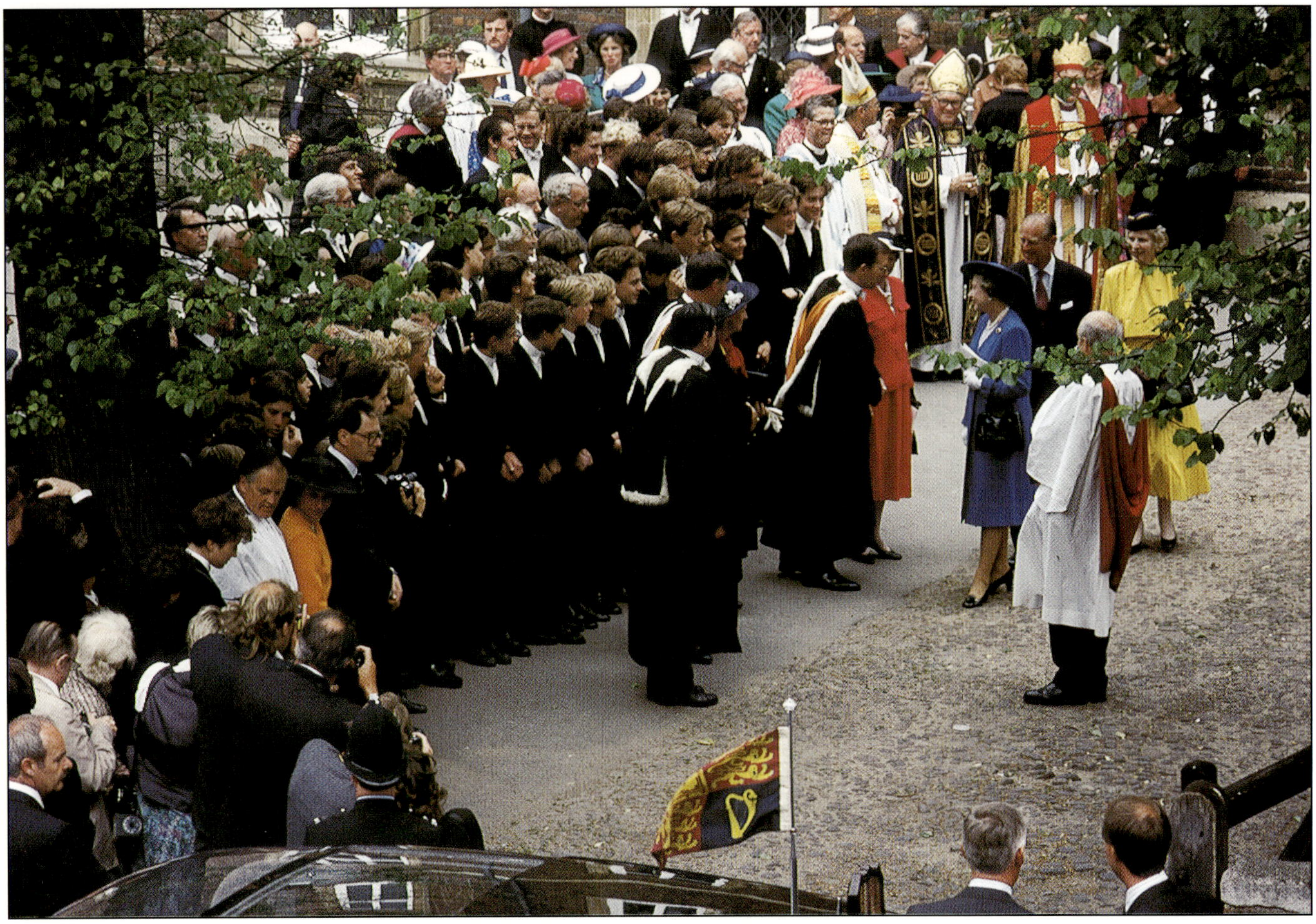

Her Majesty, Queen Elizabeth II, leaving Eton after the 550th anniversary celebrations of 1990.

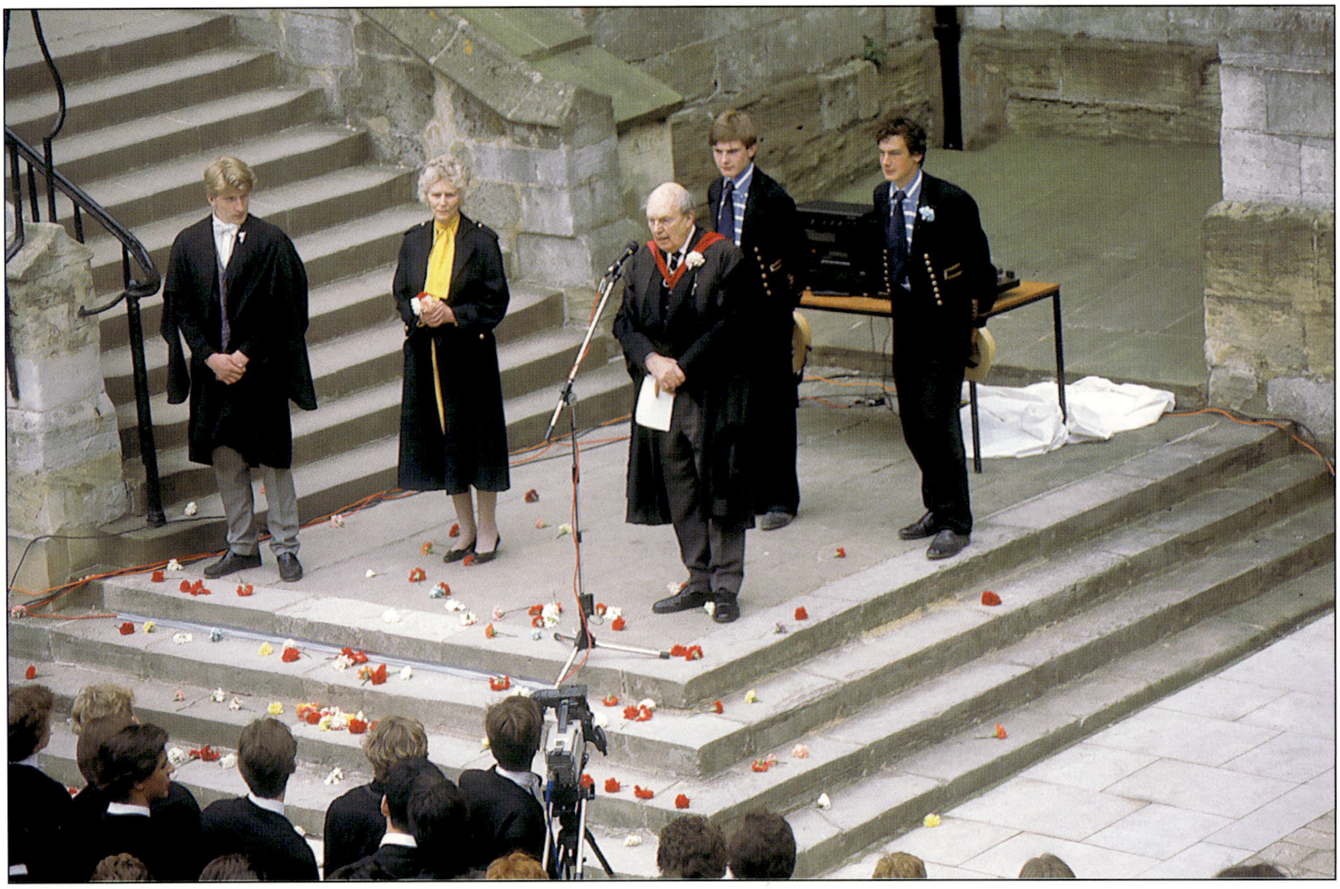

Lord Charteris addresses all boys and teaching staff on the eve of his retirement as Provost in 1991. The carnations tossed on to the steps were a sign of the affection in which he was held by the boys

Preface

"Of making many books there is no end". That is certainly true of Eton which has been well described in print over the last century and a half. This book, however, is rather different. Where others have concentrated on the history and customs of the school, or, in the case of the photographic studies, mainly on the buildings and surroundings, this volume concentrates on the most important thing in the school – the boys for whose education, in the broadest sense, Eton exists. They are seen here as they are, at work and at play, on formal occasions and in relaxed informality. They emerge from these pages as very normal young men, a long way from the tabloid stereotype of top-hatted toffs. I think the camera has caught something of the spirit of the place, something of the sense of fun which bubbles up alongside the serious business of learning.

These photographs were taken over twelve years. The book is therefore (and I cannot avoid the photographic word) a snapshot. It records one moment in Eton's history. I hope the book will give pleasure to the curious as well as to those who appear in it. It will certainly be of enduring interest to later generations within the school as a unique archive of what Eton boys were like and what they did at the start of the second Millennium.

Eric Anderson
Provost

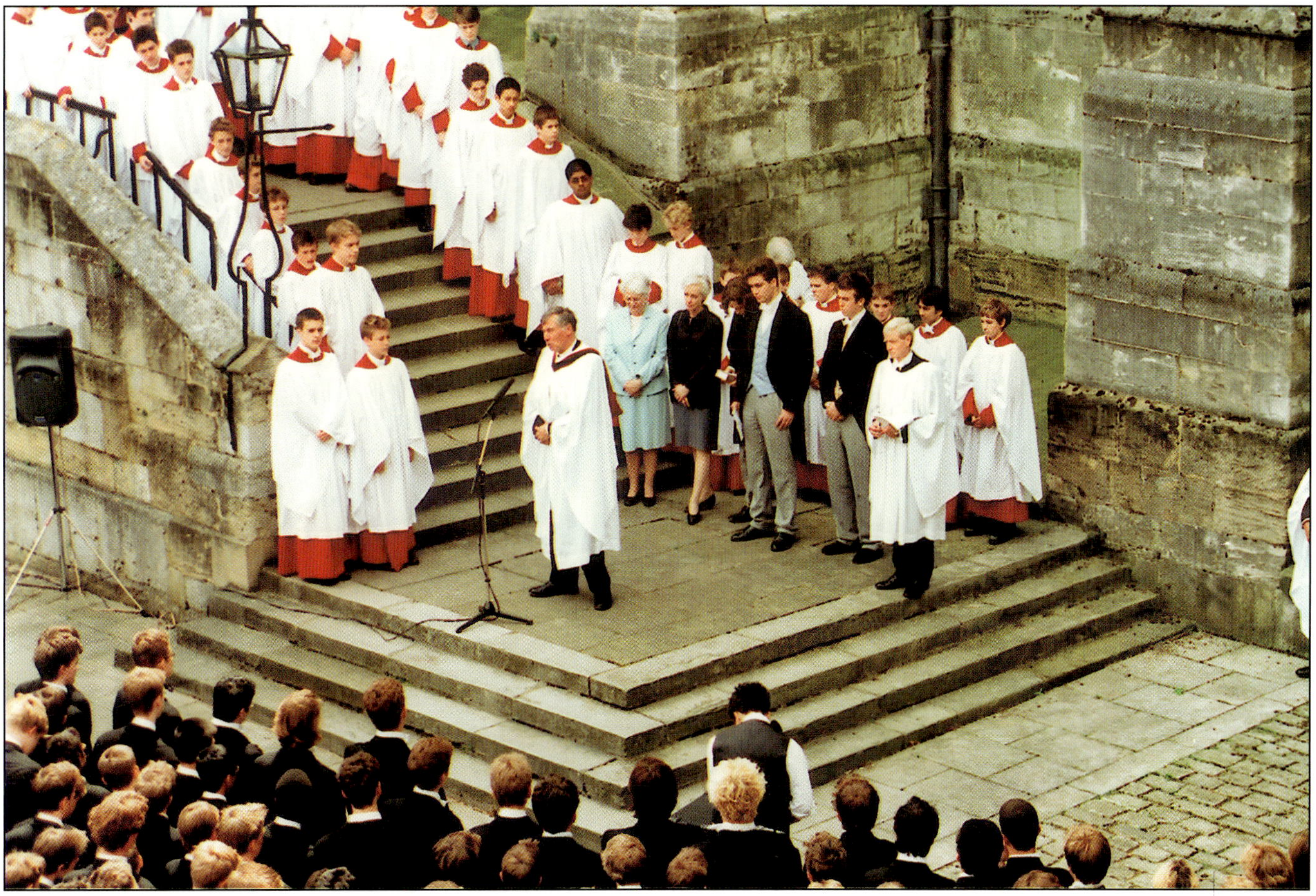

Sir Eric Anderson, Provost since 2000, pays tribute to John Lewis on his retirement as Head Master in 2002.

Foreword

My memories of Eton are dominated by the outside environment. Of course, the interior of College Chapel is amazing and the wealth of div rooms a huge asset, but it is the outside views of the School that stay freshest in my memory: the roof-lines of the oldest part of the College seen from College Field, the books wedged almost permanently in the railings of Cannon Yard, or the throng of a weekday Chambers. As a sportsman I loved the playing fields and facilities we had at our disposal and can still remember the work going on to replace the old Gymnasium. We peered through a hole in the wall and tried to imagine what an indoor hall or purpose-built weights room would look like.

When one returns, there are places that seem timeless, and one is almost surprised not to find contemporaries and beaks as they used to be. But of course, there have been huge changes. It is an illusion to think that a place stops or stands still in our absence. A new raft of pupils comes in to take over the secrets and rites that we thought would be ours for ever. Beaks who seemed steadfast age and move on, and buildings are transformed or moved. There is a new History Department building, a new laundry and a much needed extension to the Music Schools. The cadets have left the aptly named Cannon Yard for a new building beyond Lower Chapel and have decorated it with two 25-pounders!

For me, of course, the most striking and meaningful change has been the Rowing Lake. We used to run over the common for the Steeplechase each year or cycle across it in winter to get to Andrew's Boathouse.

Needless to say, it provides more pleasure now. For Eton to provide a facility so needed in the Thames Valley and make it available to the rowing world is amazing. It allows me to continue and probably end my career within a few strokes of where it started and for that and more I owe Eton so much.

Matthew Pinsent, CBE

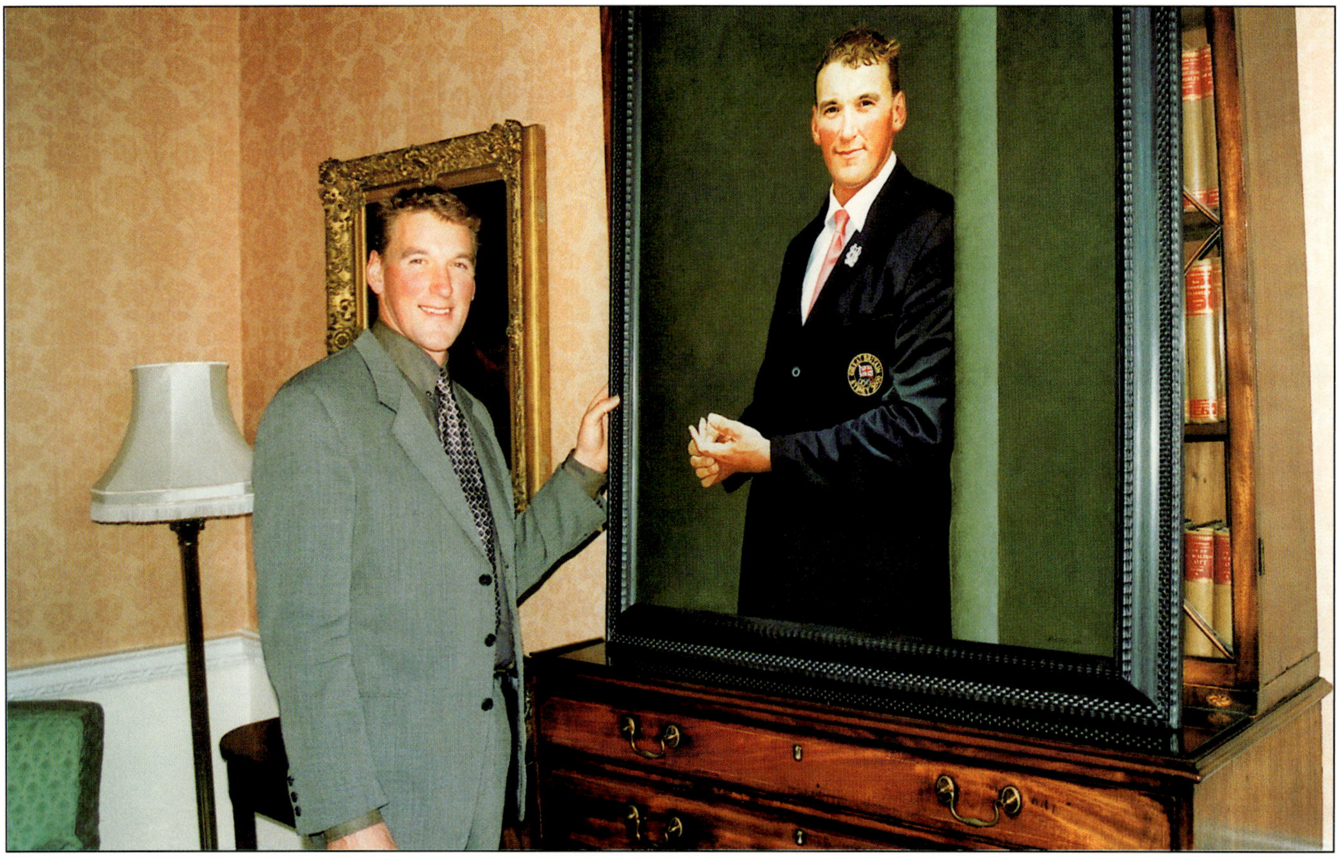

Matthew Pinsent CBE studies the portrait of himself by Paul Brason

Arrival at Eton: New Boys

The transition from preparatory school to Eton at the age of 13 may seem quite daunting, but boys settle in remarkably quickly. New boys will already have met their House Master and seen round the House, and most will have friends at the School. Although procedures vary from House to House, a new boy's first day will probably follow a common pattern. He and his parents will have tea with the House Master. He will meet his peers and sign his name in the Head Master's Chambers, in the new boys' book. With map and time-table in hand he will be shown round by his House Master, see all the main buildings and be briefed about time-table and routine. Meanwhile, his parents will go to College Chapel to be welcomed by the Head Master. Within a day or two he will know the whereabouts of his schoolrooms and the playing fields and will have no difficulty in finding them. Soccer and rugby trials take place, minor sports choices are made, and local shops are investigated. Tolerance levels are high in these opening days, and the expression 'new boy's benefit' is often used to excuse any sins of omission.

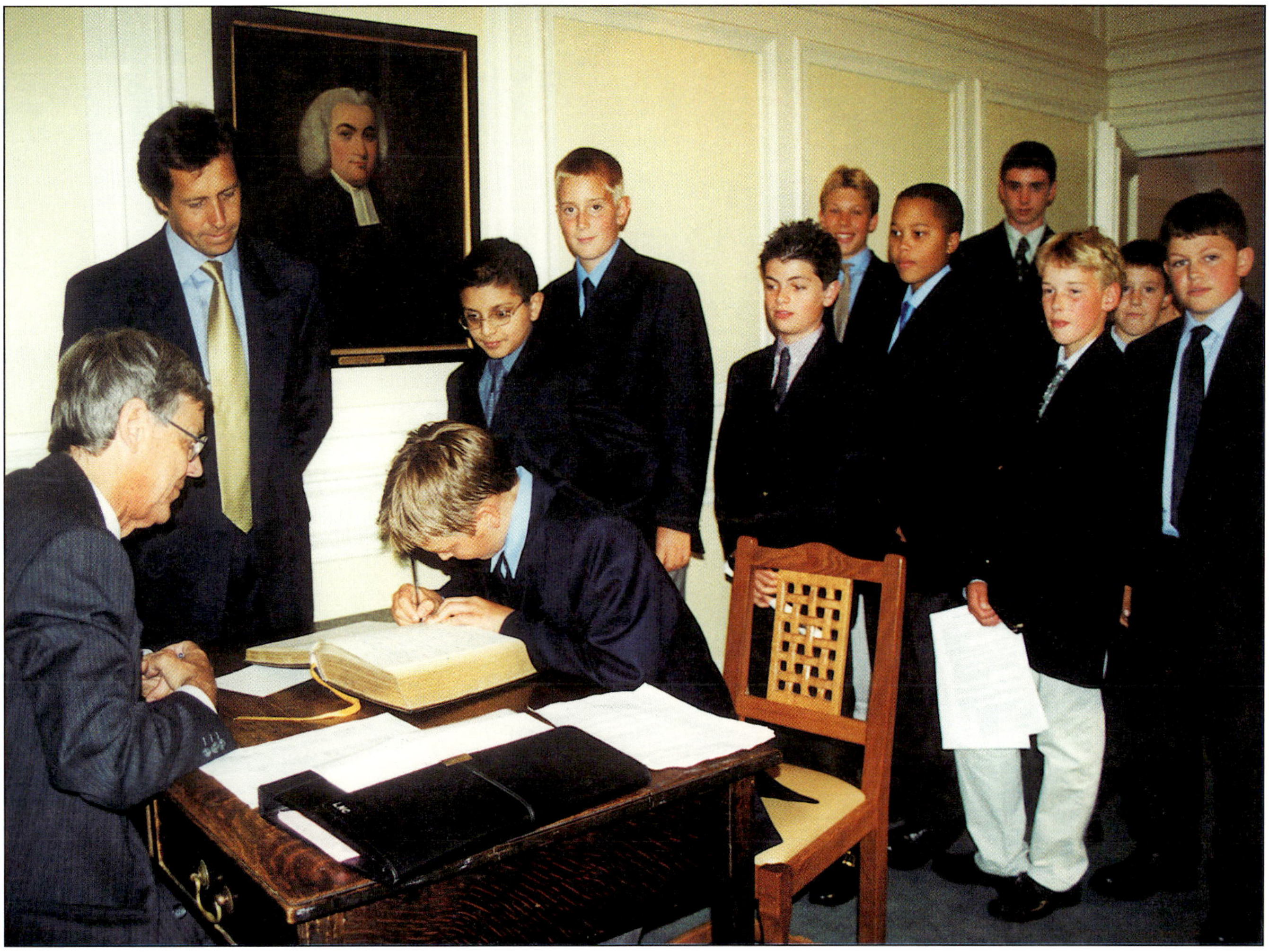

Signing the new boys' book in the Head Master's Chambers

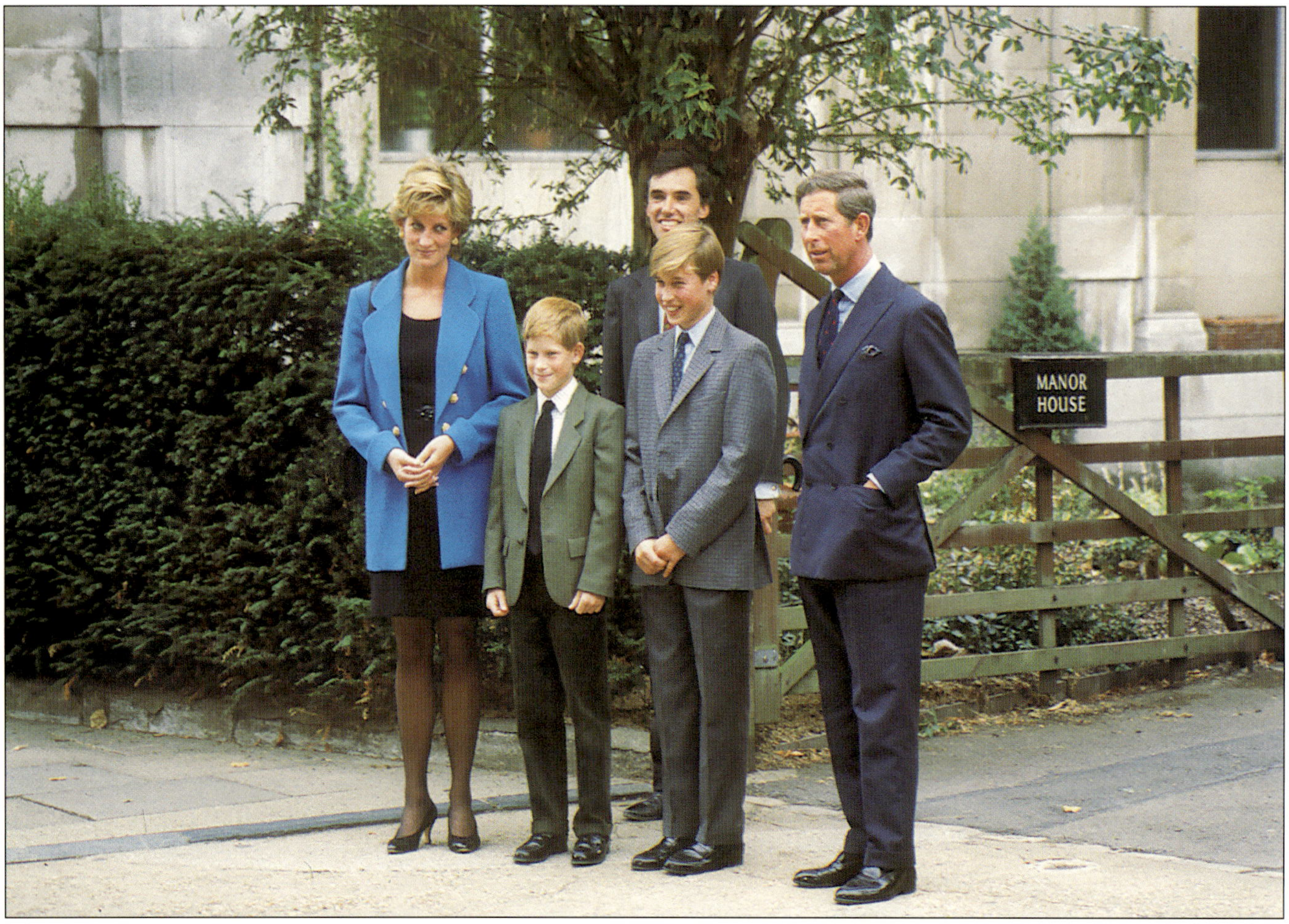

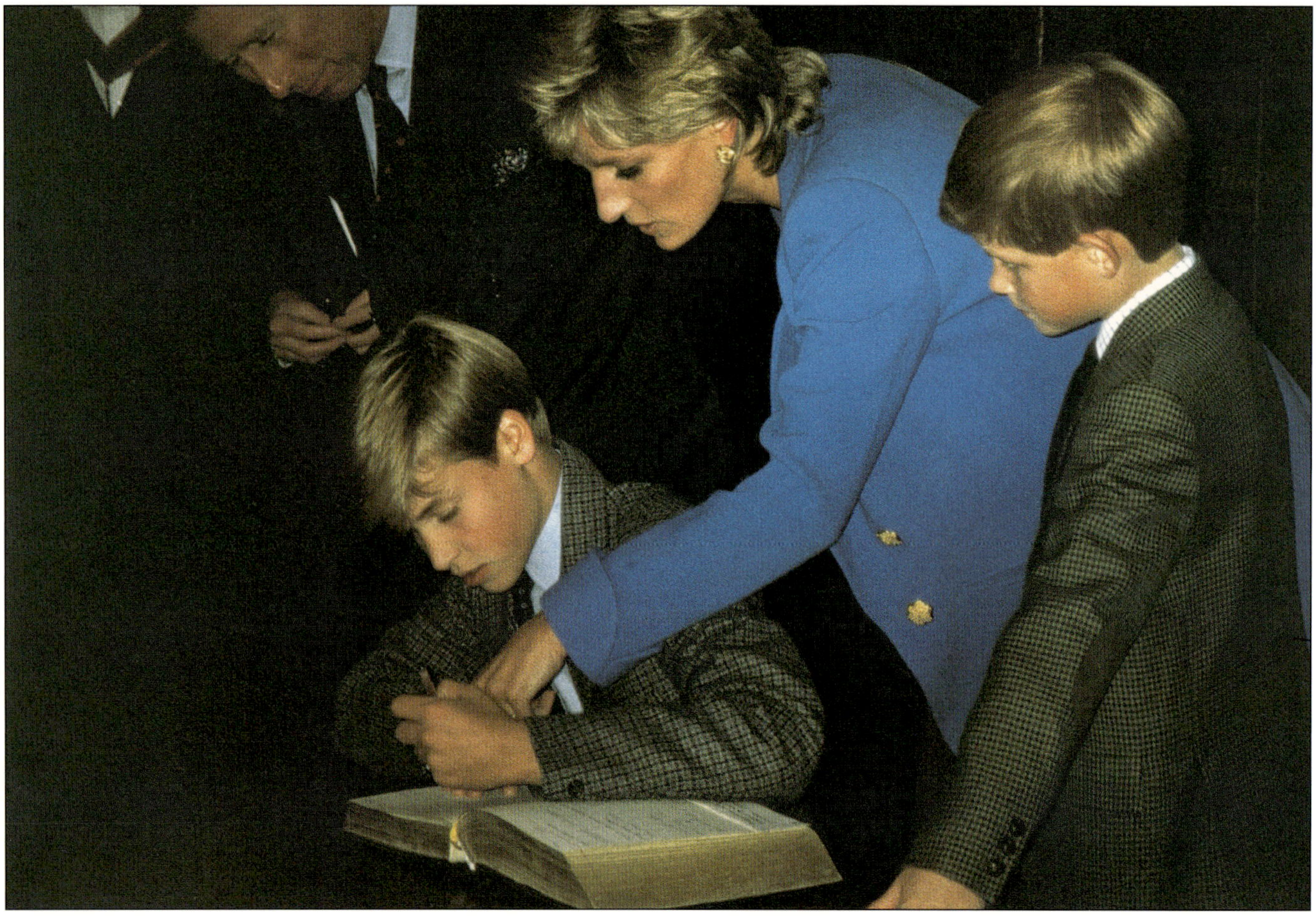

Prince William's arrival at Eton in 1995

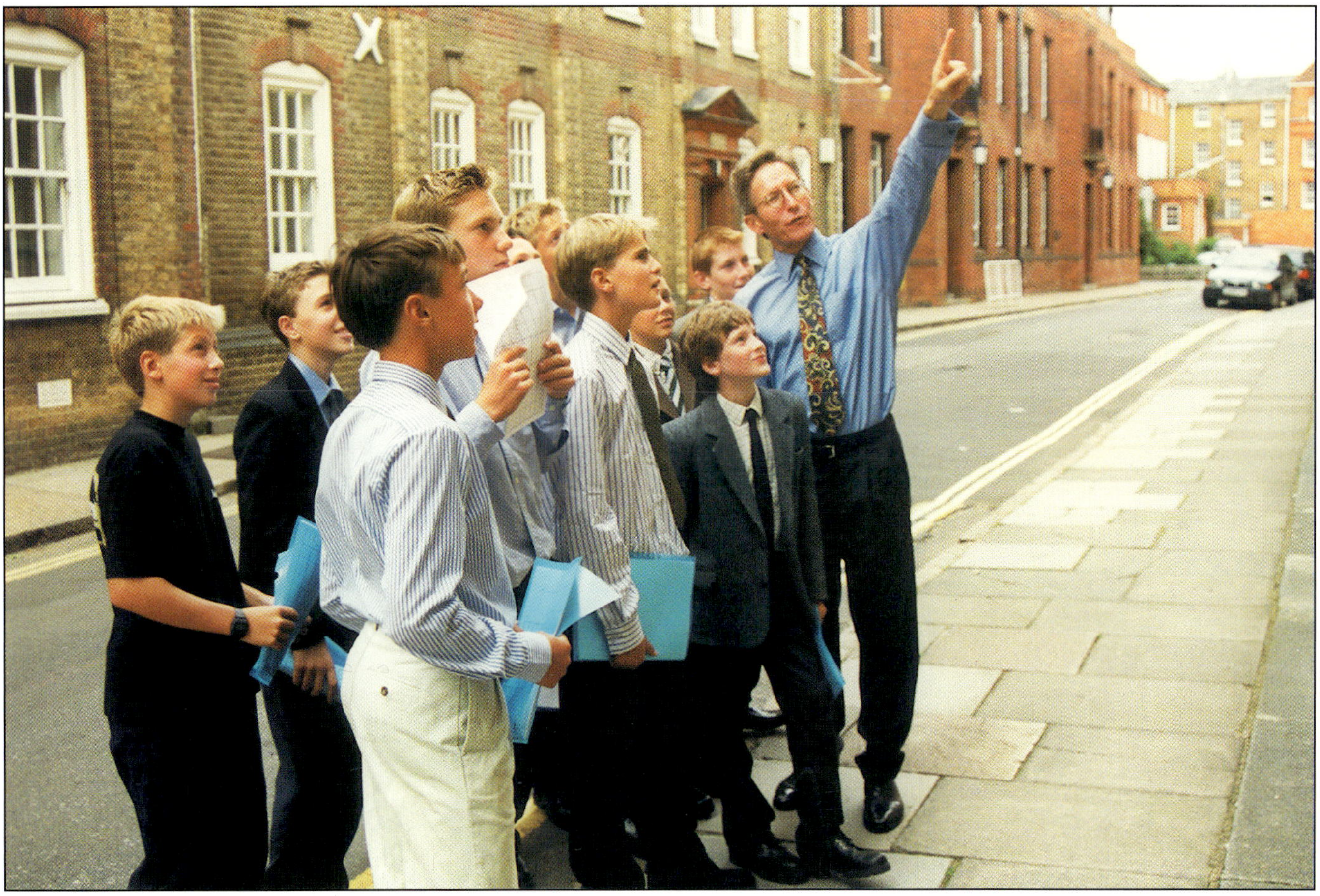

Tour of the School with the House Master

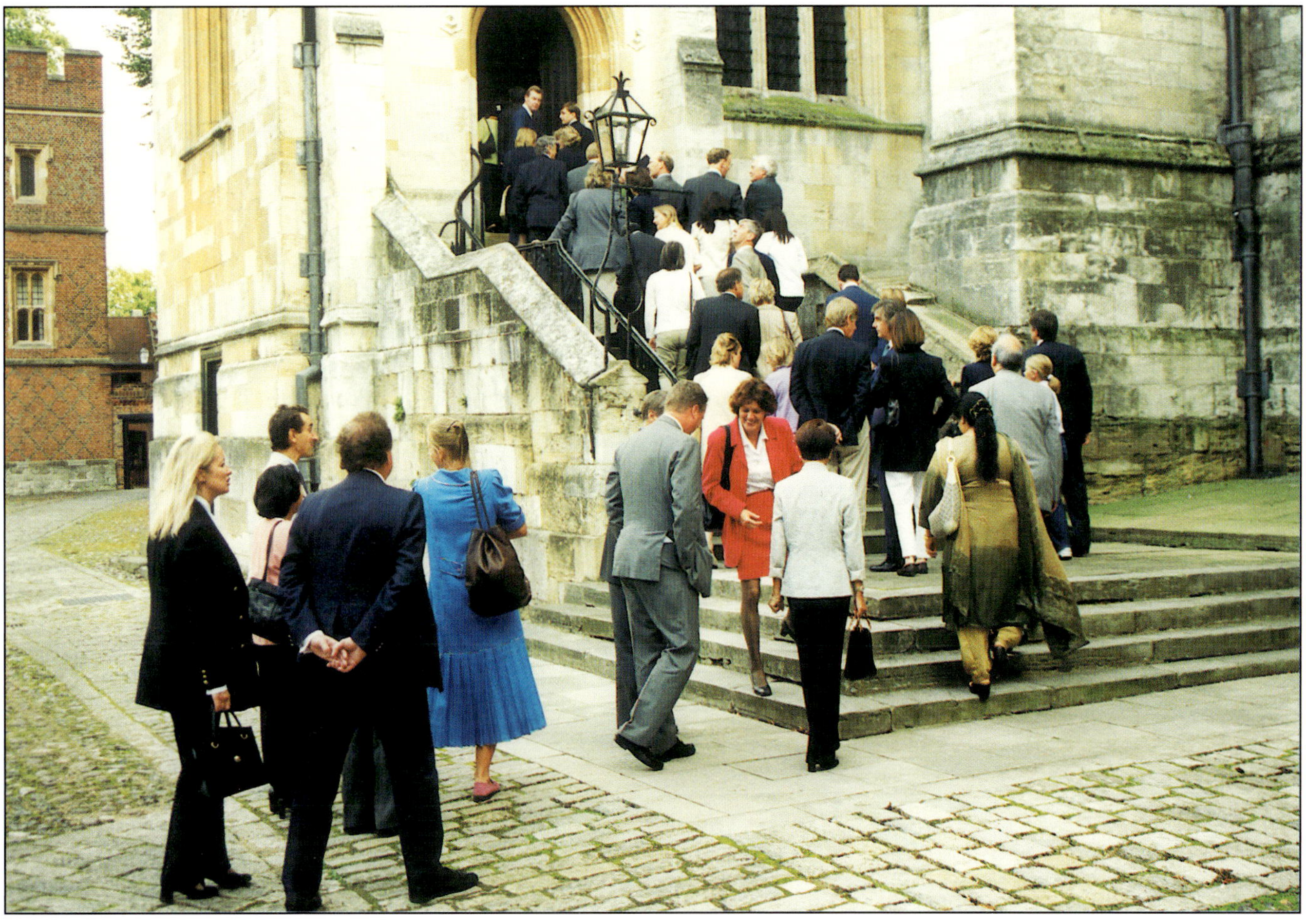

Parents entering College Chapel to be addressed by the Head Master

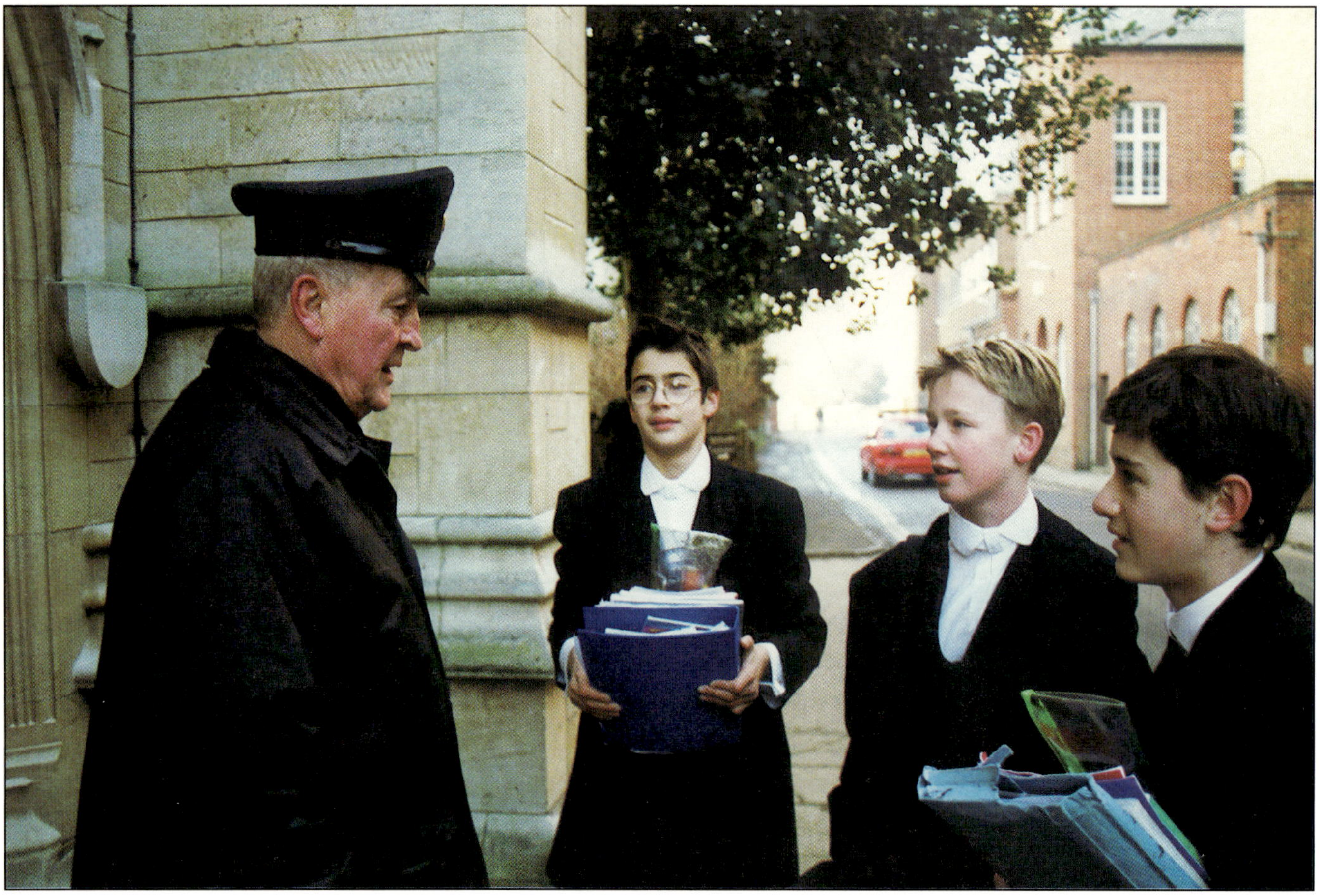

Late for Chapel? New boy's benefit!

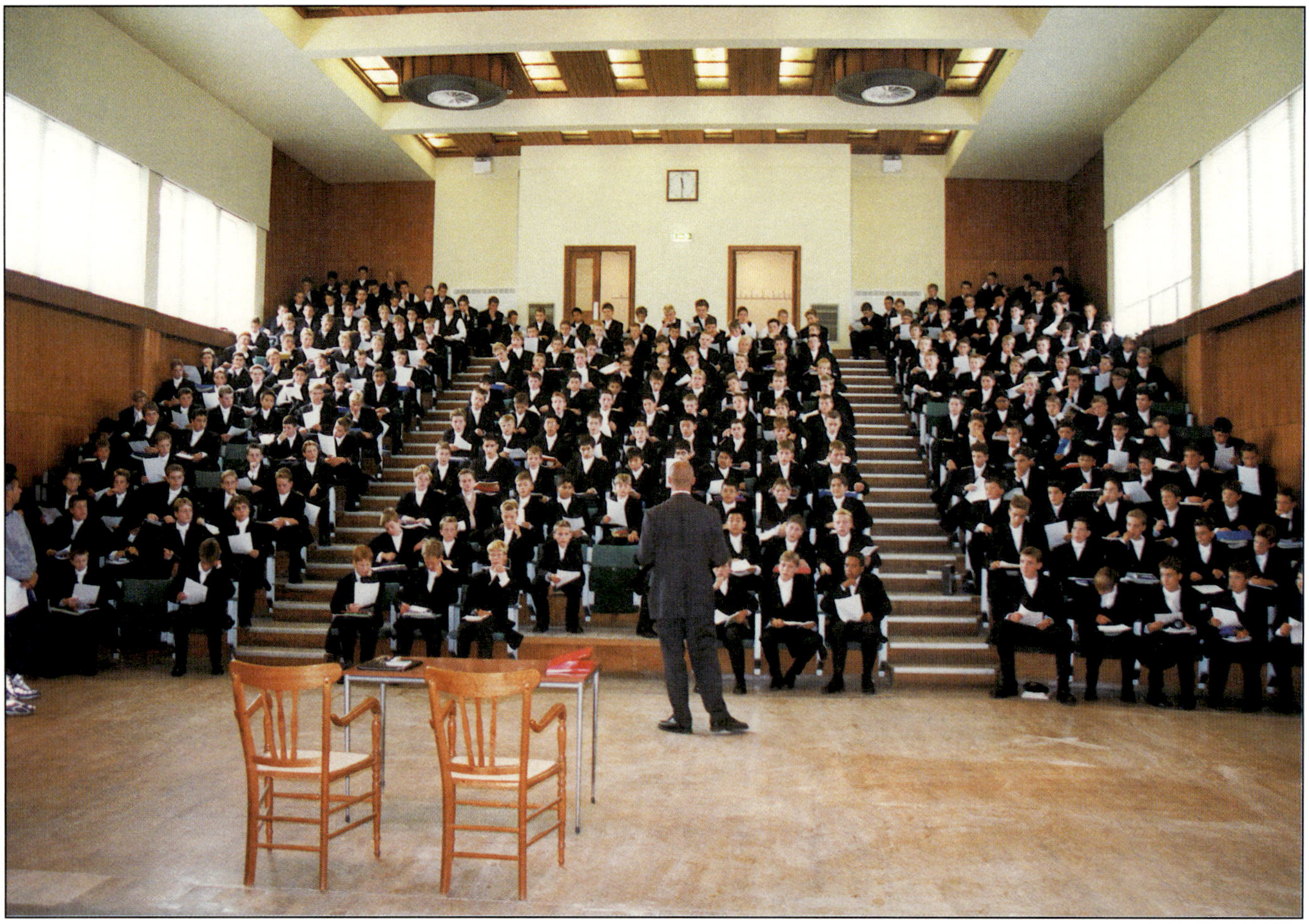

Minor sports choices being explained in the Music Schools

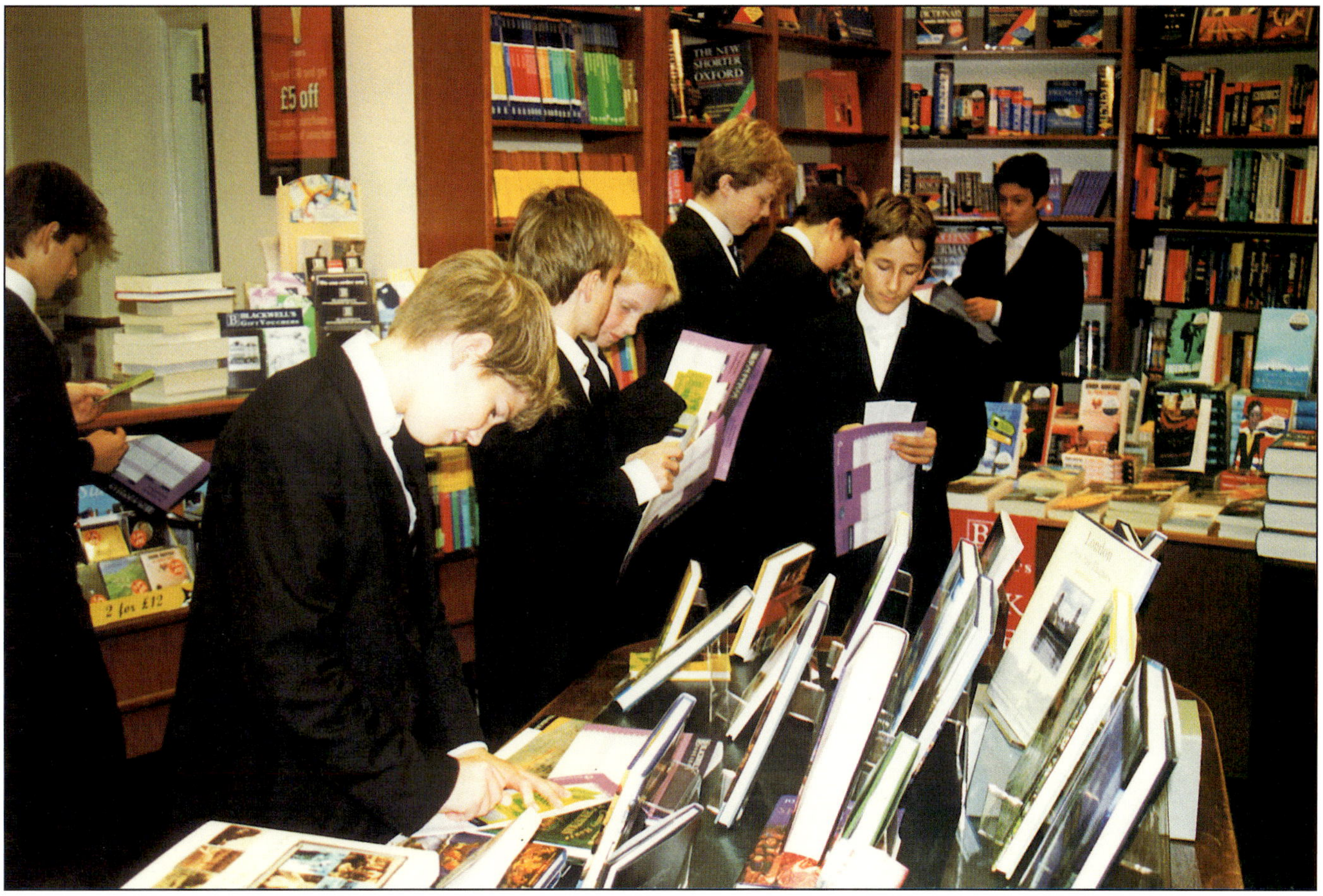

Discovering Alden & Blackwell, the School bookshop

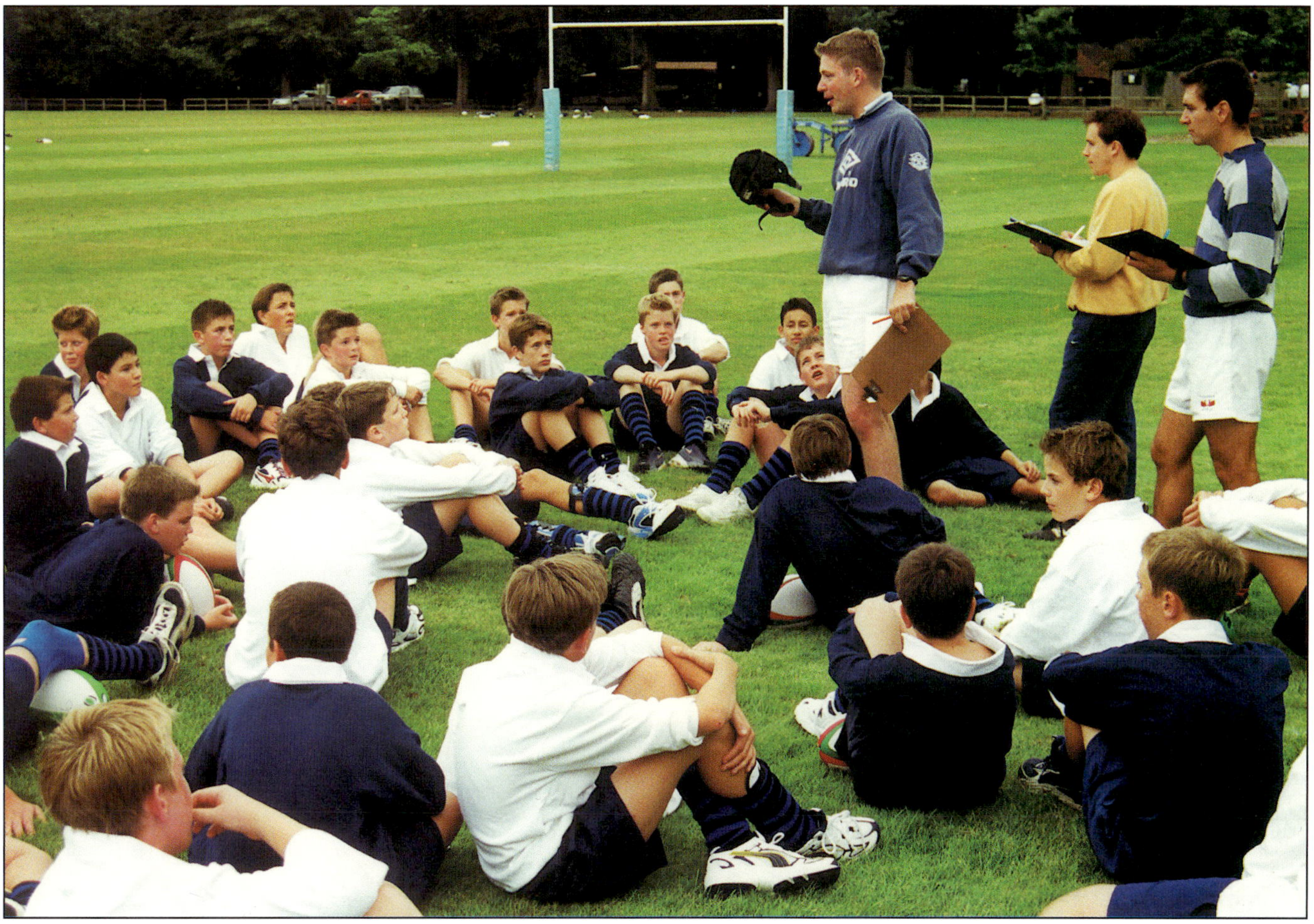

Rugby trials

School Routine

School routine is most succinctly summarised in the School Notice with that title. However, we shall follow the course of a day through photographs instead.

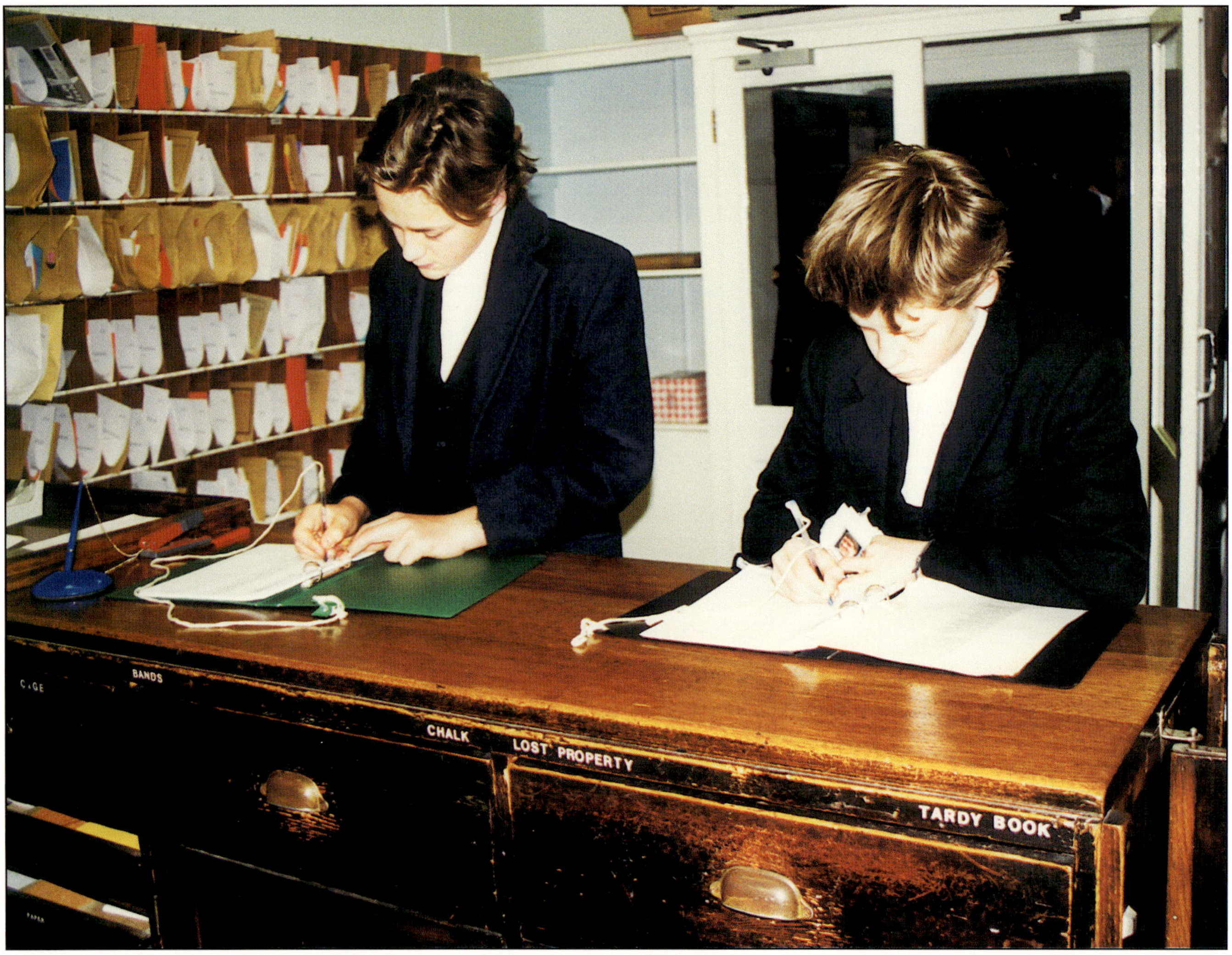

Boys signing Tardy book in School Office before breakfast. Tardy book is the punishment for persistent lateness.

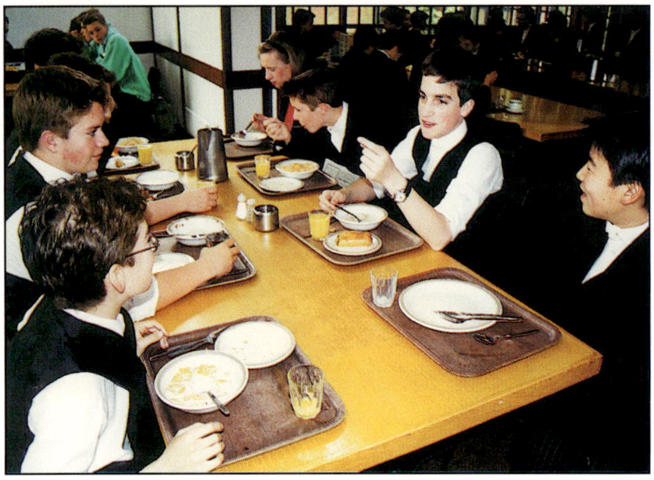

Breakfast in Bekynton

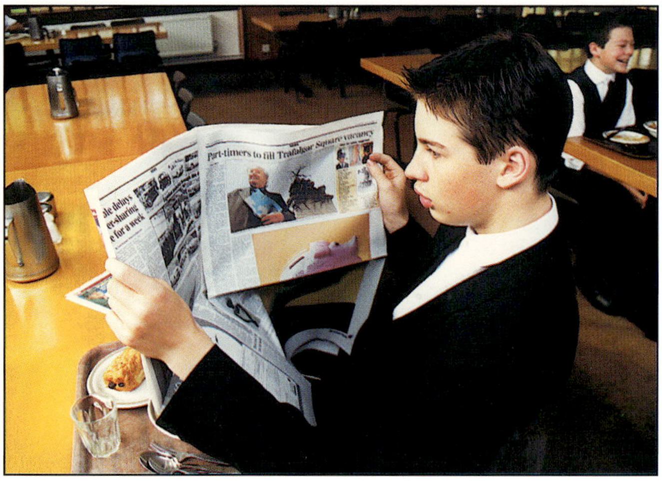

Newspapers may be read at breakfast

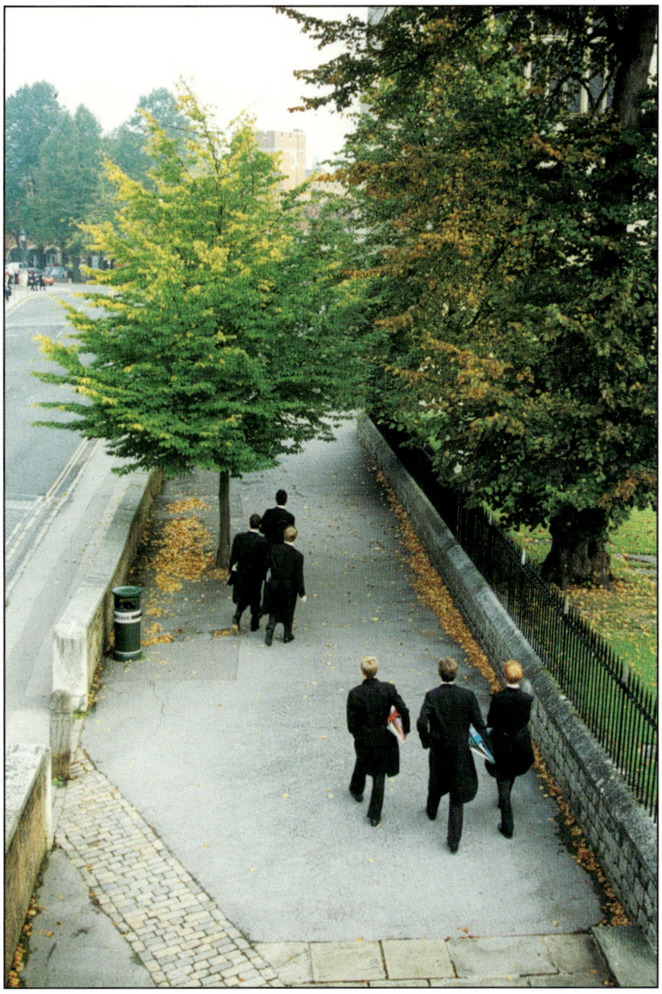

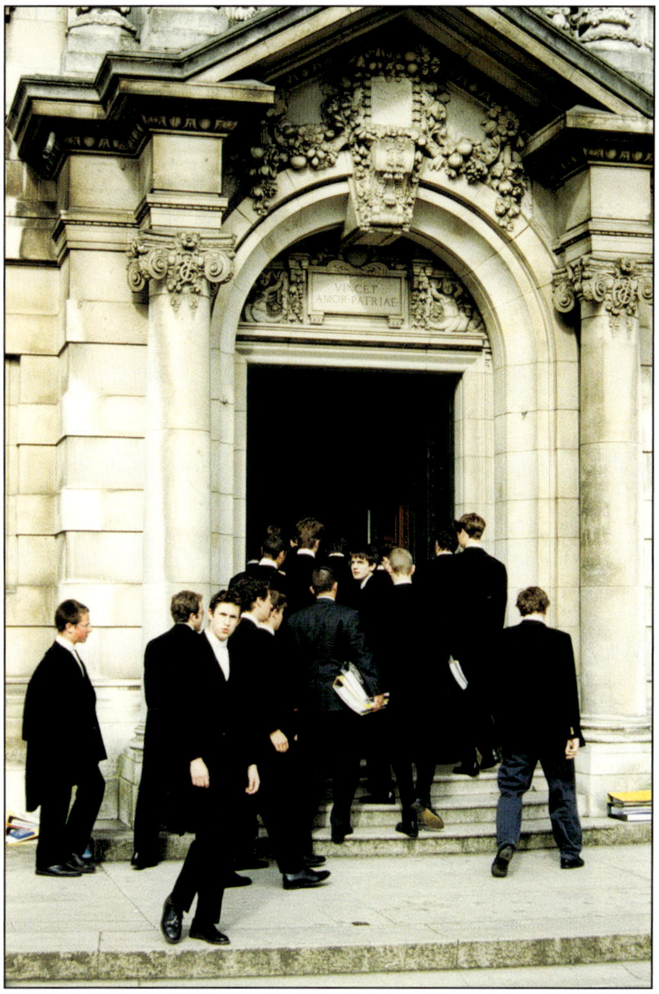

On the way to Chapel and Assembly

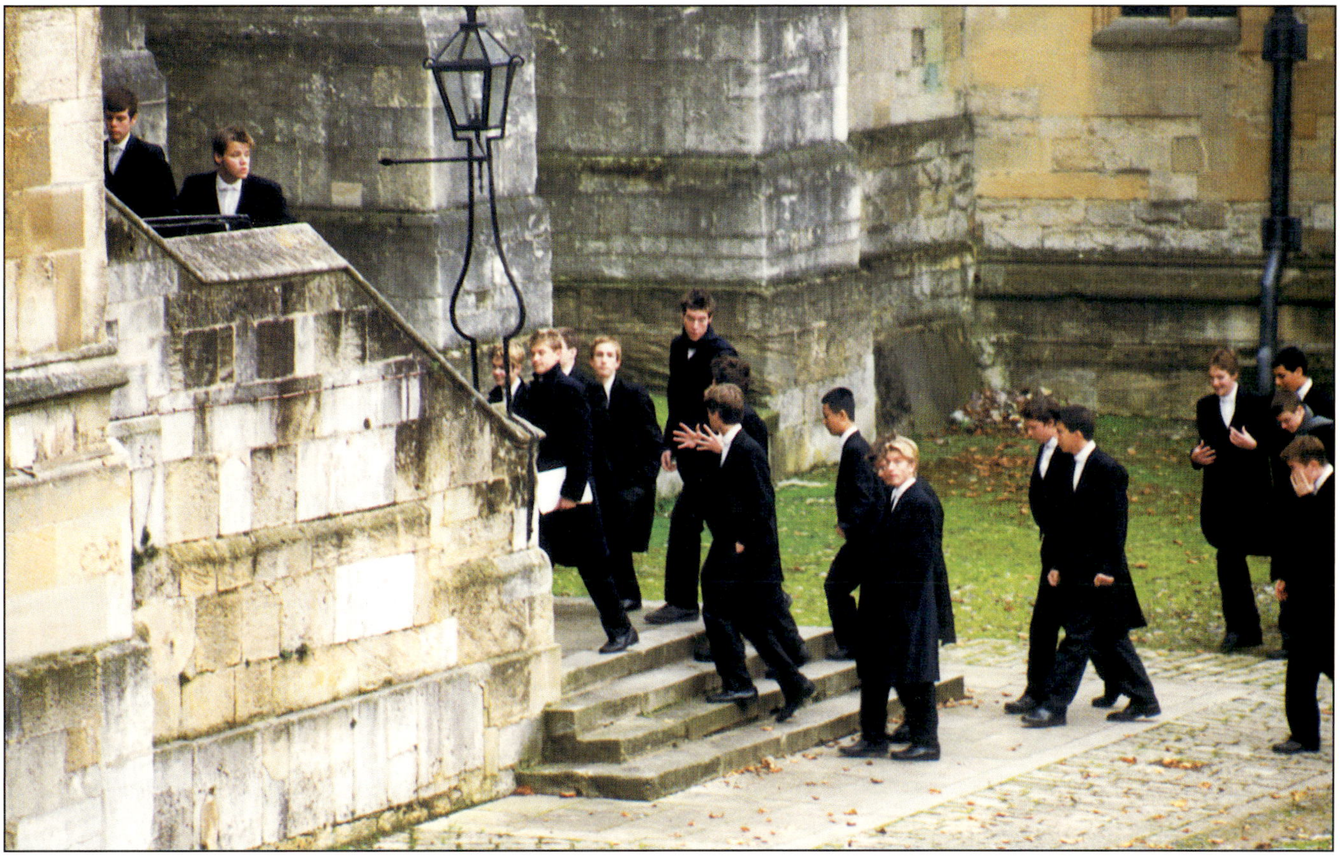

Boys entering the north door of College Chapel

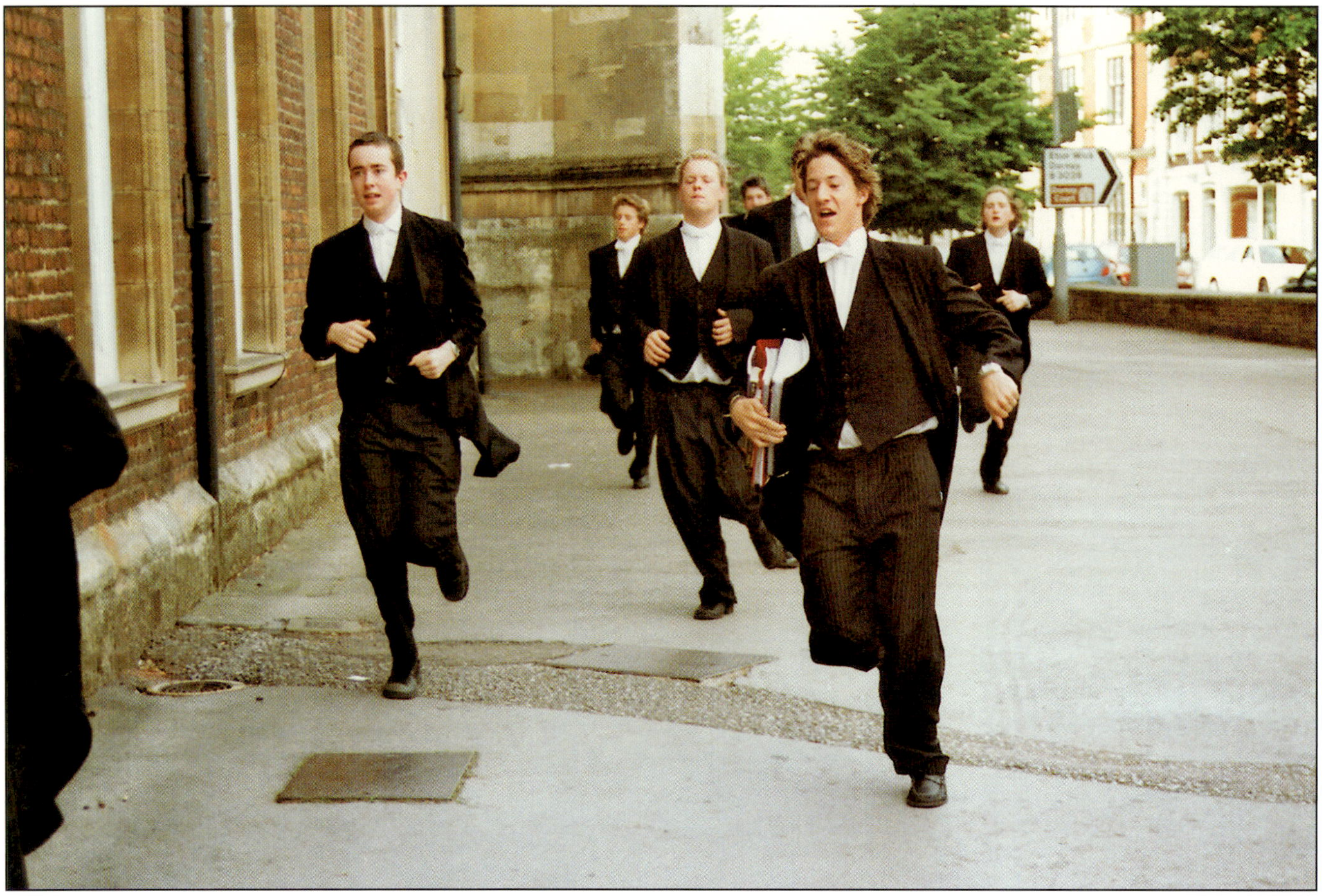

Time is running out

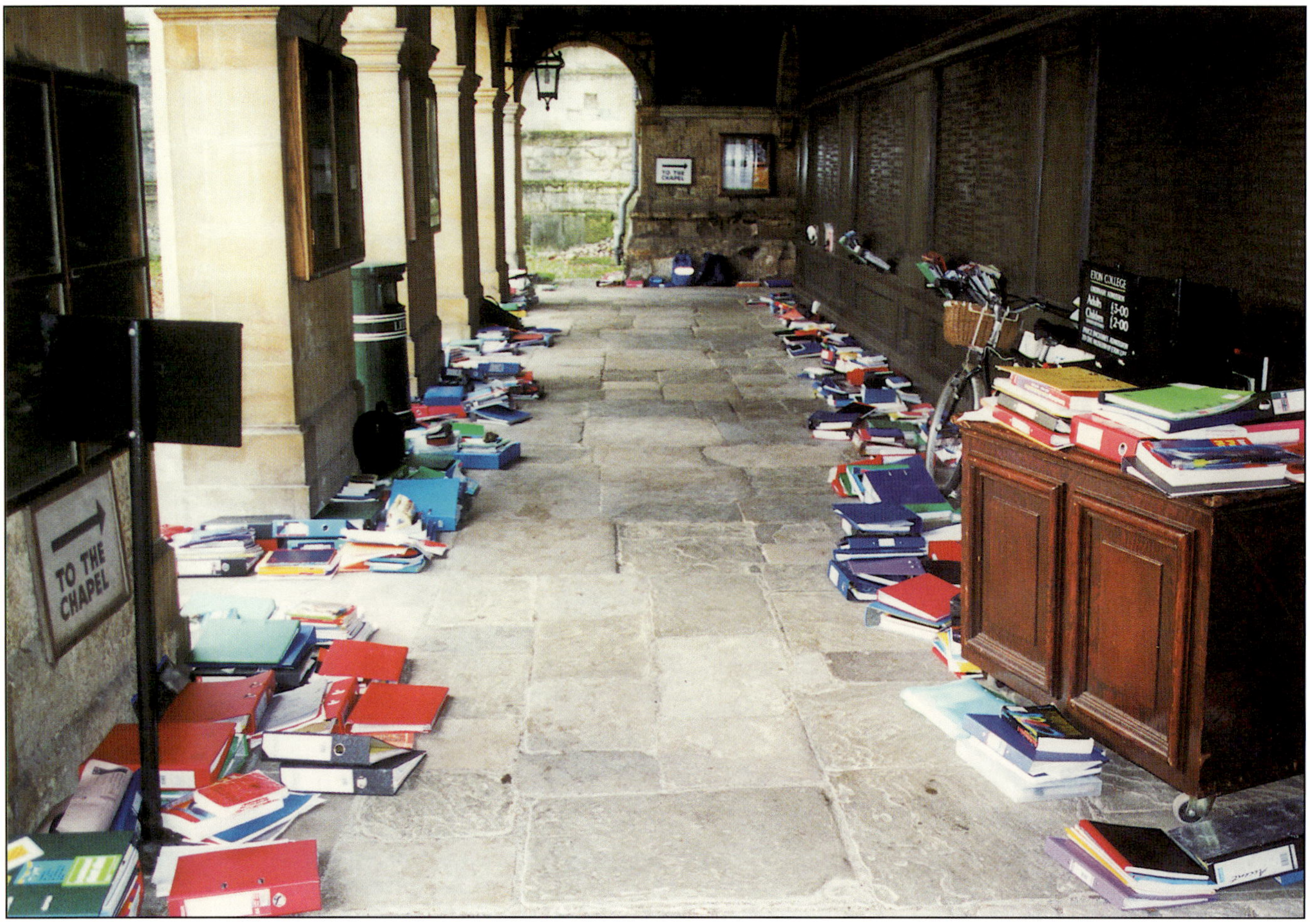

Books and files outside College Chapel during morning service

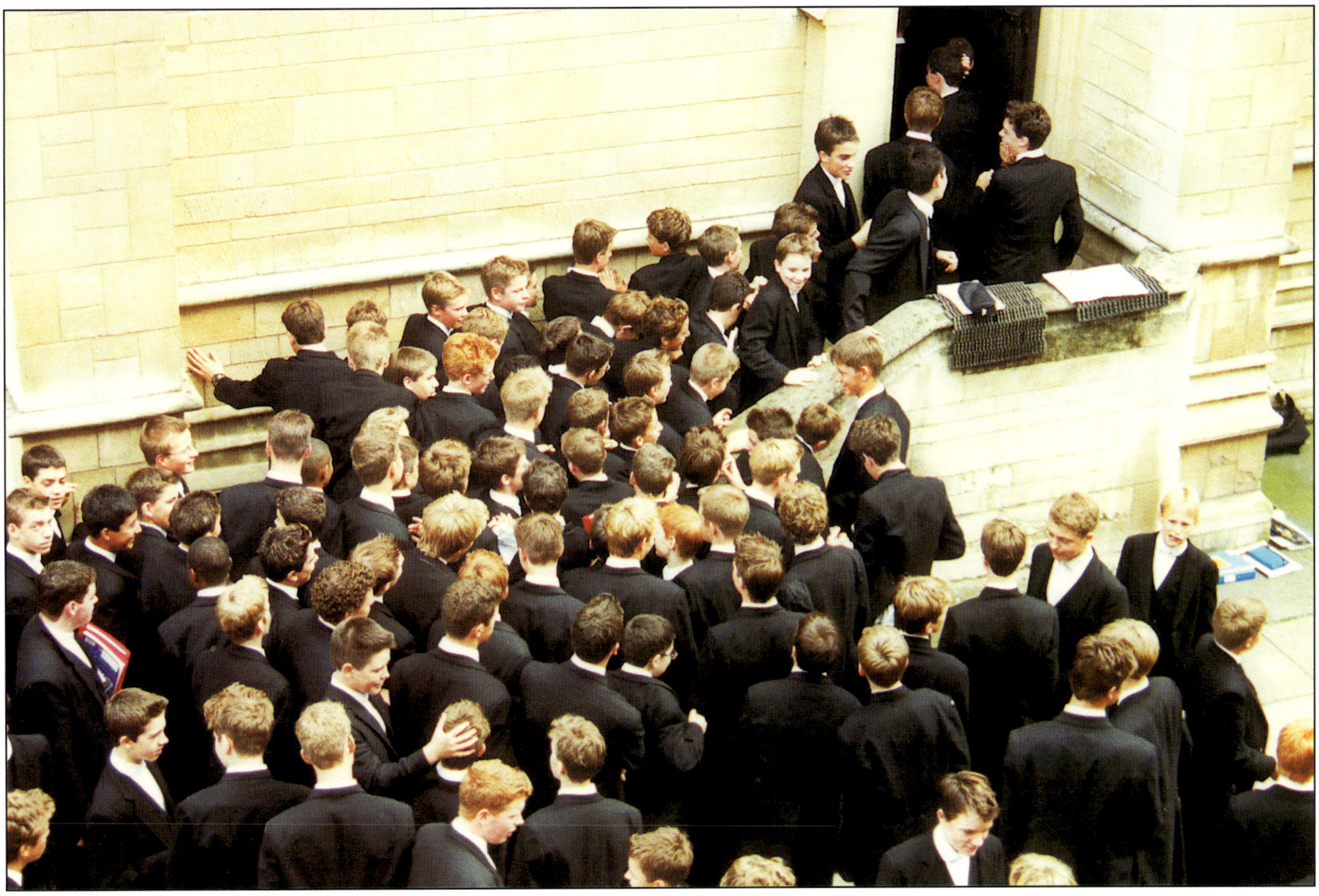

Boys in E and F Blocks go to Lower Chapel

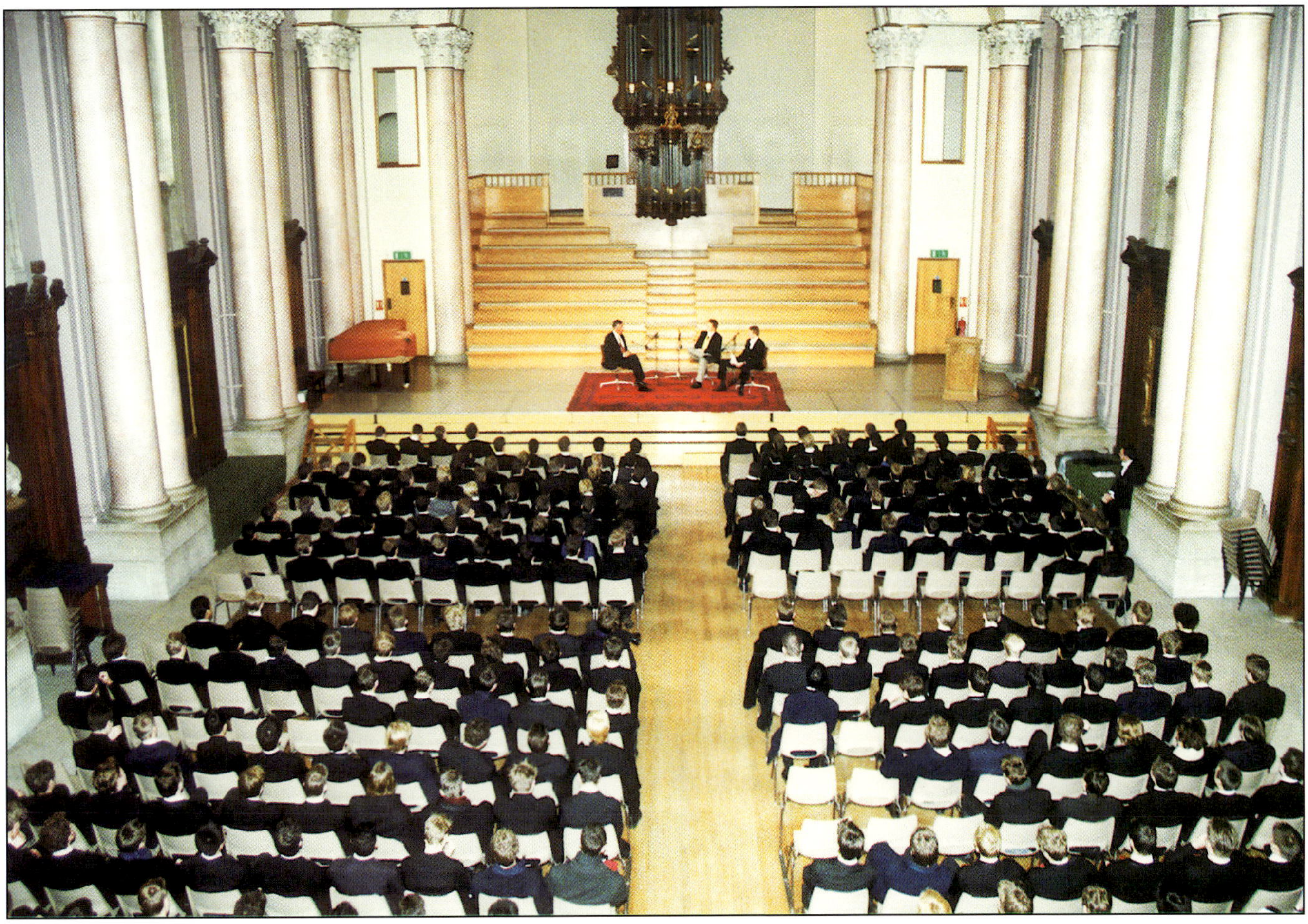

Assembly: the Provost being interviewed

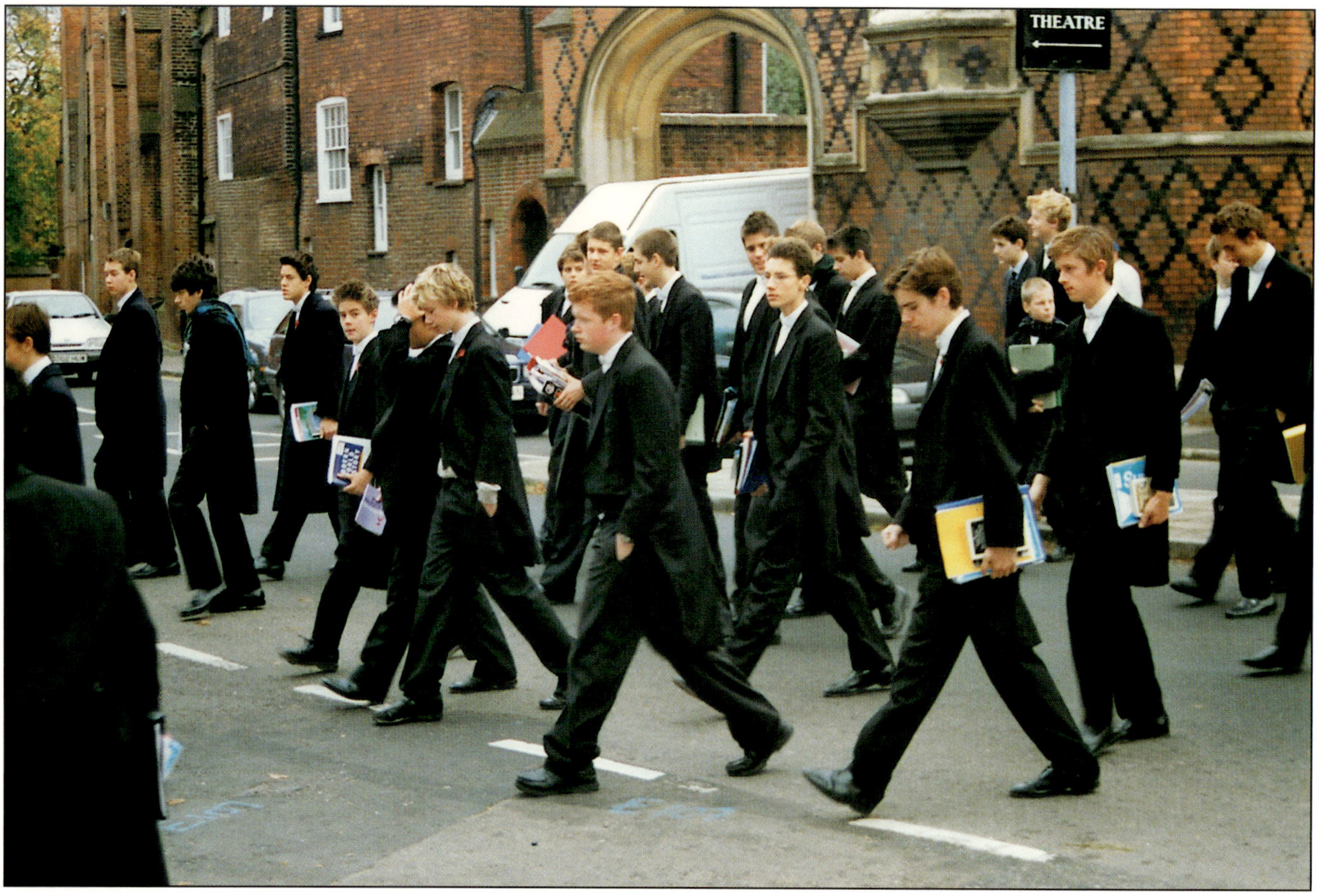

Even the traffic gives way after Chapel

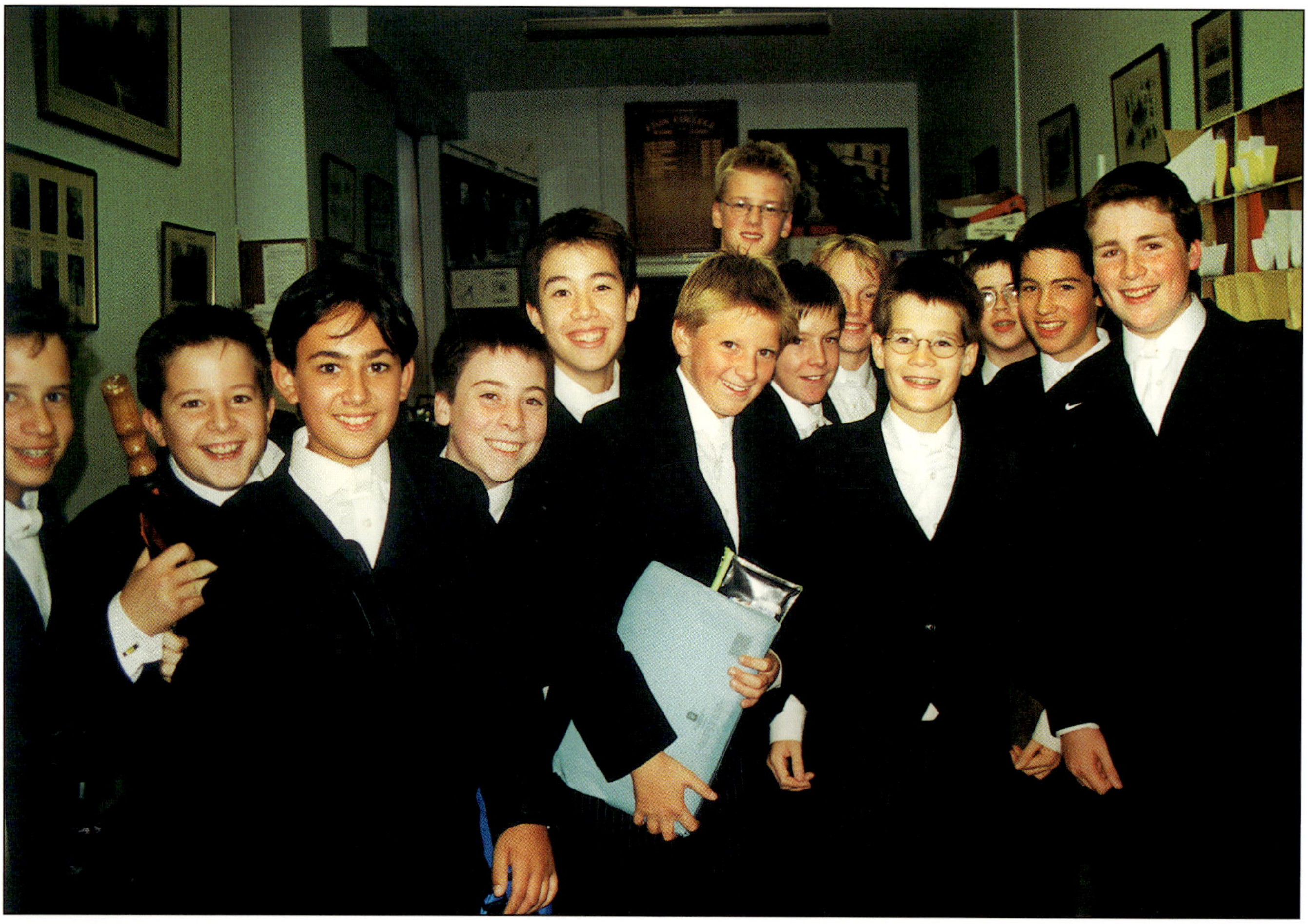

"A run!" If after 15 minutes a Master has not arrived, the boys may 'run' to School Office, report the fact and enjoy a free lesson. Triumph!

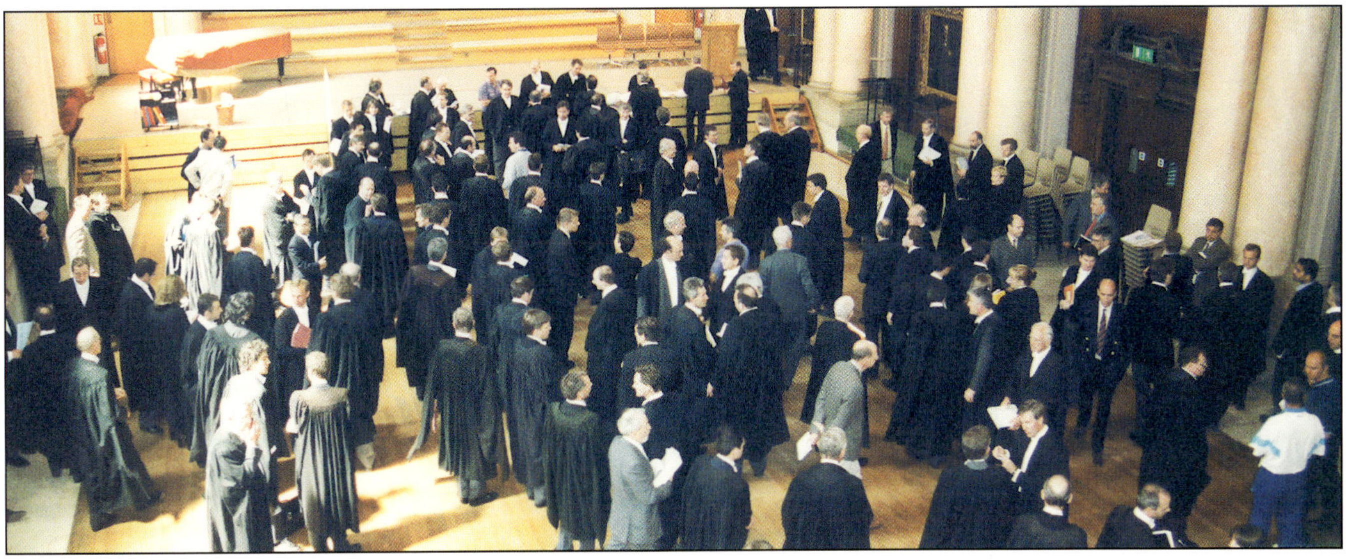

Masters assemble every day in the mid-morning break for 'Chambers', when urgent and less urgent matters can be discussed and announcements made

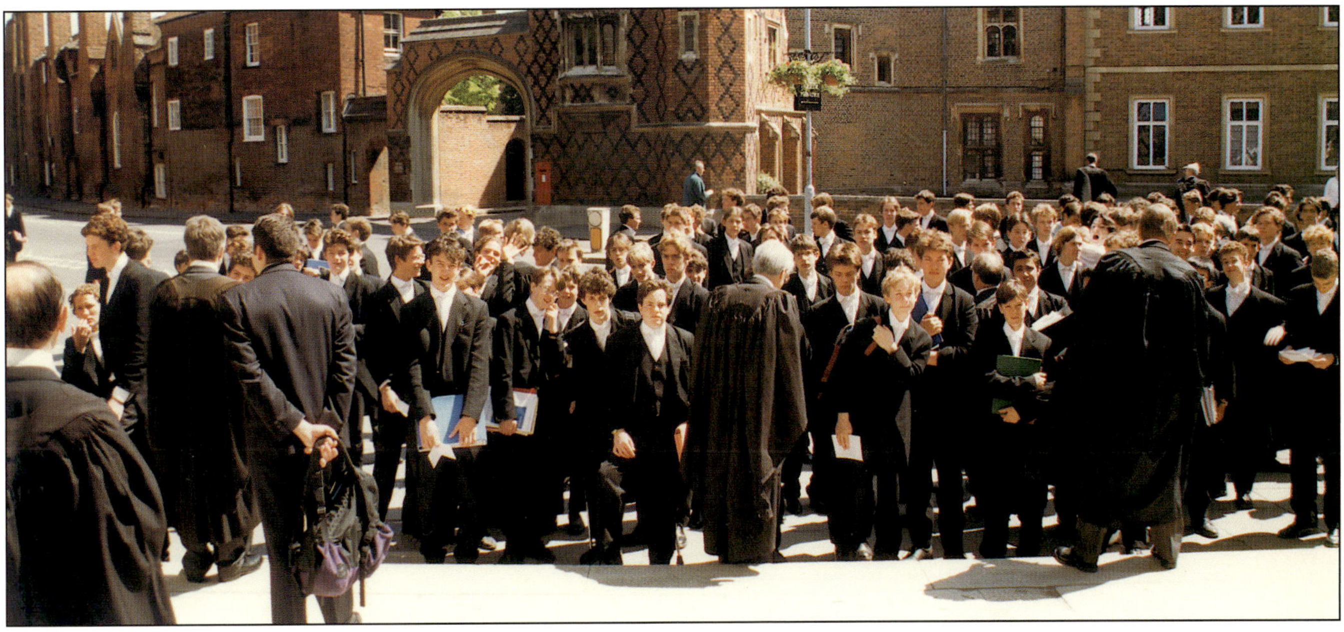

'Chambers' scene boys waiting outside School Hall to consult Masters

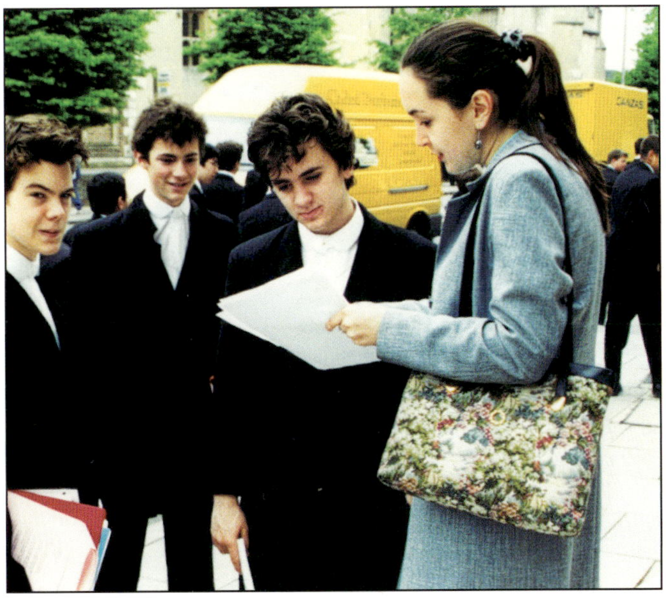

Boys with the Russian assistant

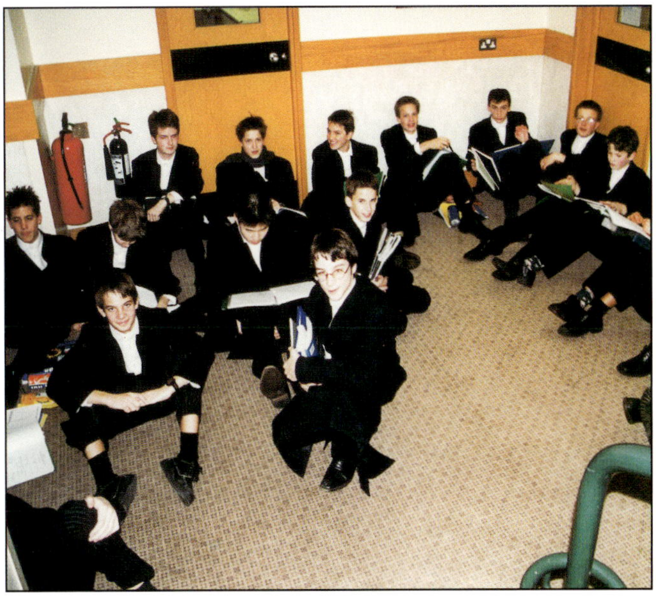

Waiting patiently

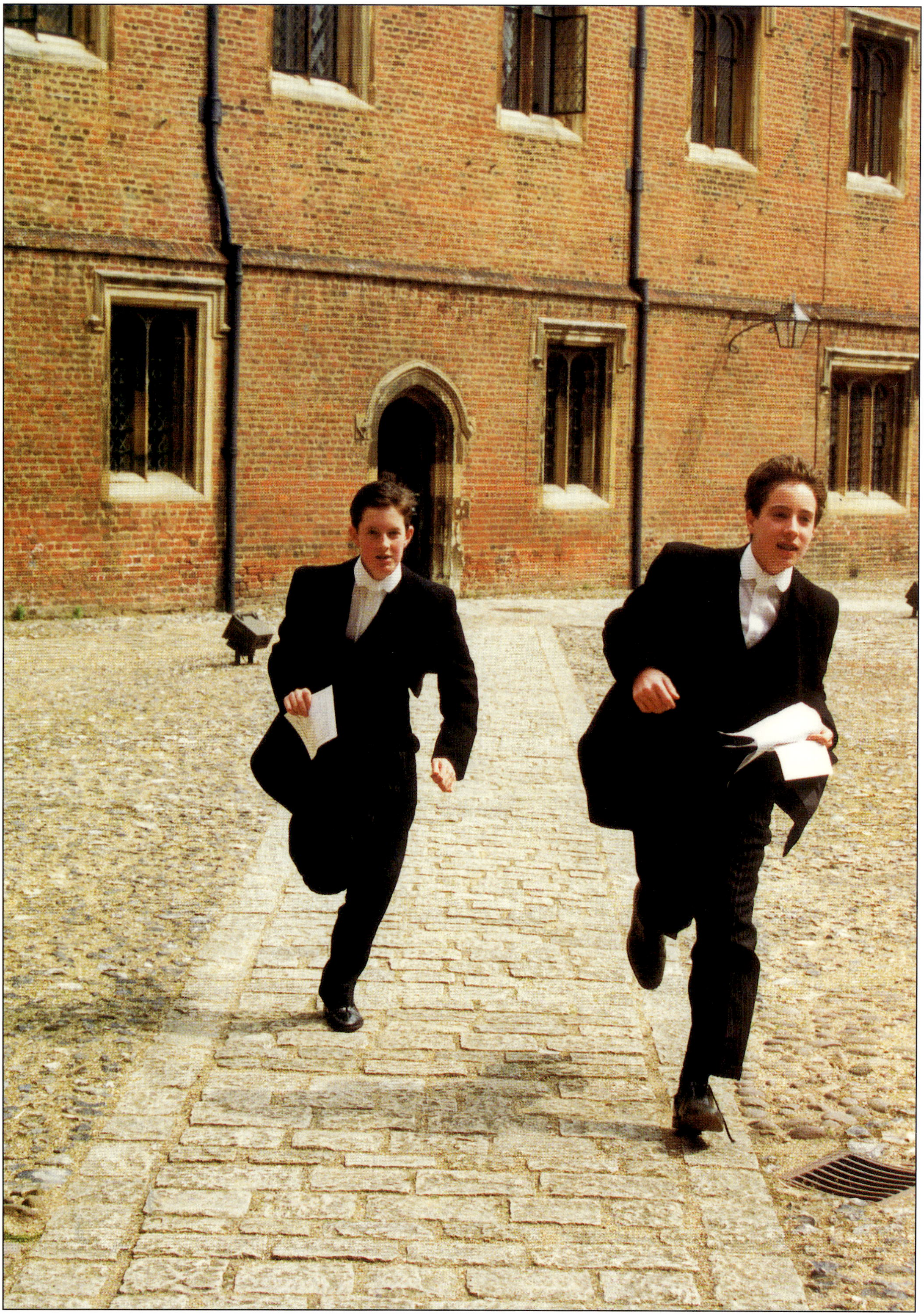

During Chambers there is often urgent business to attend to

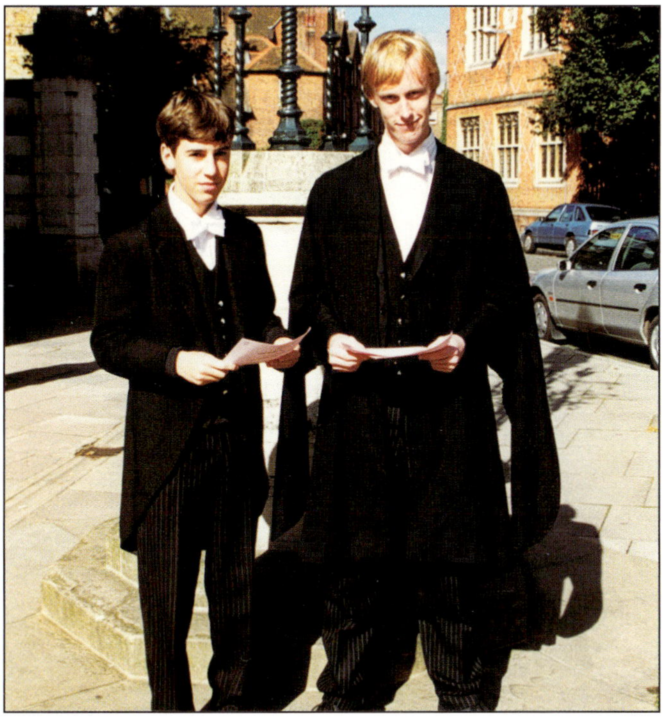

For certain infringements of the School Rules, boys are required to see the Head Master or Lower Master in the Bill. The Head Master's messengers are members of VIth. Form Select, and they summon offenders during the lesson after Chambers

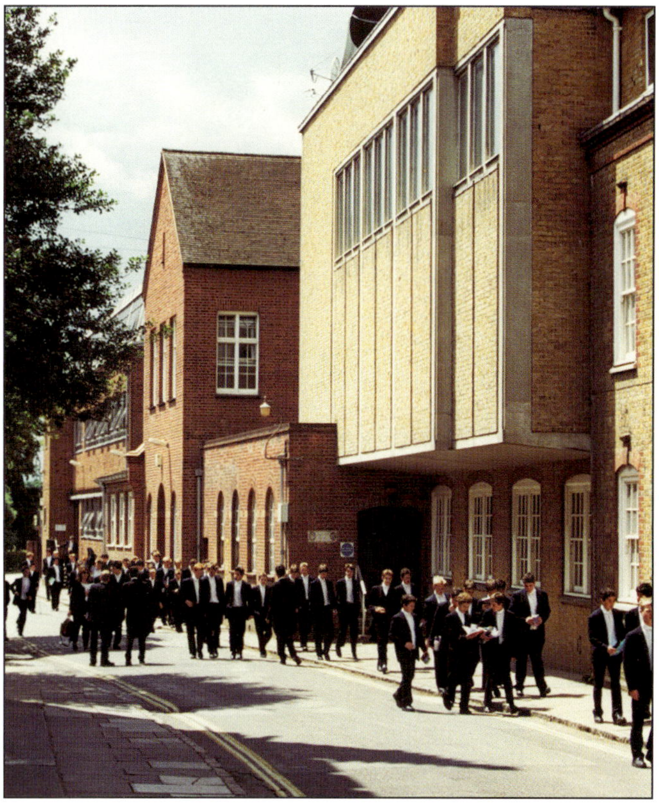

Shortly after one o'clock lessons end, and boys go to lunch

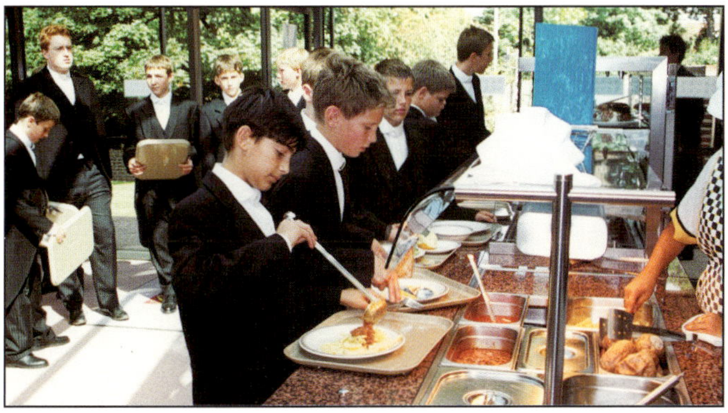

Lunch in the new servery area in Bekynton

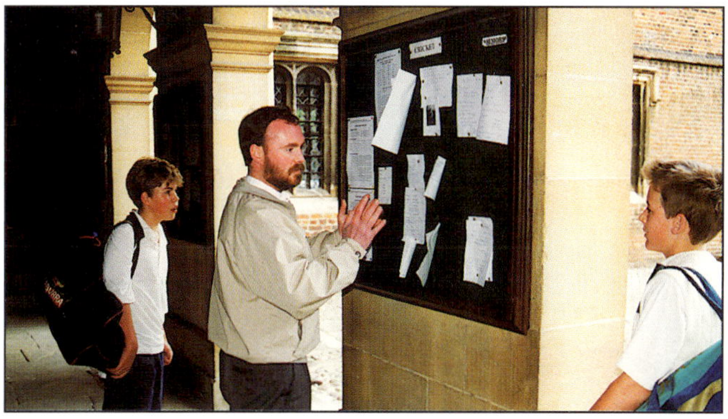

The games players consult the notice-boards

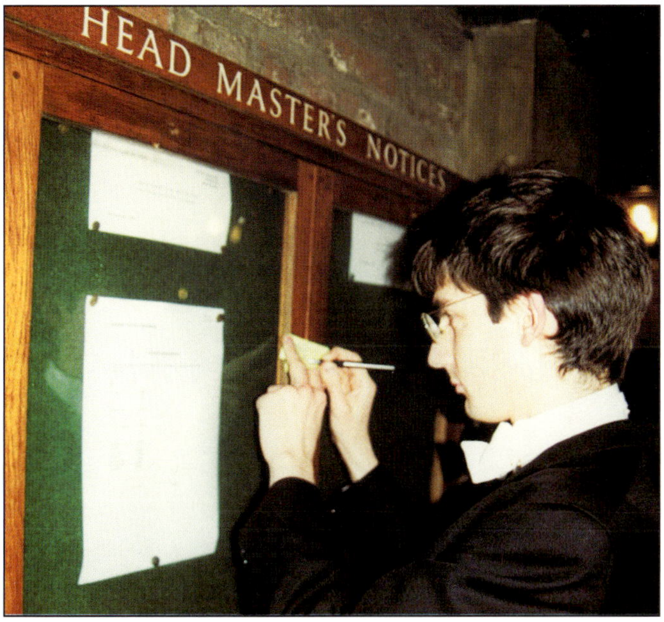

Major announcements appear on the Head Master's notice-board

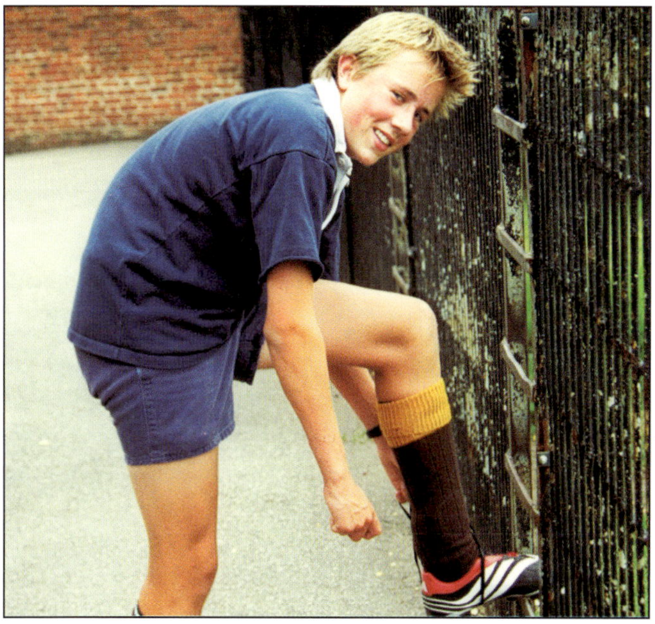

Then off to the games fields

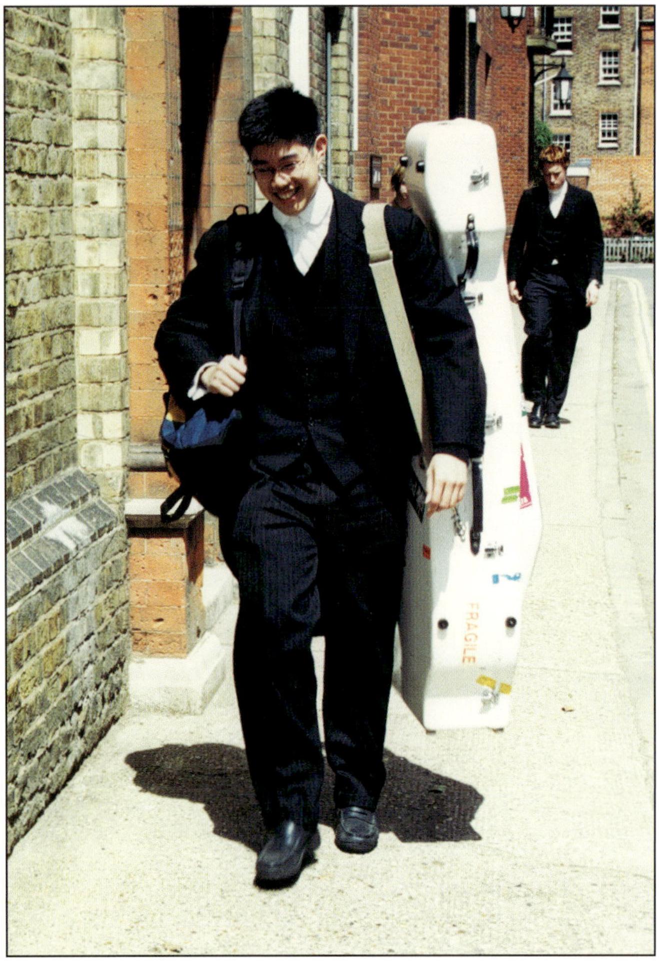

The musicians find time for practice

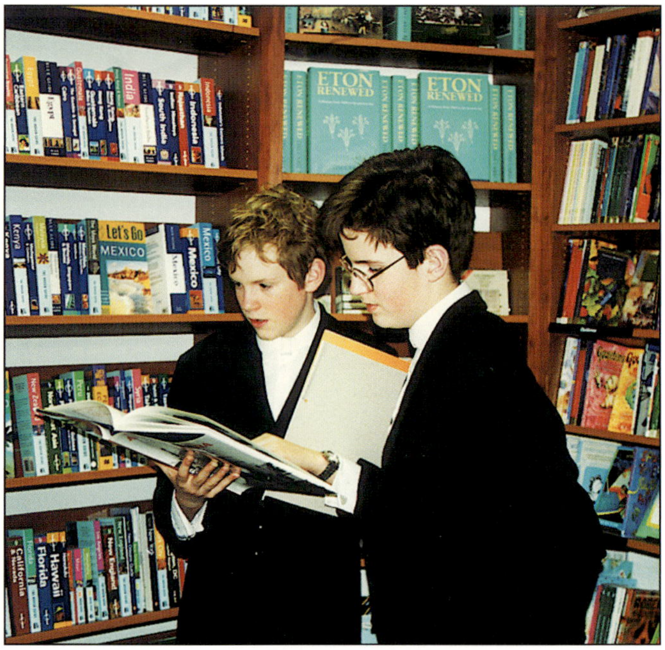

The bookshop

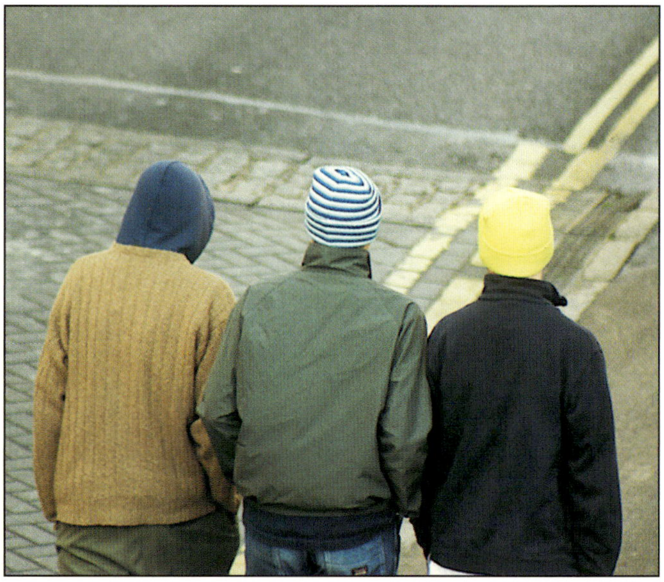

After changing out of School uniform, some boys head for Windsor

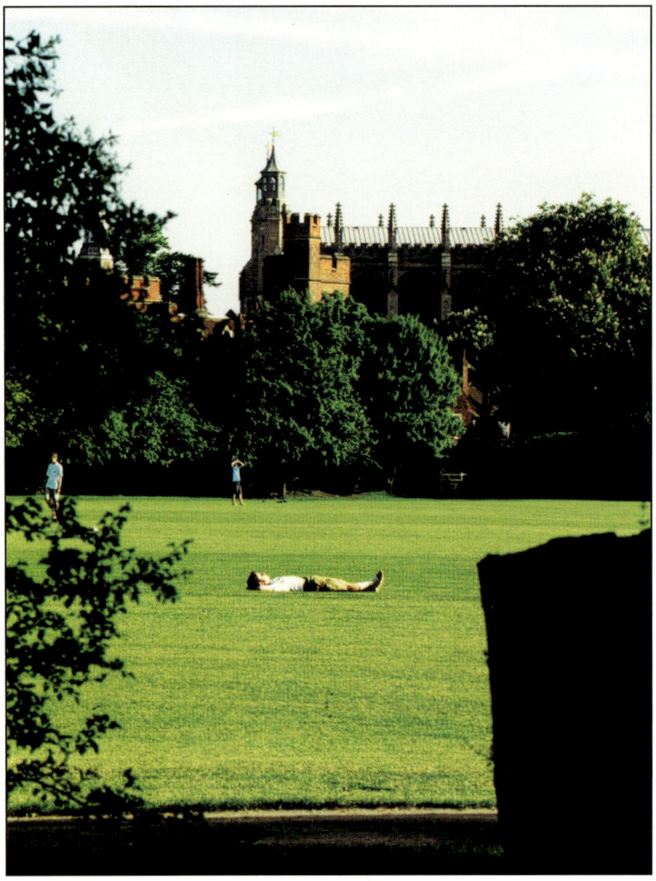

Others relax

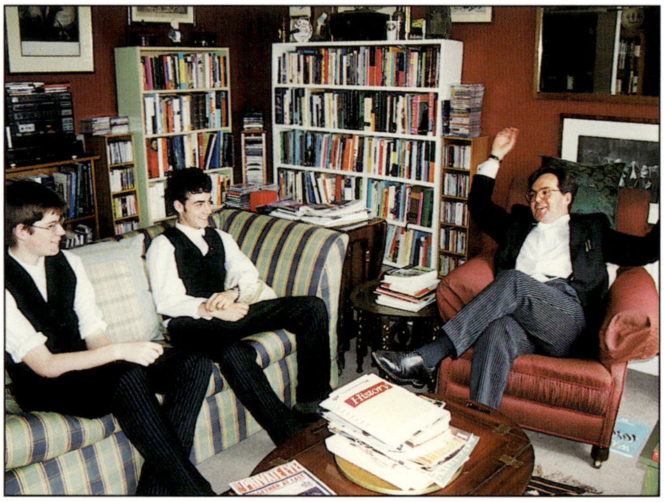

A tutorial in progress

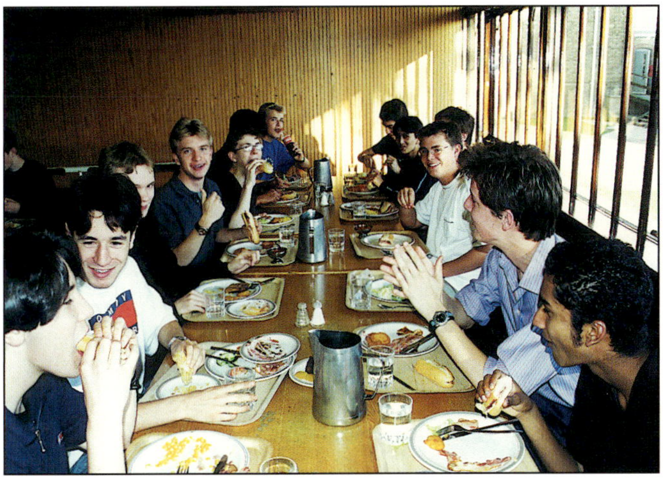

Supper is an informal meal

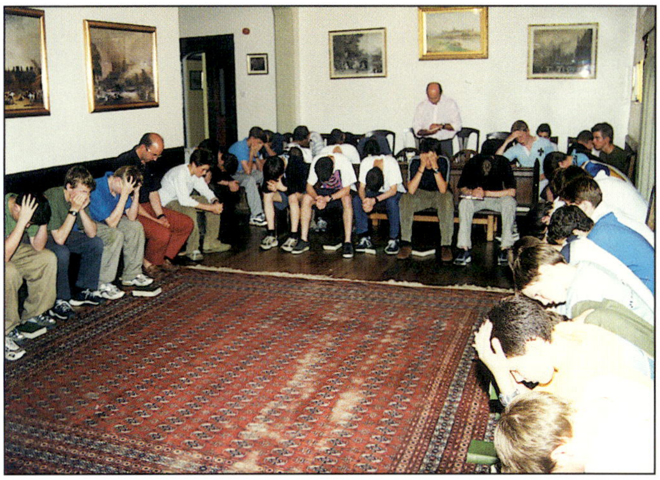

And after supper boys gather for House Prayers

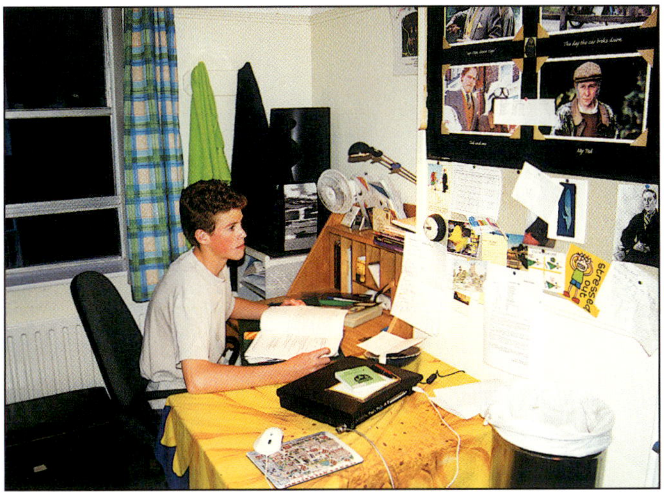

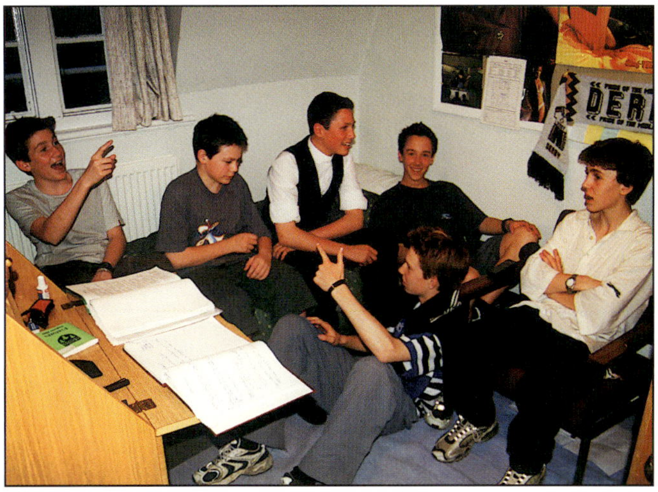

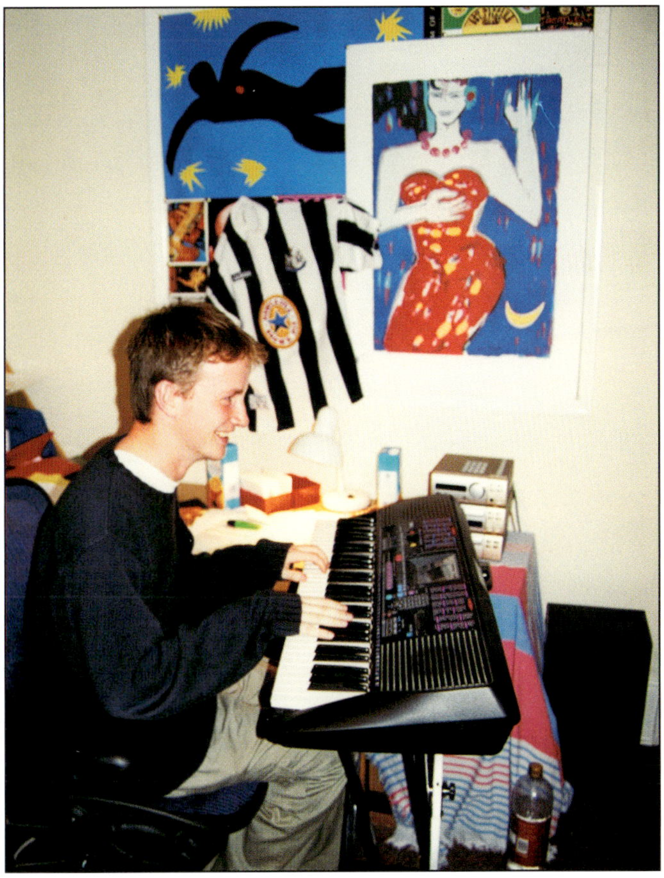

After Prayers boys usually work or they relax,

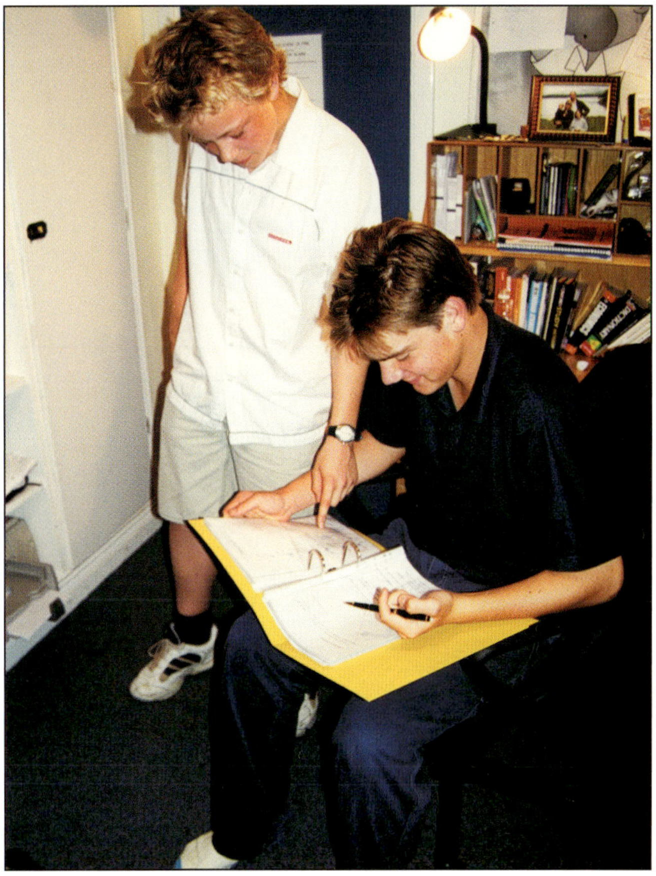

. . . or they socialize, go out to a Society, a concert or a play

Schoolrooms and Schoolroom Activity

For an independent school to survive, its academic record must be good. A high placing in the league tables, controversial though they may be, is not to be despised. Eton has long been lucky in its teachers, class sizes, good facilities and sound planning. All contribute to the pursuit of excellence. Methods vary, of course, as the photographs aim to show.

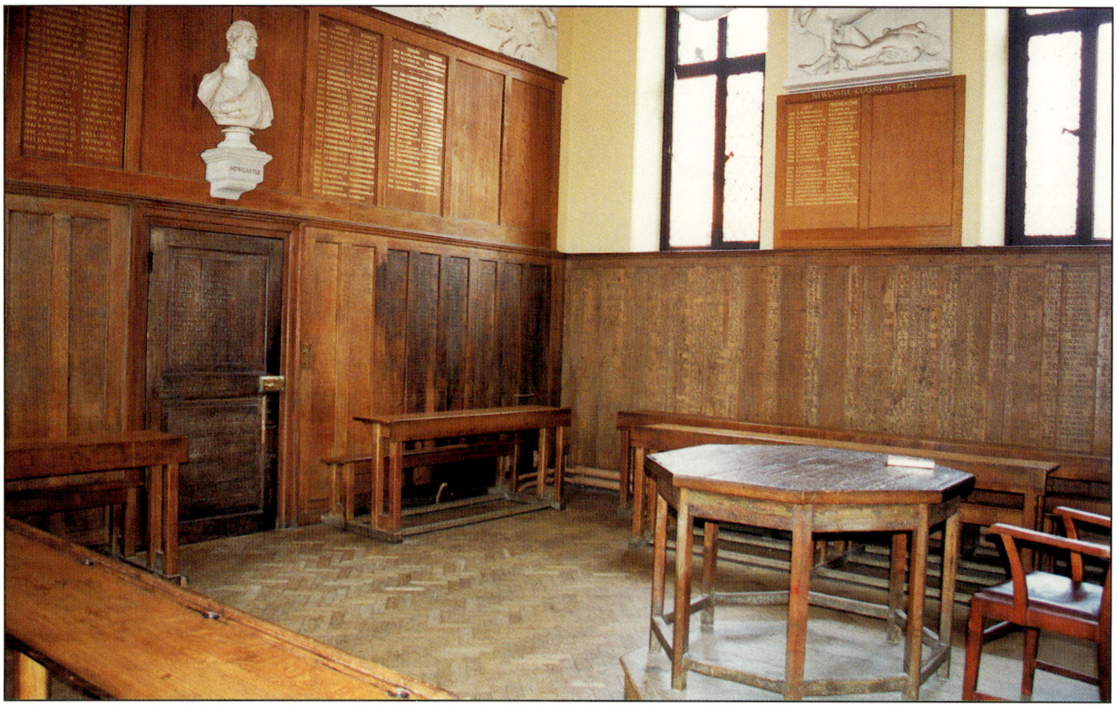

The Head Master's schoolroom. The octagonal table, honours boards, the bust of the 3rd Duke of Newcastle, who endowed the prestigious Newcastle Scholarship in 1829, and the frieze, copied from the Parthenon, give the room a character of its own

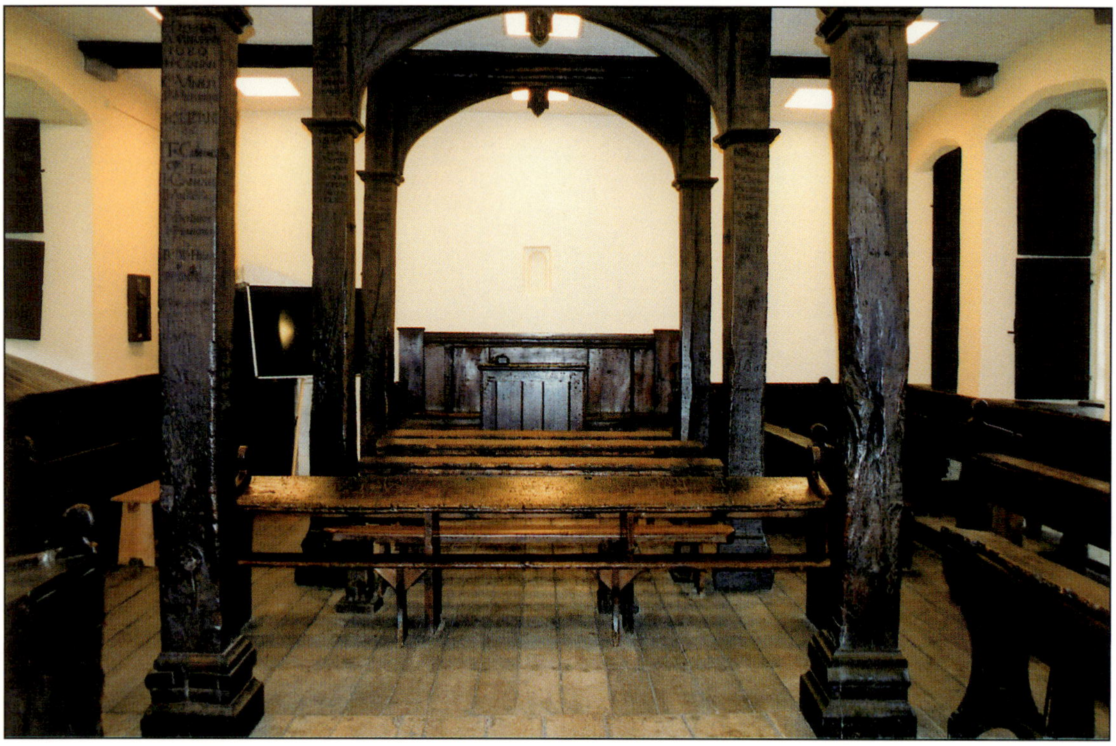

Lower School, possibly the country's oldest schoolroom in continuous use

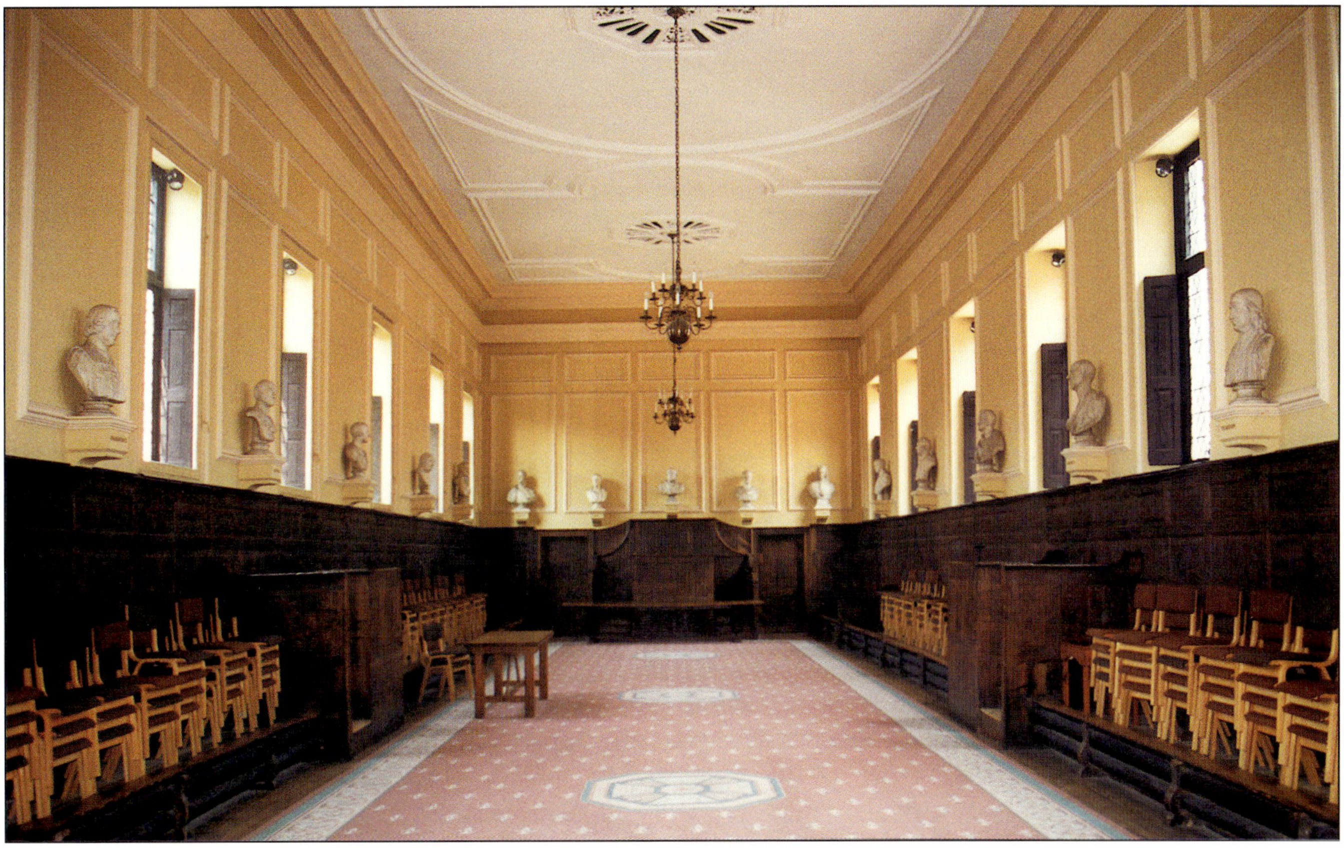

Upper School, formerly a schoolroom

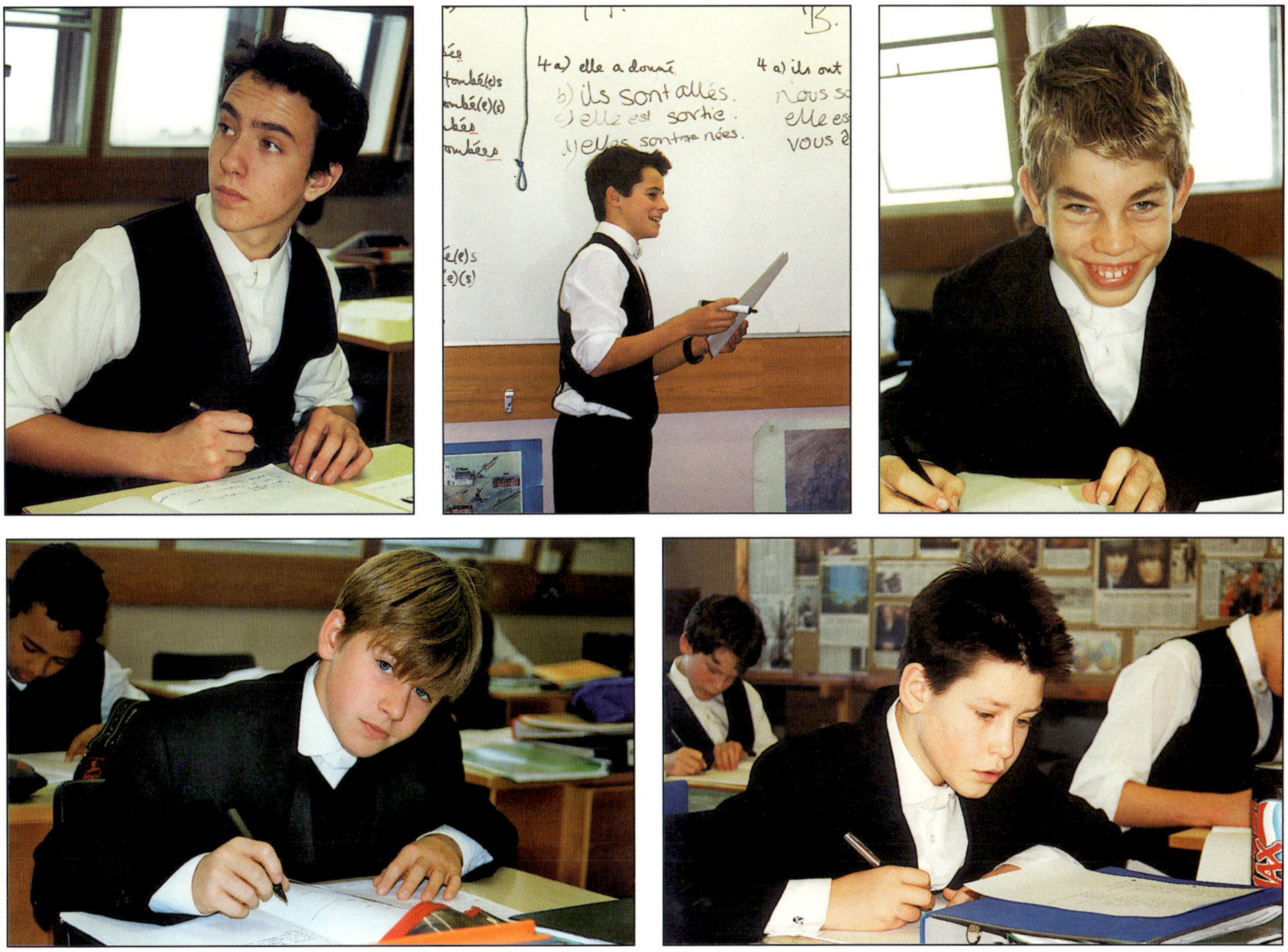

Boys at work

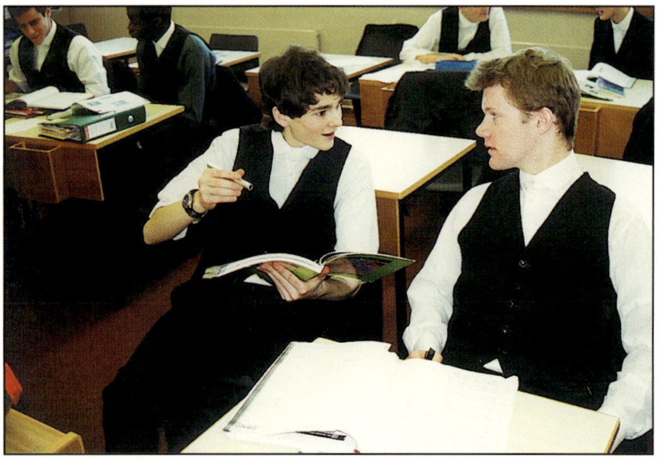

Pair-work in German

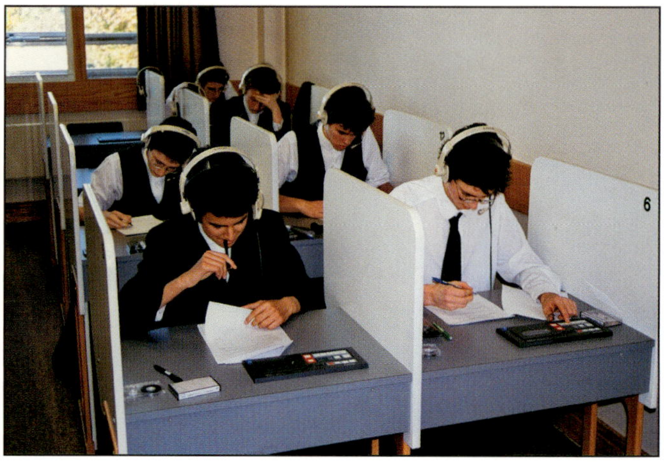

Language Laboratory

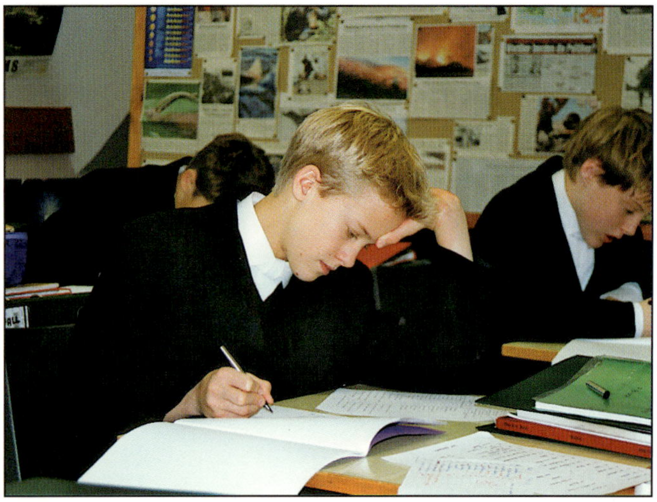

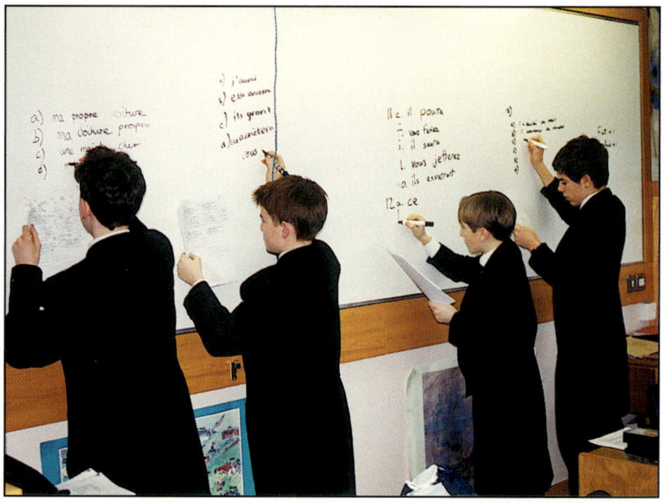

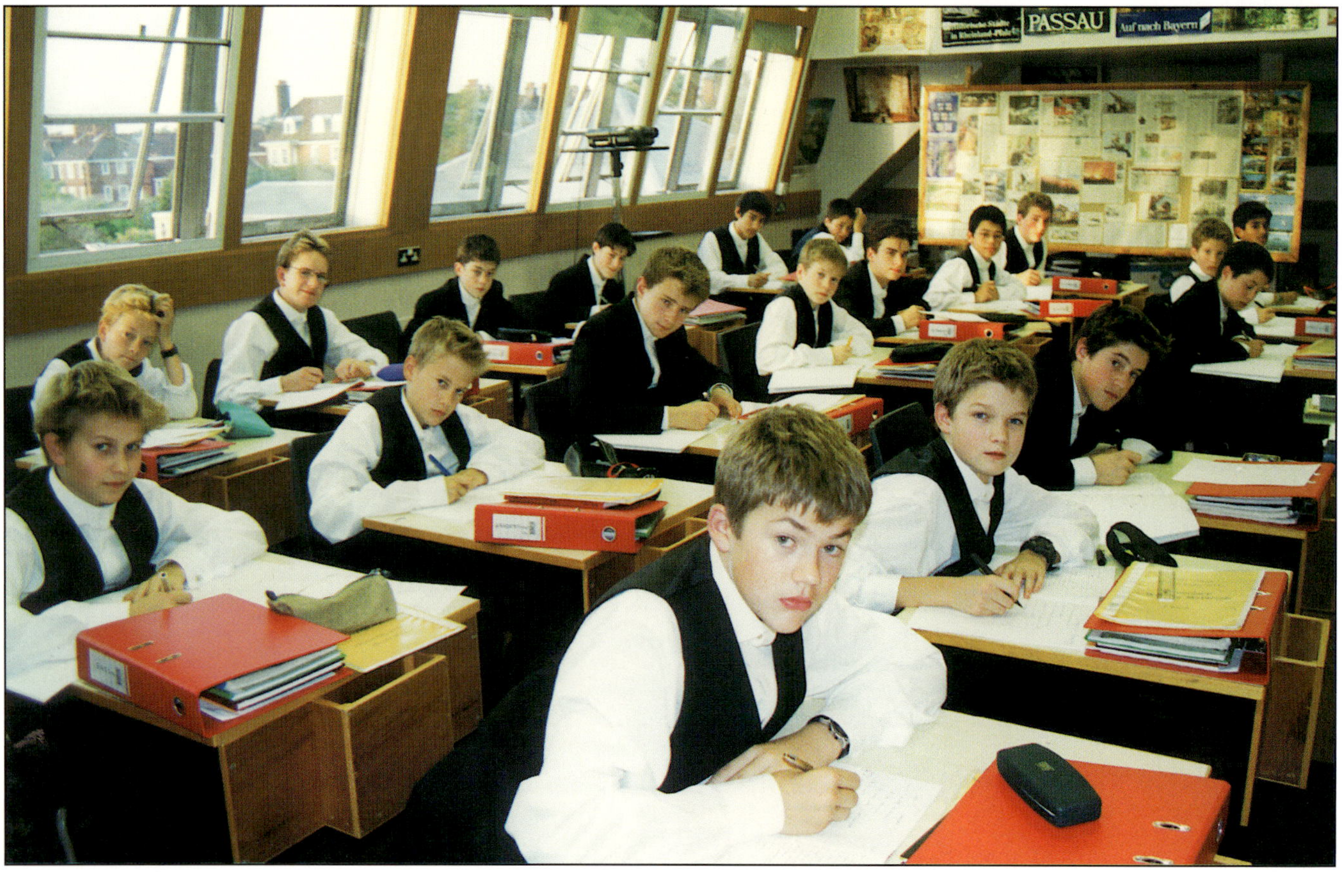

Boys at work

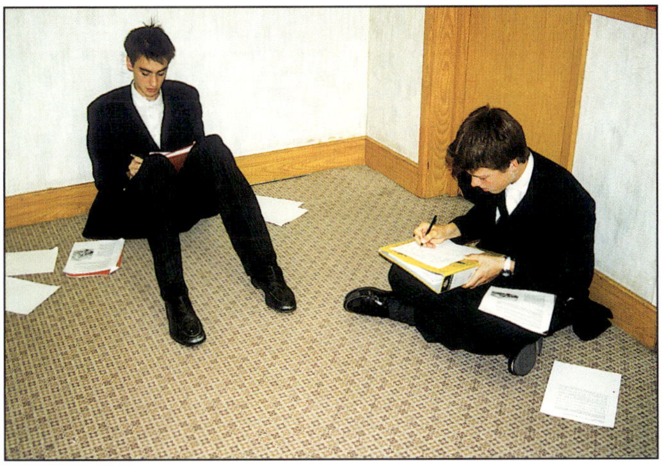

Last-minute e.w.

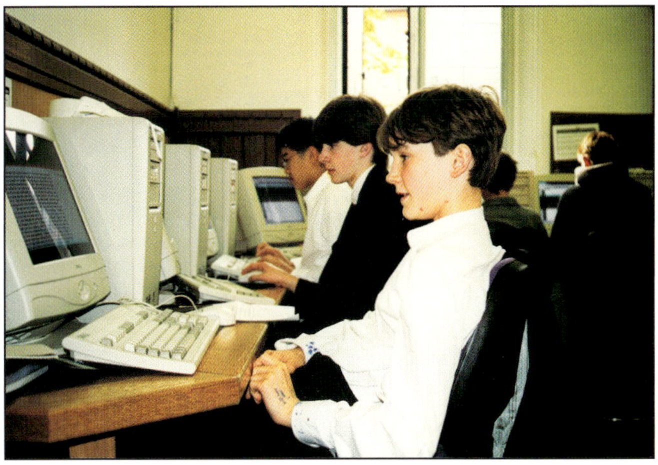

Computer Room

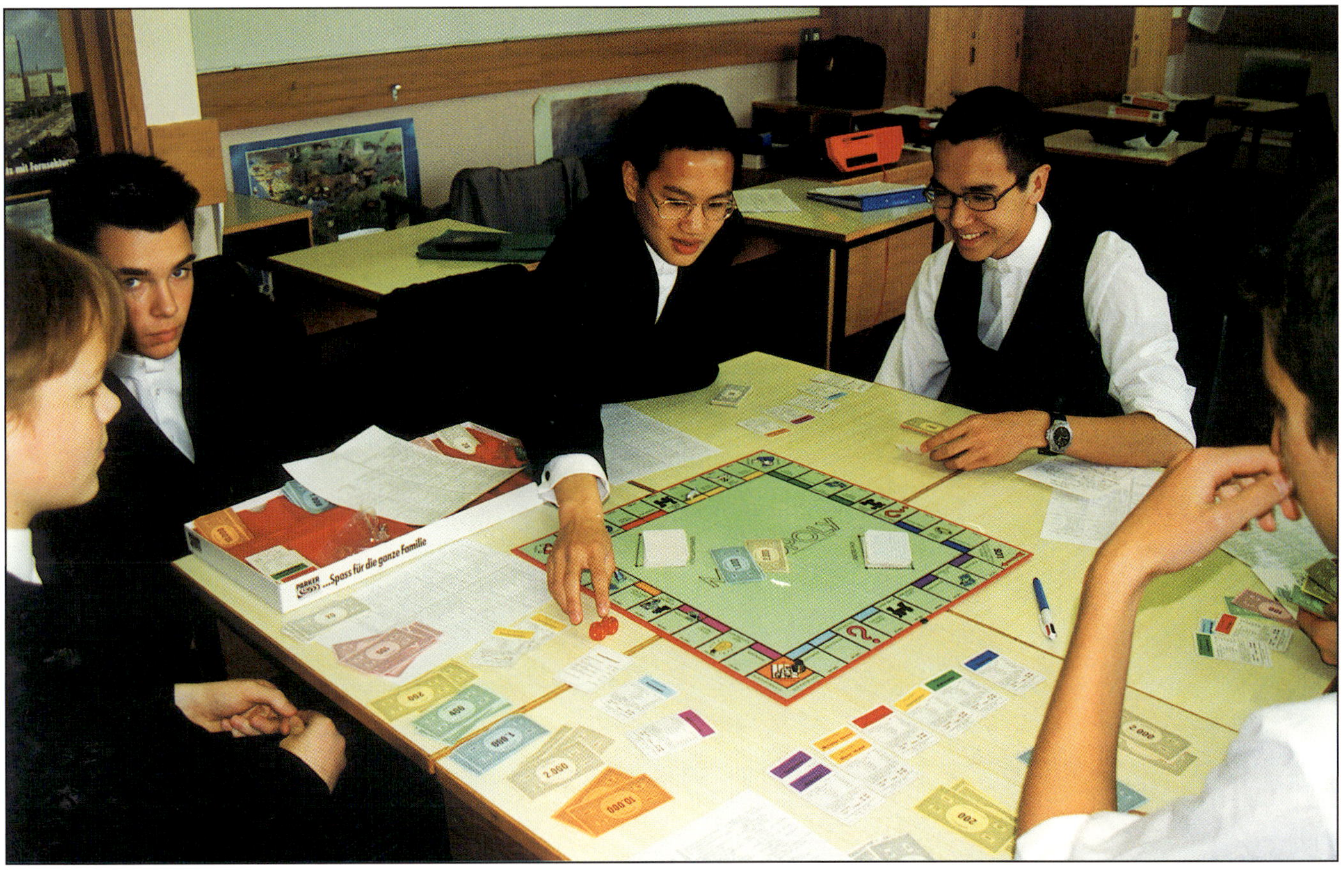

Monopoly in German

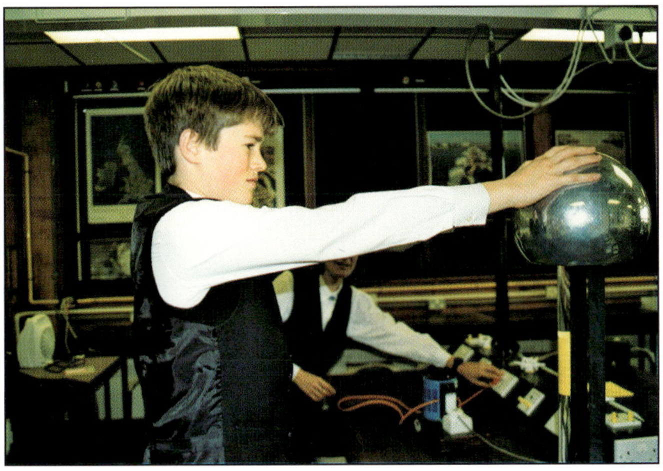

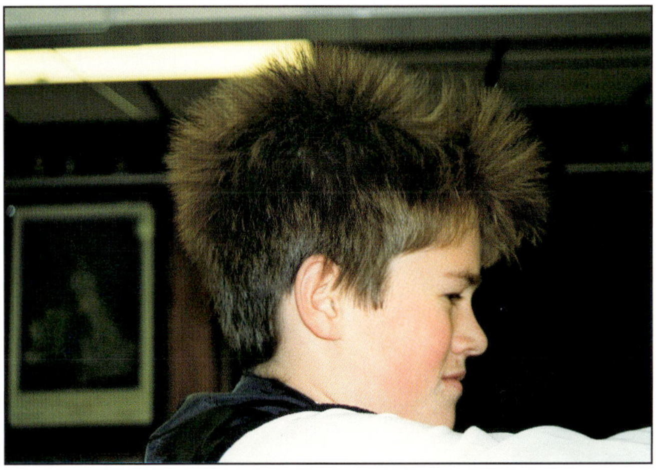

Hair-raising Physics experiment with the van den Graaf generator

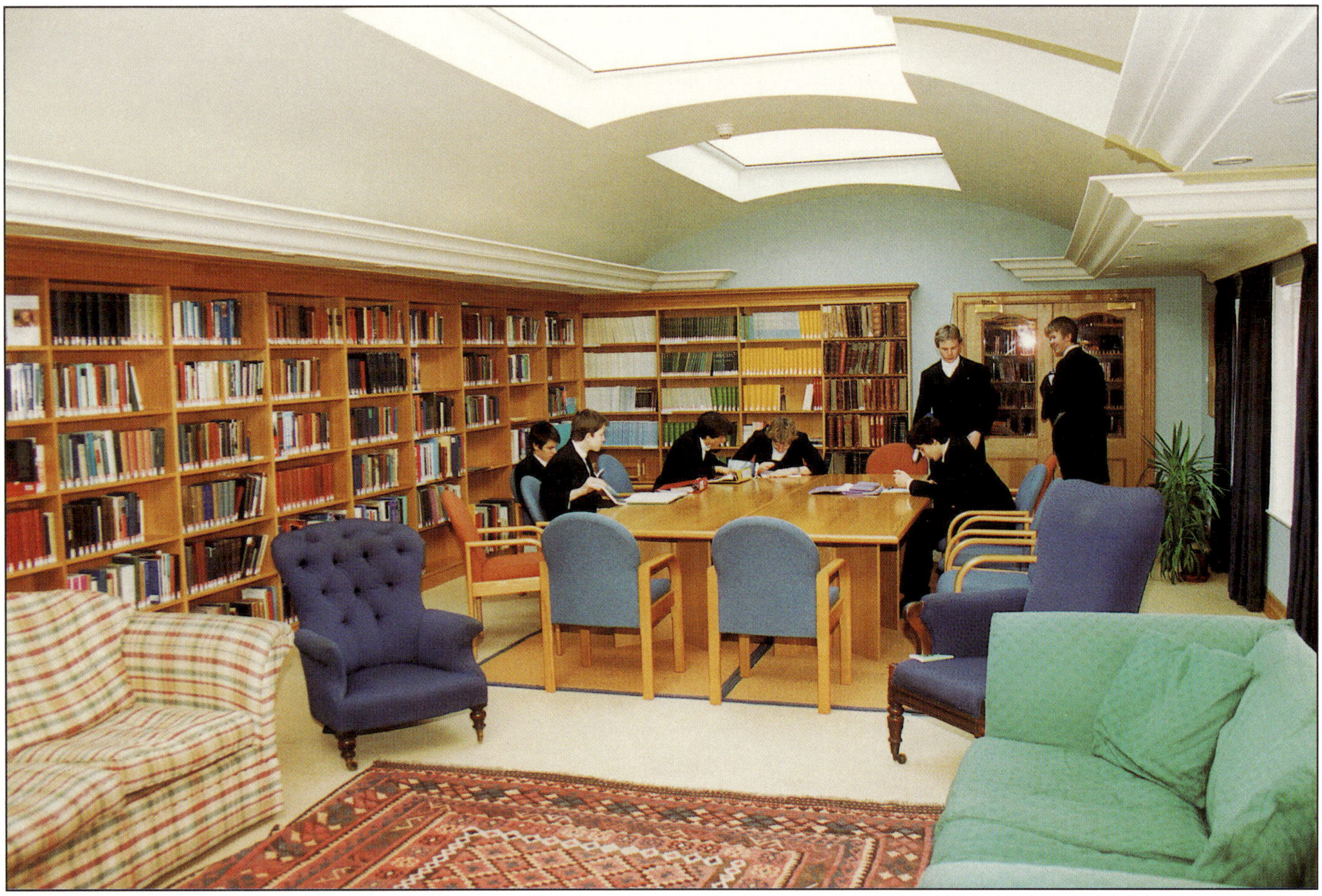

The new Marten Library

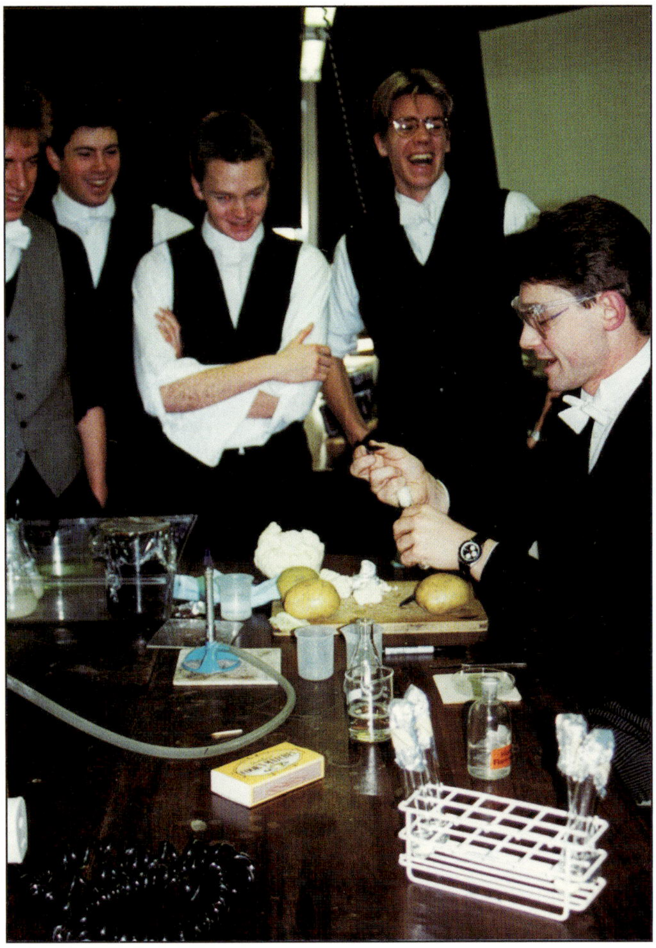

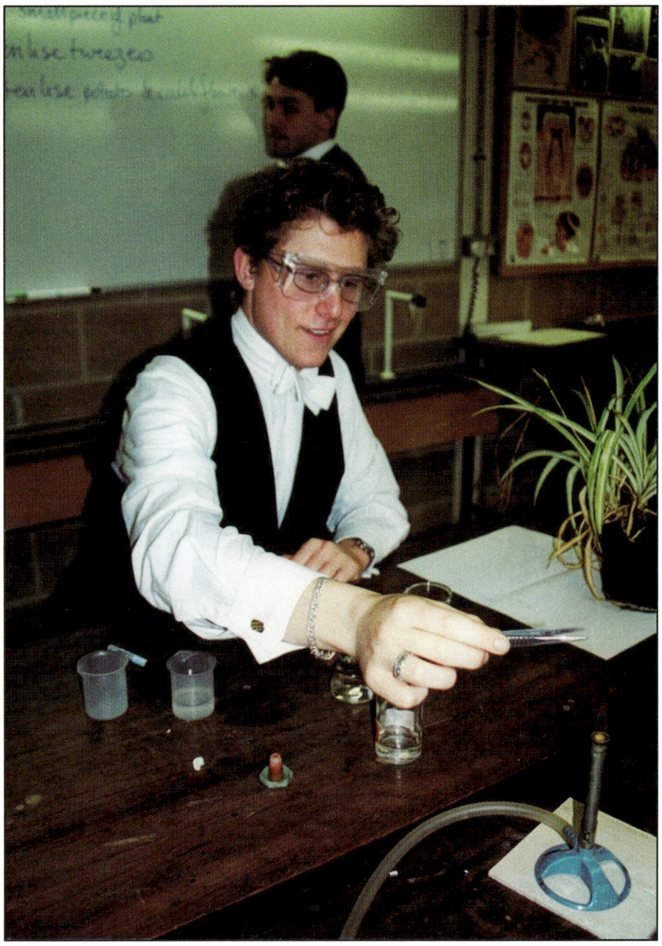

Biology practical

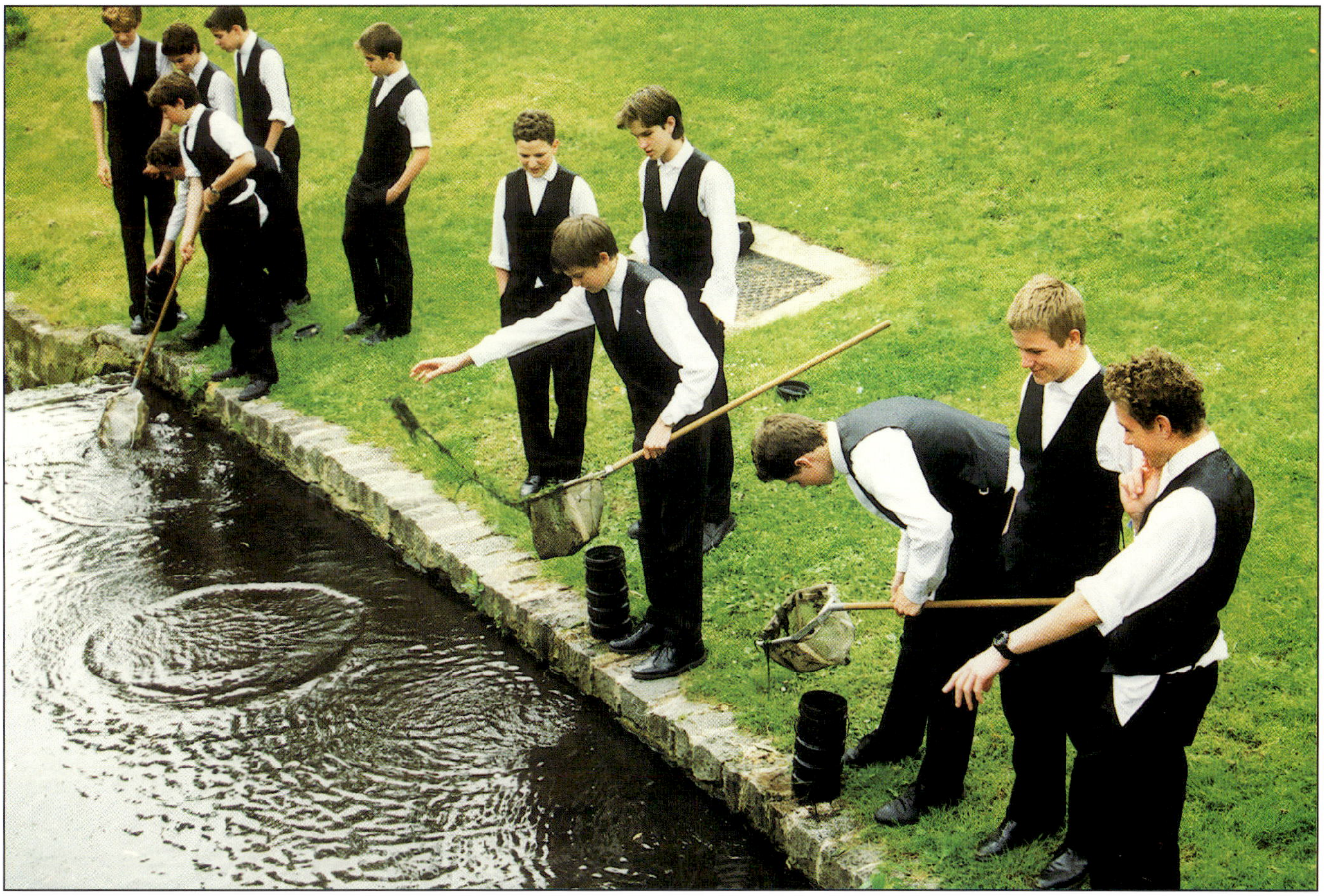

Hunting the algae

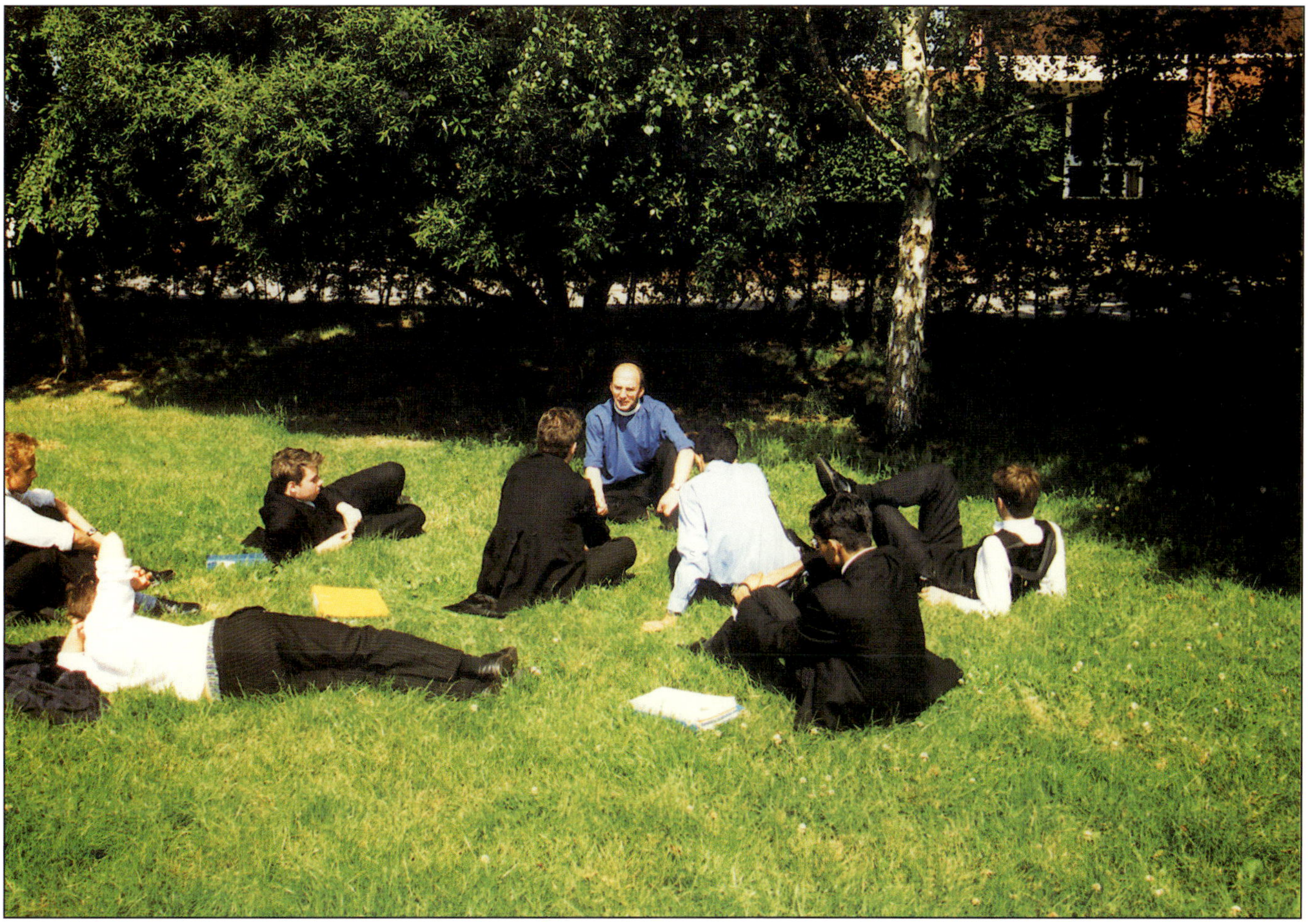

Theology 'en plein air'

Music

Eton enjoys a long musical tradition. The first purpose-built Music Schools were constructed within a former rackets court in 1903. They were extended substantially in 1966 to include more practice rooms and a concert hall that seated 220. The new Music Schools were opened in 1998 by Lord Armstrong of Ilminster. Joined by a covered walkway to the original building and stretching into the former Rackets Court Field, this extension contains a new concert hall (the Parry Hall), recording and computer facilities, teaching and practice rooms for brass and wind players, and a sound-proof rotunda where pop groups can rehearse. In 1903, 150 boys had music tuition, but by the year 2003 this number had risen to over 600 being taught by more than sixty music teachers. The School's many instrumentalists can be heard performing in groups large and small. These include the first and second orchestras and bands, and a number of pop groups. Generous music scholarships attract many promising young musicians to Eton.

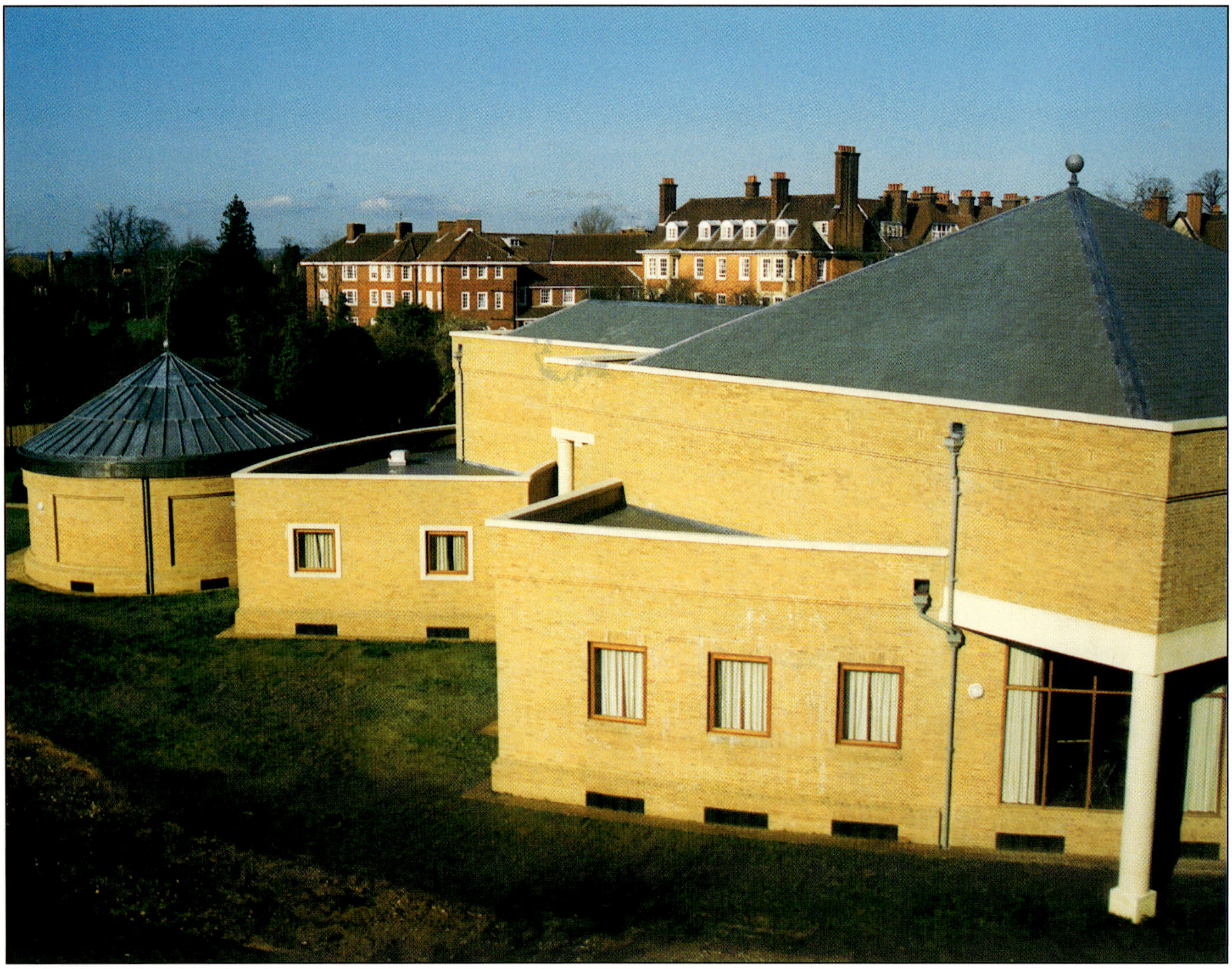

The new Music Schools: Parry Hall (right), the rotunda (left)

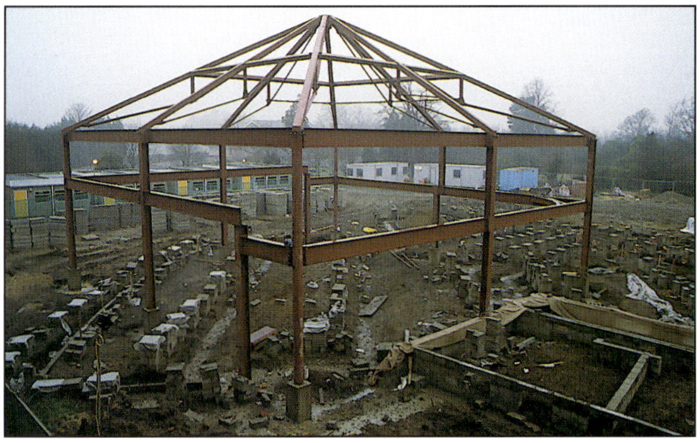

The new Music Schools under construction

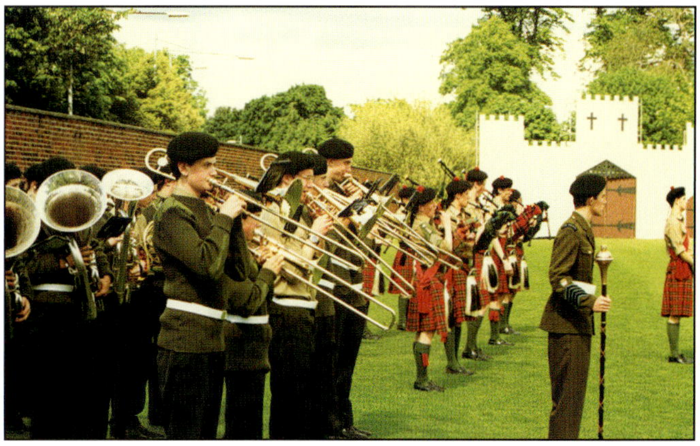

The corps band

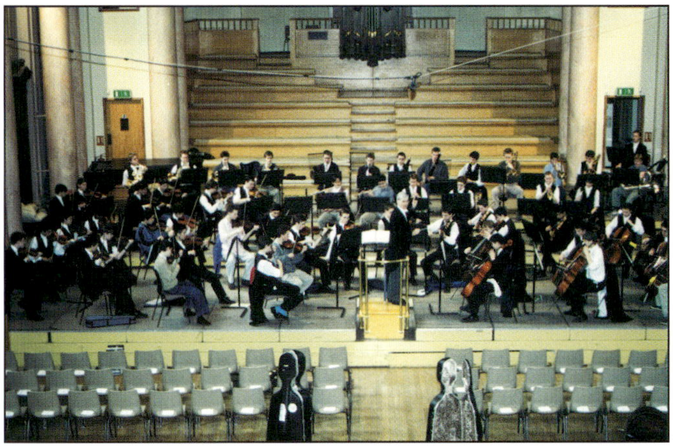

The School Orchestra

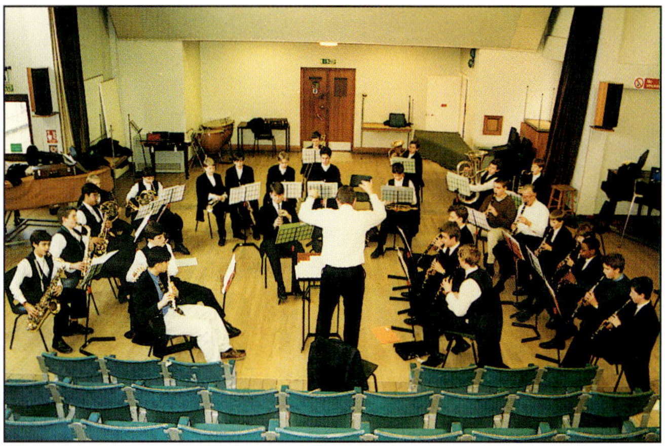

The 2nd Band

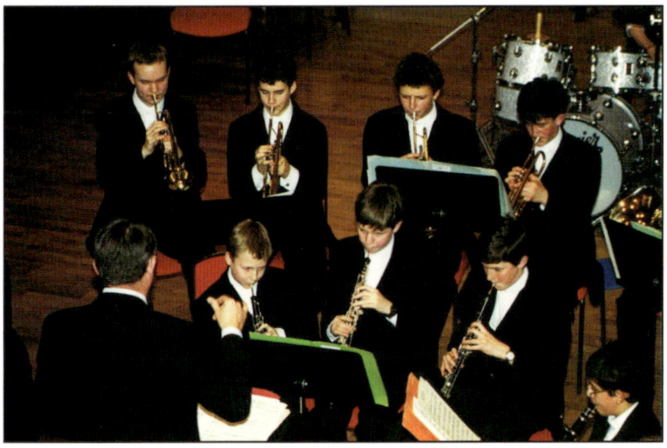

Wind and brass

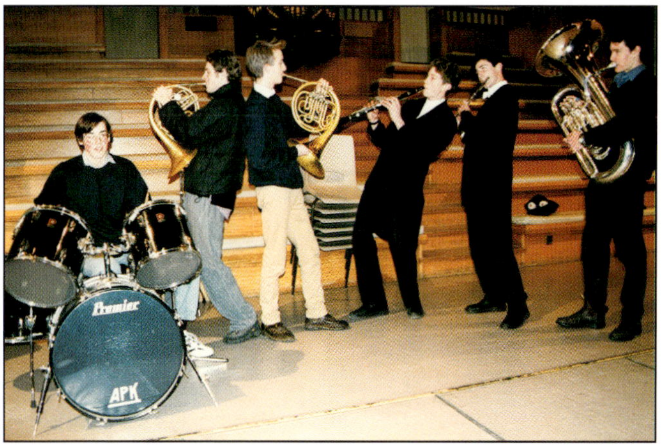

An independent band

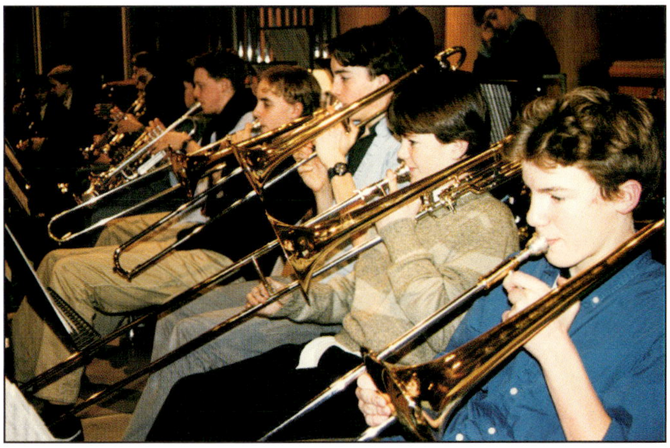

The trombone section

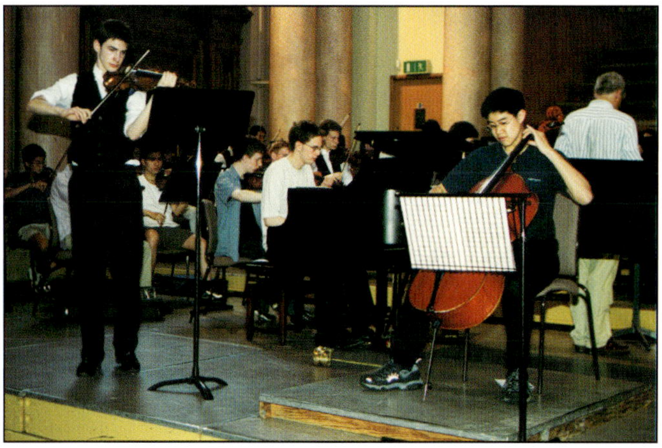

Rehearsal for the Beethoven Triple Concerto

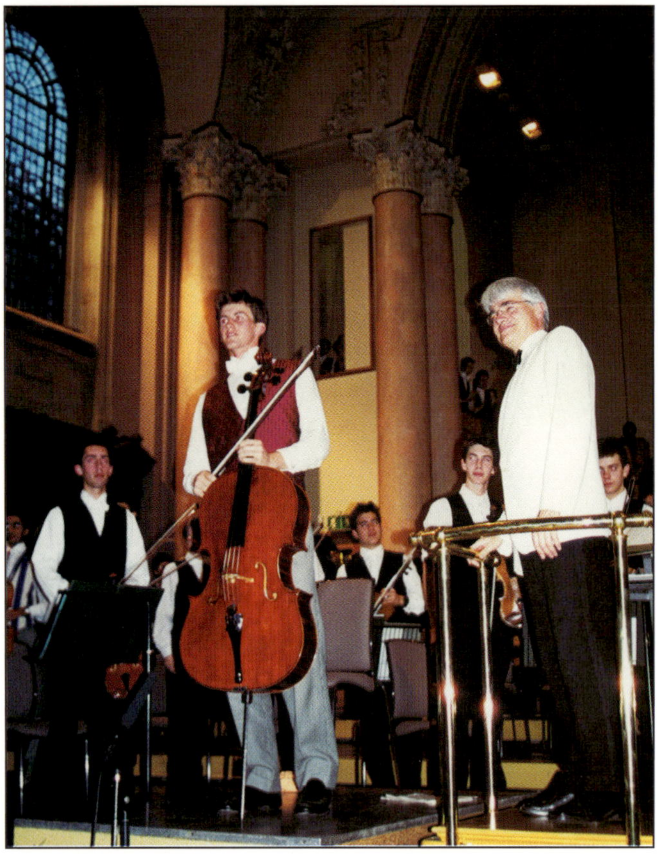

Applause for 'cello soloist, conductor and orchestra

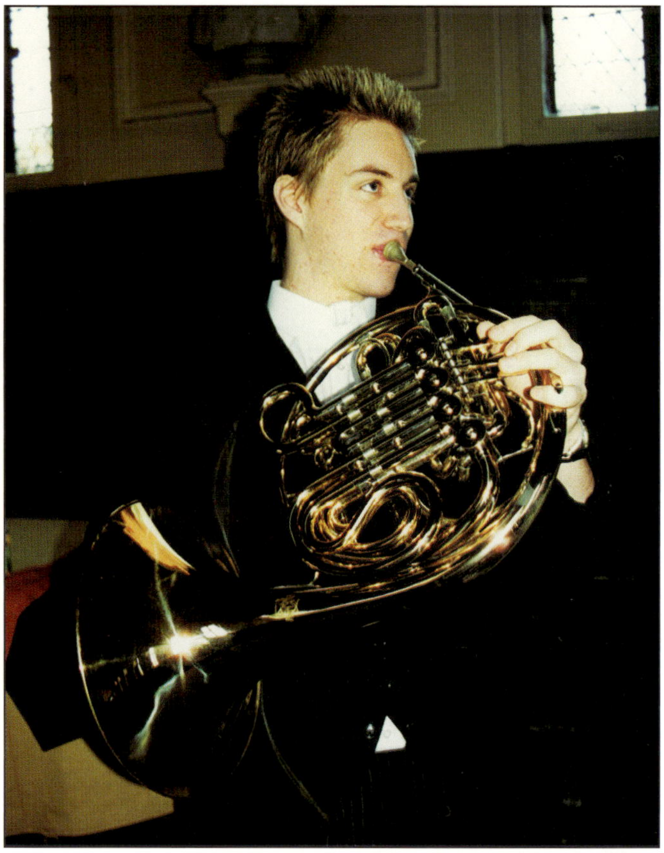

French horn

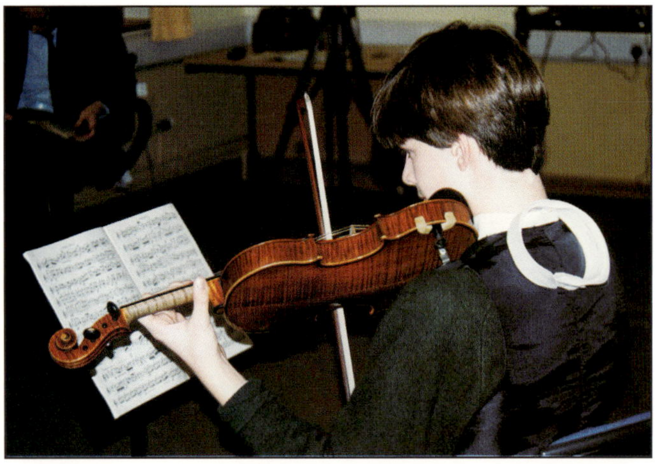

Violinist in rehearsal

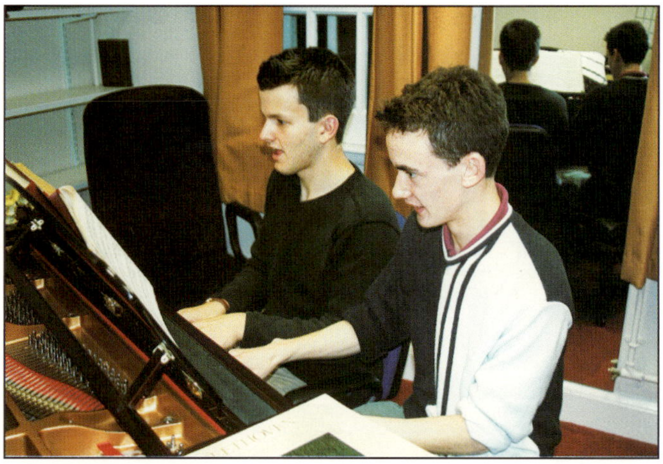

Piano duets

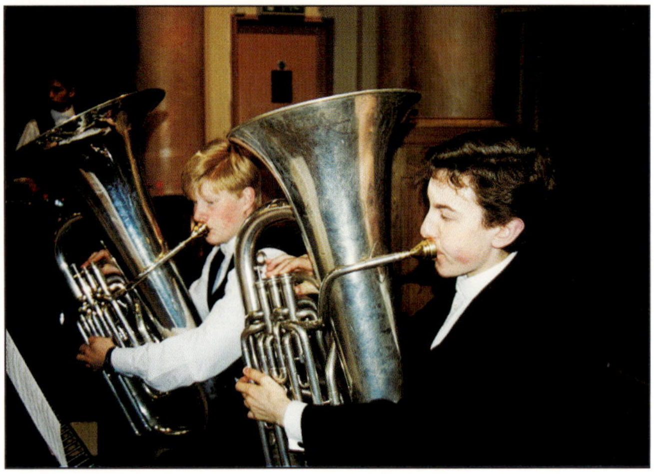

The tuba section

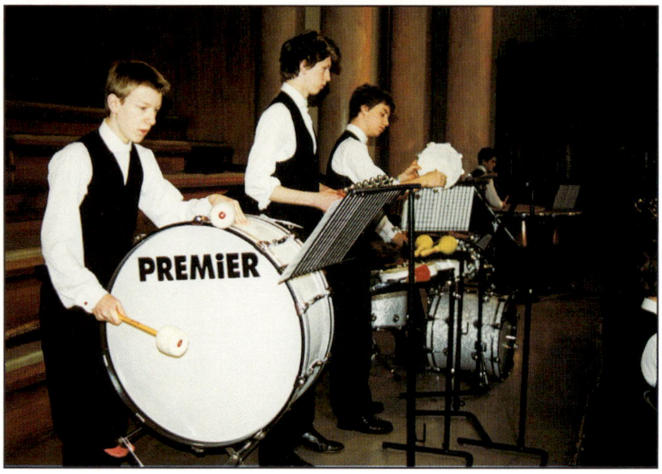

Percussion

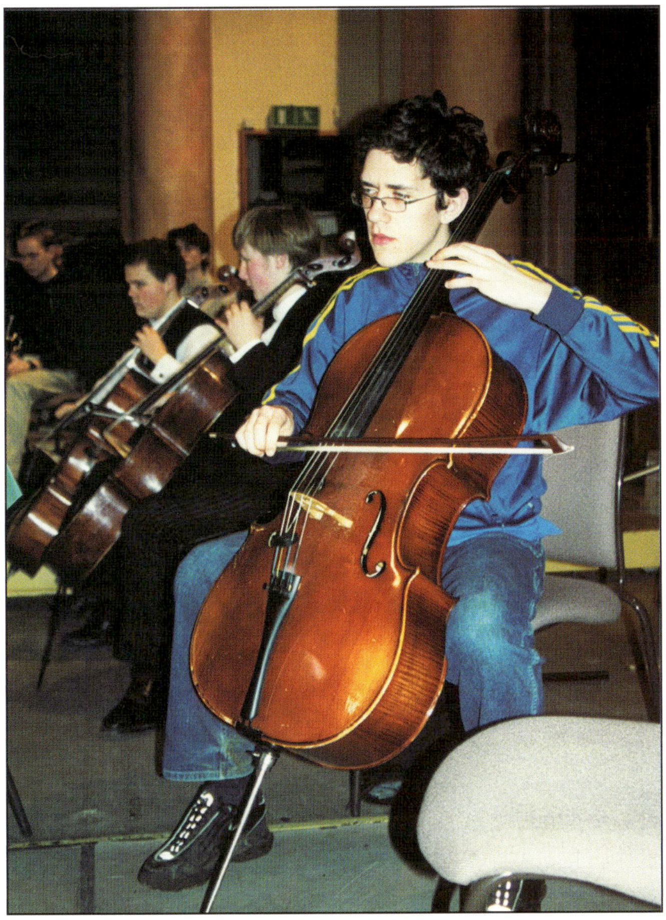

Studious 'cellist

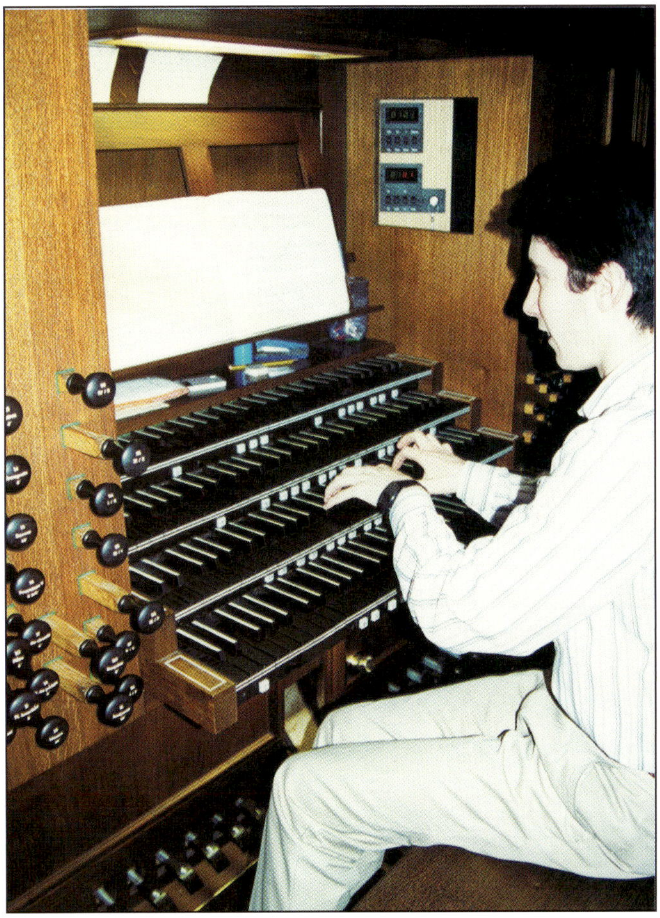

Organ scholar

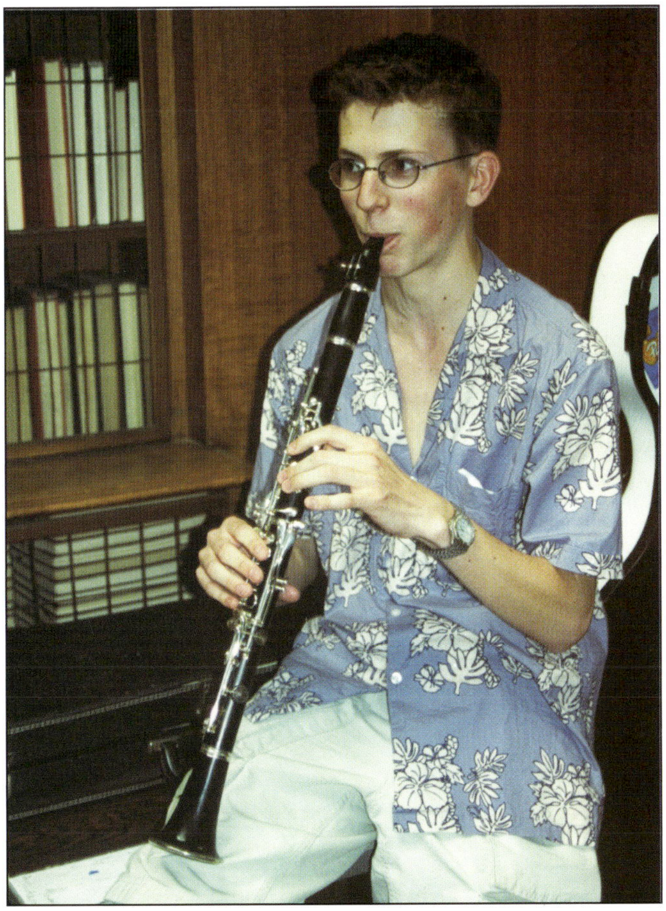

Clarinet soloist

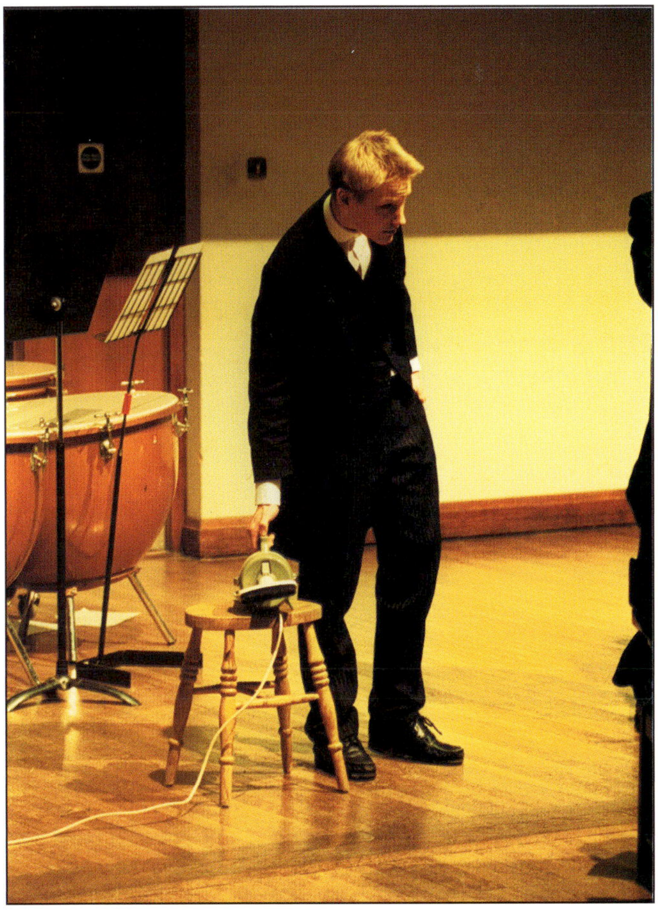

One boy's composition required the hum of a vacuum cleaner playing the note of G

Choral Music

Provision for the College Chapel Choir was made at the time the College was founded in 1440 by Henry VI. It was only towards the end of the 19th century that secular music became a part of the School curriculum. Eton has three principal choirs: the College Chapel Choir, the Lower Chapel Choir and the Eton College Music Society Chorus (E.C.M.S.). The College Chapel Choir is made up almost entirely of boys in the School. It sings at all major services and has a wide repertoire. It makes an annual concert tour, most recently to Japan, USA, Cuba, China and Hong Kong, and has produced a number of impressive recordings. One CD entitled 'Eton Choirbook' has recordings from the 15th century Eton Choirbook, one of the most significant manuscripts of early church music in existence and now one of the treasures in College Library. The Lower Chapel Choir is made up of boys in E and F Blocks and leads the singing in Lower Chapel. The E.C.M.S. Chorus performs a major choral work in the Lent Half each year. Any boy or Master may join this choir, which is usually supported by the soprano voices of a local girls' school. In addition to the three official choirs there is a small choir organised by a senior boy that rehearses in its spare time and performs close harmony songs, often as dinner party entertainment. In the context of choral music mention should also be made of the summer holiday choral courses for 16-20 year olds from any schools. These were founded by Ralph Allwood, the Precentor, and by 2002 were being attended each year by over 300 young singers in four different courses at Eton and elsewhere. There are many internal music competitions, but none more popular than the inter-house Unison Song competition commonly called 'The House Shout'. This is a very lively occasion, which takes place in School Hall. As most Houses participate, the majority of boys in the School will be in action on that particular evening. It is hard to think of any other event in which so many boys are involved, and in so short a space of time, two hours.

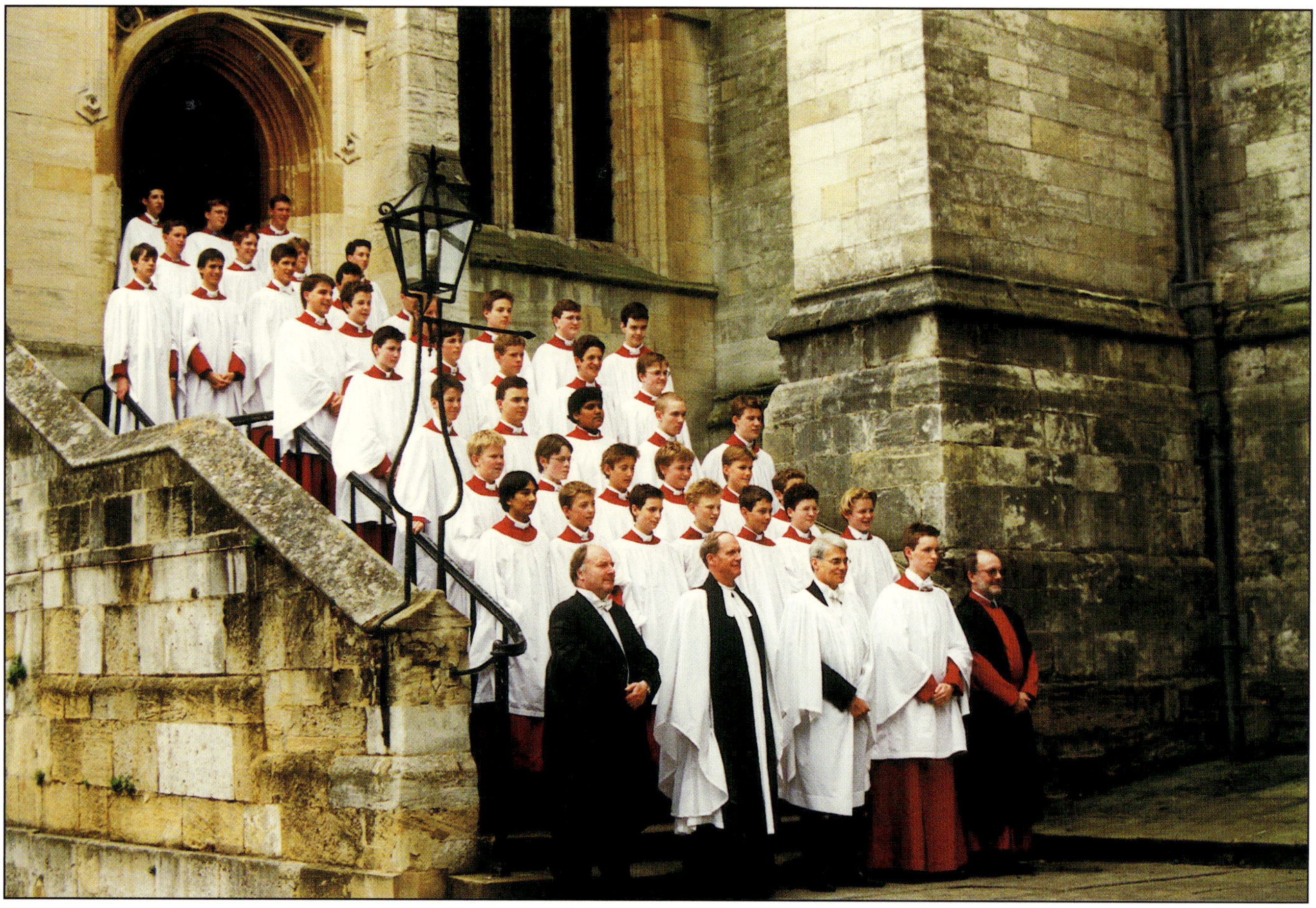

College Chapel Choir on the steps of College Chapel

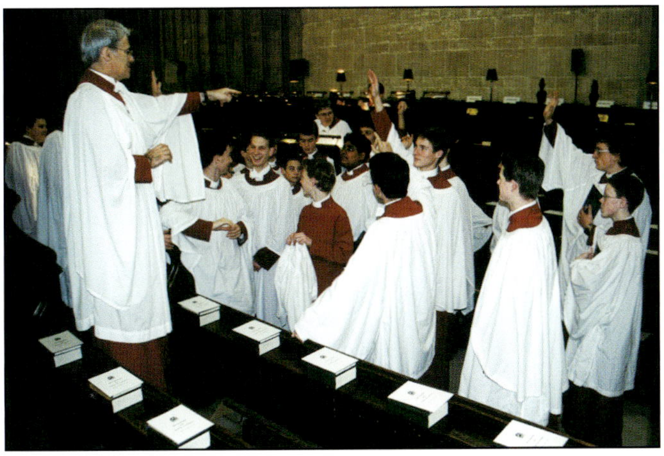

The Precentor with the College Chapel Choir before morning service

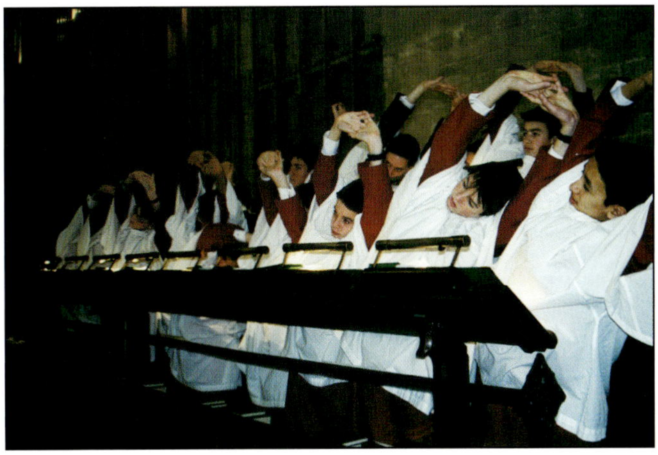

Warming up

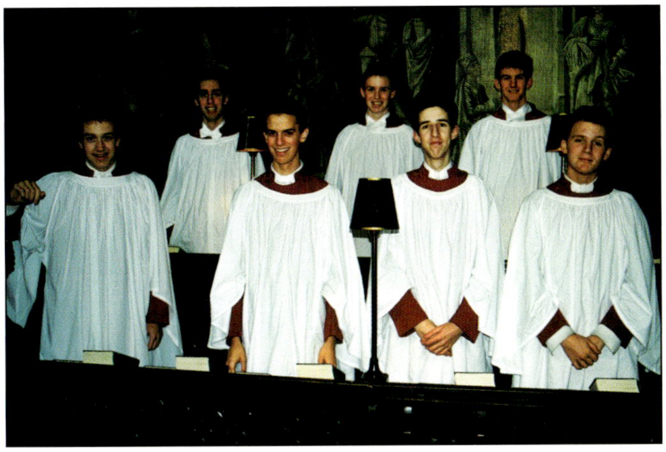

In front of the 15th century wall paintings

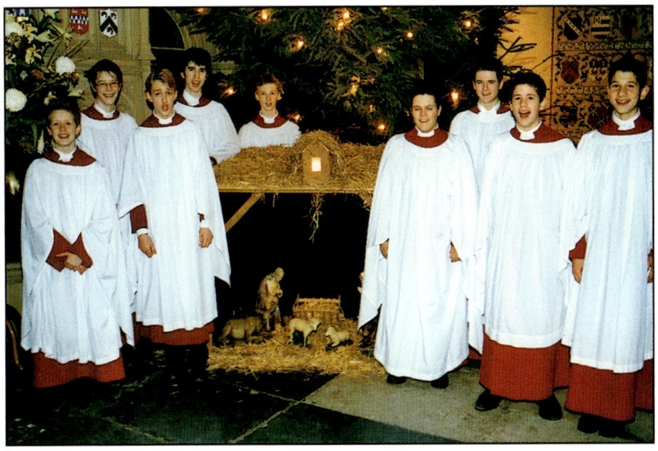

Members of the Choir by the Christmas crib

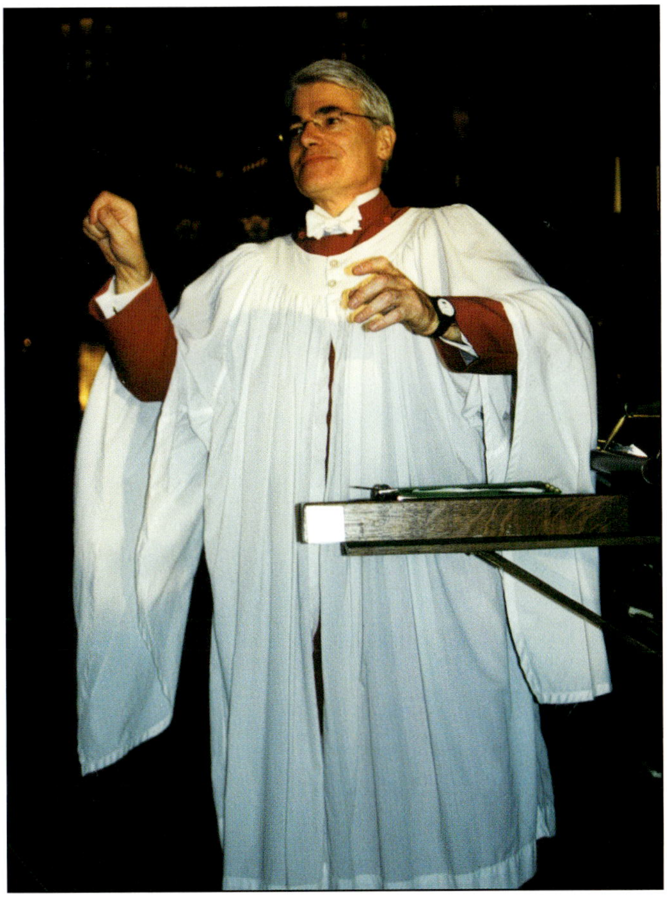

The Precentor in action

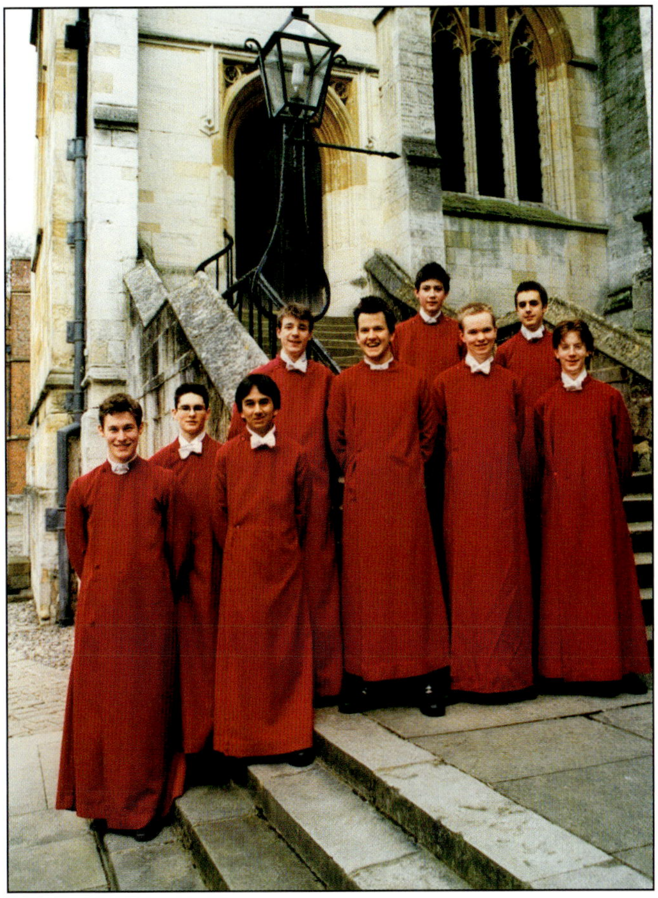

Leaving members of College Chapel Choir in 2002

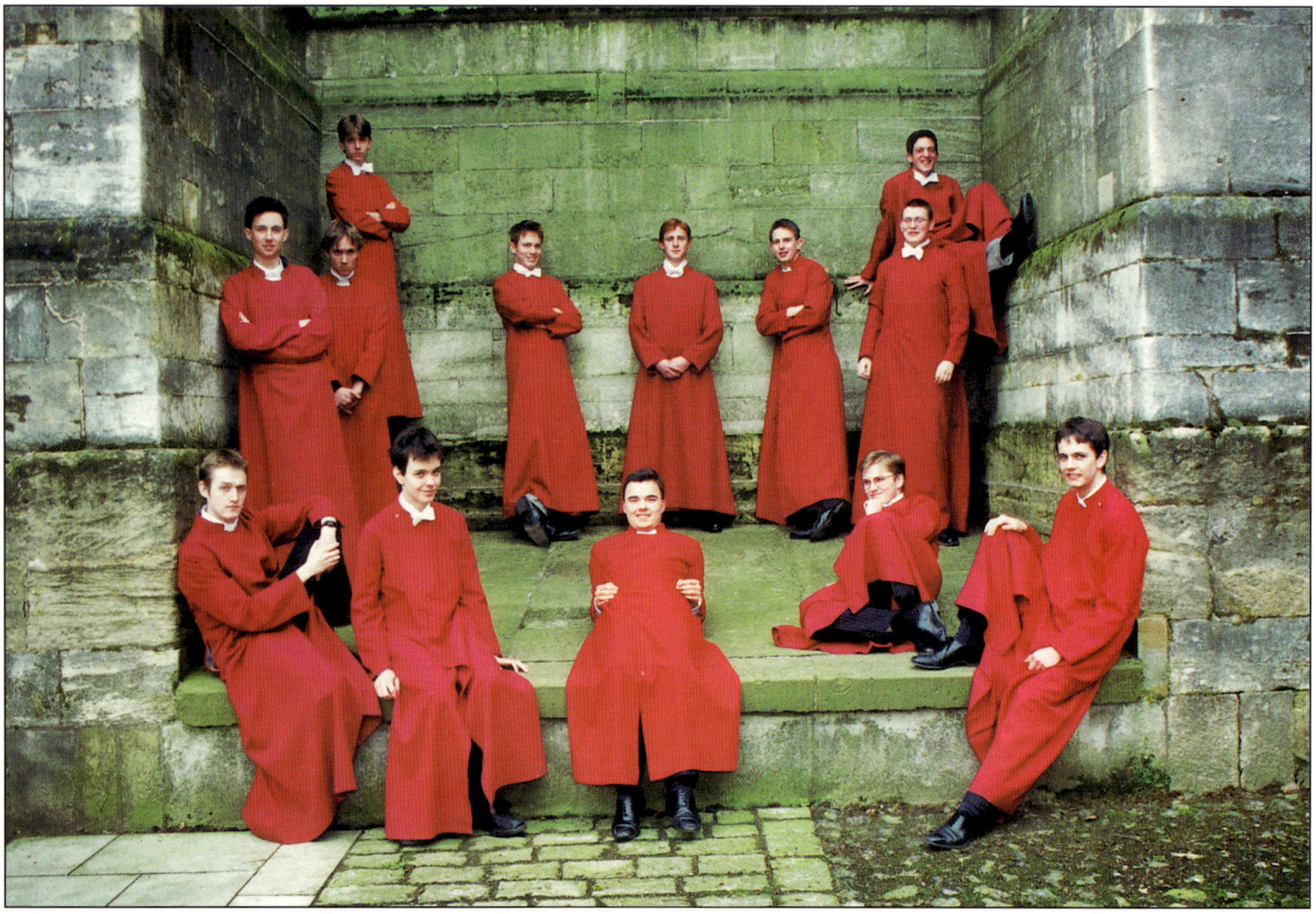

Leaving members of College Chapel Choir in 2001

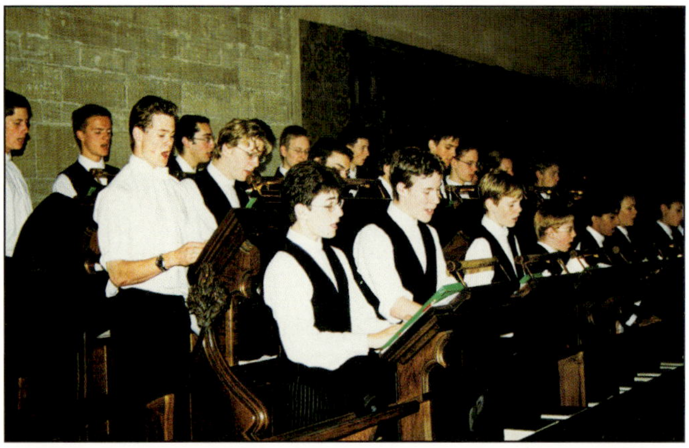

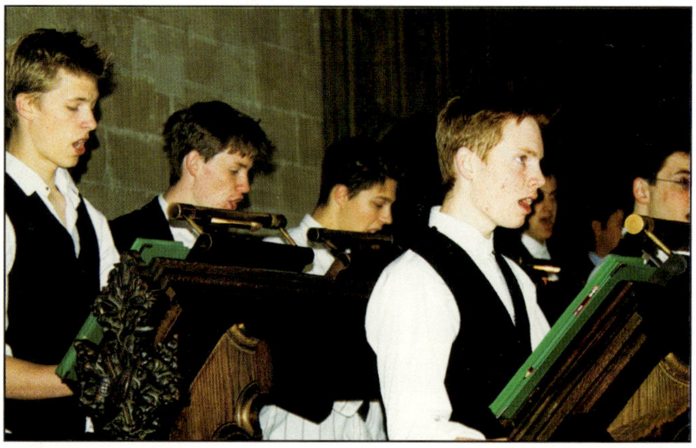

College Chapel Choir in rehearsal

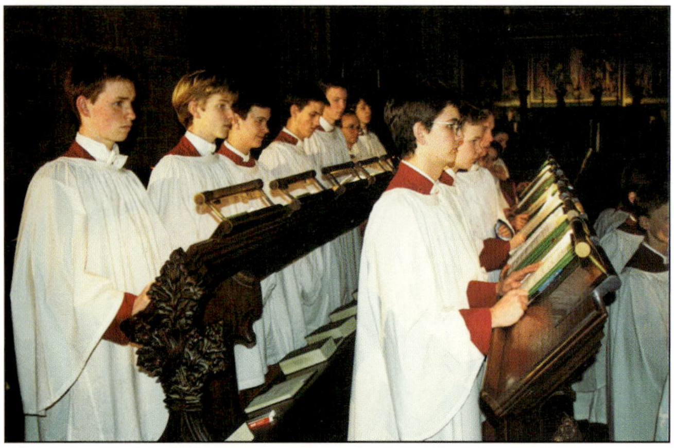

College Chapel Choir fully robed

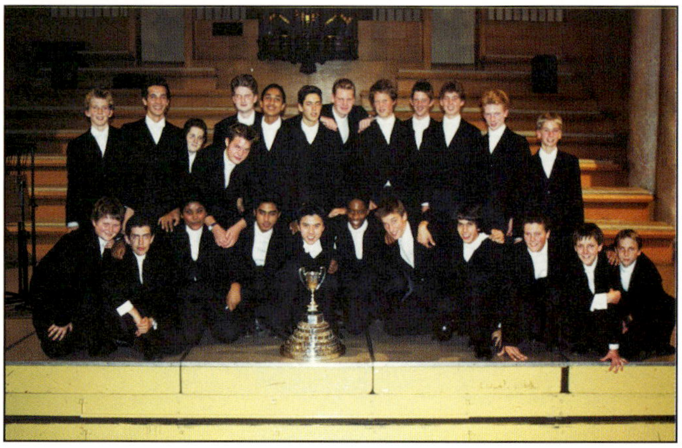

Members of the winning House after the House Unison Song competition

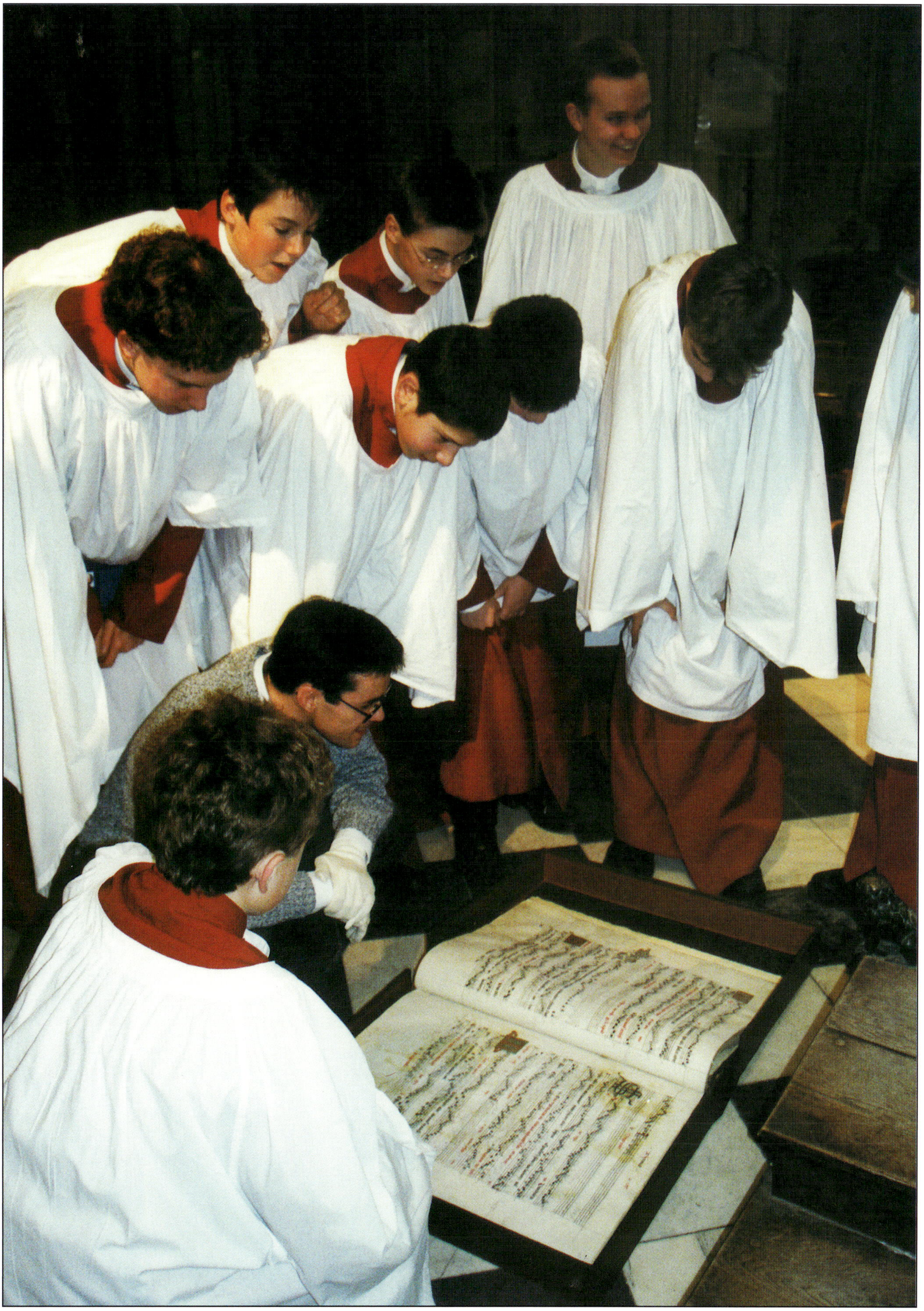

Members of the Choir inspect the 15th century Eton Choirbook

School of Mechanics

The forerunner to the School of Mechanics was first proposed by Edmund Warre in 1879 and was opened as a free-time hobby centre in the same year. Its location has moved, most recently in 1978 from beside the Parade Ground to its purpose-built workshops facing South Meadow. There are facilities for Electronics, Woodwork, Engineering, Graphics, Computer Aided Design and Silverwork. The Design course is now part of the Lower School Curriculum, and boys can go on to GCSE, AS and A2 courses, or merely take Design as an option. There is an impressive list of trophies won by boys working in the School of Mechanics, ranging from BP 'Build-a-car' competitions to Commonwealth Young Designer of the Year.

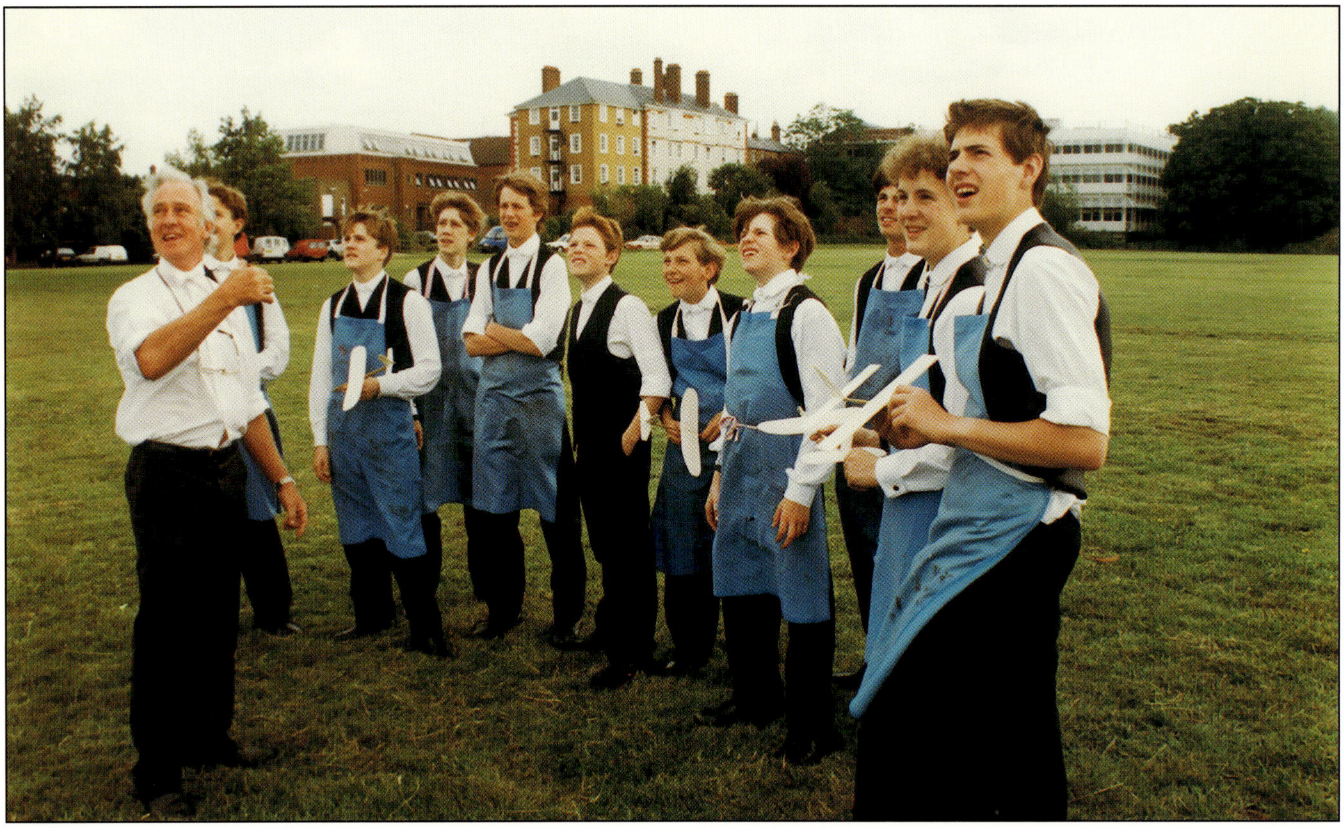

Test flight in progress

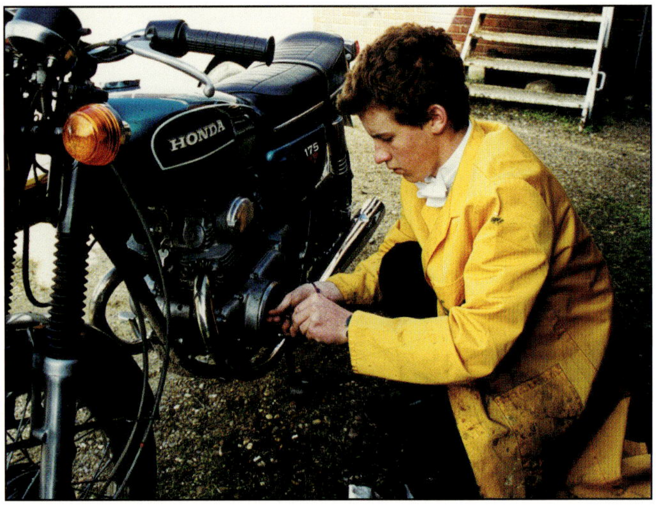

Motorcycle restoration

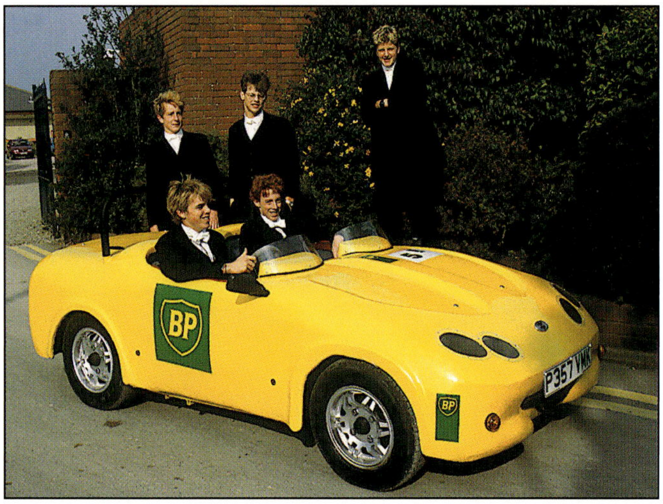

The BP 'Build-a-Car' competition

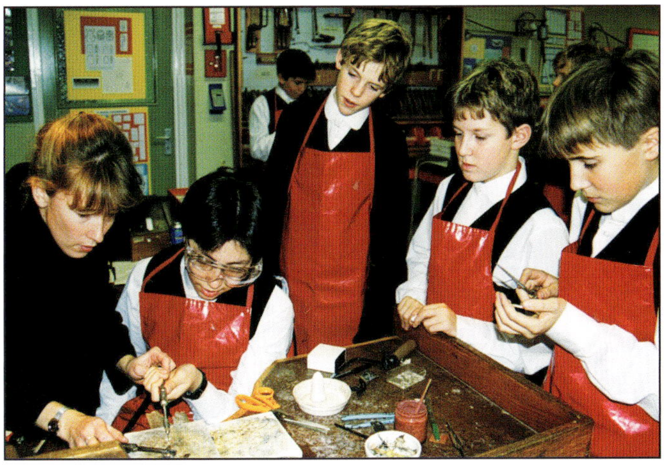
Silverwork class

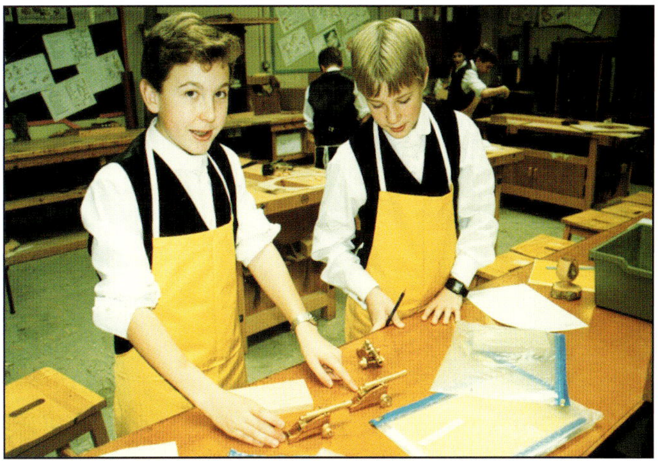
Cannon fire

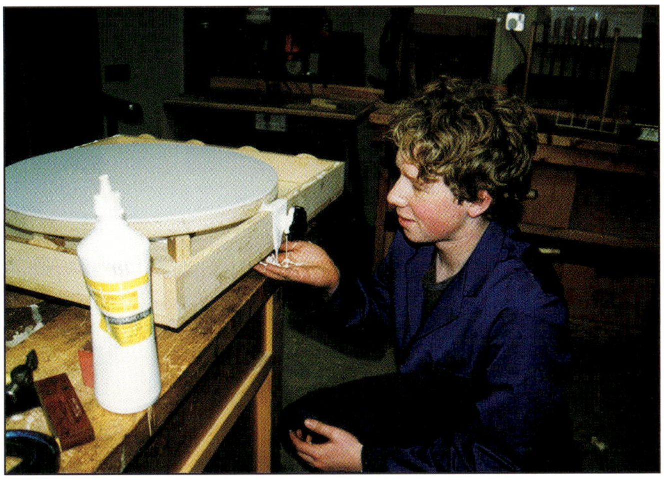
Excess adhesive

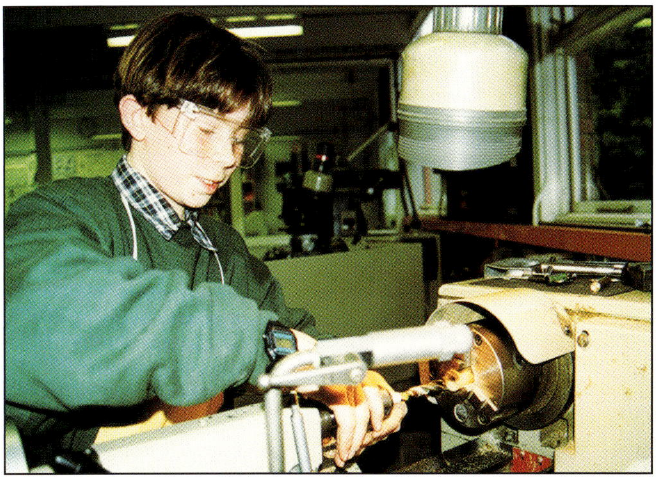
Turning on a lathe

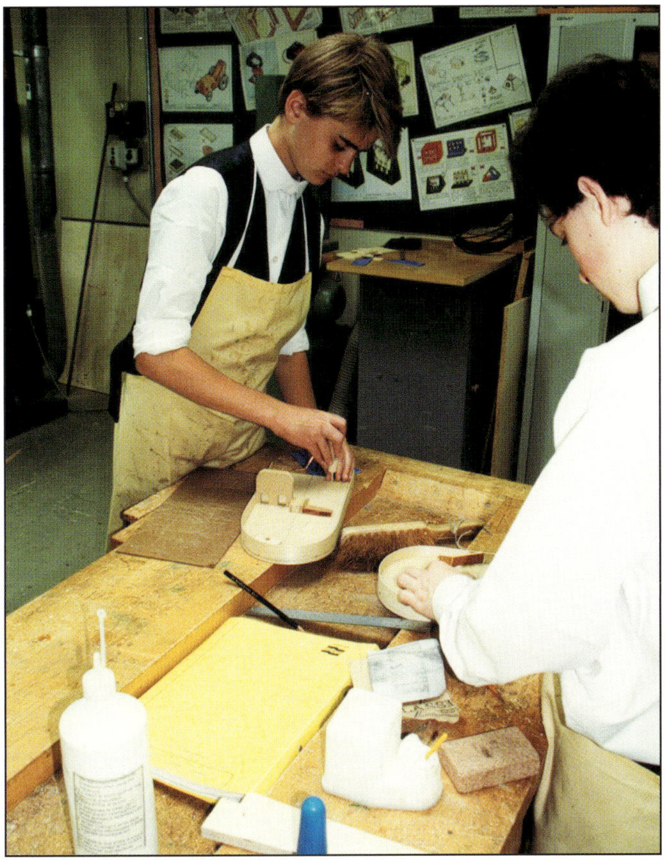
Woodwork class

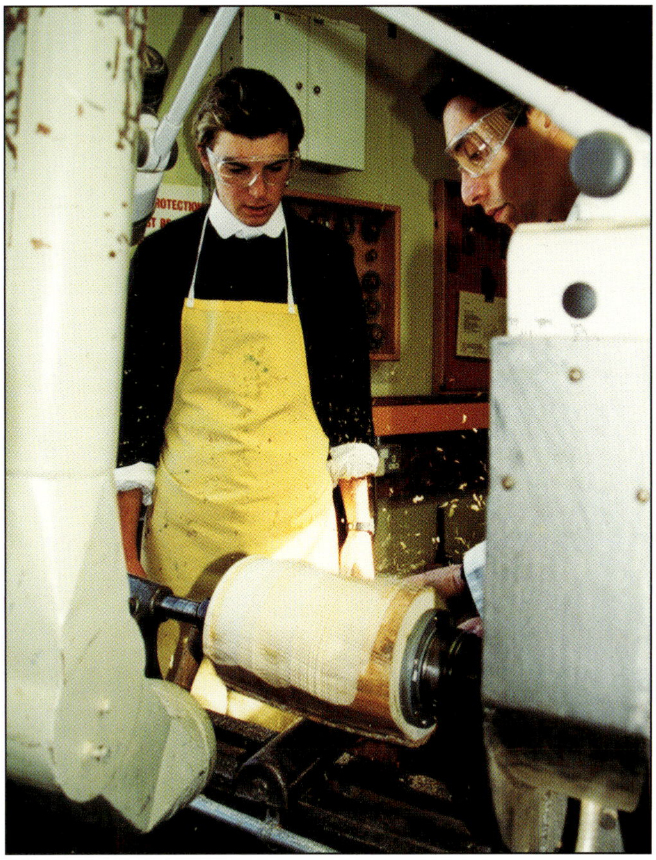
Chips off the old block (wood turning)

The Drawing Schools

The Drawing Schools were opened in 1926 by King George V and Queen Mary. The studios are arranged round an entrance colonnade and a large exhibition area. An ambitious refurbishing and rebuilding programme was completed in 2002. Phase 1 provided new studios for painting and printmaking. Phase 2 provides new studios for pottery and sculpture as well as a new library, workshops and a computer room. The subject is taught through the disciplines of Painting and Drawing, Printmaking, Sculpture and Ceramics. It is taken by all boys in their first year, but thereafter it is optional and can lead to AS and A2 level examinations. Exhibitions of work by boys and Masters punctuate the School year.

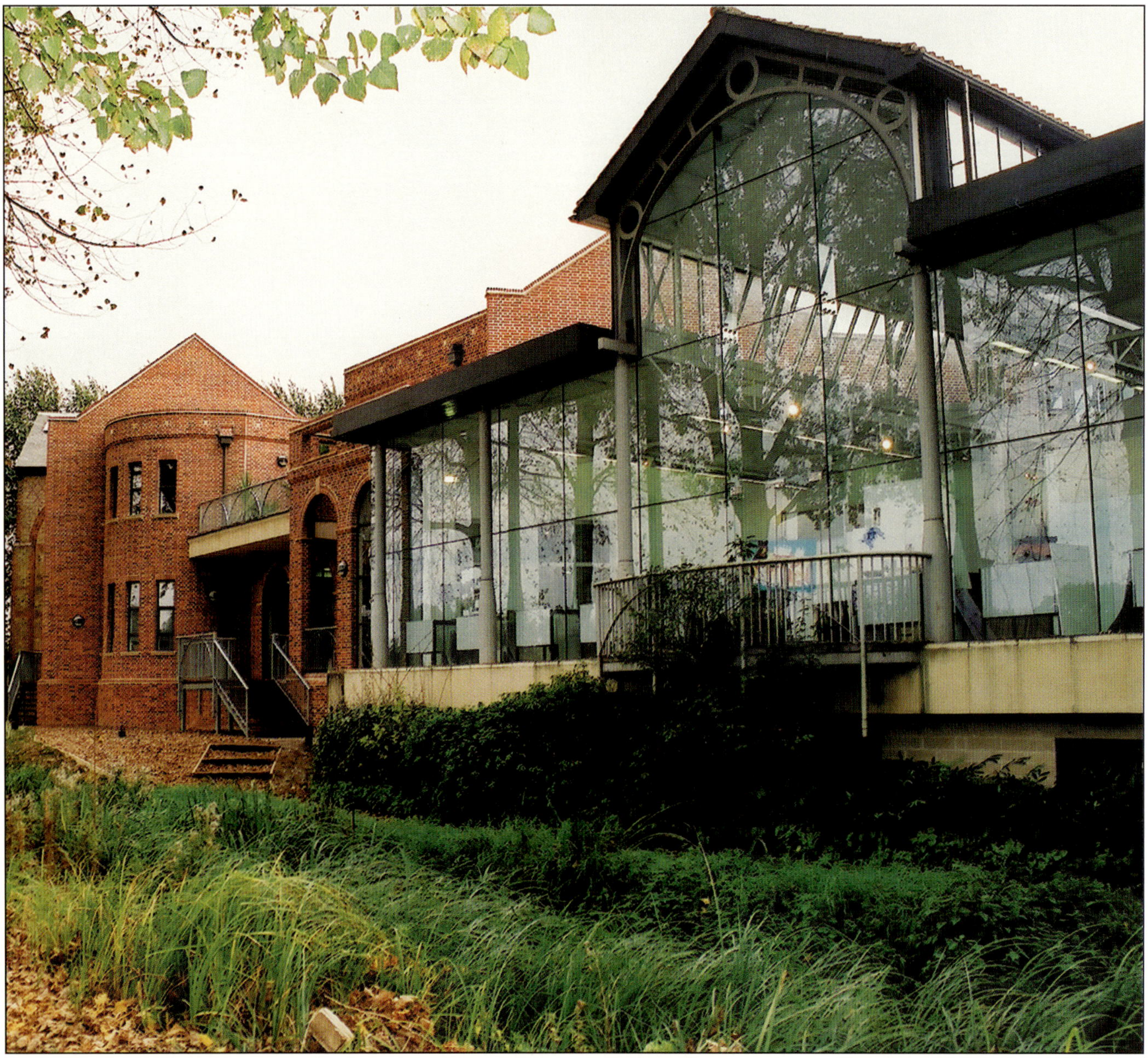

The completed Drawing Schools

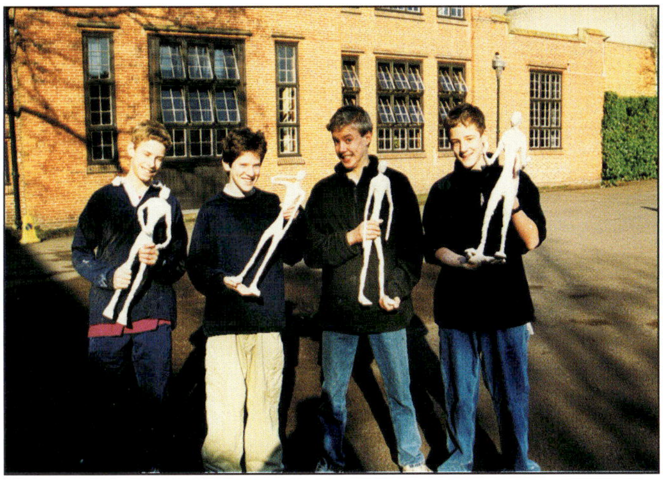

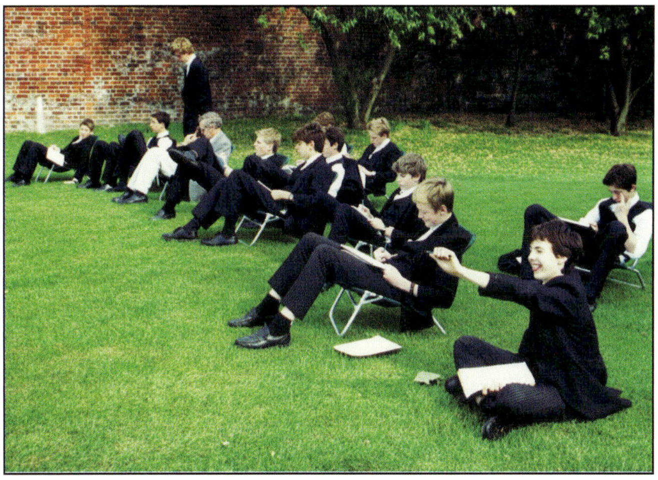

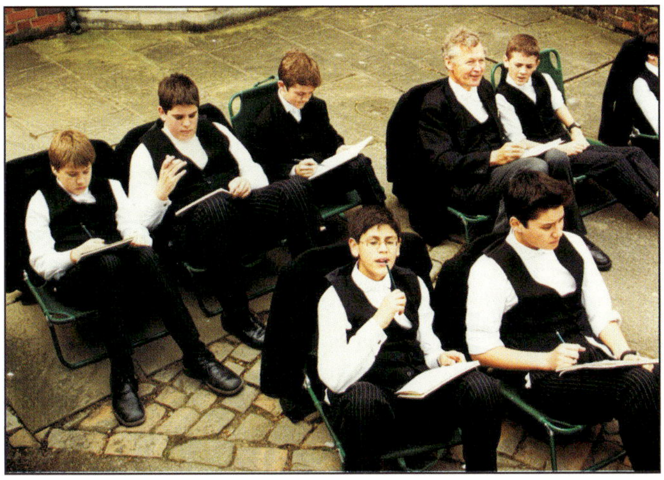

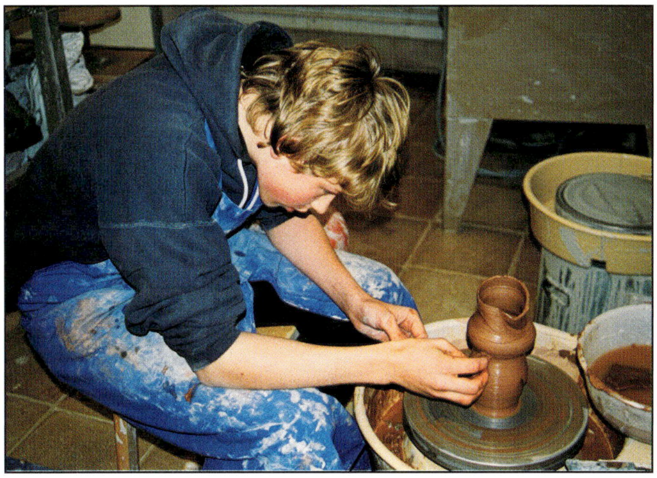

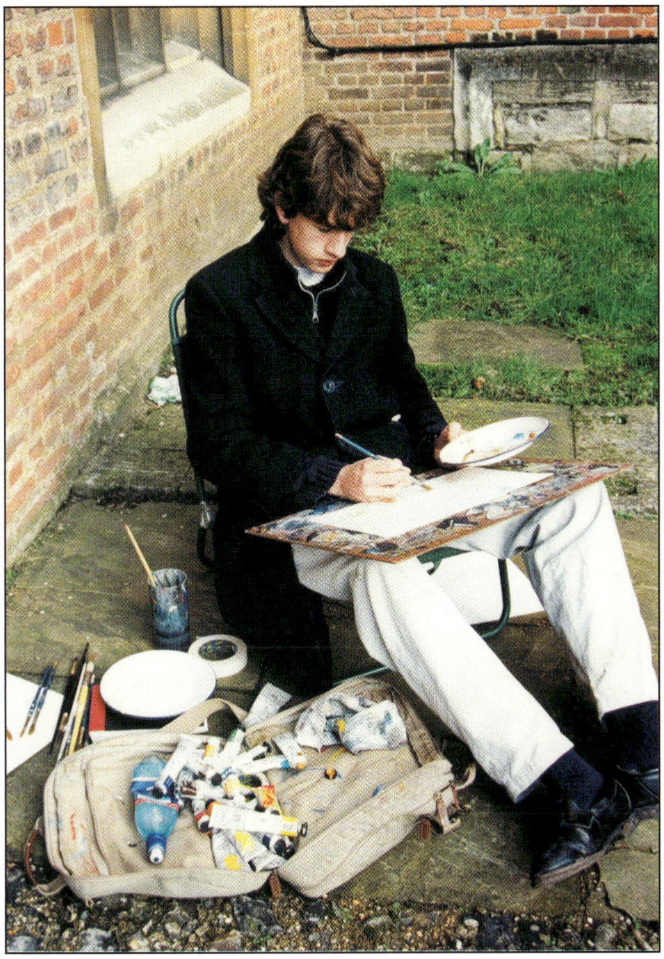

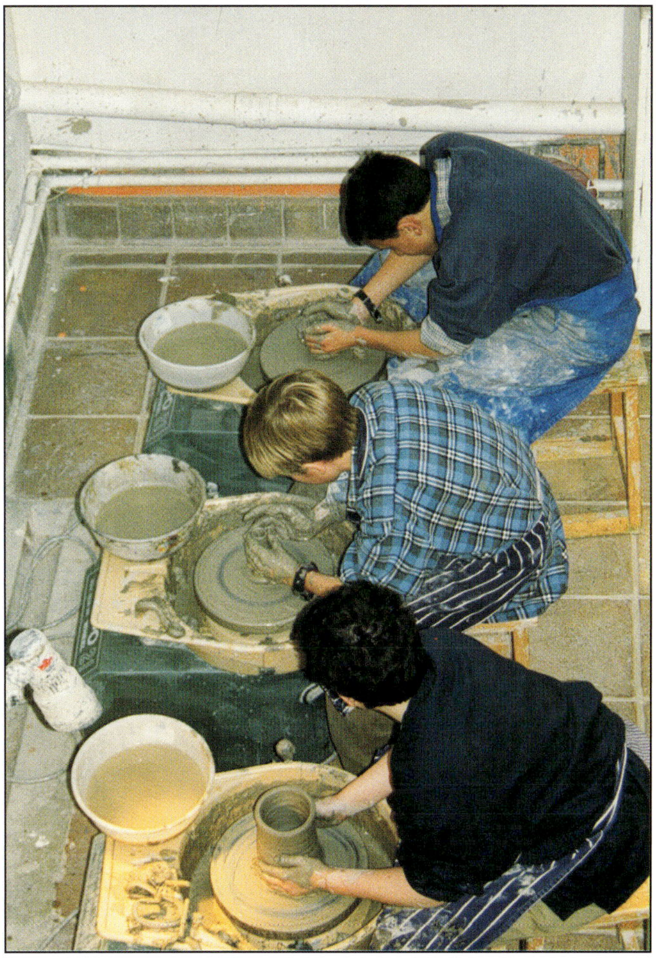

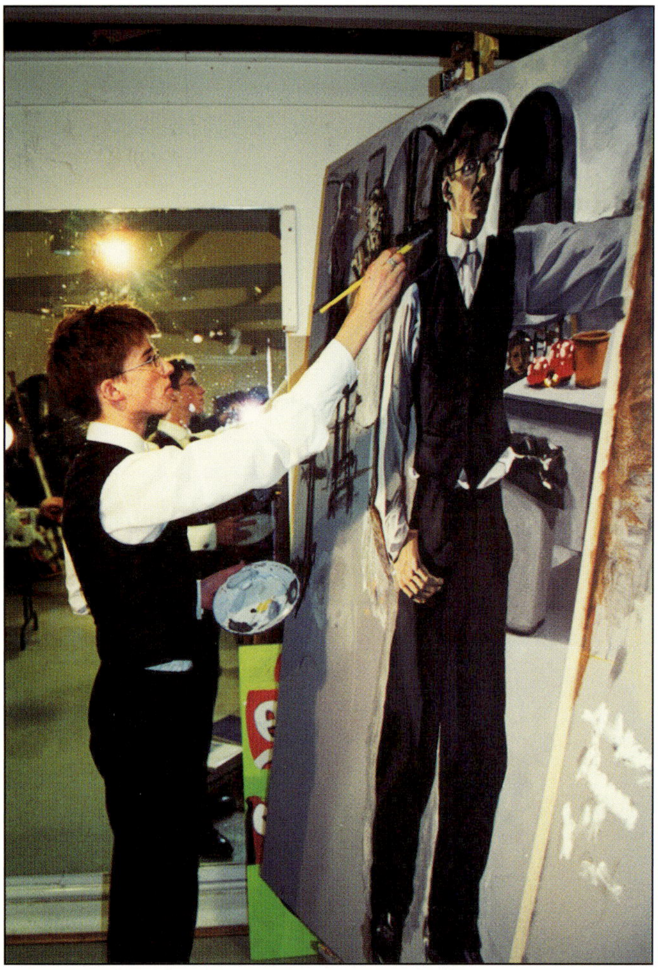

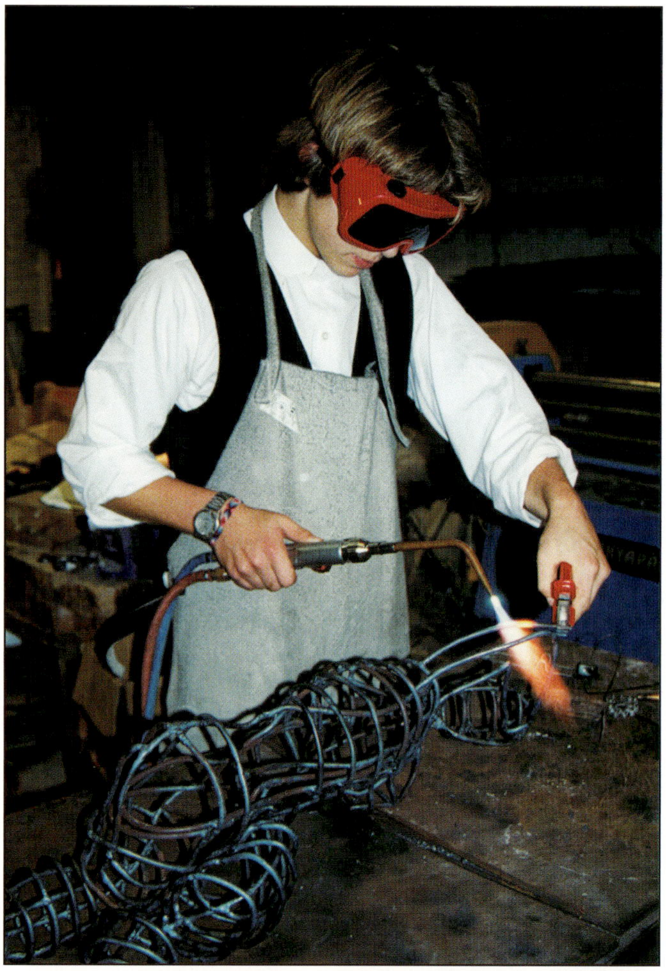

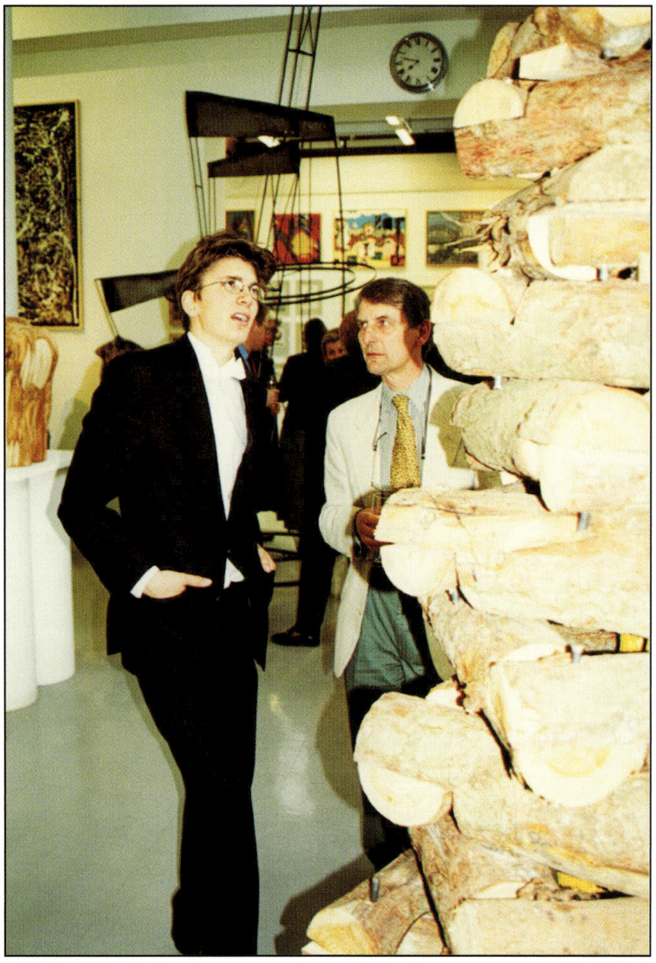

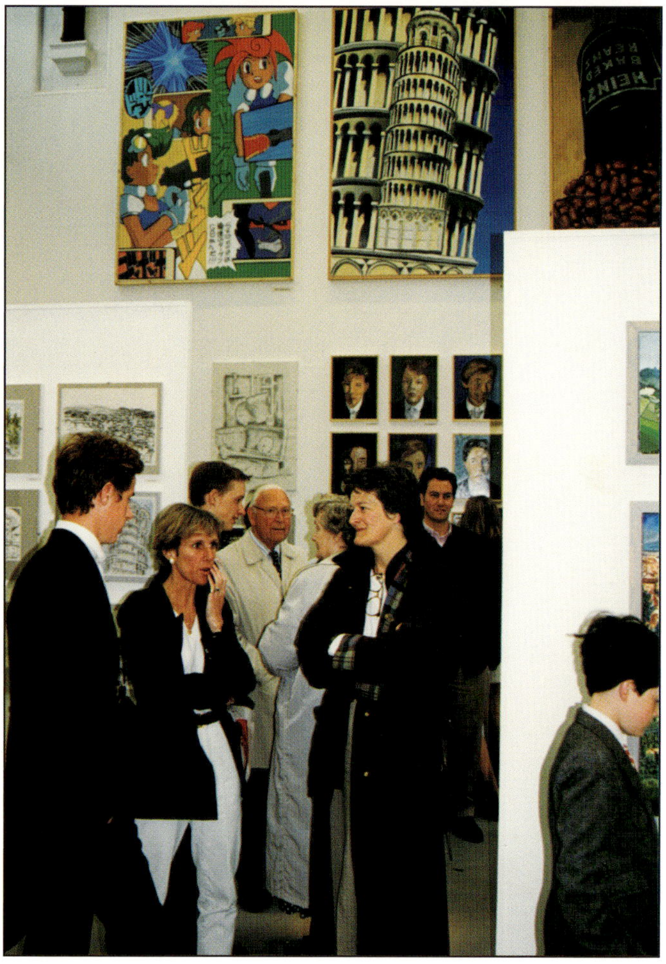

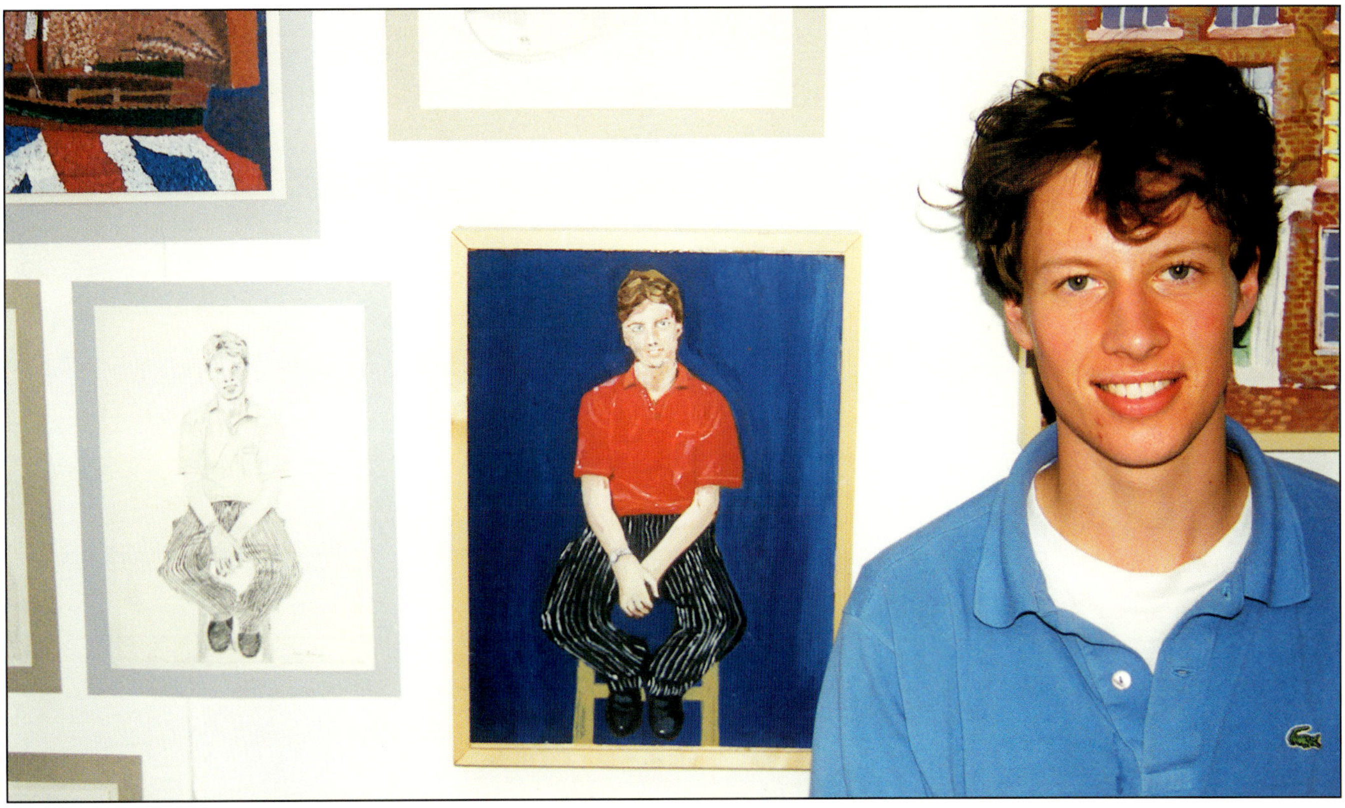

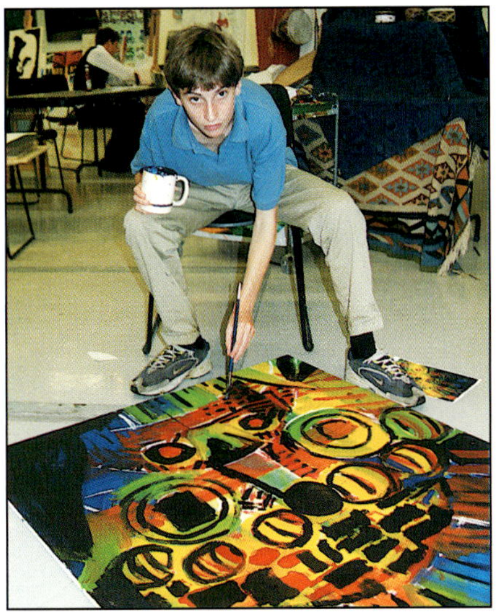

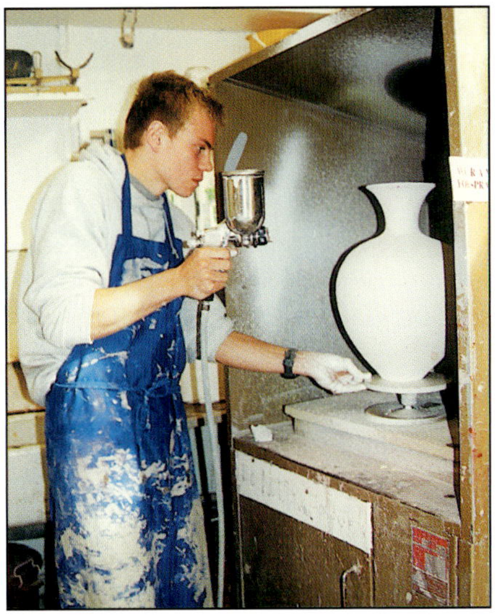

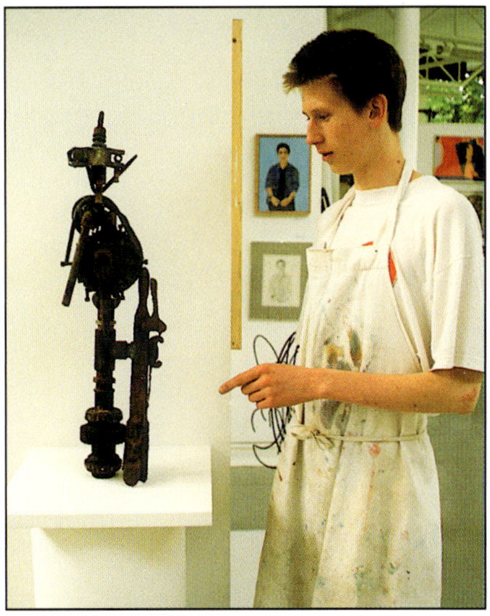

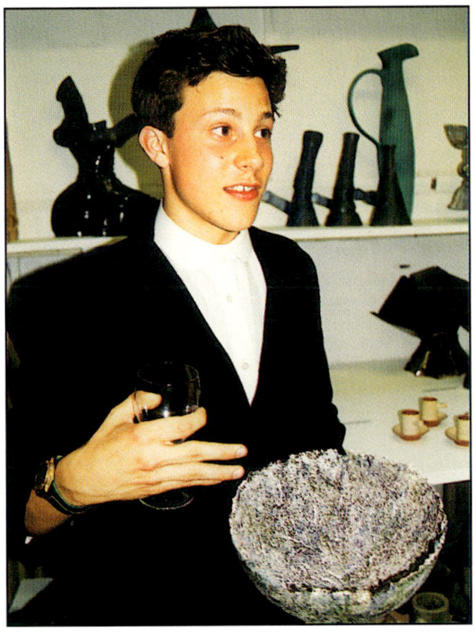

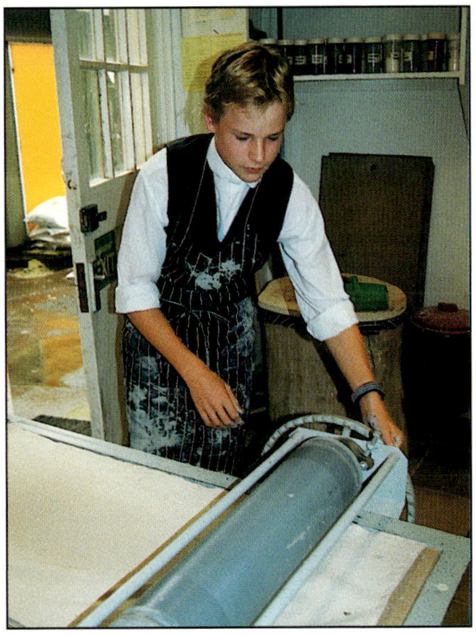

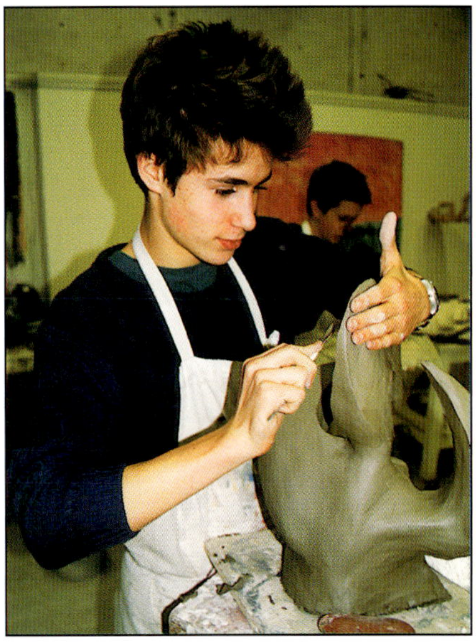

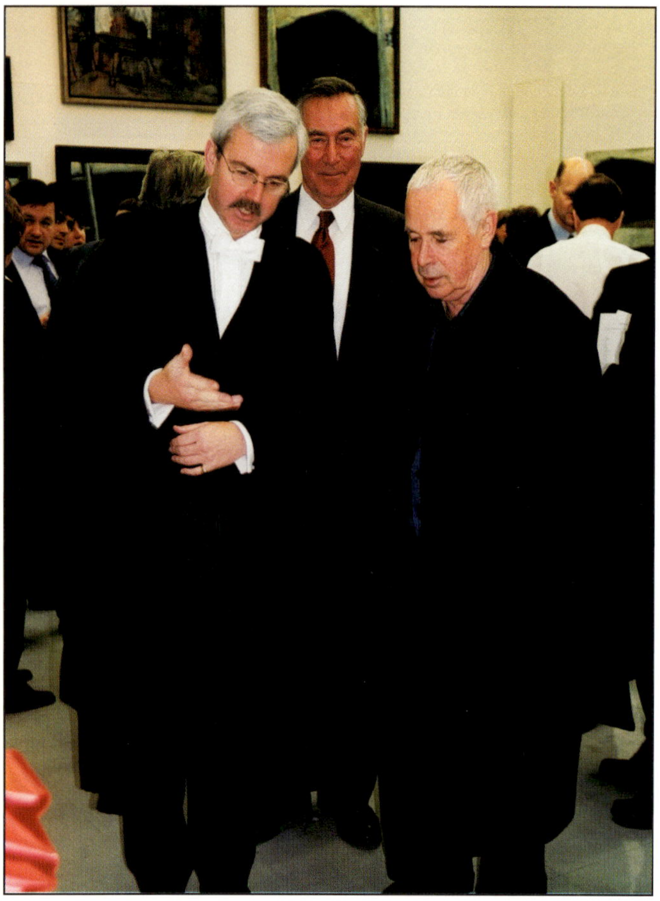

Tony Little, Sir Eric Anderson and Sir Howard Hodgkin at the opening of phase 2 of the Drawing Schools

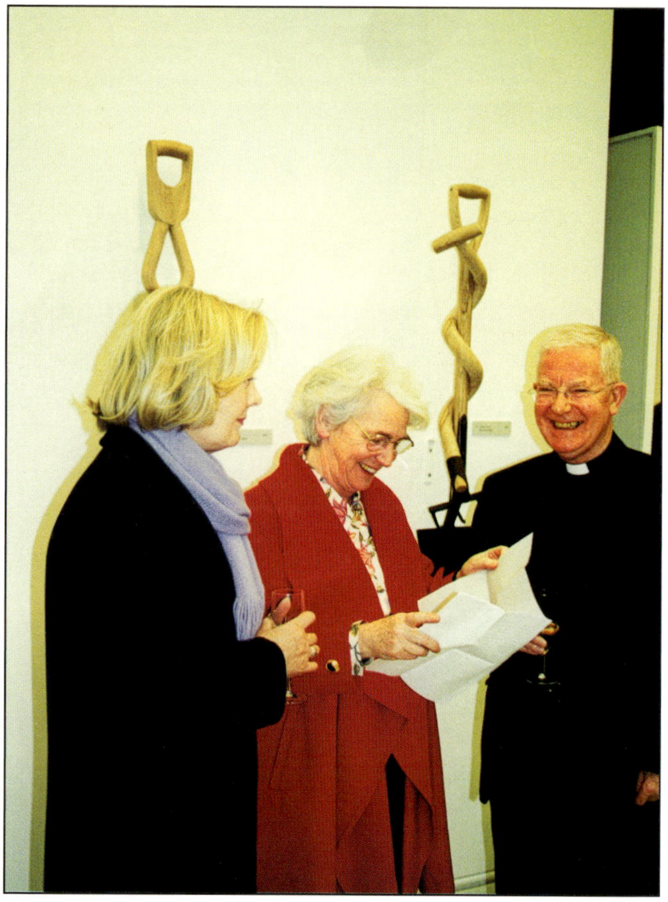

Lady Anderson consults the catalogue of exhibits

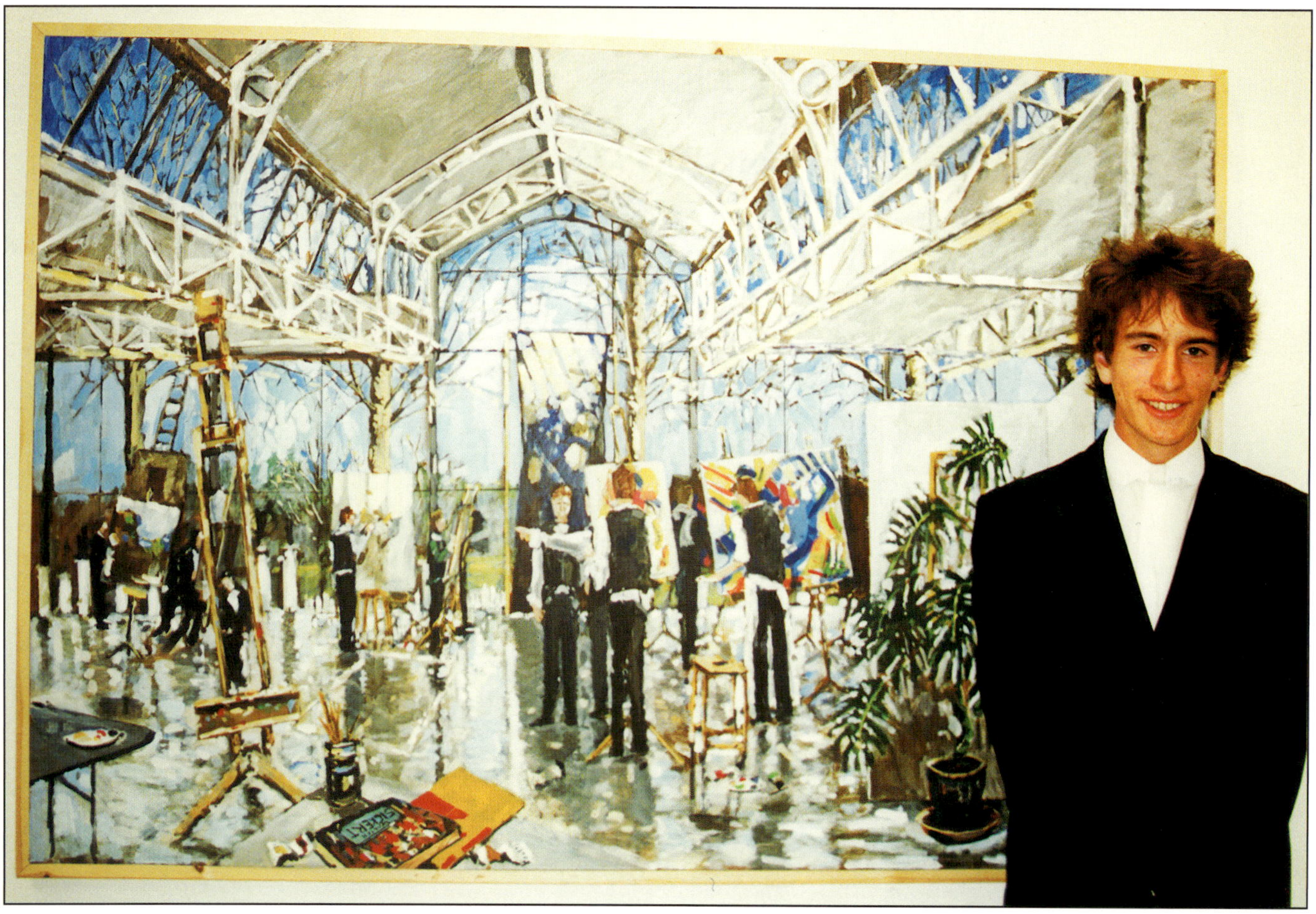

An artist's own view of the interior of the refurbished Drawing Schools

Drama

The history of drama at Eton has been expertly recorded by Michael Meredith in his recent booklet "Five Hundred Years of Eton Theatre". There have been rises and falls in the fortunes of drama over this time, including a total prohibition for part of the nineteenth century. However, with the building of the Farrer Theatre in the 1960s and the construction of the Caccia Centre in 1978, standards rapidly improved. The appointment of the first director of drama in 1979 gave the process added momentum. Nowadays, in the winter halves, it is rare for any week to pass without either a School, House or independent play being performed, such is the popularity of drama. Indeed producers have to look beyond the Farrer Theatre and the Caccia Centre for a venue – to the 'Empty Space', boys' Houses, the Chapel, the barn on Agar's and outdoor locations in the summer. However, major productions take place in the Farrer Theatre. With its rehearsal room, its Green Room, dressing rooms, make-up rooms, fly tower, computerised lighting system and its thrust stage, it can accommodate even the most ambitious of productions, including musicals..

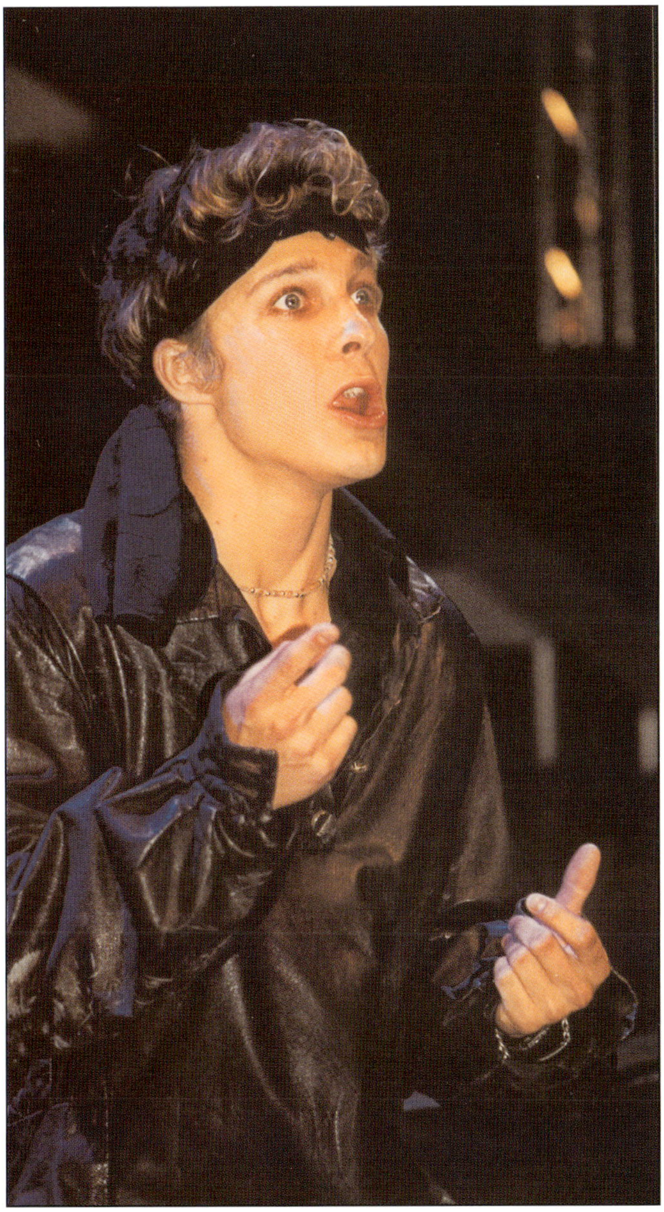

Jesus Christ Superstar: Judas

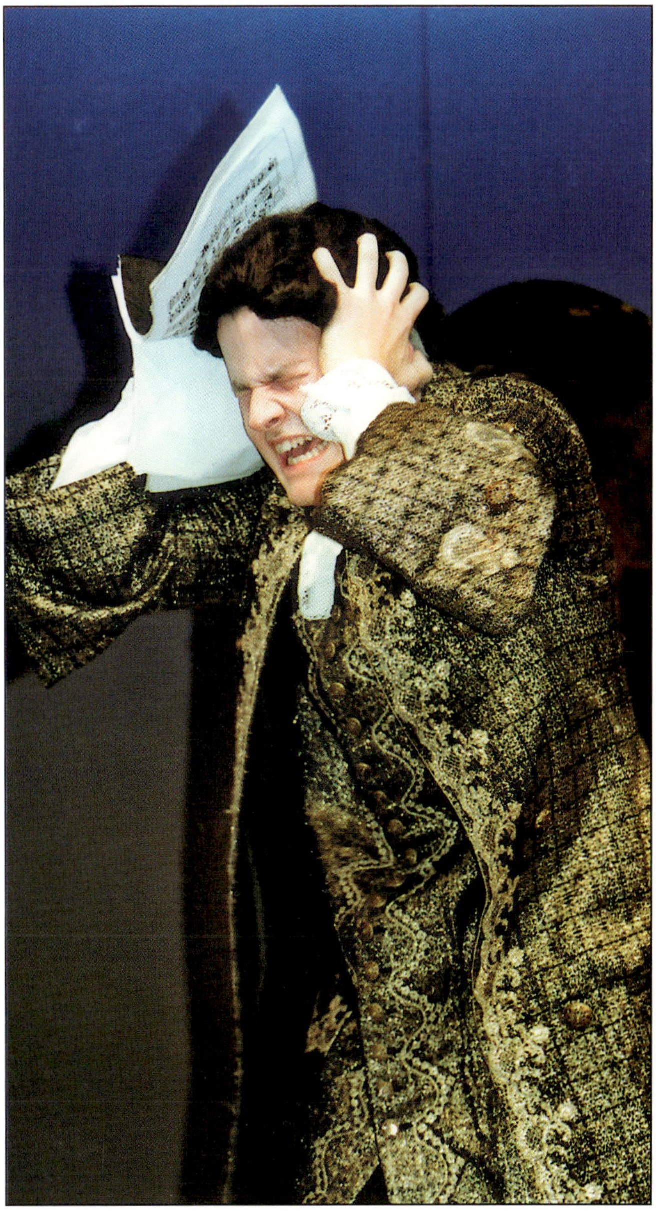

Amadeus: Salieri

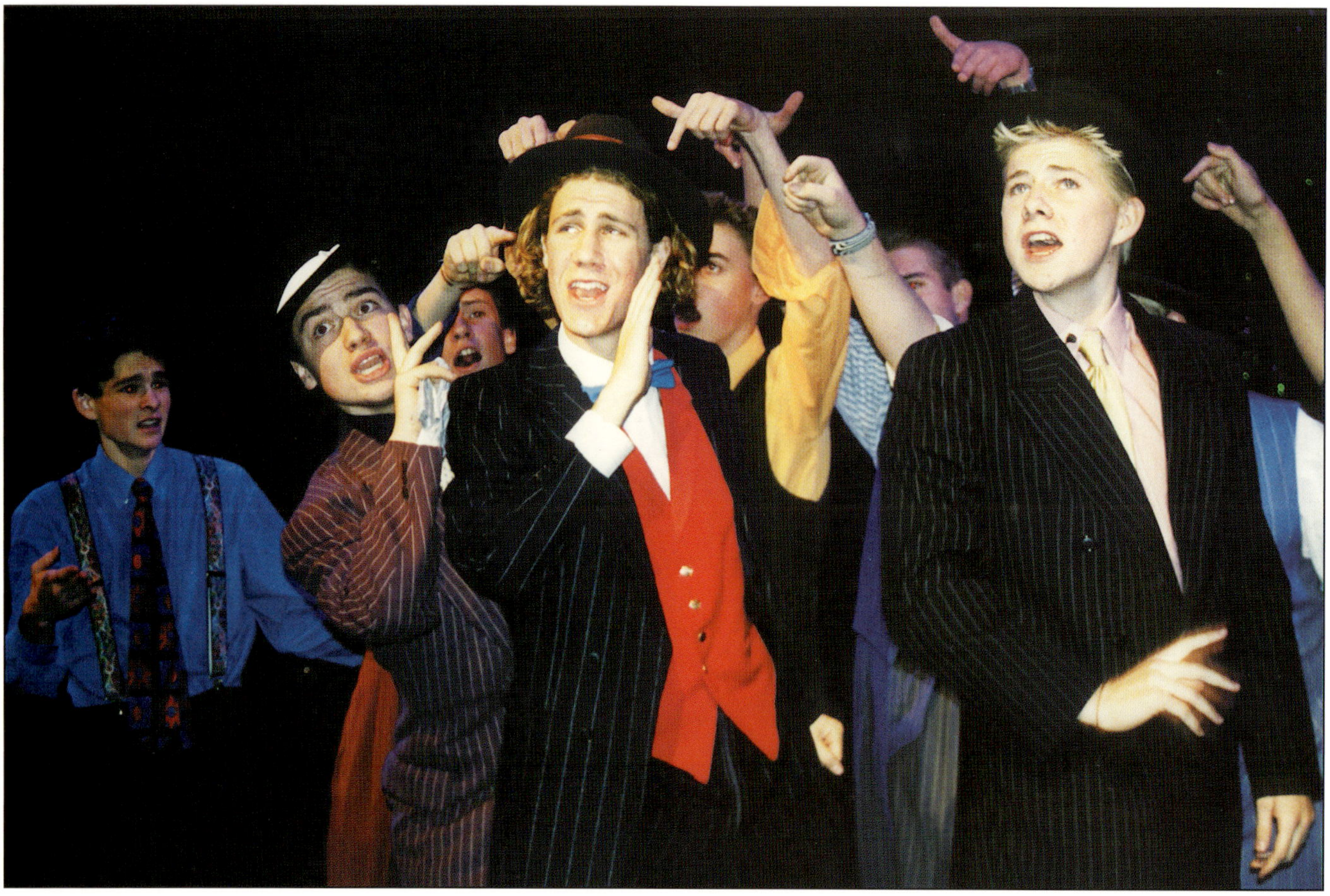

Me and my Girl

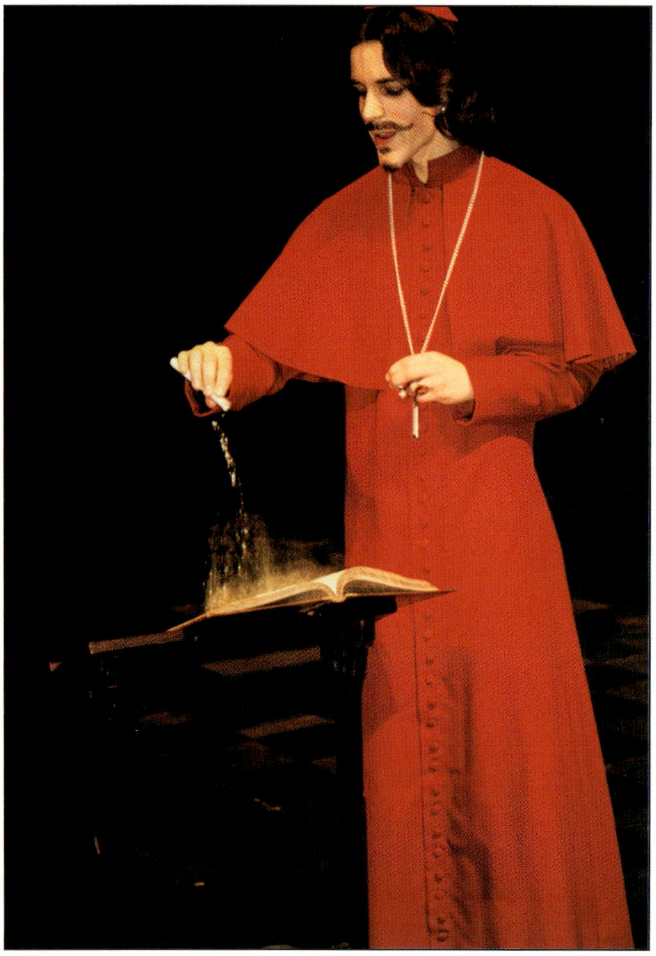

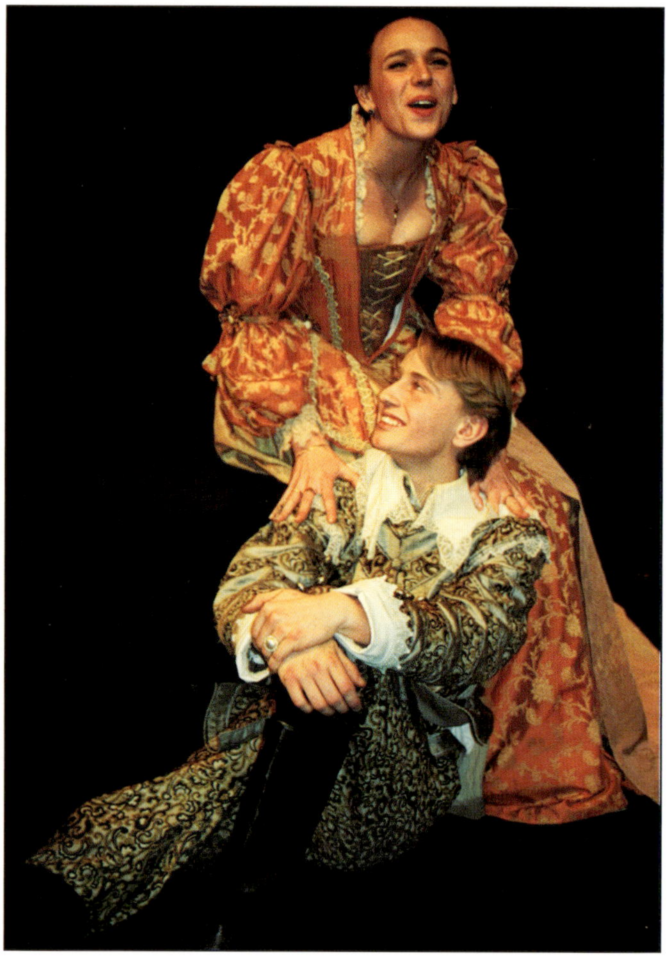

The Duchess of Malfi

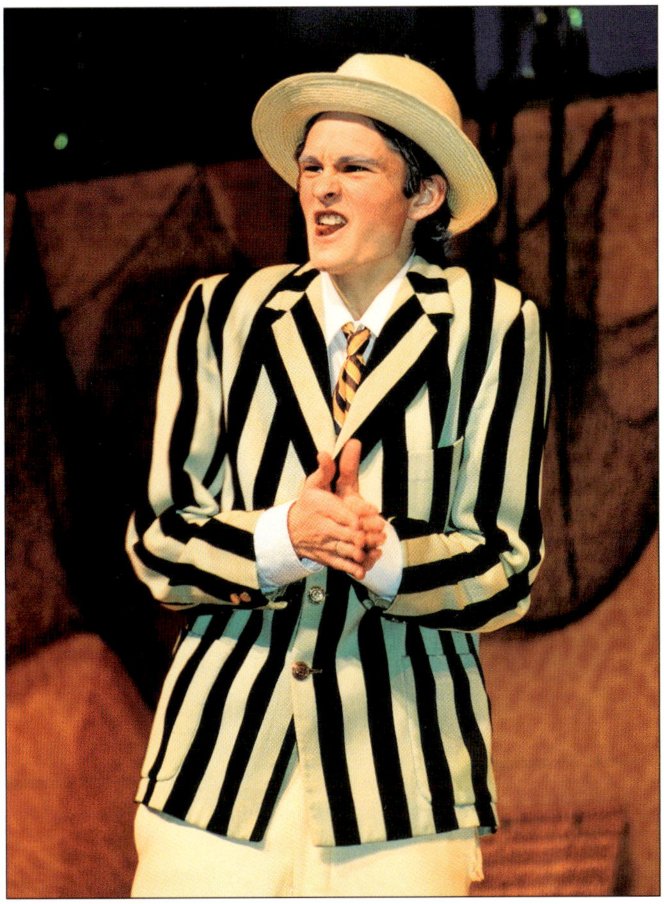

"It's never too late to fall in love"

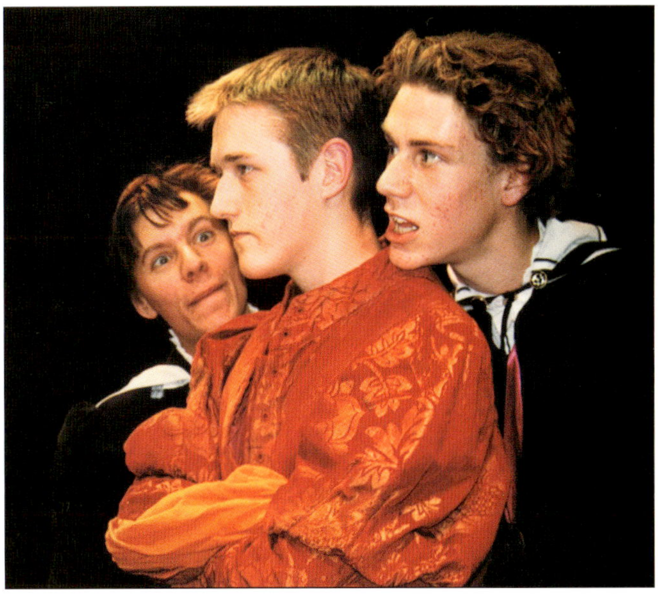

Rosencrantz and Guildenstern

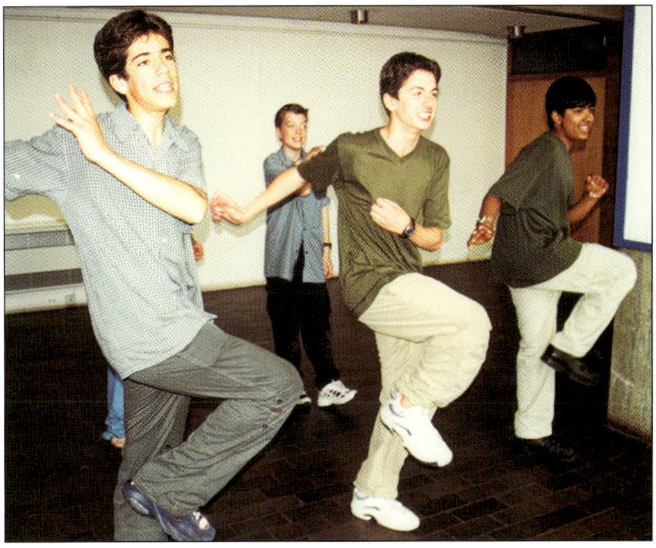

Rehearsal in the foyer of the Farrer Theatre

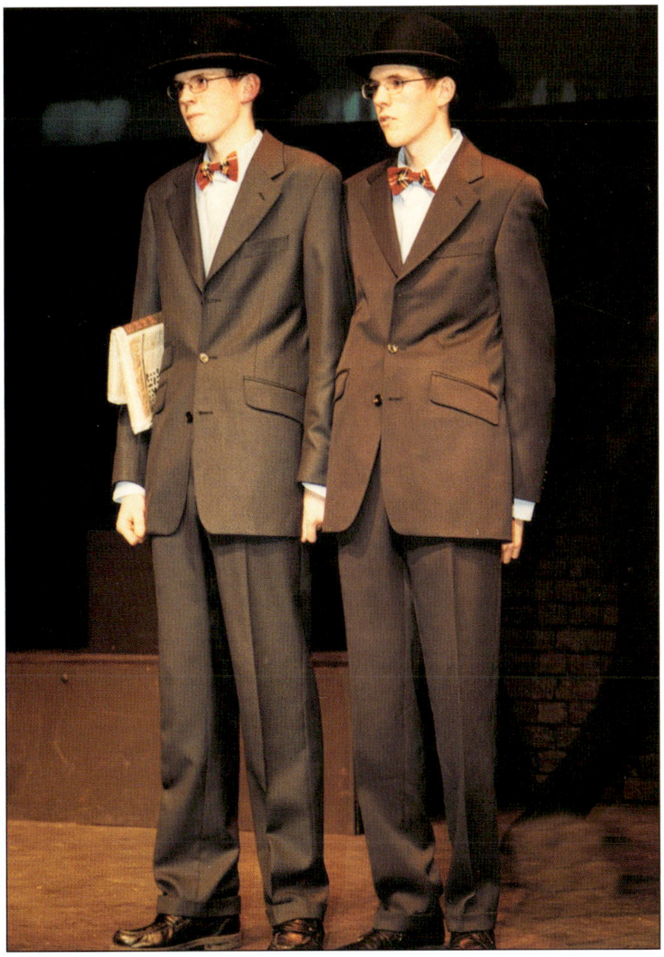

Arturo Ui

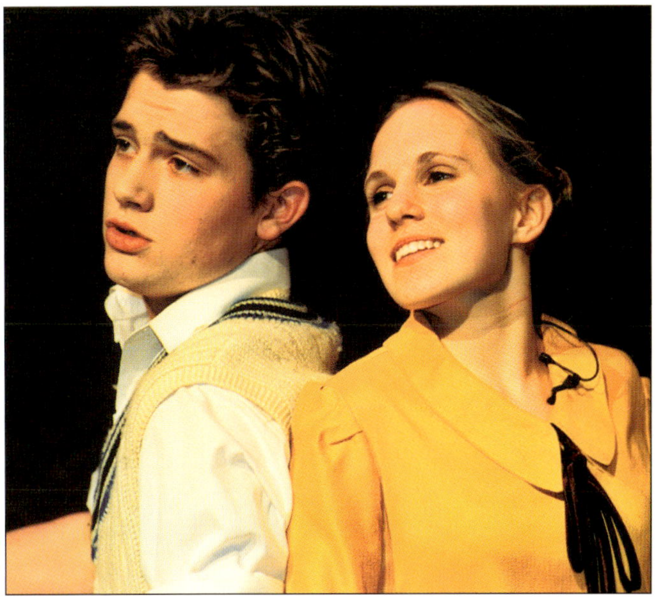

The Boy Friend

The Corps
and its Musicians

Membership of the corps is open to all boys in B and C Blocks. The average membership is about 30 boys from B and 90 from C. Each half there is a week-end training scheme, and the year's activities build up to two summer events.

First, there is the Tattoo that takes place on the eve of the Fourth of June. It is then that the Band and Pipe Band show off their musical and marching skills; there are mock battle scenes; martial arts are demonstrated, as are weaponry skills; teams compete for supremacy in various races, and occasionally the evening ends in a firework display. The Sword of Honour is awarded to the best first-year cadet, and the Acland Trophy is awarded for leadership in the second year. All takes place under floodlights in the presence of an inspecting officer and a vast crowd of families and friends.

Secondly, there is corps camp that takes place at the end of the Summer Half. Recent locations for this have included Snowdonia, the South Coast (sailing), and the Pembrokeshire Coast (sea kayaking) in the UK, whilst destinations abroad have been Belize, Oman and Germany.

In the year 2000 the Orderly Room was moved from Cannon Yard to a new site between the Laundry and Walpole House. Larger in size, it has greater storage space and many practical benefits.

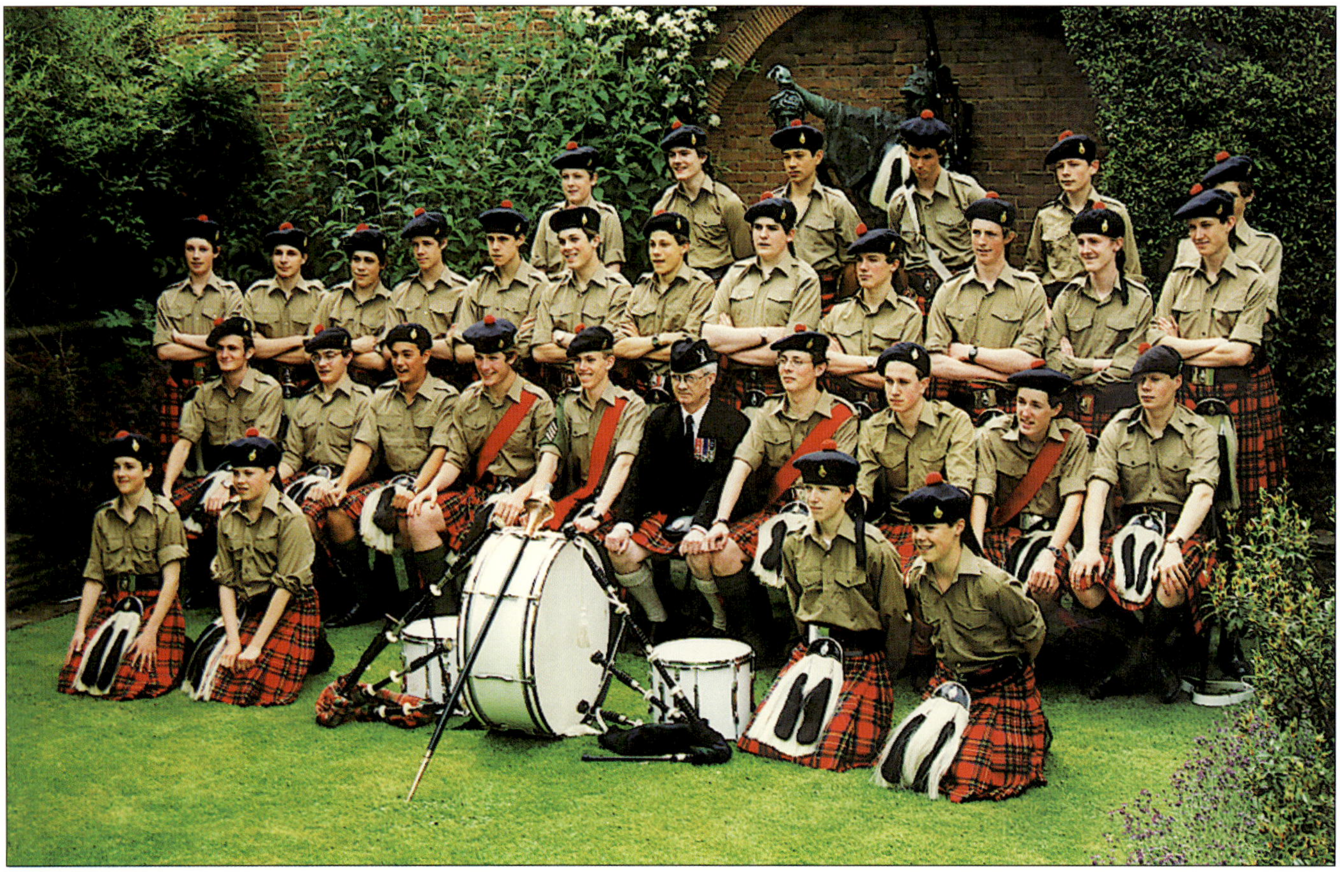

The Pipe Band

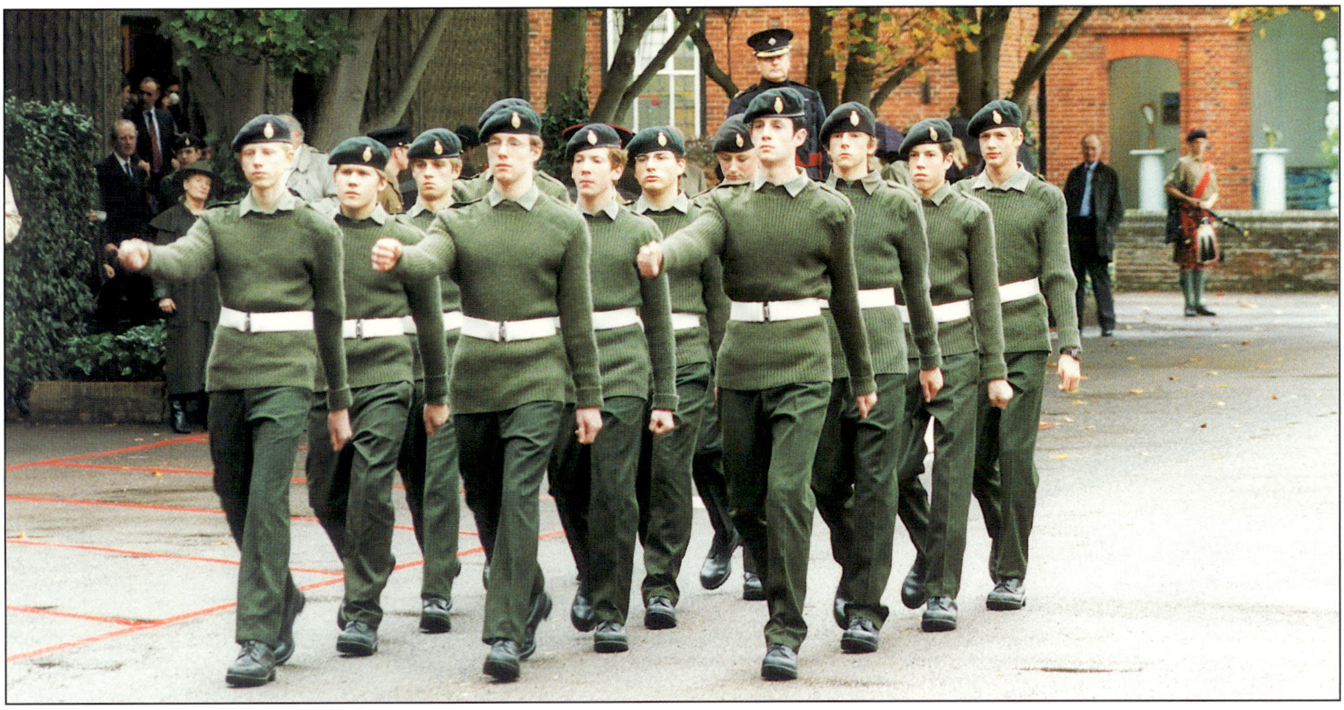

Passing-out parade for new recruits

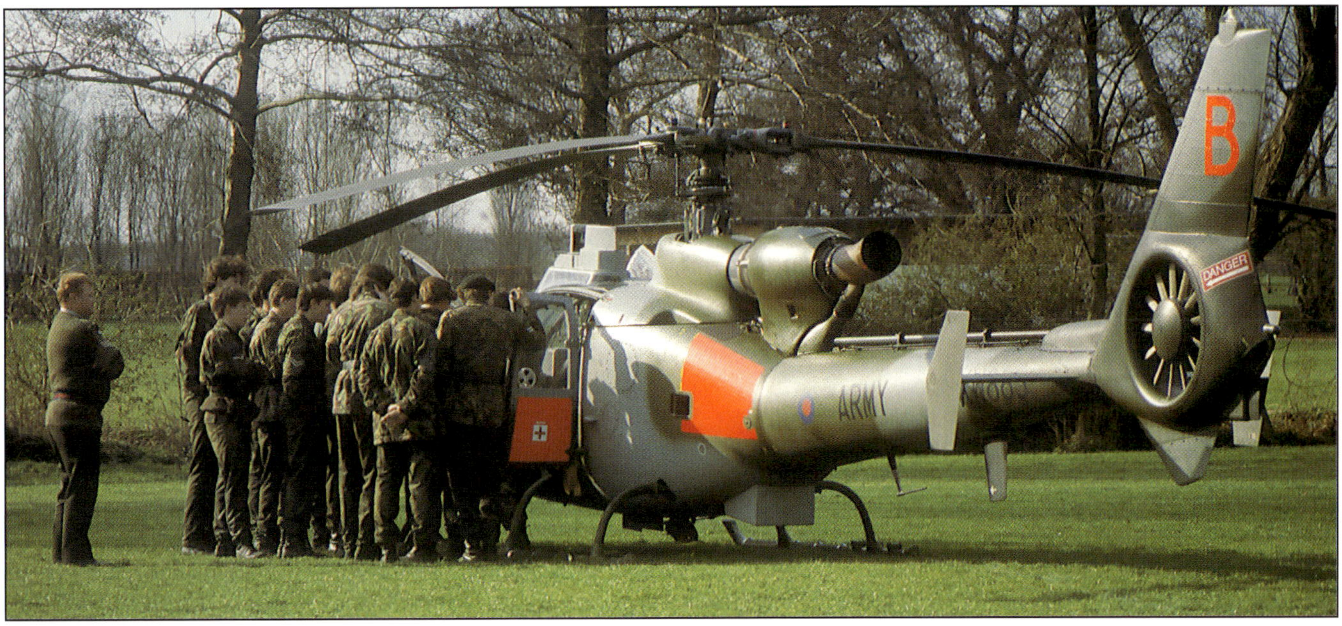

Helicopter training

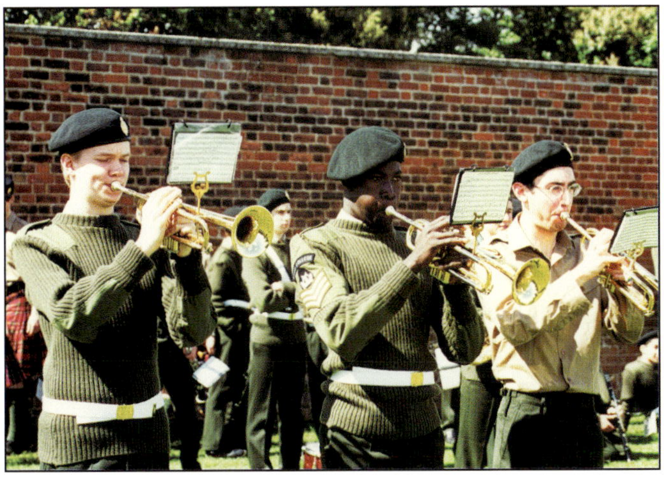

The Band in rehearsal

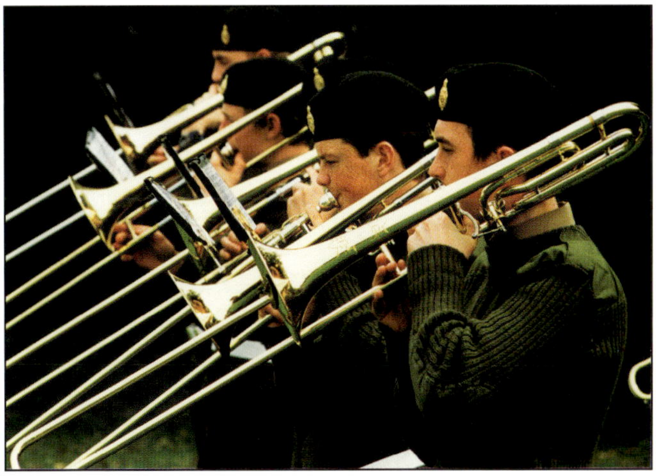

Trombone section

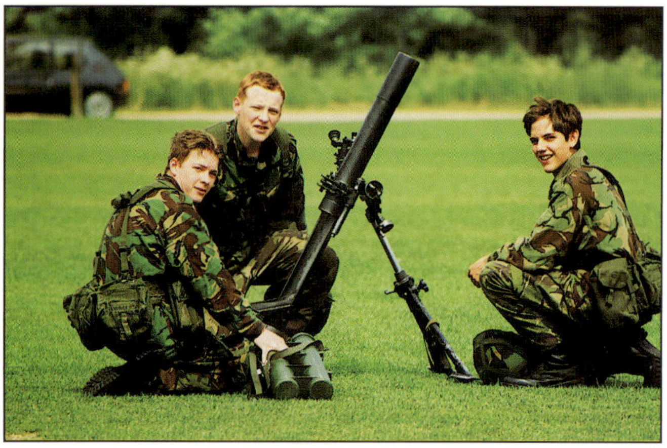

Simulated mortar firing

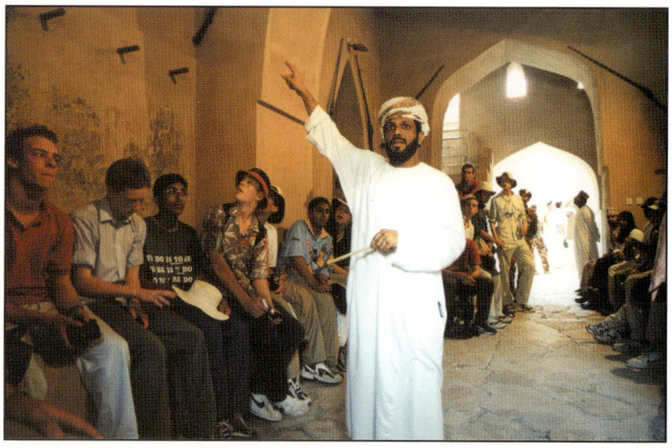

In Oman

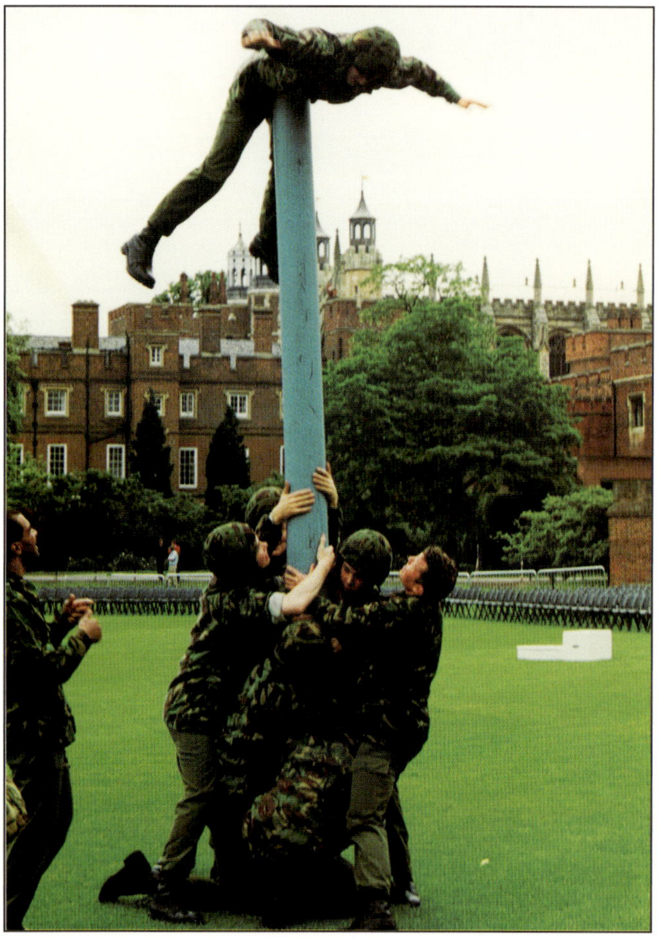

Borne aloft

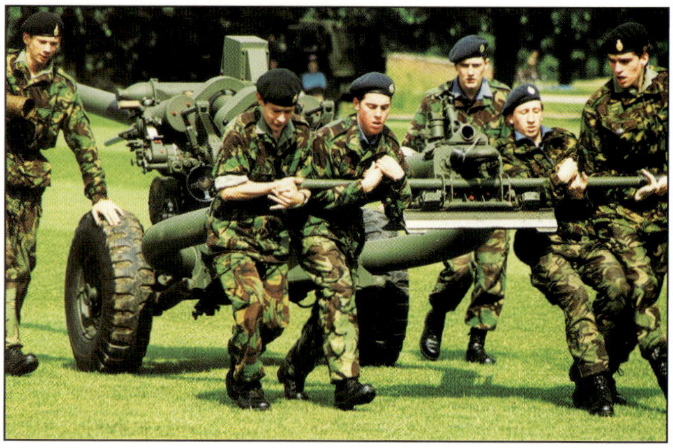

It's a race!

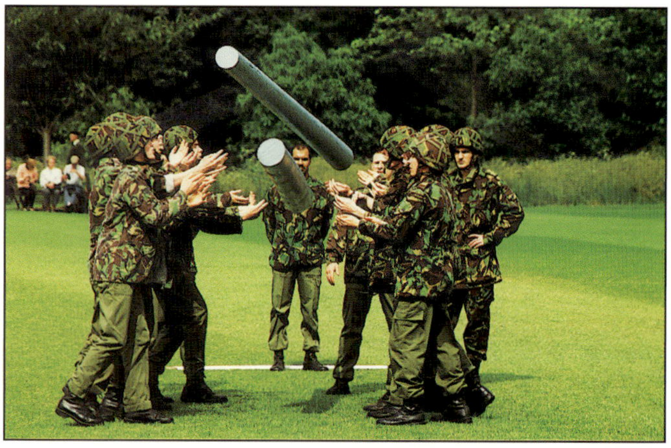

Log exercises

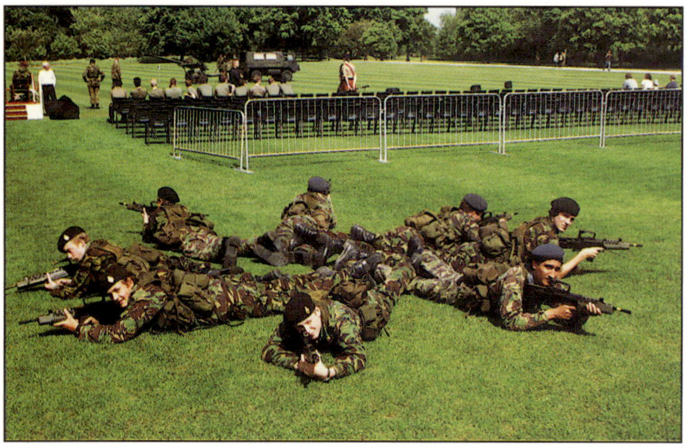

Preparing for action

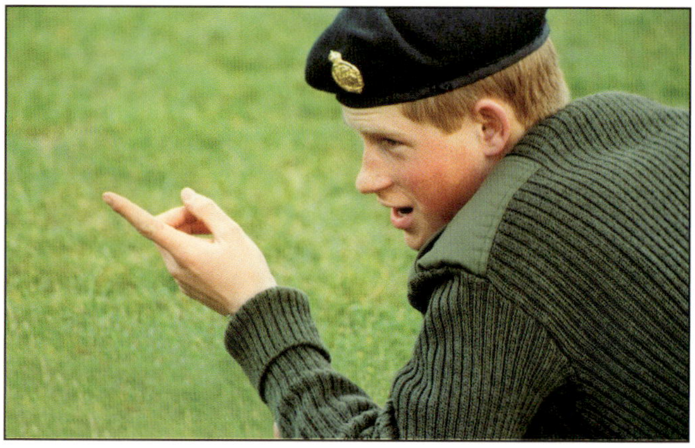

Prince Harry

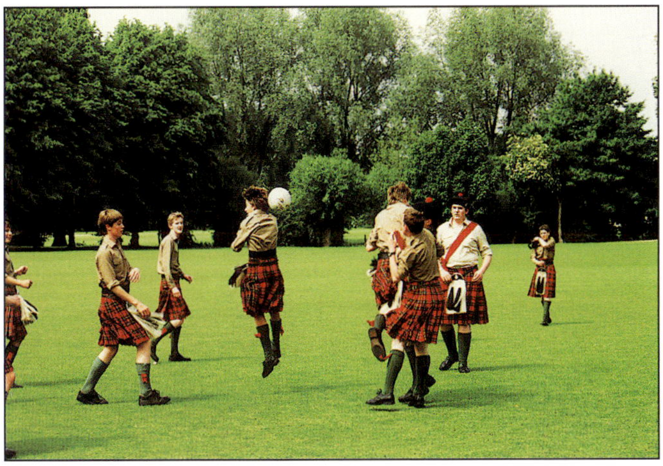

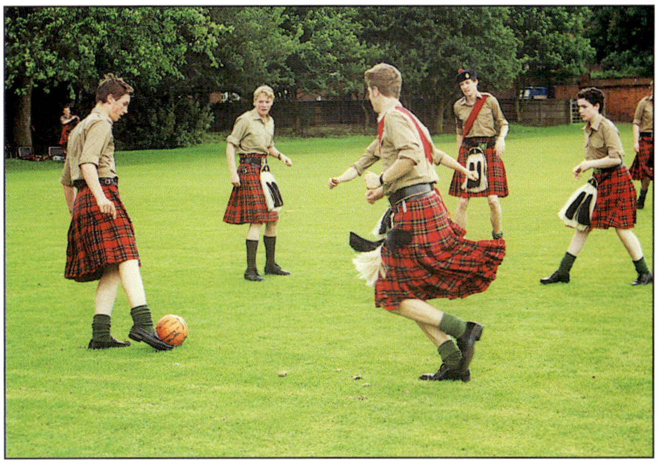

Pipers relax awaiting their call to parade

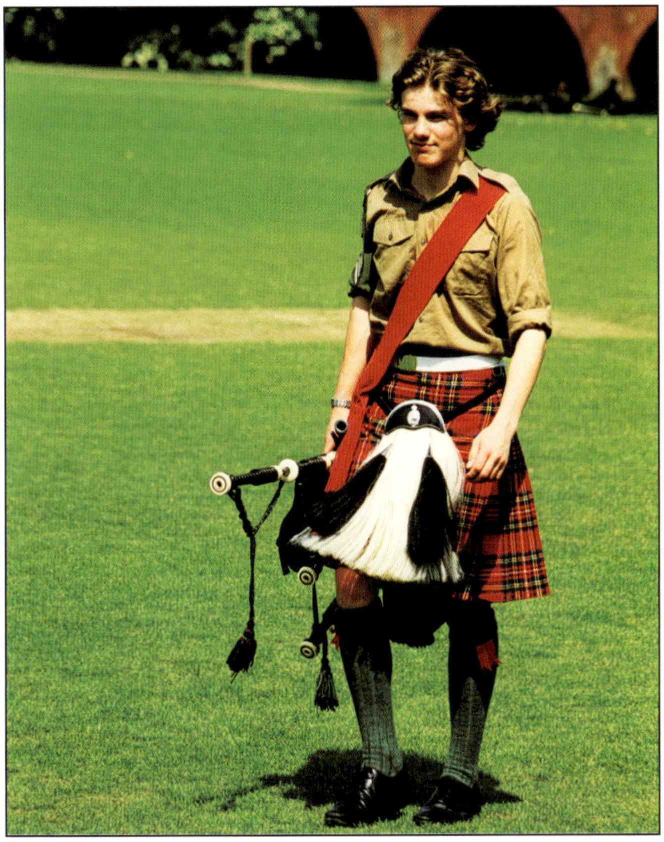

Off to parade

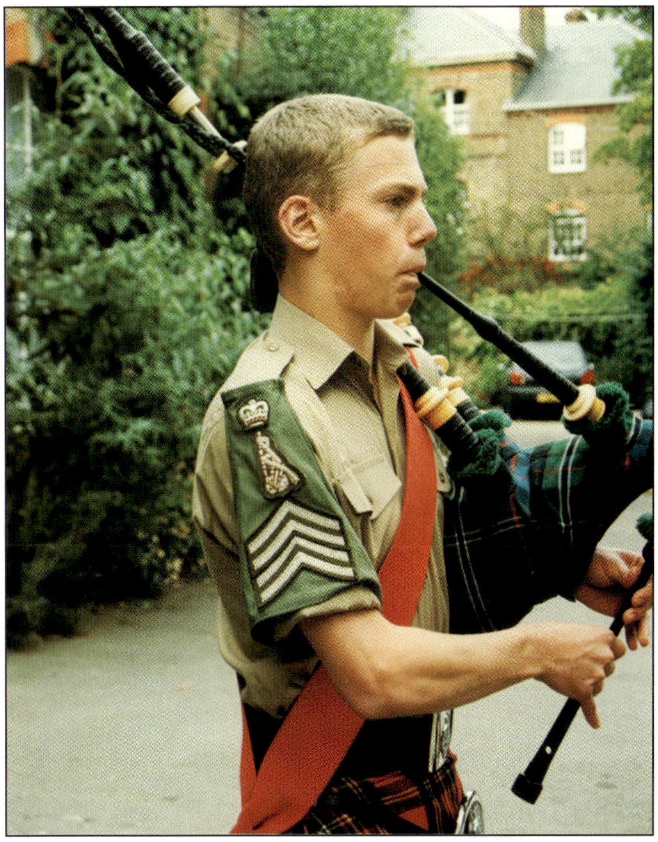

The Pipe-Major

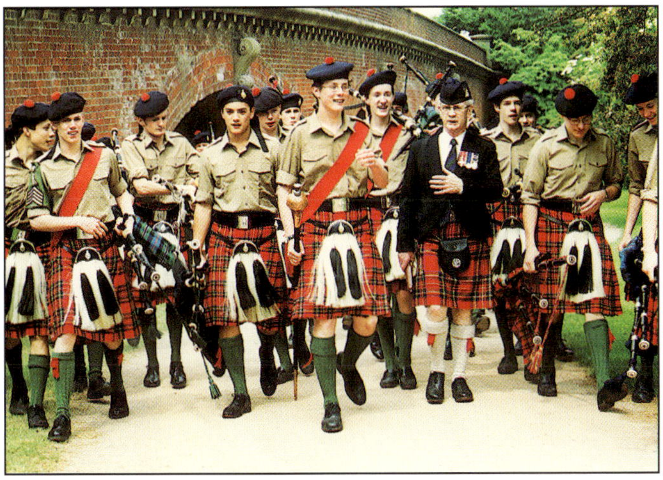

Pipe-Major with his men

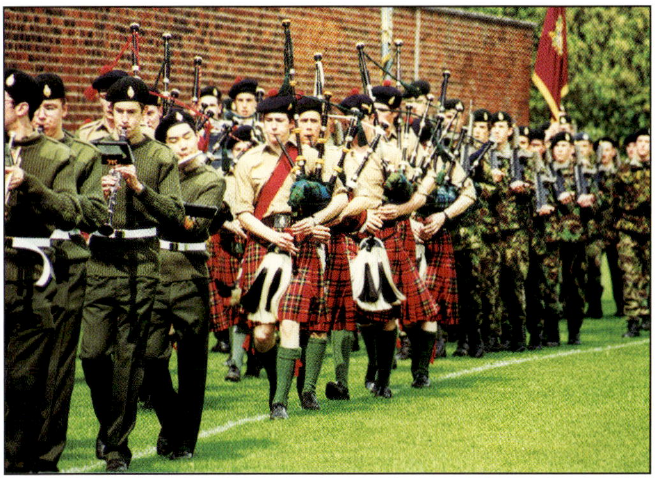

Marching on to parade for the Tattoo

Grounds, Playing Fields, Trees

Eton is fortunate in having extensive grounds with many fine gardens and trees. The trees suffered badly from Dutch elm disease in the 1970s and from the great storm of 1987, but through imaginative replanting and hard work by ground and forestry staff they have recovered well.

At the northern end of the campus lie Agar's and Dutchman's – over 100 acres of mown grass, fringed with chestnuts and planes, and divided by an avenue of limes. In the winter football and rugby are played on some 24 pitches here, whilst 15 cricket pitches take their place in the summer. Closer to the School is Upper Club, surely one of the most picturesque cricket grounds in the country, lined with horse chestnuts and limes. Along the river bank are willows and alders, and nearby is College Field. On one side of College Field is the famous Wall, and on two others are mixed plantings of flowering trees, among them a fine euodia. At a cheerful and informal ceremony attended by staff and boys shortly before her 100th birthday, HM the Queen Mother planted a liriodendron here. It complements the mature tulip tree that stands at the entrance to College Field.

Outside the Cloister buildings are grouped three formal gardens, the Provost's, the Head Master's and the Fellows'. These are open to the public on a Saturday in June under the National Gardens Scheme. Towering above the Fellows' Garden is Eton's noblest tree, a massive plane, possibly planted before 1700. Across Fellows' Eyot on an island in the Thames is Luxmoore's Garden, laid out by Henry Luxmoore, Master and Housemaster, between 1890 and 1926. It is now approached over the elegant Kingfisher Bridge, built in 1990 for the 550th anniversary of the founding of the College. With its happy combination of wild areas and formal borders and its views of river and Chapel, this is an idyllic spot.

In central Eton attractive gardens stretch behind many of the boys' houses, and there are some colourful trees in the grave-yard beside College Chapel. Sadly the line of old lime trees in Long Walk had to be felled in 1993, but the hornbeams that replace them are already growing well. A very extensive arboretum is being planted beside Dorney Lake.

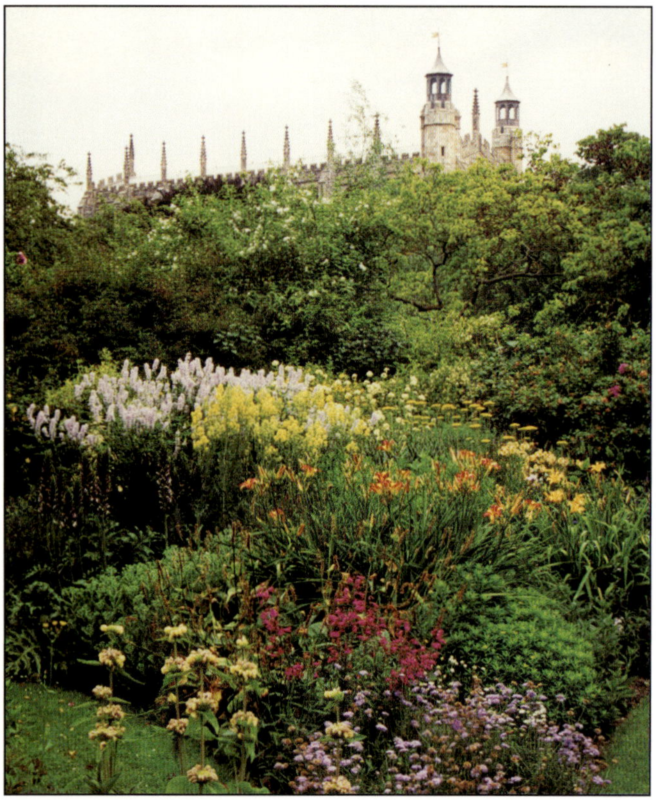

Luxmoore's Garden

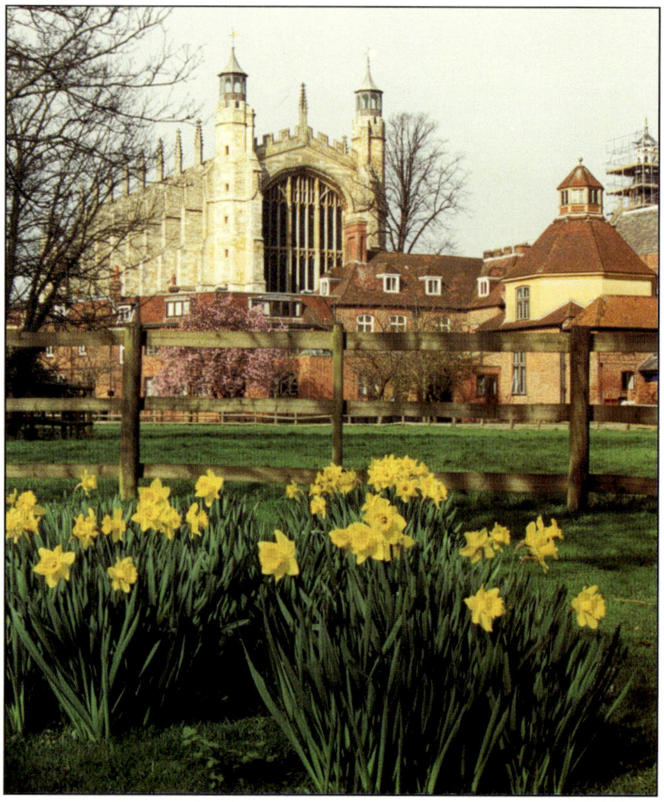

East end of College Chapel and the octagonal College kitchen

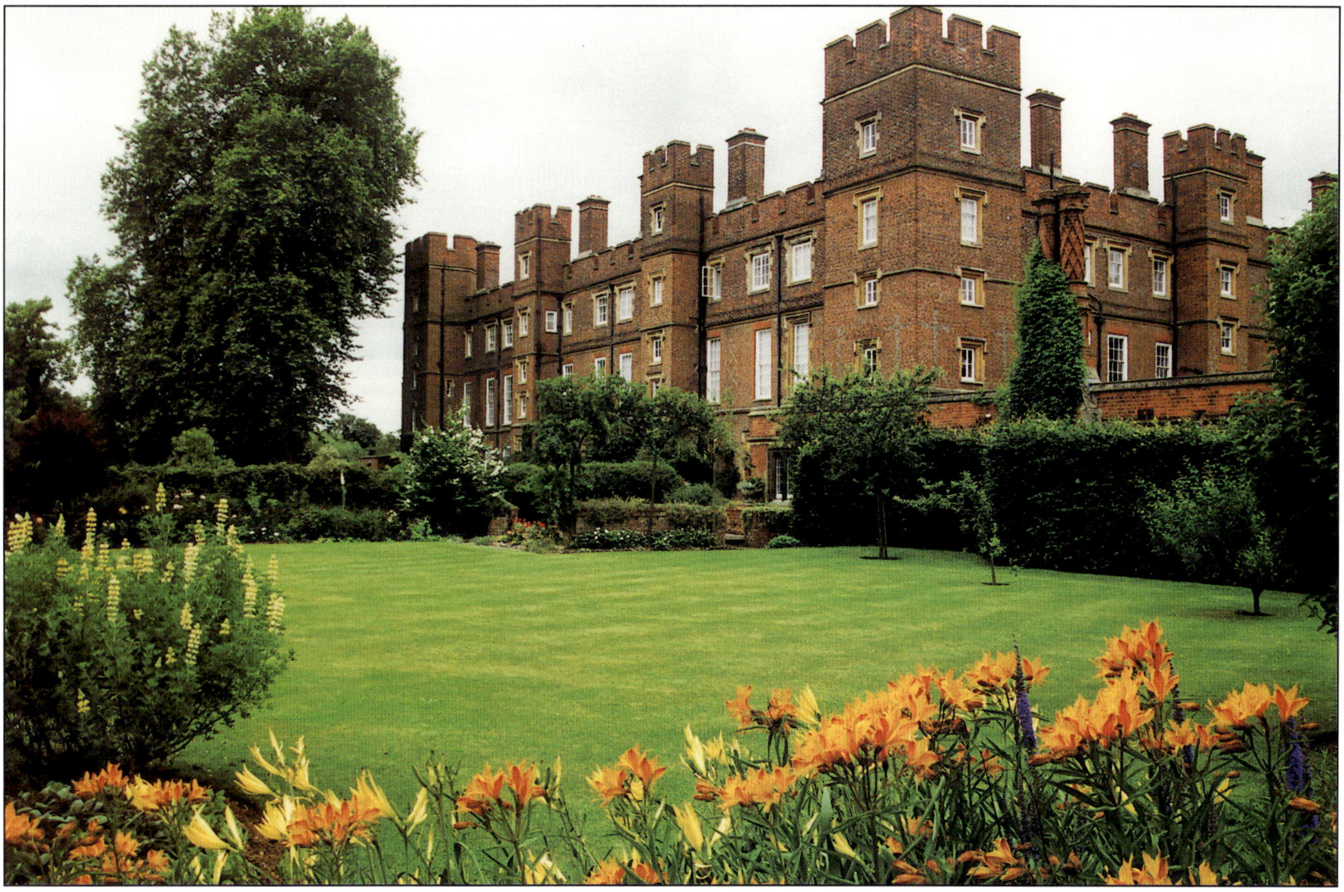

The Head Master's Garden

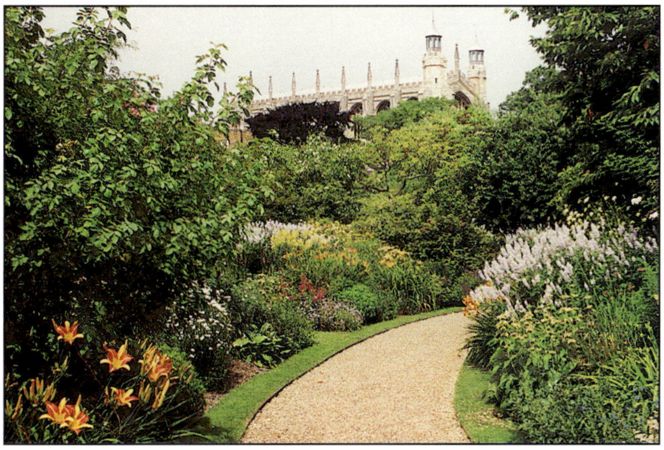

Luxmoore's Garden

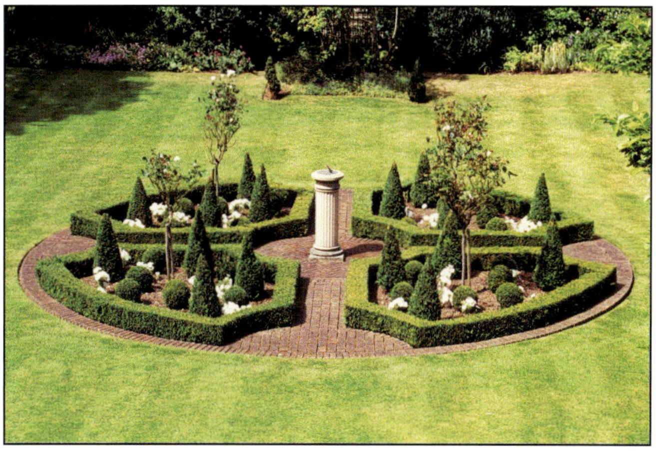

The Provost's Garden

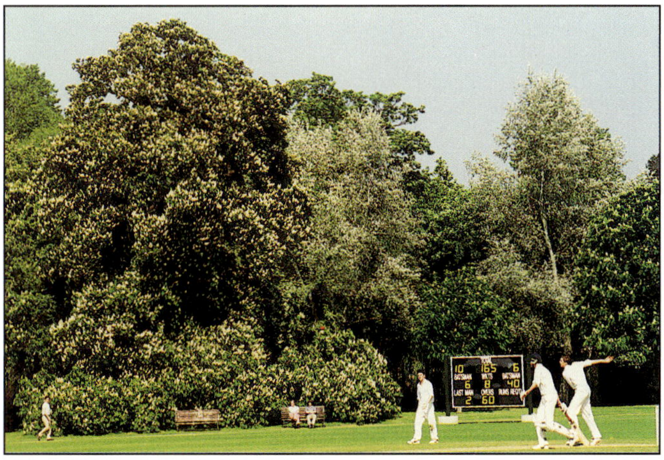

Summer on Upper Club

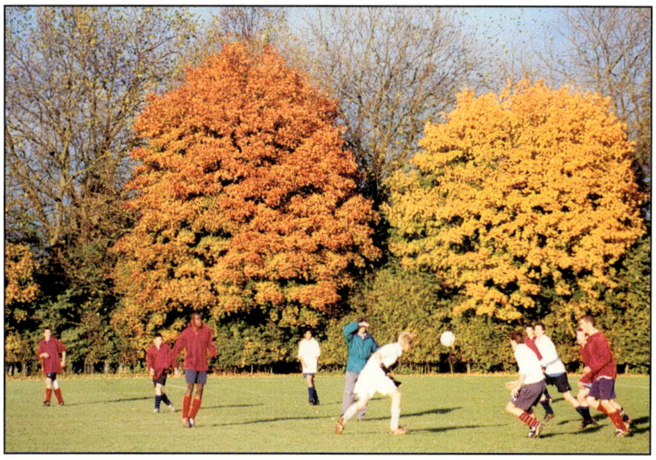

Autumn colours on Agar's

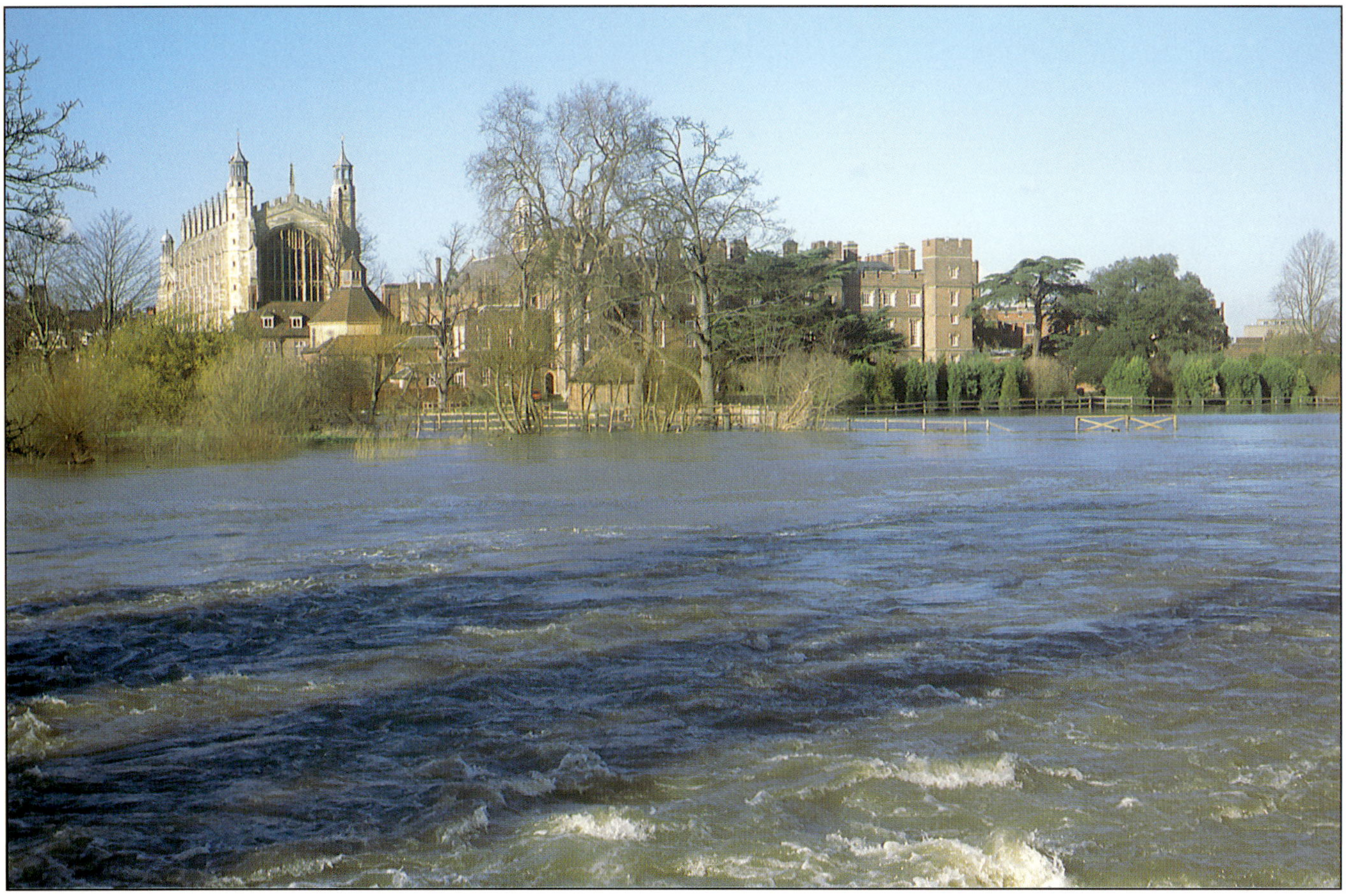

Winter floods seen across the Thames from Romney Island

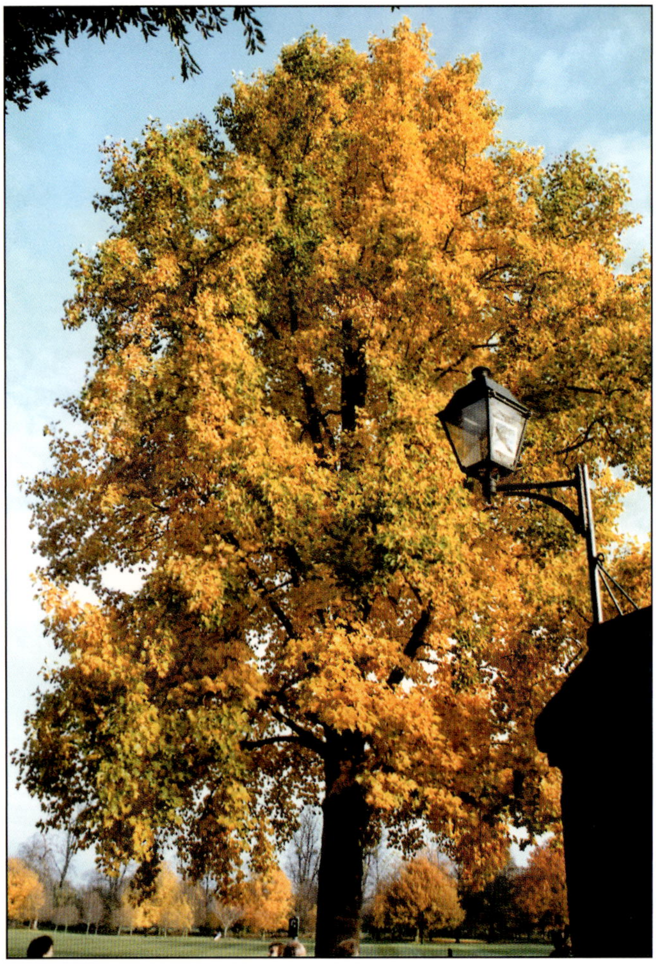

The tulip tree at the entrance to College Field

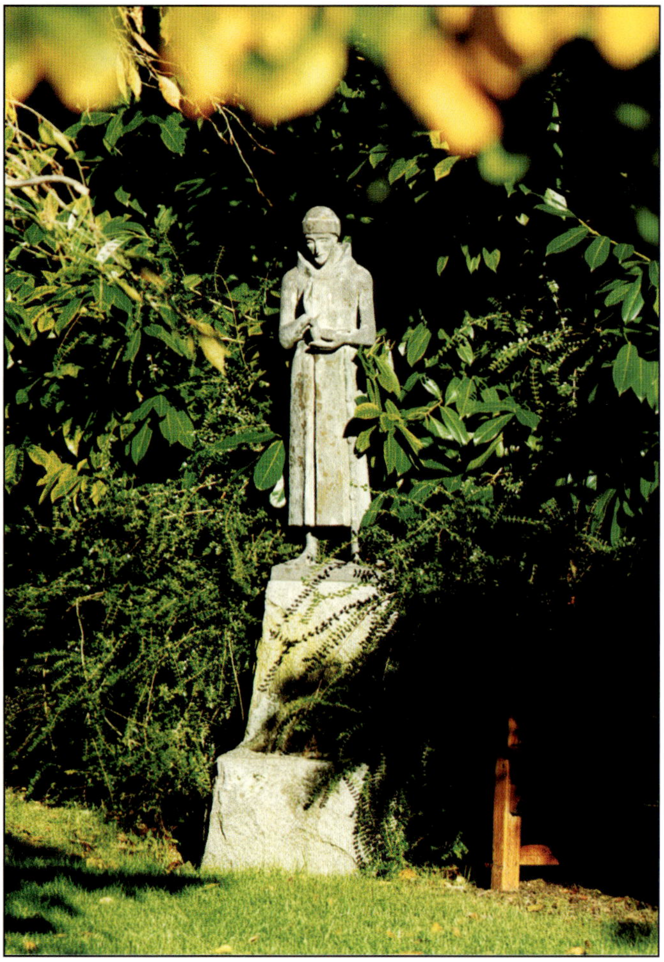

The statue of St. Francis in Luxmoore's Garden

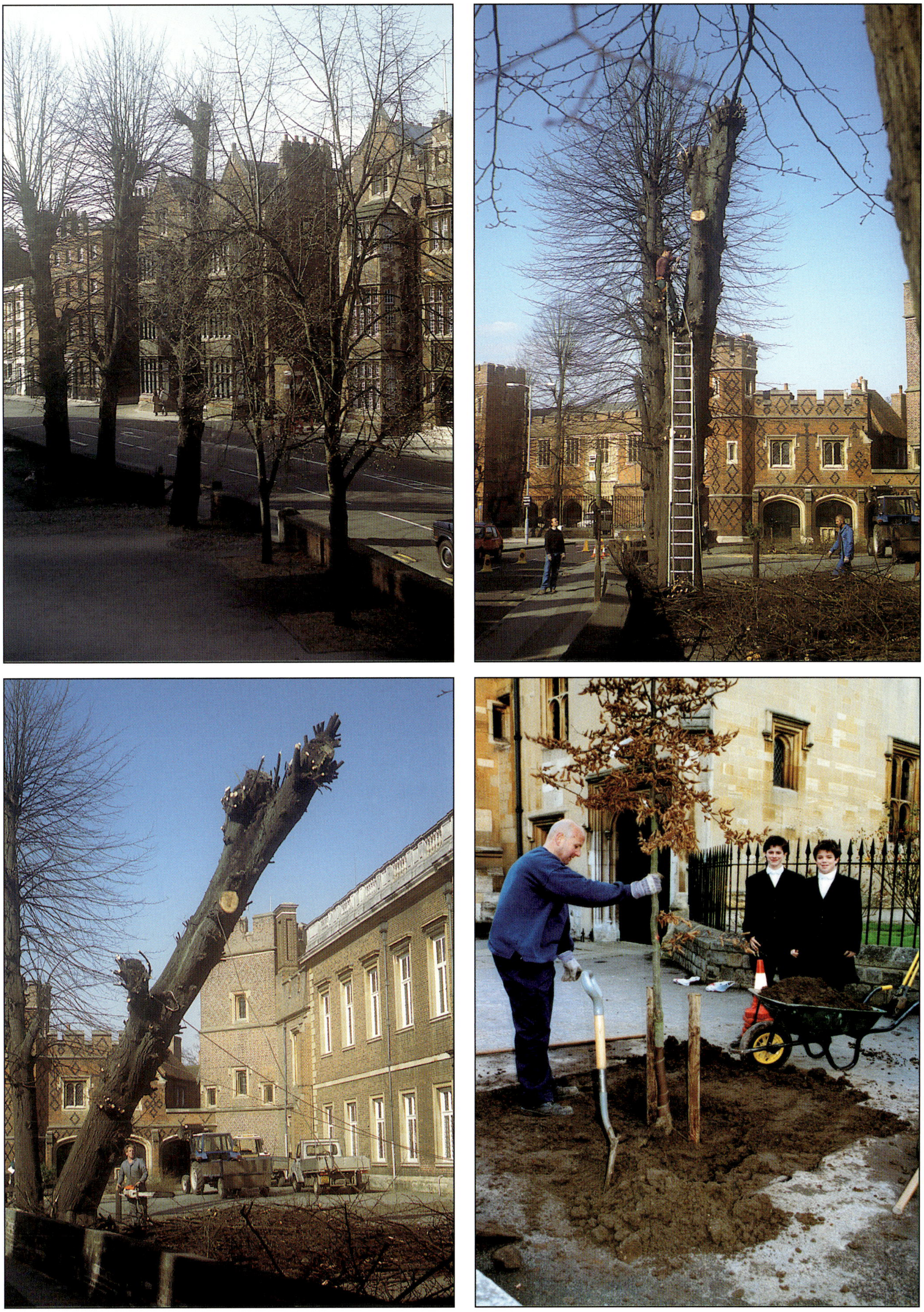

The felling of lime trees in Long Walk in 1993, and the planting of hornbeams to replace them

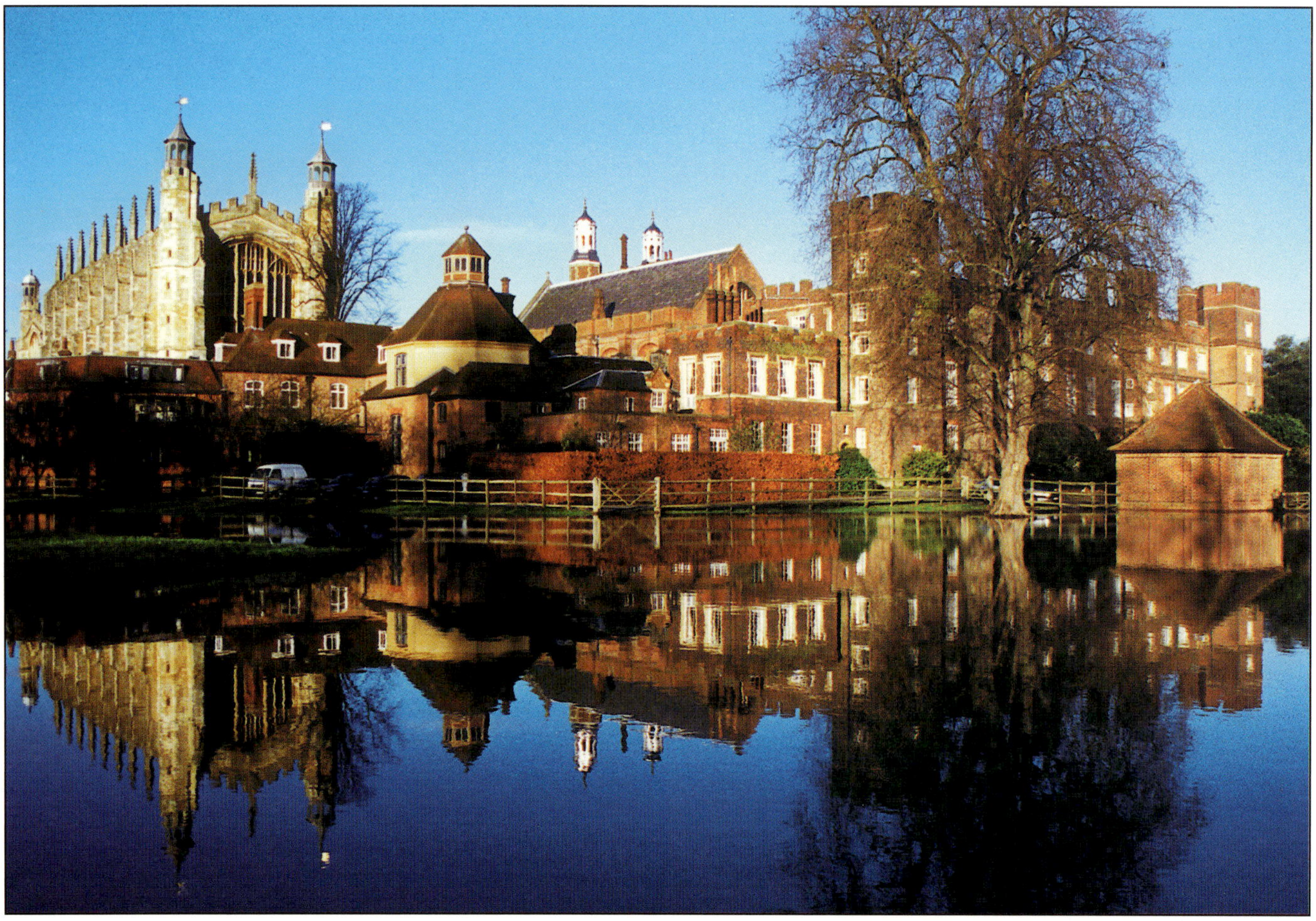

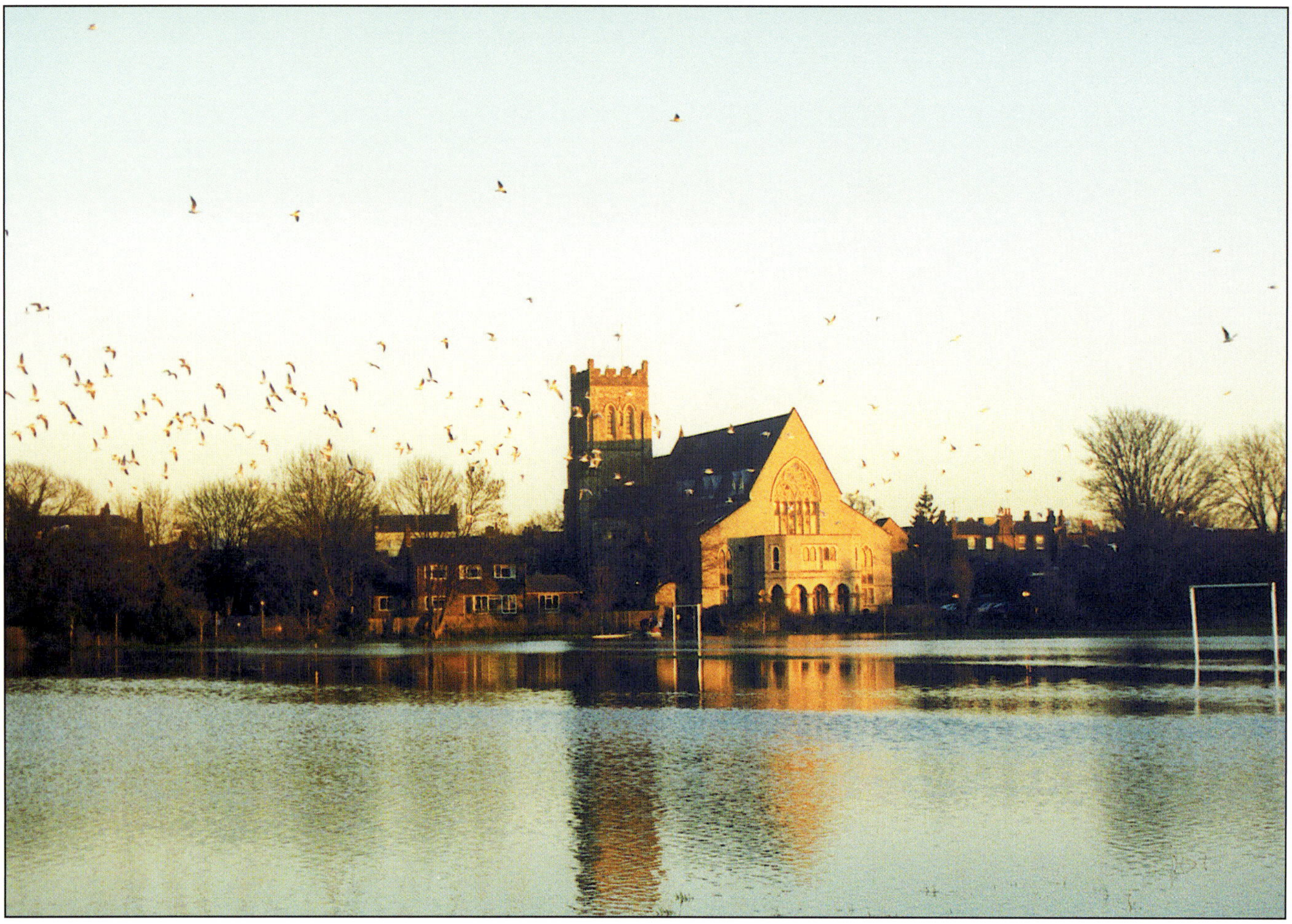

The floods of December 2000. Fellows Eyot and South Meadow under water

Sport at Eton

In many respects sporting life at Eton is no different from that of any other similar school. Teams train hard for all the popular sports, receive expert coaching, compete fiercely against other schools, and the best players enjoy considerable kudos. Inter-house competitions are keenly contested, and passions are roused when they reach their final stages. In addition to popular sports, there are two games that are played only at Eton, the Wall Game and the Field Game, and one that originated here and spread, Eton Fives. Several of the rarer sporting activities are also available to enthusiasts, so overall the boys have remarkable breadth of choice.

Thames Valley Athletics Centre

Planning for The Thames Valley Athletics Centre originated from a request by the Royal Borough of Windsor and Maidenhead to permit Windsor, Slough and Eton Athletic Club to have access to Eton's six-lane track. Consent in principle was readily granted, but improvement was needed to the College's track to bring it up to the required standard. During the feasibility study it became apparent that there was a need for an eight-lane track and indoor facilities. This promoted a highly successful partnership between an independent school and two local authorities, and the Sports Lottery Fund provided the finance. Eton College's use of track and hall amounts to less than ten per cent of the total use. Opened in May 1999 by the Duke of Edinburgh, track and hall are used by athletes of all abilities from Olympic champions to local schoolchildren.

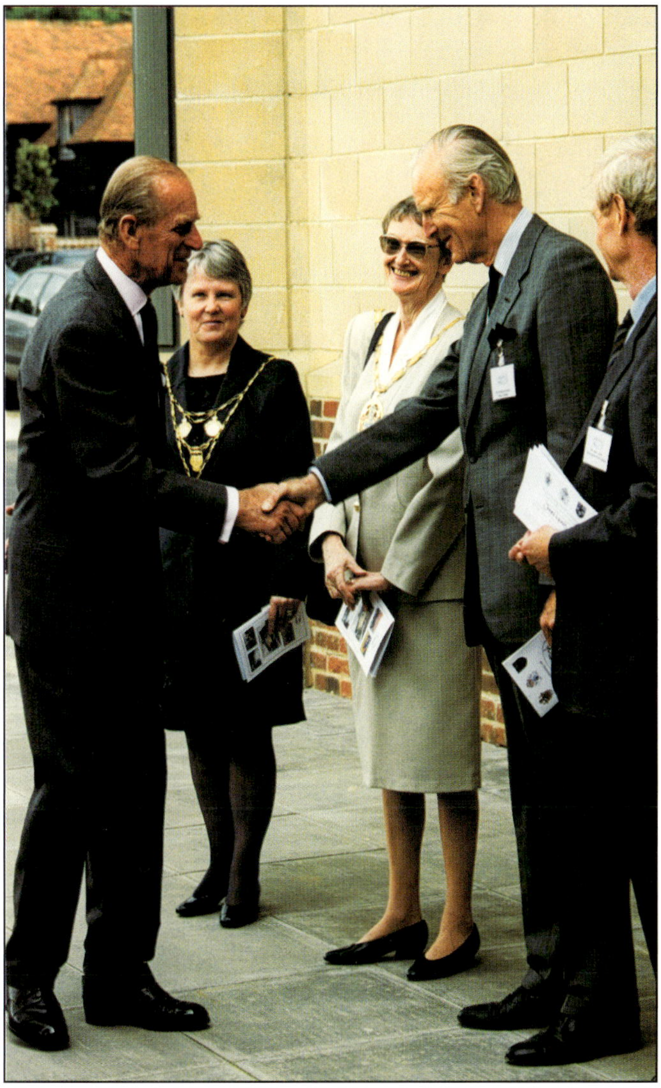

The Duke of Edinburgh at the official opening

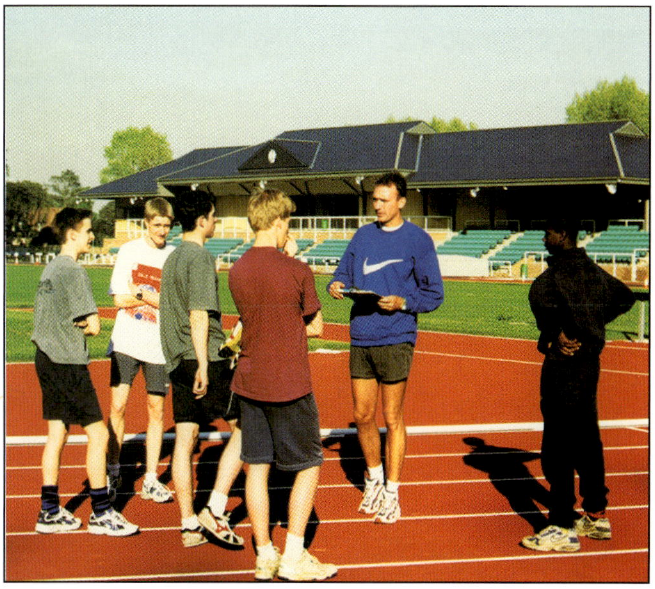

Eton boys training on the new track

Athletics

The athletics season spans the Lent and Summer Halves. The Lent Half programme is domestic. In often arctic weather conditions, the boys battle for the various individual and inter-House trophies in track and field events. Even if a competitor is eliminated in the heats, he can still contribute towards his House's points total by reaching one of three set standards in his event. A running tally of House points adds excitement to finals day, for the House with the highest total wins the coveted athletics shield. In the summer boys opting for athletics compete in matches against many other schools, and the best boys are entered for the Berkshire county championships. The new facilities give athletes every chance to train hard and perform to the best of their abilities.

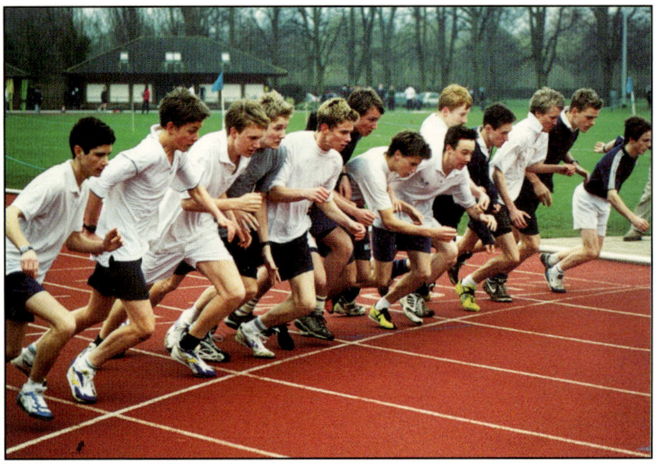

Away they go

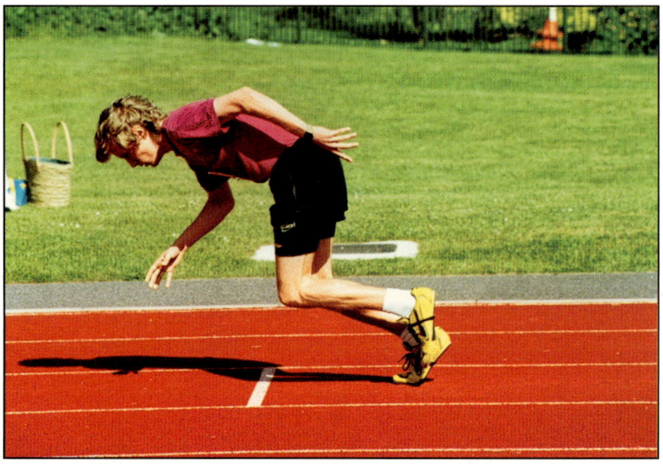

A horizontal start

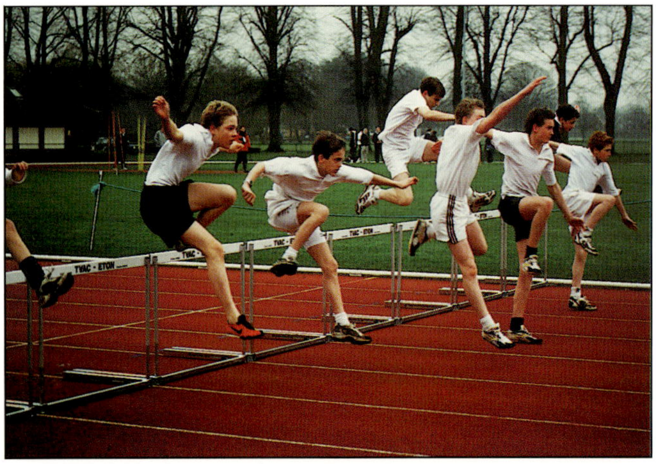

Contrasting styles

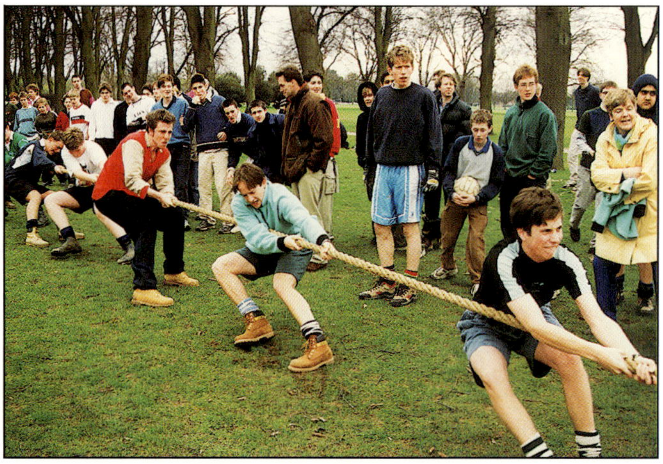

Tug-of-war

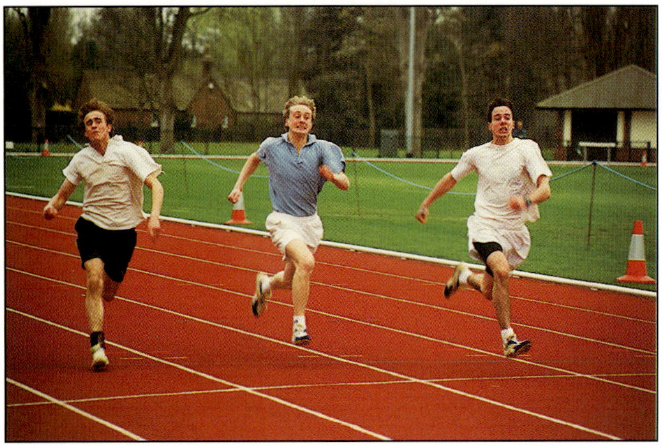

Approaching the tape

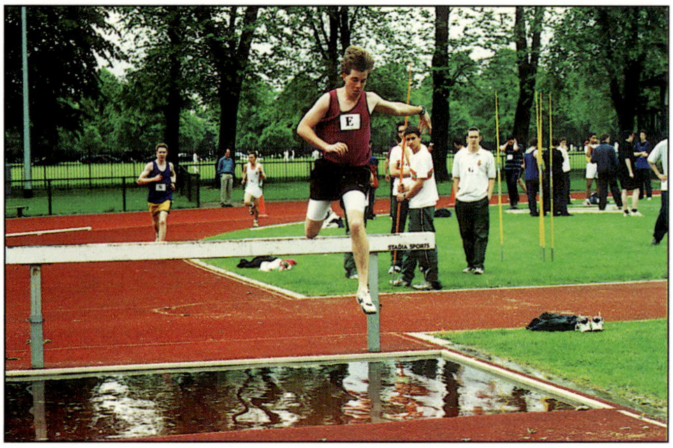

Steeplechase

Beagling

Beagling – the hunting of hares with dogs by man – is an ancient pursuit. The Eton College Hunt has officially been in existence since 1899. Beaglers hunt with a pack of about 16 'couple' (i.e. 32 hounds) drawn from the total of 33 couple. The Masters will have visited the land to be hunted in advance and discussed with the land-owner or host which areas to hunt and which to avoid. About 15 boys accompany the hunt, fewer mid-week, more on Saturdays. The hounds are kennelled in new buildings, the old ones having been taken down to make way for the flood relief channel, now known as the Jubilee River. The hounds are exercised twice daily by the Kennel Huntsman and boy volunteers, and they can be seen passing through the School grounds before breakfast and after lunch. The hunting season runs from September to March.

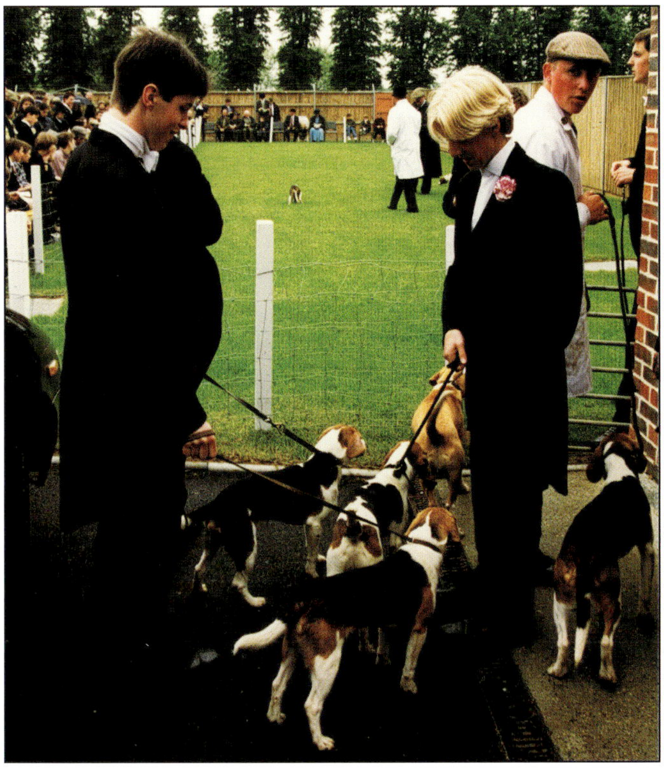

The puppy show

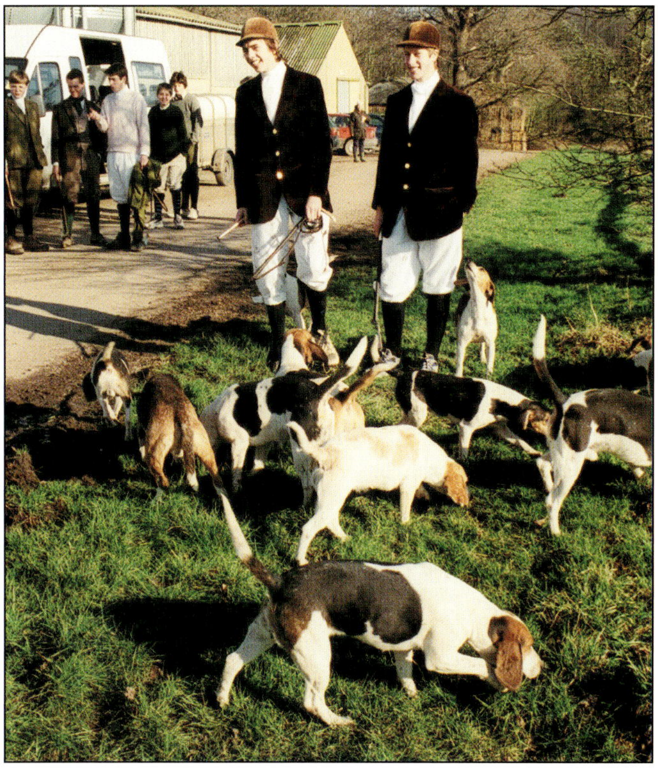

Preparing for the hunt

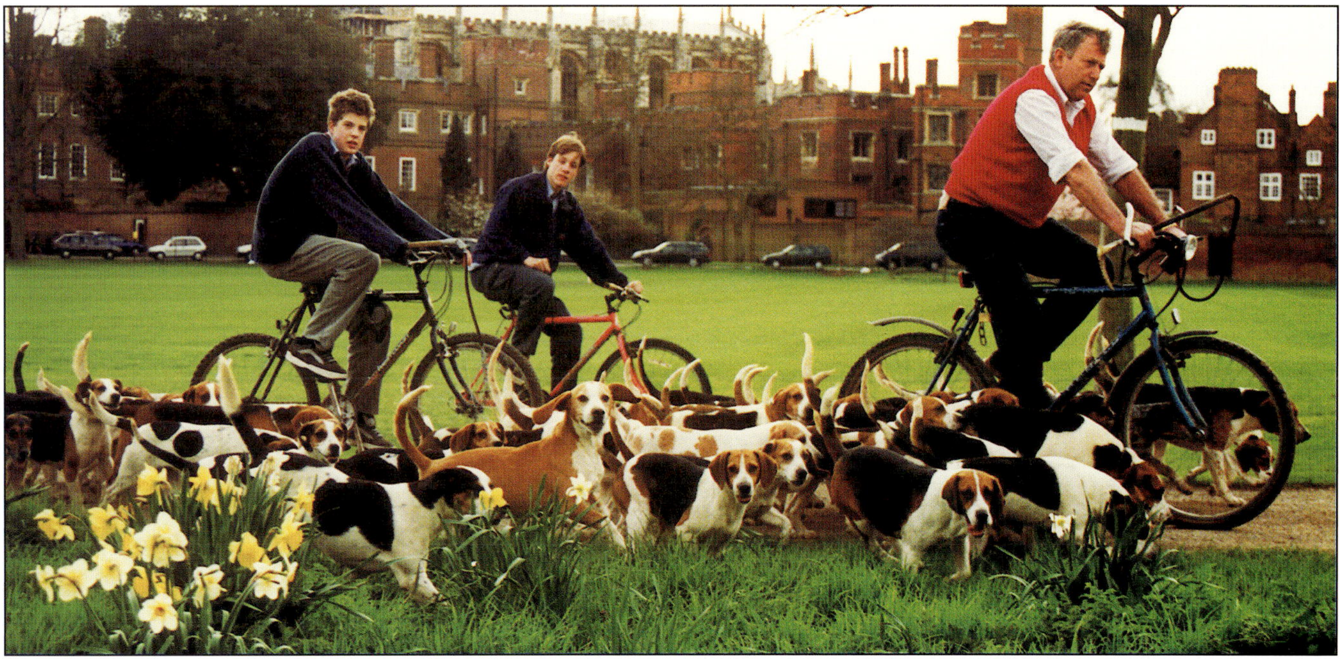

Exercising the beagles

Cricket

A watercolour by William Evans from the 1830s and a lithograph by C.W. Radclyffe of 1844 remind us that cricket has been popular at Eton for more than 150 years. No one could wish to play the game in more idyllic surroundings than Upper Club, the 1st XI pitch. Surrounded as it is by chestnut and lime trees, it provides a picturesque backdrop to a game played by a large number of boys. There are twenty-one regular School teams and, of course, internal league and knock-out competitions between the twenty-five houses. One development of recent years is that limited-over cricket has largely taken the place of the more traditional game that so often ended in a draw. The highlight of the 1st XI season remains the match against Harrow at Lord's. This fixture is no longer a two-day match, nor does it attract the crowds of former years. In 1914, for example, the two-day attendance at Lord's was estimated to be 38,000. In 1994 and 2001 the Eton Under 15 XI won the final of the national knock-out competition for that age-group in matches played at Trent Bridge. Recent Etonians to win honours at cricket have been John Barclay (Sussex) and Matthew Fleming (Kent and England).

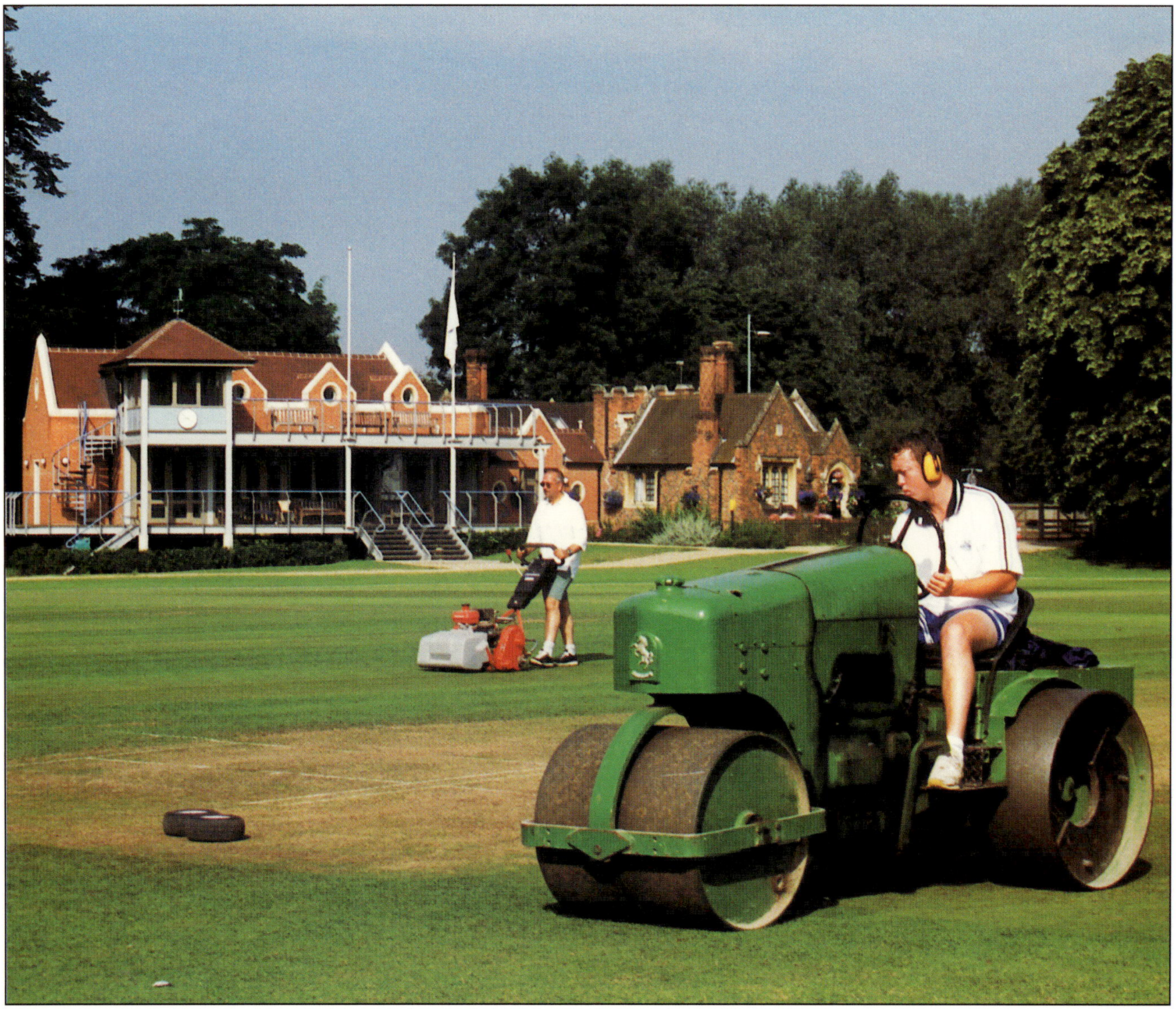

Groundsmen preparing the square on Upper Club, early morning. The new pavilion (*left*) was opened by Lord Bramall in 1998

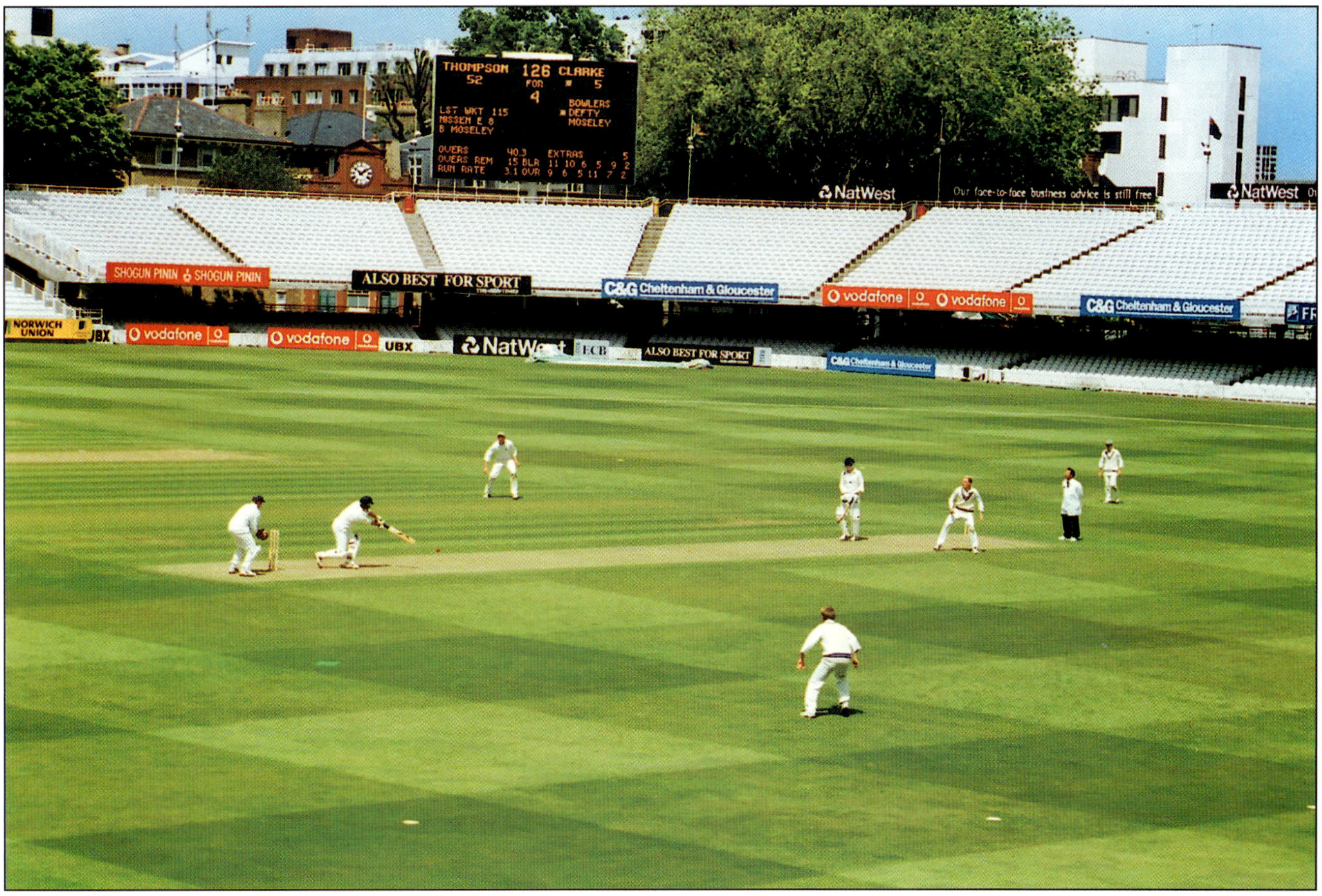

Lord's, 2002

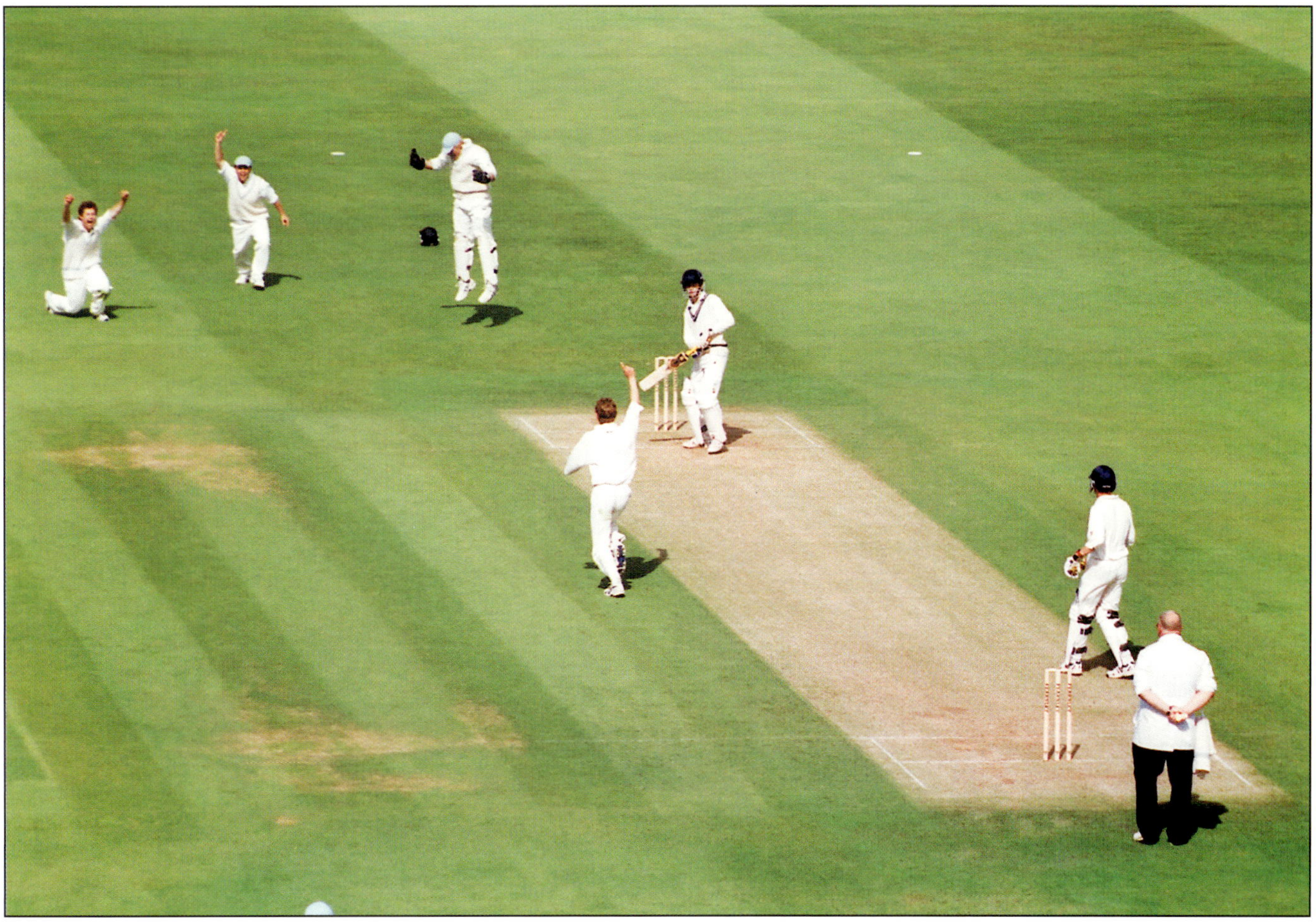

Another Harrow wicket falls!

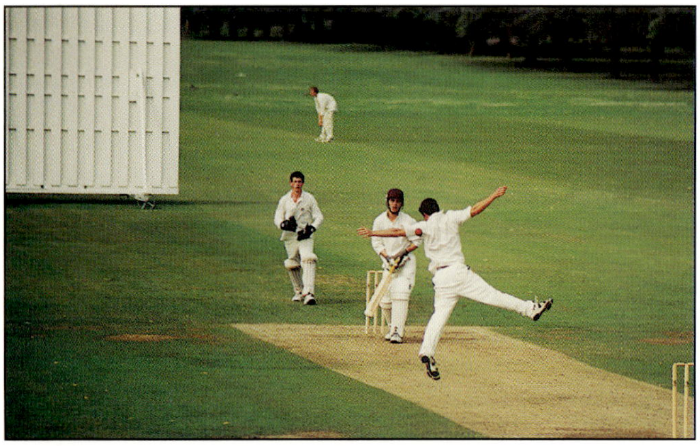

Almost caught and bowled!

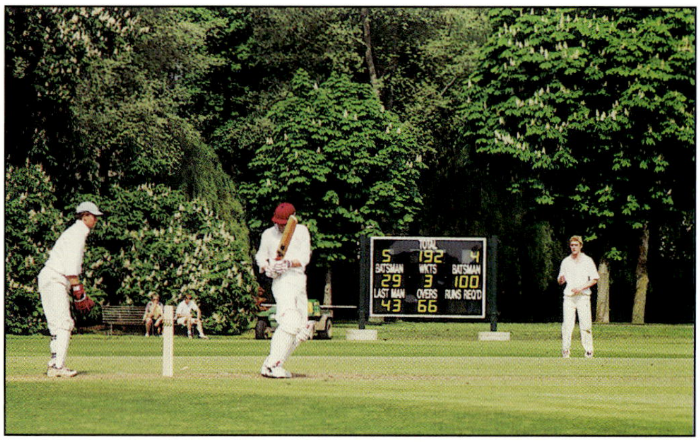

Batsman 4 bowled for 100

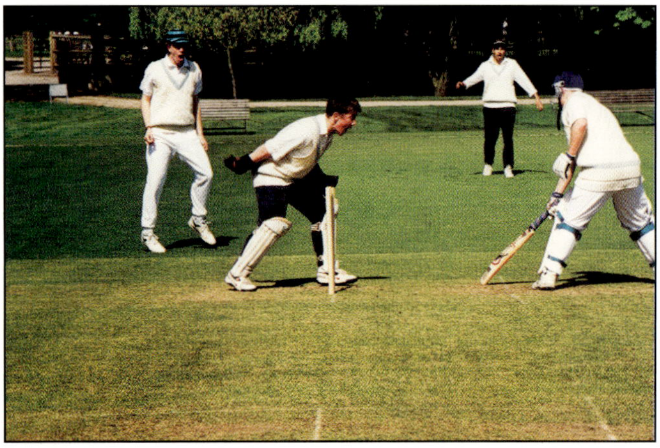

Middle practice – no bails

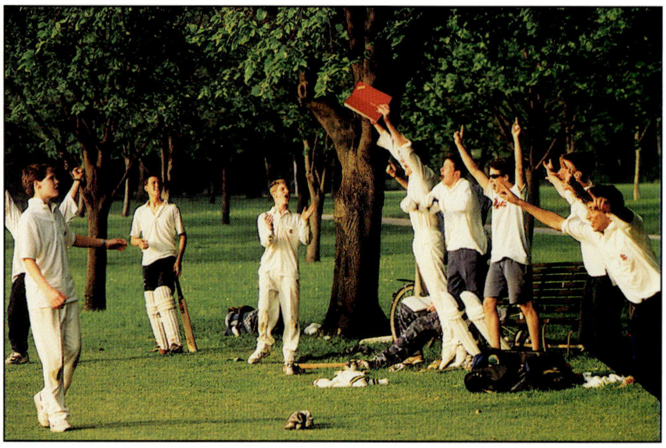

A narrow victory is celebrated

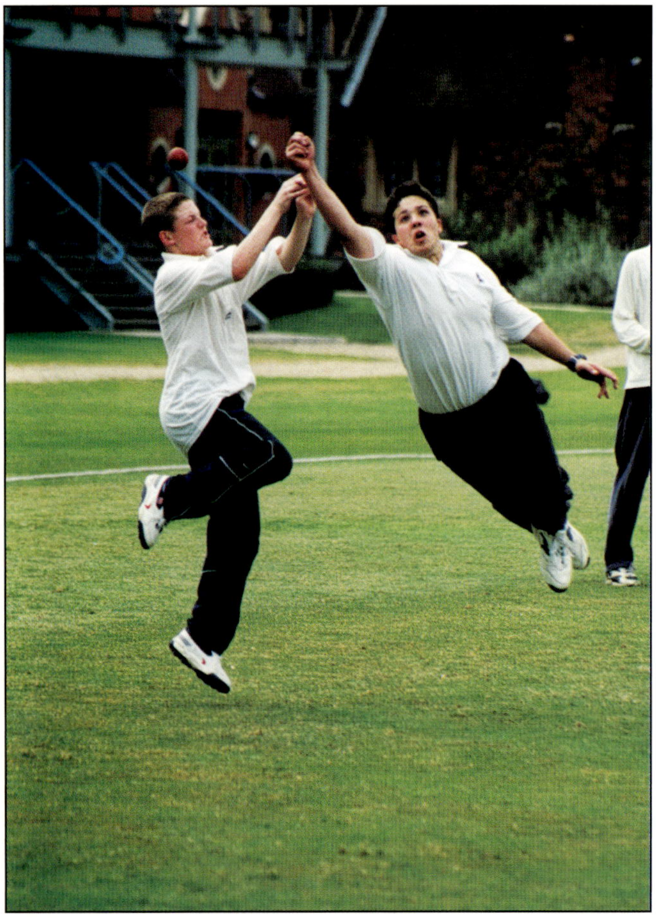

Fielding practice

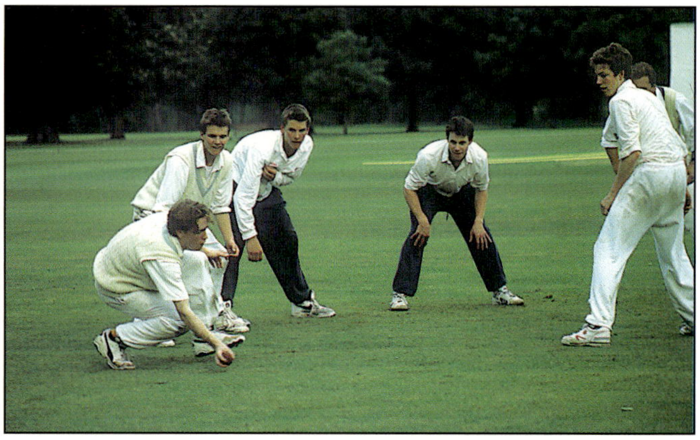

Slip catch

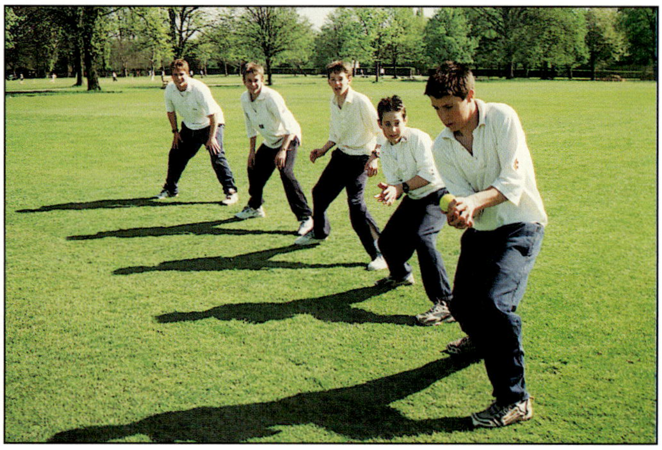

Fielding practice with a tennis ball

Eton Fives

Eton Fives, as the name suggests, originated at Eton. Boys, probably Collegers, gradually developed a ball game between two of the buttresses by the steps that lead up to the north door entrance of College Chapel. By 1848 the game had become so popular that four purpose-built courts were constructed. In the heyday of the game there were over 60 courts at Eton which were packed with players every day in the pre-lunch hour. Sixteen courts remain, and the game continues to flourish with internal competitions and matches against about twenty other schools. There is an Eton Fives Association, and the game has spread outside the UK to countries such as Switzerland and Nigeria. The court resembles its ecclesiastical prototype with the step, buttress and ledges clearly visible. Even the pepper-pot has its forebear in the angle between buttress and step. Unlike squash, this is a game uniquely for pairs, so cannot be played as a singles event. With gloved hands and a hard ball, just larger than a golf ball, the players hit the ball above the upper ledge on the front wall. As most shots are aimed at the protruding buttress on the left-hand side of the court, left-handers are at an advantage.

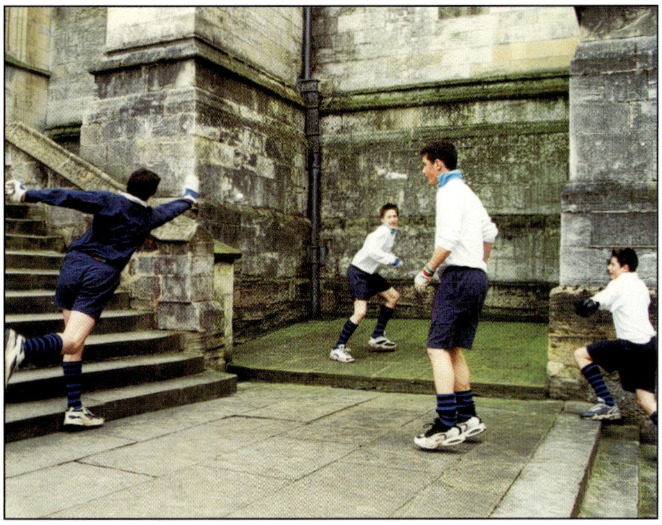

The original fives court between the buttresses of College Chapel

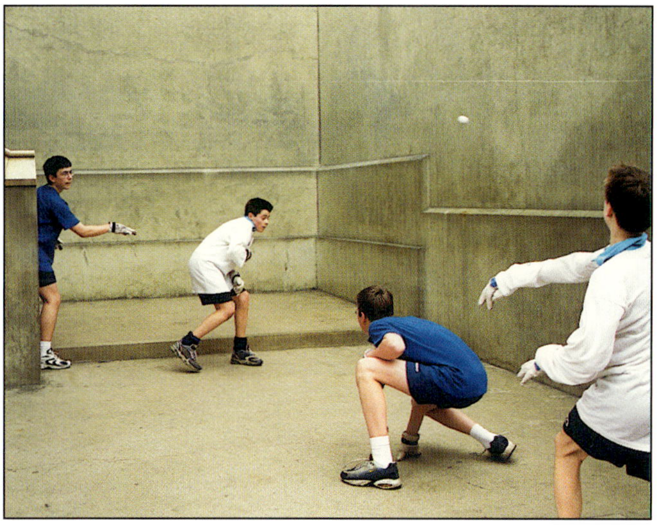

Purpose-built fives court

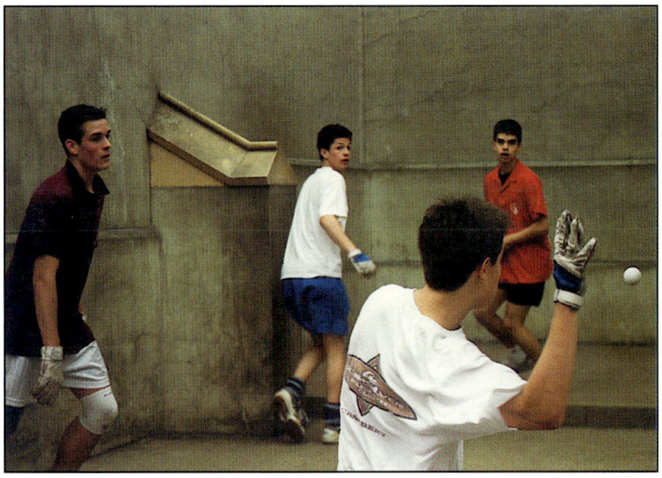

All eyes on the ball

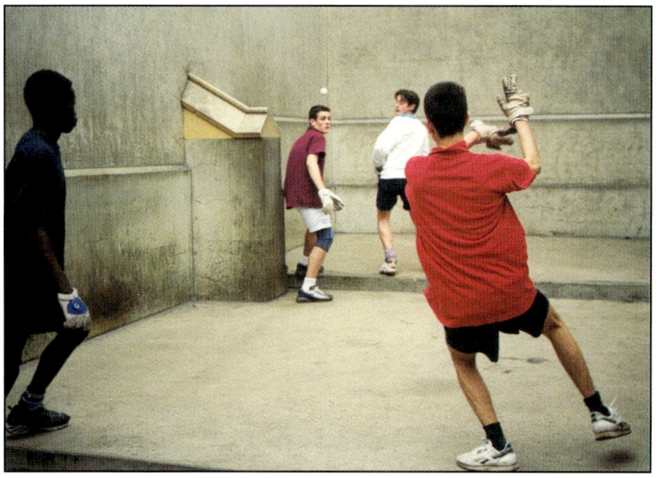

The buttress on the left-hand side adds an element of chance to the game, as the ball flies out at unexpected angles

Field Game

One of the two games unique to Eton is the Field Game. By contrast to the Wall Game, this is played by nearly all boys. It is a complicated game, and, unless one knows the rules, it is hard to spectate with any insight. The pitch resembles a football pitch, but with smaller goals. The ball, a size-4 football, cannot be passed, as in soccer. Seven players in a team of eleven form what is called a bully, the equivalent to a rugby scrum. The remaining four stand behind the bully at five to ten-yard intervals. The foremost of these is usually the star of the team, the 'fly', who is meant to perform heroic dribbling feats when he gets possession of the ball. The other three are the 'behinds' whose task it is to punt the ball over the opposing bully for their own bully to run on to. If the ball ricochets off a defender and over the goal line (which in football would mean a corner kick), a member of the attacking team should touch the ball down, as in rugby, and a rouge worth five points (three points until 2002) is scored. The conversion of a rouge used to be achieved by a ram, but in recent reforms to the game, a conversion is now achieved by taking the ball along the line (see photographs) and aiming for another touch-down. It may seem like organised bedlam to the uninitiated, who will be none the wiser if they hear the terminology of the game: a rouge, sneaking, cornering, furking and the like. However, once conversant with the rules and tactics of the game, boys play with great enthusiasm and commitment, and many Etonians say that the Field Game is the best team game they have ever played. One of the advantages of the game is that boys who are not natural footballers can still be useful team members.

Almost all matches are inter-House matches, the exception being when former pupils or Masters organise teams to play against four senior School teams.

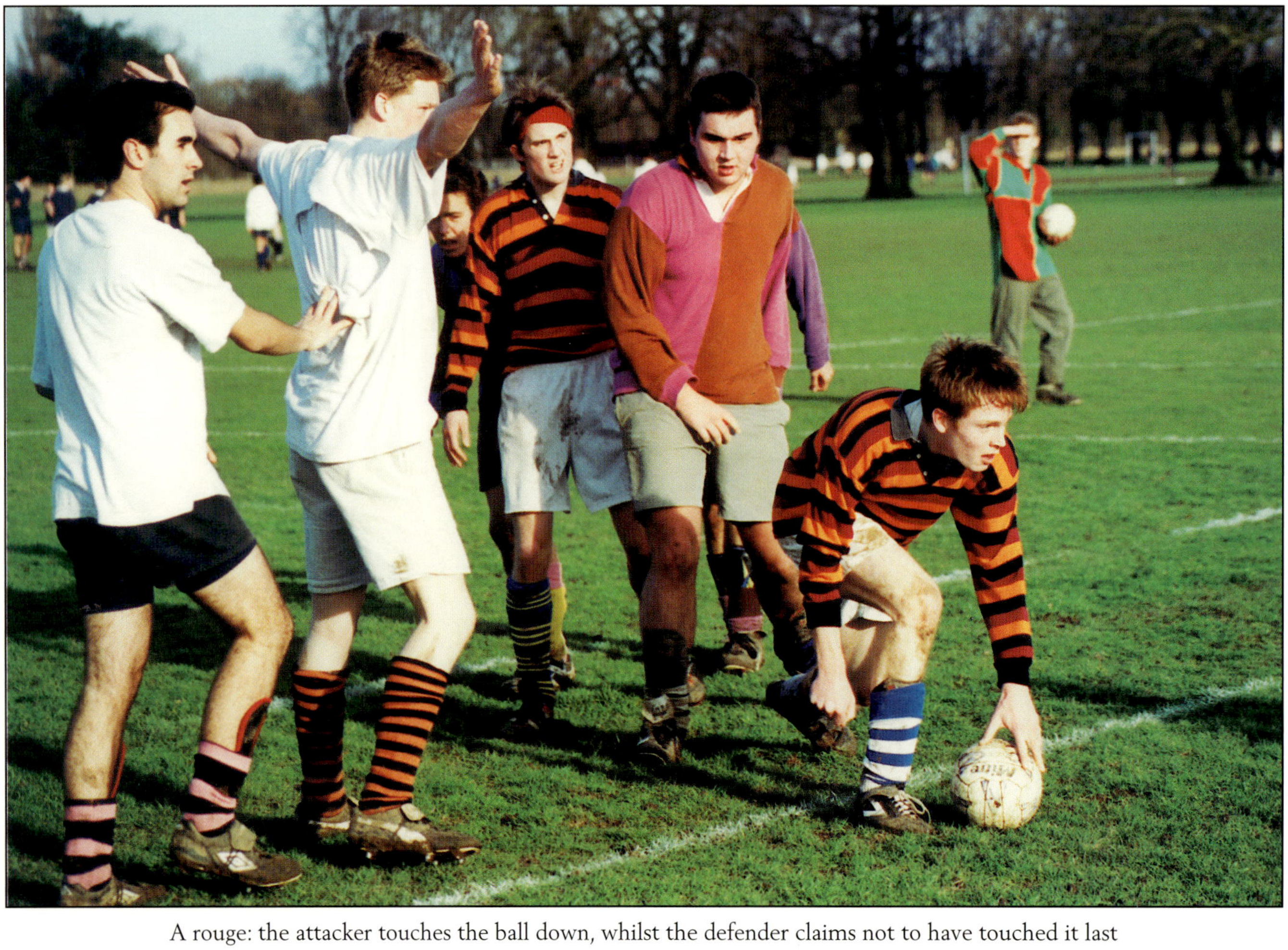

A rouge: the attacker touches the ball down, whilst the defender claims not to have touched it last

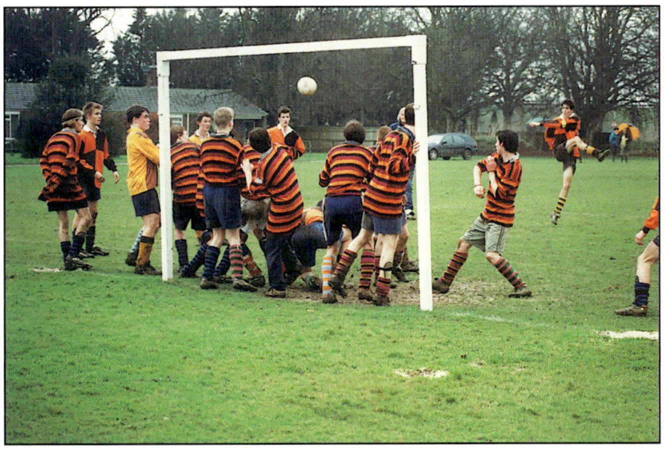

Shot on target

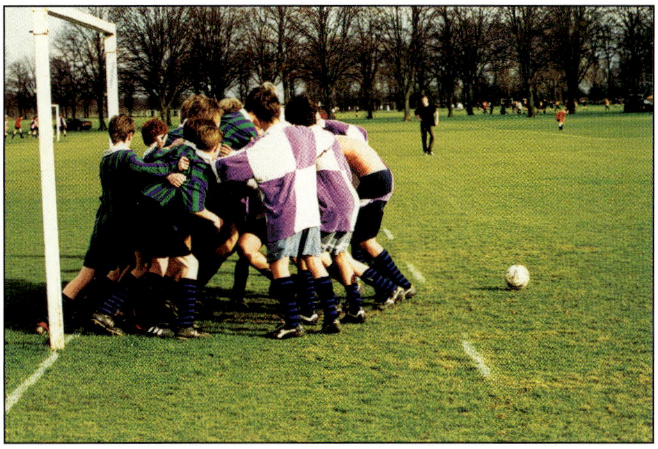

Yes, the ball is needed!

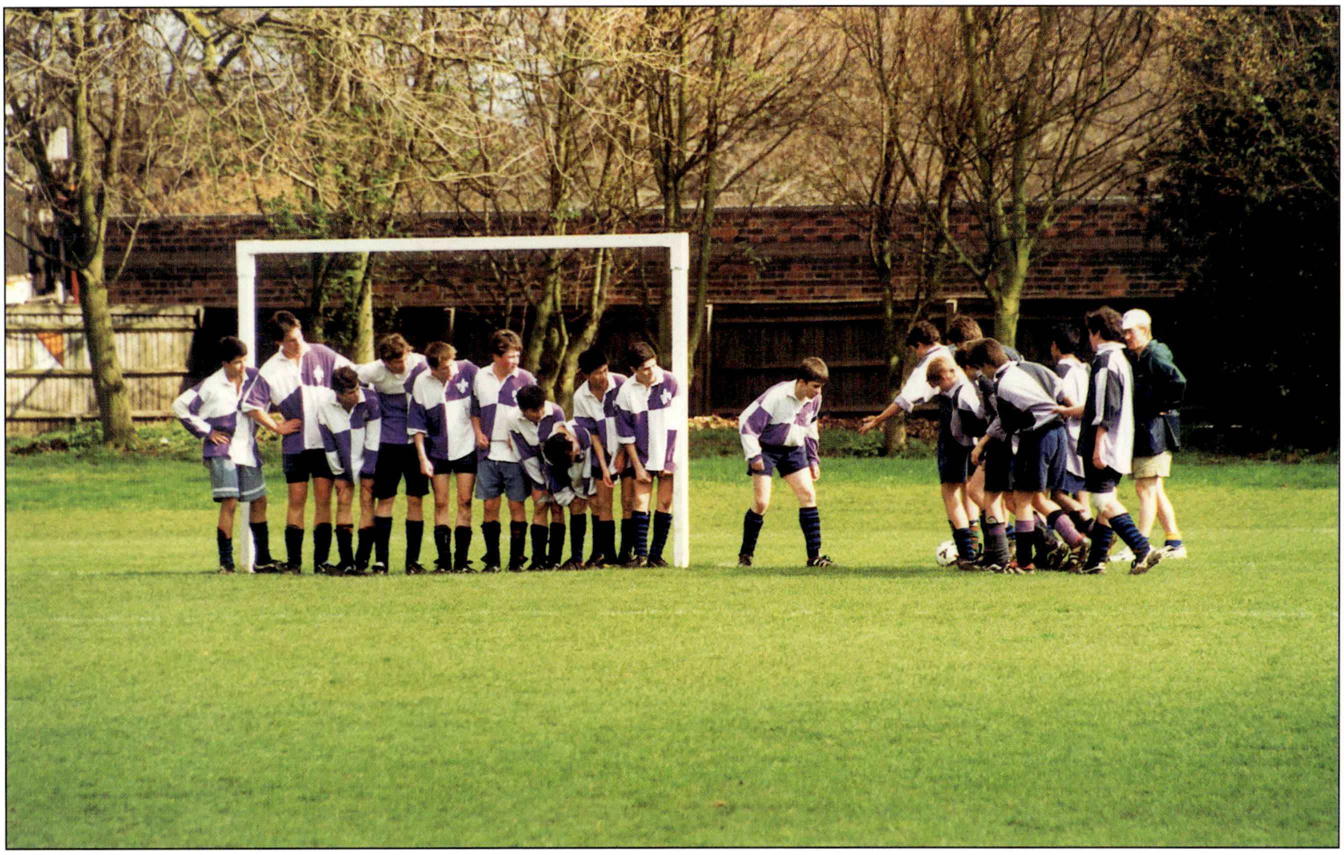

Going along the line

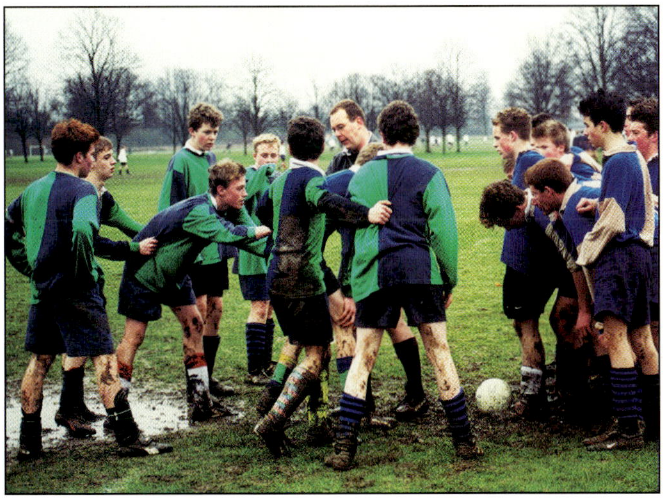

A ram: the greens are about to charge

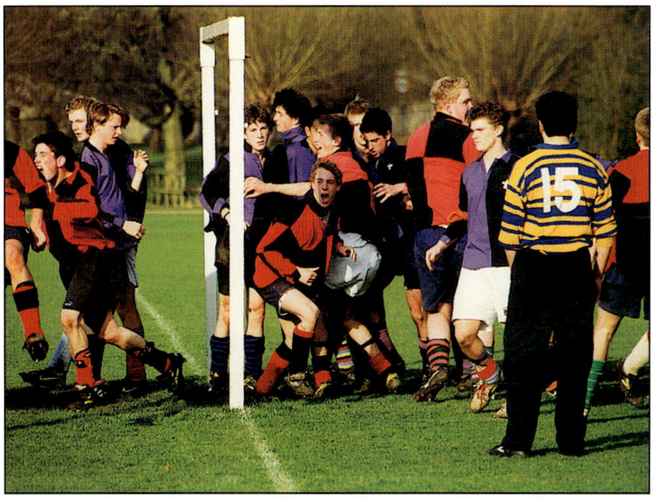

A ram converted: the reds have forced the ball through the goal

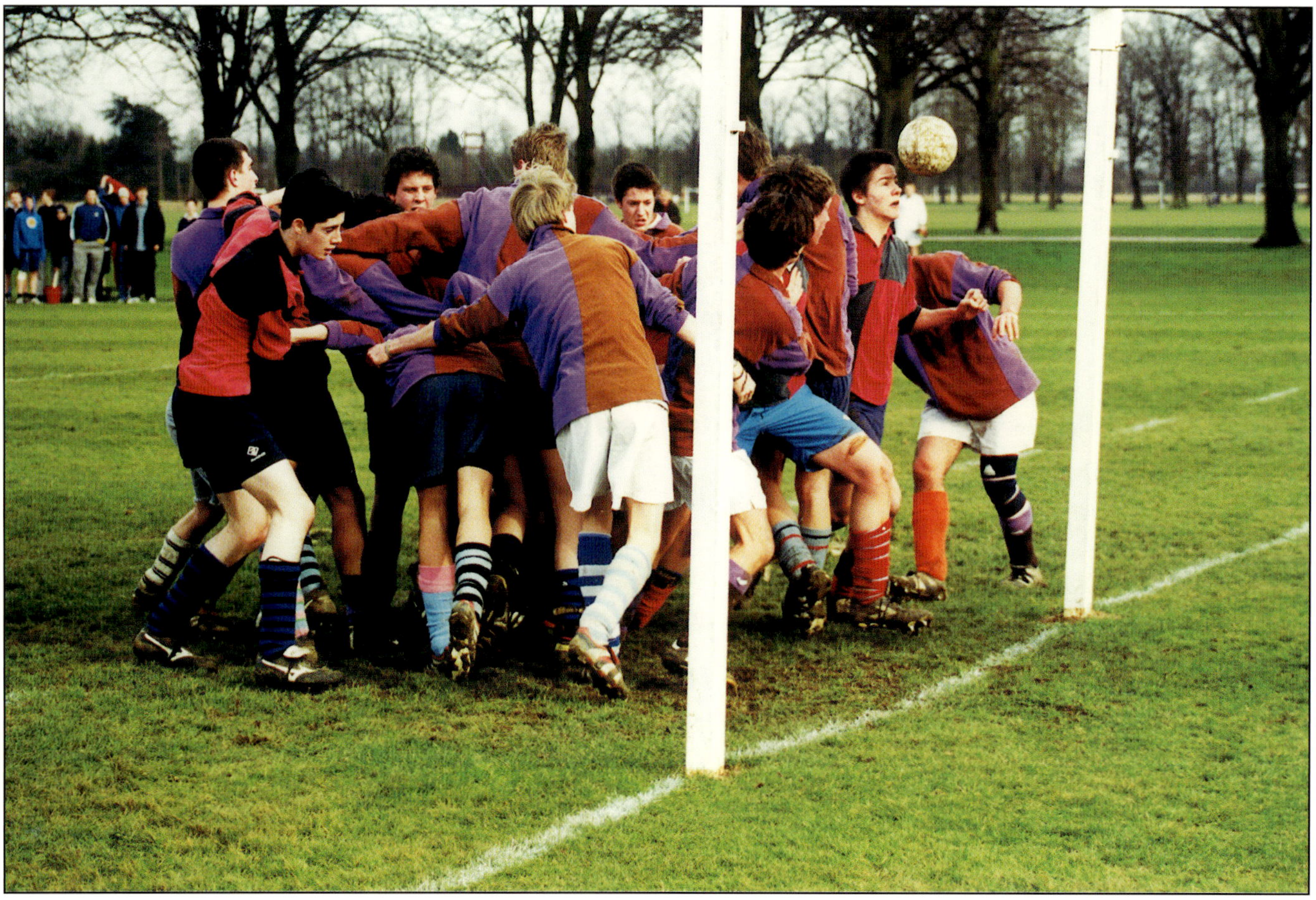

Goals can be scored, as in football, but are worth only two points

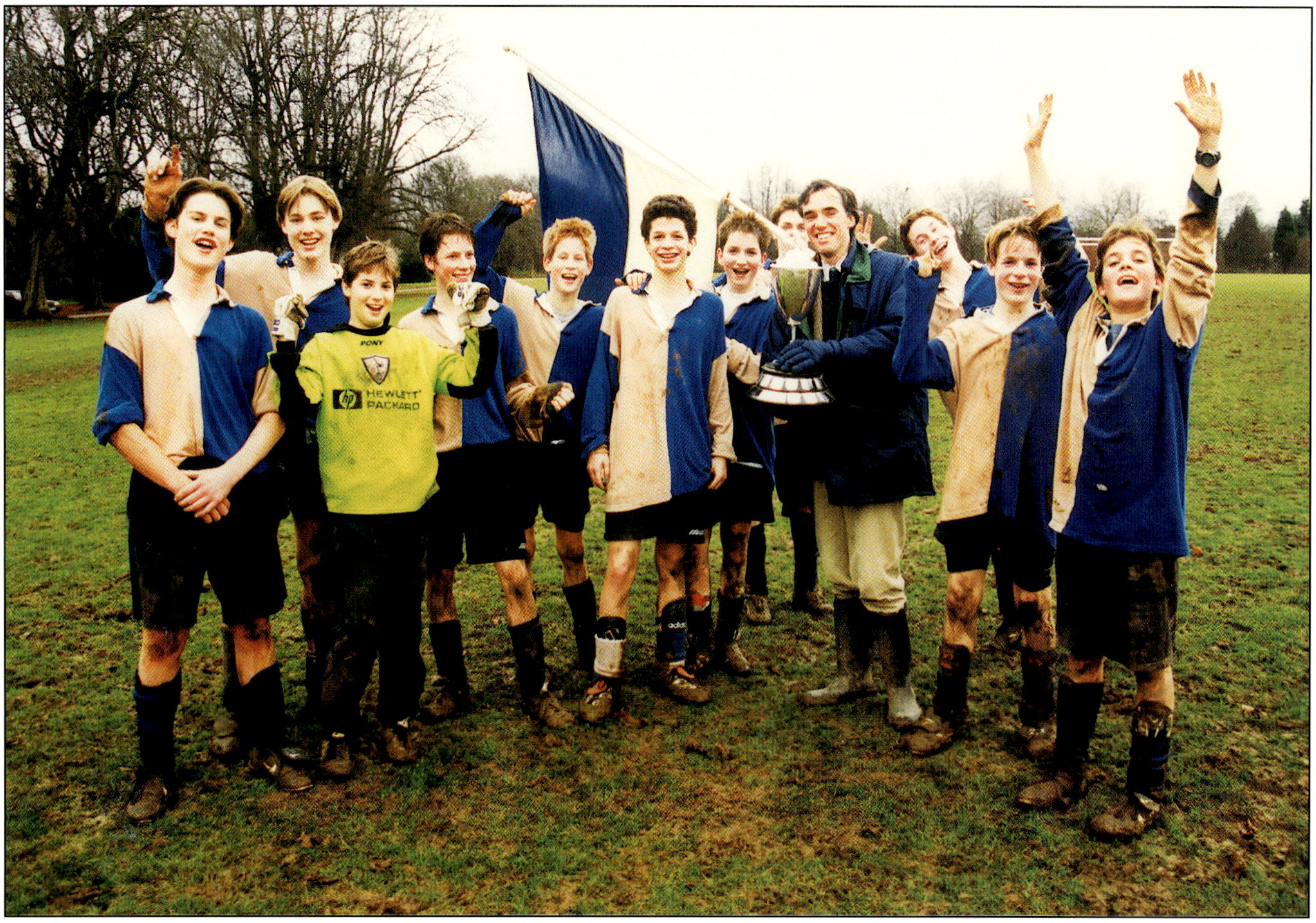

Victorious team in an inter-House knock-out competition

Golf

Since 1972 Eton has enjoyed the luxury of a nine-hole golf course, and this has contributed towards raising the profile of the game in the School.

Carefully avoiding a passing train, Provost Caccia inaugurated the course with a fine drive off the first tee. There are a 1st team and an Under 16 team who play matches throughout the year against other schools and clubs. The high points of the season are the Gerald Micklem independent schools tournament and the Golf Foundation's annual schools event, not forgetting the more relaxed family foursomes on the Fourth of June.

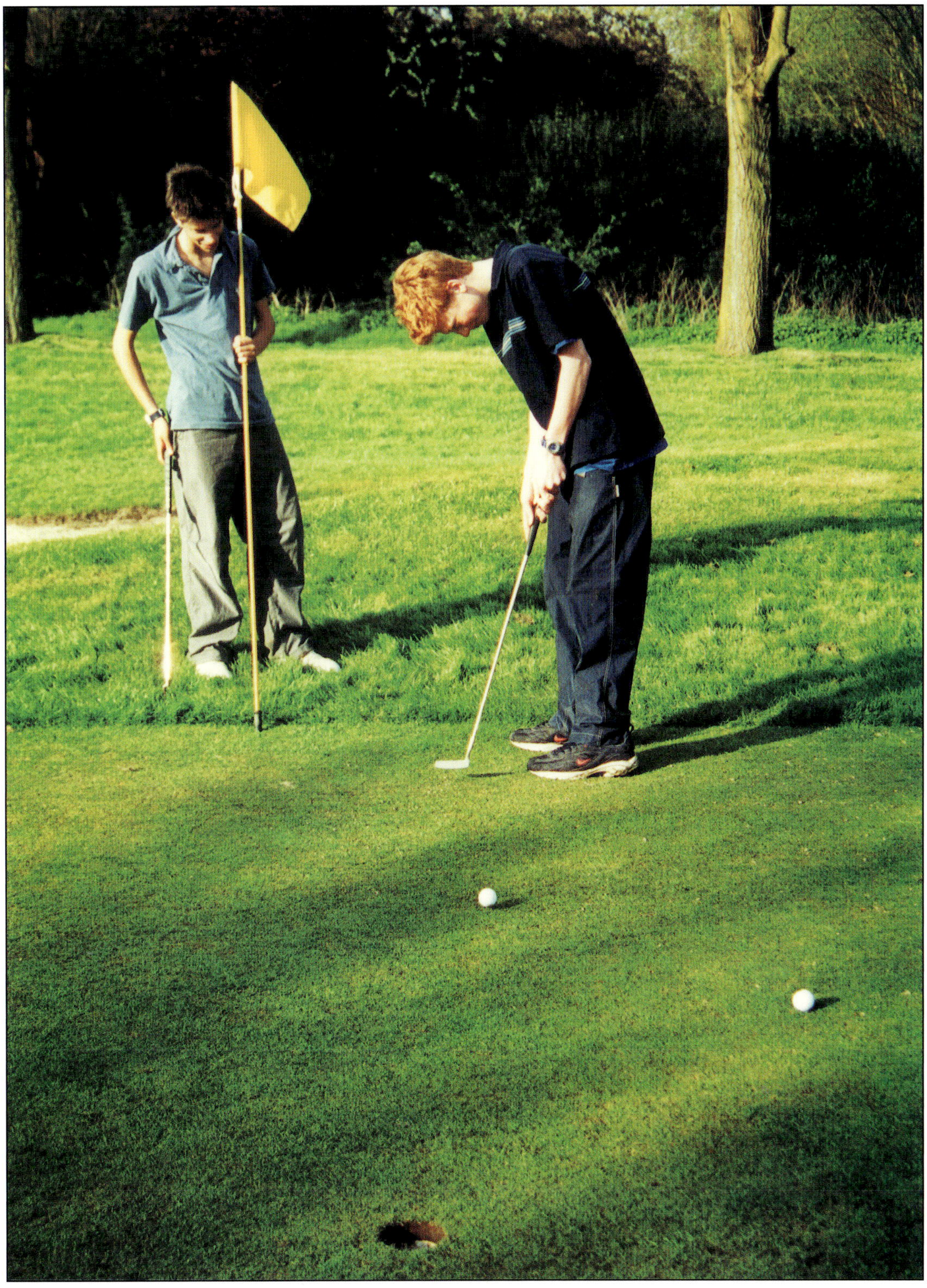

Putting on the School golf course

Gymnasium

The gymnasium complex caters for sports of all sorts. The sports hall is used for many purposes, including cricket nets and indoor soccer. Elsewhere, there are a shooting range, a badminton hall, a weight-training room, a fencing salle and a martial arts room, and all these are adjacent to the squash courts and the indoor swimming pool. PE is compulsory for a boy's first two years, and AS-level Physical Education is a new subject in the curriculum for Specialists.

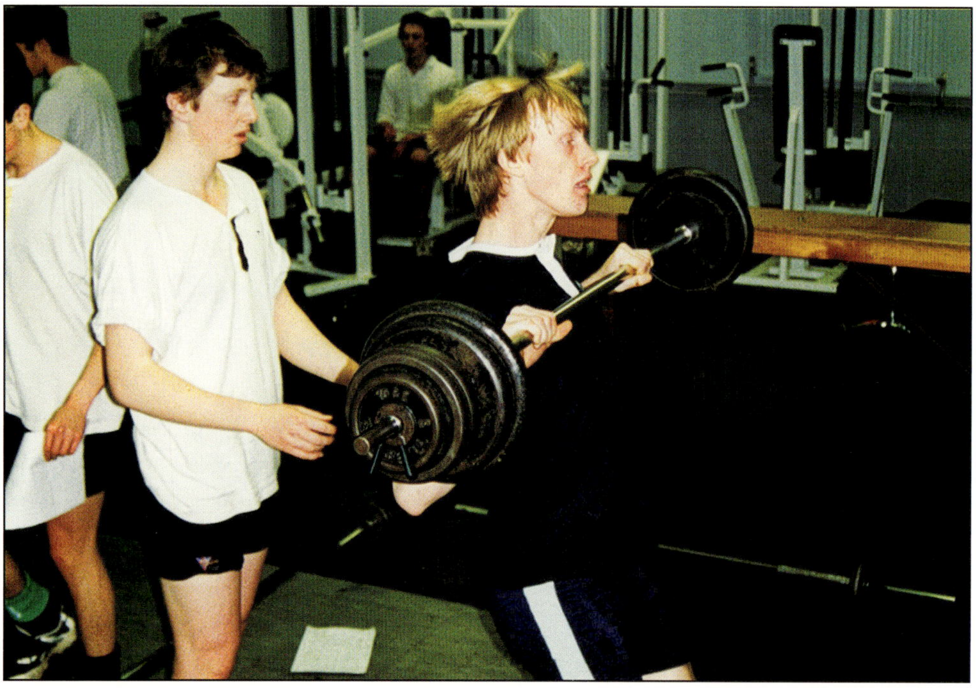

Weight training

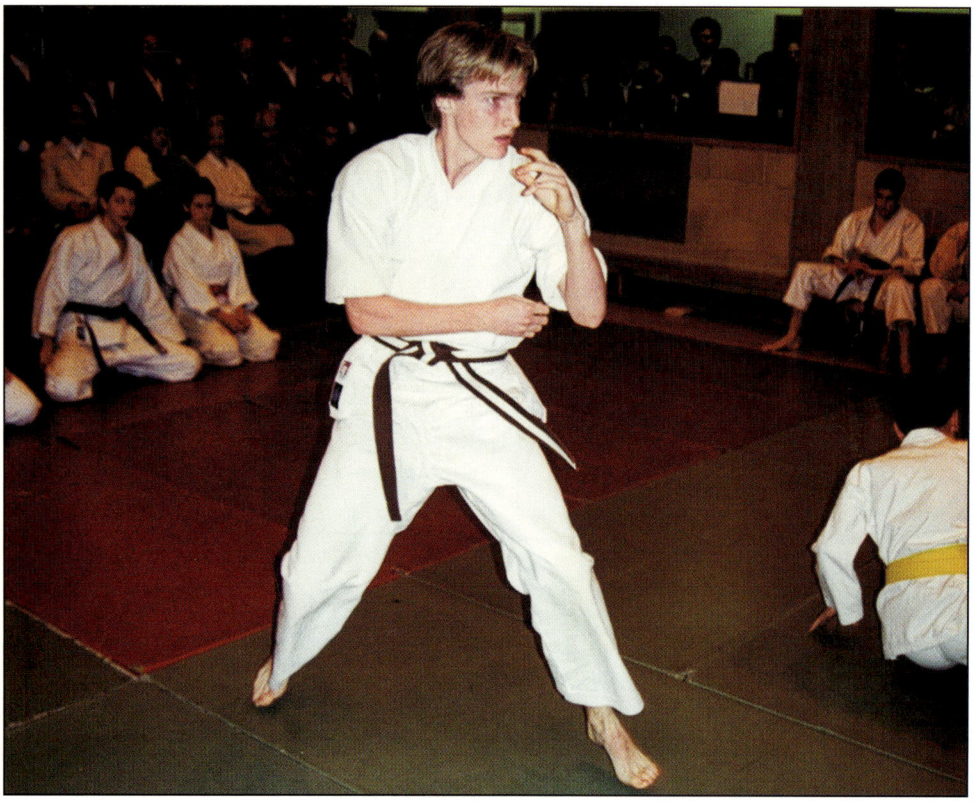

Martial arts

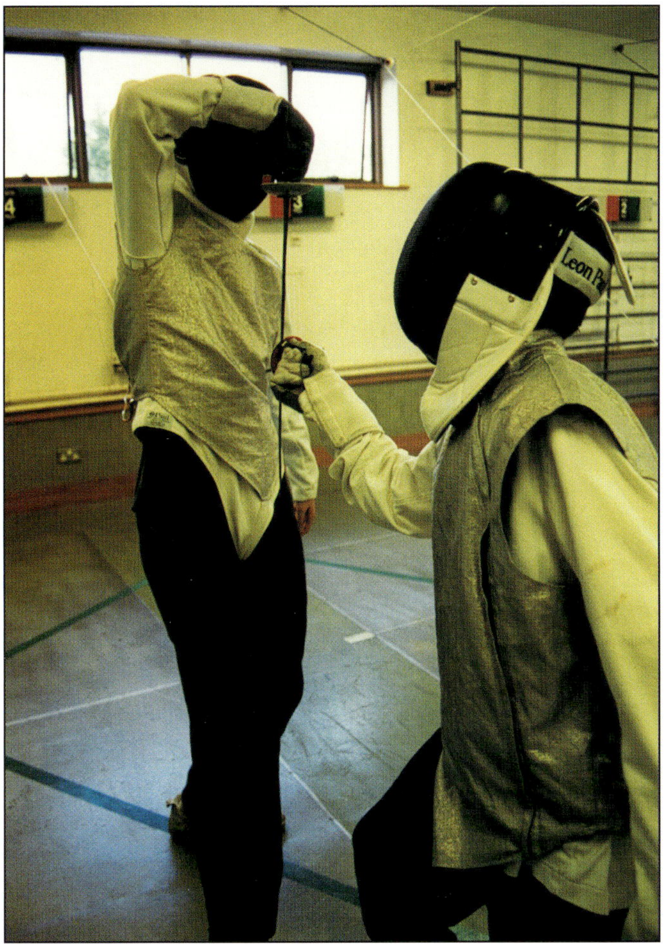

Fencing

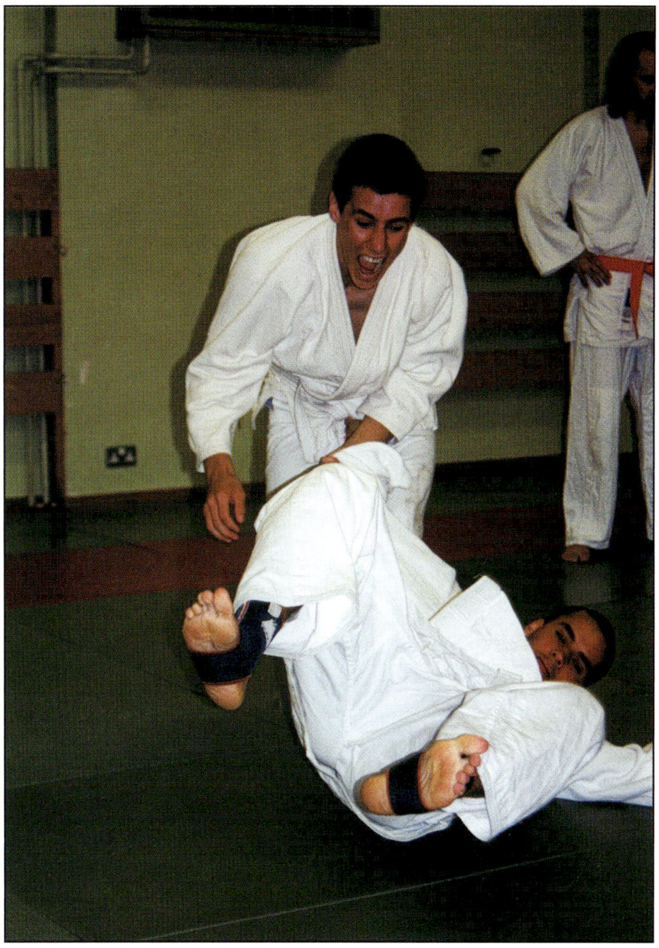

Martial arts

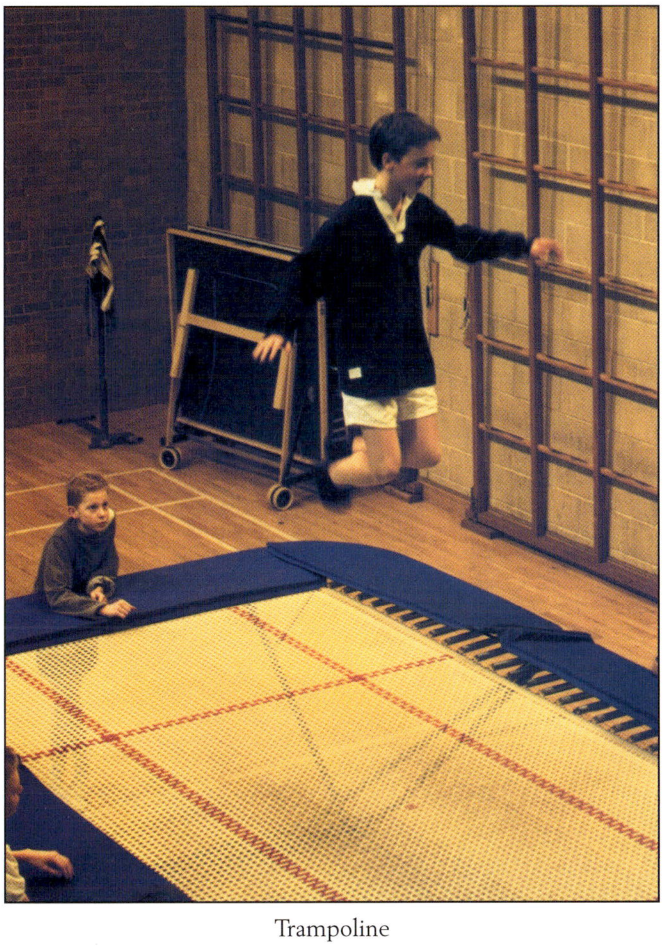

Trampoline

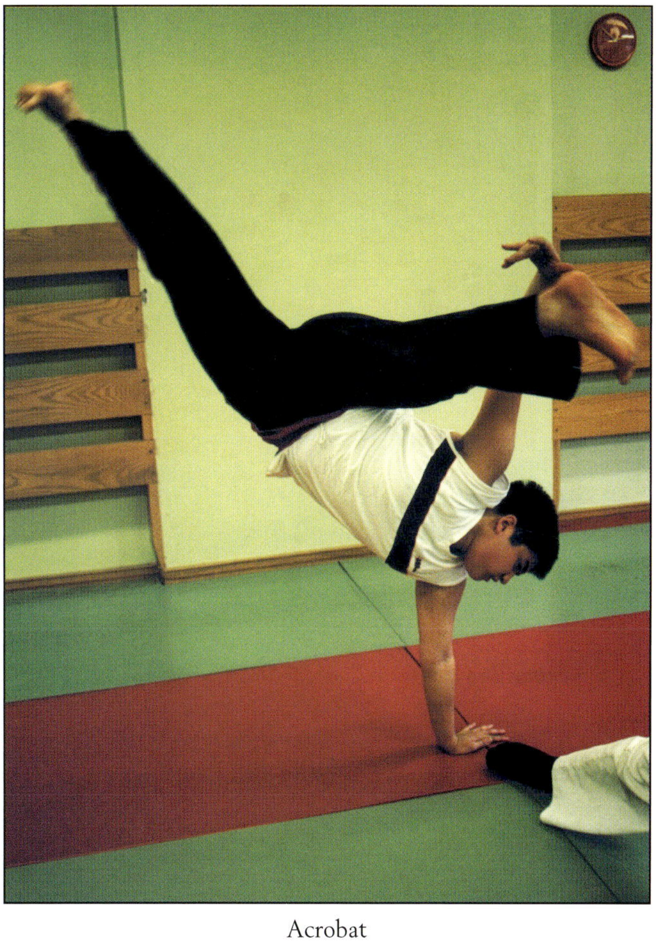

Acrobat

Hockey

Hockey is a relative newcomer to Eton's sporting programme. Played at the outset on the grass pitches of Dutchman's, it quickly grew in popularity when the two all-weather pitches were built on Masters. Hockey is played in the Lent Half with a full inter-school fixture list, and also senior and junior House competitions. About 200 boys compete for places in School teams.

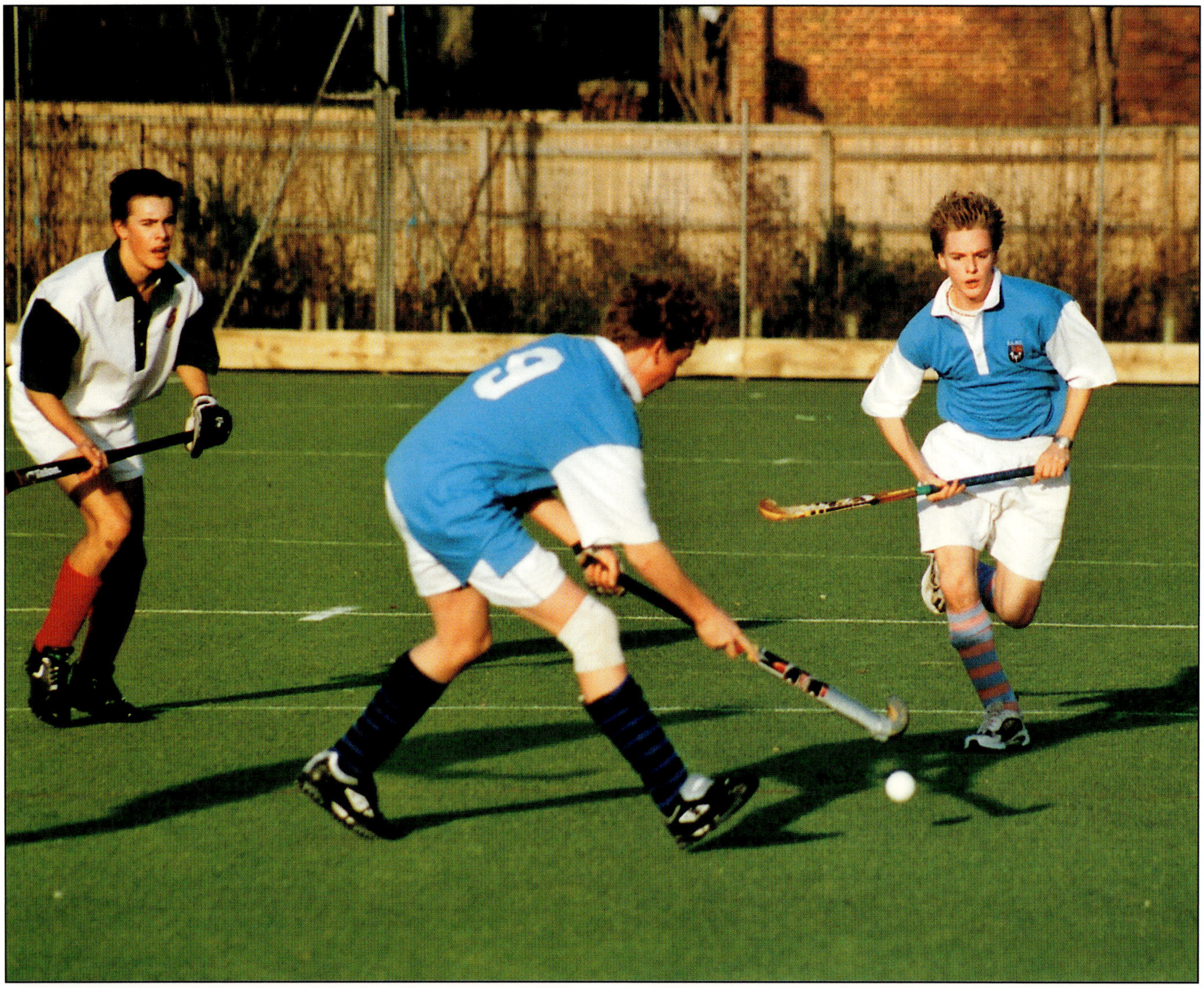

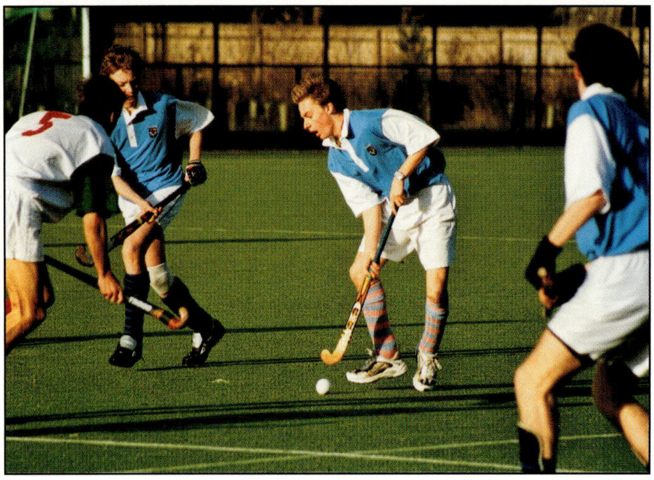

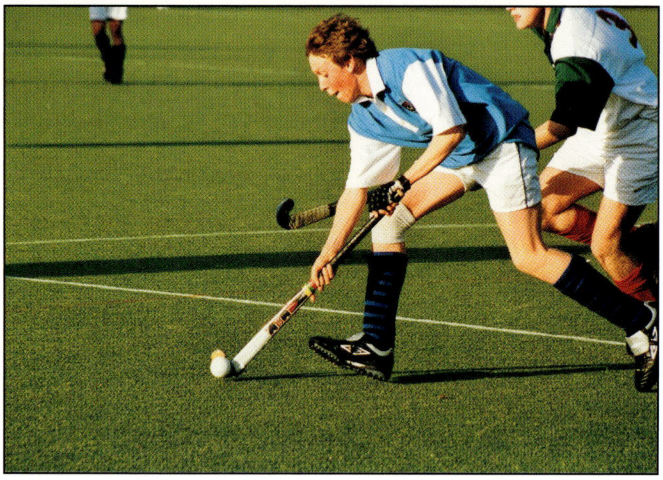

Hockey in progress on the new all-weather pitches

Polo

Polo is a minority sport, played by between twenty and thirty schools. It is rare for more than ten or so Etonians to be involved in any one season, but those boys who do play take part in about twelve matches during the Summer Half. Home matches are played on the Flemish Farm pitch of the Guards Polo Club. Away matches are played at many other clubs in the South of England.

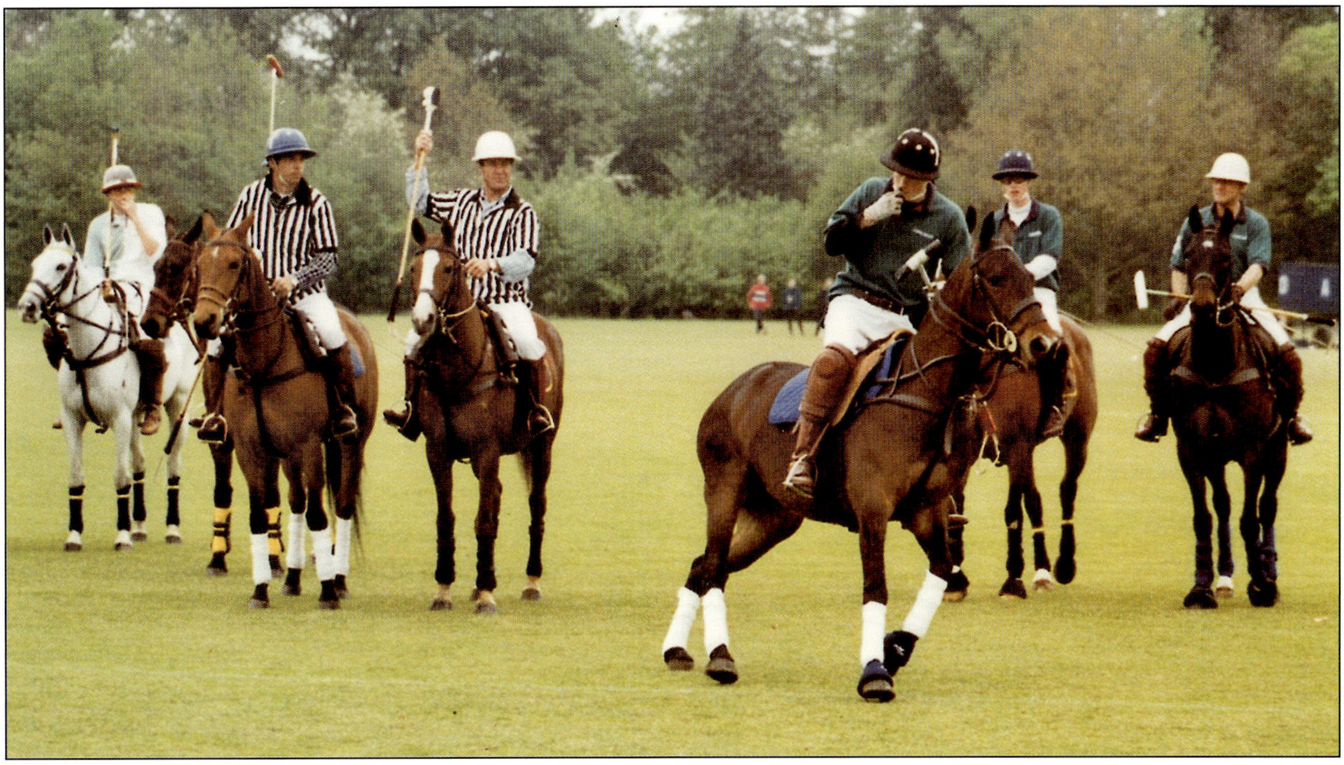

A rare sight: polo on Dutchman's

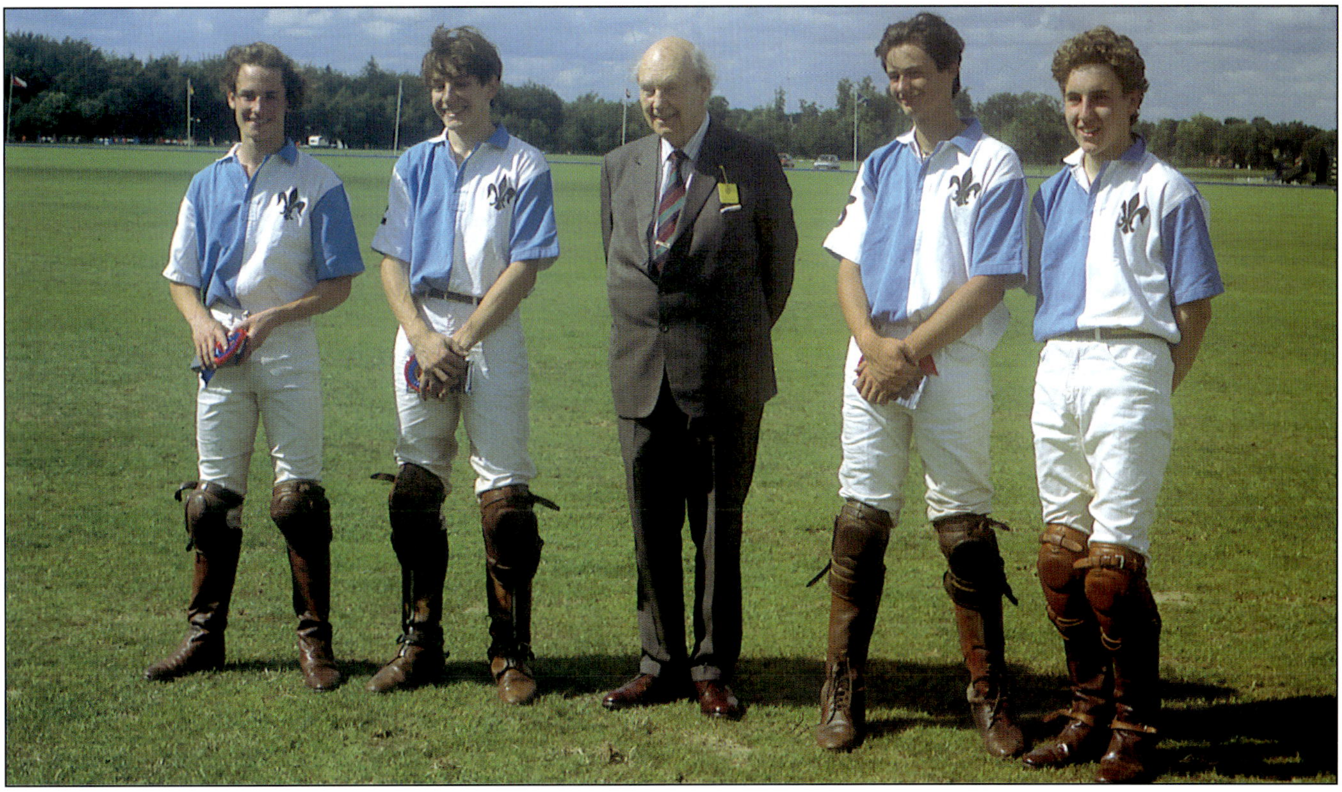

The School team with Lord Charteris, Provost from 1978 to 1991

Rackets

It is said that rackets originated as a pastime for inmates of two debtors' prisons in London. By the time the game came to Eton in the 1860s the rules had been refined and defined. The first rackets court was on the site now occupied by the older part of the Music Schools, which is why the land now taken up by the Music Schools extension and Bekynton was once called Rackets Court Field. The two "new" rackets courts date from 1902 and are to be found at one end of the Field, partially shielded from view by a row of poplar trees. A rackets court is twice the size of a squash court, and the game is played with a hard ball, marginally larger than a golf ball. About 50 boys play the game. The season builds up to the Public Schools Championships at Queen's, the singles tournaments taking place in December, and the doubles in March. Eton is fortunate to have had the services of Ronnie Hawes, Jim Dear and Norwood Cripps, fine coaches and skilled exponents of the game, and Eton's record of championship victories has been impressive.

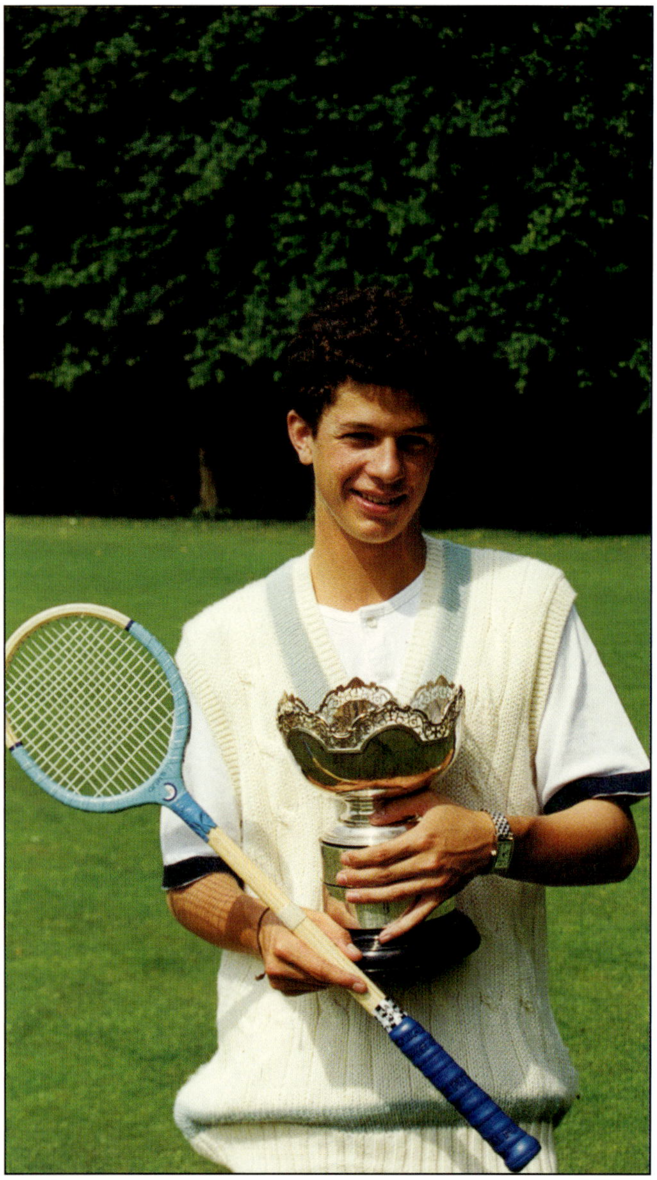

Winner at Queen's

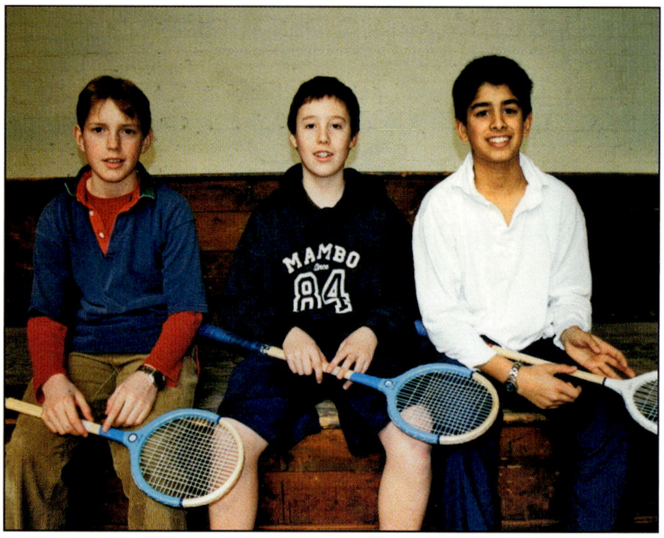

The rackets are sturdier than those used for squash

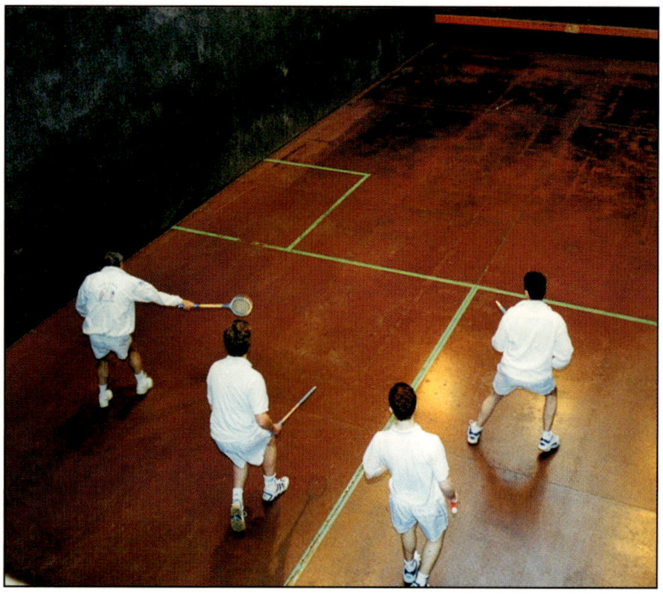

Coaching session

Dorney Lake

Among the new facilities for Eton's sportsmen, Dorney Lake, the Thames Valley Athletics Centre and two all-weather hockey pitches take pride of place. The idea of constructing a rowing trench goes back to the early sixties. The present concept of a national training and regatta course dates from the re-appraisal of the project in the eighties. The Fellows accepted the need for safer conditions than are often available on the Thames and the desirability of Eton providing for the needs of the rowing community at large. This fitted in with Eton's policy of sharing its facilities whenever this is practical. Construction of the Lake, now called Dorney Lake, began in 1996. The boat-house and the first 1000m of lake were opened in 2000. The full eight-lane international course is scheduled for completion in 2005, and the World Rowing Championships will take place here in 2006. When the main lake is complete in the spring of 2003, work will then start on a parallel channel, along which crews will row to reach the start-line. Eton College is on its own financing and building this international rowing and canoeing lake, park, arboretum and nature reserve. All levels of oarsman from beginner to top performer are welcome, with the emphasis on junior rowing. By the end of 2001 several events of significance had taken place here. These included an international sprint regatta that welcomed back our rowers from their success at the Sydney Olympics, the Wallingford and Marlow regattas, as well as several inter-school events. The official opening of the new boathouse took place on 10th June, 2000, when the Minister for Sport unveiled a plaque during the School's rowing championships, at which Steve Redgrave presented the prizes.

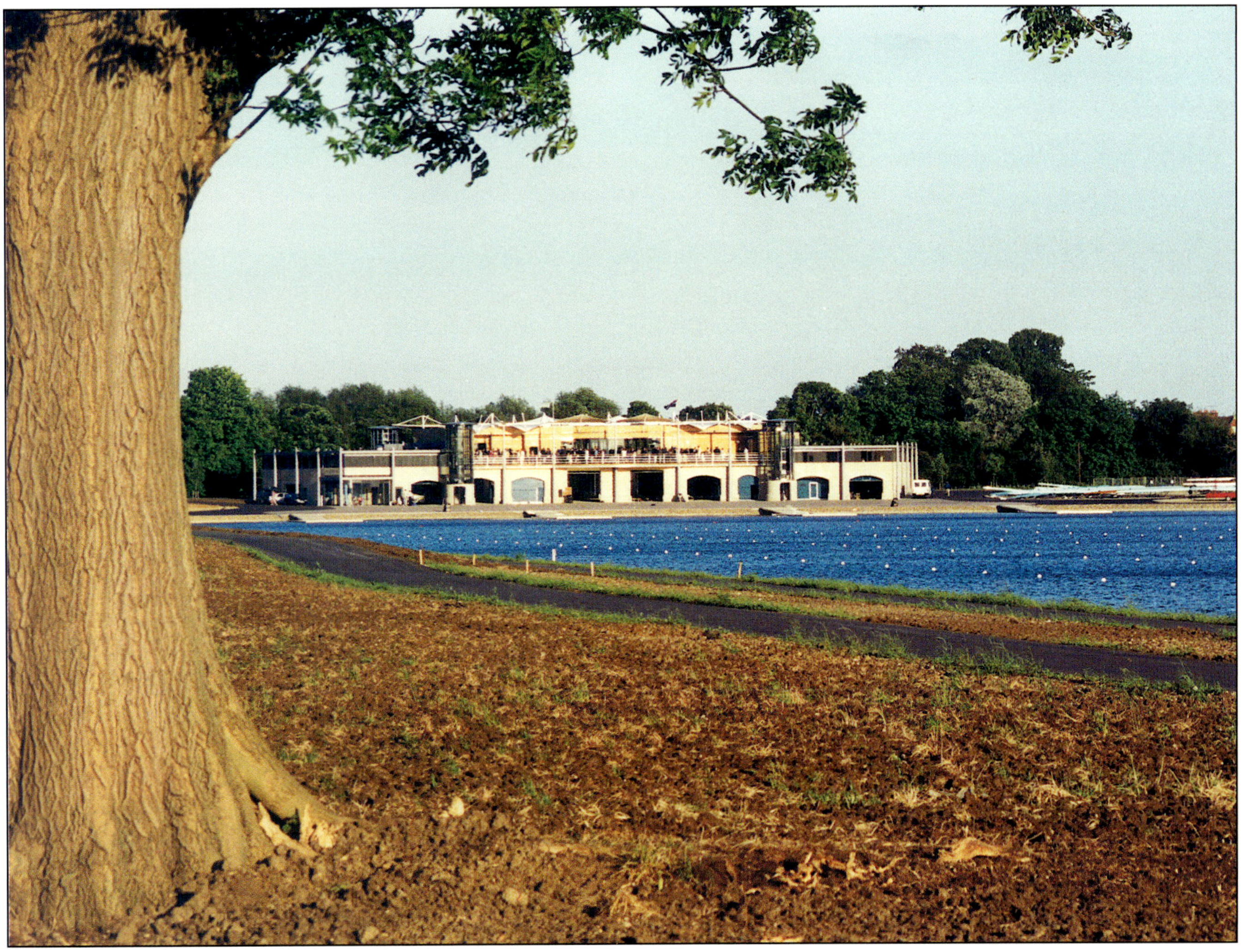

View of the new Boathouse on Dorney Lake

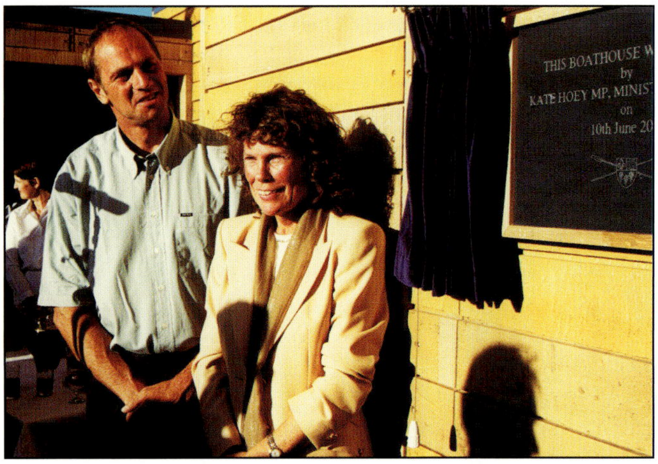

Kate Hoey declares the Boathouse open

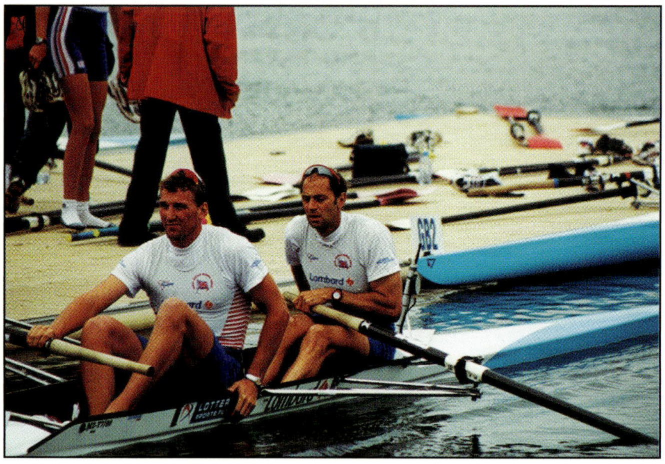

Matt Pinsent and Steve Redgrave

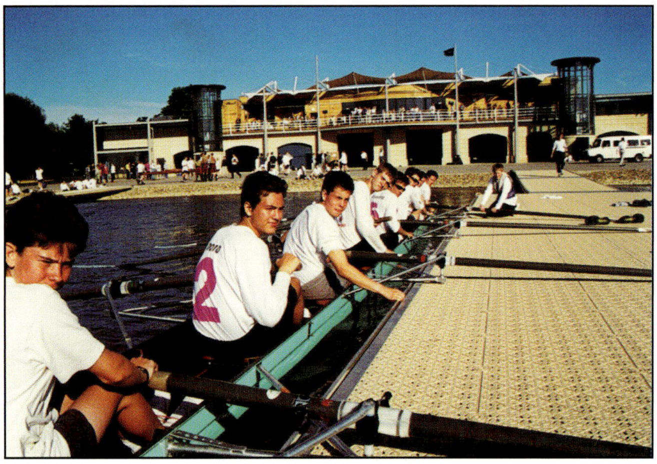

An Eton VIII leaves the pontoon

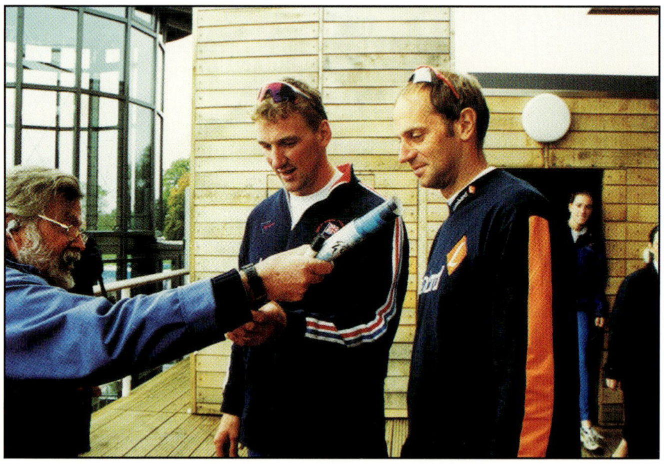

Matt Pinsent and Steve Redgrave prepare for interview

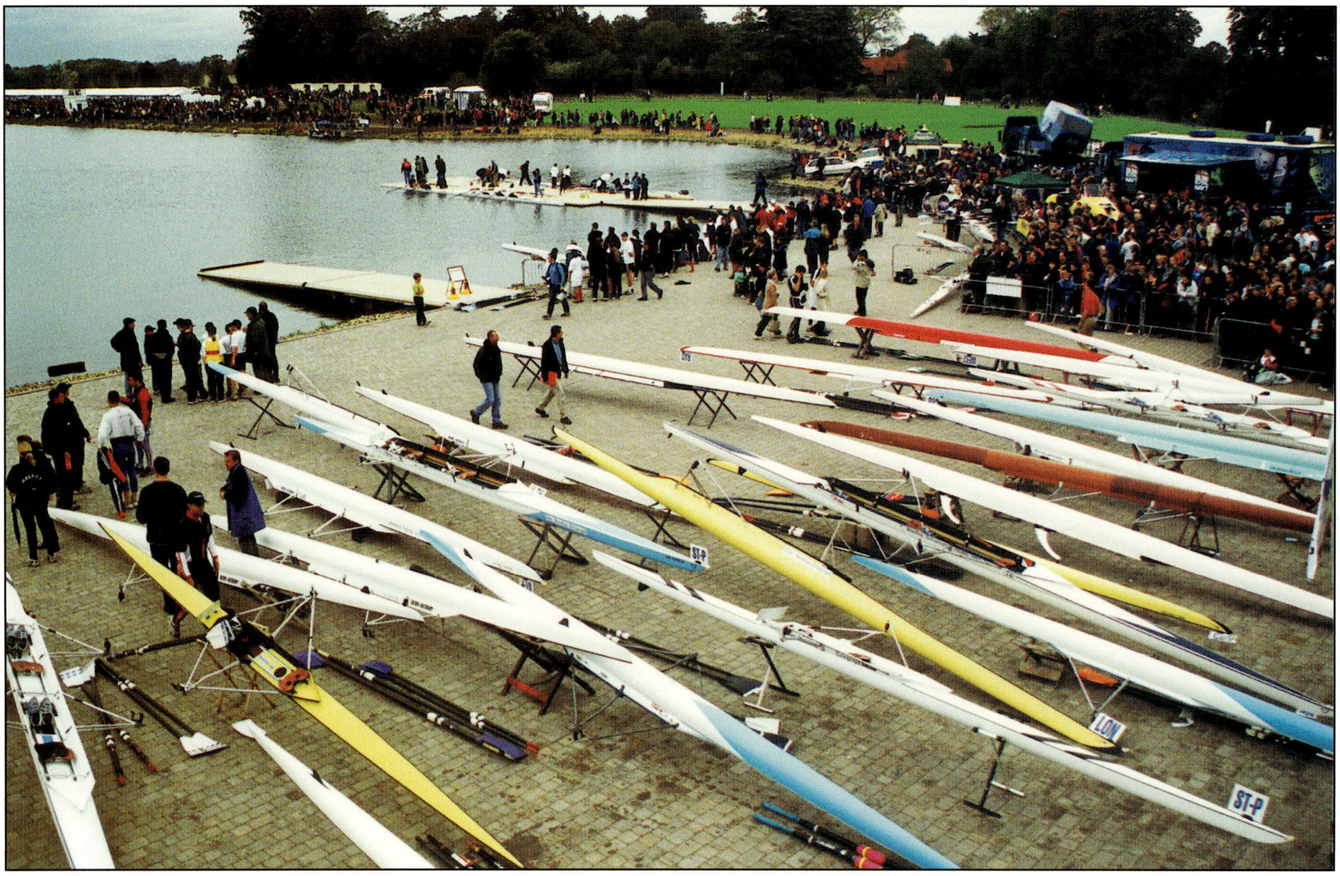

Dorney Lake on regatta day

Rowing

Boys in their first year, F Blockers, may opt for rowing, cricket, tennis or athletics as a summer sport. Those who choose rowing are called 'wetbobs' as opposed to 'drybobs' who play cricket. F Blockers are introduced to rowing in the Summer Half. For those who take the sport seriously, the aim is to be selected for the best VIII in their age group. By one's final two years one might hope to row for the VIII and represent Eton at head races and regattas, the most prestigious of which is Henley. It is not unusual to see Old Etonians rowing for Oxford and Cambridge, and even internationally. The most successful recent Old Etonian rowers are Matthew Pinsent and Andrew Lindsay, both of whom won gold medals at the Sydney Olympics, and Ed Coode, world champion in 1999 and 2001. There are many internal rowing competitions, and since 2001 these have led up to finals on one single day at the Dorney Rowing Lake. The internal regatta seems likely to become one of the highlights of the year for oarsmen and their parents.

Not all rowing activity has been transferred to Dorney Lake. School VIIIs still have outings on the Thames at Masters and Andrews. Bumping IV races, the F Quad competition for boys in their first year, dragon boat racing and casual sculling still start from Rafts, and boys row up the Thames to Queen's Eyot on half-holiday afternoons as a form of relaxation.

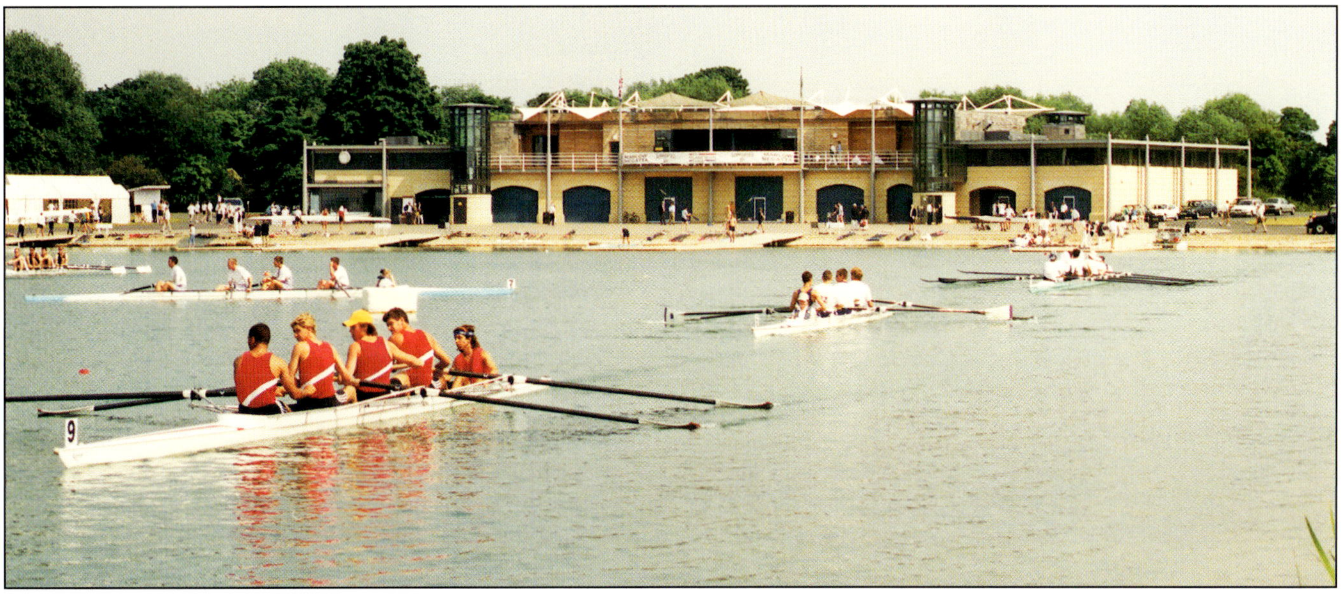

Inter-schools IVs

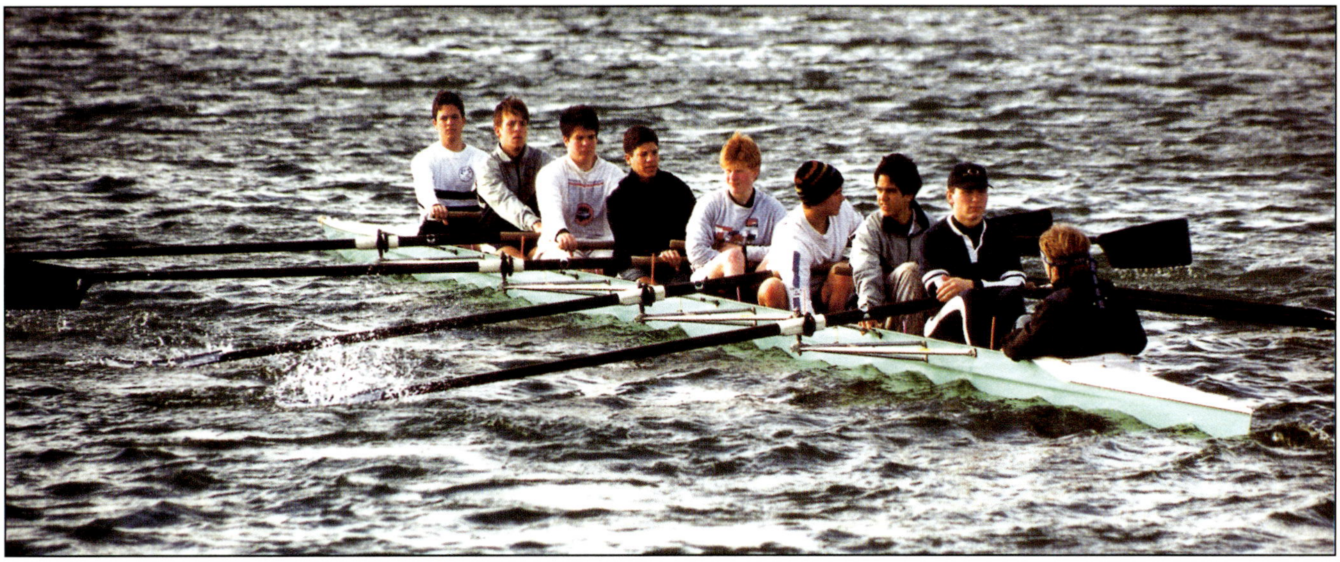

An VIII on choppy water

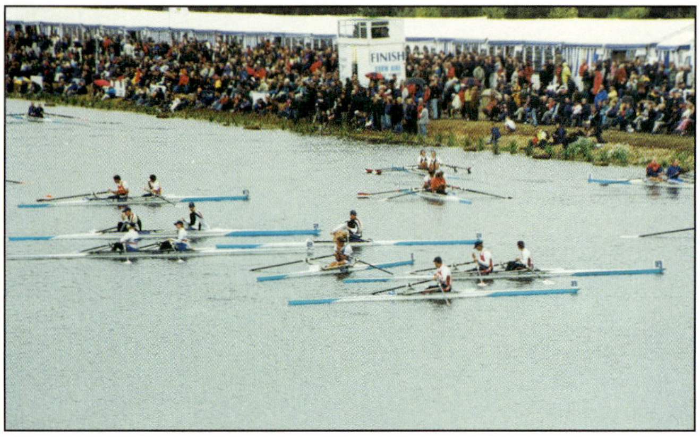

Crowds at the finishing line

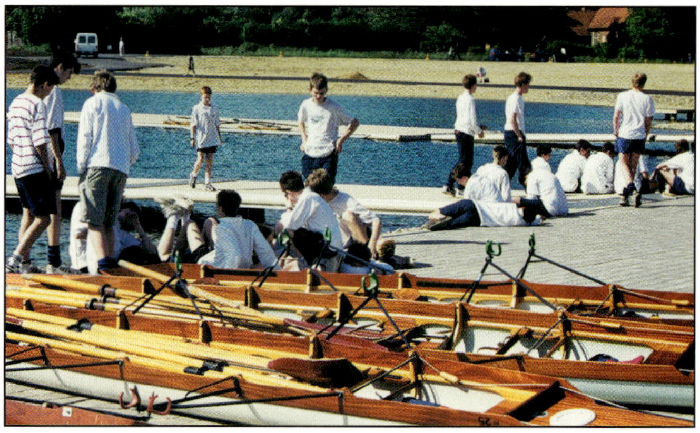
Waiting for action

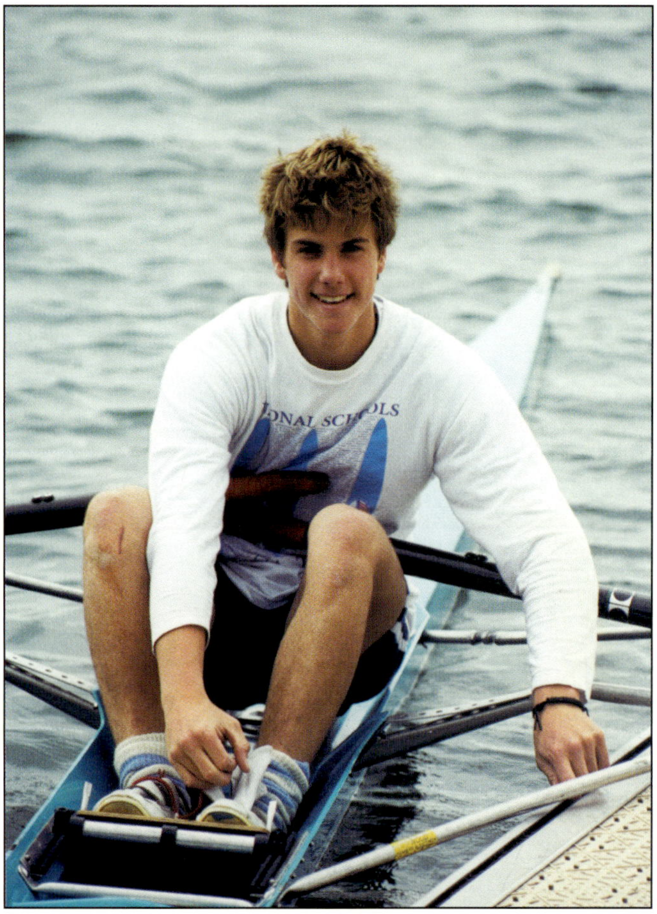
Single sculls

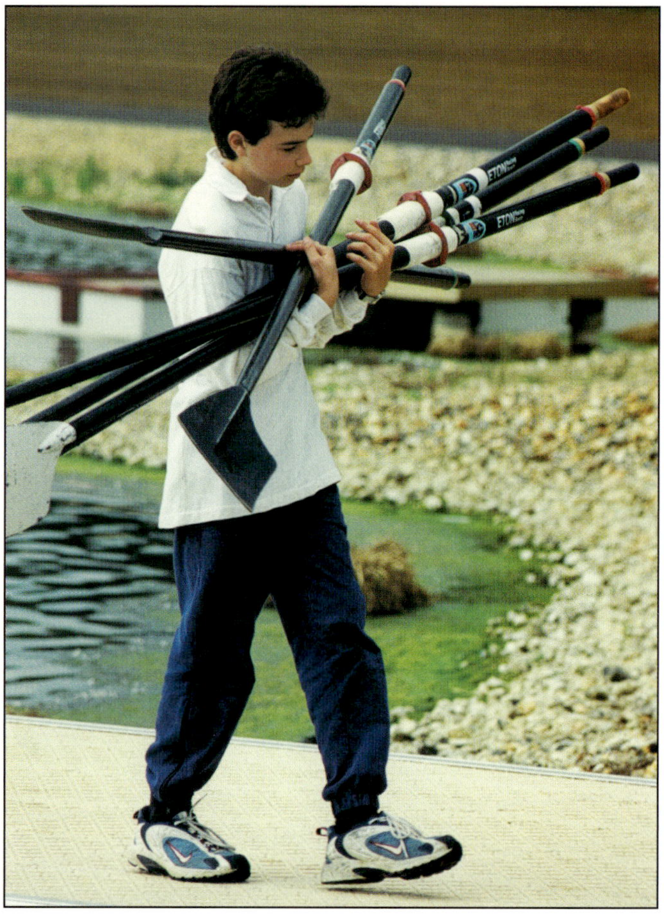

Juggling oars

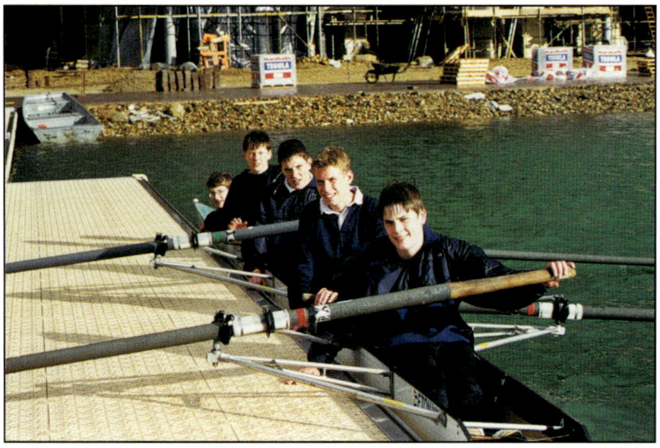
One of the first IVs to use the Lake. The Boat House still under construction

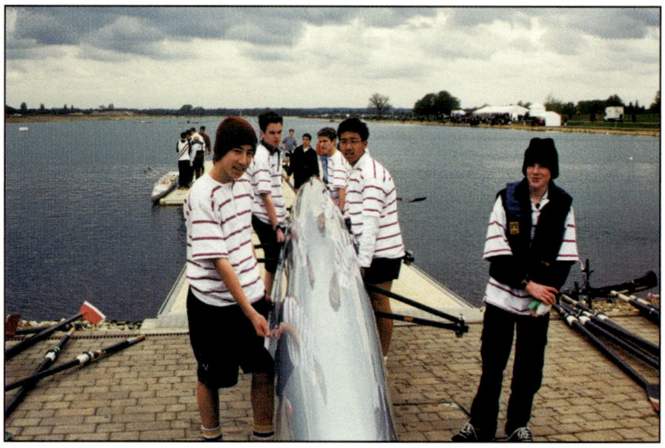
Coming ashore

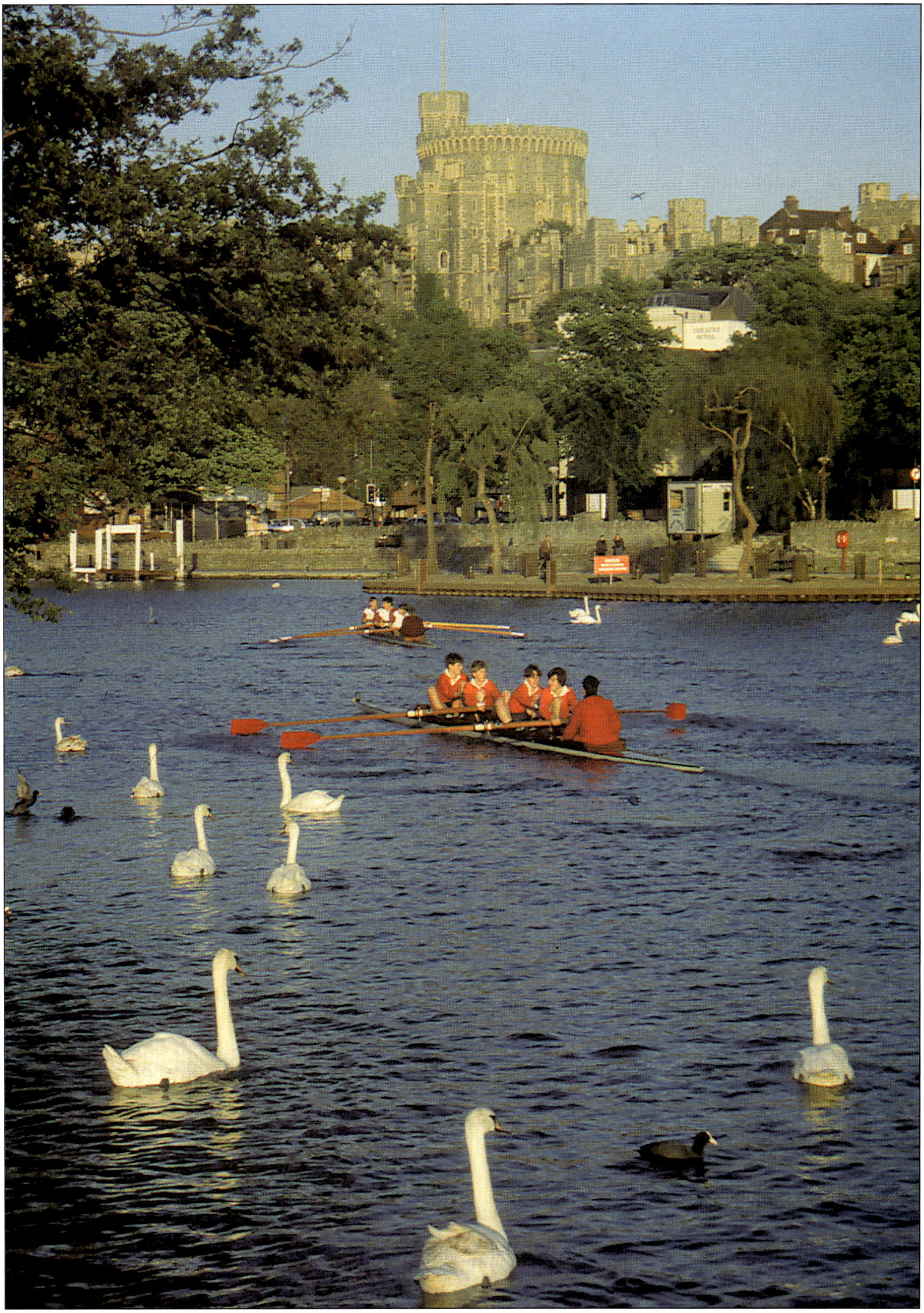

Bumping IVs on the Thames in the shadow of Windsor Castle

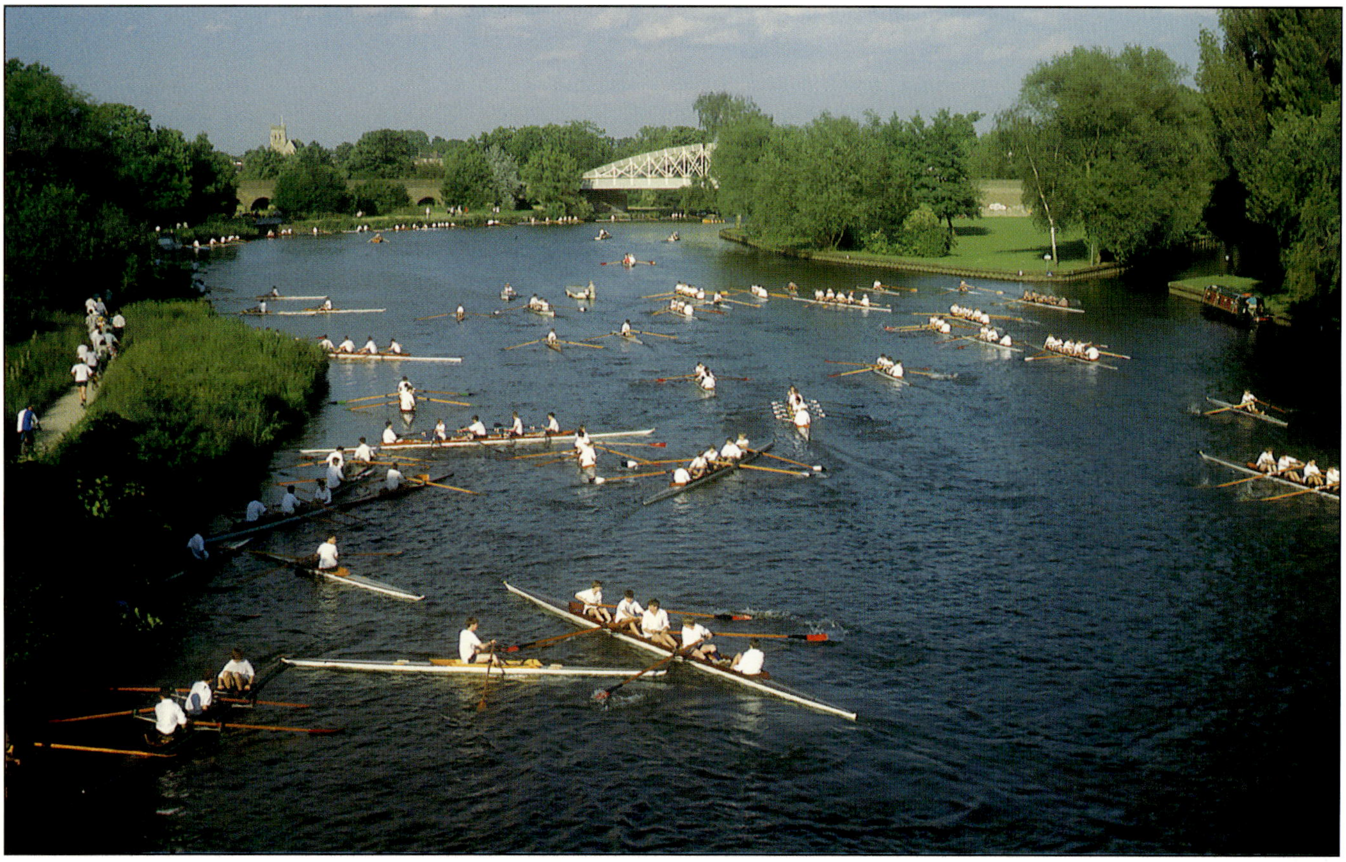

The Armada that marked Eric Anderson's retirement as Head Master in 1994

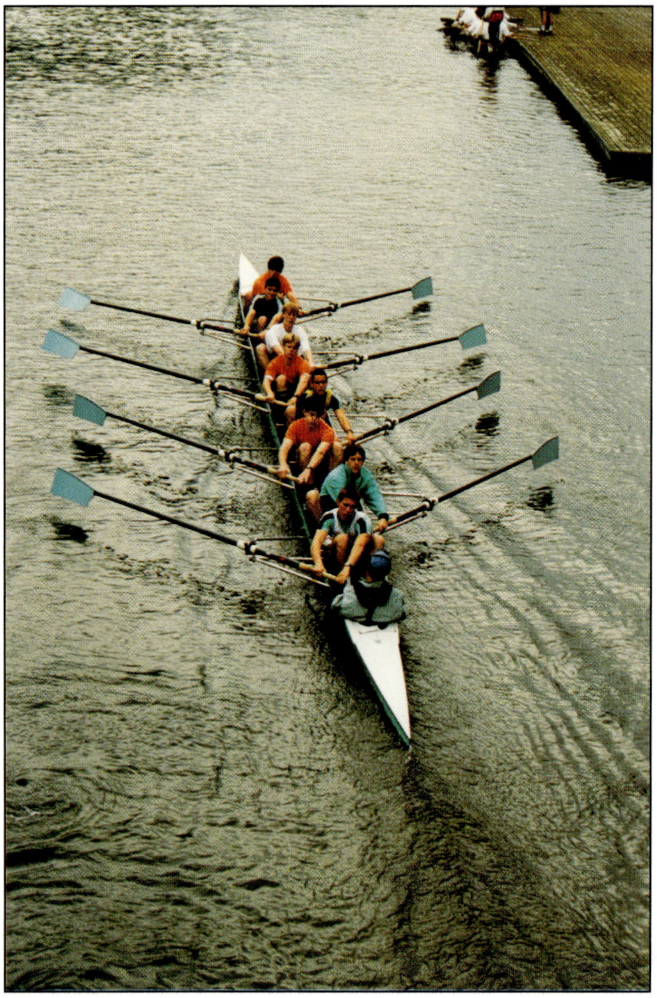

The 1st VIII rowing past Rafts

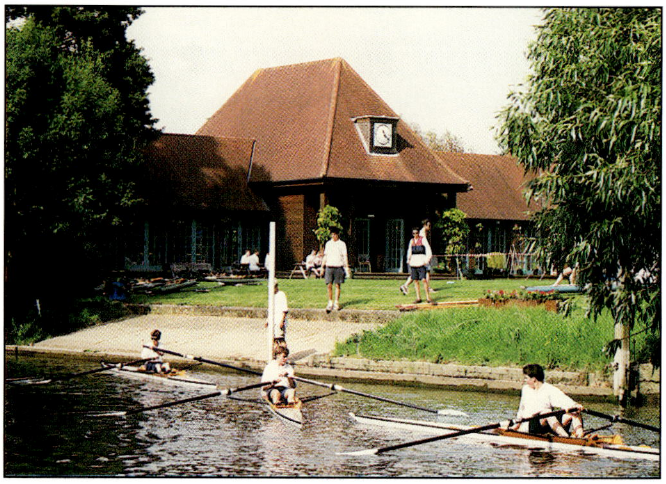

Landing at Queen's Eyot

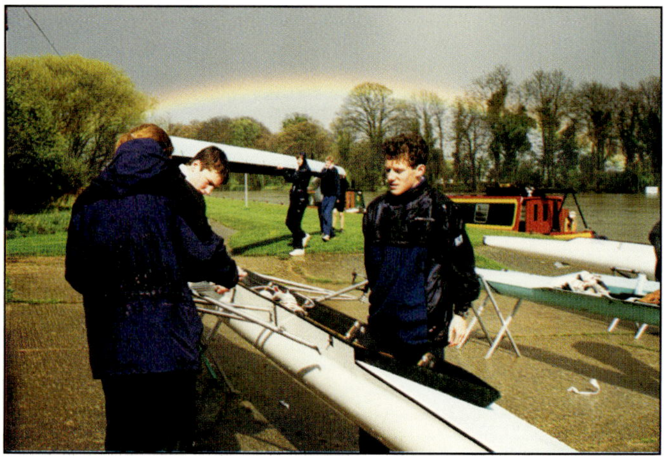

Training goes on in all weathers

Bumping IVs

The Bumping IVs probably attract more spectators to the river-bank than any other internal rowing event. The Houses are divided into two divisions according to the previous year's results. For the start of the race the boats line up behind each other with an equal gap between each crew. The cox is required to hold on to a bung at one end of a rope secured to the river-bank. When the starting gun is fired, the cox drops the bung, and away go the crews. The object is to touch or overtake the boat in front and thereby move up one place in the league table for the following evening's race. Dramatic, full of incidents and unexpected twists of fate, these races are a popular event. They take place on four successive evenings in mid-May.

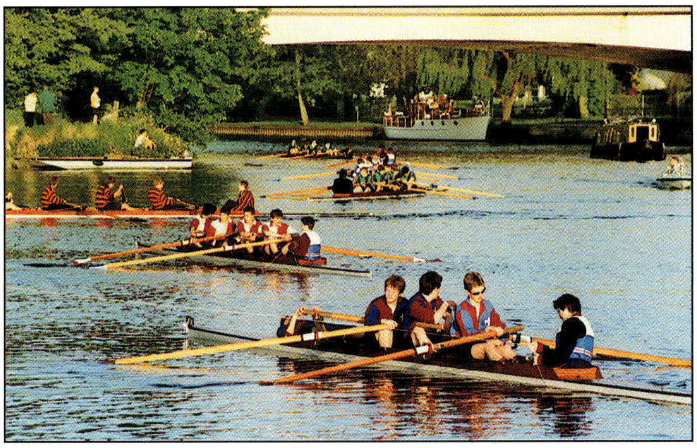

Five minutes before the starting gun

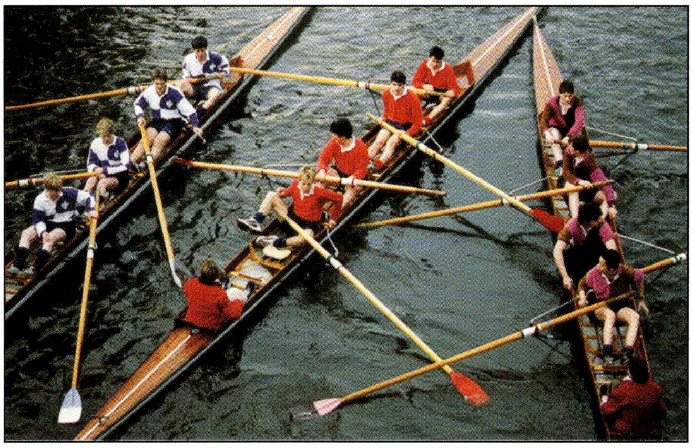

Fluvial pile-up

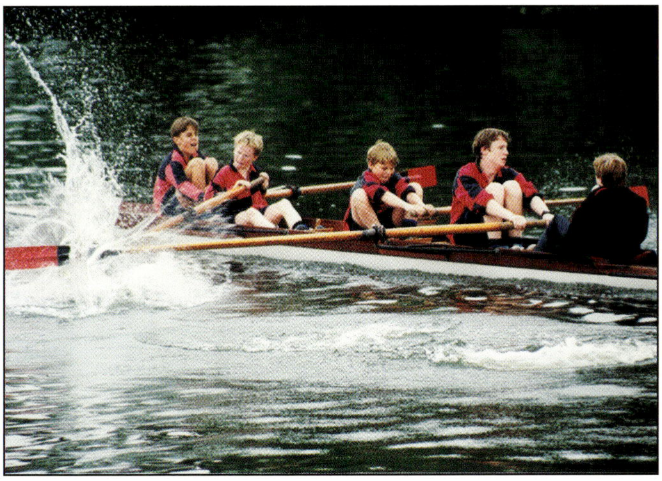

Catching a crab

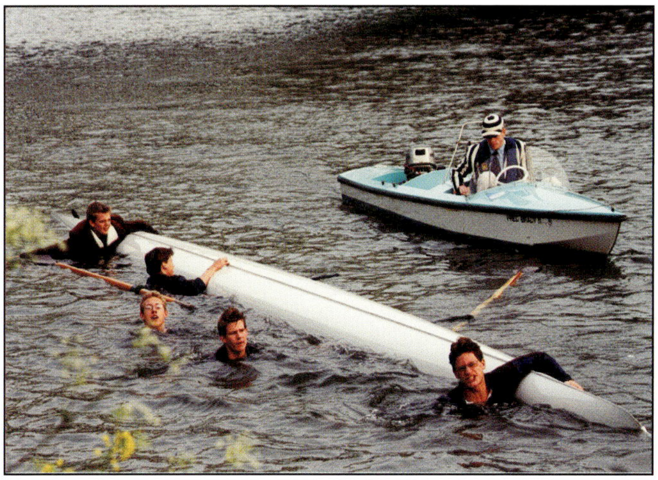

Capsize, but help is at hand

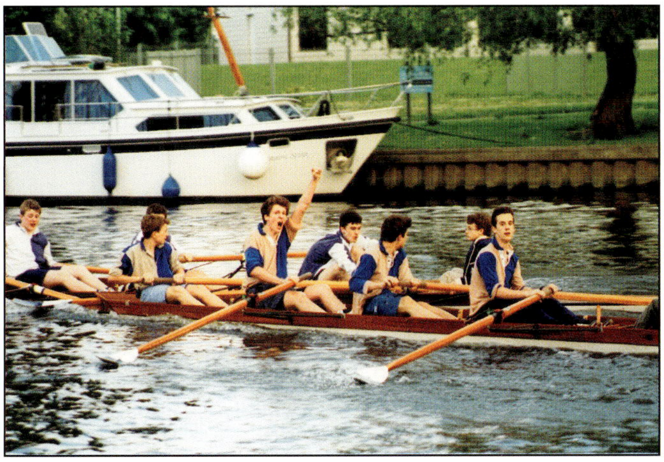

Triumph . . . a bump

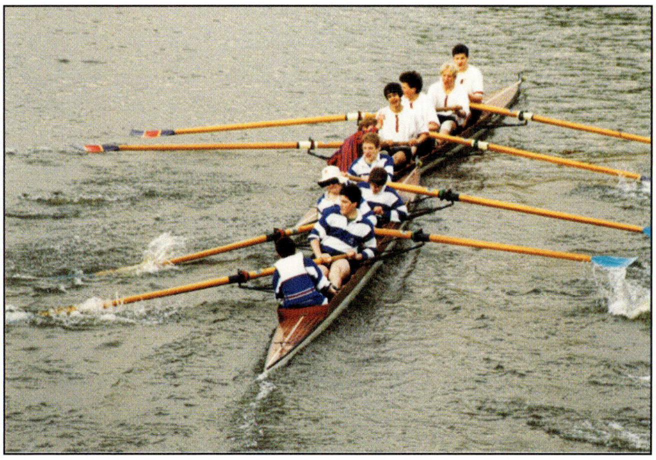

Another Bump!

Dragon boats

Dragon boat racing was an innovation of the late nineteen-eighties. After a fire sadly destroyed the old clubhouse five miles up the river on Queen's Eyot, a magnificent new pavilion was built there. It was felt that this was a facility that should be accessible to all boys, not just wet-bobs. Bill Masser, the river-master, asked the question, "How can we easily transport boys five miles up the river to Queen's Eyot?" "Dragon boats," replied the senior boatman, John Cork. The matter was researched and resulted in the purchase of two such boats, resplendent with their dragon heads. The original purpose of the boats for mass transport was soon forgotten, and instead they have been used for racing.

At this level little skill is required to paddle in a dragon boat, apart from the ability to keep in time with the drummer. The House crews do not train for the competition, but, once on the river, they participate with tremendous enthusiasm and minimal finesse. The temptation to fool around has to be resisted, for individuals can be drenched and boats can capsize. But there is no doubting the overall enjoyment gained!

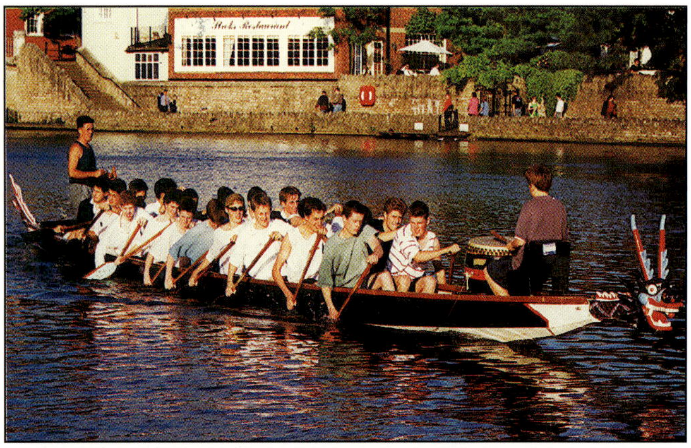

Dragon boat sets off for the starting line

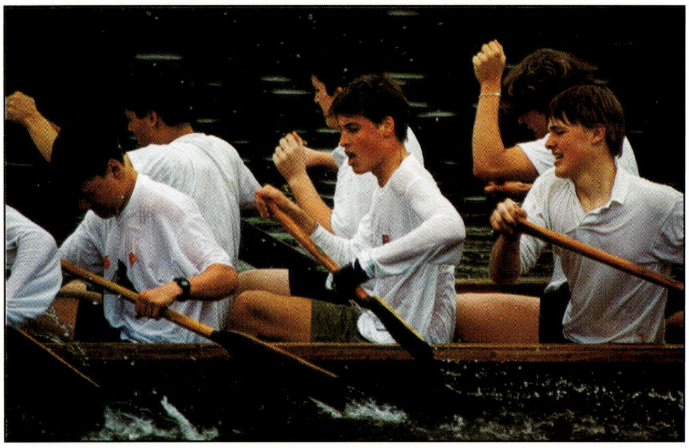

Perfect timing

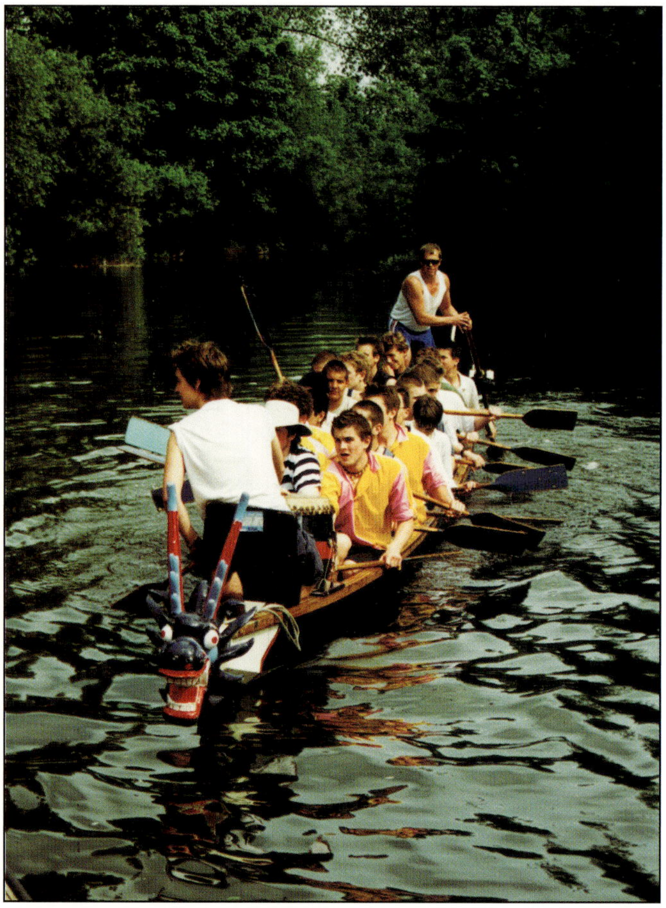

Coming in to land

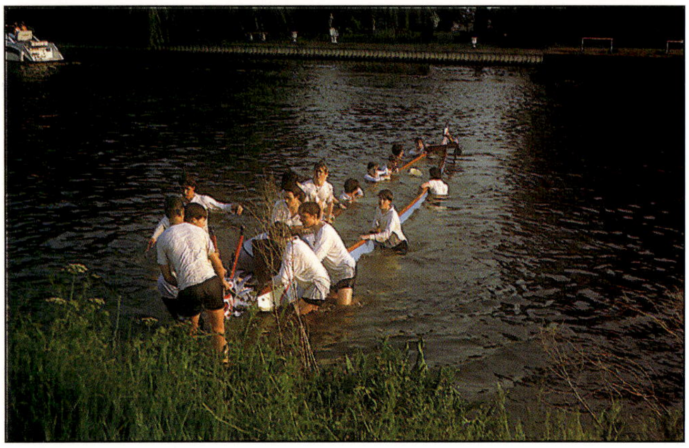

Capsize

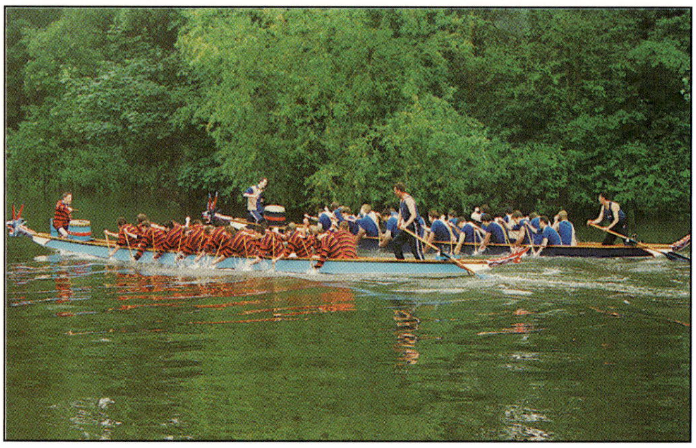

A close race

Rugby

Rugby shares the Michaelmas Half with soccer. Numbers fluctuate, but about 450 boys opt for rugby in any year. This enables the School to field twenty XVs on the busiest day of the season. There is a strong fixture list and, in addition, a hard-fought inter-house VIIs tournament at the end of the Half. Some talented players continue to play VIIs in the Lent Half, and the season reaches its climax with the Rosslyn Park National Sevens at the end of the half. It was heartening to see an Old Etonian score all Oxford's points in the 2001 Oxford and Cambridge match.

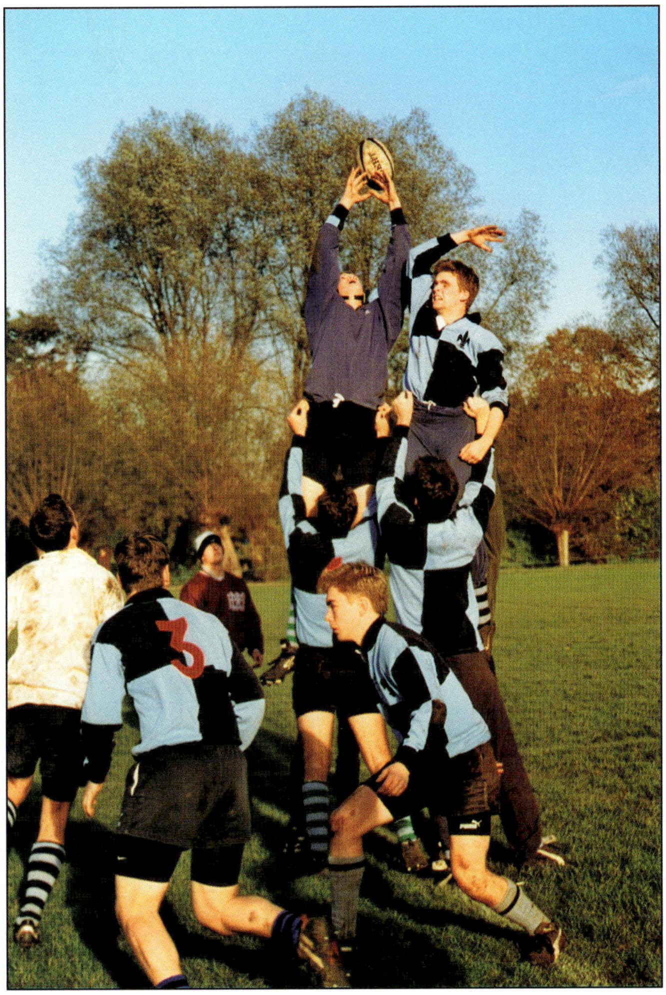

Line-out training

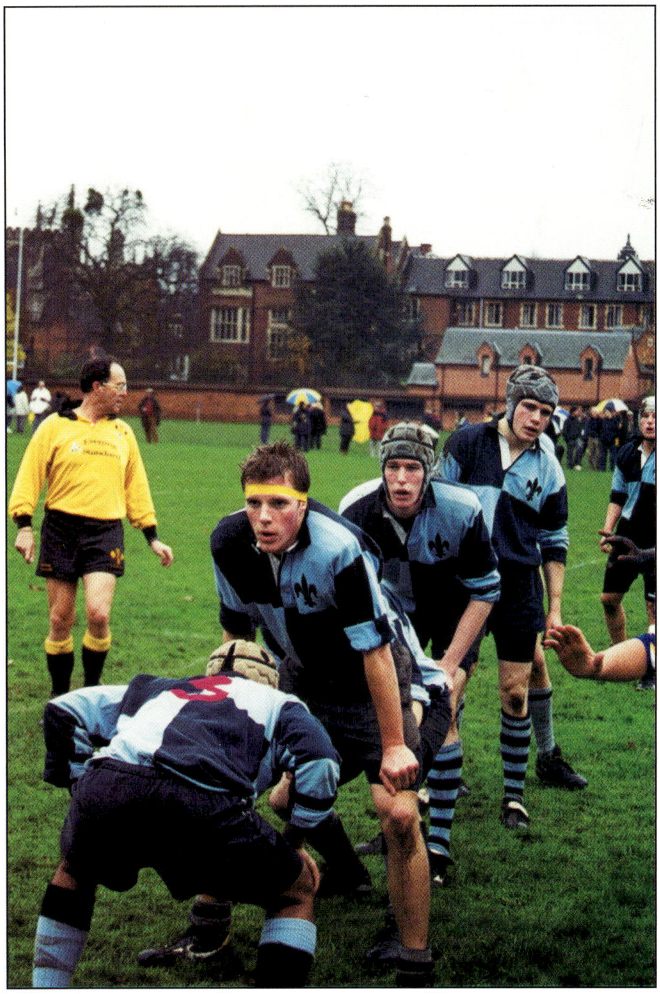

Now to put training into practice

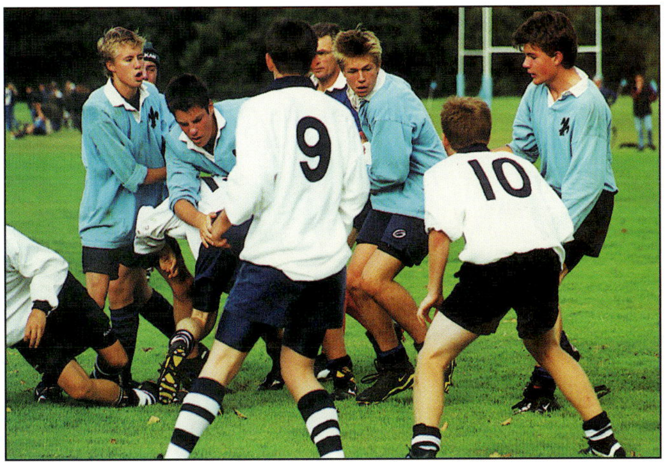

Colts team on the attack

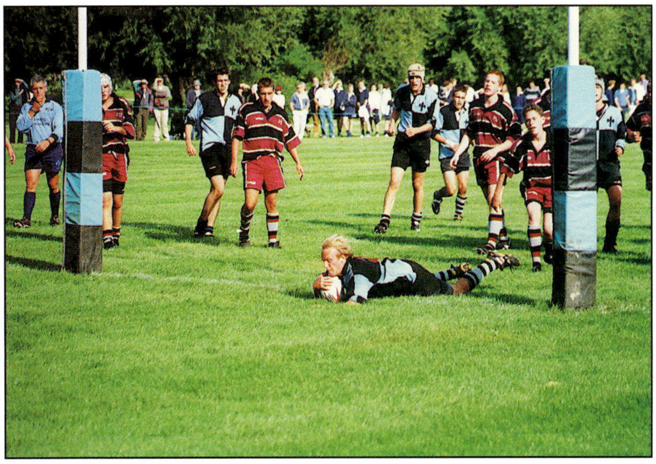

A try between the posts

Soccer

In the Michaelmas Half boys choose either football or rugby as their major sport. This inevitably means that both sports can draw from about half the School for their teams. Eton can field up to twenty-three soccer XIs on any one day, but usually they will be competing against two or more schools. Since 1979 the 1st XI squad has made an annual tour abroad before the season starts, although the first recorded tour was in 1950. Between September and December they play seventeen inter-school matches, and more if they are successful in the two knock-out competitions, the Boodle & Dunthorne Independent Schools Cup and the Berkshire Cup. The two inter-house knock-out competitions bring the season to an exciting close. It seems unlikely that Etonian footballers will ever emulate the performances of the Old Etonian teams of 1879 and 1882 who were F.A. Cup winners, but it is pleasing to report that the game continues to thrive at Eton.

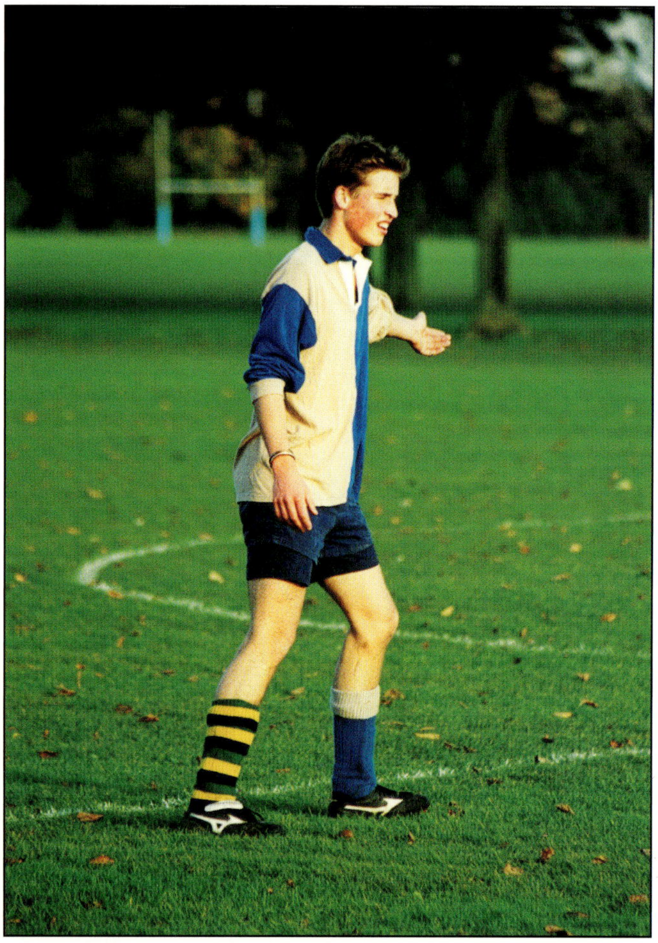

Captain of the Senior House Side encouraging his team

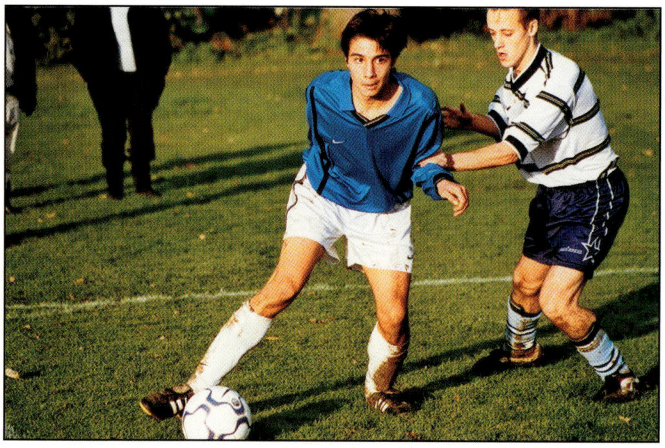

The 1st XI in action

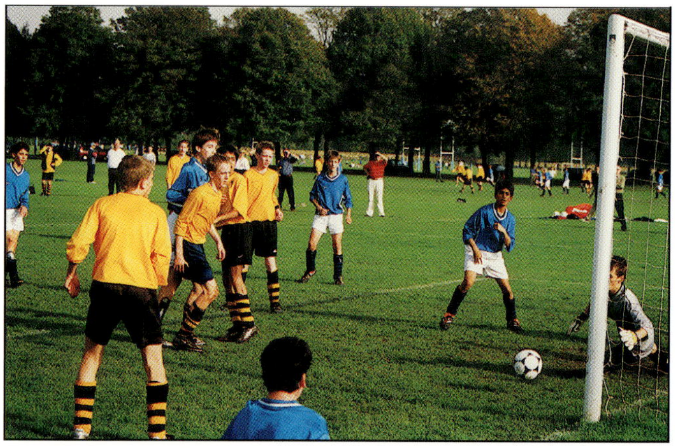

Under 14 XI on target

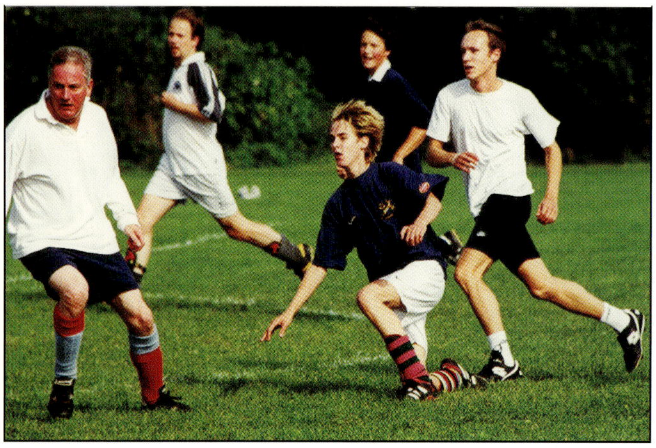

Beaks v. Boys

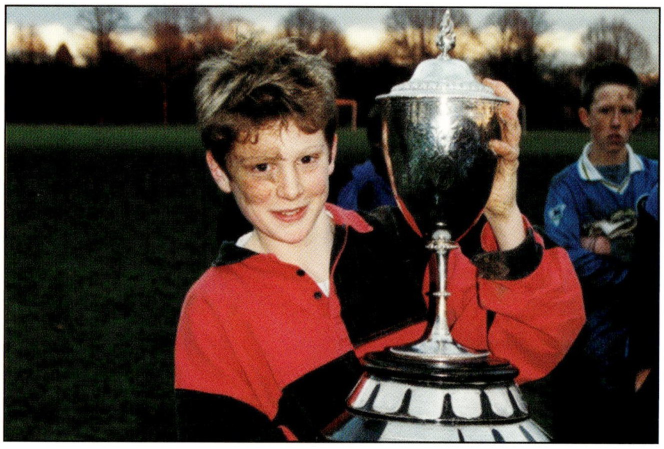

Winning captain of the Junior inter-house knock-out

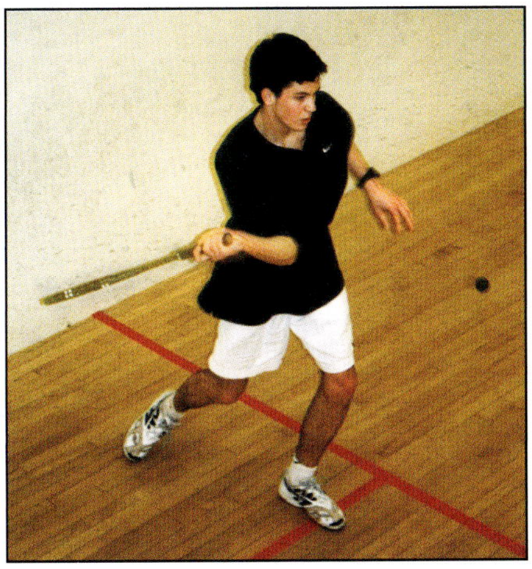

Service from the left-hand court

Squash

Squash enjoys great popularity. There is a full fixture list at all levels, and three outside coaches come in to train the squads. The School has twelve courts in blocks of eight and four at either end of the indoor swimming-pool. In addition to the normal internal competitions there is a Master-and-Boy doubles competition, which creates considerable interest. A recent Keeper of Squash went on to captain Cambridge, and in recent years there have been tours to the USA and Italy.

Steeplechase

In 2001 the course for the internal steeplechase was changed for reasons of safety. Previously, competitors had started from Mesopotamia and had completed their race on the Field. The climax for the seniors had been a glorious leap across (or into) the Jordan to reach the finishing line. But crossing of the Eton Wick Road became increasingly dangerous, so in 2001 a new course was marked out, which starts and finishes outside the Sanatorium on South Meadow. Winners in 2001 inevitably hold the course records, as there is no certainty as to the actual length of either old or new courses! The race is compulsory for D, E and F Blocks, but queues for the doctors' surgery on the eve of the race suggest that not all boys enjoy the occasion. A cross-country team, made up of a group of dedicated athletes, competes in a number of inter-school and inter-county events with considerable success.

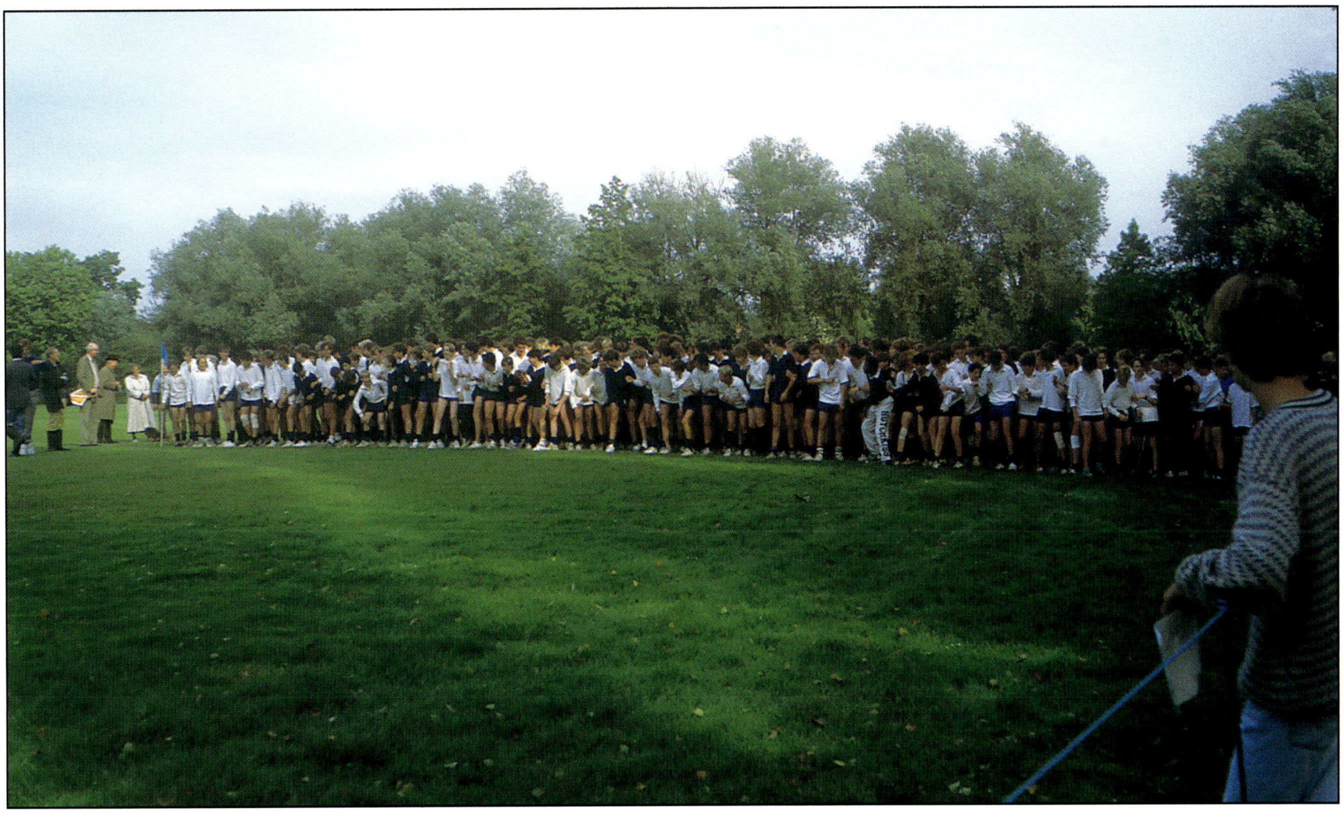

Lining up for the start

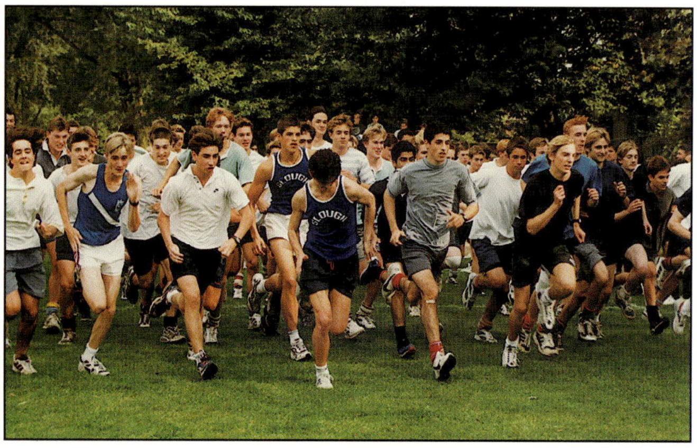
They're off

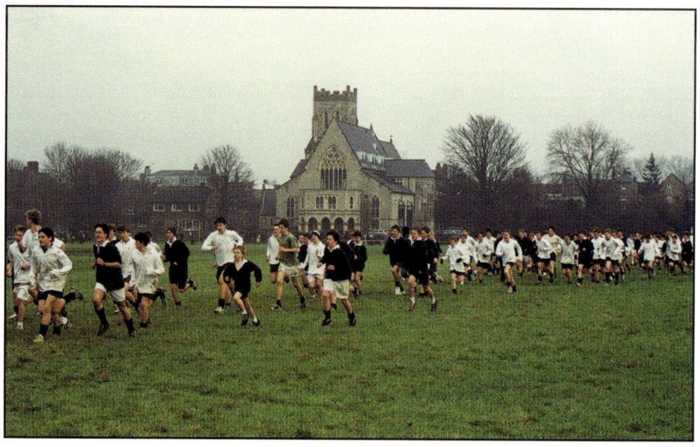
The new starting point outside the Sanatorium on South Meadow

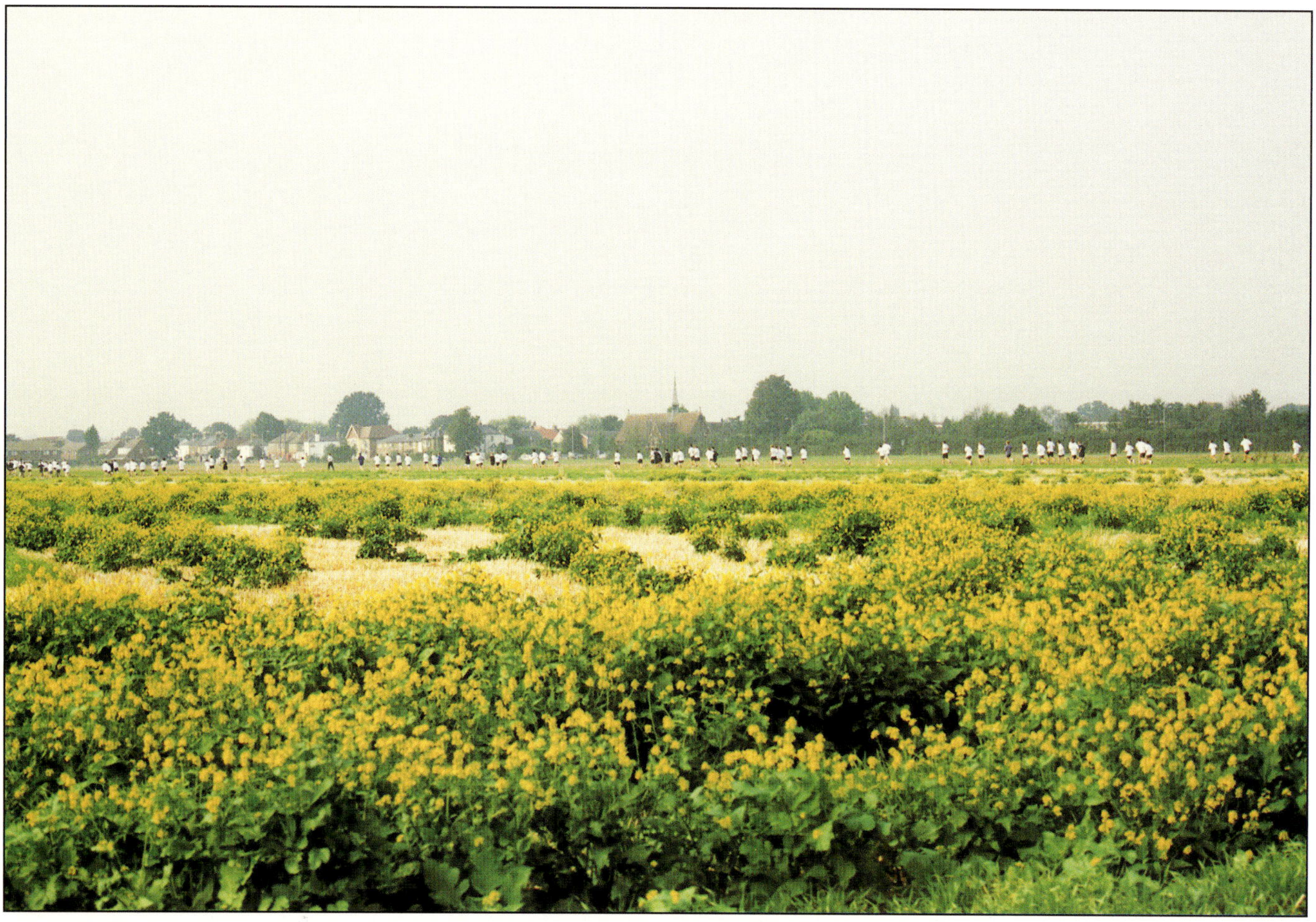
Runners strung out making for Eton Wick

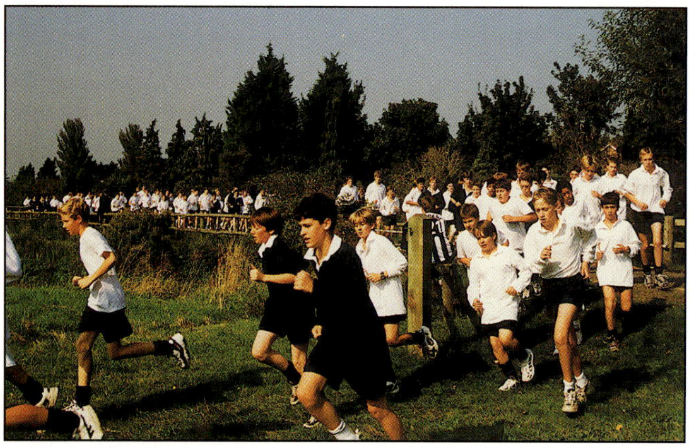
Runners on the old course approaching the Eton Wick Road

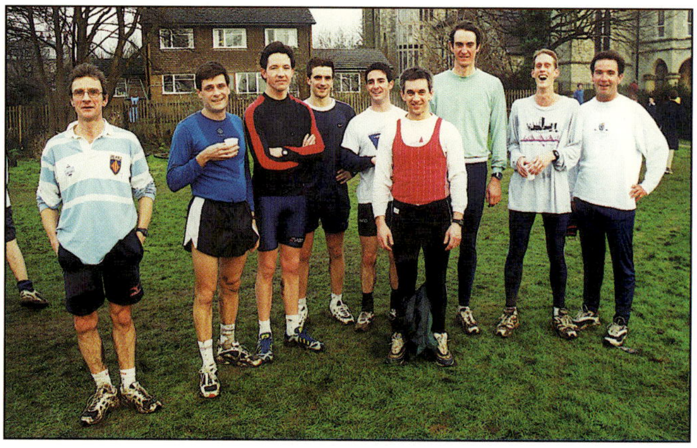
Many fit Masters run in the event

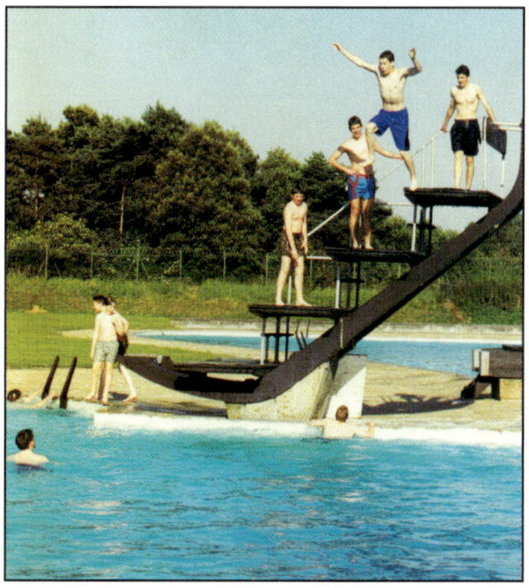

The outdoor pool

Swimming and Water Polo

The School has one indoor and one outdoor pool. The former has taken the place of the fives courts that used to face the Field. It is well used for recreational and competitive swimming, water polo, sub aqua training and kayaking. It is another of the School's facilities that is made available to outside clubs. Squads train regularly for both swimming and water polo matches, and there have been tours to China and America in recent years. The very best water polo players have made their mark at county and even national level. The outdoor pool, shaped like a distorted figure of eight, is vast, but associated with leisure rather than competition. It is eagerly sought late in the Summer Half, when temperatures rise and boys are in need of relaxation.

Tennis

Tennis at Eton enjoyed a rapid growth in popularity when boys were given greater freedom of choice over their summer sports. Nowadays the busiest day for tennis fixtures might see some fifteen VIs on court. The general standard of tennis has probably never been higher than it is now, though it was in 1970 that an Eton team last won the Youll Cup, the inter-schools team tournament for independent schools. The team at that time was led by Robin Drysdale who later became a leading figure in the national game. Since 1993 there has been a pre-season training camp at the Harry Hopman Tennis Academy in Florida, and the season itself leads up to the Youll Cup and Thomas Bowl competitions. These Independent Schools Championships used to take place at Wimbledon, but were transferred to Eton, when public examination dates were brought forward. For many years there has been talk of building indoor courts at Eton. The School would undoubtedly benefit and awaits a generous gesture from a kind benefactor!

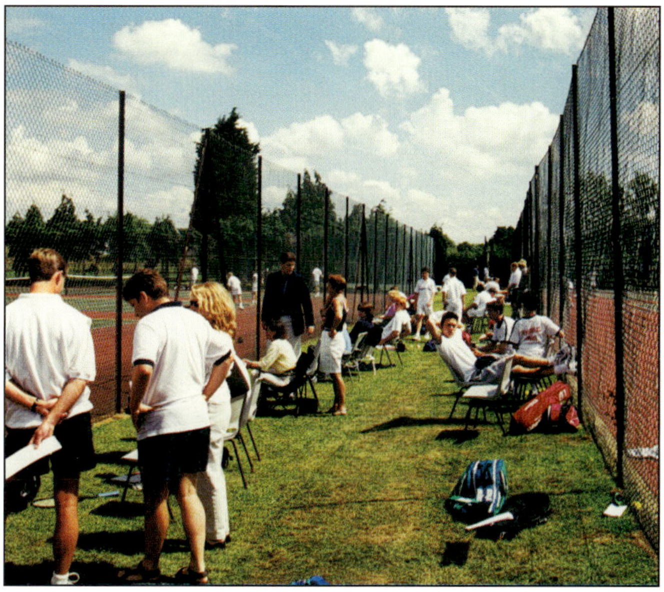

The Independent Schools Championships at Eton

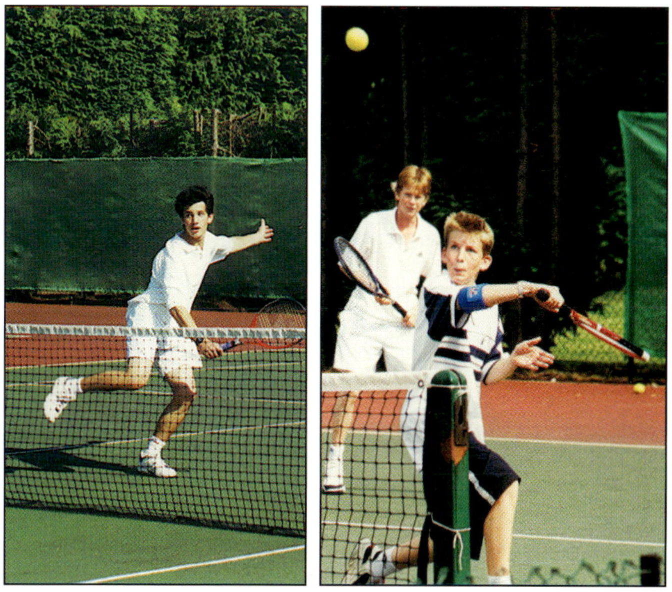

Eye on the ball

Wall Game

Few boys actually play the Wall Game, in part because there is only one suitable wall! In a school of just under 1300 boys it would not be practicable to give all boys a chance to play, nor would they necessarily wish to do so, as it has the reputation of being even rougher than rugby. By tradition, the Wall belongs to College, the House made up of some 70 boys who have won academic scholarships to Eton. So College provides one team, and their principal rivals are the Oppidans, a team made up of boys from all the other houses. Opponents are hard to find and usually consist of Masters and Old Etonians. Dedicated proponents of the game teach the rudiments to younger boys, and in this way the game is kept alive. There are two significant contests between Collegers and Oppidans in the School year, a serious one on St Andrew's Day in late November, and a more light-hearted one at day-break on Ascension Day. A large crowd will spectate on St Andrew's Day, mostly ignorant of the rules, but still determined to see it. On Ascension Day the early risers are present, and, as early-rising is not popular, the crowd is small. To the non-initiated the game looks like a permanent rugby scrum formed against the Wall with each team trying to make ground towards the elusive end-zone, known as calx, at either end of the Wall. If successful, the attacking team may then have a throw at goal, a door at one end and formerly a tree at the other. The ball is often hidden from view, but when it does appear, there are loud cheers. Yes, it is true that the last time a goal was scored on St Andrew's Day was in 1909. *(see also Ascension Day and St Andrew's Day: pages 113–115, 121–122)*

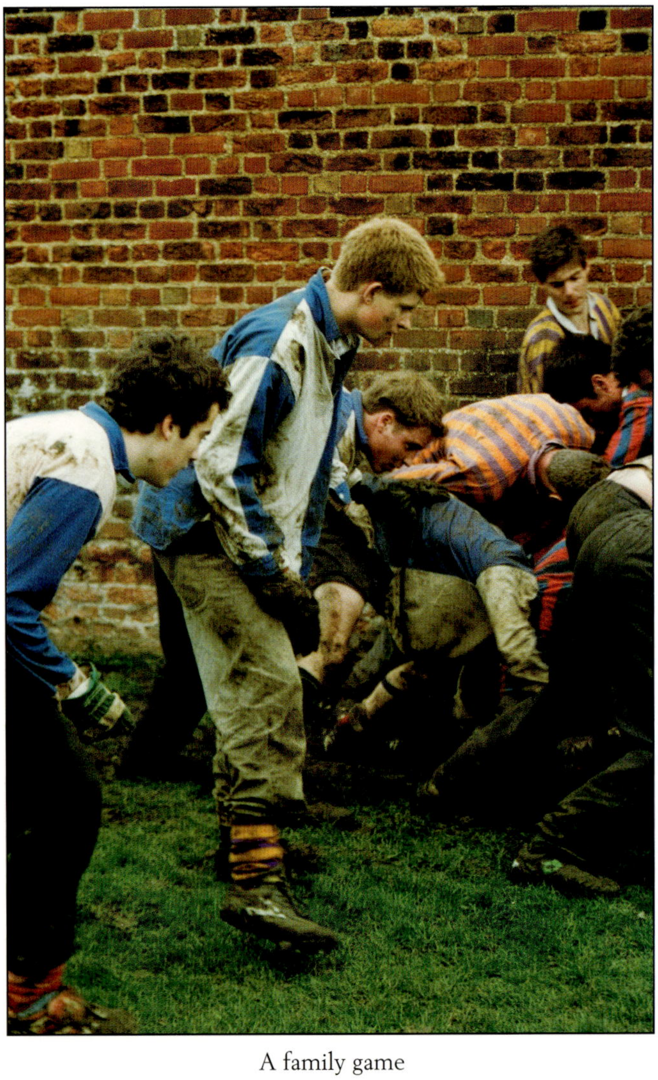

A family game

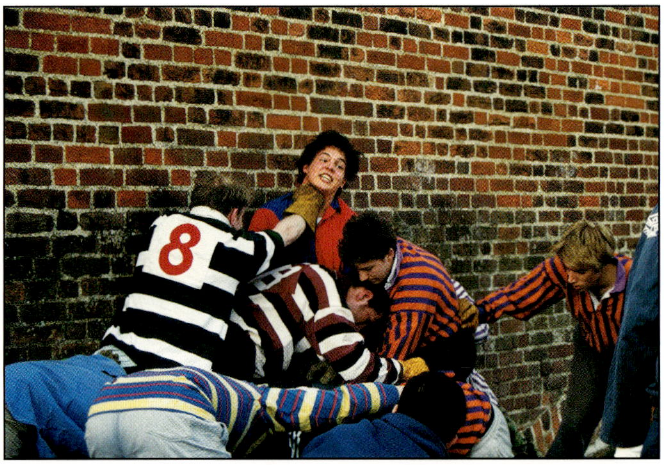

This unusual tactic surprises the uninitiated

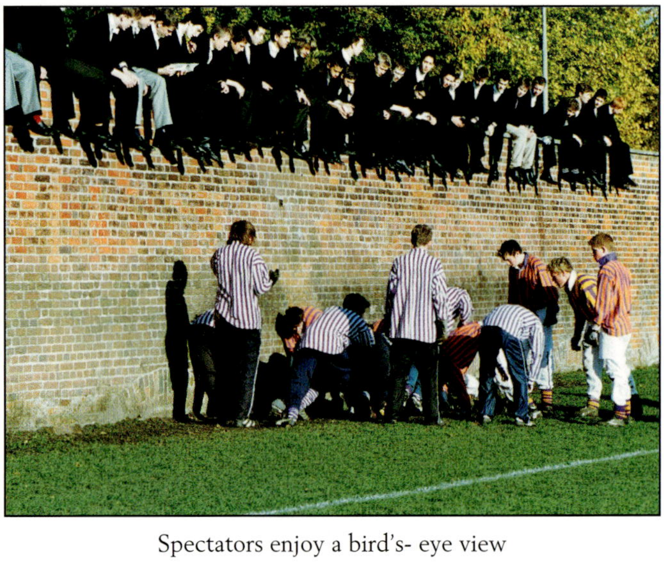

Spectators enjoy a bird's- eye view

Give a boy a football . . .

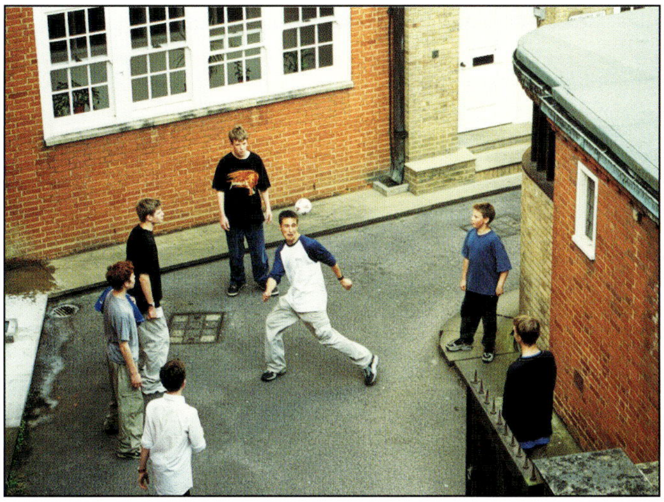

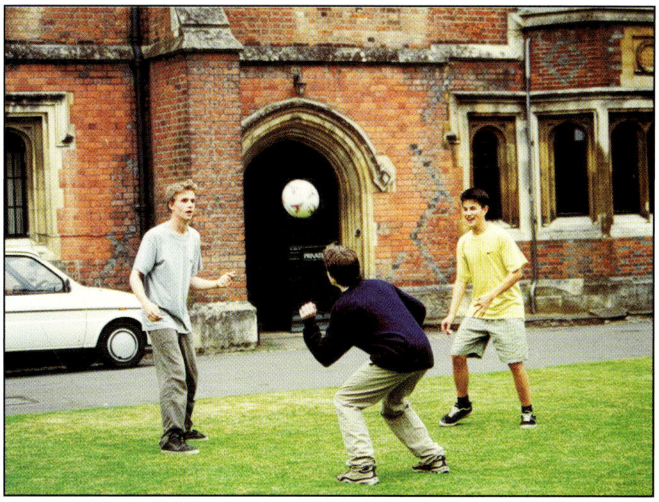

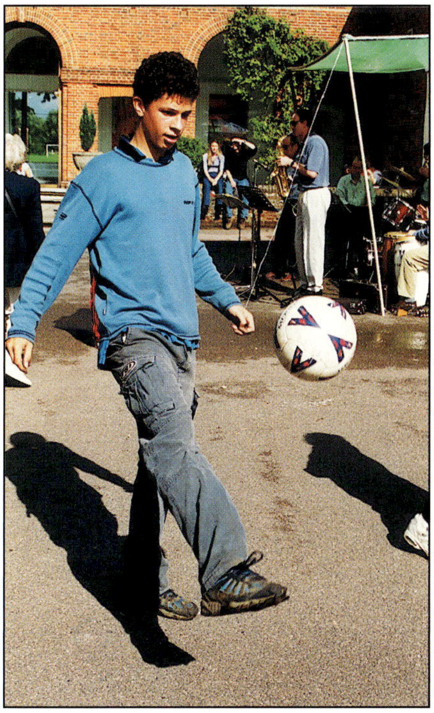

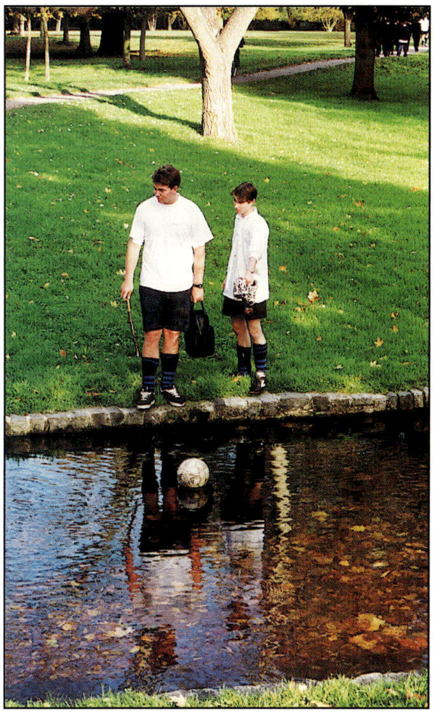

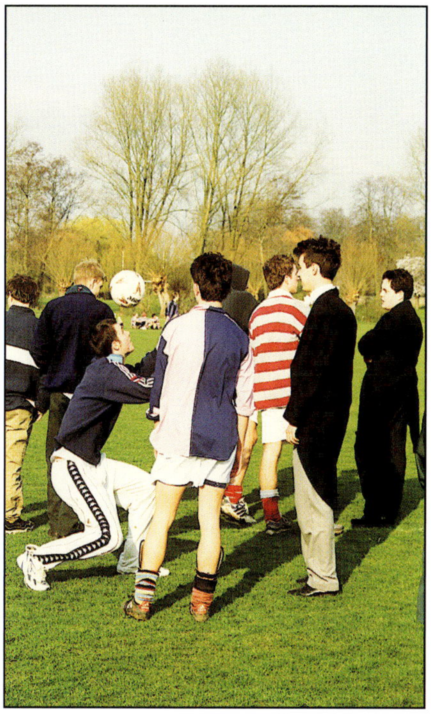

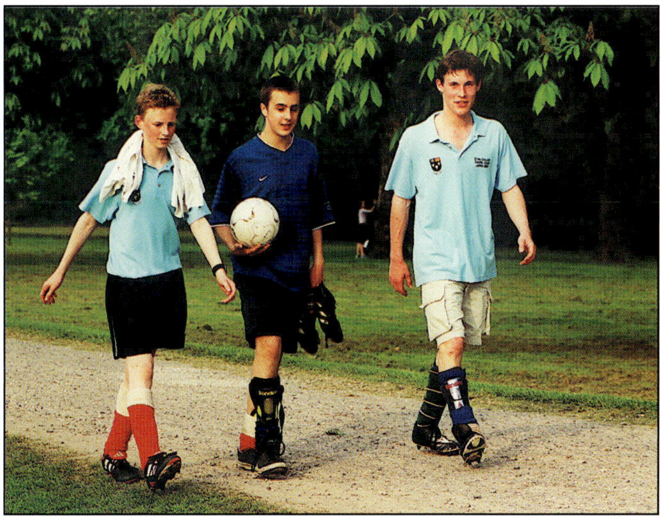

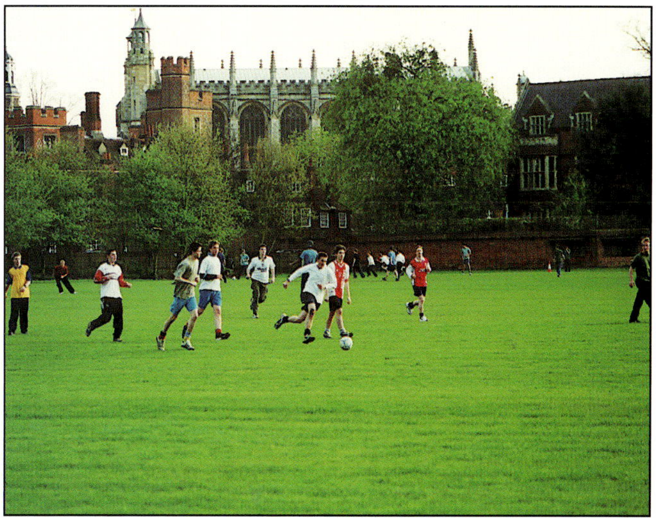

Boys will be boys

The Etonian is nothing if not resourceful! His mind can wander from the serious matter of schoolwork, and his sense of fun takes over. Some deviations from the norm derive from forgetfulness, whilst others are carefully premeditated.

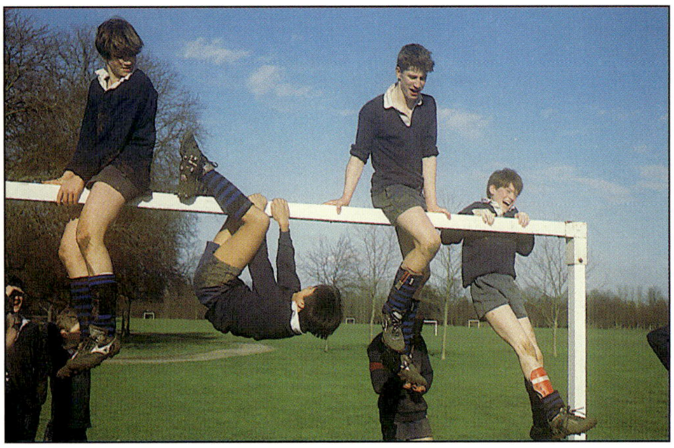

Pleasure at victory

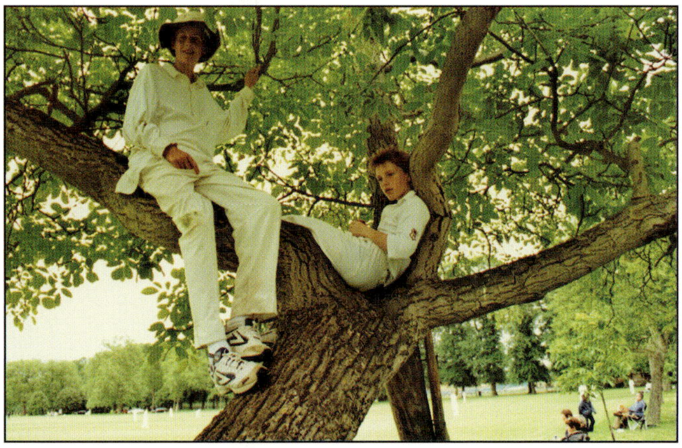

Good vantage point

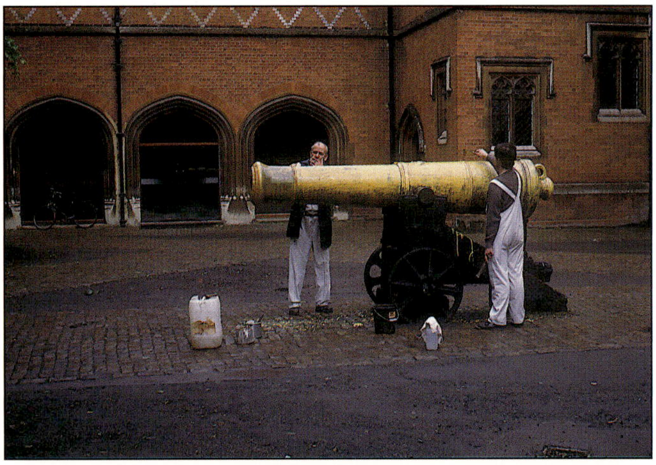

A yellow cannon

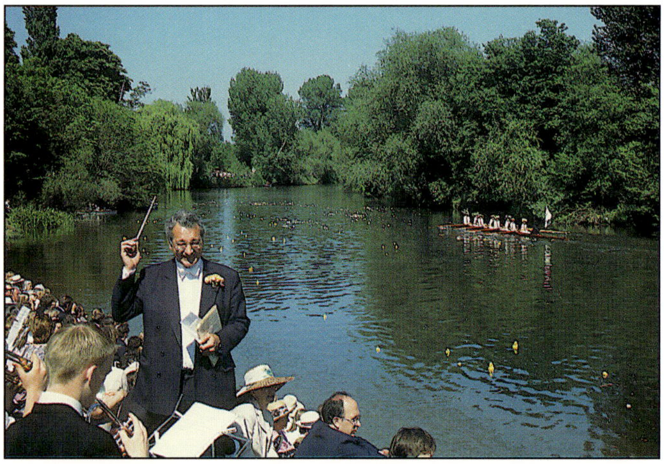

Yellow plastic ducks are not part of the tradition

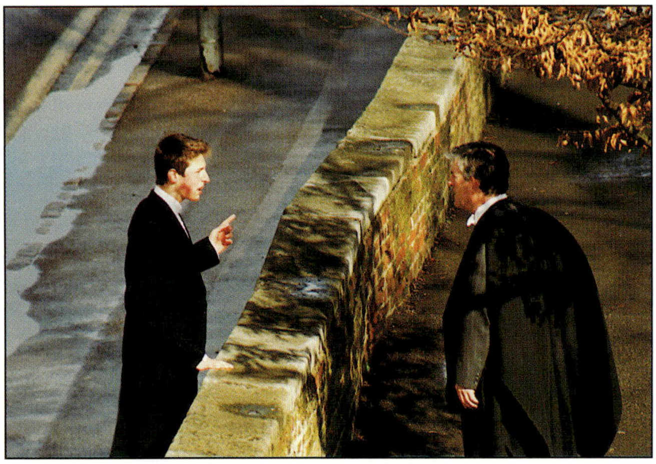

It was him, Sir!

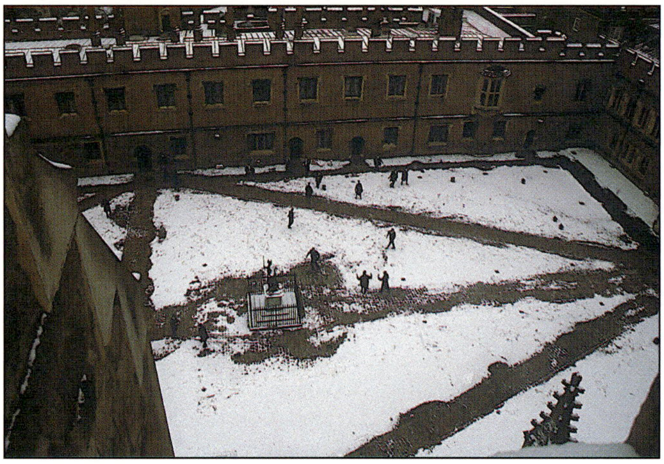

Collegers snowballing in School Yard

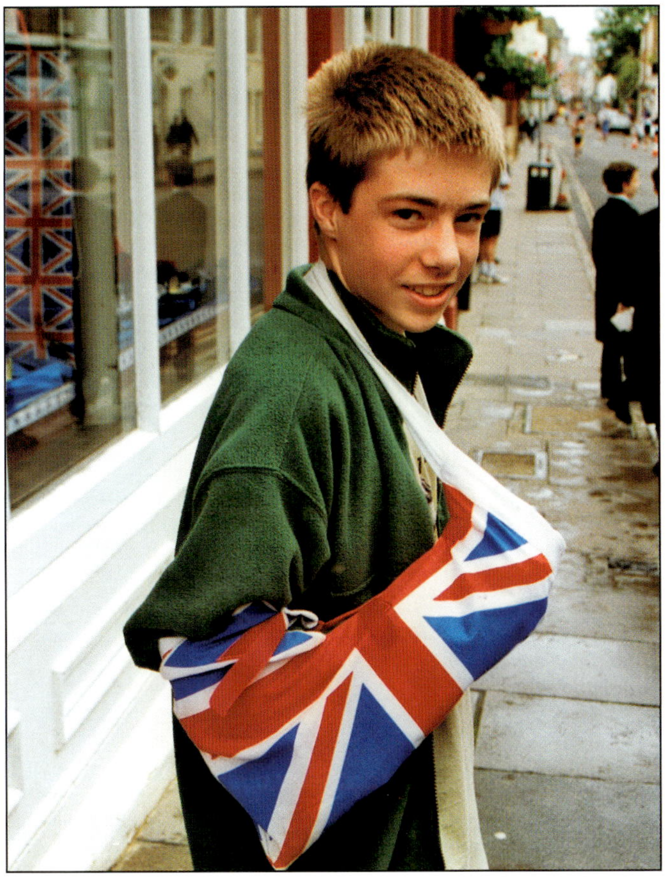

Slinging the flag

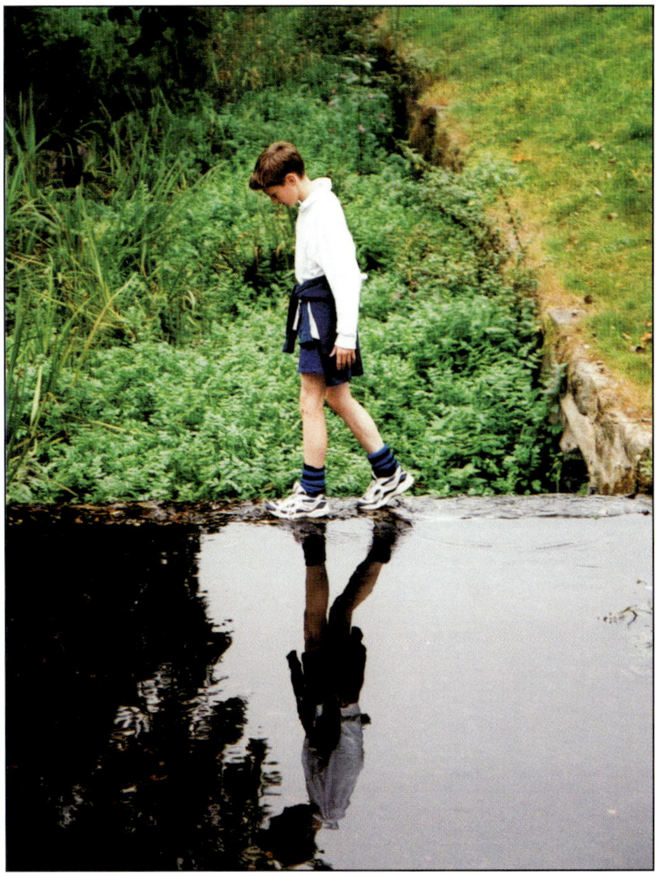

Crossing the Jordan

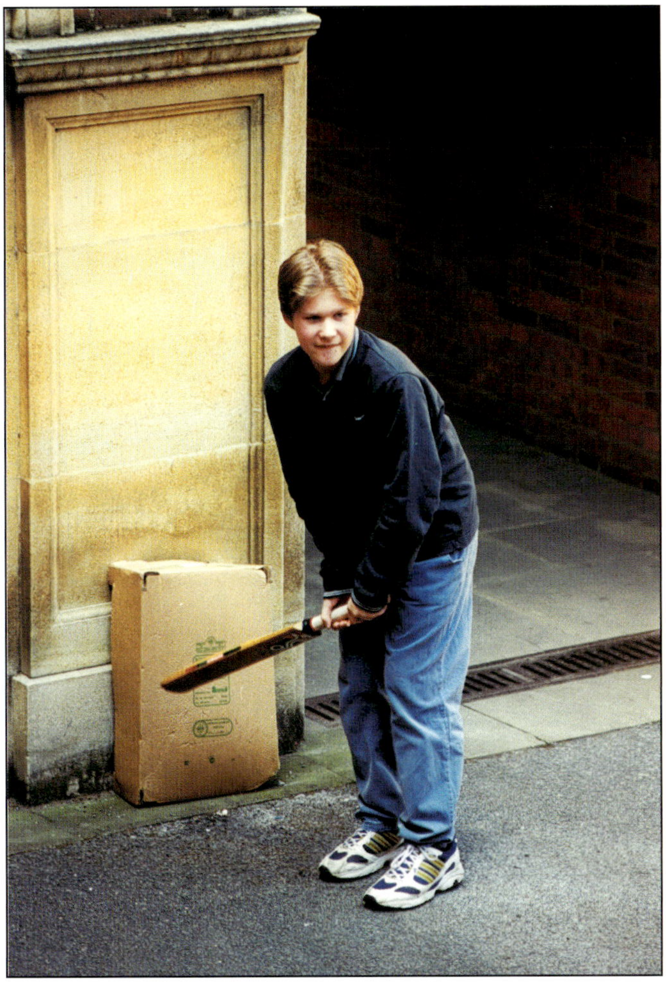

Improvised court-yard cricket

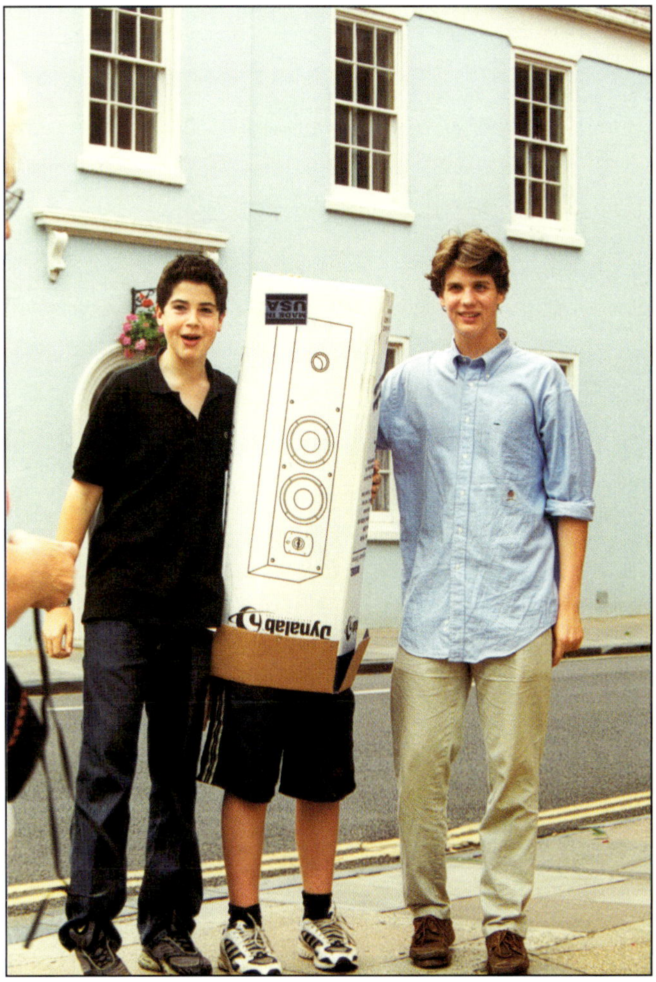

All boxed up

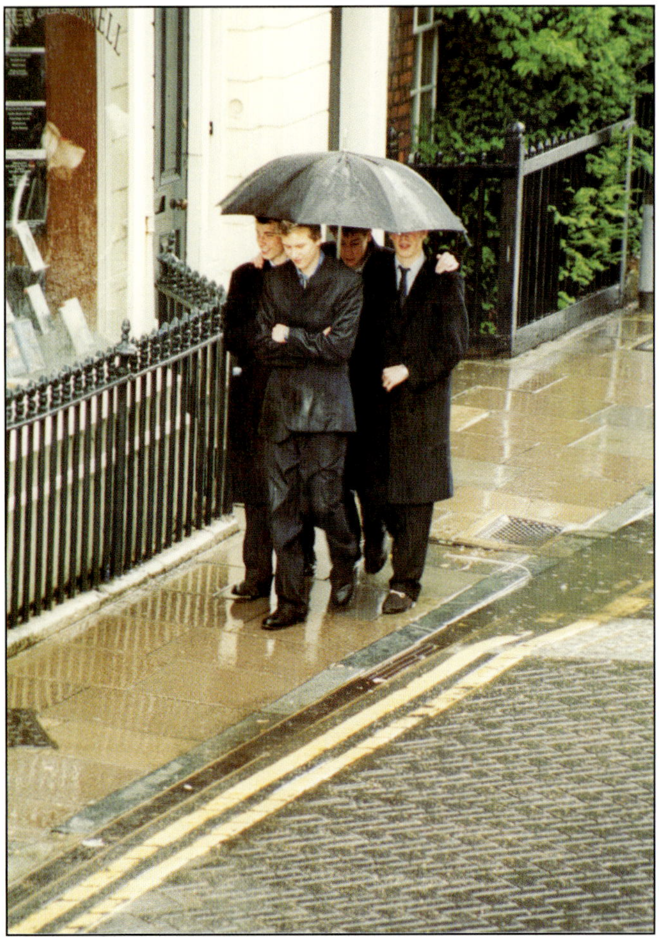

Four boys under one umbrella

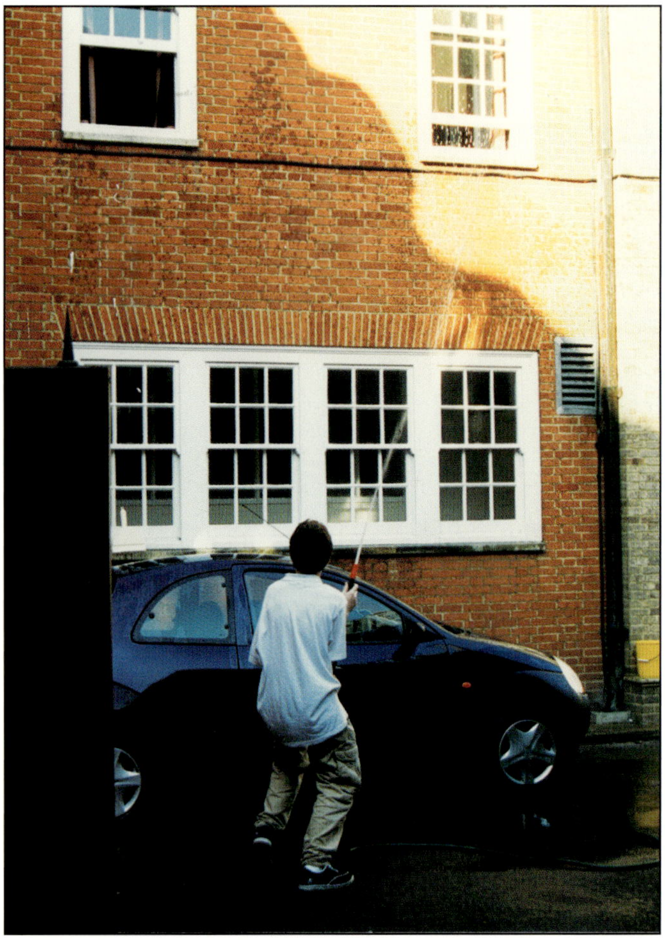

Cleaning m'Dame's car

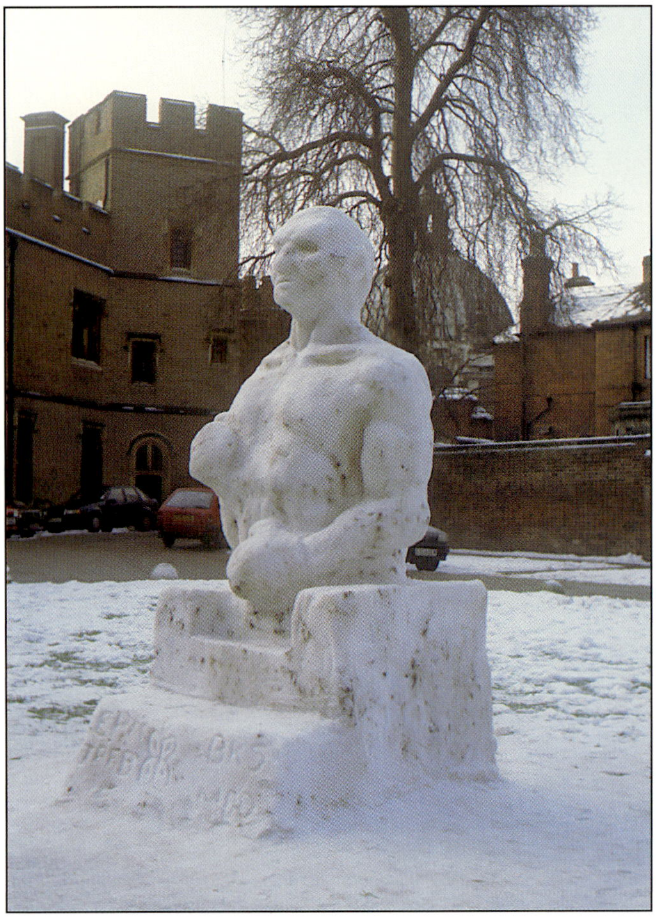

Collegers' snowman

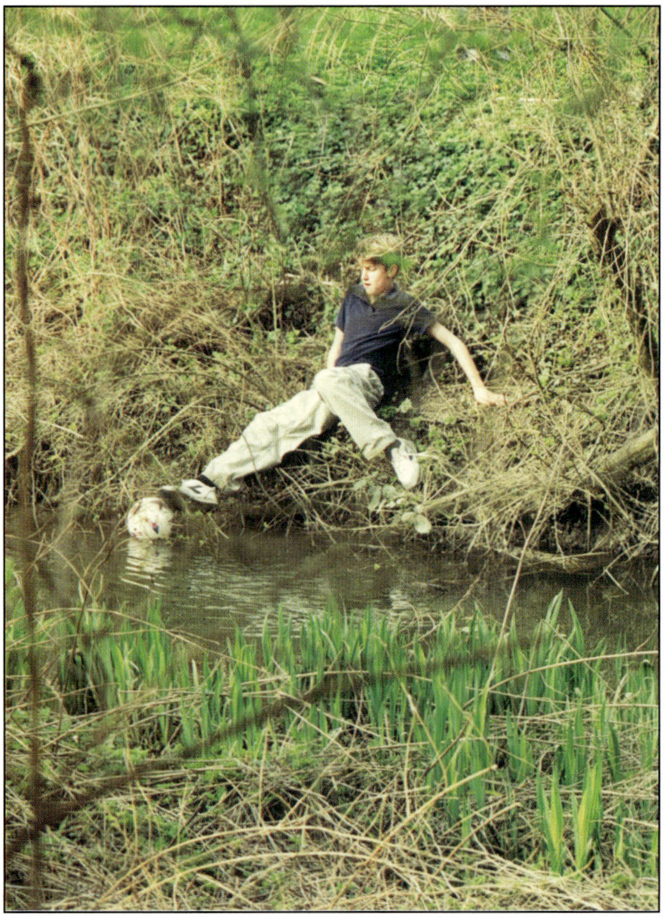

Lost football

Food

More attention is paid to healthy eating and balanced diet than perhaps was traditionally the case. Ask any schoolboy about school food, and the answer is predictable, but any objective outsider would be impressed by the quality of current menus. Of Eton's twenty-five houses, fourteen are self-catering, and the boys from the remaining eleven houses eat in Bekynton. Bekynton is a large central feeding complex opened in 1974 by Lady Home. Originally it catered for four houses, but has since expanded in size and capacity and now also includes the Masters' Dining Room. Long queues were once a problem, but a recent extension of the serving areas has largely solved this problem. Probably the most popular meal of the year is the Founder's Feast or 'sock supper' that takes place shortly before the Christmas holidays. On this occasion a Christmas meal is served, and it is followed by speeches and entertainment of some sort. Between routine meals Rowlands and Tudor Stores are Mecca for the hungry boy.

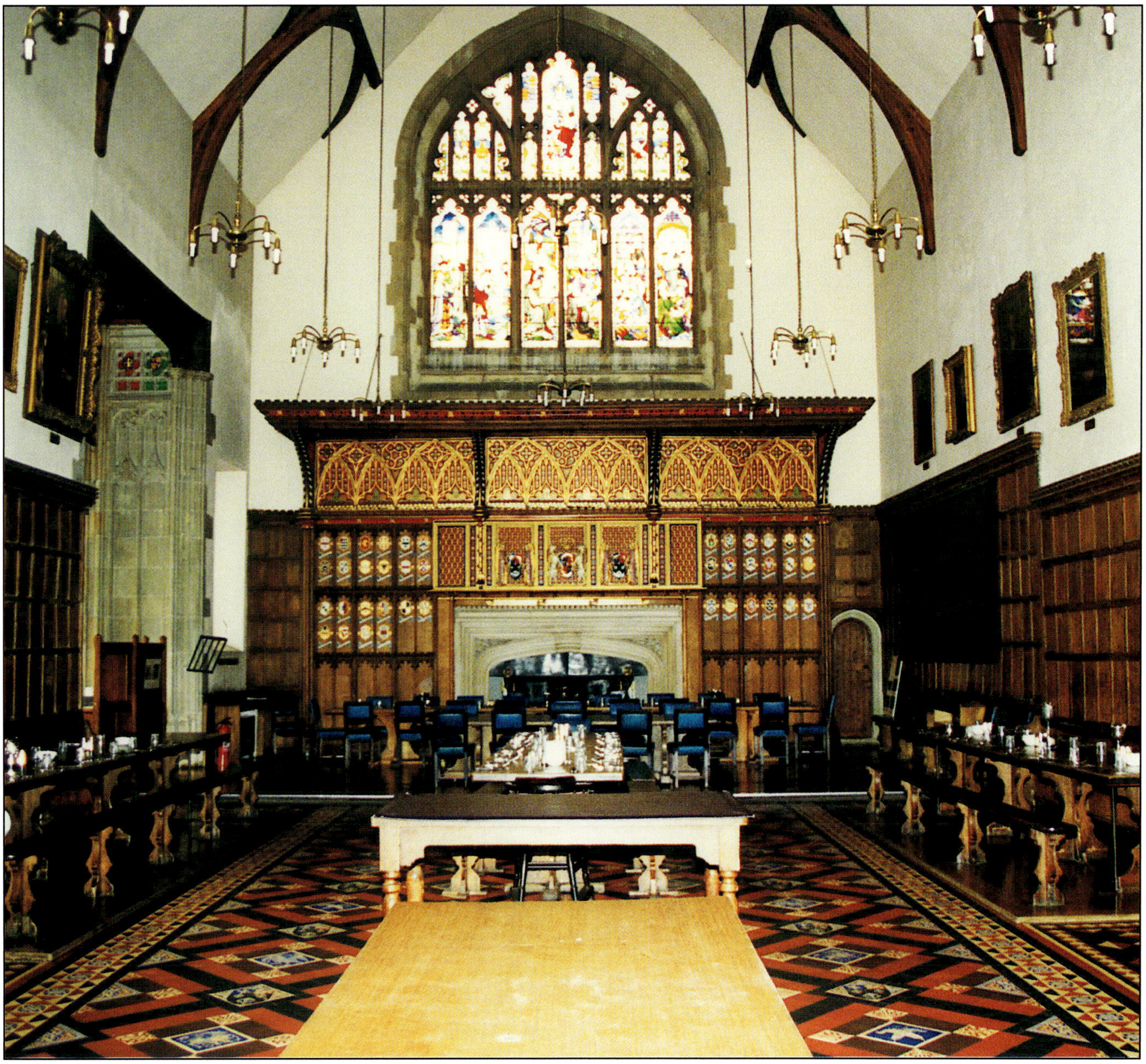

College Hall

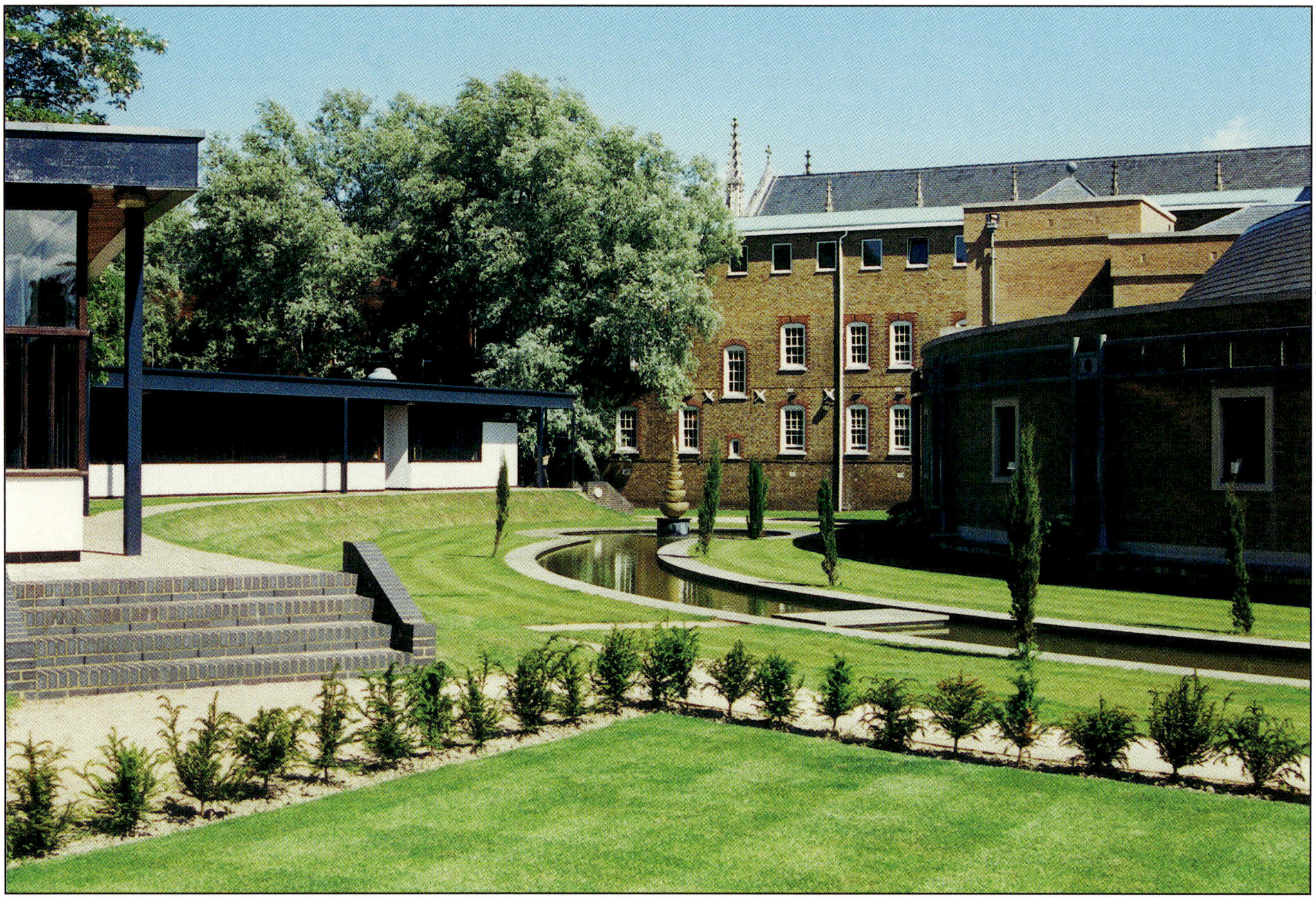

Bekynton (*left*) and the Music Schools extension (*right*) have been built on the former games field, Rackets Court Field

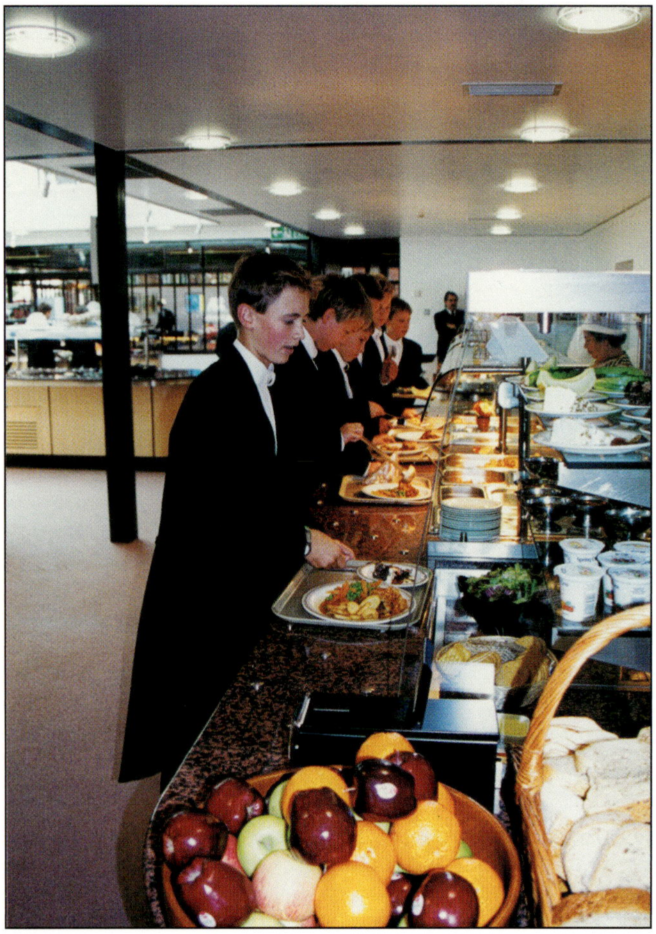

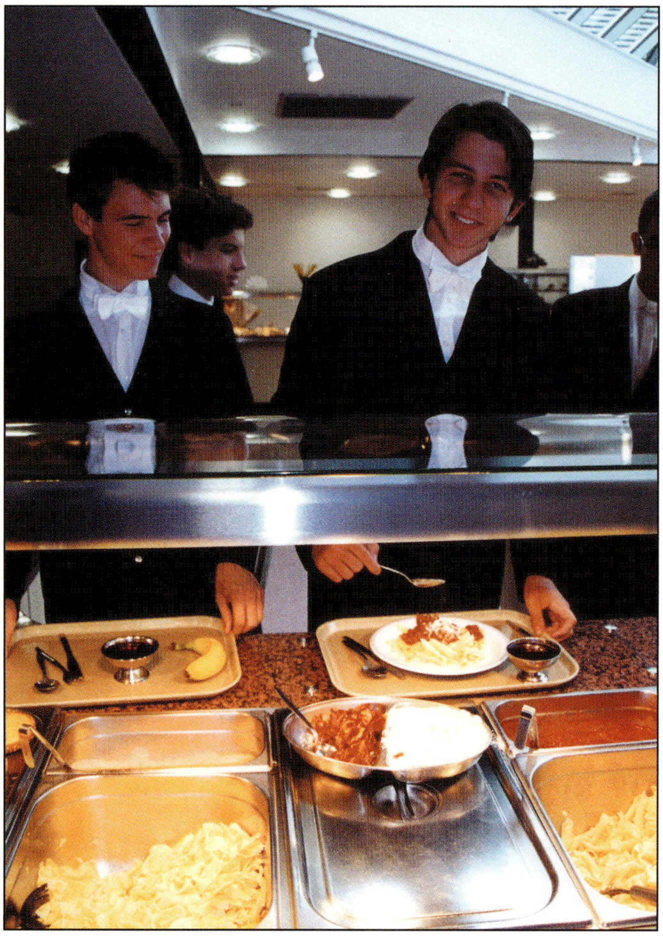

New servery areas in Bekynton

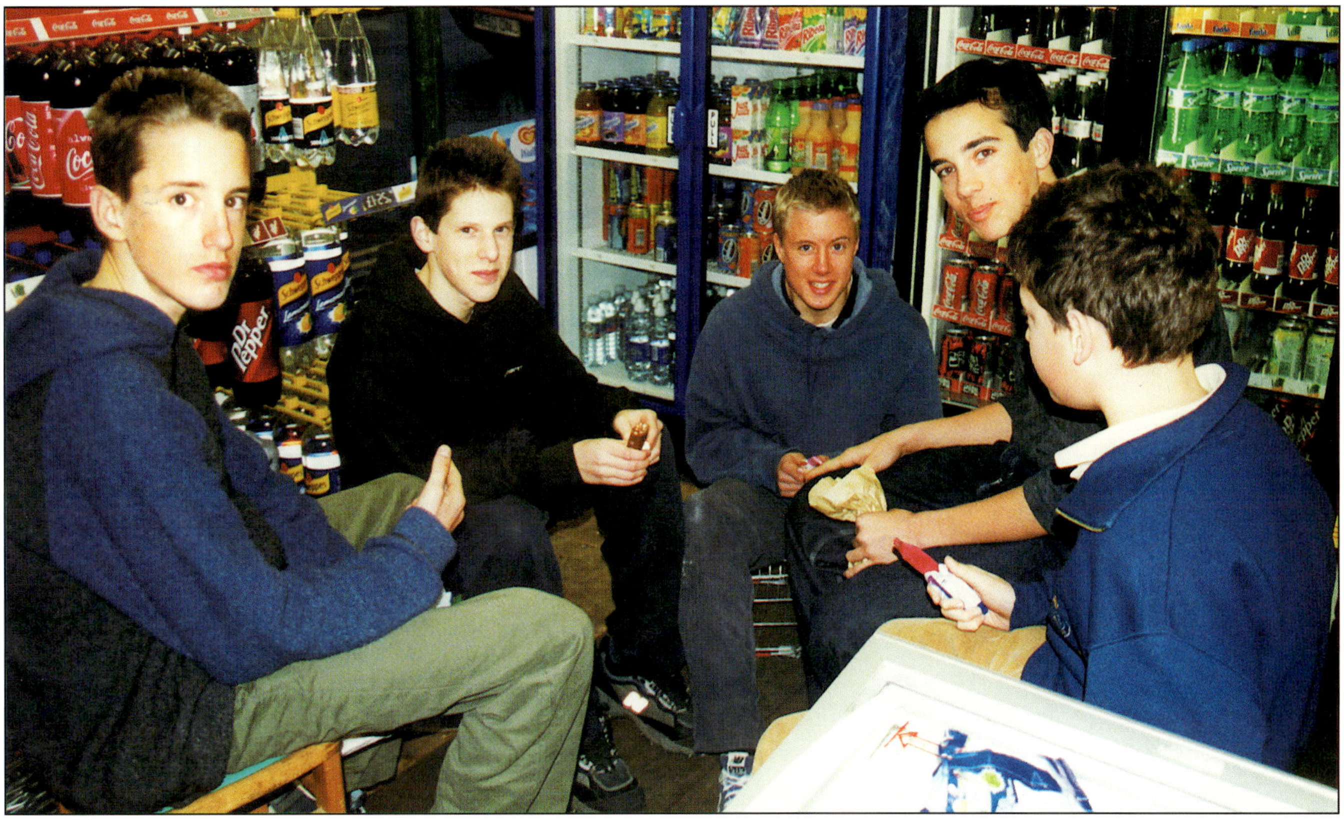

Time to relax in Tudor Stores

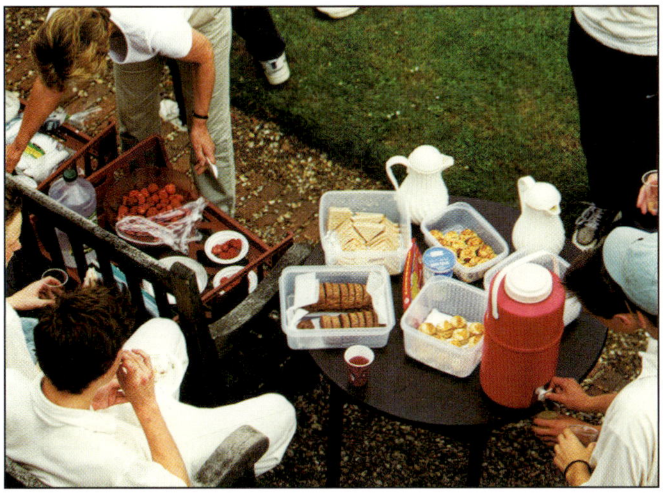

Cricket teas are always popular

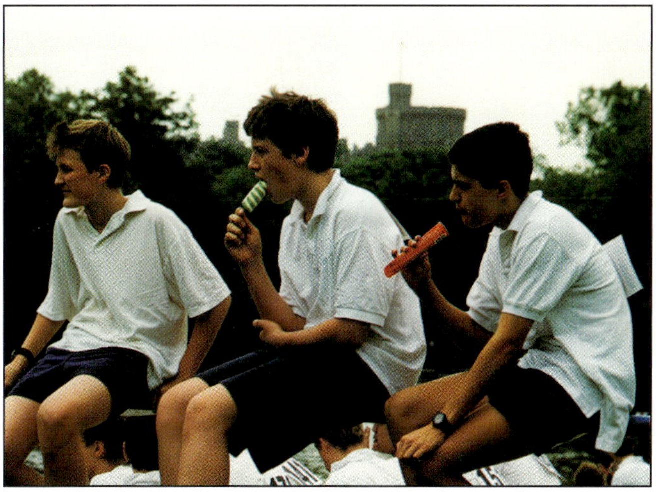

On the river bank

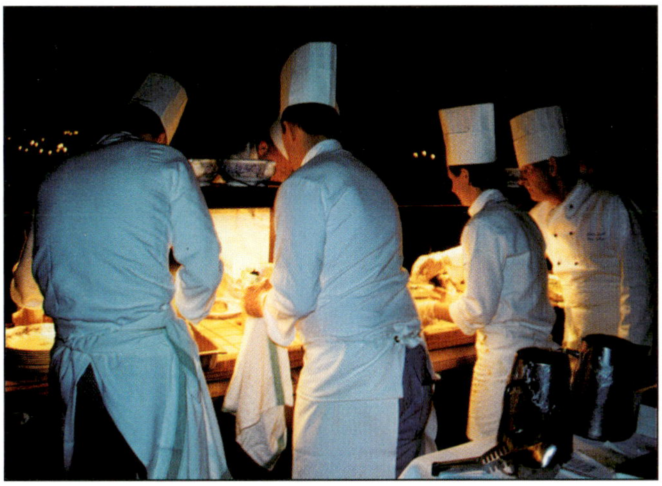

Chefs serving in College Hall

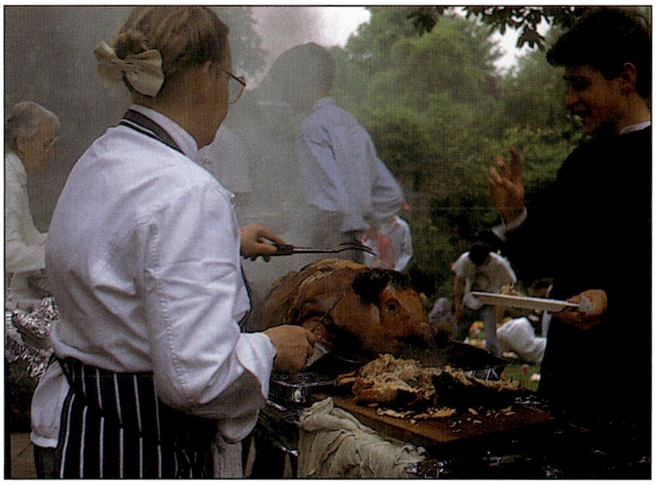

Barbecue time

Health

The new Sanatorium, housed within the converted parish church, was opened in 1991. The building contains a fourteen-bed sanatorium, a boys' day room, GP practice for three doctors and their staff, physiotherapy rooms, a fully equipped treatment room and flats for three nurses. The two School doctors have daily boys' surgeries starting at 8.15am. Some boys hurry down to the Sanatorium at first light to head the queue; others take their time, hoping possibly to miss first school which usually starts at 9.00 am!

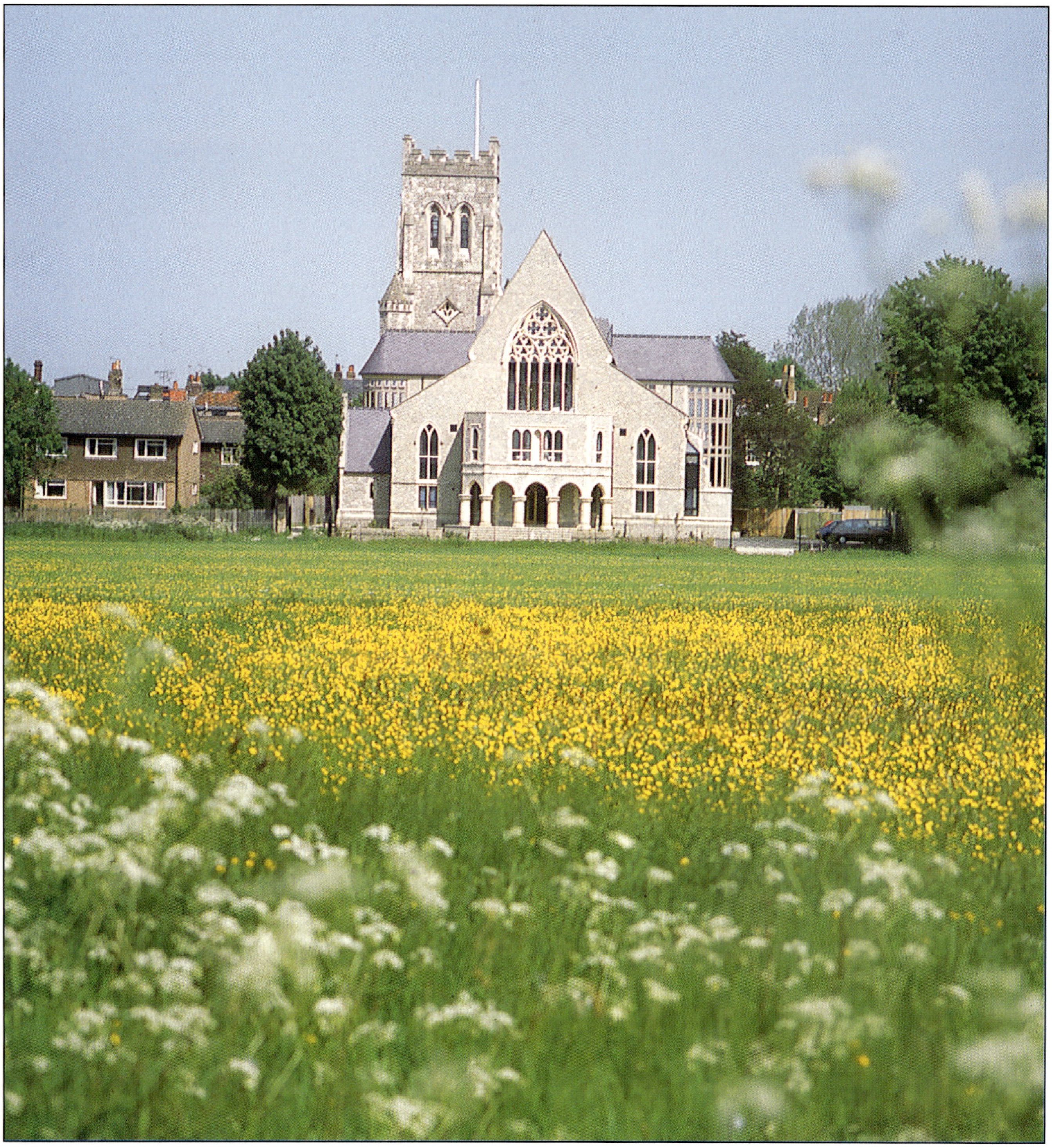

The conversion is complete

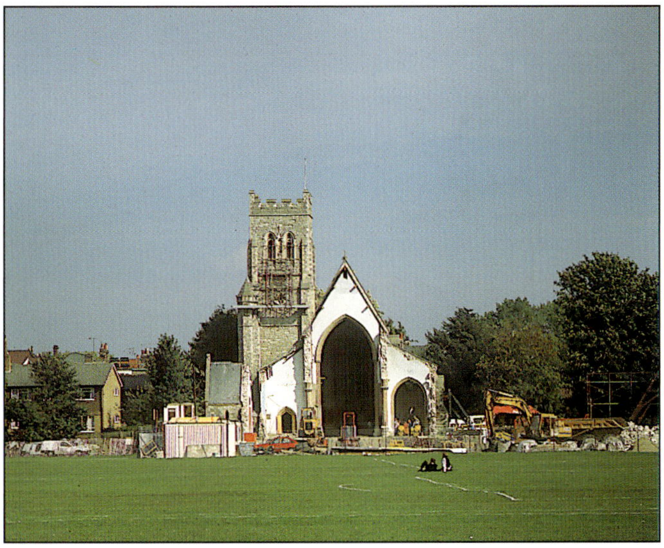

Conversion of Parish Church to Sanatorium

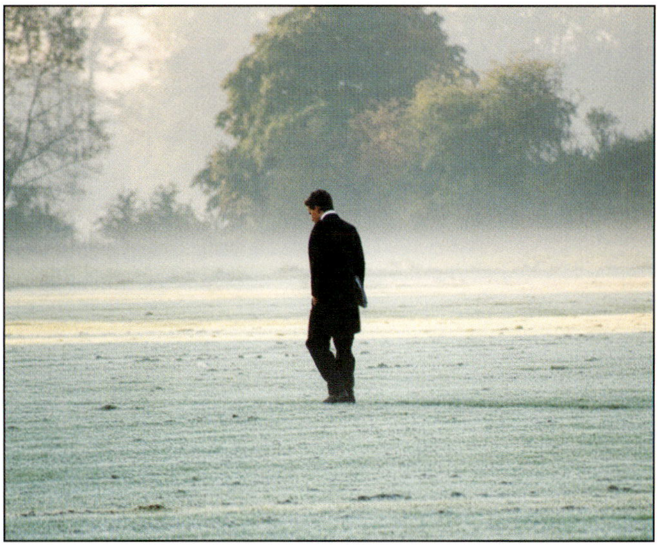

Off to the San through the autumn mist

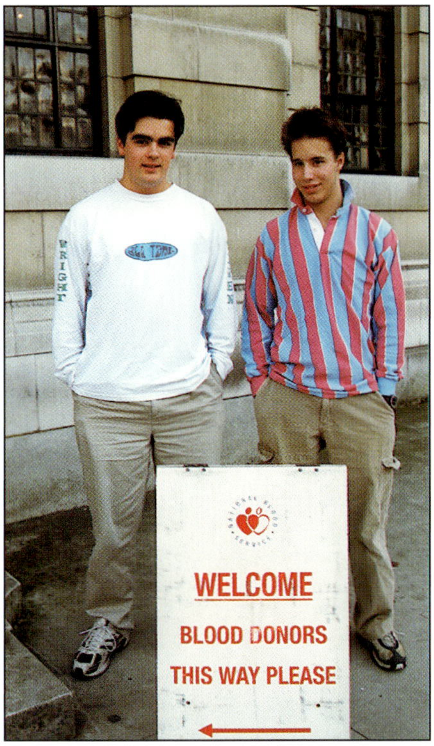

Blood donors

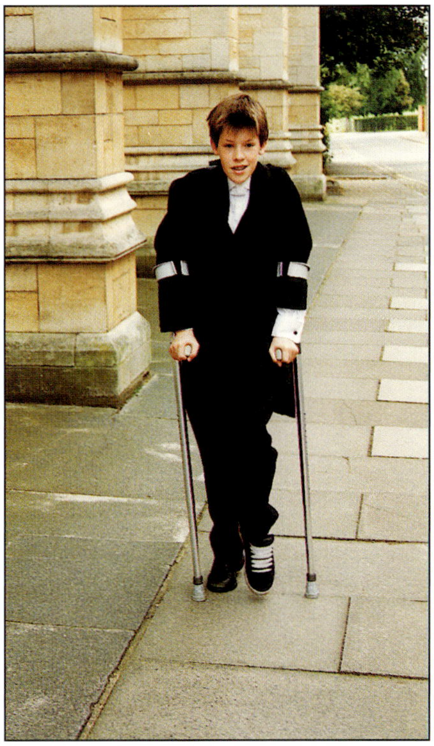

The football season is here!

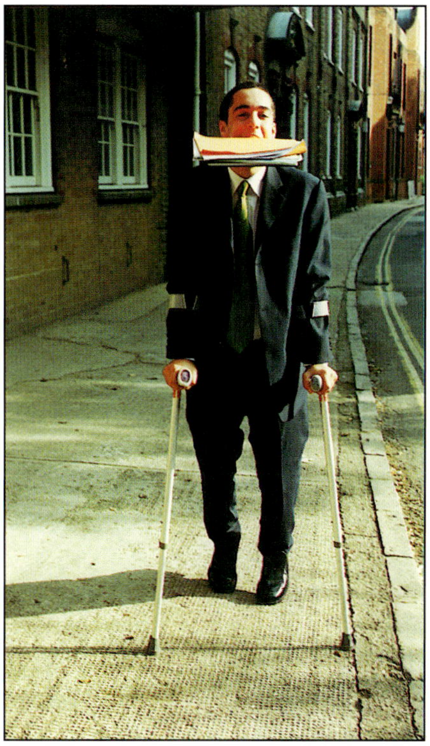

The rugby season is here!

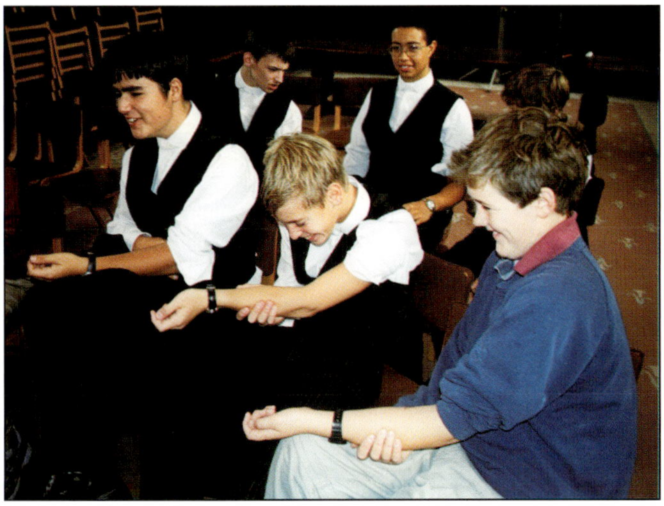

The Heaf test prior to the BCG injection

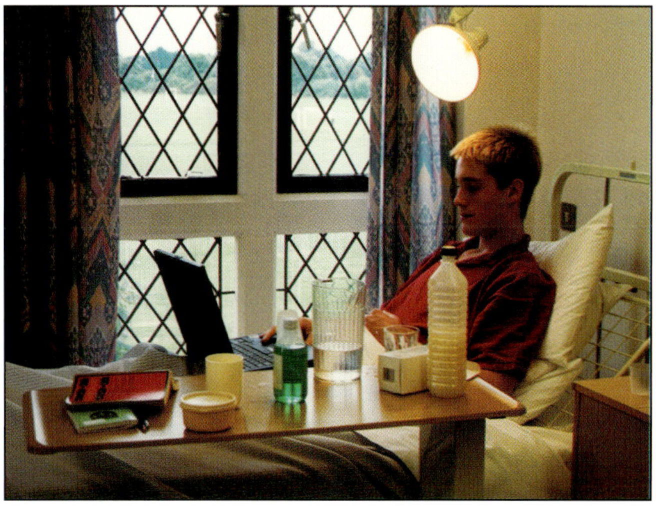

Sanatorium patient close to full recovery

School Yard

School Yard is the historical and architectural centre of Eton. All new boys catch a glimpse of it as they come to sign the new boys' book in the Head Master's Chambers on their first afternoon, and all visitors begin their tour of the College buildings here. As one enters the quadrangle through the arch under Upper School, the eye is caught by the fine bronze statue of the Founder, a tribute from an 18th century Provost to King Henry VI who founded Eton in 1440. To right and left are buildings whose 15th century origins King Henry would recognise, College Chapel, and the living quarters of the first King's Scholars, today's Collegers. The east end of School Yard is dominated by Lupton's Tower of 1517, whose clock, chiming four times an hour, controls Eton's working day.

School Yard still plays a daily part in the lives of the Collegers, as they walk across it on their way to classes and to take their meals in College Hall. But Oppidans pass through less frequently. Boys seated at the east end of College Chapel will walk up the steps to the North Porch; a few will pass through on their way to the playing fields; any who have business with the dignitaries in the Cloisters will approach the Cloisters across School Yard and under Lupton's Tower.

There is no single building nearly large enough to accommodate all boys and Masters, so on ceremonial occasions School Yard comes into its own. For example in 1990, as part of the 550th anniversary celebrations, The Queen addressed the whole School from the Chapel steps. When a new Provost is to be installed, he is only admitted once he has knocked on the gate to School Yard. Farewell ceremonies for retiring Provosts and Head Masters are also held here. Finally, on each Fourth of June an old practice is revived when the Head Master calls Absence from the Chapel steps. Senior boys answer their names here, and other boys do so elsewhere in School Yard and beyond, before they depart with their parents for Long Leave.

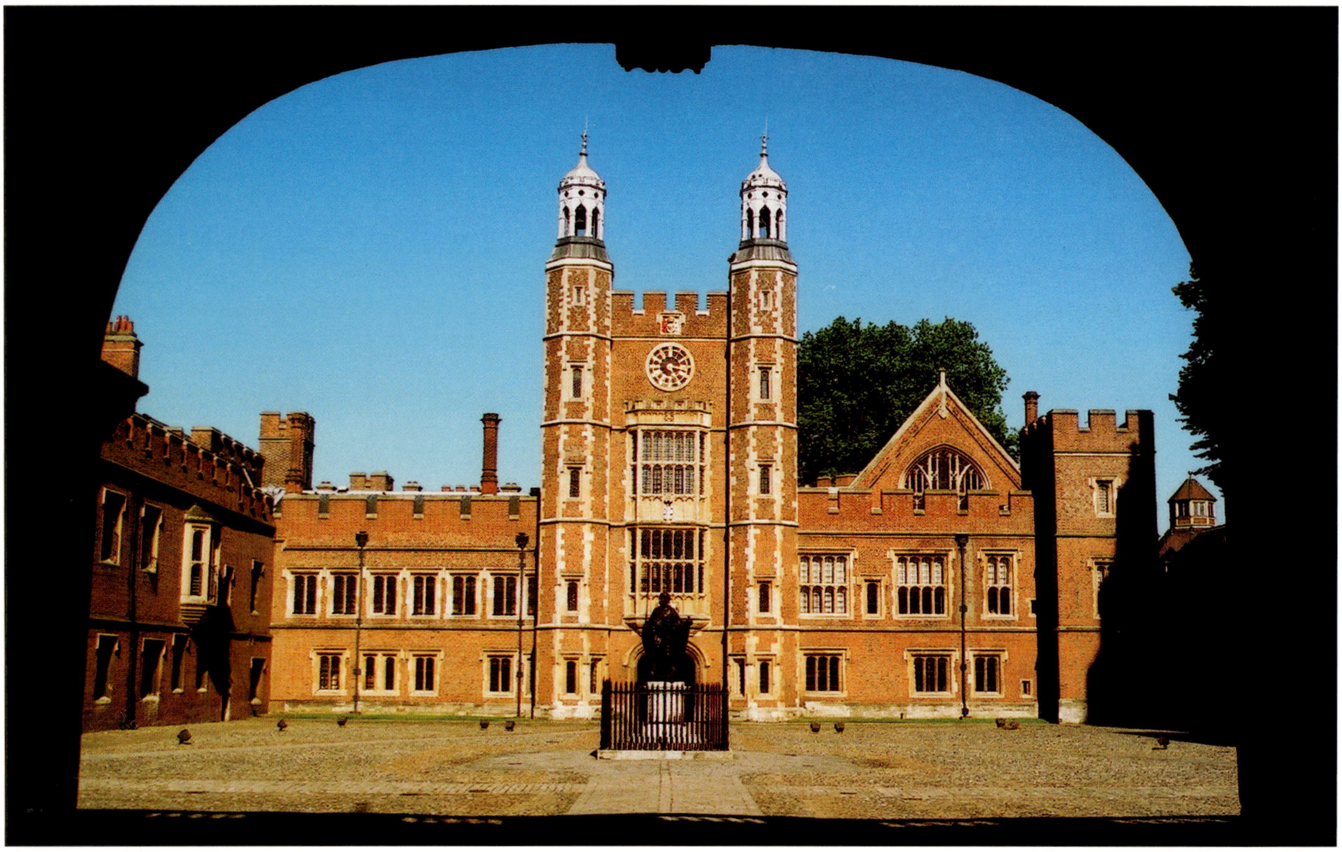

Lupton's Tower and the Founder, Henry VI

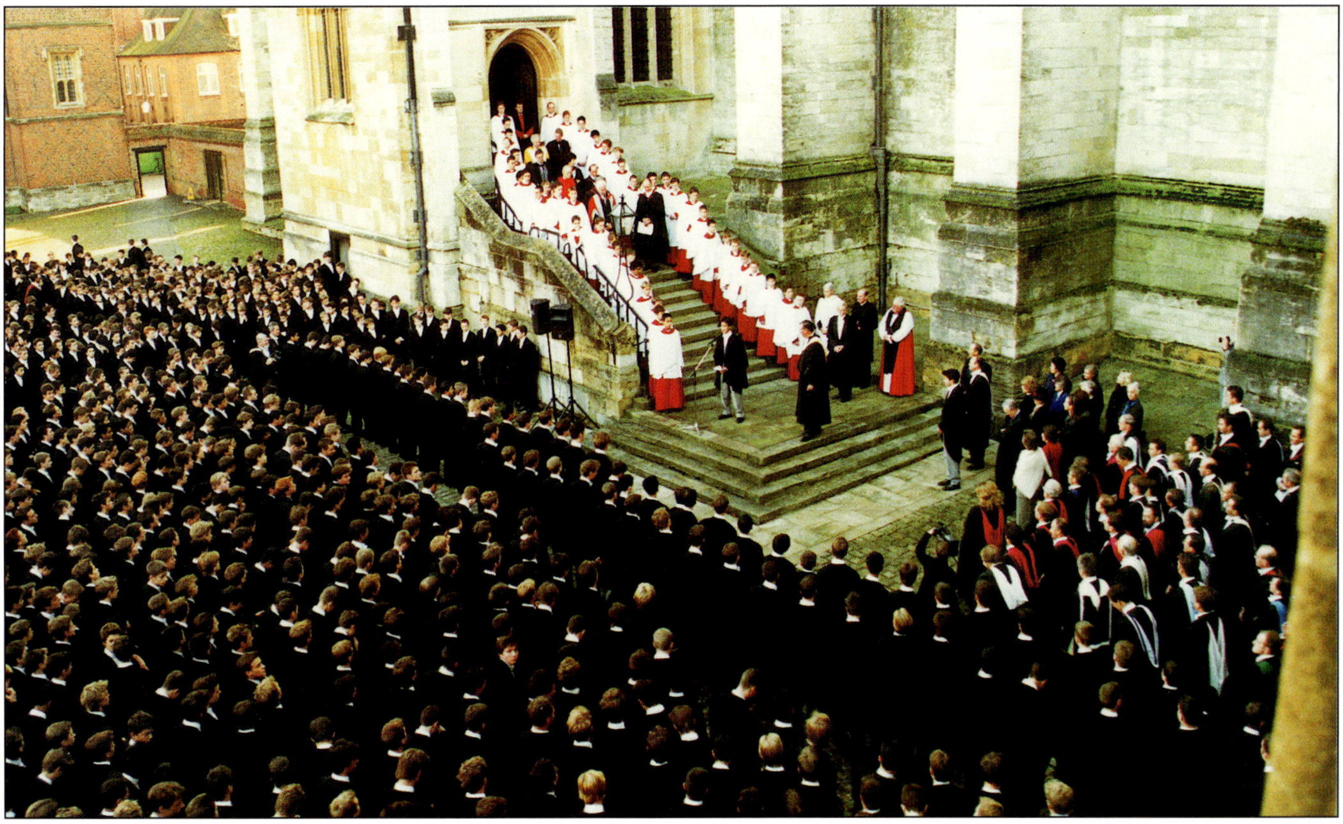

The Captain of the School welcomes the new Provost

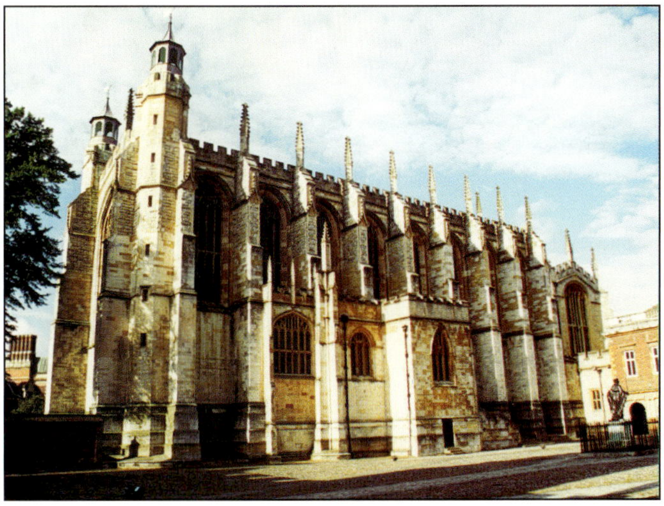

College Chapel and the Founder's statue

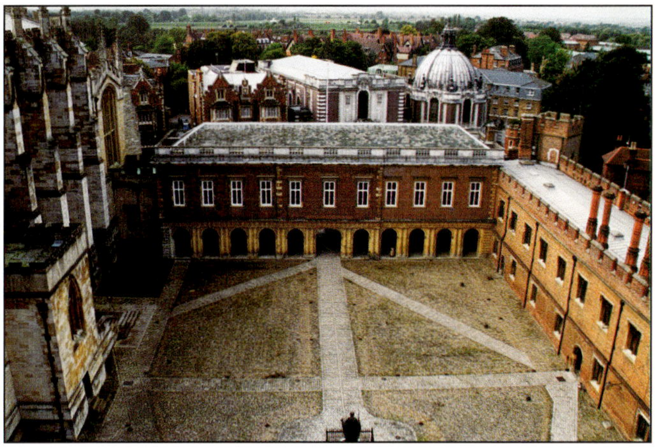

From scaffolding above Lupton's Tower, one sees Upper School in the foreground and beyond, from left to right, Durnford House, School Hall and School Library

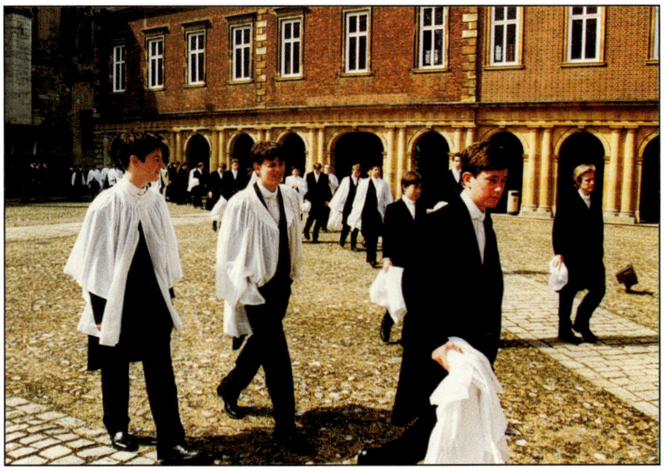

Collegers return to College across School Yard after Chapel

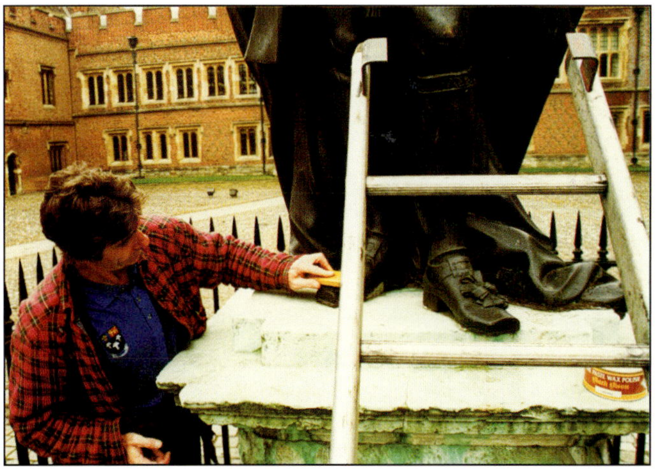

Polishing the Founder's shoes

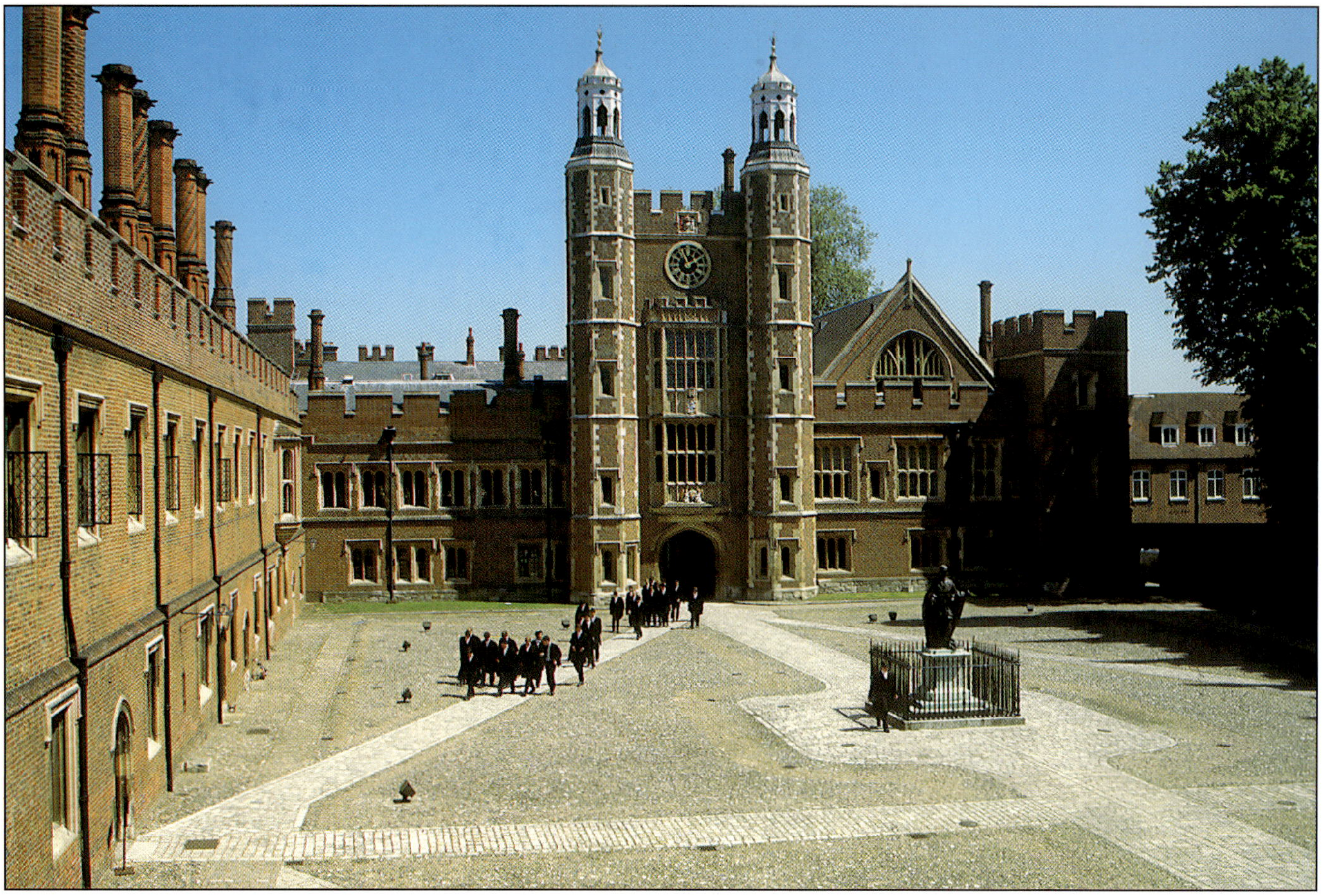

Collegers returning from College Hall after lunch

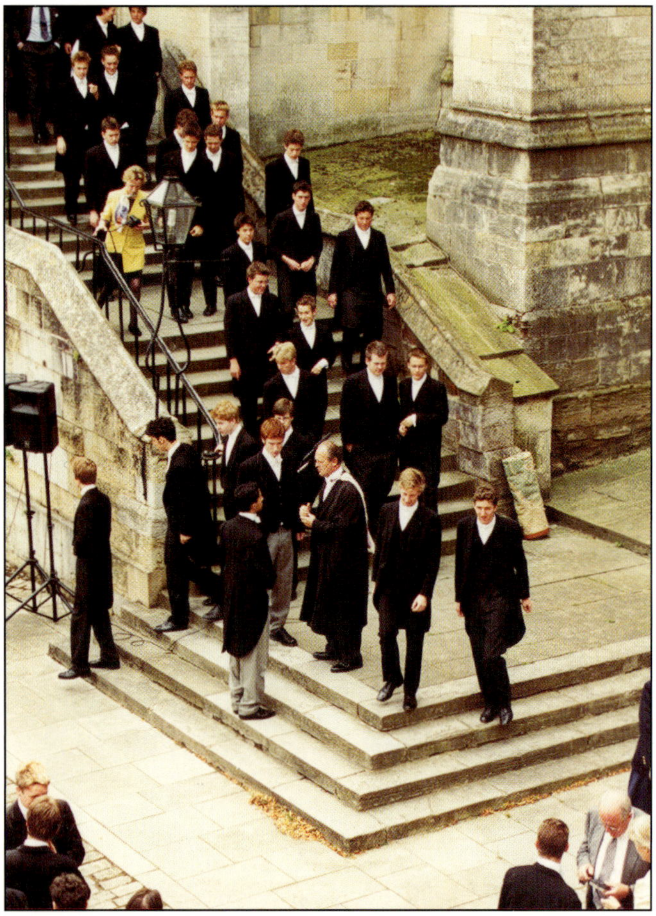

The congregation leaves Chapel by the north porch

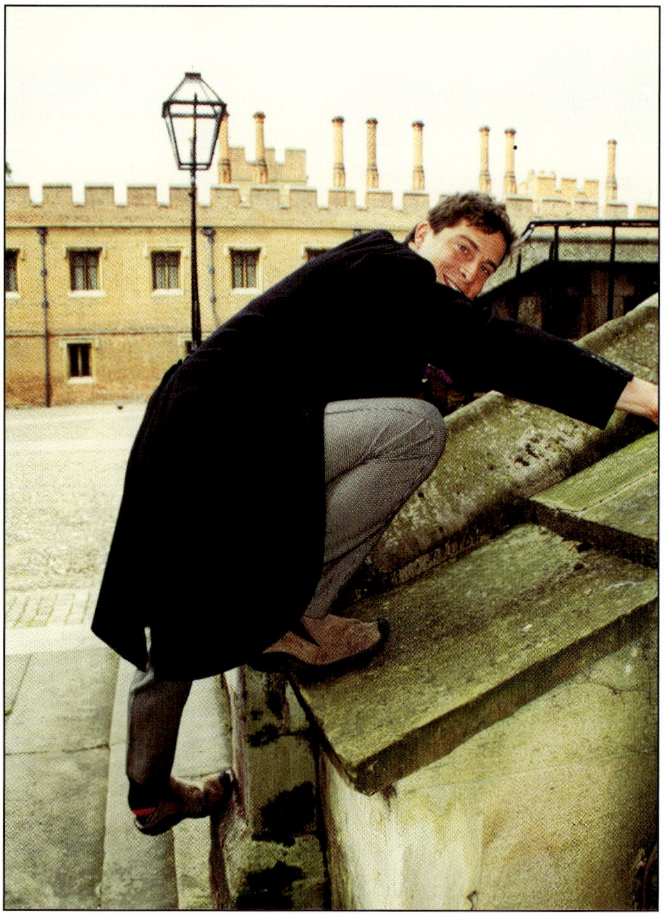

Bear Grylls, the youngest successful climber of Mount Everest, tries his skills on a College Chapel buttress

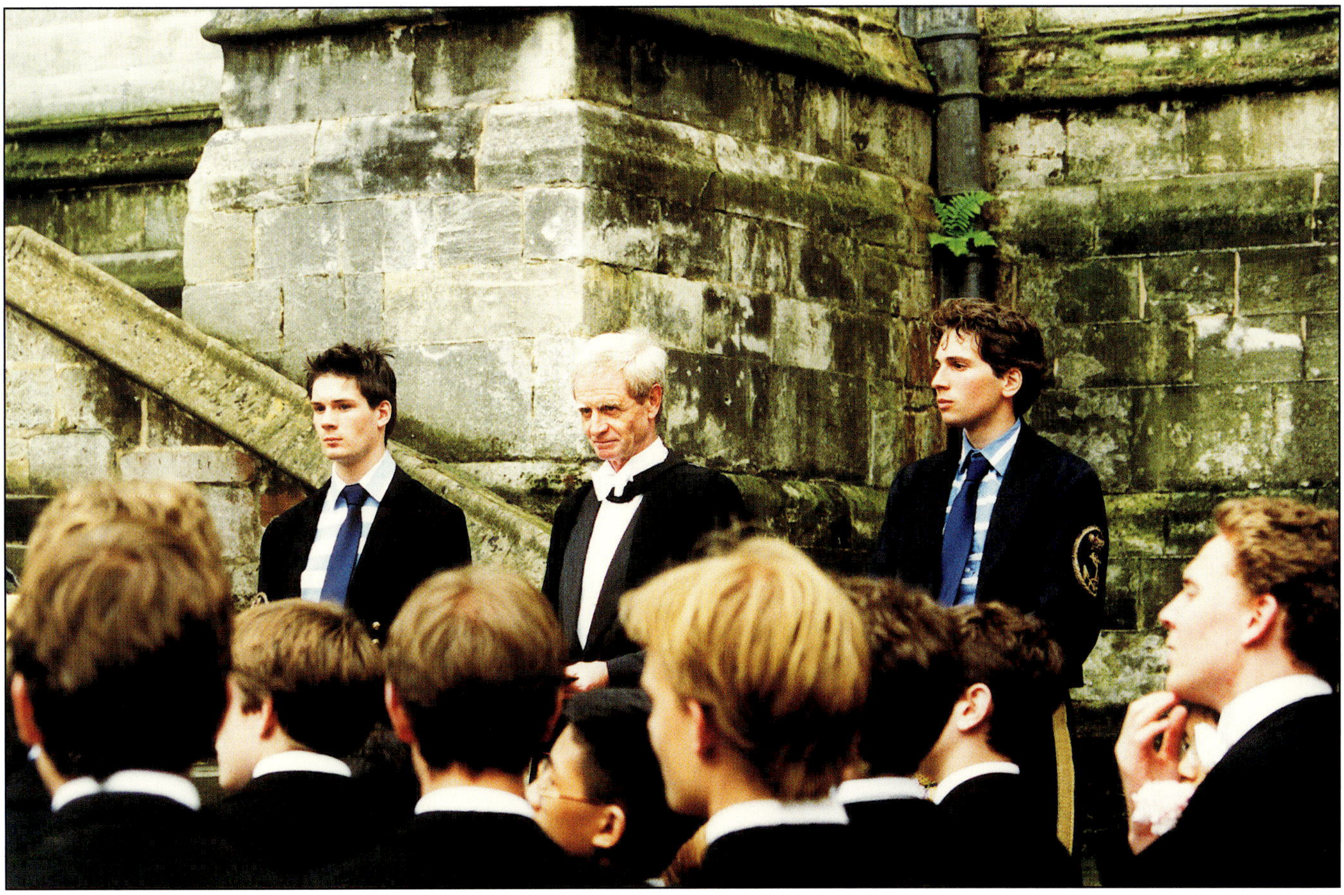

The Head Master calls Absence on the Fourth of June. He is flanked by the Captain of the School and the Captain of the Oppidans who are dressed for the Procession of Boats

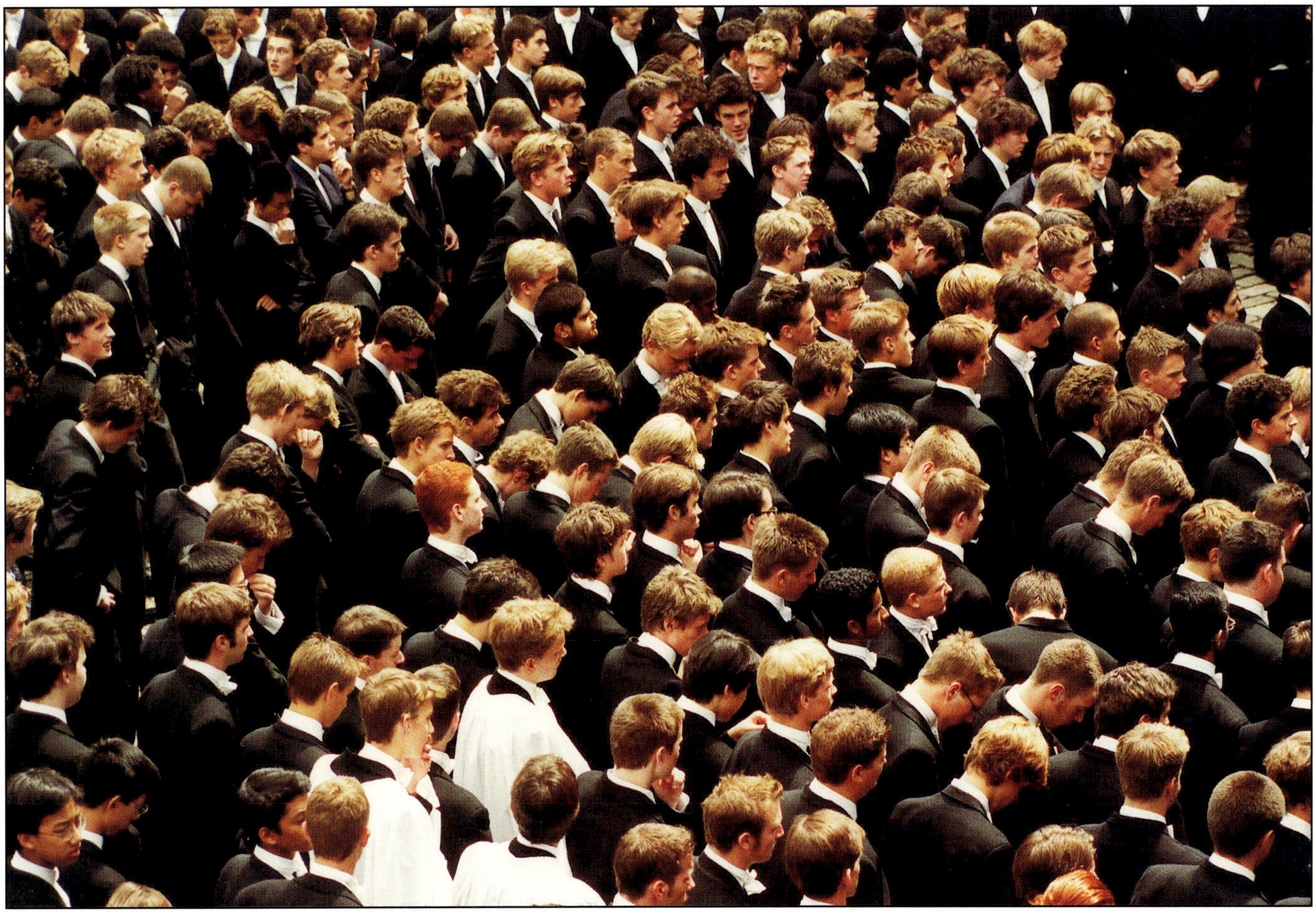

A ceremonial occasion: only in School Yard can the whole School assemble

Cloisters

If one leaves School Yard under Lupton's Tower, one reaches a haven of comparative calm, the Cloisters. The Cloister buildings were originally inhabited by members of the Foundation, including the scholars, but now only the Provost, Vice-Provost and Head Master reside here. On the west side at first-floor level is Election Hall built as a library in 1517, but now used for formal occasions. On the south side are the steps leading to College Hall, and, at first-floor level, College Library, built between 1725 and 1729 and replacing the original south section of the Cloisters. Of the remaining rooms some are Bursary offices, whilst others house the O.E.A. Office, the picture collection and the Photographic Archive. If one compares David Loggan's print of 1690 with the current Cloisters, it is apparent that, on the north and east sides, an extra floor in stone has been added to the largely red-brick ground and first floors. This was carried out in the 1760s, since when little has changed in external appearance except perhaps the addition of a fountain.

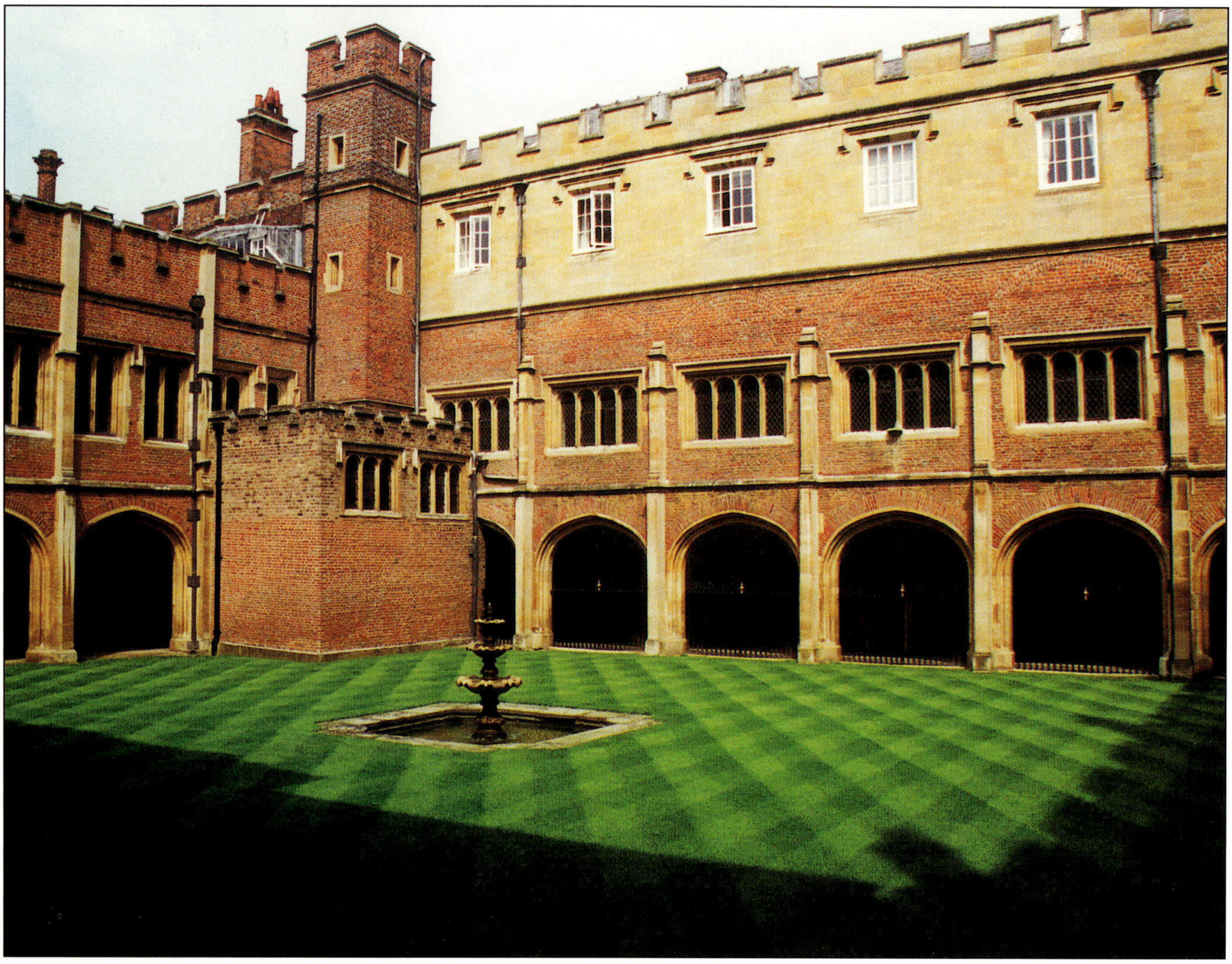

The west and north sides of the Cloisters. On the first floor of the north side is the Blue Corridor, from which there is access to all first-floor rooms

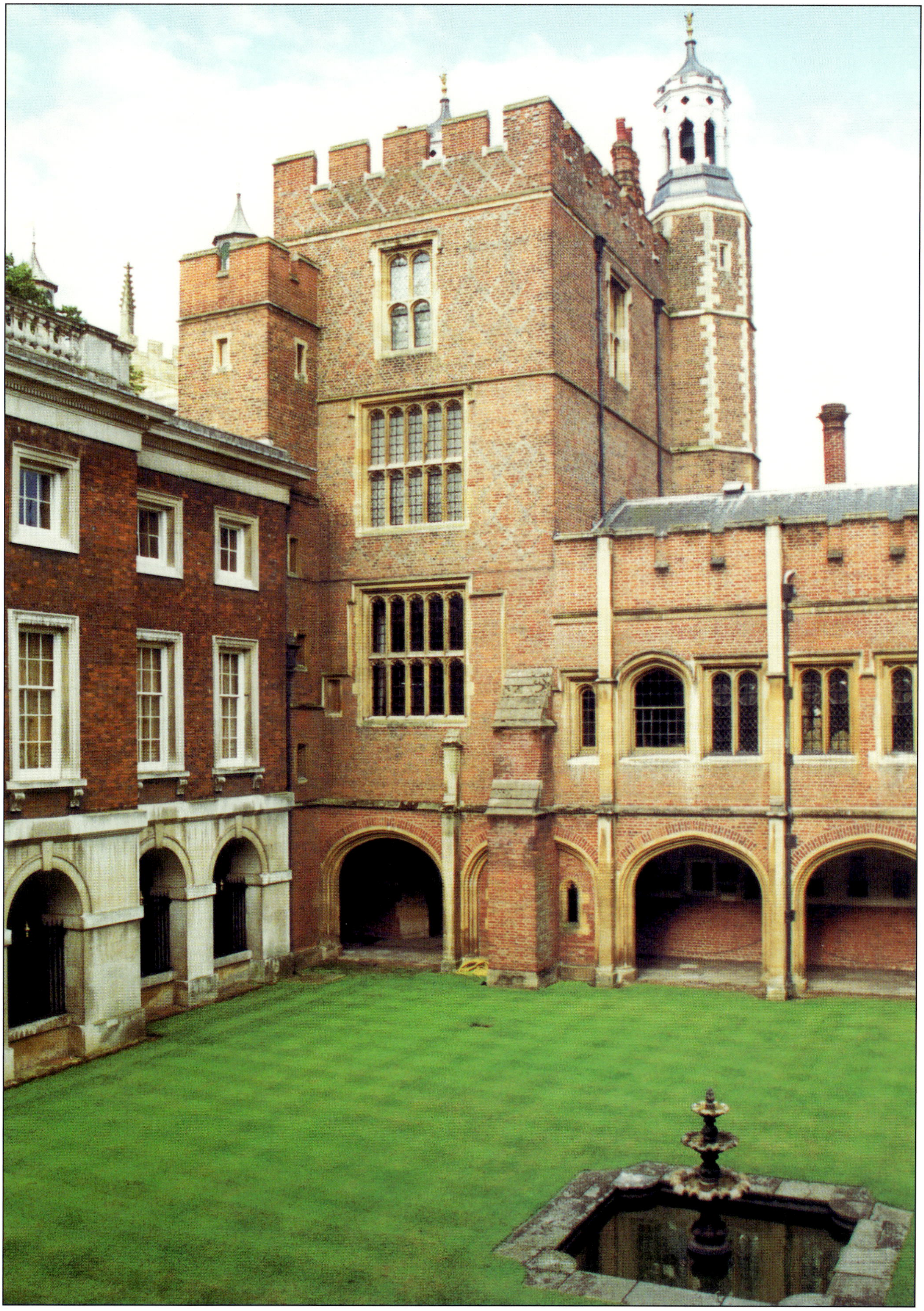

The south and west sides of the Cloisters with College Library (left), a rear view of Lupton's Tower (middle), and Election Hall (right)

College Chapel

It is College Chapel that catches the visitor's eye as he approaches Eton over 15-arch bridge from Slough, its lime-stone walls, buttresses and pinnacles rising majestically above the red brick of other College buildings. Vast and imposing though it is, it can accommodate only two-fifths of the boys at any one time. True, had the Chapel been completed as planned, its nave would have stretched across the road, as the white cross on the wall of Carter House reminds us, and then possibly all 1288 boys might have been able to attend services together. Instead of Henry VI's projected nave, it is Provost Waynflete's ante-chapel, completed in around 1480, that squares off the west end of the Chapel.

At week-day Chapel time E and F Blocks go to Lower Chapel, D Block to College Chapel or the Farrer Theatre, whilst B and C Blocks have some choice. There are days when Chapel is compulsory for all senior boys, but on many weekdays they may choose between Chapel and an Alternative Assembly.

Boys enter the Chapel through the north door or via the ante-chapel. The Chapel bell starts tolling a full ten minutes before the start of a service, falls silent after five minutes, then rings four more times when the service is about to start. As this moment draws closer, boys can be seen quickening their pace and even breaking into a reluctant, but dignified run *(see page 8)*. Tardiness could have its repercussions. It will be noted that there are twenty-four steps up to the north door of College Chapel. Henry, it seems, must have been well aware of the possibility of floods, hence the floor of College Chapel at first-floor level.

Despite all additions to the School's buildings College Chapel remains the most striking and significant building in the School, tall and conspicuous at the very heart of Eton.

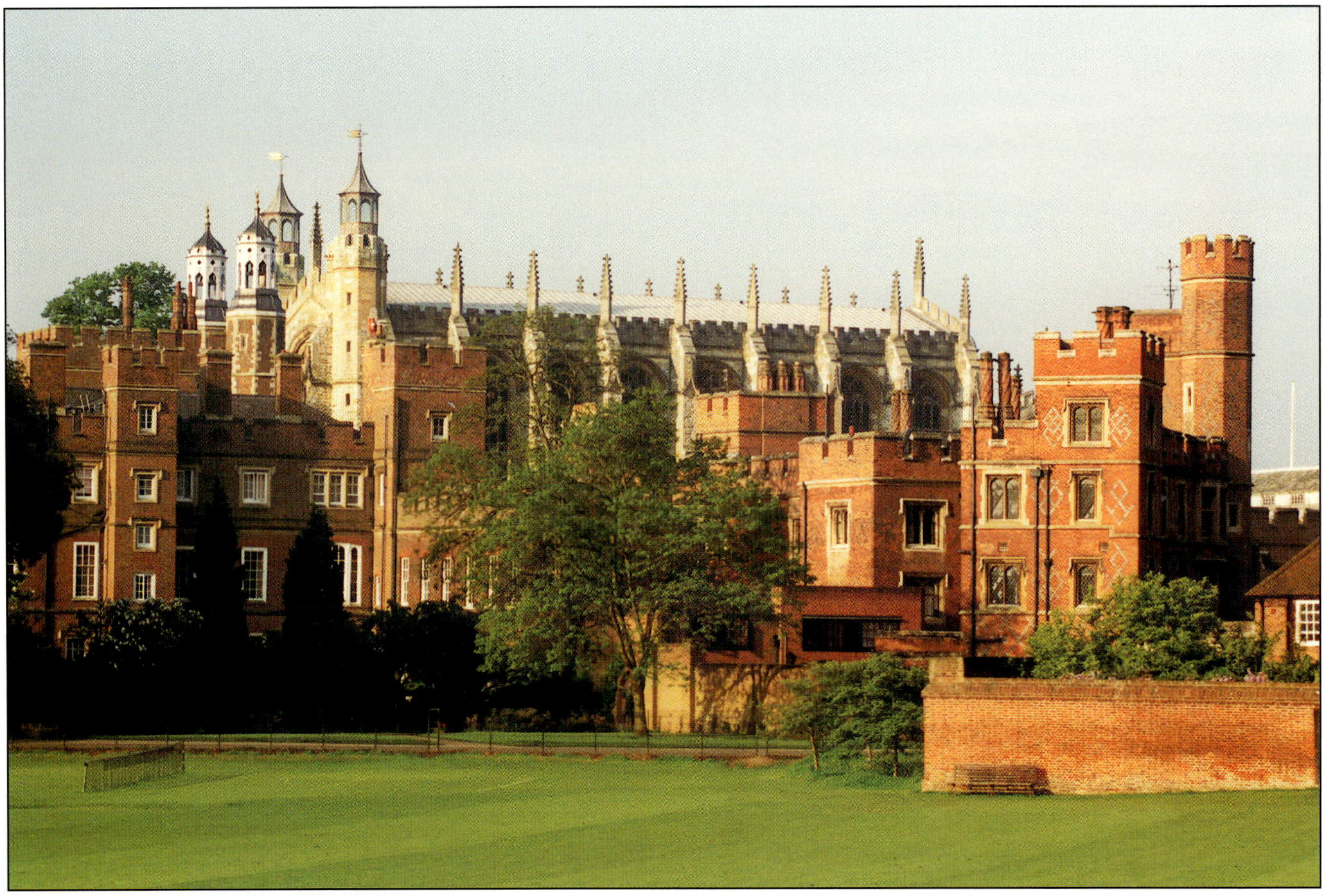

Chapel and College buildings from College Field

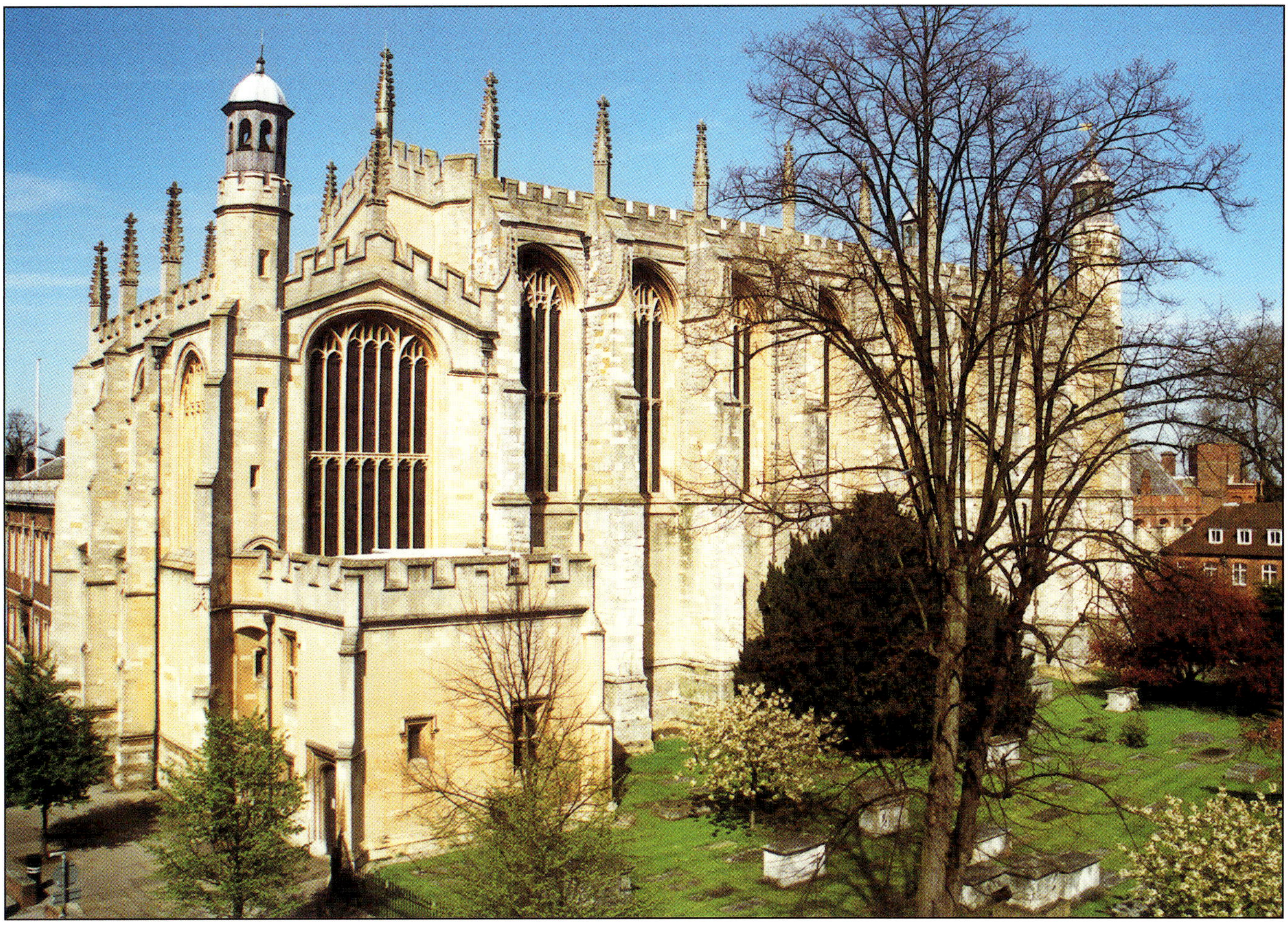

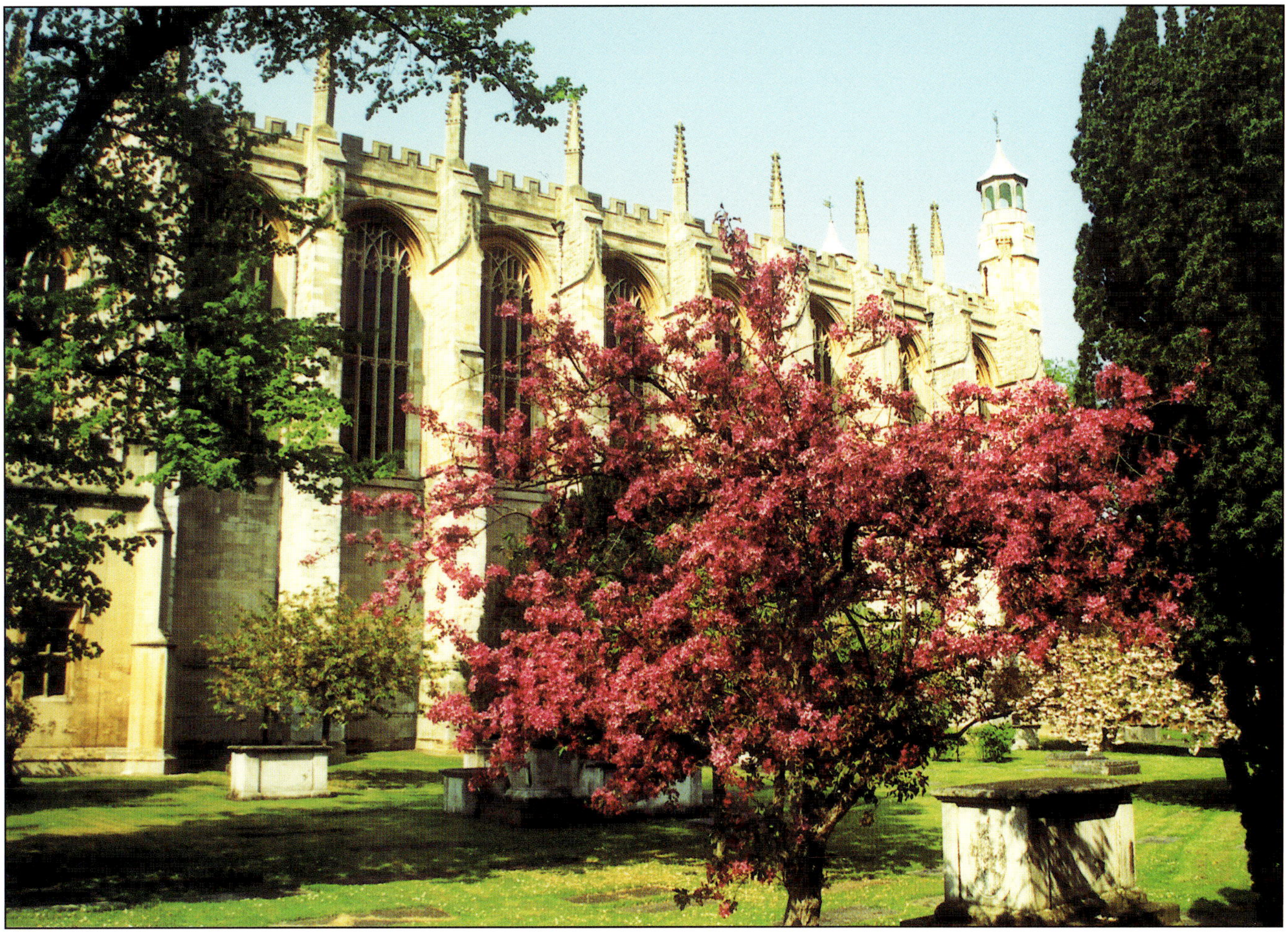

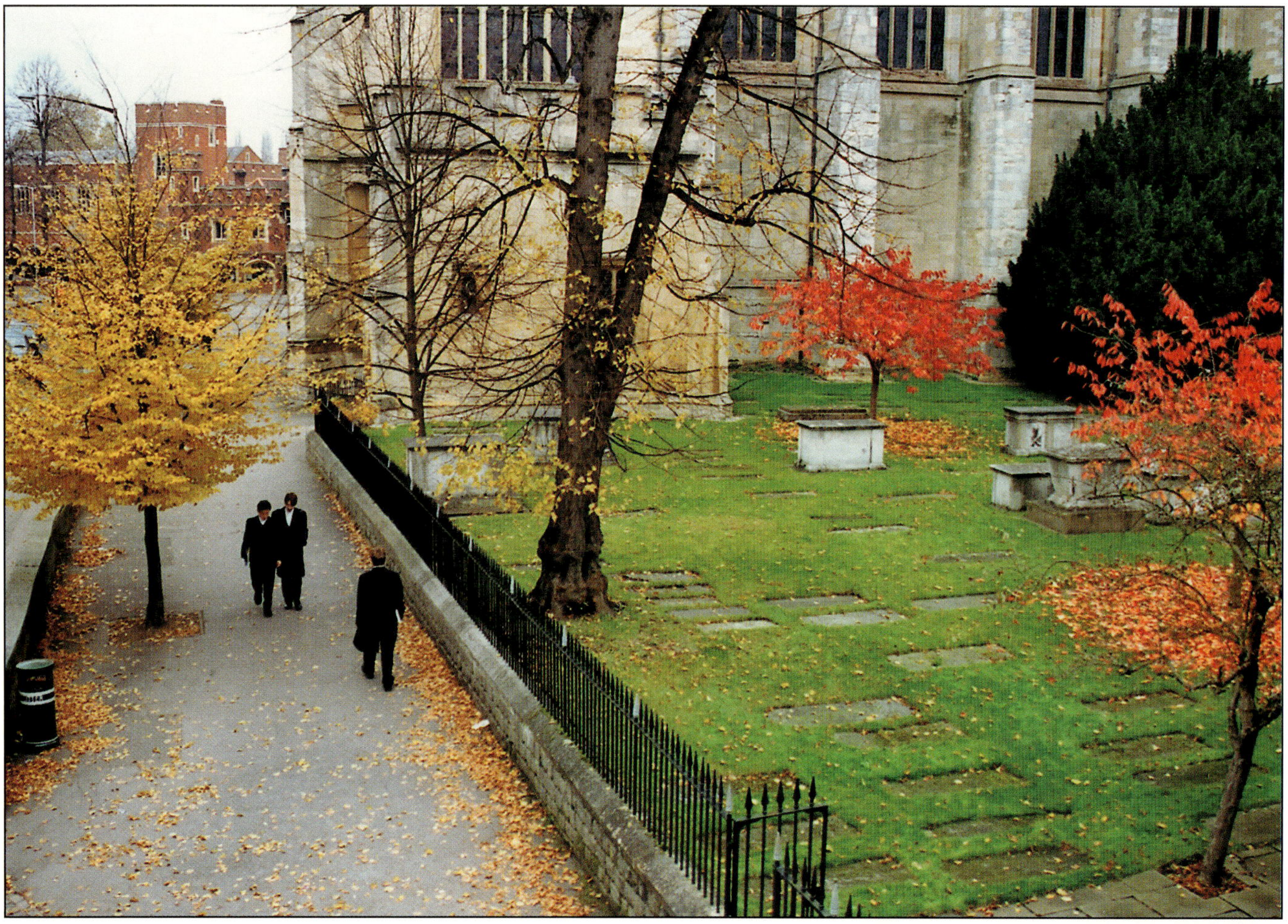

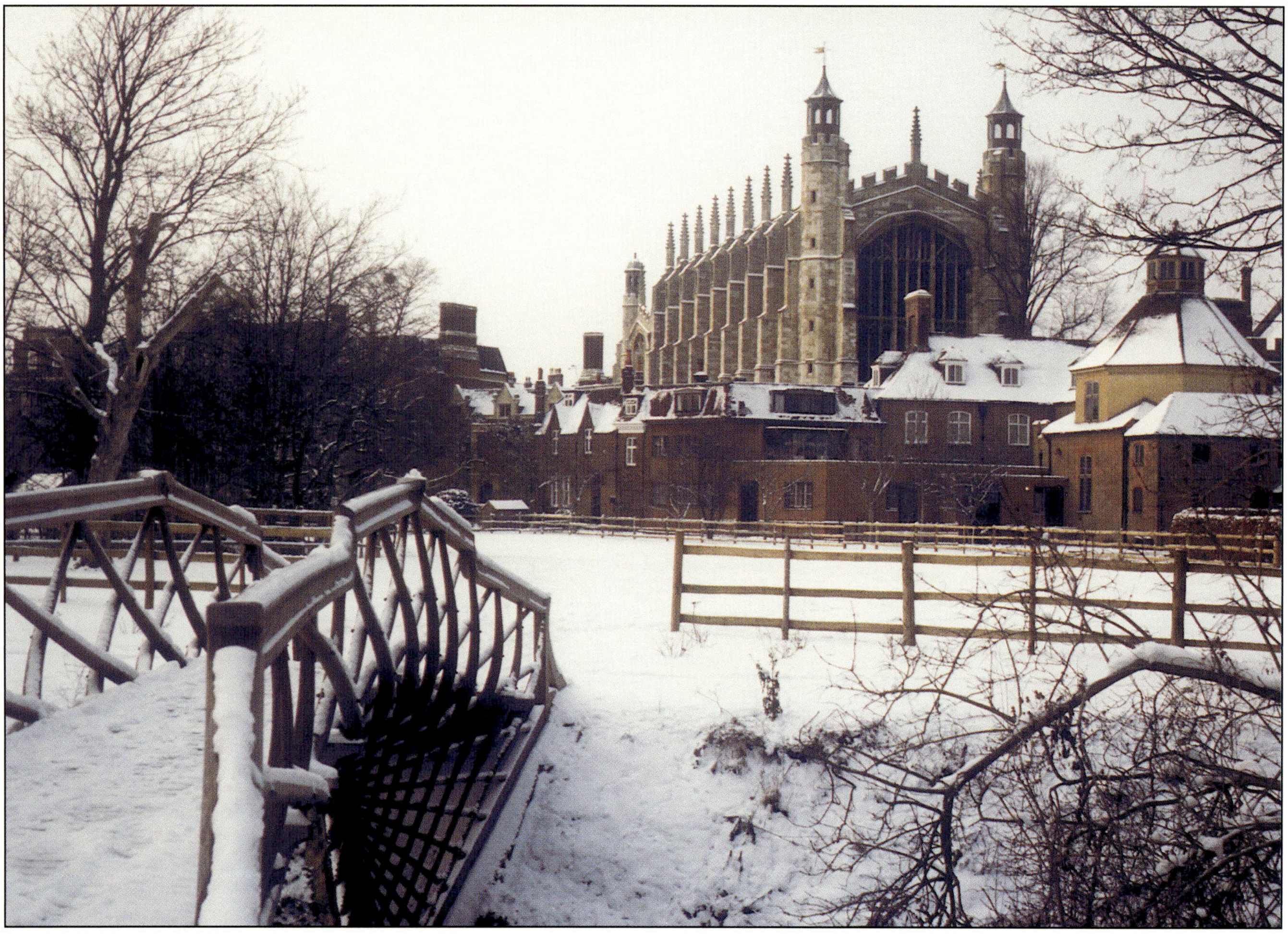

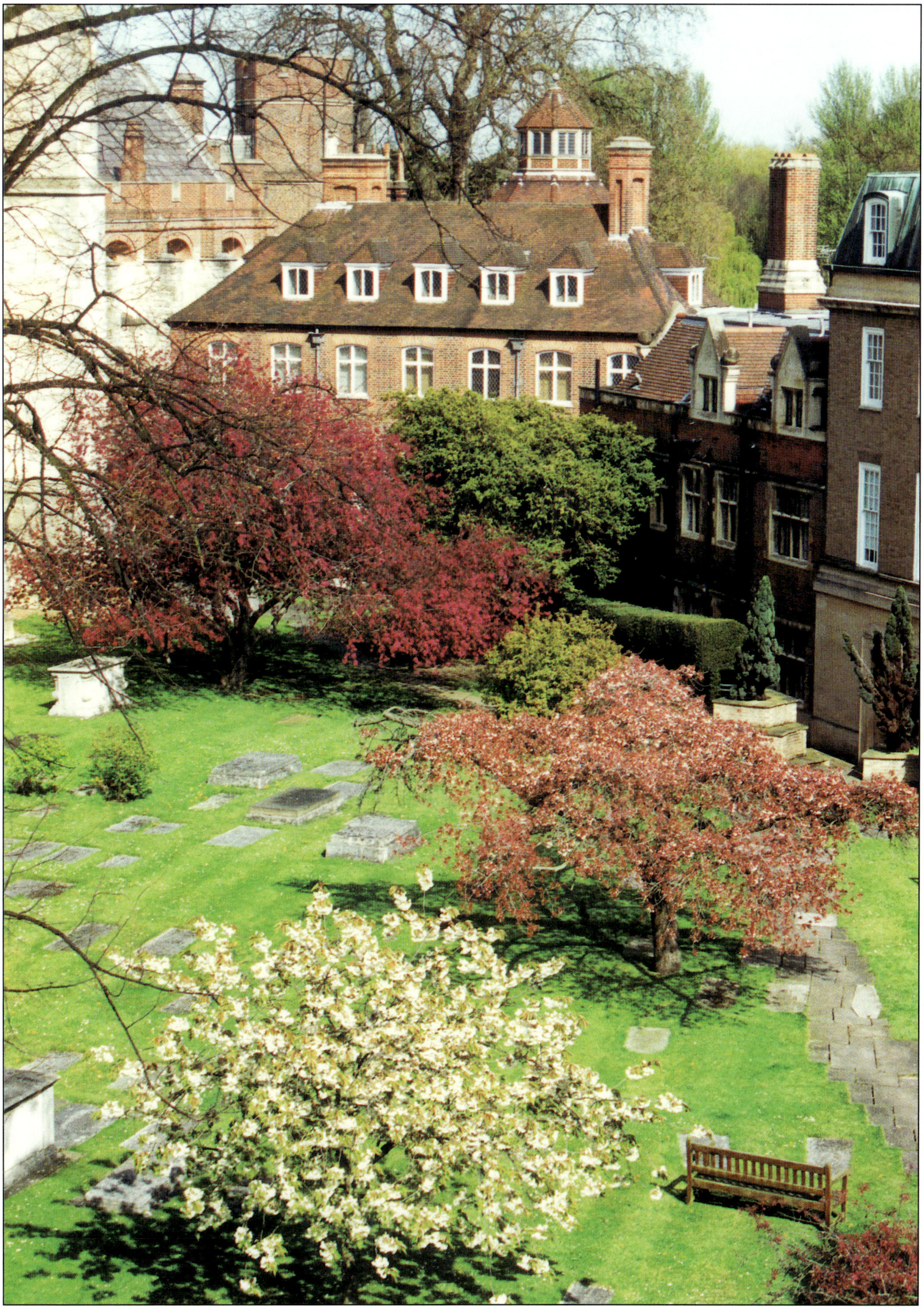

View across the grave-yard to the Brewhouse

College Chapel Interior

The busy Etonian may well not appreciate the glories of College Chapel until later years. Only if one has time to stand, stare and reflect can one fully appreciate the happy fusion of worship, architecture and art. The colour of the stone, the perpendicular pillars, the15th century wall paintings, the organ pipes, the stained glass windows, the wall of glass above the High Altar, and fan-vaulting (a 20th century replacement for a wooden ceiling) combine to marvellous effect. Only about 550 boys can comfortably be seated in College Chapel, and those seated in the pews might well dispute the word 'comfortably'. Full College Chapel services are impressive occasions, enhanced by a choir of some 58 boys. C Block are seated at the altar end, B Block in the choir. There are Confirmation services four times a year, on successive days in the Michaelmas and Lent Halves. The carol services are particularly popular occasions, as are concerts of church music performed here.

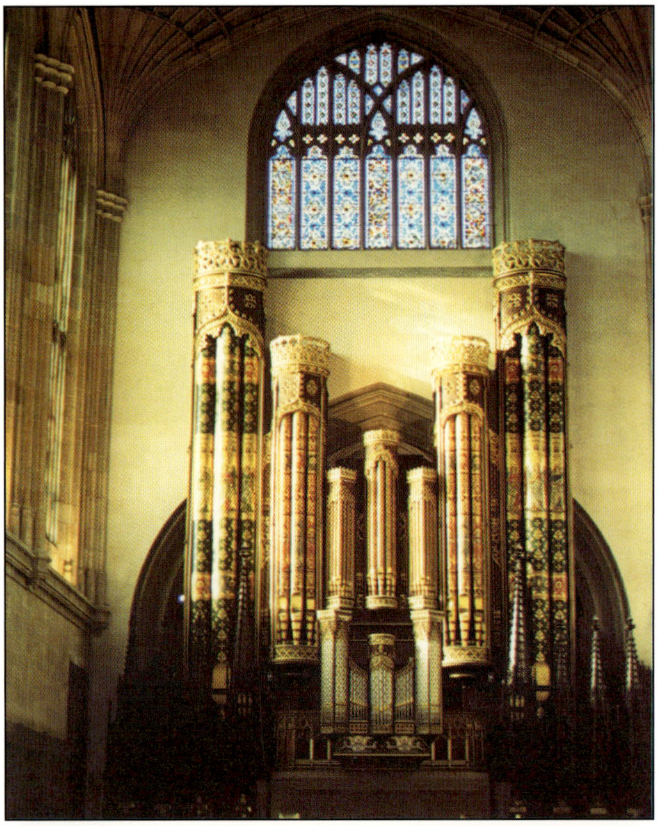

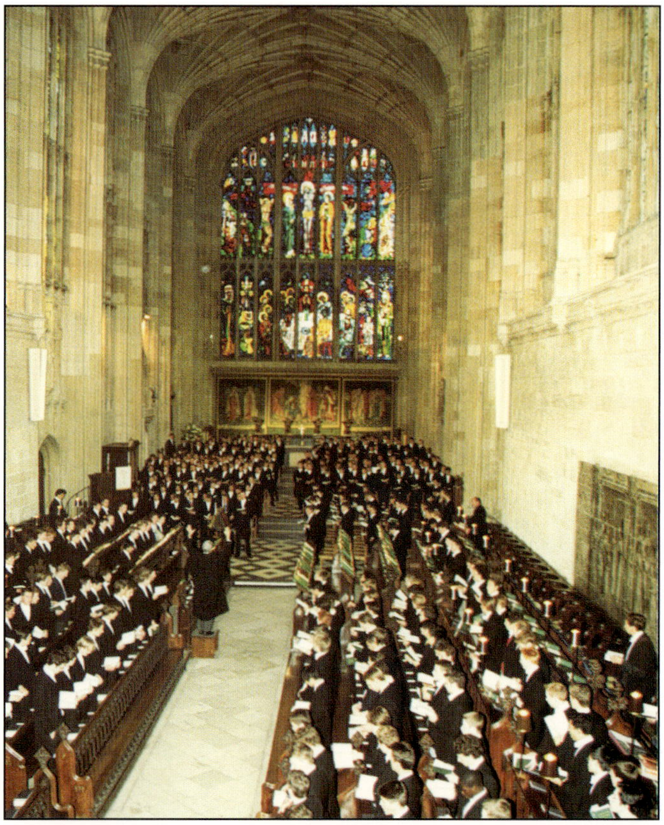

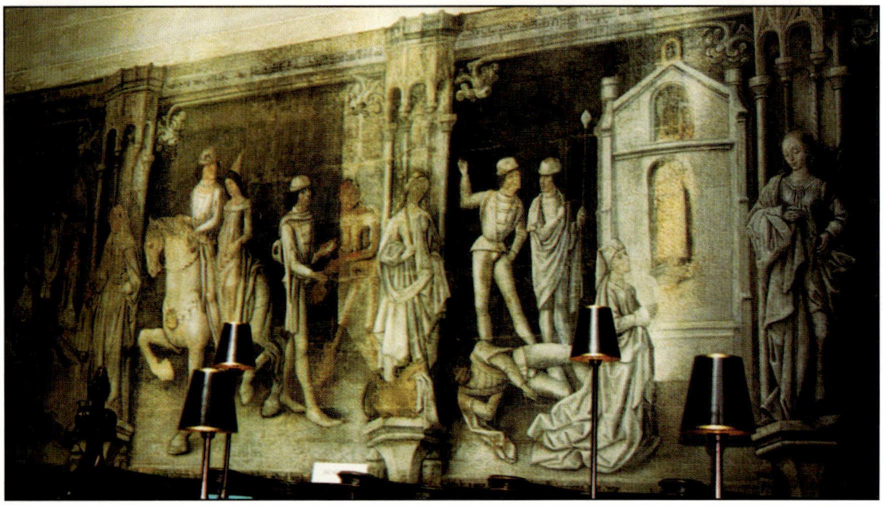

The 15th century wall paintings

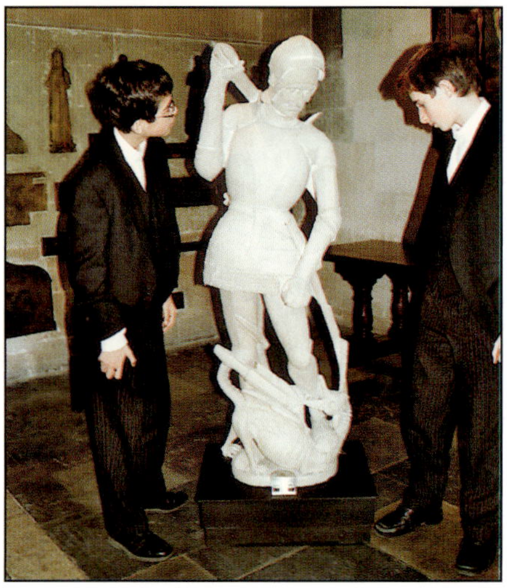

St George and the Dragon c1510

Lower Chapel

Lower Chapel was completed in 1891 and is the place of worship for E and F Blocks, about 560 boys. The new organ built by Kenneth Tickell was installed in 2000.

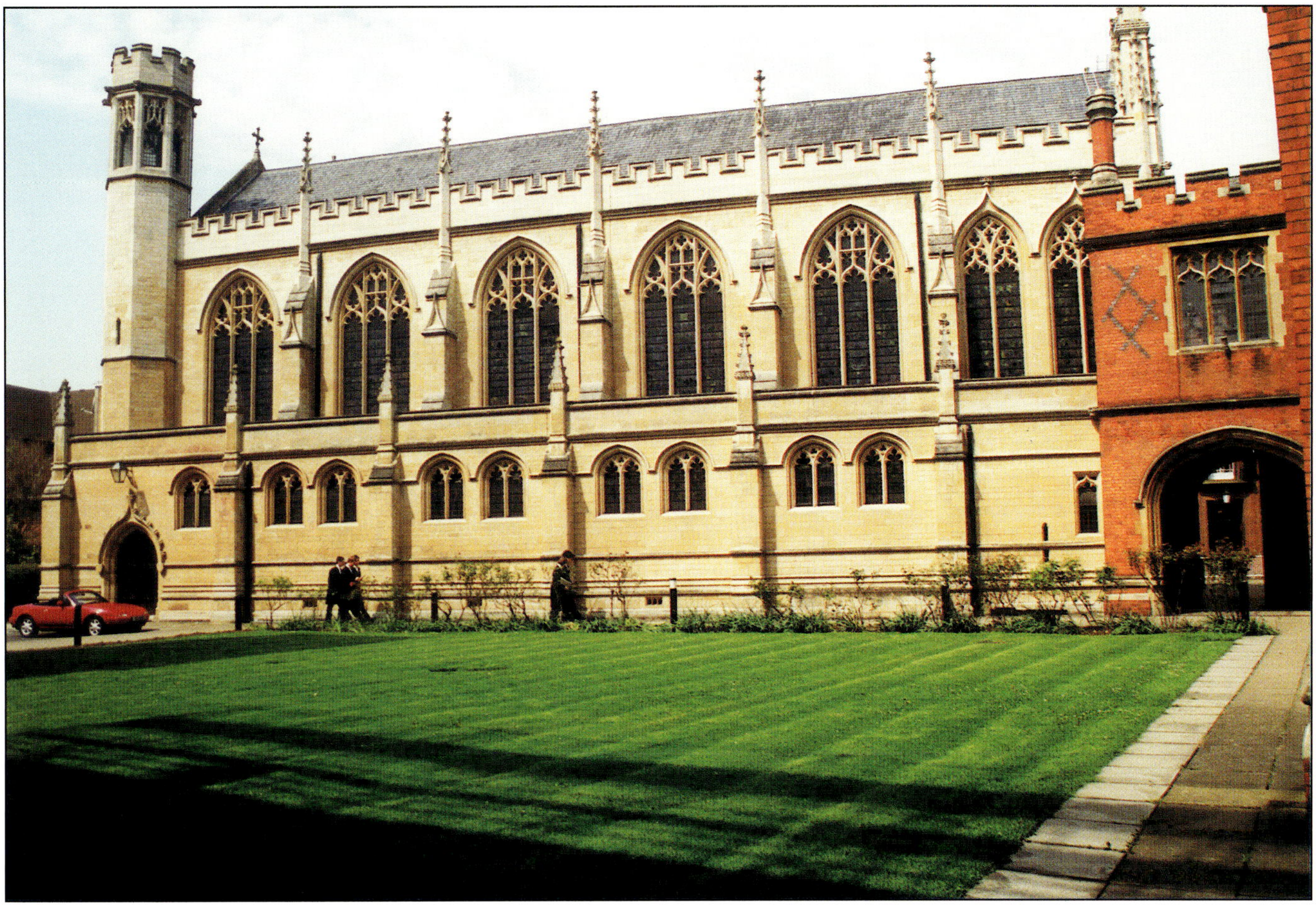

The south side of Lower Chapel from Queen's Schools quadrangle

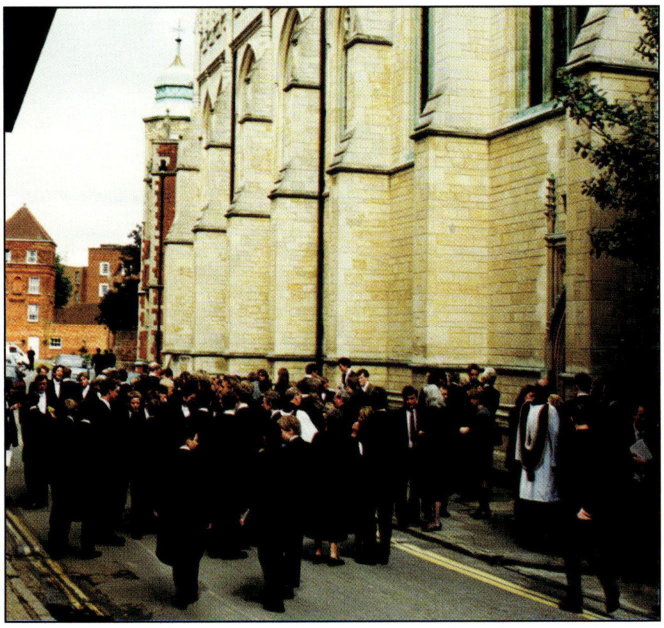

The north side of Lower Chapel

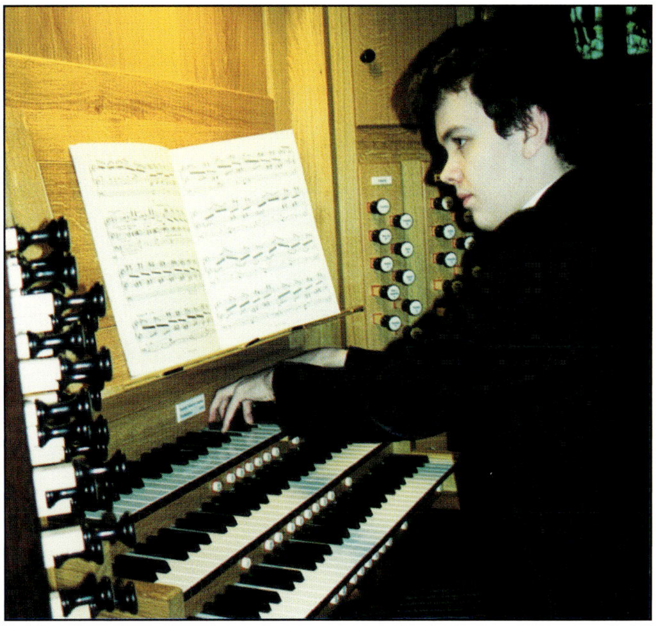

Music scholar in the new organ loft

School Hall

School Hall is the venue for assemblies and many other major and minor events. Masters meet here daily for mid-morning Chambers; the Head Master and Lower Master address the boys here in formal assemblies; the Alternative Assembly takes place here, likewise concerts and some lectures. The old wooden chairs have given way to the modern stackable alternative, and the custodian is a busy man adjusting the seating daily to suit the next event on the agenda. A balcony over the pillared vestibule and tiered seating behind the stage provide extra seating for unusually large audiences. Whilst stylistically it is reminiscent of the baroque and contains a fine Dutch baroque organ, it was opened in 1908 as part of the Memorial Buildings in honour of 129 Etonians who lost their lives in the Boer War. *(see also page 9)*

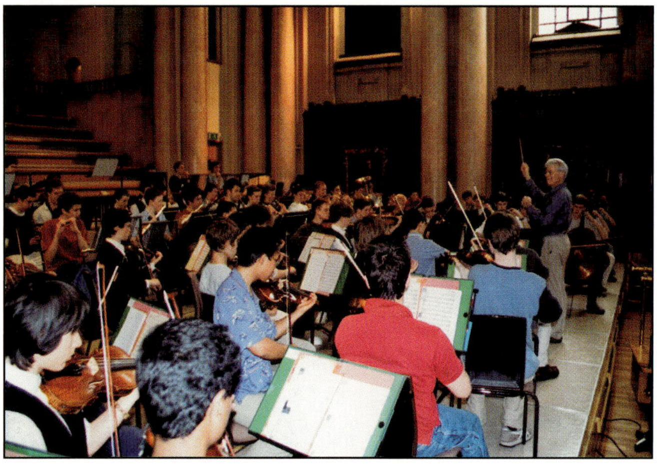

The School Orchestra rehearses before the School Concert

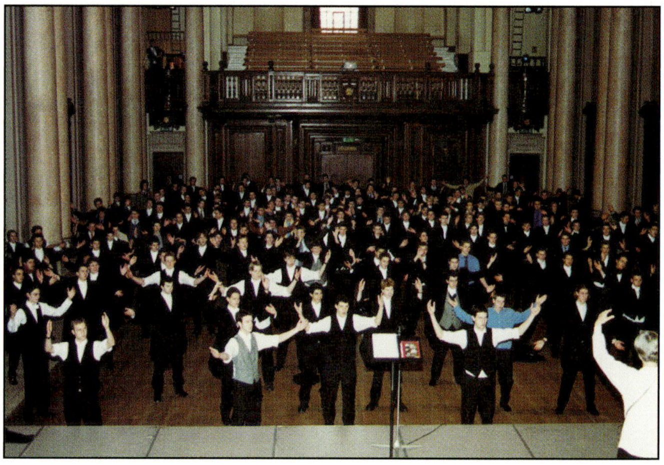

Some relaxation exercises in the Alternative Assembly

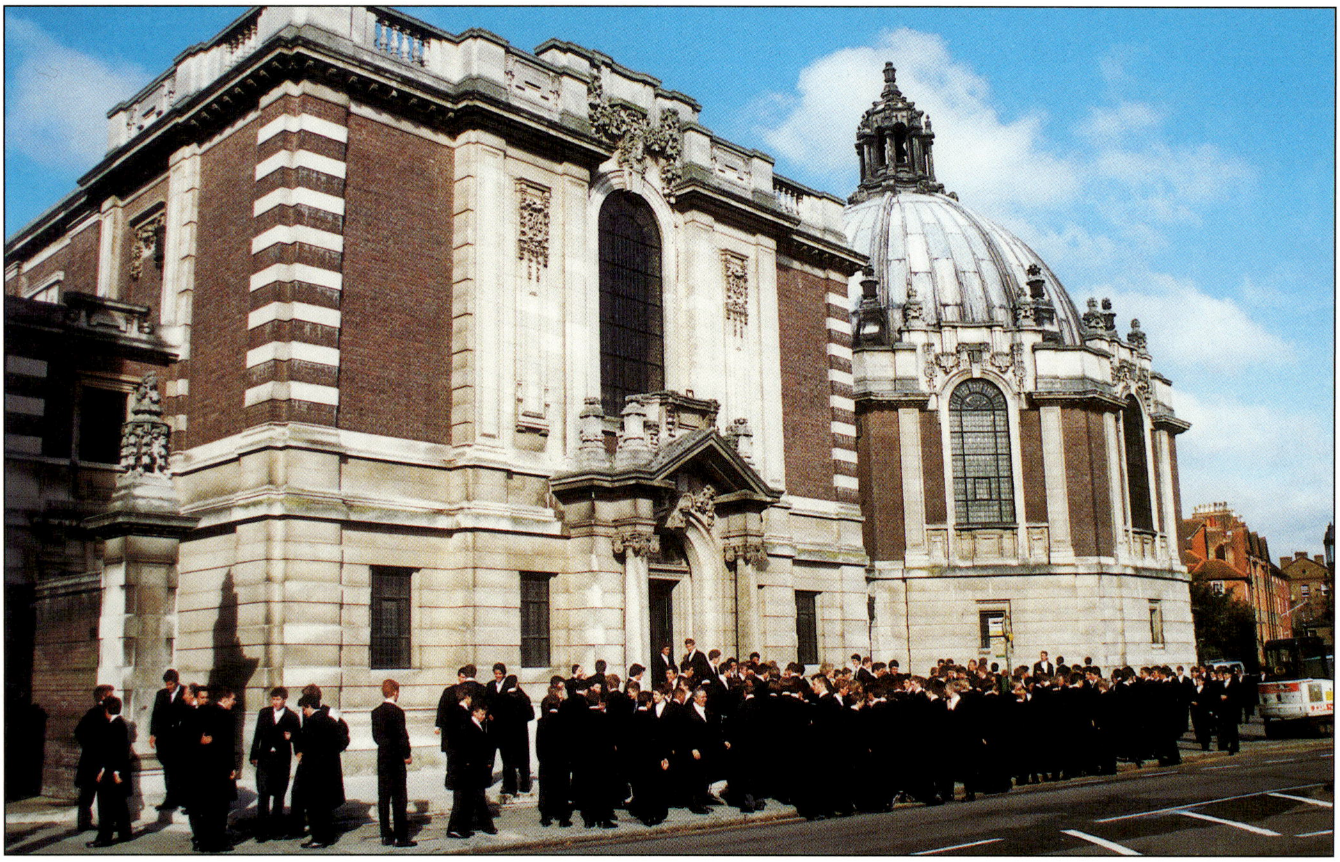

Boys awaiting Assembly

School Library

School Library has a central location and is therefore within easy reach of all School buildings. Beneath its impressive dome boys are able to read, research and write on almost any topic. Its resources are wide-ranging: 36,000 books, several thousand videos, CD's, cassettes, newspapers and magazines. Via the computers boys have access to the Internet, newspapers, periodicals and encyclopaedias. On average between four and five hundred members of the School use the Library each day, but numbers swell when School and public examinations approach. Borrower cards have recently been replaced by a finger-print recorder!

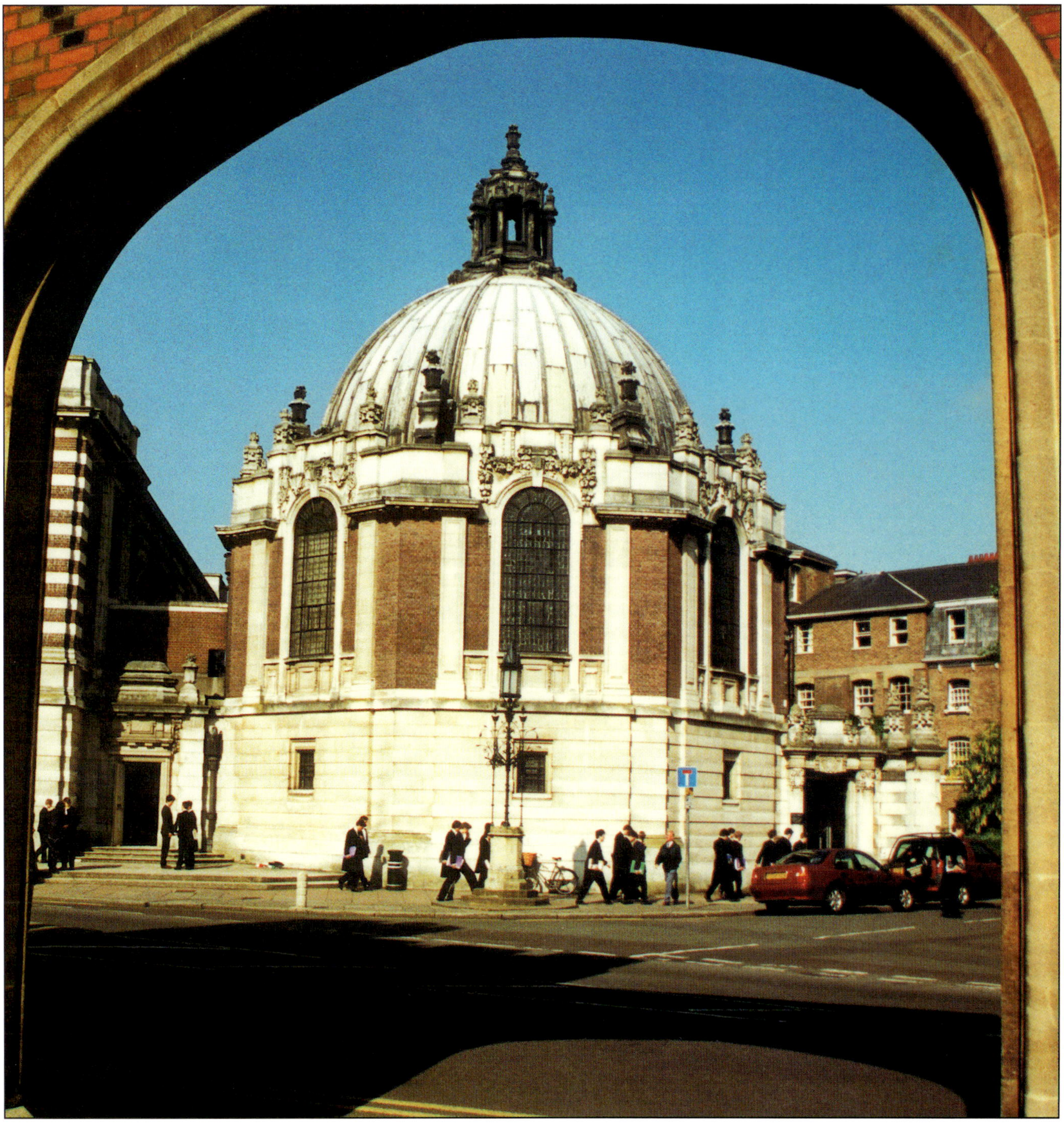

School Library from the entrance to Weston's Yard

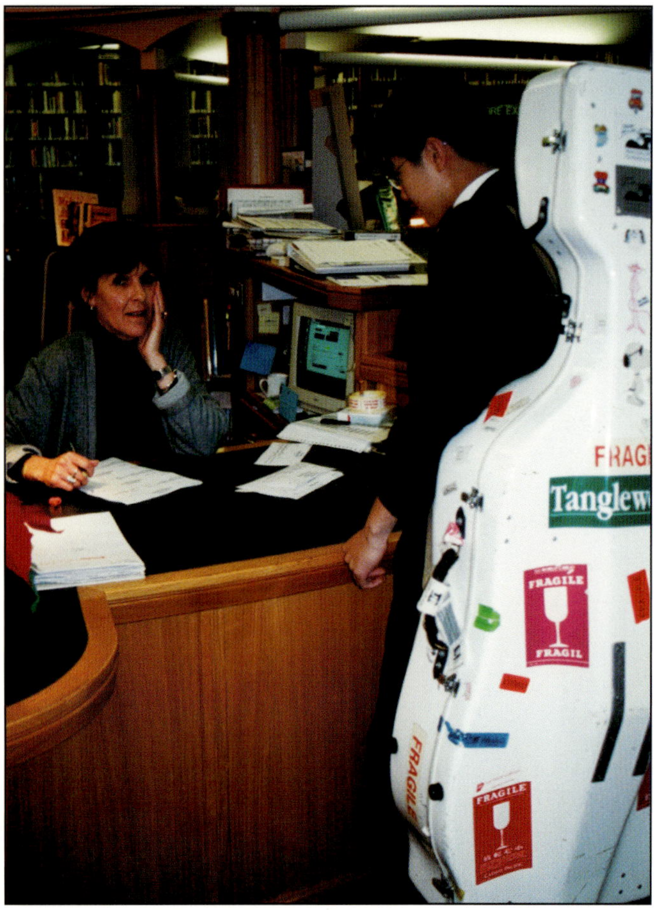

School Librarian answering questions

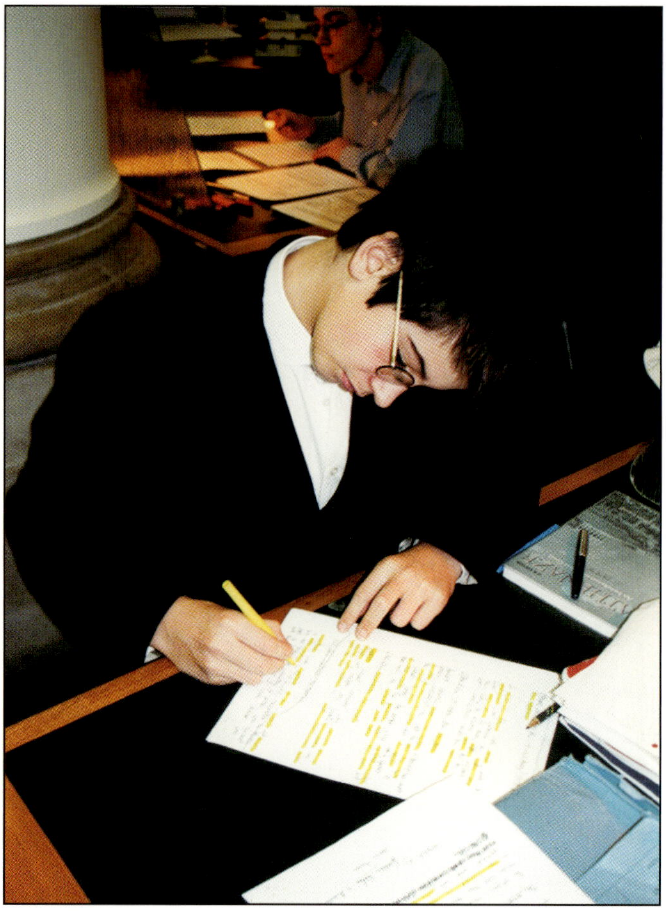

Boy(s) at work

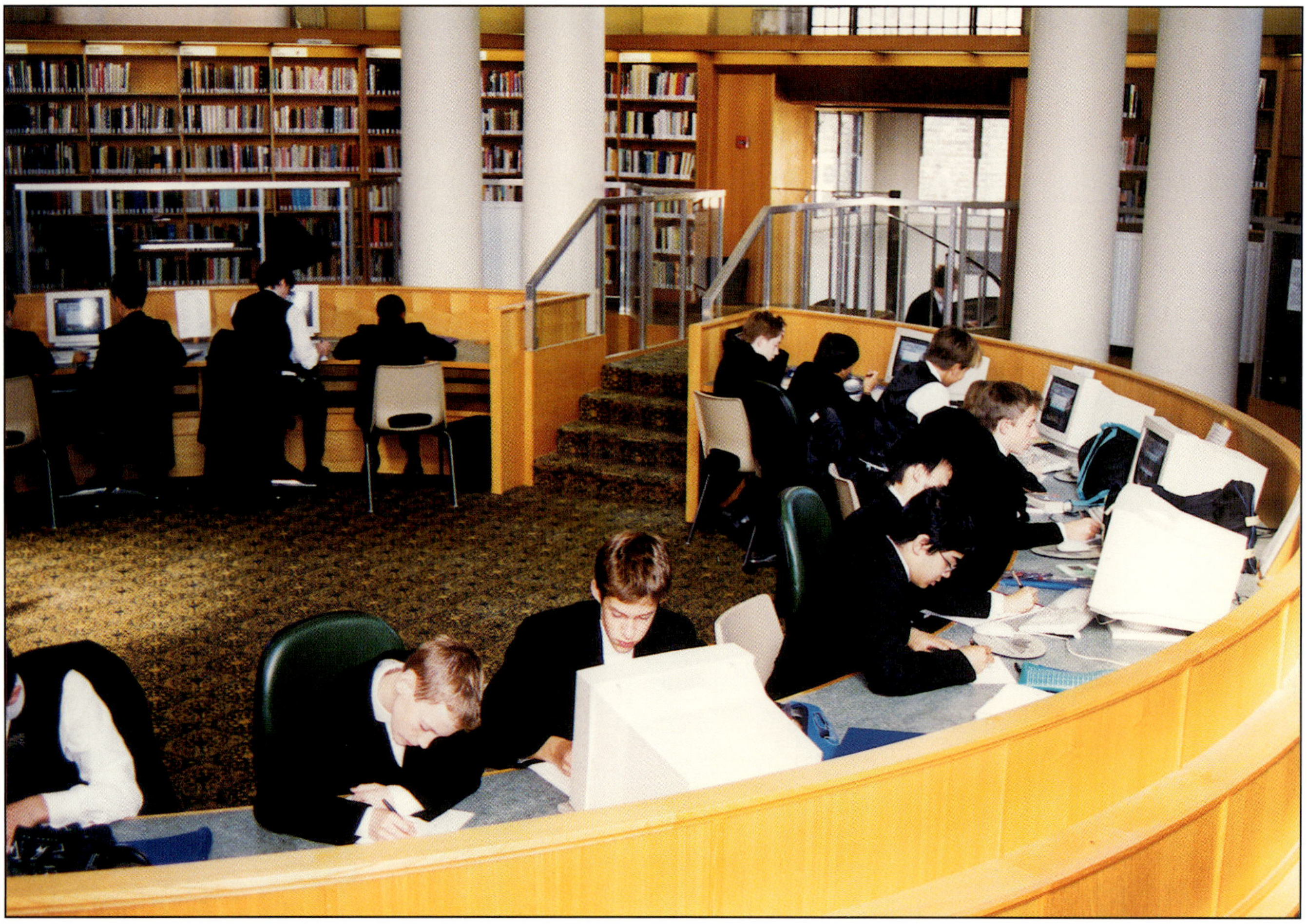

Working at the Library computers

The College Collections

Over the centuries many benefactors have given generously to Eton. A combination of gifts and acquisitions has led to the accumulation of several impressive collections, the most recent being the modern art collection. College Library has a fine collection of manuscripts and rare books (including a Gutenberg Bible) and is the Mecca for many a scholar researching his particular field. There is a large collection of paintings, watercolours and prints, the source of many interesting exhibitions in the Brewhouse Gallery and outside Eton, most recently at Christie's. The Myers Egyptian Collection is so significant that it was recently on display in the Metropolitan Museum, New York. The silver collection dates back to the 15th century and boasts the names of many famous silversmiths including Paul de Lamerie, Francis Nelme and Paul Storr. The Natural History Museum, recently renovated, is a useful extension to the activities of the Biology Department. A College Archivist looks after records and manuscripts relating to the College, whilst the gift of his private collection of photographs by a former Eton House Master, Peter Lawrence, led to the founding of the Photographic Archive, from which the photographs for this book have been taken. A Collections Committee under the chairmanship of the Provost is responsible for looking after these collections and adding to them, if circumstances allow.

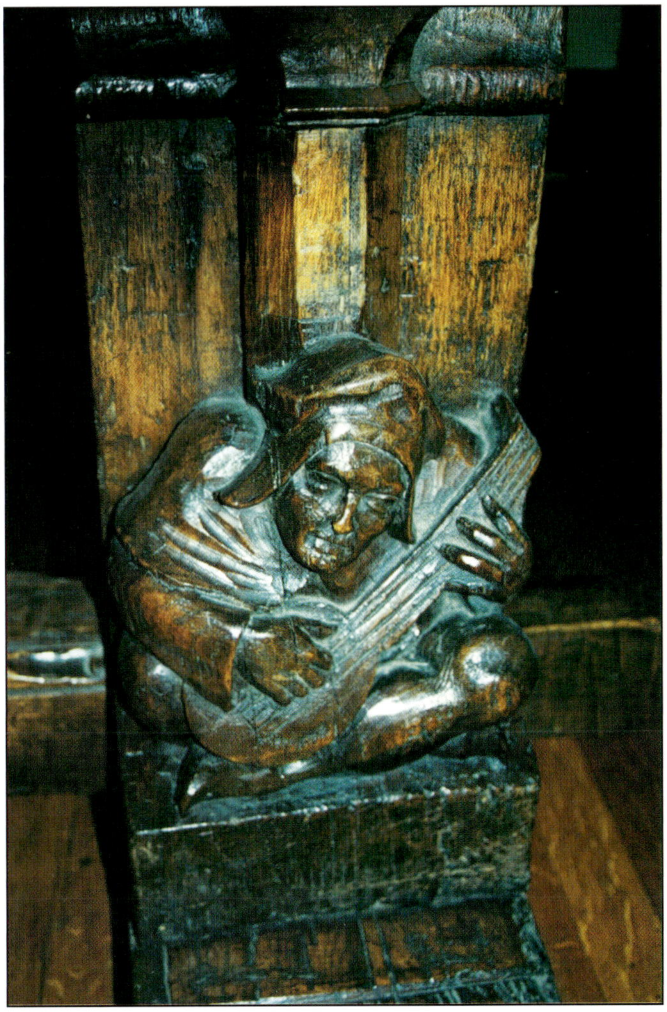

16th century Flemish carving on a pedestal table in Election Hall

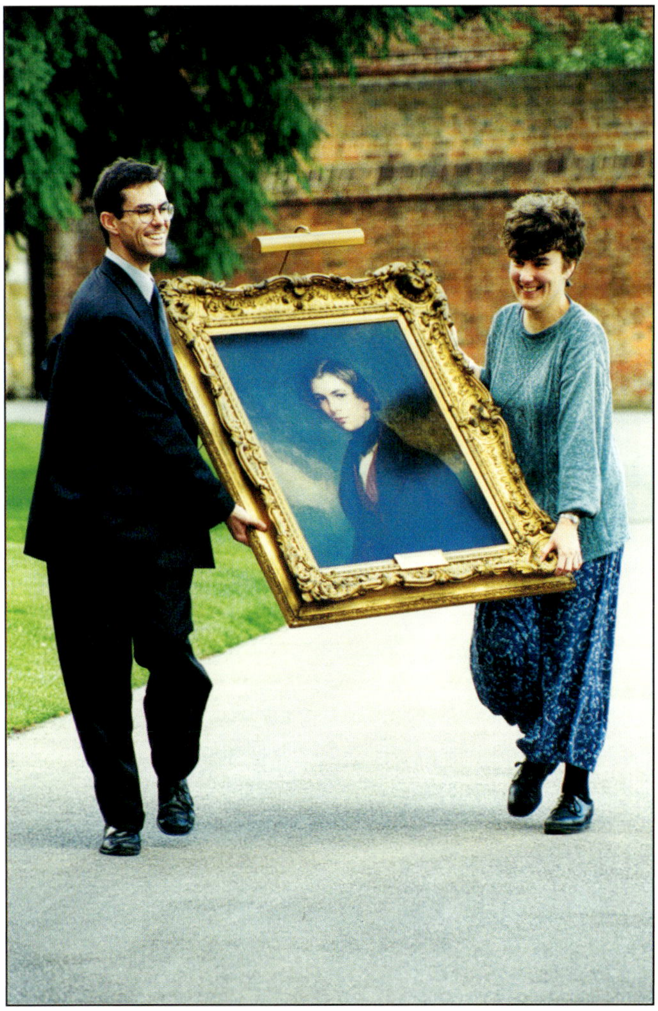

A leaving portrait on the move

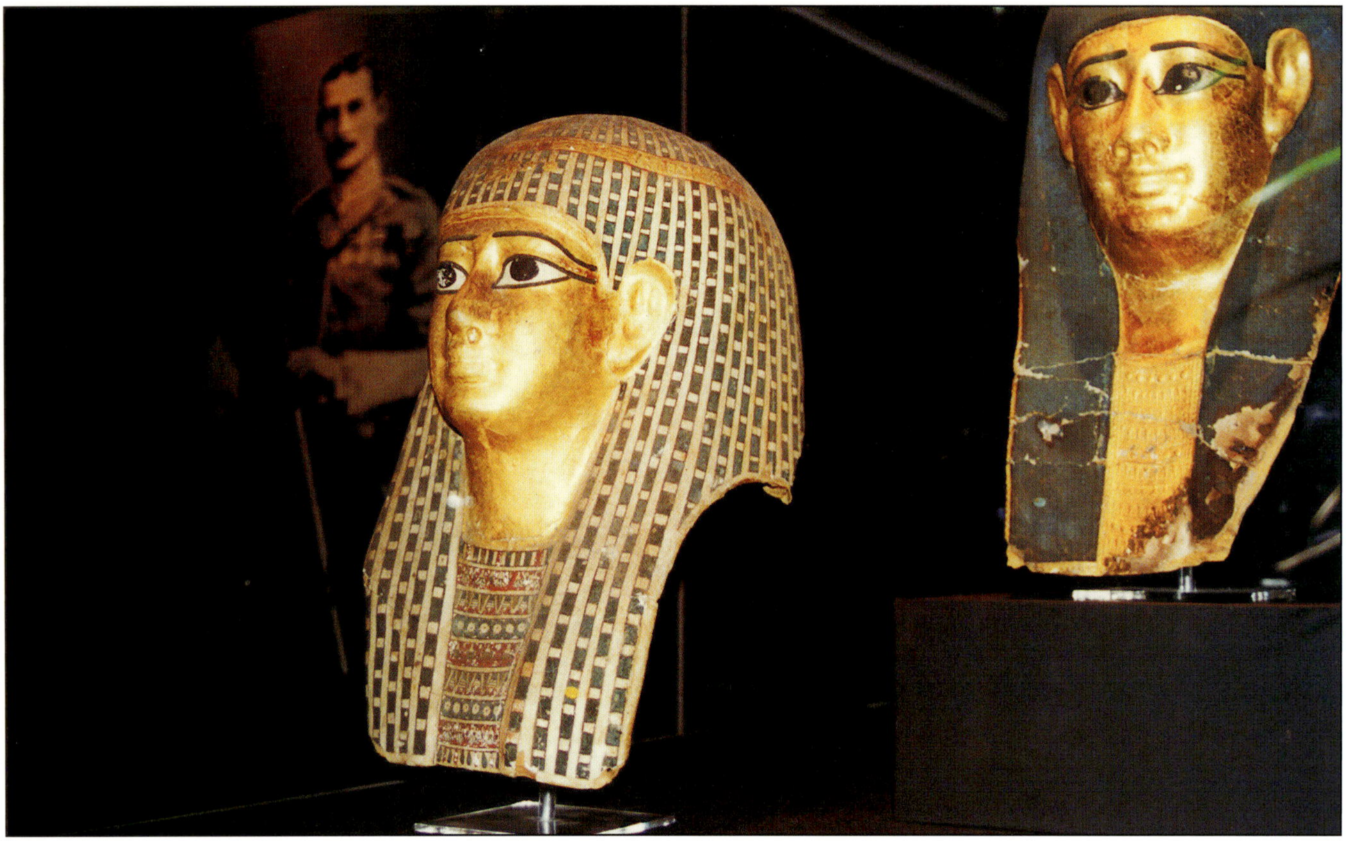

Colonel Myers looks down on his collection

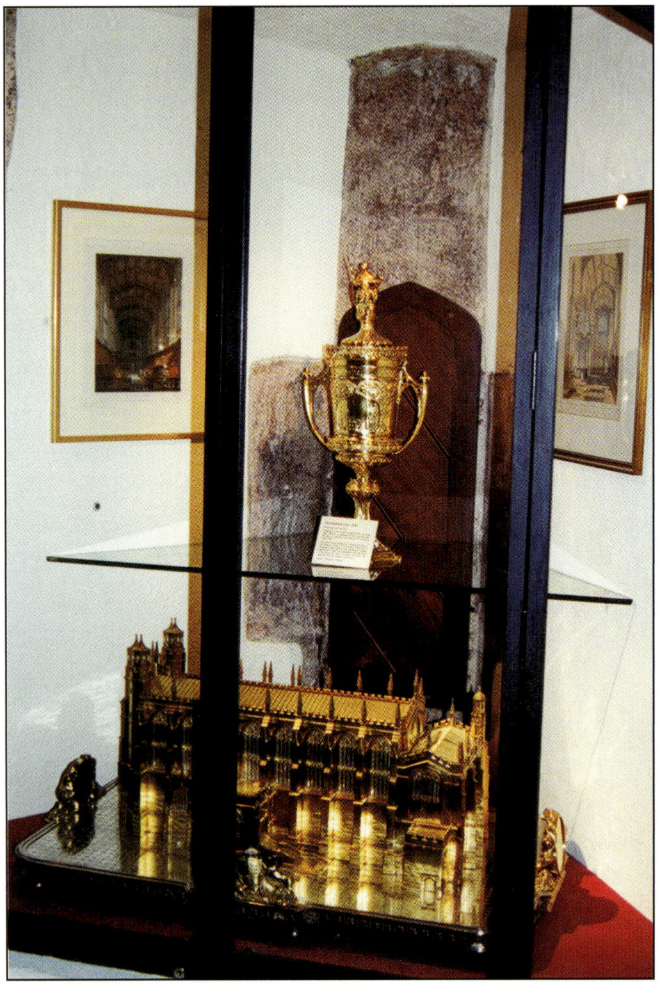

William IV presented this silver model of College Chapel to the College

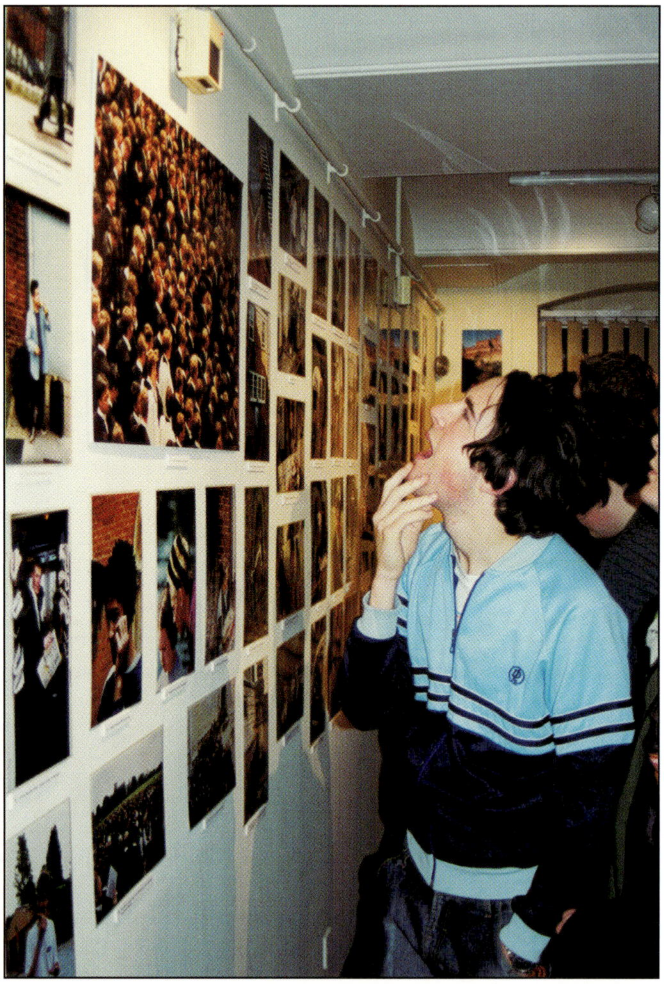

Boys inspecting a photographic exhibition

College Library

College Library, the home of Eton's rare books, was originally the province of the Provost and Fellows. In about 1900 its doors were opened to the Masters and boys, and today it is used regularly for teaching and for research. In 1996, with the addition of a readers' room, an exhibition room, new stacks and offices, College Library became equipped to deal with the demands of a major rare book collection.

The present main library was built in 1728 to contain the books acquired by Eton since its foundation. Generous bequests during the eighteenth century meant that by 1800 the Library was full. The range of books and manuscripts (mostly gifts from Old Etonians) is remarkable. The earliest manuscript, which includes part of Ovid's Heroides, dates from 950A.D., and there are over 200 incunabula. The four Shakespeare folios and a number of early quartos form the centrepiece of an outstanding collection of Elizabethan, Jacobean and Stuart plays. There are major scientific works, including a first edition of Copernicus, as well as important books on theology, architecture and Roman antiquities. In 1834 the Library received a Gutenberg Bible from the bequest of John Fuller, the only copy surviving in its original signed binding.

Since 1965 Eton has collected nineteenth and twentieth century rare books and manuscripts, all of which were transferred to College Library in 1996. Among these are major archives of Elizabeth Barrett Browning, Thomas Hardy and Edward Gordon Craig. In 2000 the Macnaghten Library of World War I books came under the care of College Library, and recent acquisitions include papers relating to Field Marshal Montgomery, as well as substantial collections of rare books about China and Russia. Today boys may attend meetings of the Book Collectors' Club and develop their own interests in the Library. College Library also organises public lectures and welcomes visits from other schools.

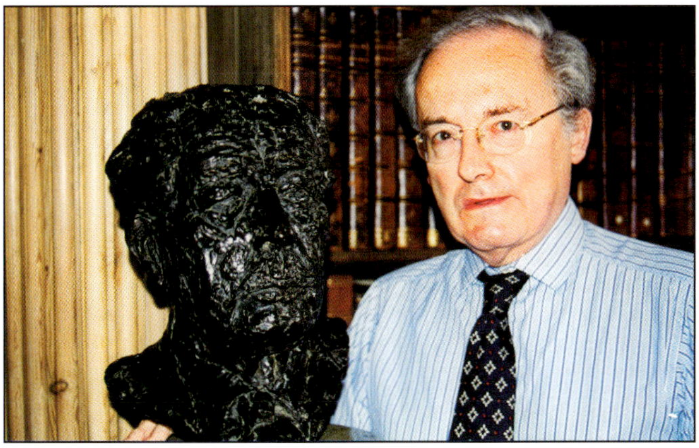

The College Librarian beside a bust of Harold Macmillan

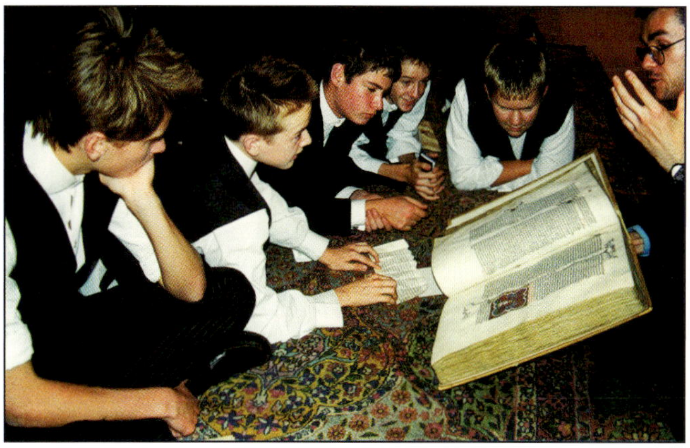

The Collections Administrator introducing boys to a 14th century French Bible

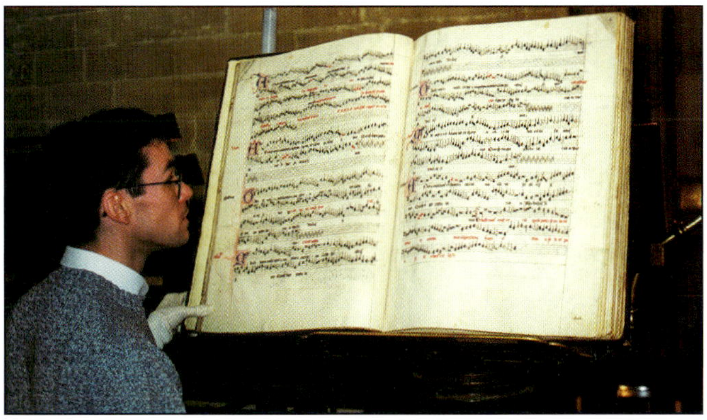

The Eton Choir Book

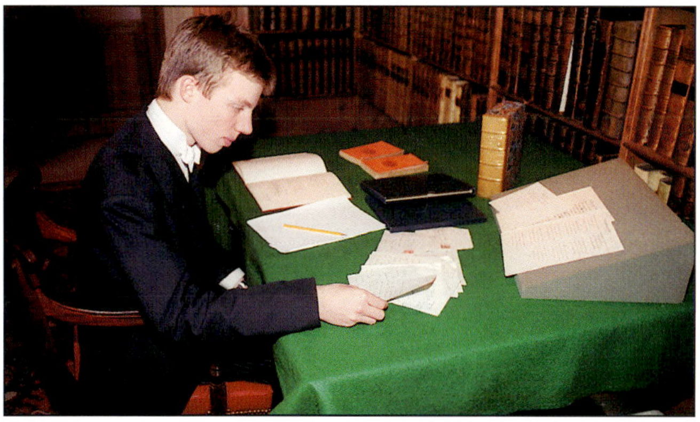

Boys are encouraged to do their own research

Eton in the Community

Eton is very much aware of its obligation towards the local community. Whilst the College's first duty is to look after the boys in its care and to further their education and upbringing, it also looks outside its confines to the wider world and its needs. For example, when the School sanatorium was moved to the former Parish Church, a skilful conversion, space was also provided for the South Meadow surgery, the local medical centre. The Farrer Theatre and School Hall are used for plays and concerts put on by local societies and orchestras, whilst many of the sports facilities (swimming-pools, athletics centre, squash courts and rowing lake) are used by outside clubs and individuals. There is an old people's Christmas Party, which is much appreciated by those who attend. Guests are fetched from their homes, given Christmas hospitality and then driven home after the party. The boys are active in two ways. First, they raise money for many outside charities. Twenty-four hour events (football and squash, for example), a swimathon and concerts have been organised for fund-raising purposes. And secondly, they go out into the community and give help, where help is needed.

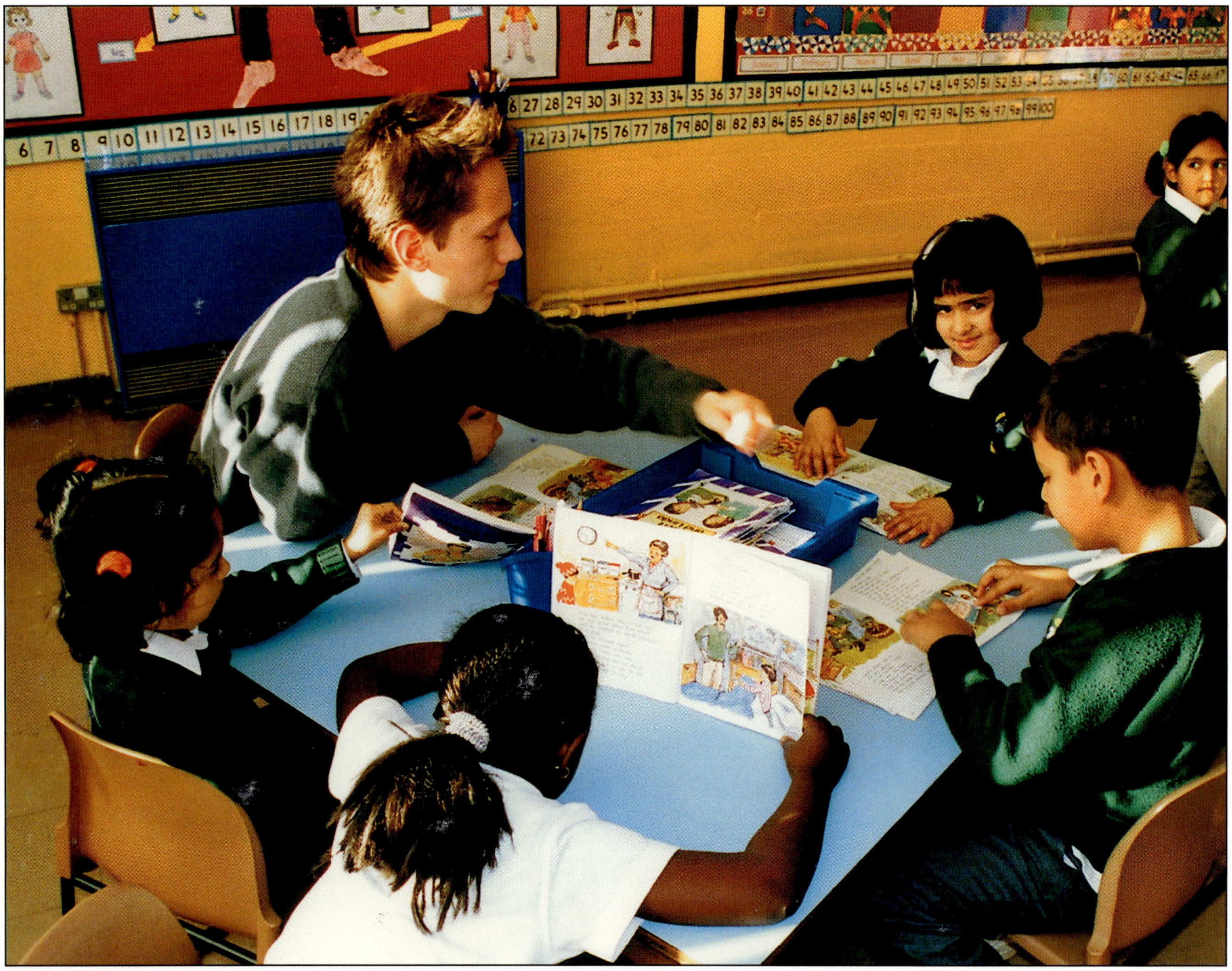

Boys help in local primary schools

Mufti Day

Mufti Day is a recent innovation. It was introduced in May 1999 and was the idea of the then Head Master, John Lewis. In return for a small donation, Masters and boys abandon School Dress for the day and attire themselves in any acceptable way they please. Tourists, expecting to see Etonians in their traditional uniform, are astonished to see yogi bear, a lion, the Loch Ness Monster, Father Christmas, Grecian priests, space men and the like walking through the streets. The contrast with School Dress could not be more complete and is the cause of much enjoyment and mirth. On average, the day raises about £3,000 which is donated to charities, many of them children's charities.

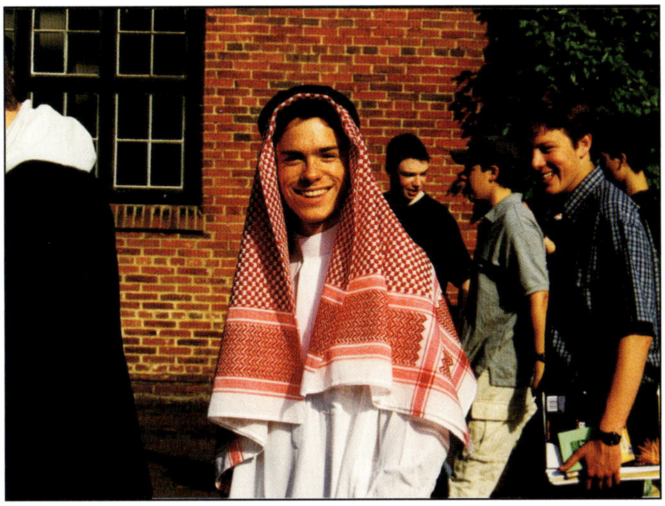

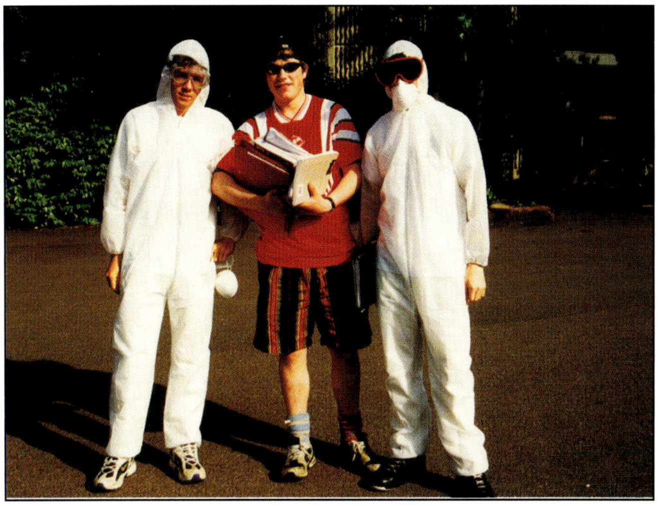

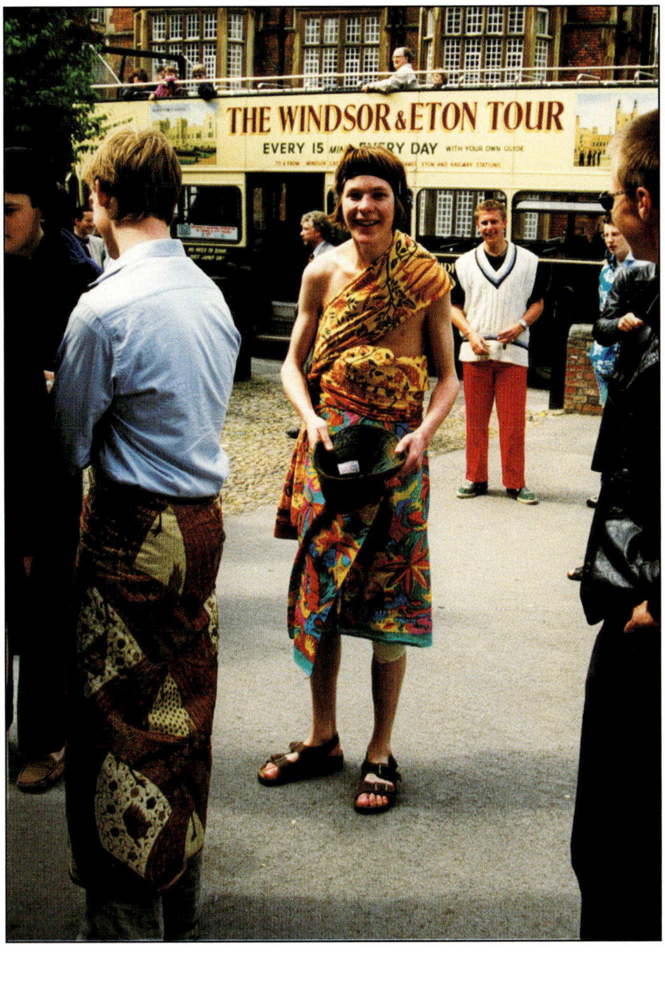

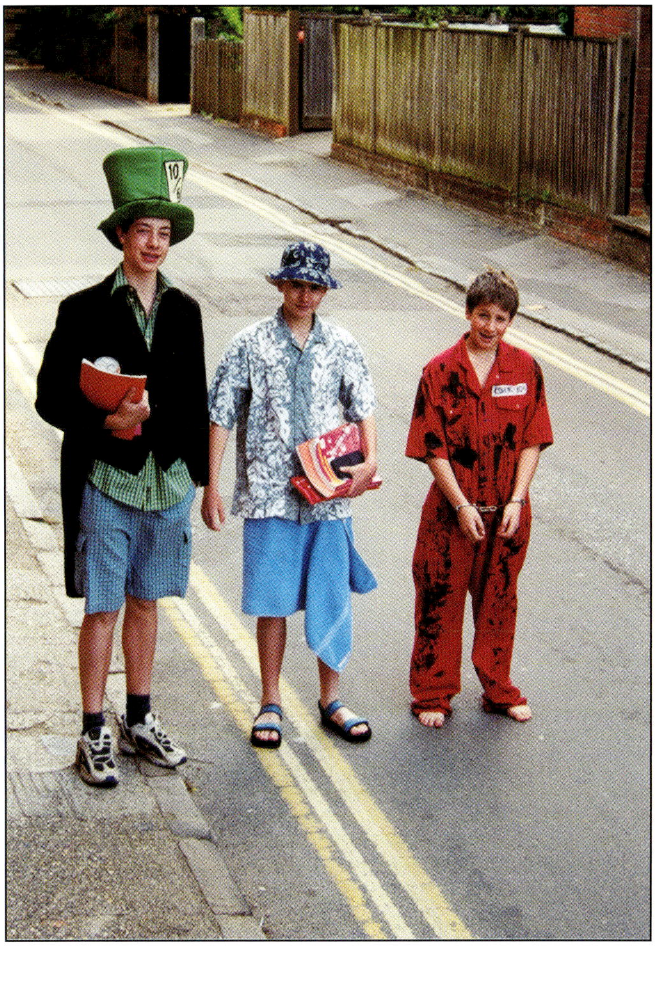

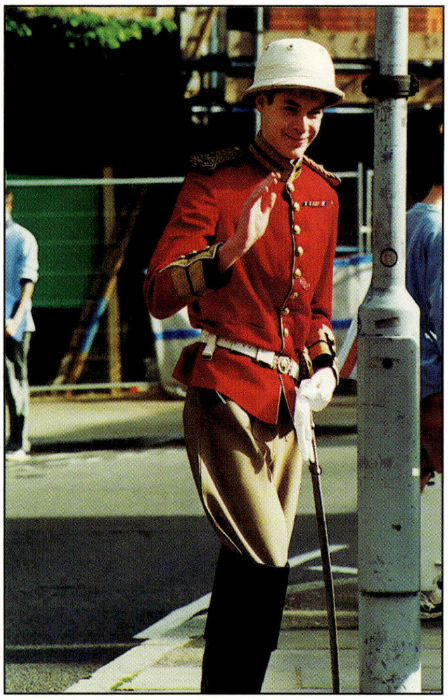
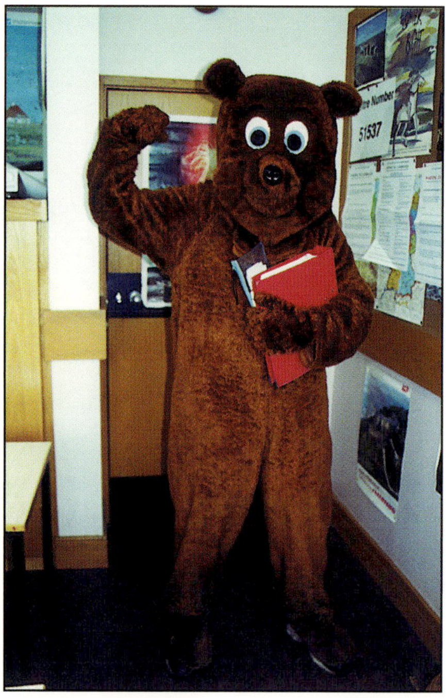
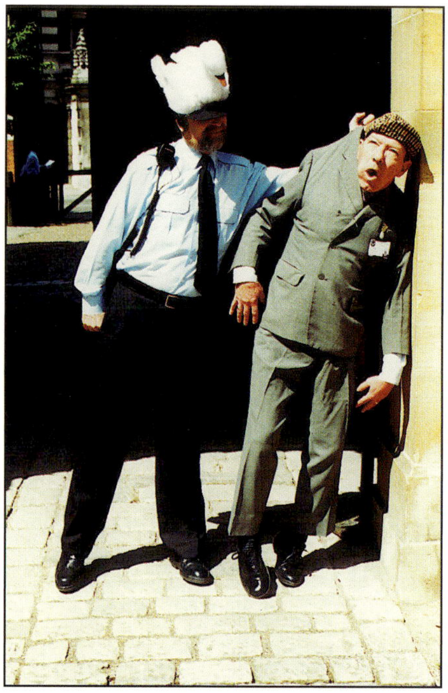
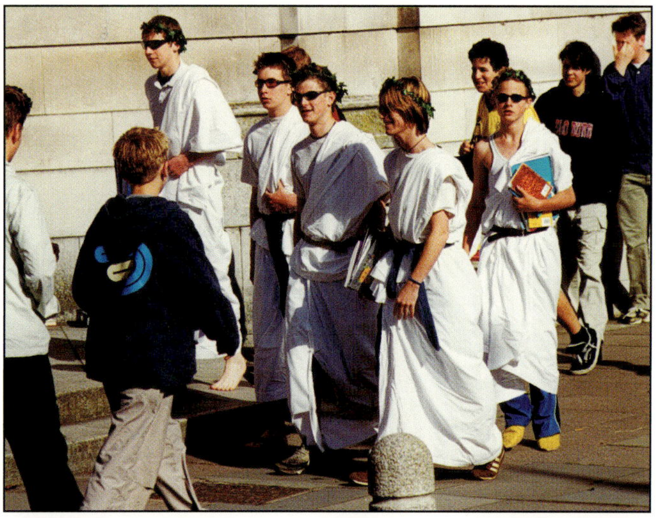
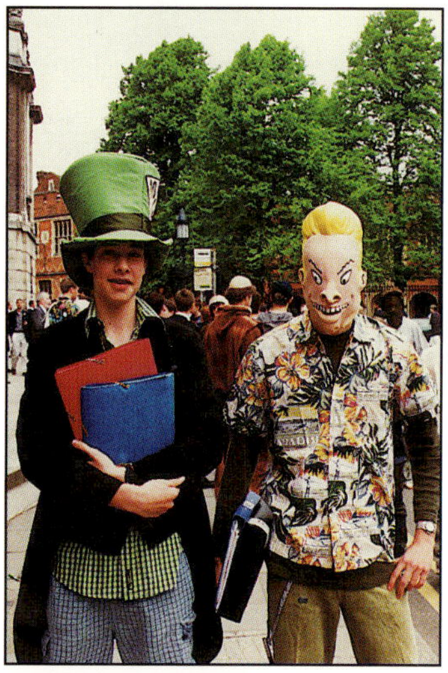
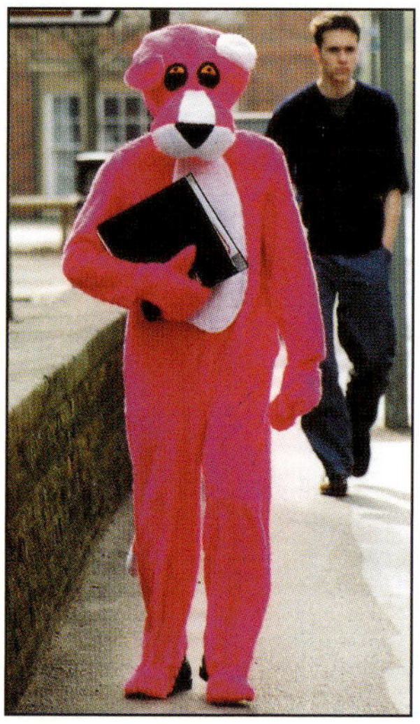
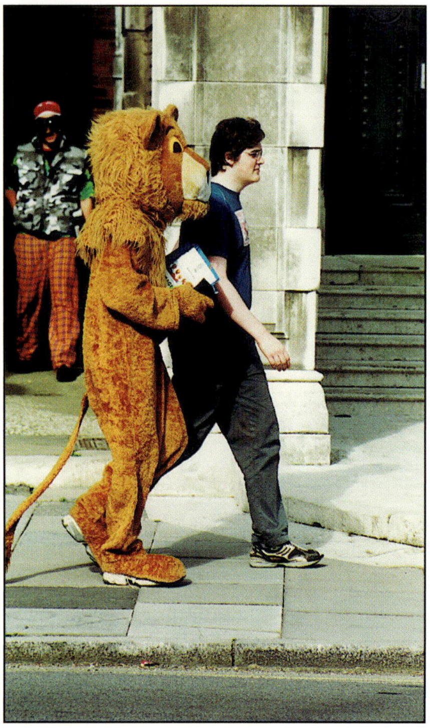
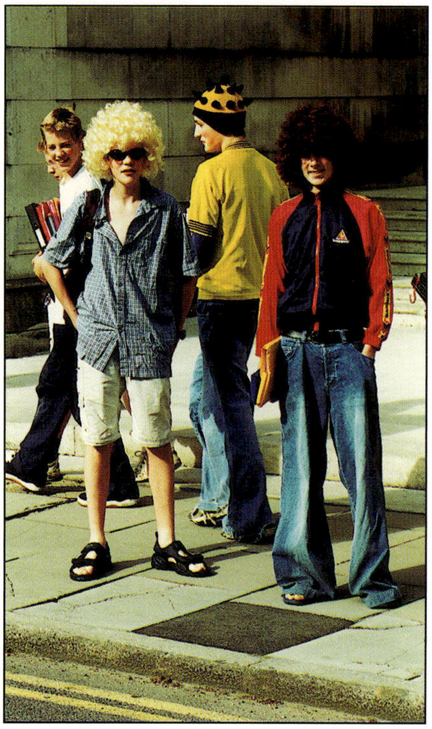
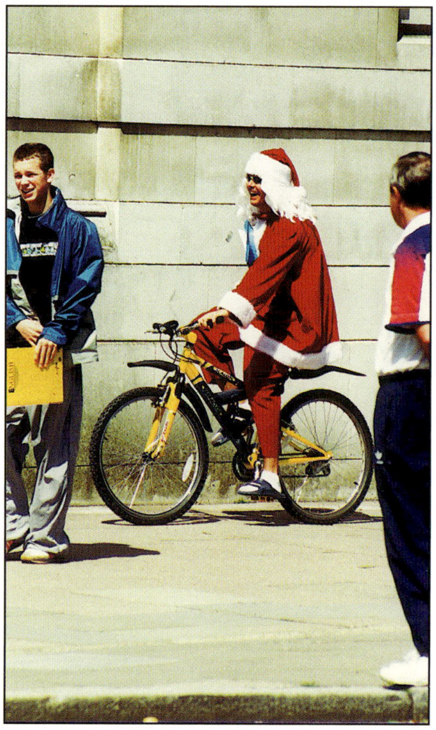

Eton Action Fair

The Eton Action Fair takes place on a Saturday in late September and always seems blessed with fine weather. The event starts at 11.00am and closes at 4.30pm. The School welcomes local charities who put up their own stalls on the Parade Ground and in the Fives Courts, and there is a large jumble sale in School Hall. Each Boys' House devises its own methods of raising money, which range from the staid and steady to the weird and wonderful. At the one extreme there are raffles, guessing games, sales of refreshments and charity Christmas Cards. At the other one sees boys crawling from Windsor Castle to Eton accompanied by pail-rattling money collectors, or one can douse a Colleger with cold water or smother an Etonian's face with shaving foam. The individual charities swell their own funds, whilst the money raised by the Eton boys is given to charities voted for by the boys.

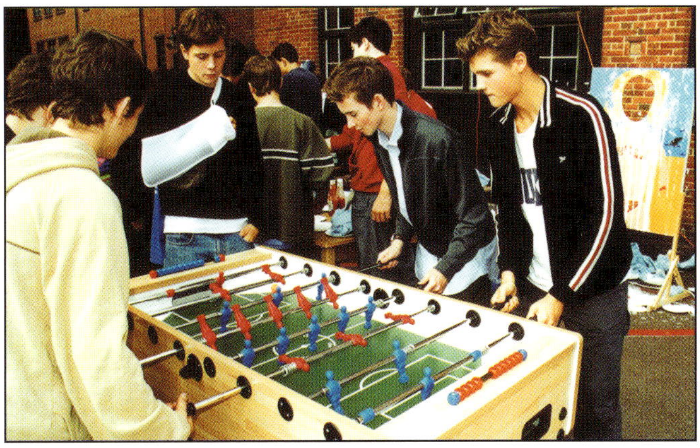
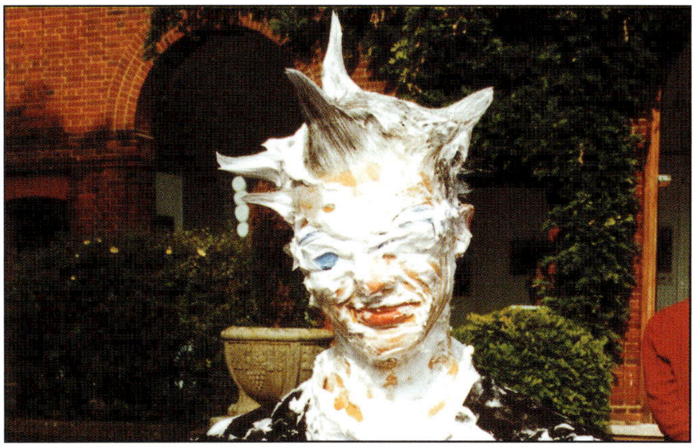
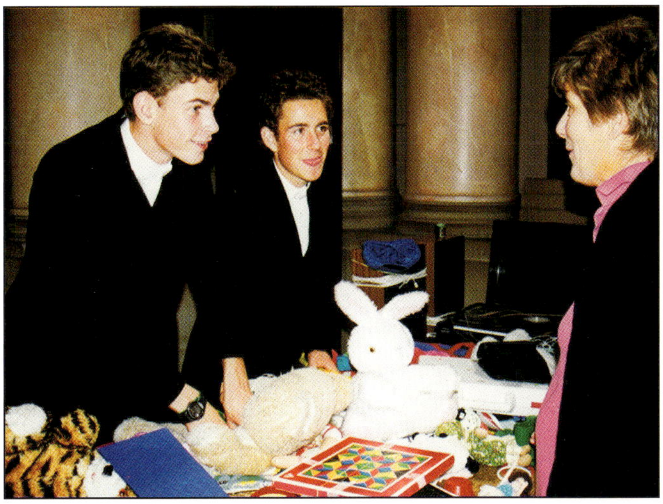
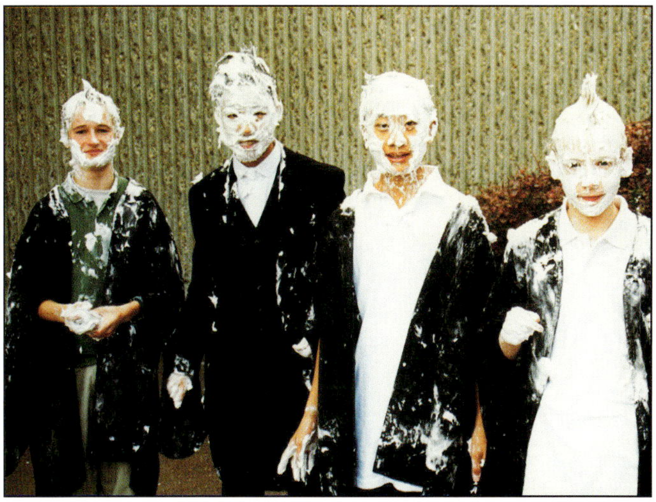
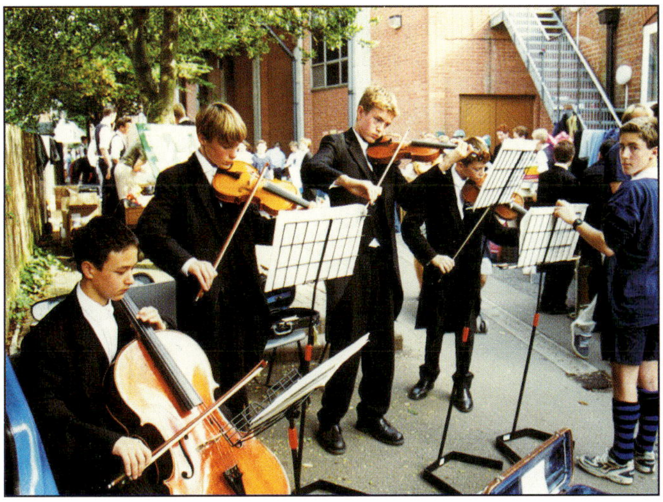
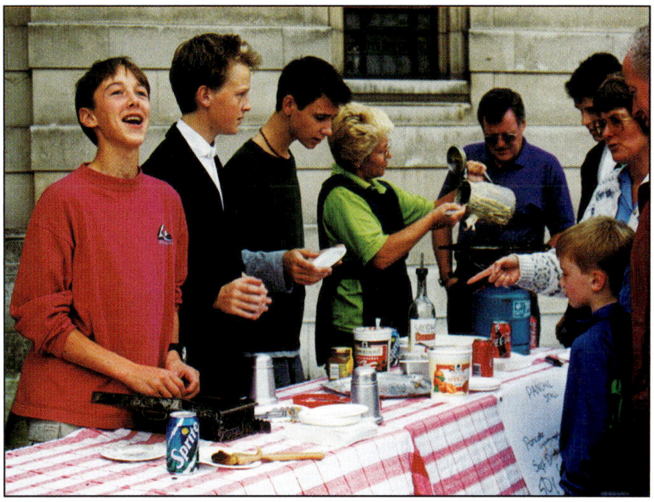

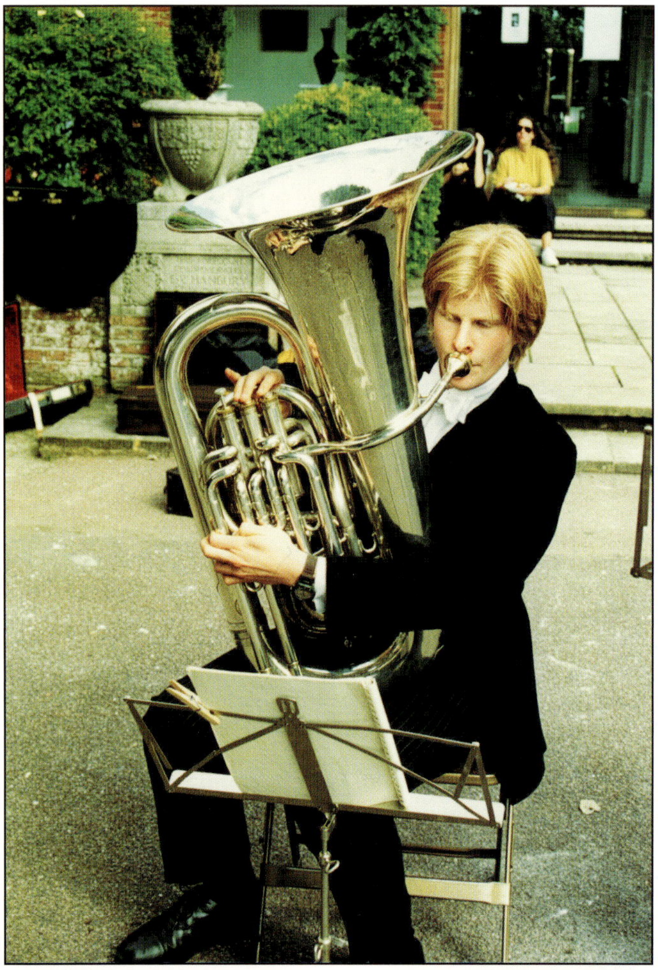

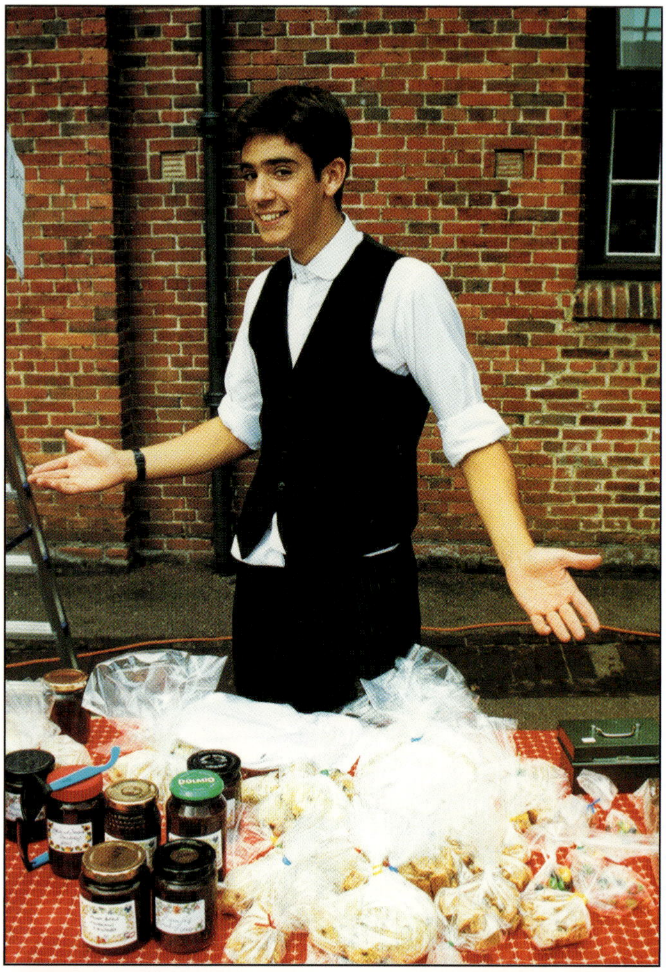
DOLMIO

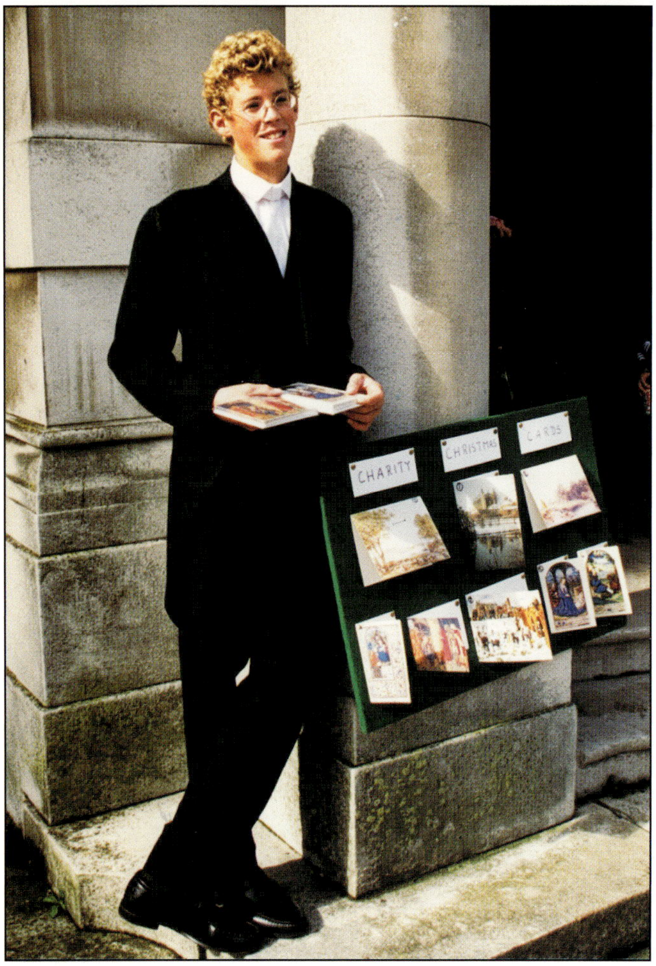
CHARITY
CHRISTMAS
CARDS

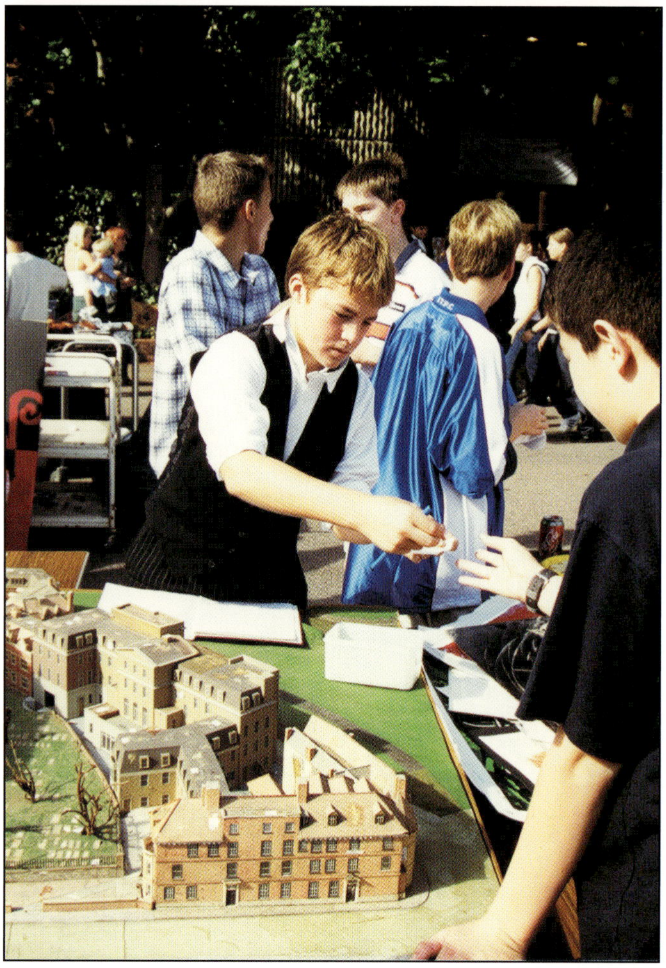

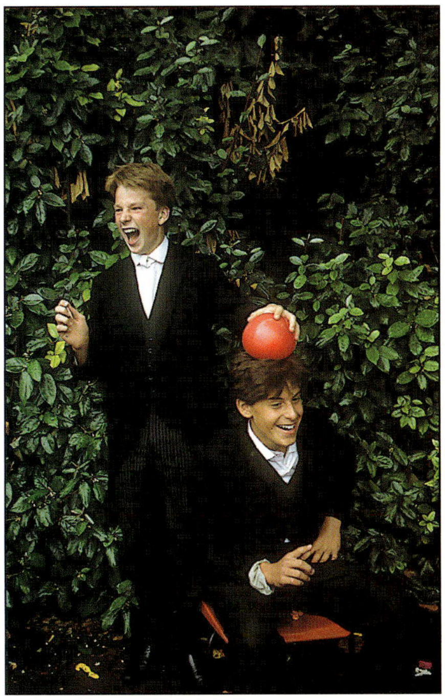

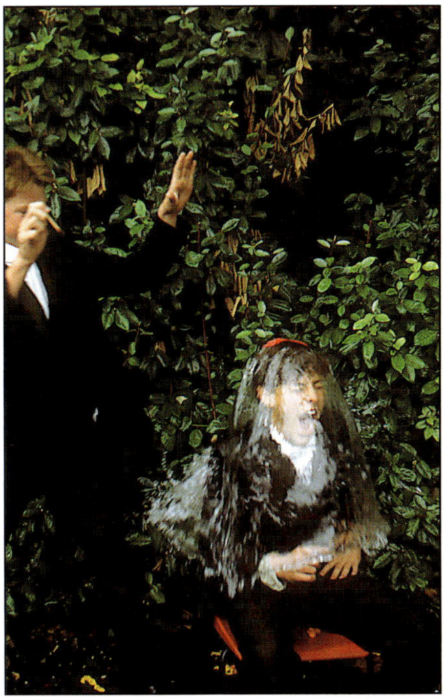

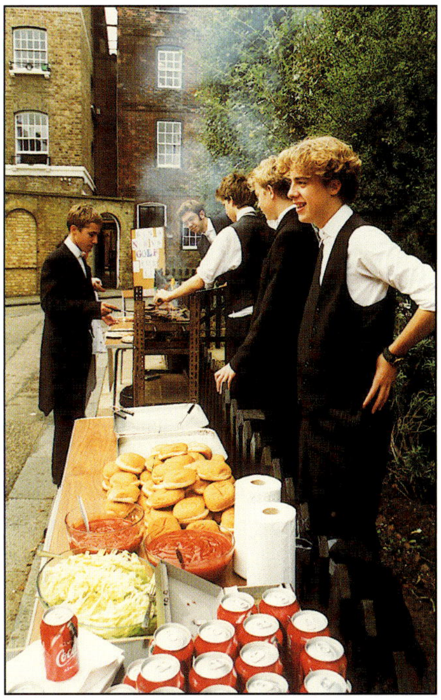

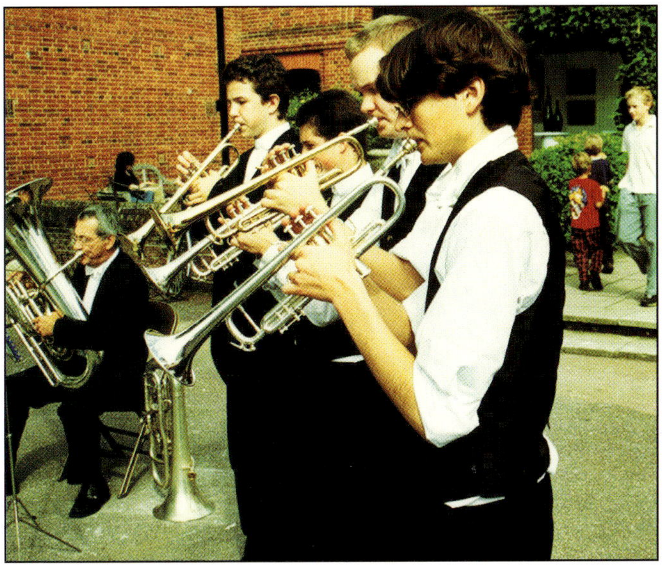

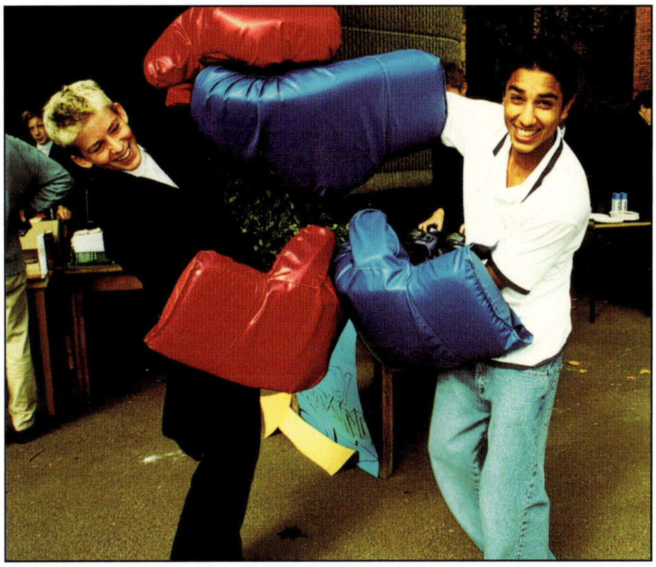

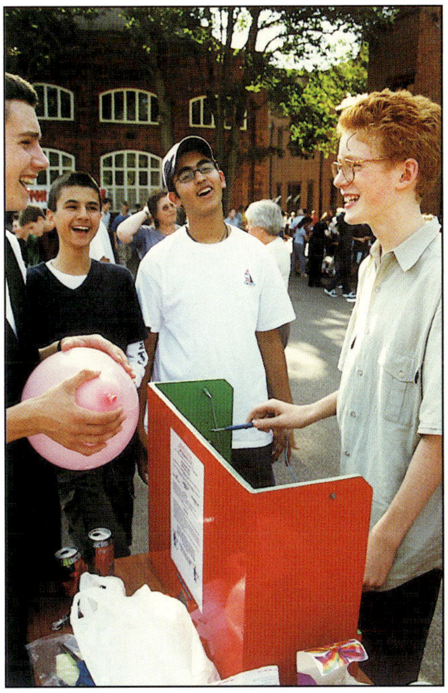

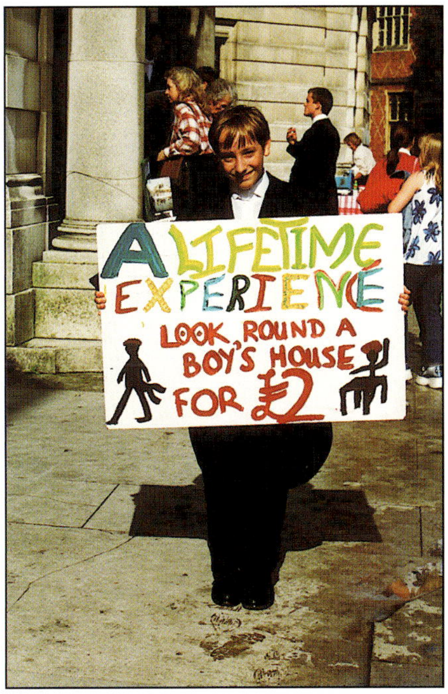
A LIFETIME
EXPERIENCE
LOOK ROUND A
BOY'S HOUSE
FOR £2

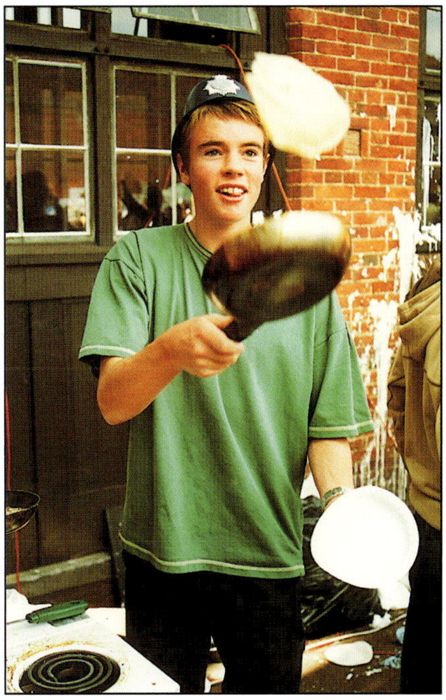

Community Service

Social Service involves about 150 boys from C Block. It enables them to contribute constructively to the life of the local community. There is a wide variety of activity. Boys visit the elderly in their homes and in hospital. They help in local primary schools and in a school for children with learning and physical disabilities. Volunteers join in the activities of the Friendly Club, and others call out the bingo numbers at the Charteris Day Centre. Some help in Windsor charity shops, and their contribution ranges from taping and pegging clothes to creating displays and working at the till. A small group helps the local Swan Lifeline, feeding swans, mending cages and cleaning out pens. Many of these activities are illustrated, but in one case it would be inappropriate to take photographs, and this is for the so-called Slough Run. Under the experienced guidance of Mrs Phyllis Wallbank boys go to Slough once a week to an unofficial gathering in the shelter of a multi-storey car park. How does Mrs Wallbank describe this work? "We take food, clothes and blankets to a group of people who are in need of help. About twenty to thirty people of all ages who are lonely and lost in our society meet together every Monday evening. Some are literally killing themselves on drugs and alcohol; some are mentally fragile; some come for food, others for friendship. Volunteers bring anything that they think is needed and try to be there on a regular basis, especially when the weather is bad. Thank you, Eton, for playing a part in helping those who are often outside society."

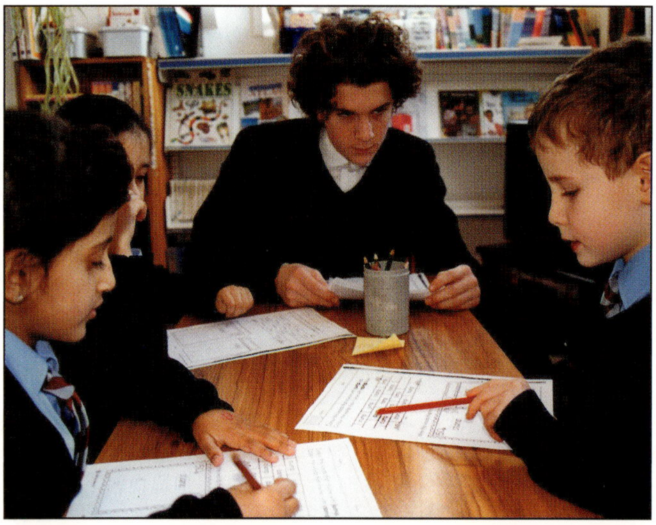

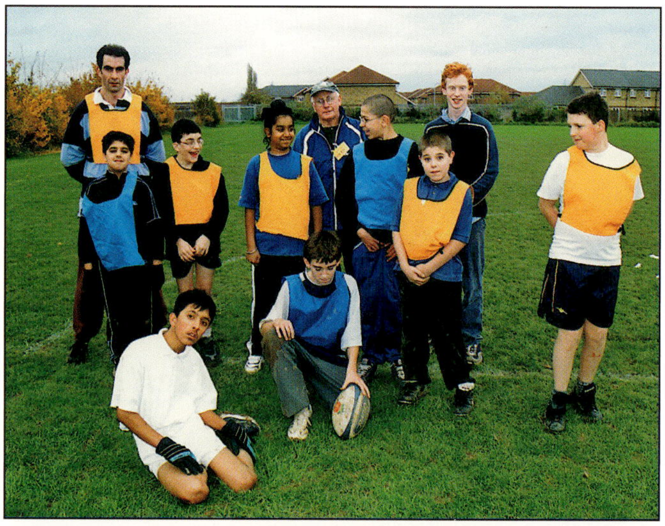

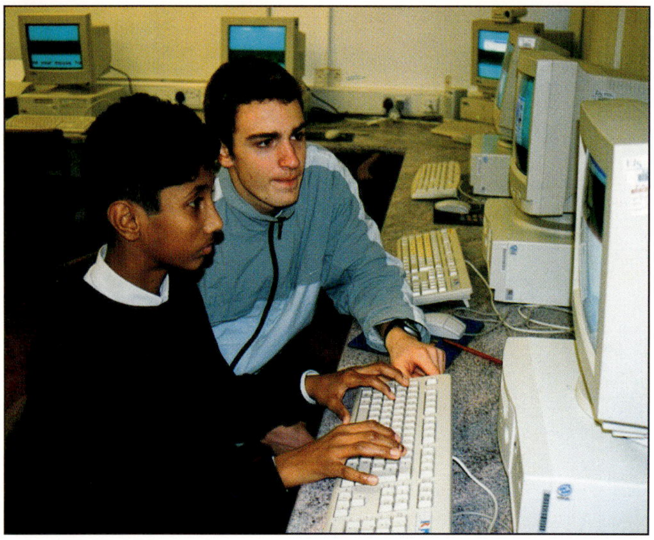

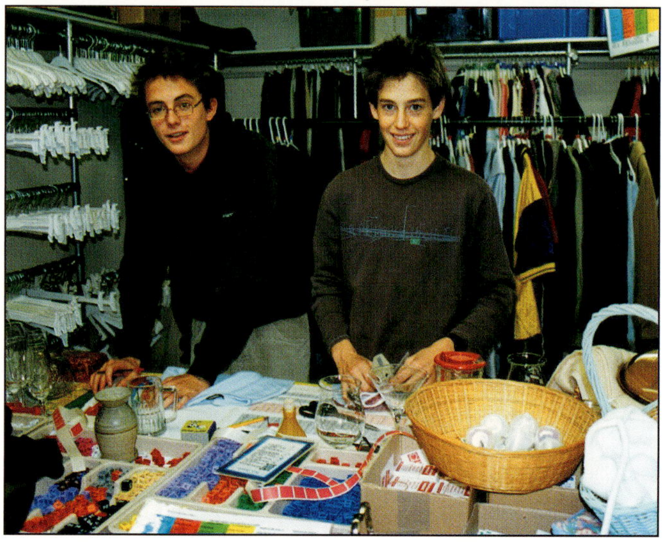

Ascension Day

Ascension Day celebrations start early with a service on College Chapel roof at 6.00am. Access to the roof is up a spiral staircase in the north-east corner of College Chapel. Despite the early start many boys are keen to attend, but for the reasons of safety and lack of space numbers have to be limited. The choir in red cassocks and white surplices, the College and Oppidan wall-game teams in their coloured sports gear, and the boys in School Dress present an unusual mixture of attire. As the sun rises, prayers are said and a hymn is sung before all descend into the Chapel for the remainder of the short service. Members of the congregation then become players and spectators of the Ascension Day wall game encounter on College Field. The early hour and the summer climate make this fixture less serious than the St Andrew's Day equivalent. After an hour at the Wall all return to their houses for a well earned breakfast.

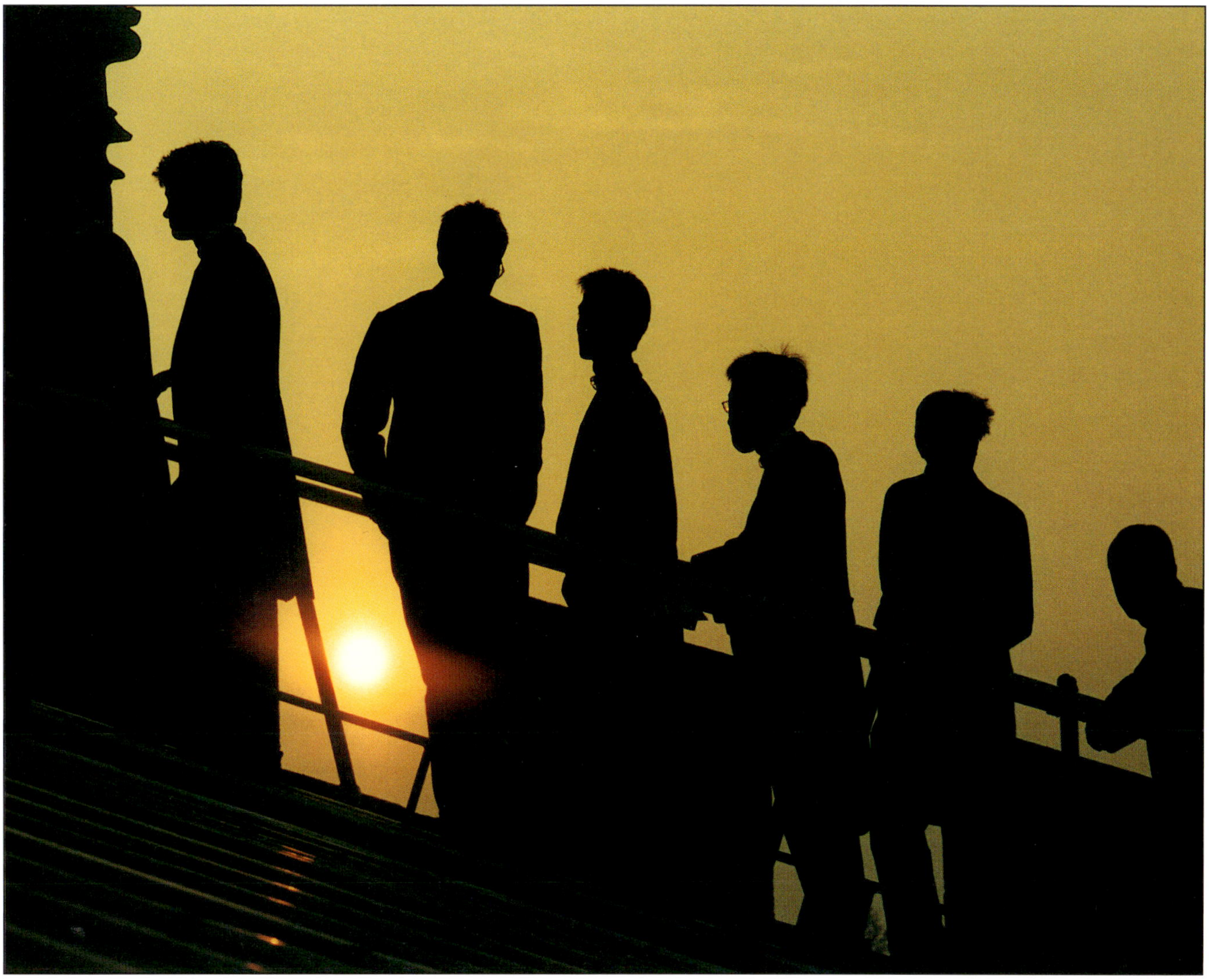

Sunrise on Ascension Day

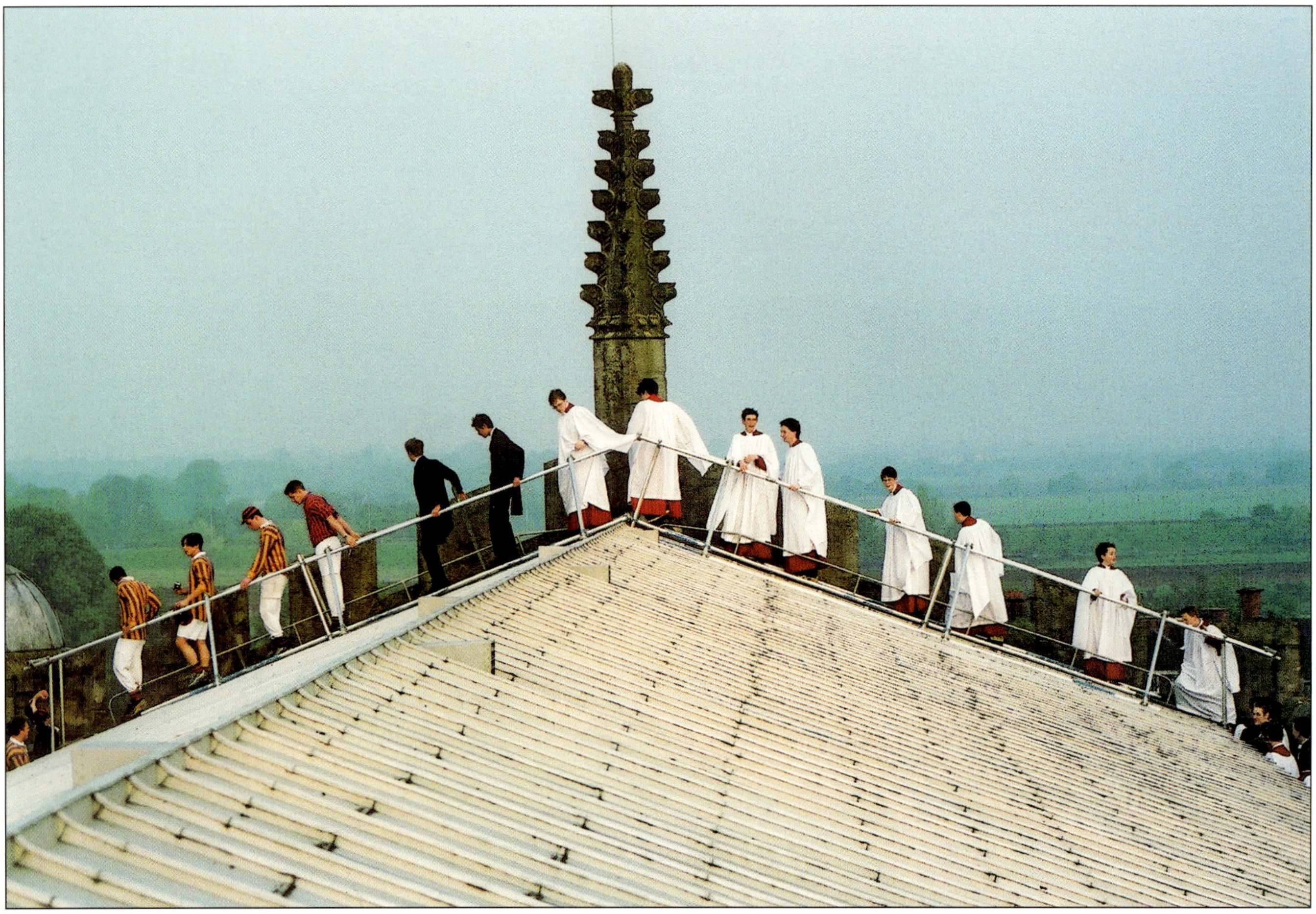

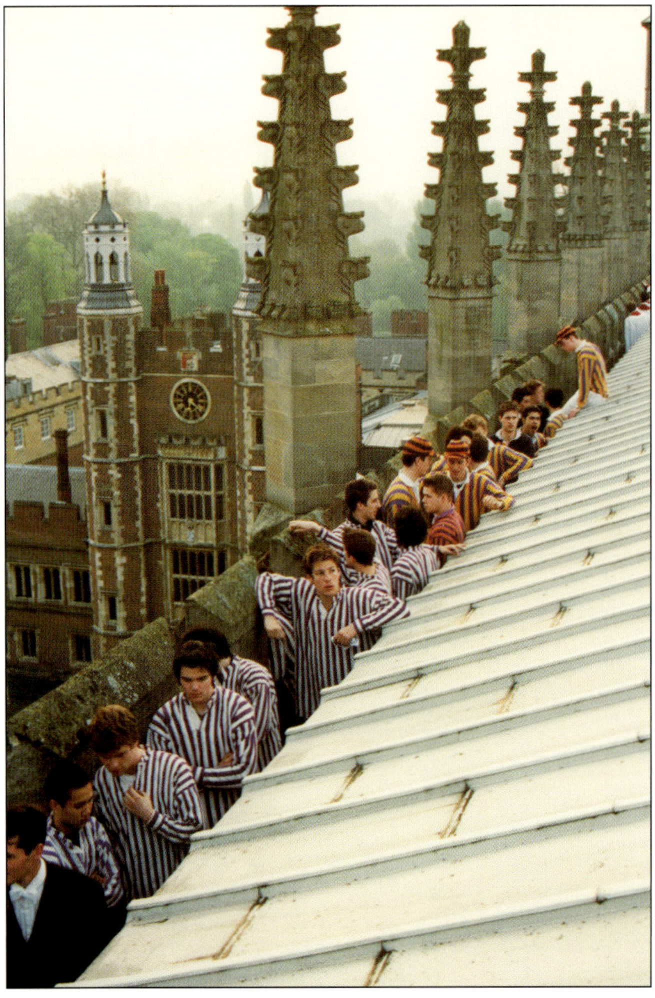

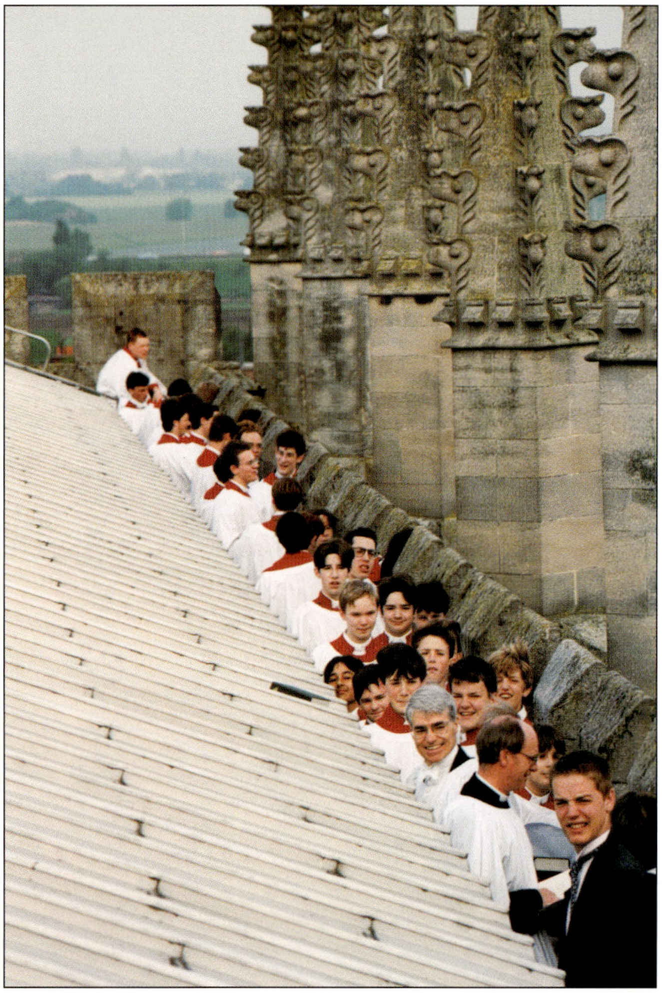

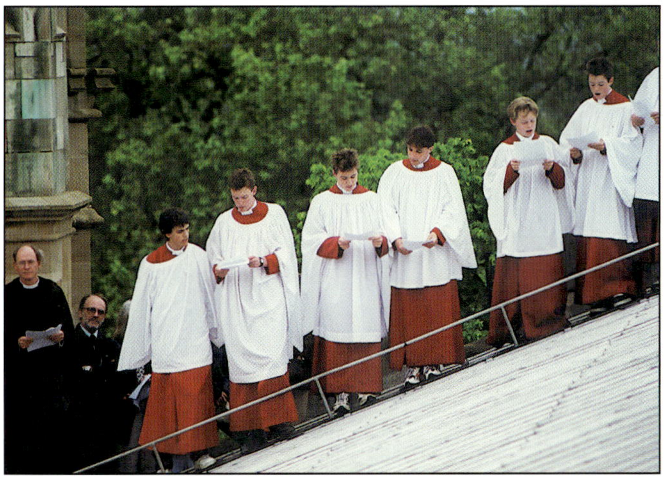

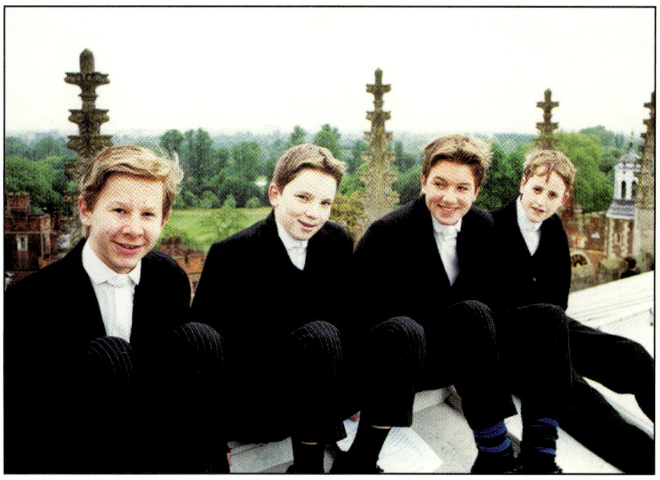

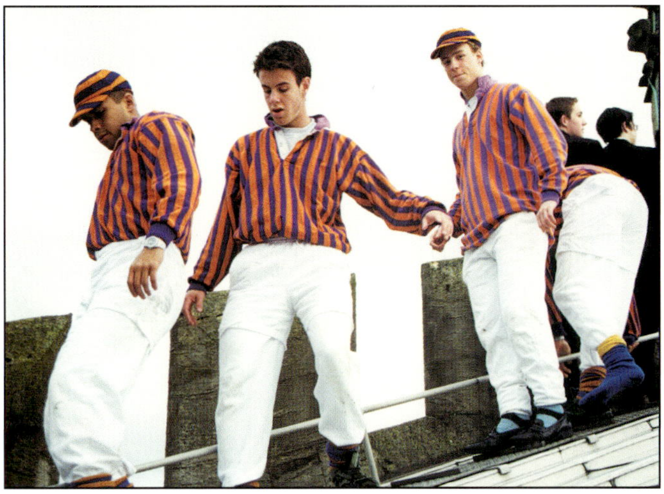

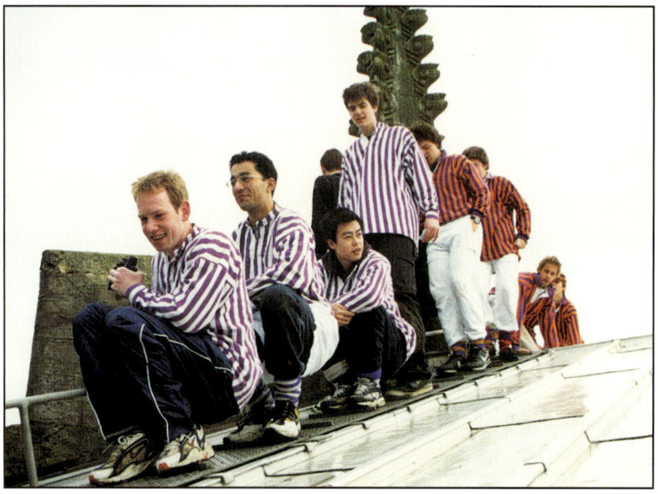

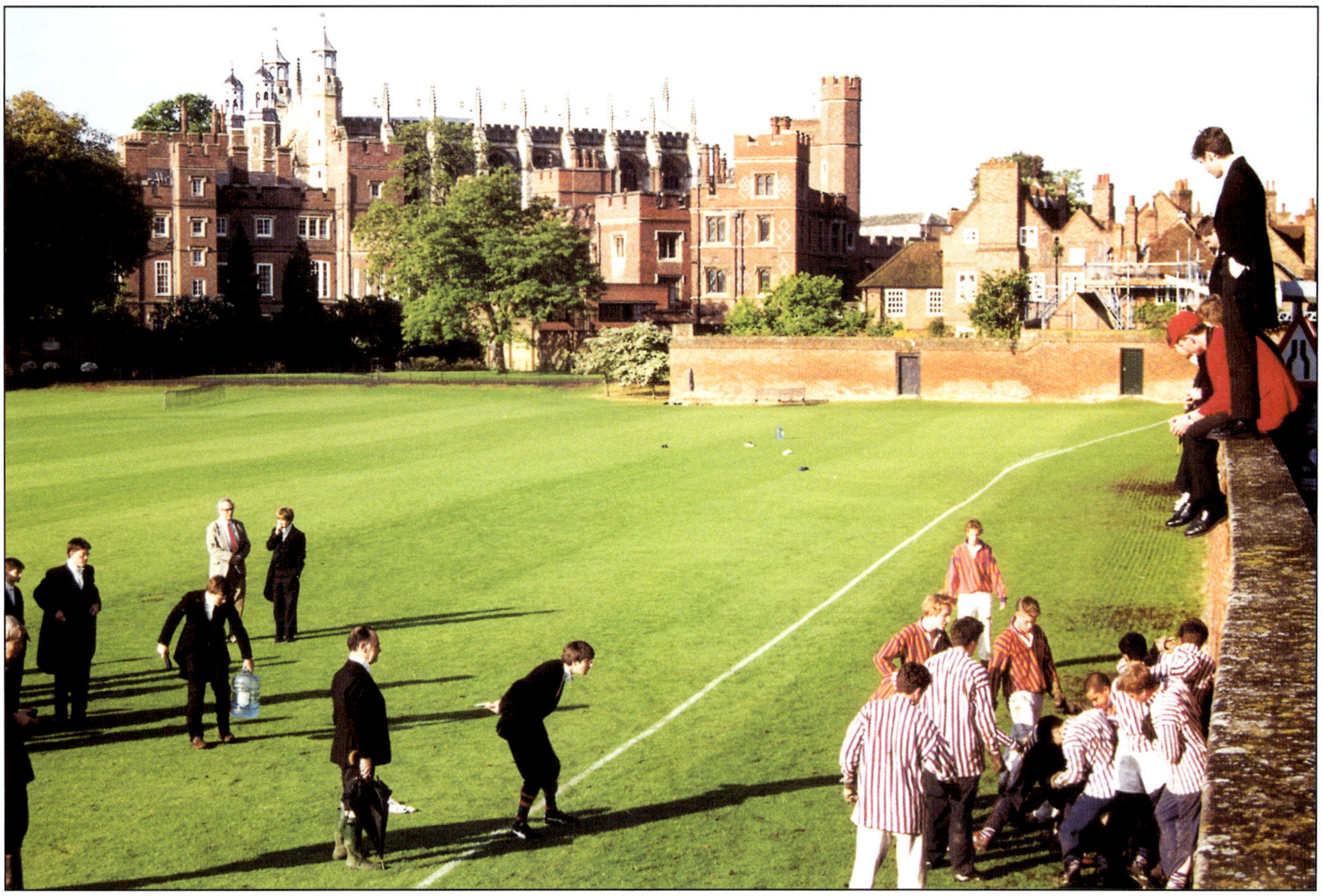

Participants have moved from top left (roof of College Chapel) to lower right (foot of the Wall)

The Fourth of June

The Fourth of June has become a quaint misnomer, as it is seldom celebrated on that date. In recent years it has taken place on the Wednesday after the so-called spring Bank Holiday, so the actual date can be in late May or early June. The Fourth of June was the birthday of George III, a good friend to Eton, and has become the name used to describe the Summer Half Parents' Day. There are no lessons, but instead a series of events and displays. The day begins with a Chapel service. Then follow concerts, sporting fixtures, displays and exhibitions. At 11.00am there are speeches in Upper School, at which members of VIth Form declaim prose and poetry on a particular theme. Prior to lunch parents attend a reception given by their sons' House Masters before picnicking with their sons on the playing fields. The Procession of Boats is the highlight of the afternoon. Then all boys attend absence in School Yard at 4.00pm, after which they are free to go home for Long Leave.

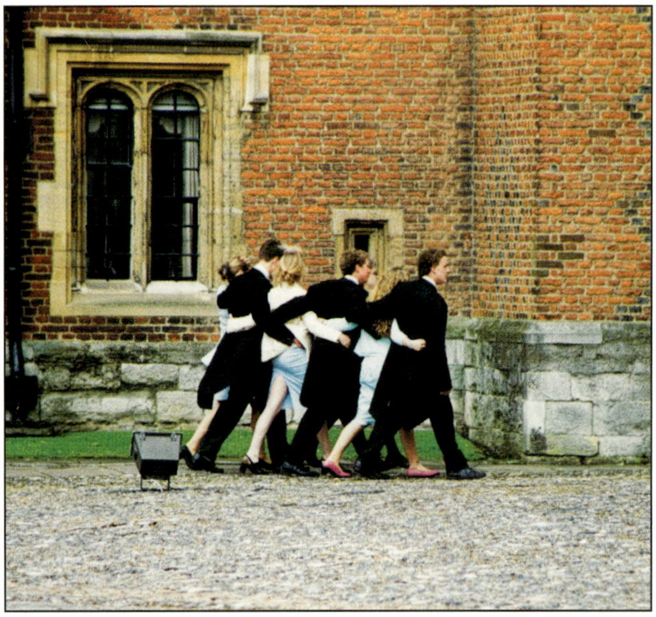

Boys' girl friends are made very welcome!

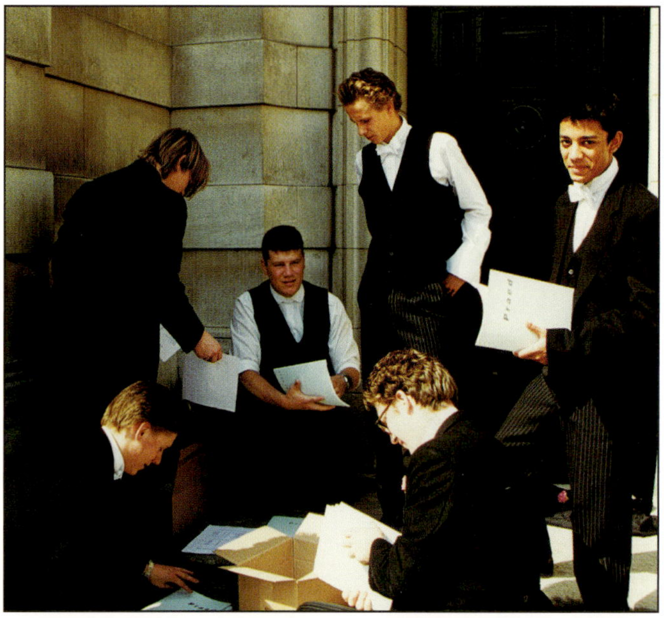

Magazines are on sale

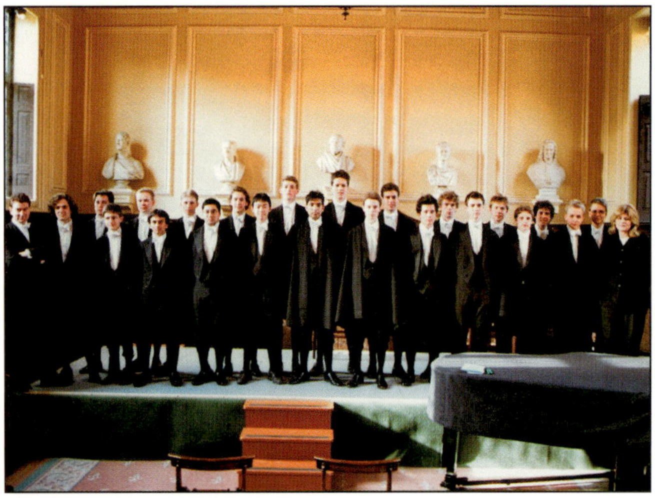

Speeches in Upper School

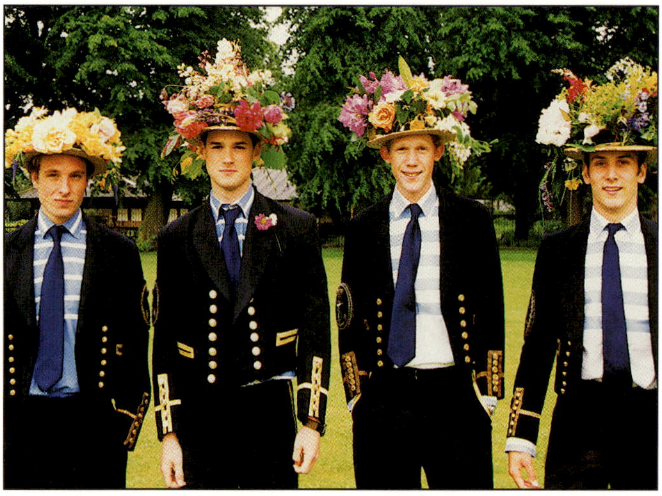

Boys taking part in the Procession of Boats wear historical naval uniform and decorate their boaters with flowers

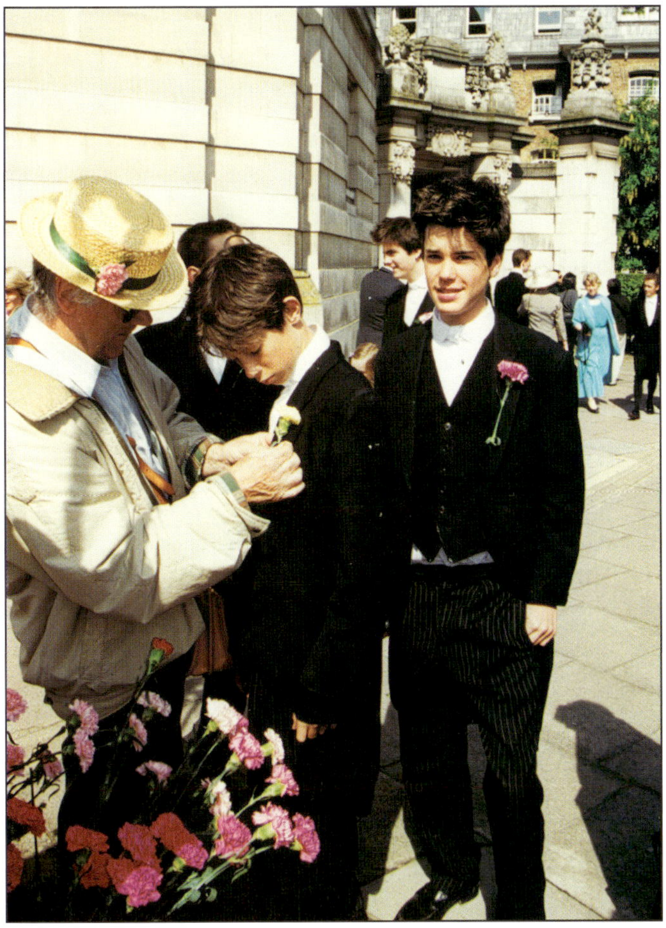

Most boys have a carnation in their button-hole

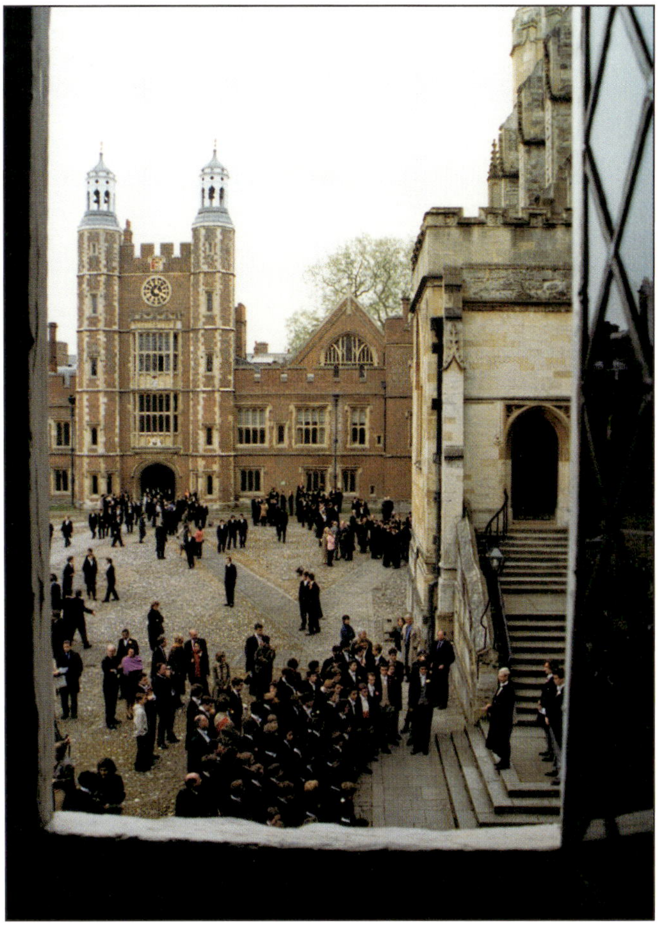

Absence in School Yard as seen from Upper School

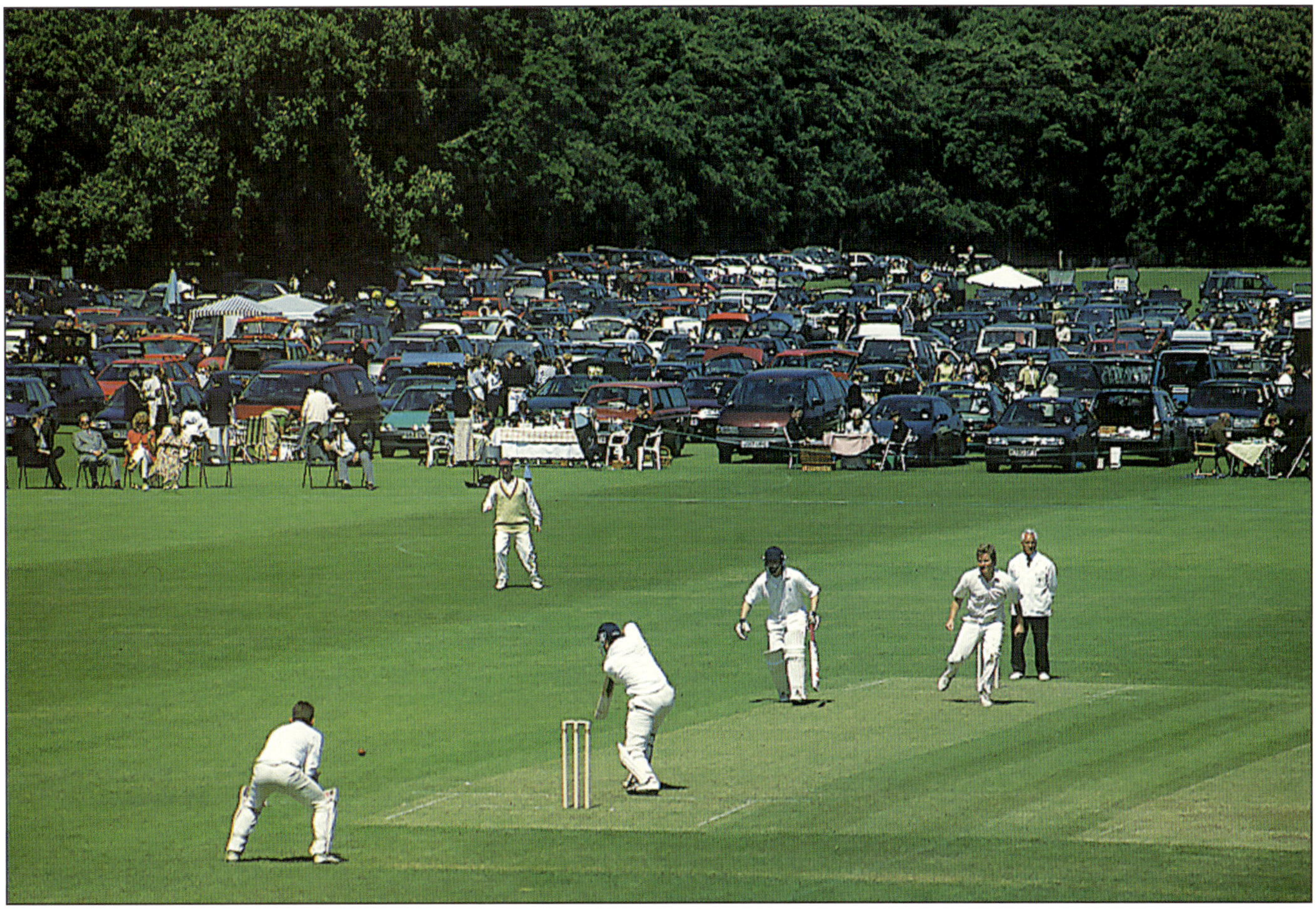

Cricket and picnics on Agar's

Procession of Boats

The first documented Procession of Boats took place in 1793 in the presence of the King, and it soon became a feature of the Fourth of June celebrations. The naval attire was adopted in about 1841. The names of the boats belong to ships in Nelson's navy and have remained the same since 1877. The boats were not made for racing, but specifically for this activity. The leading boat is called the Monarch and is propelled by ten oarsmen. It replaced its predecessor in 1990 and was dedicated by Her Majesty Queen Elizabeth, The Queen Mother, during the 1990 celebrations. Ten boats take part in the procession. Each boat slows down as it reaches the main enclosure and, on the cox's instruction, members of the crew stand up in pairs (one and eight, two and seven etc), until all eight are standing, and then they doff their boaters to Eton and to Windsor. The Lower Boats also raise their oars, a difficult manoeuvre that requires a good sense of balance. It is necessary to rehearse this skill several times in advance of the real occasion, for 'falling in' in front of such a large crowd is considered unacceptable!

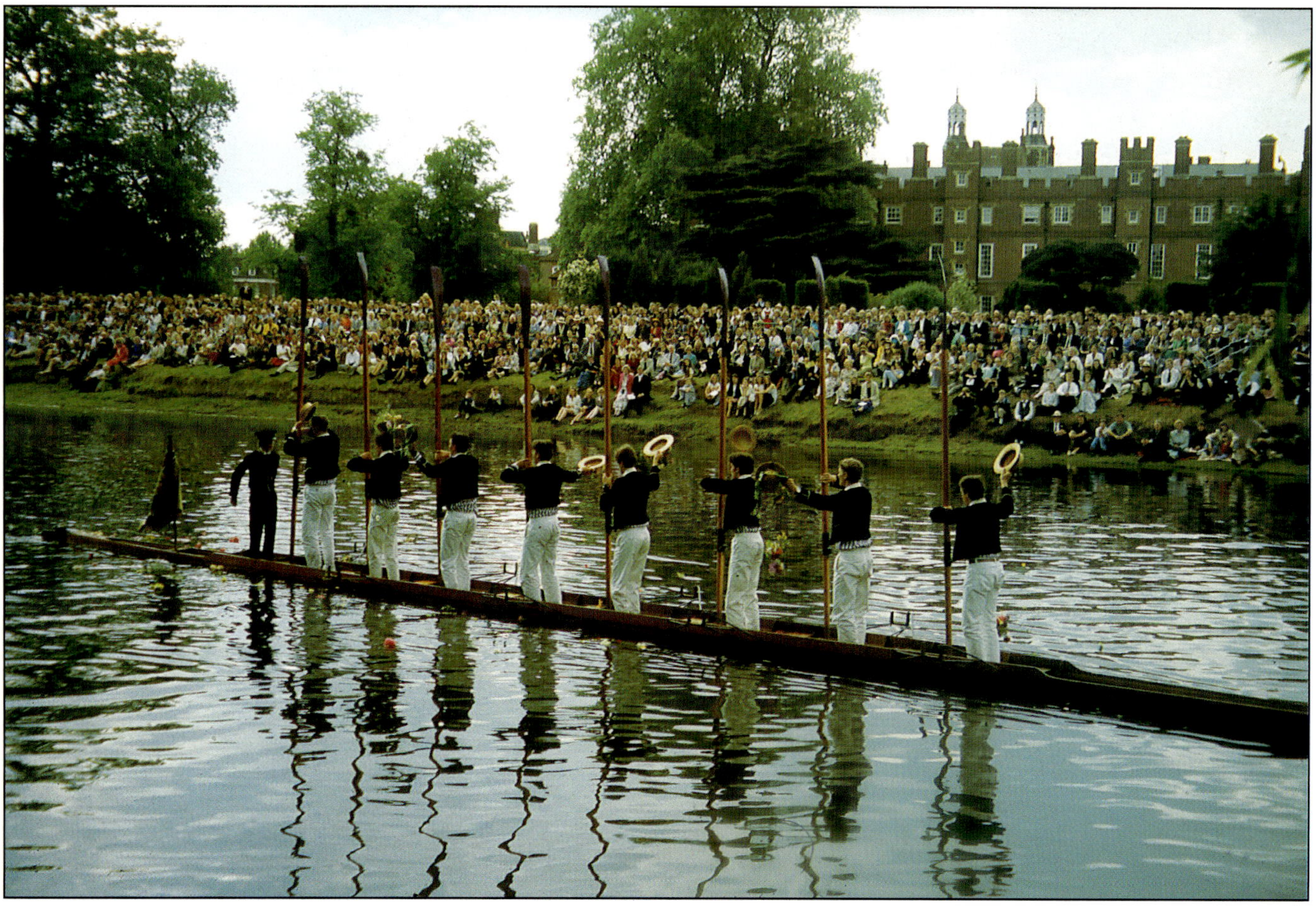

View from Romney Island

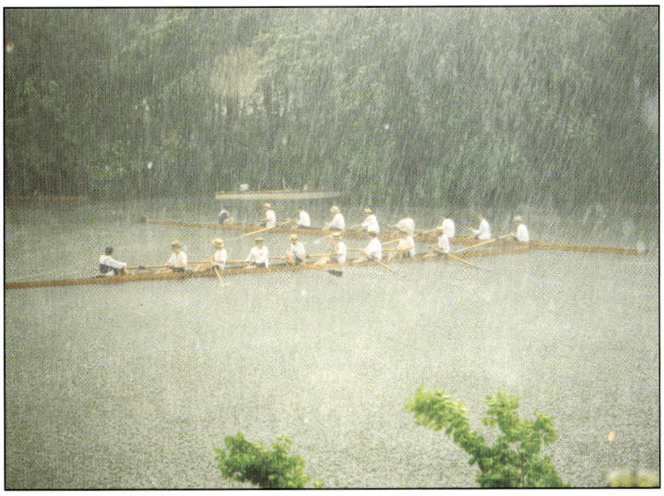

Rehearsal in a downpour

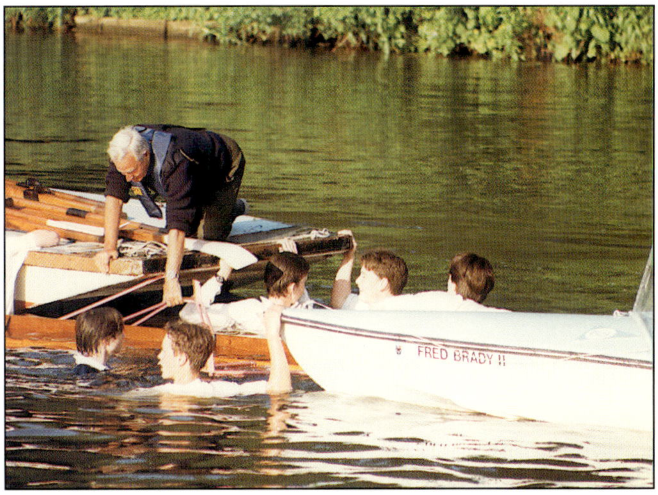

This crew shows the need for practice

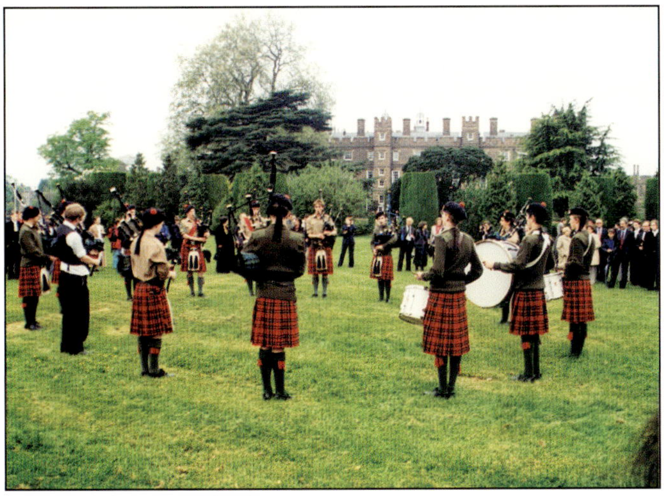

The Pipers attend the Procession of Boats

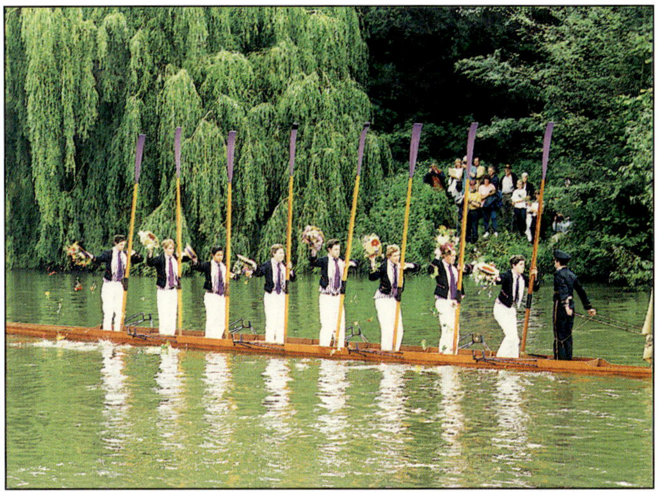

Oars aloft; crews stand, raise their oars and salute by raising their boaters

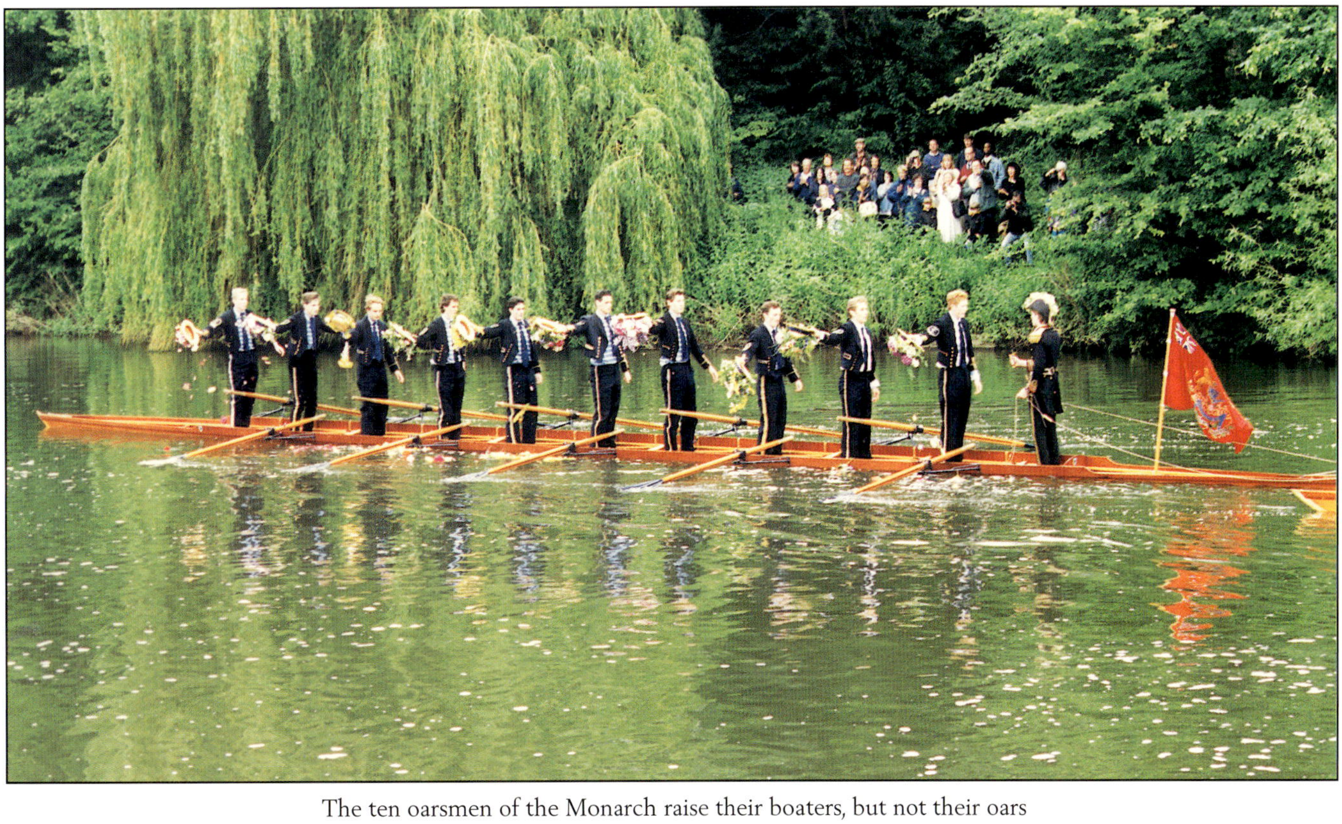

The ten oarsmen of the Monarch raise their boaters, but not their oars

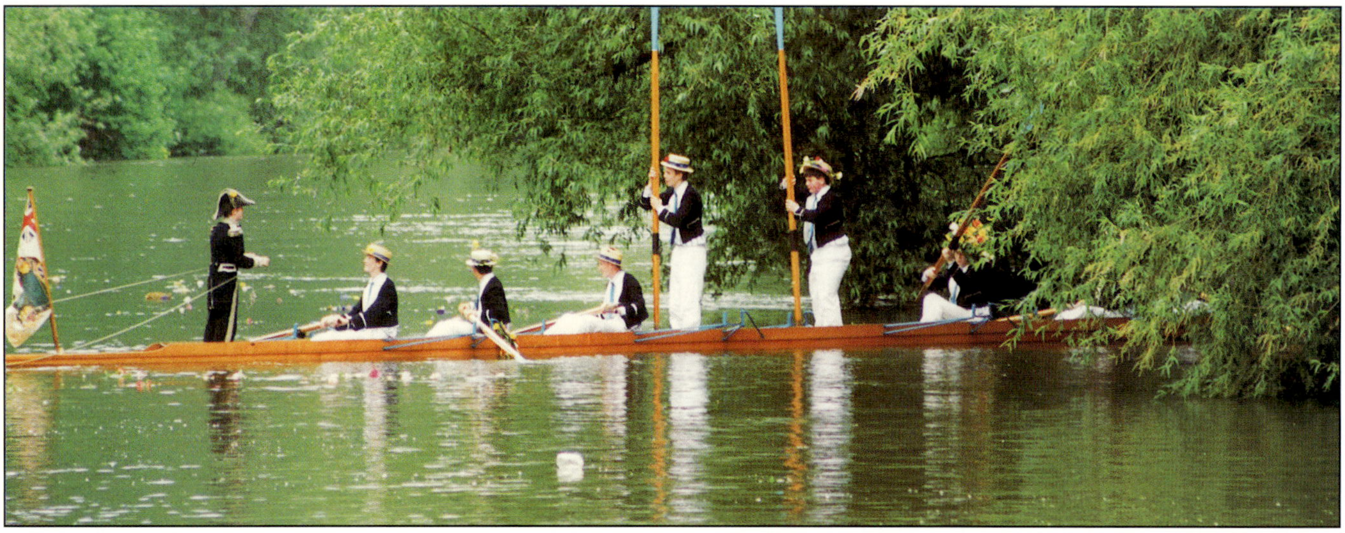

The cox has lost his sense of direction, it seems

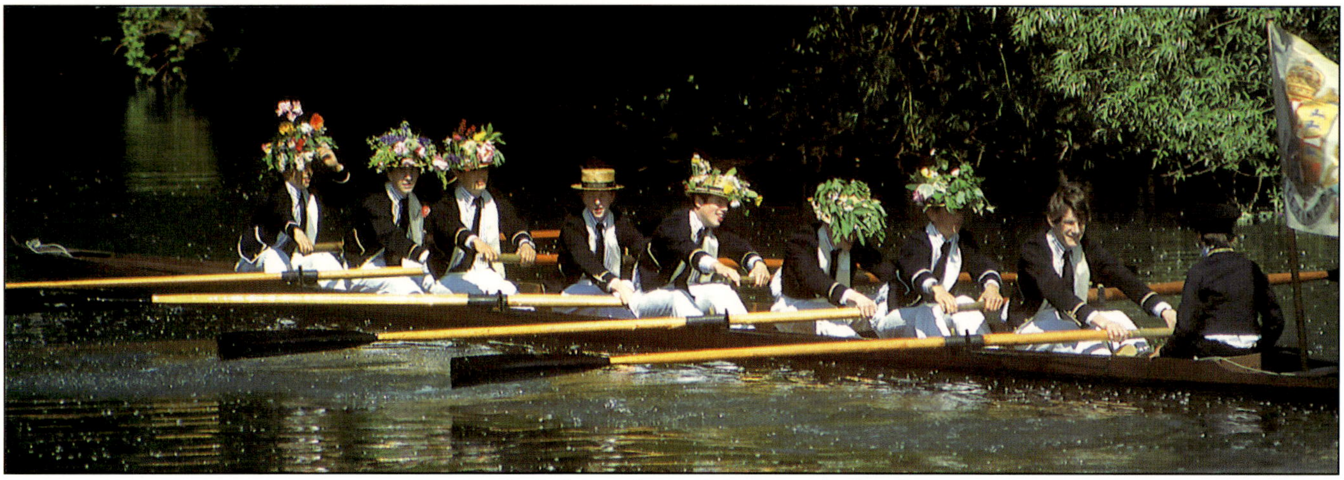

Sense of relief that *almost* all has passed off well

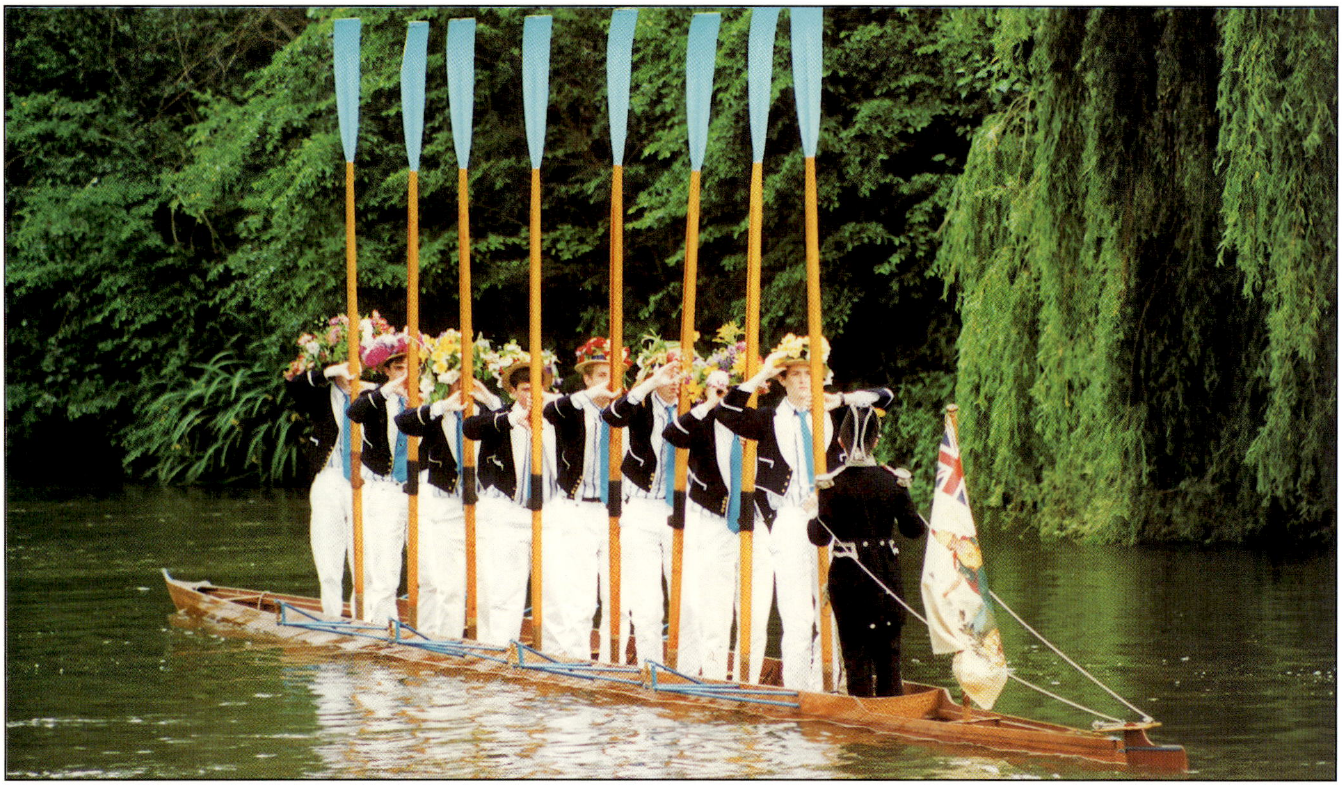

Crew and oars are safely vertical

St Andrew's Day

St Andrew's Day is the winter equivalent to the Fourth of June except that the celebrations last only until just before lunch, and it is the prelude to a week-end exeat. A number of sporting fixtures, concerts and exhibitions are arranged, but the focal point has long been the Wall Game fixture between Collegers and Oppidans. Few spectators understand the game, and the ball rarely emerges from the heaving mass of players positioned against the wall of College Field. Boy spectators often perch on the wall itself and look down on the sparring gladiators. If it is a cold day, parents are grateful for a glass of mulled wine with their son's House Master. But soon it is 12.30pm, and they depart with their sons for the week-end exeat.

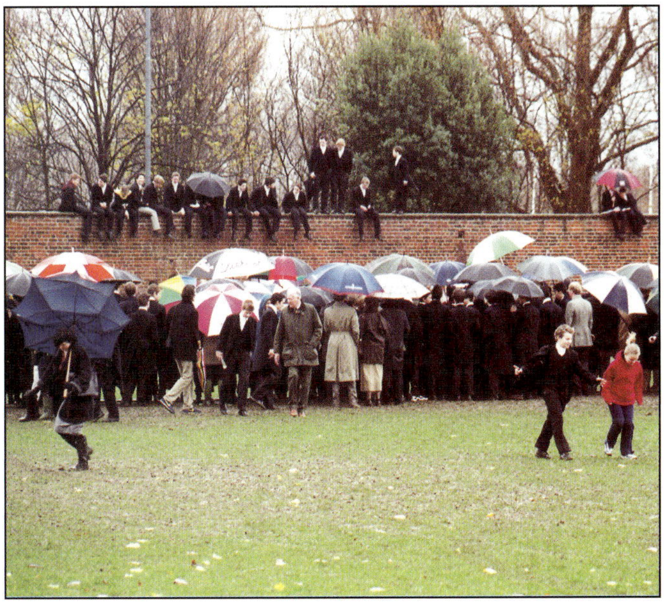

Rain does not deter the hardy spectators

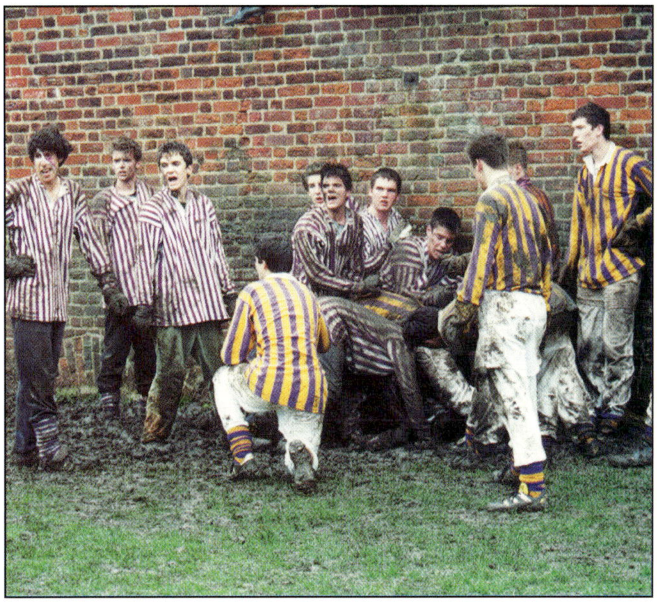

Appealing to the umpire

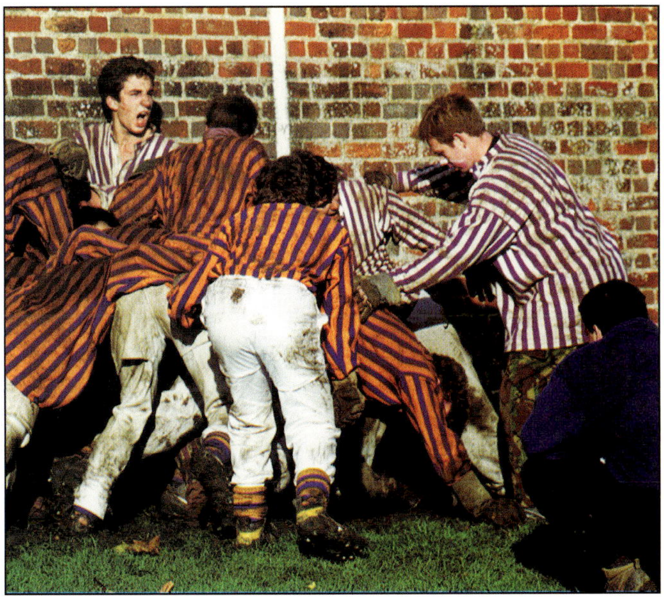

It can be painful

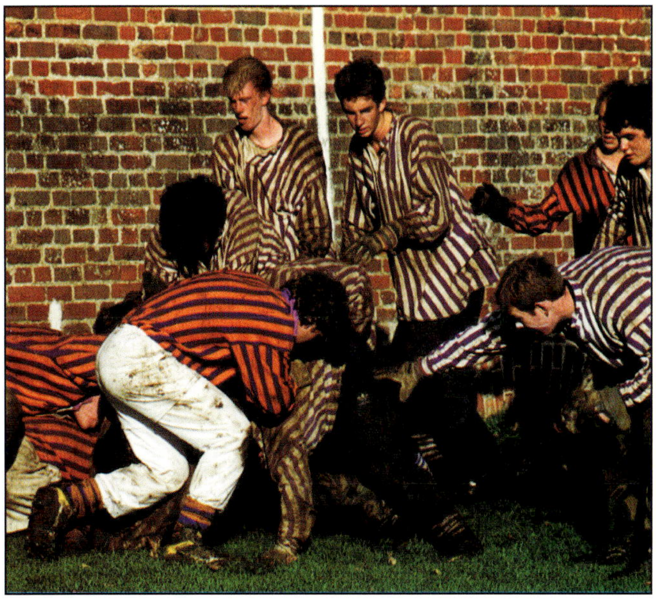

College on the defensive

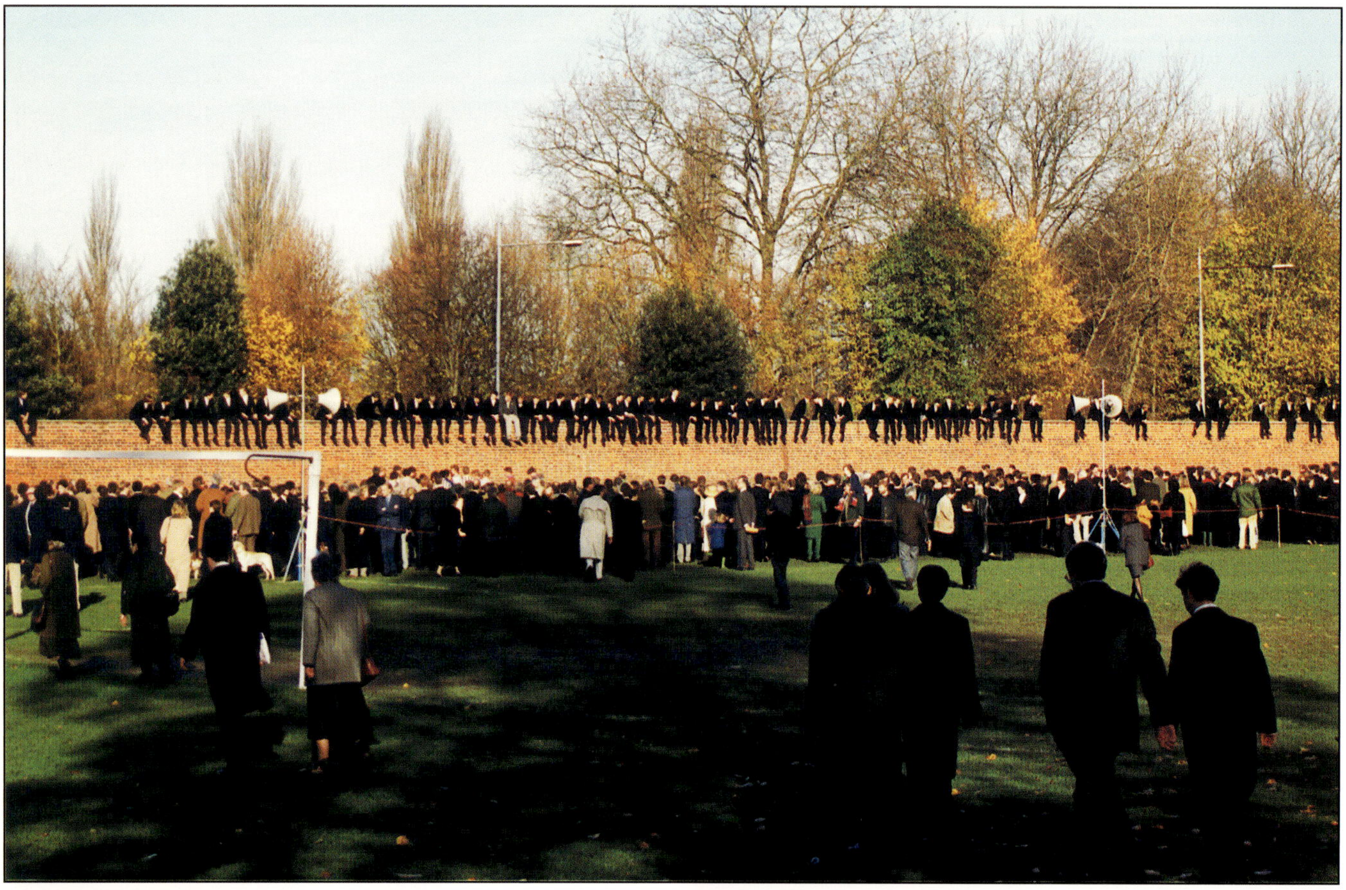

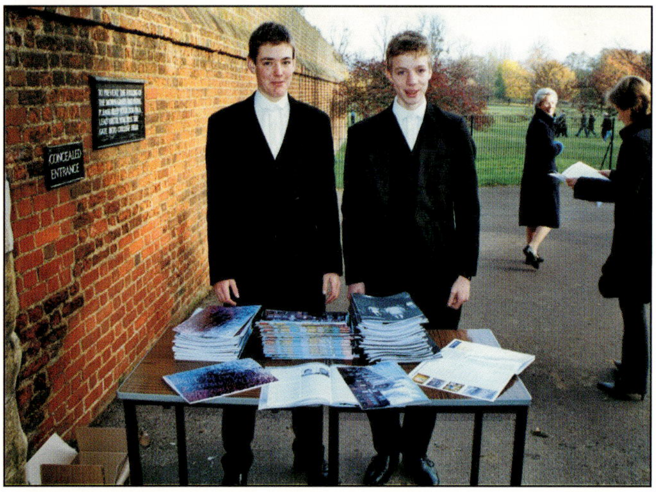

Magazines for sale, including the St Andrew's Day Chronicle

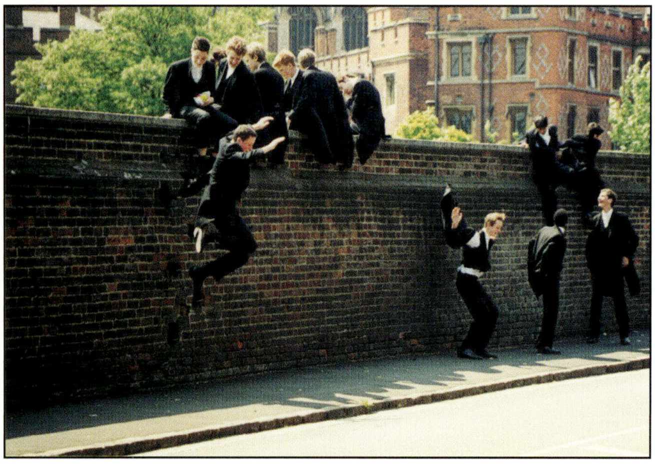

Game over!

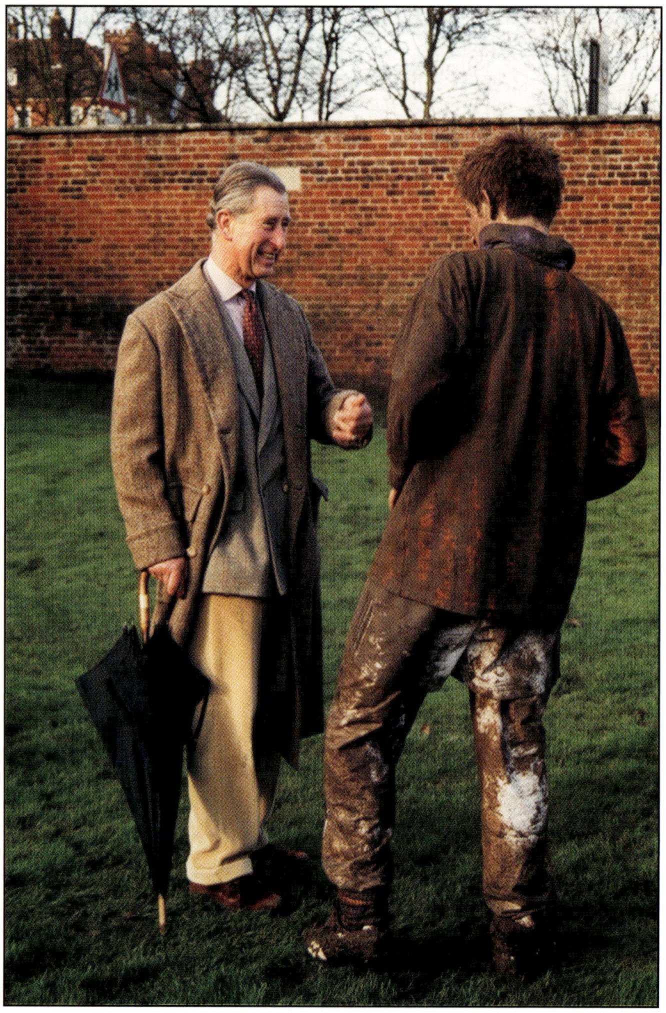

Paternal interest in the Wall Game

A Very Special Guest

A frequent and welcome guest at Eton was Her Majesty Queen Elizabeth, The Queen Mother. She clearly enjoyed meeting all members of the community. Whether it was attending Chapel or a play, unveiling a plaque or a bust, or planting a tree, she was in her element. On each occasion after her departure all would agree that they had been cheered by her radiance and charm.

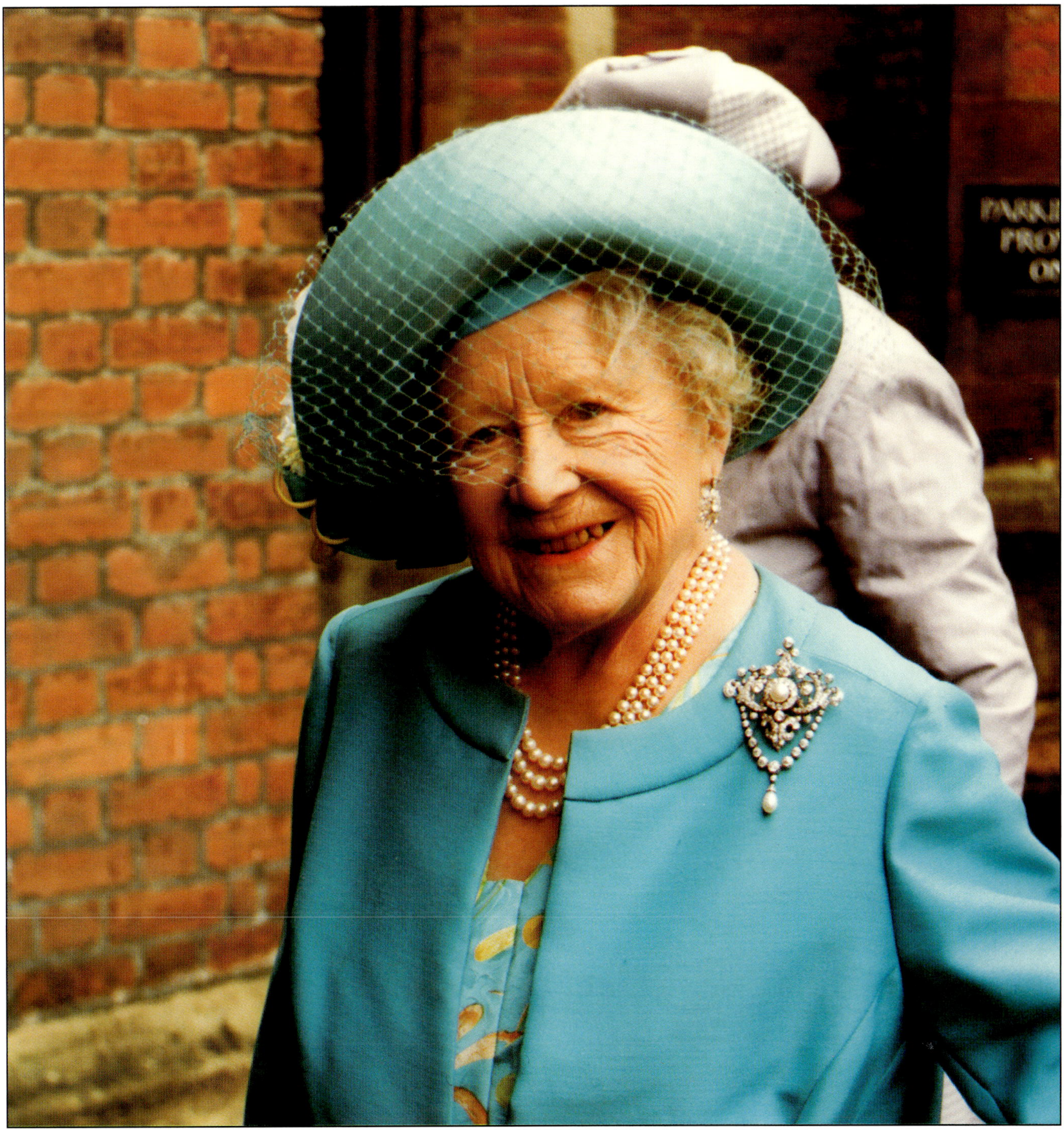

On her way to the Provost's Lodge

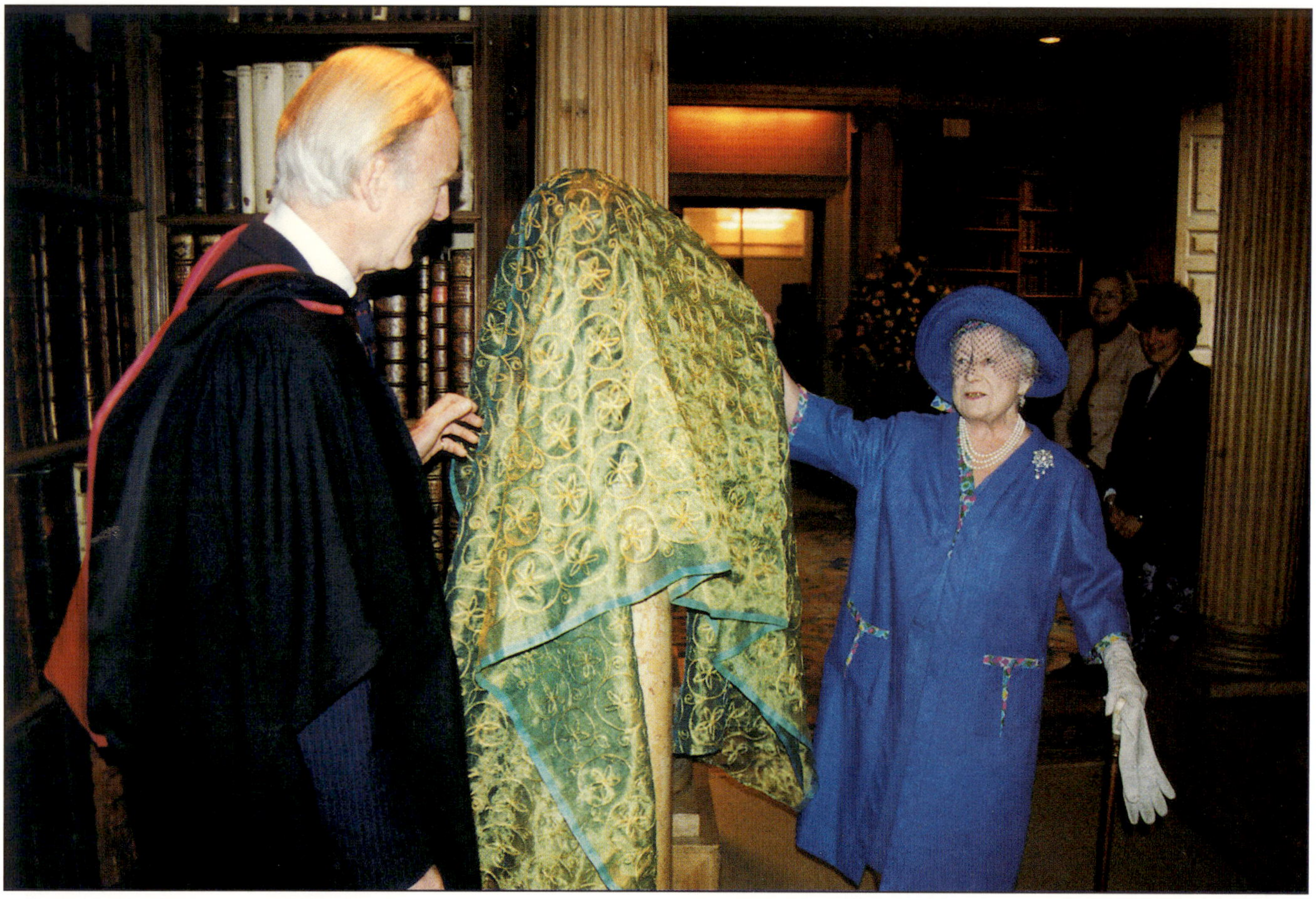

After a short speech Her Majesty The Queen Mother prepares to unveil a bust of Sir Alec Douglas-Home in College Library

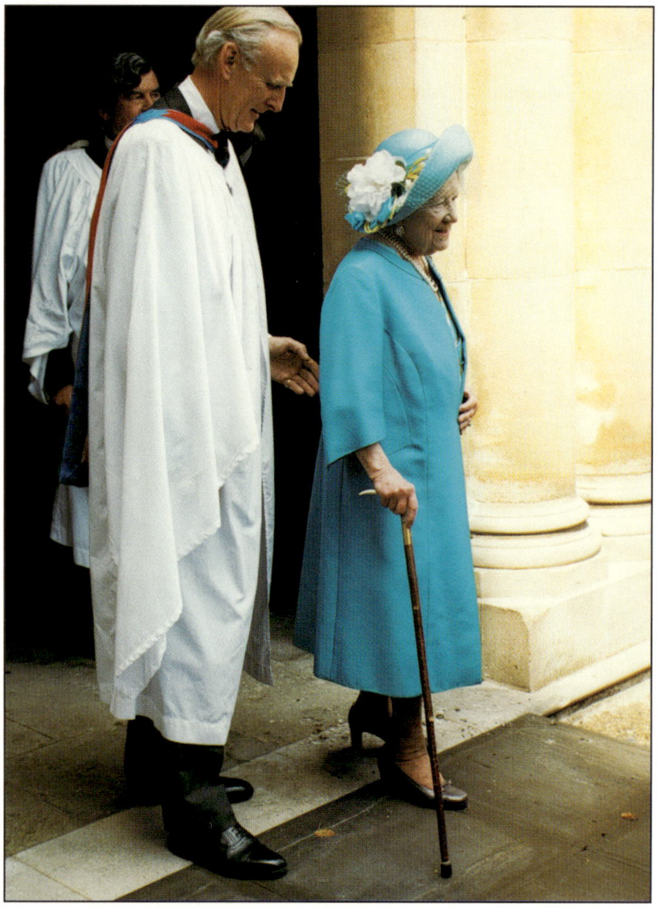

Leaving College Chapel, accompanied by the Provost, Sir Antony Acland and Vice-Provost, Tim Card

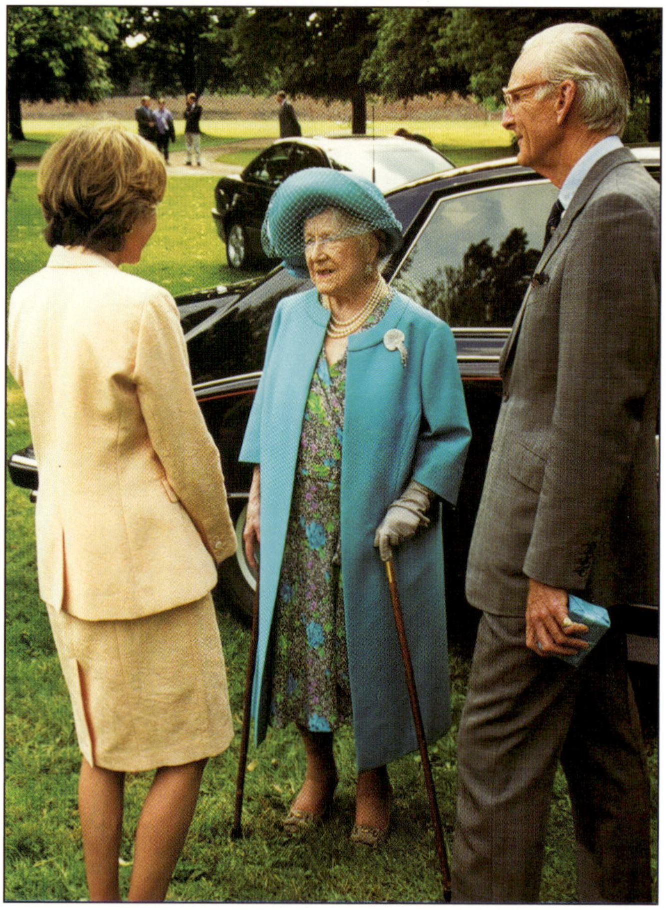

Arriving in the playing fields and welcomed by Sir Antony and Lady Acland shortly before her 100th birthday

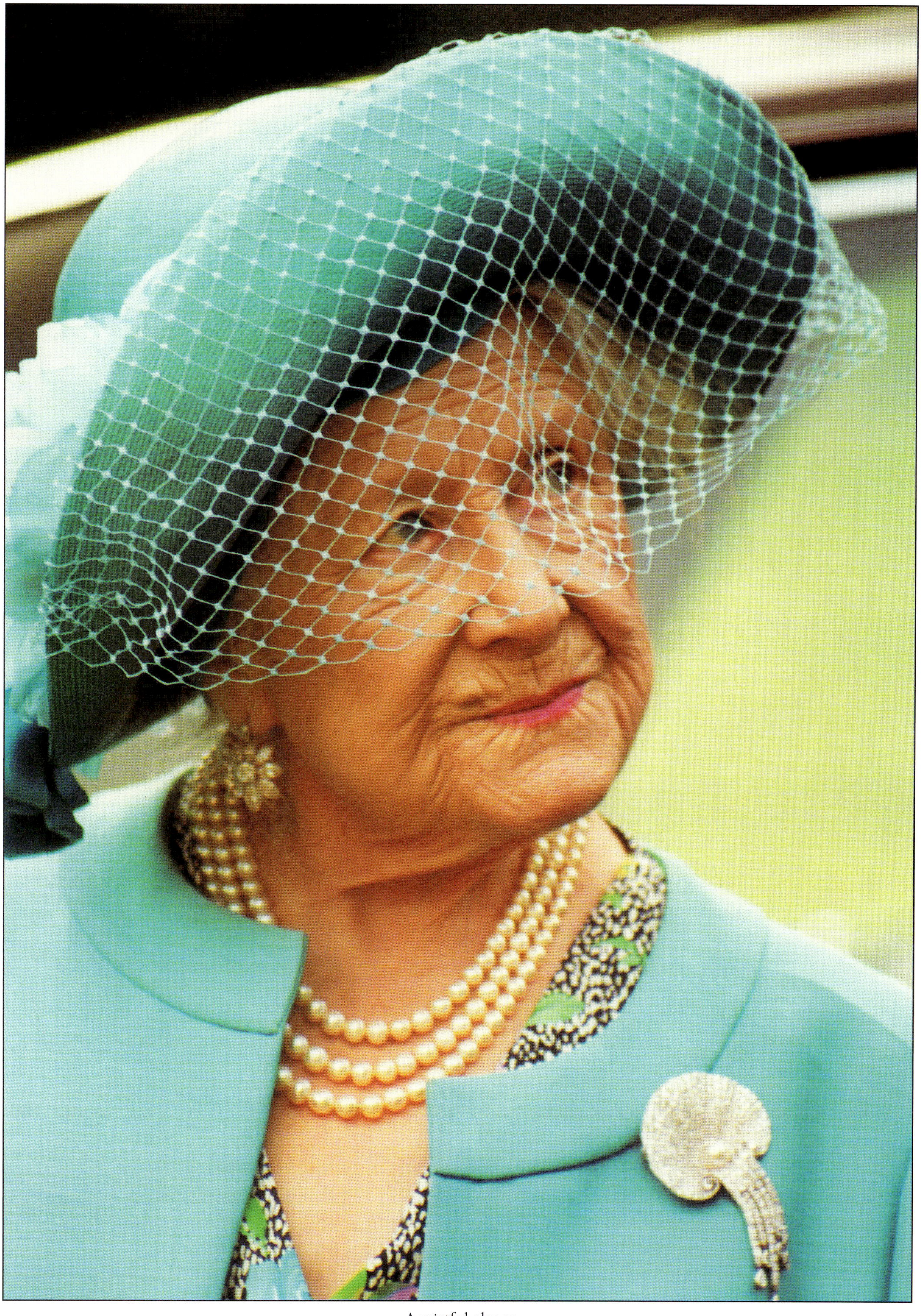

A wistful glance

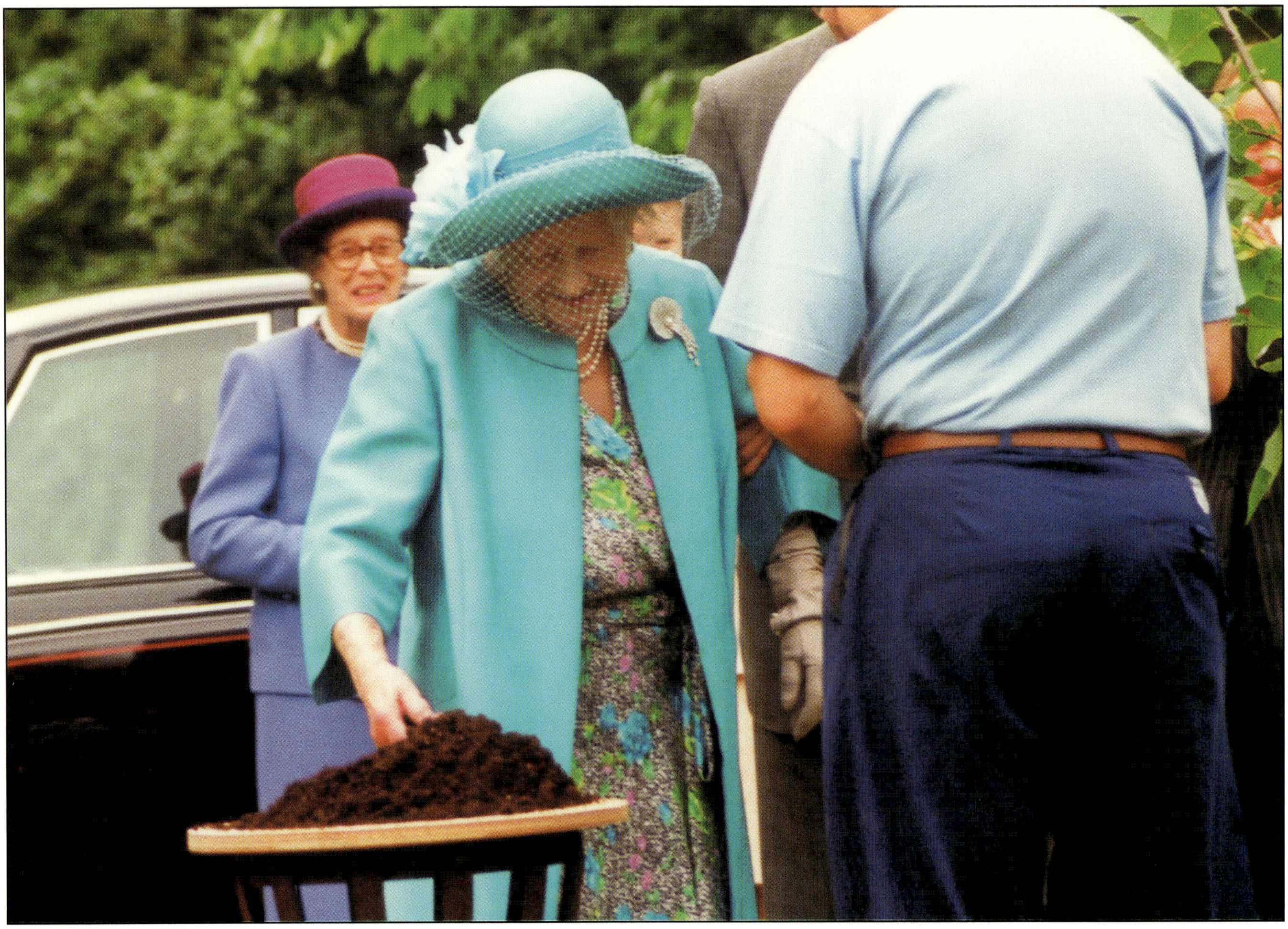

Planting a tulip tree

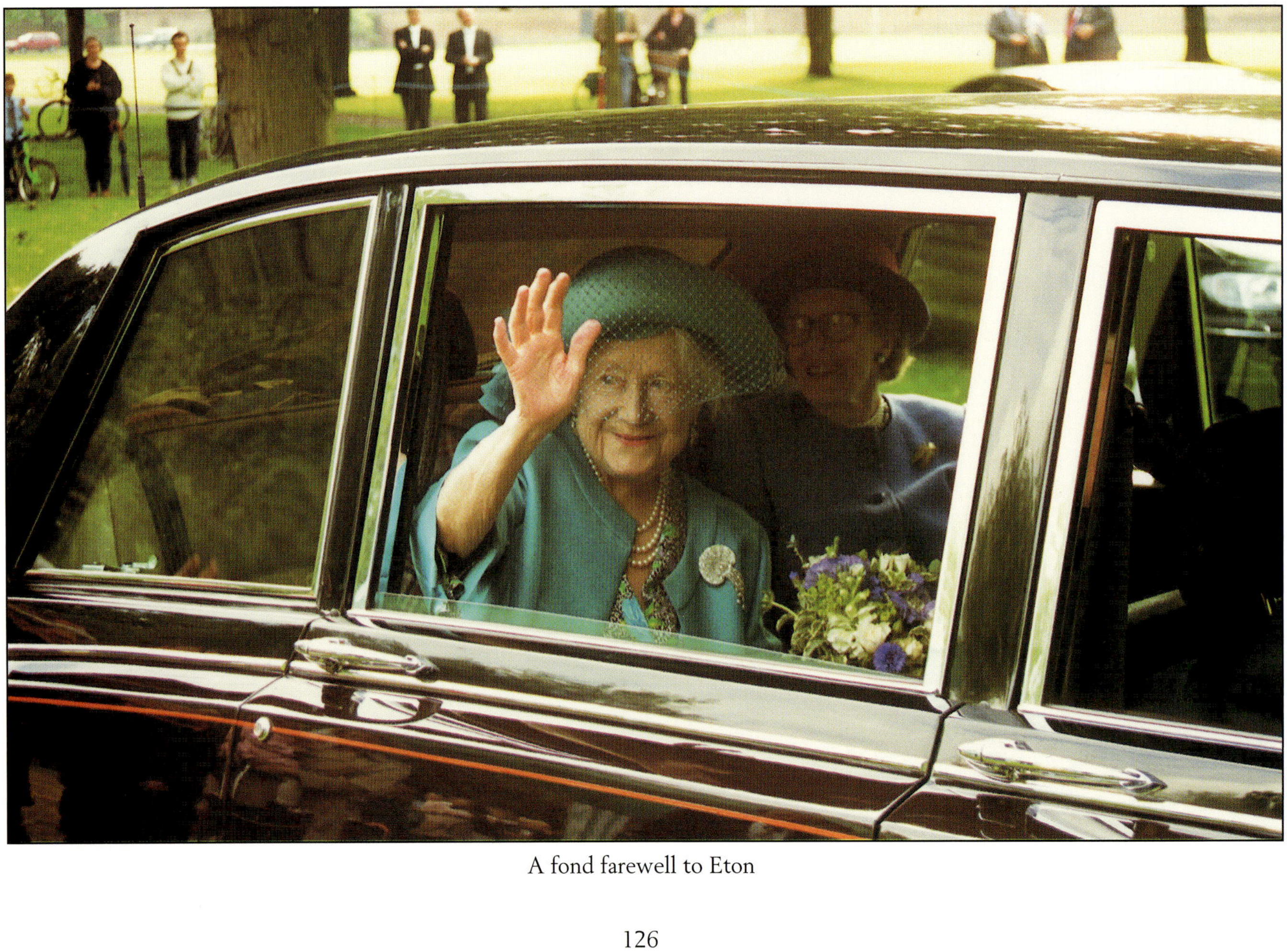

A fond farewell to Eton

Miscellaneous

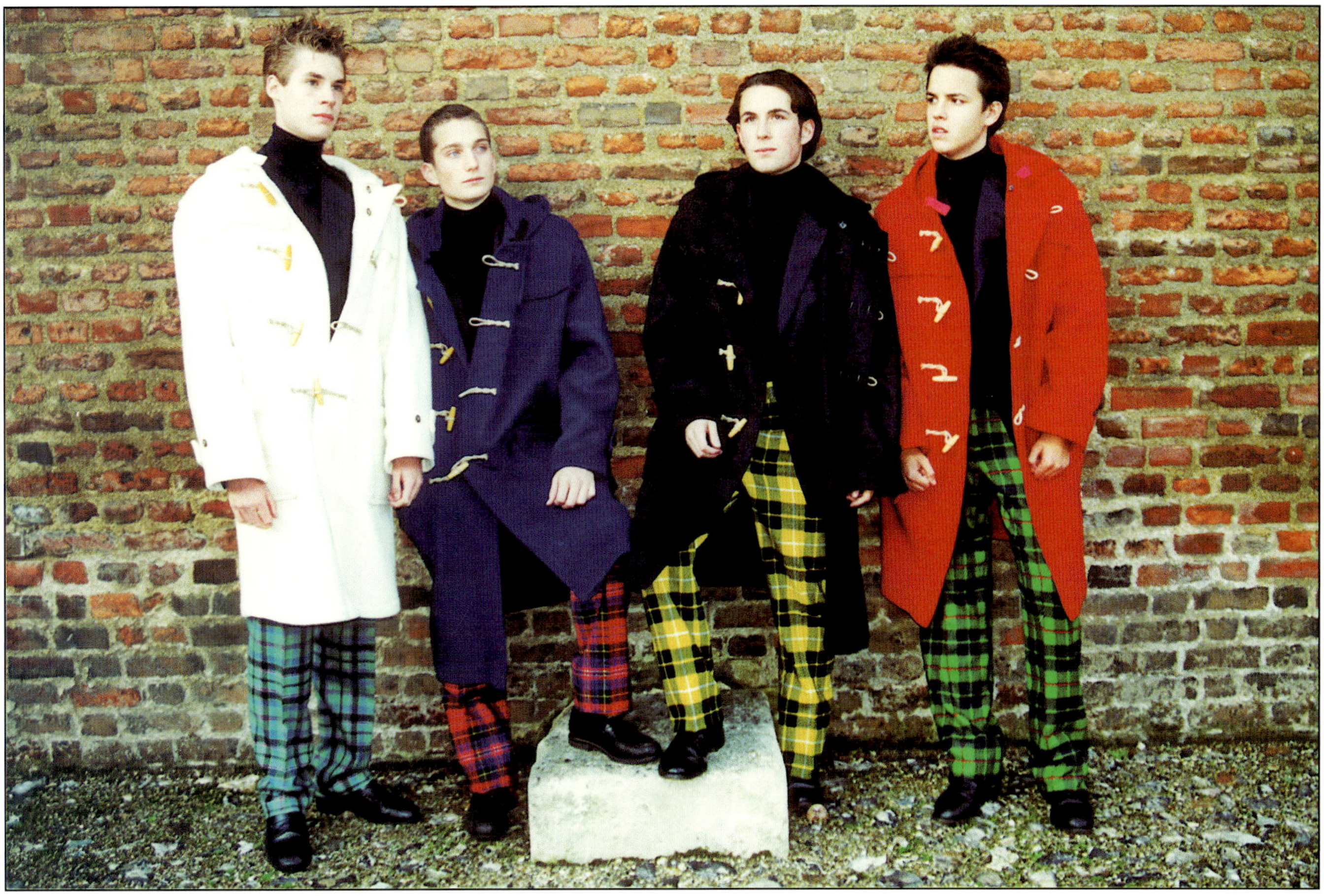

Fashion Parade

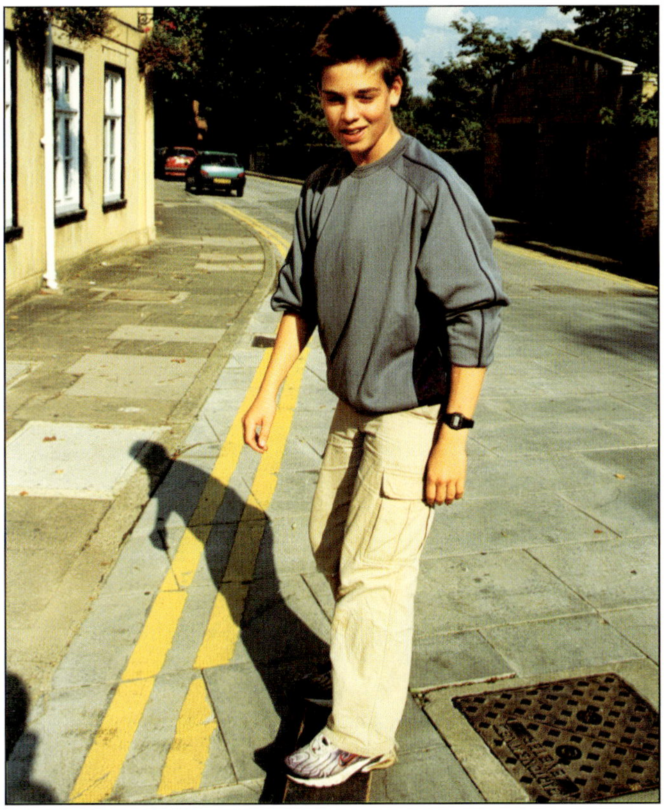

Skateboarding

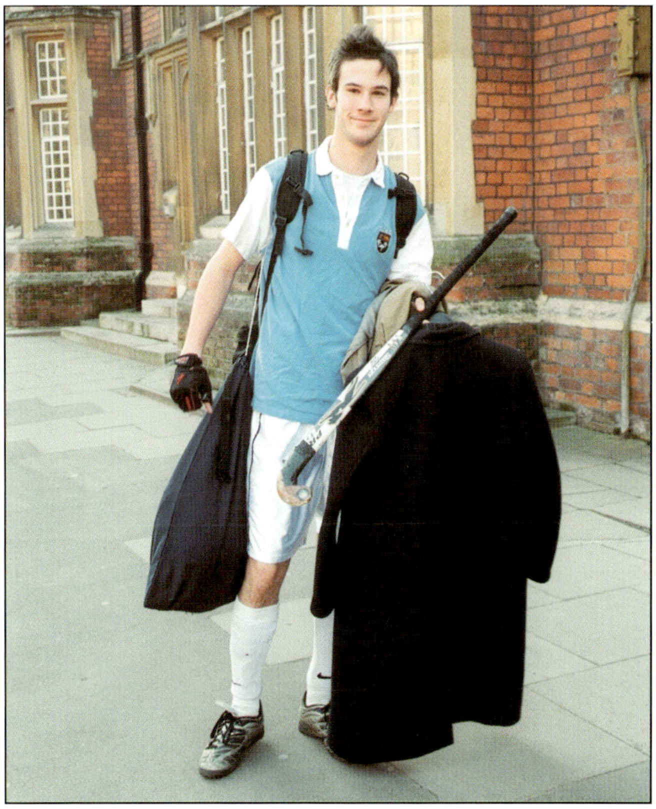

Prepared for any occasion

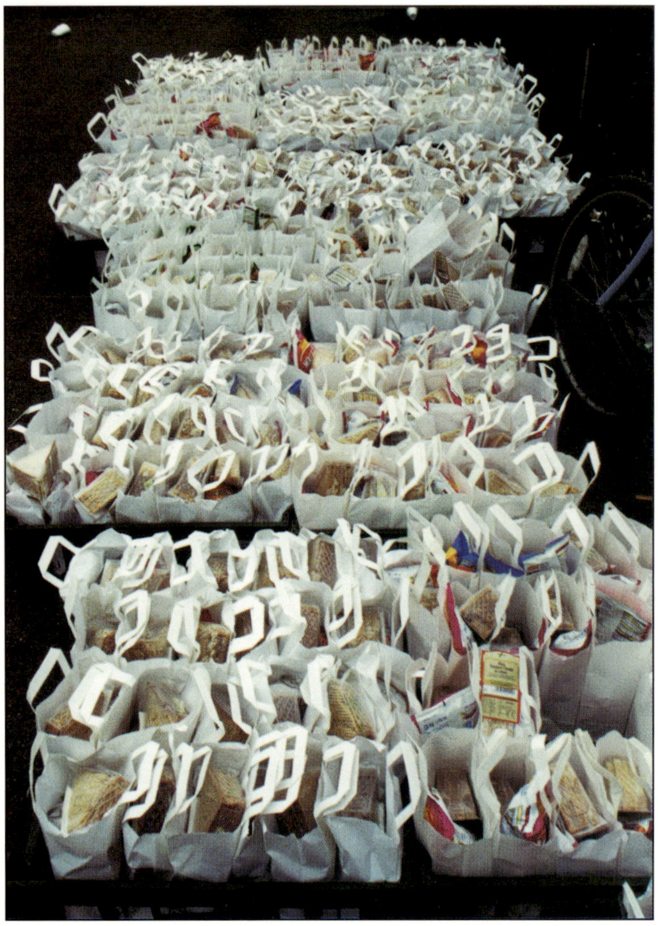

Packed lunches

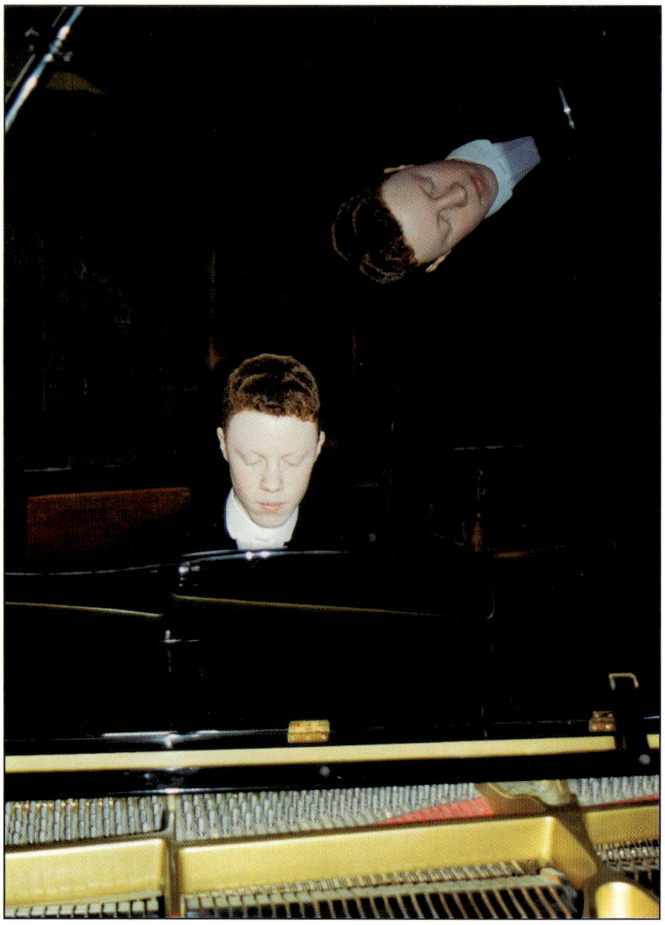

Reflective music

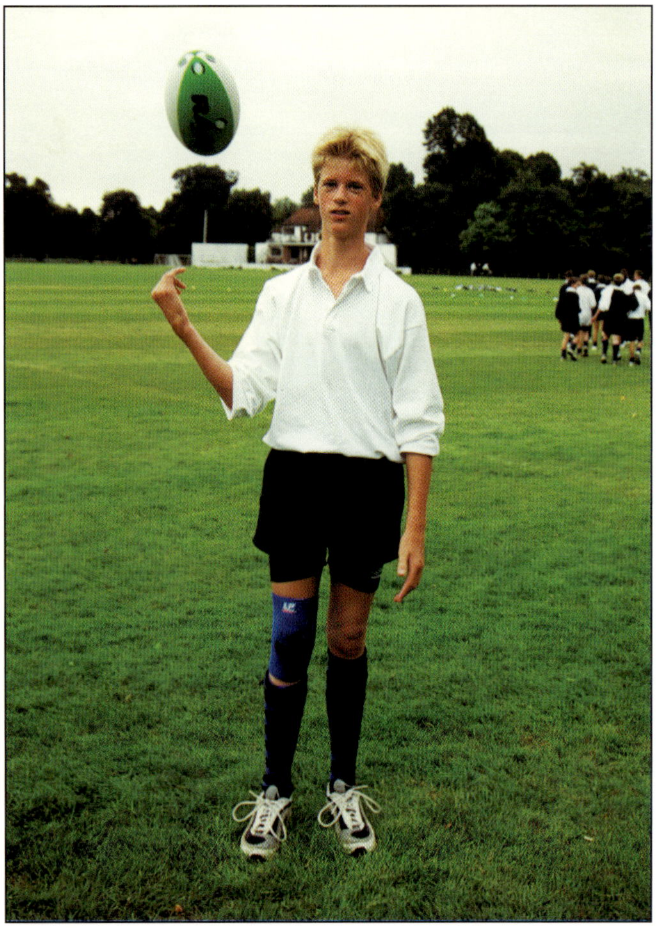

It's a toss up

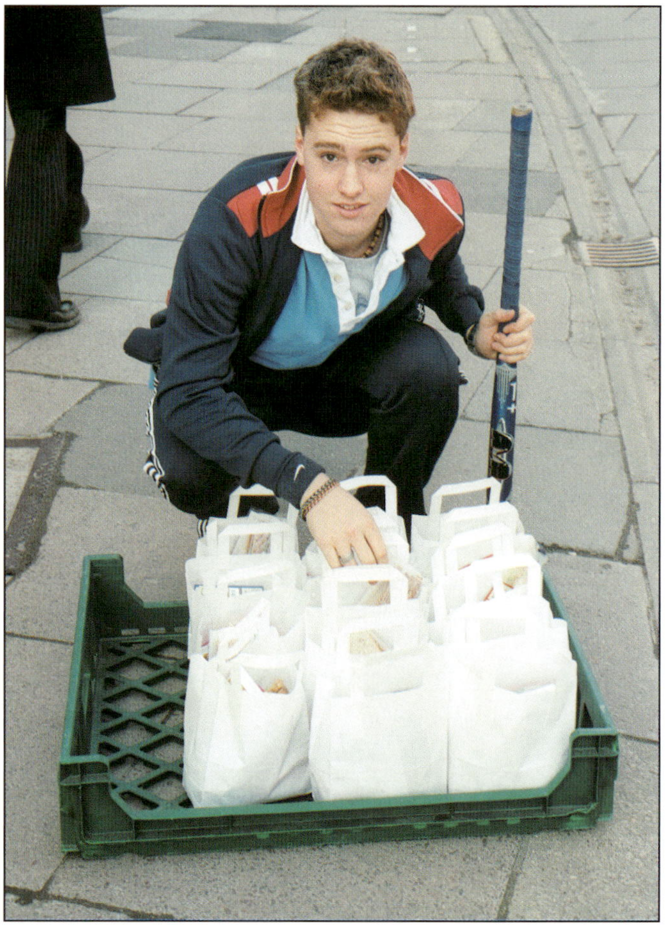

Where's the Mars Bar?

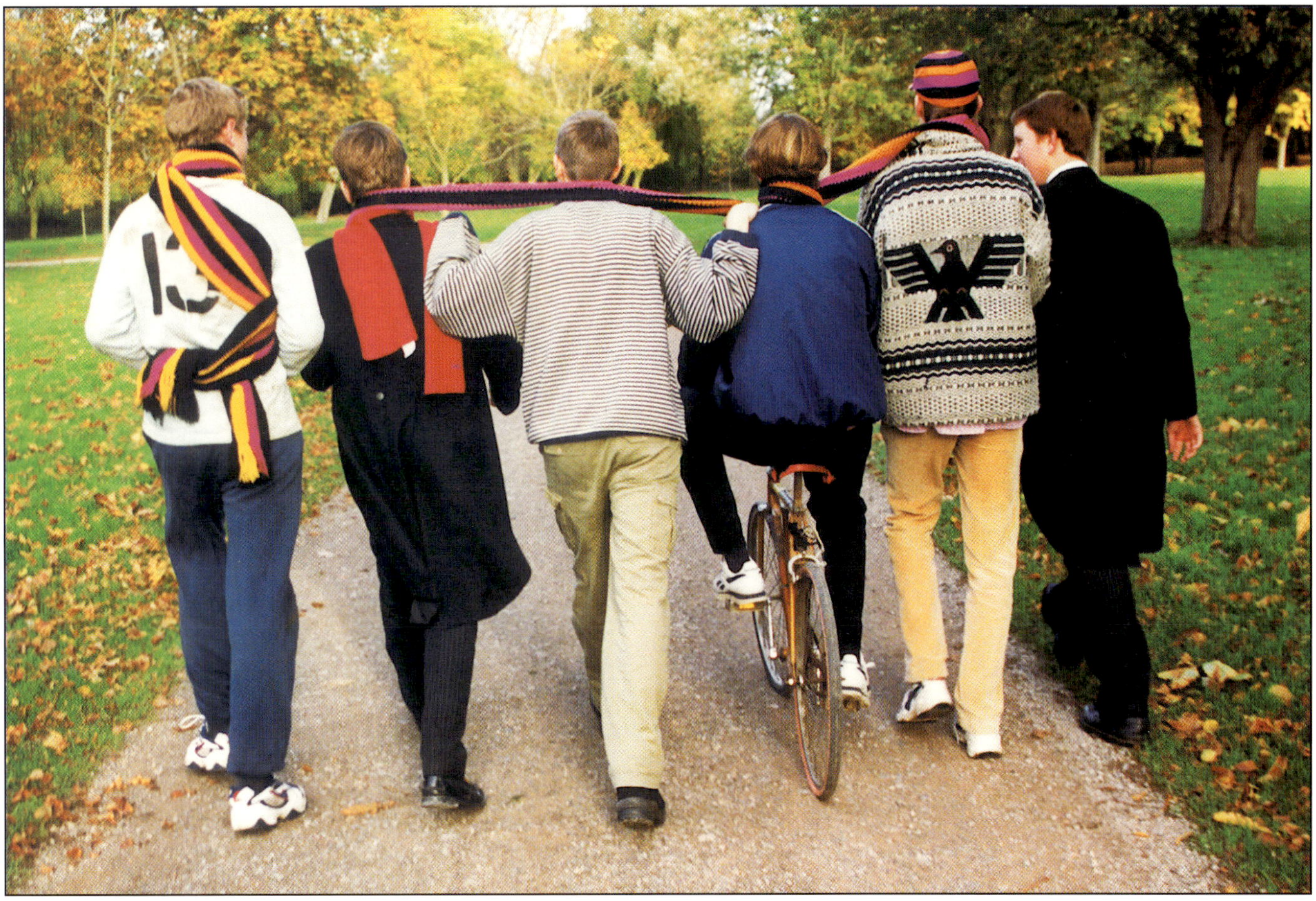

Supporting the House Side

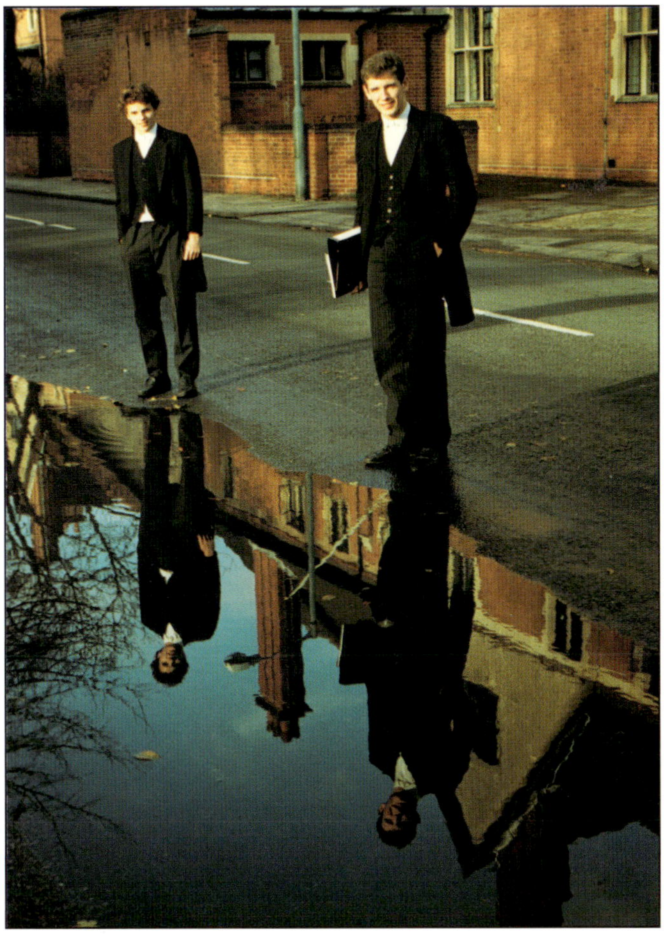

After the storm

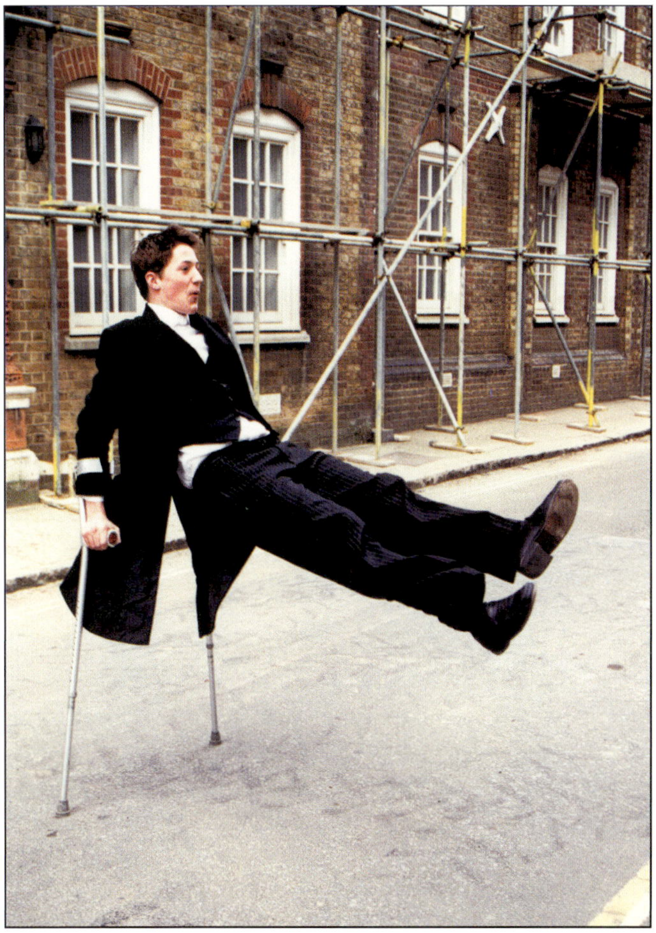

Well on the road to recovery

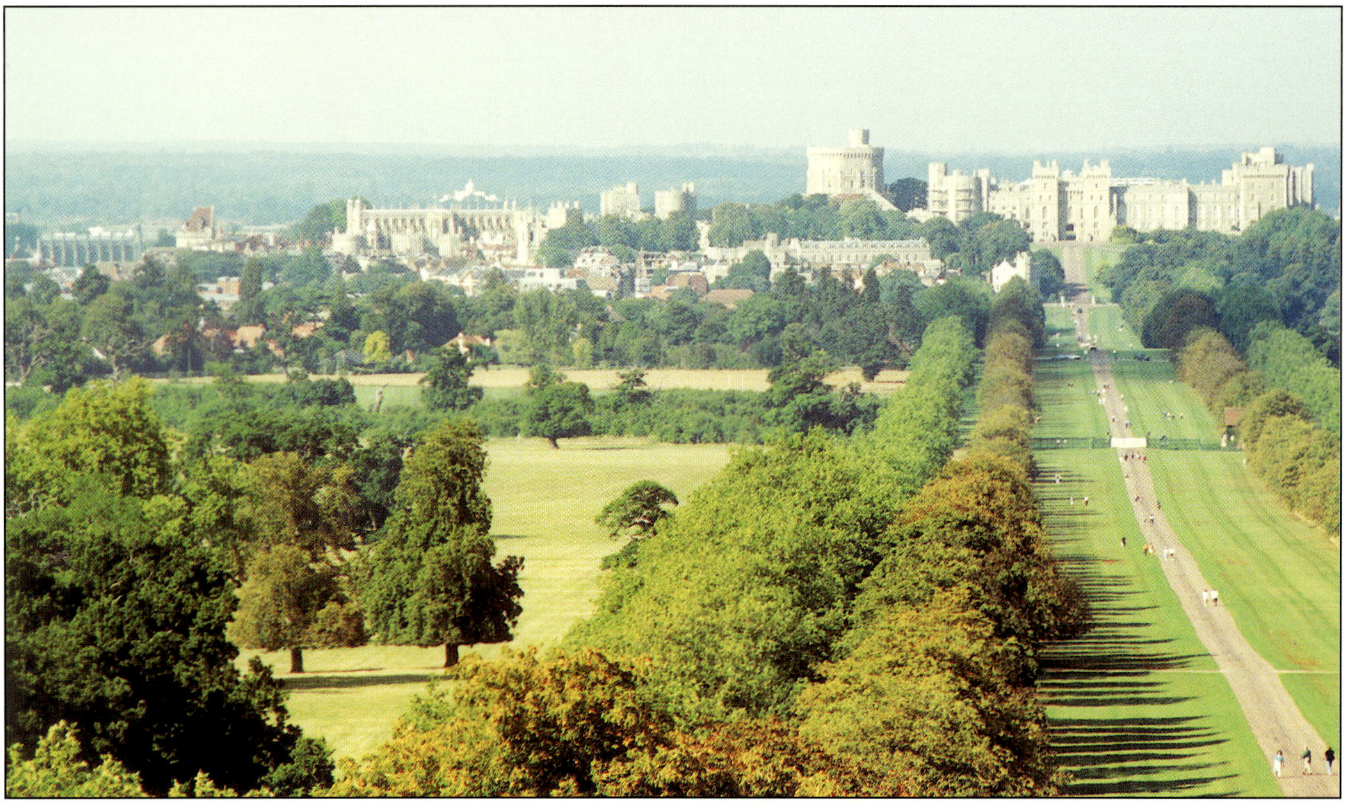

From left to right: Eton College Chapel, St George's Chapel, Windsor Castle

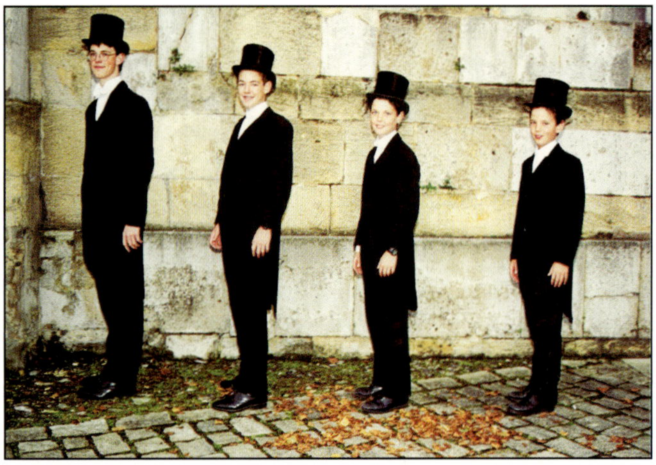

Four brothers max, ma, mi, min

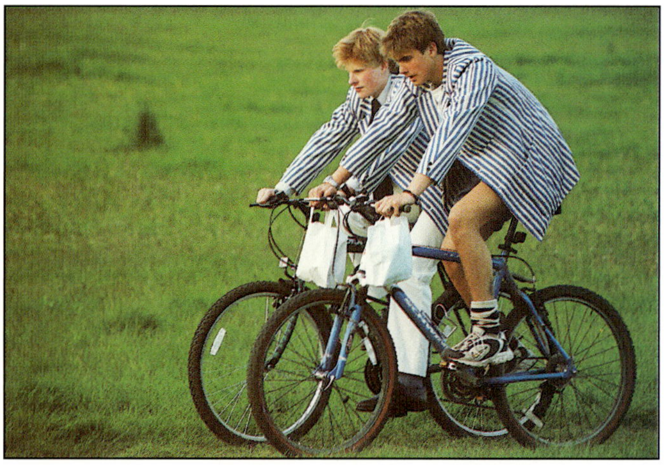

Boy officials at the Bumping IVs

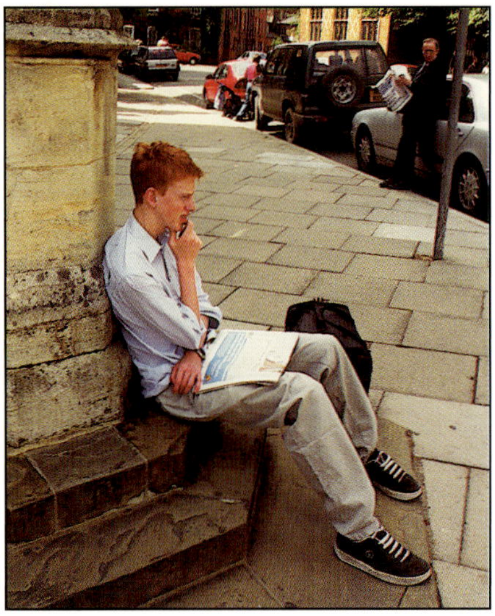

Waiting for parents at the Burning Bush

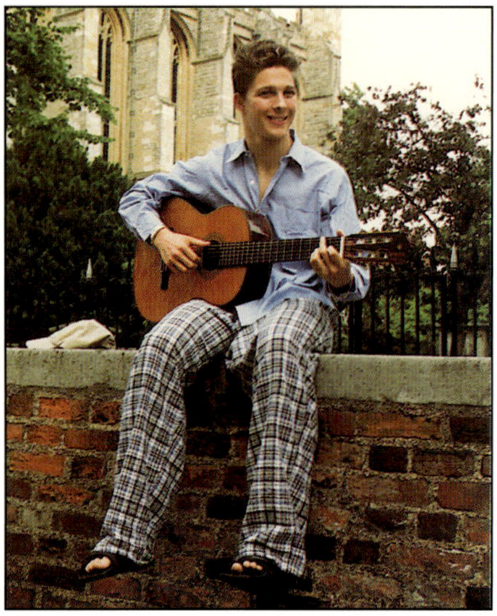

Keen guitarist

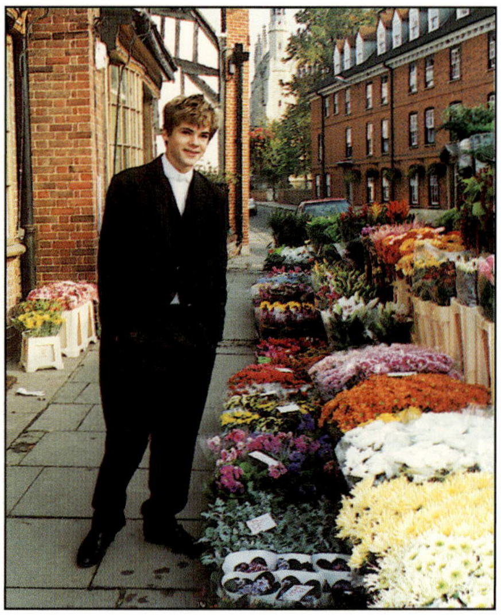

French market

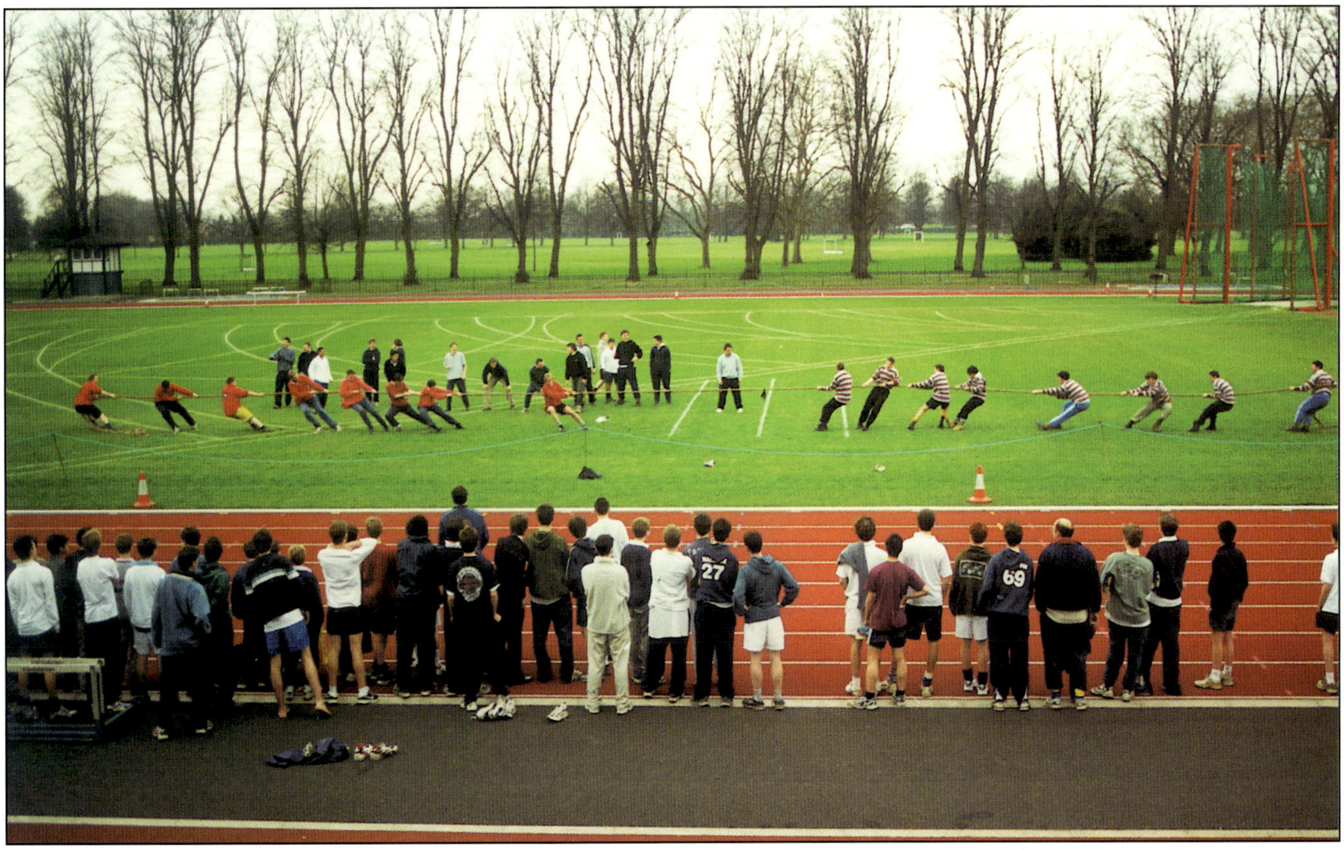

Tug-of-war

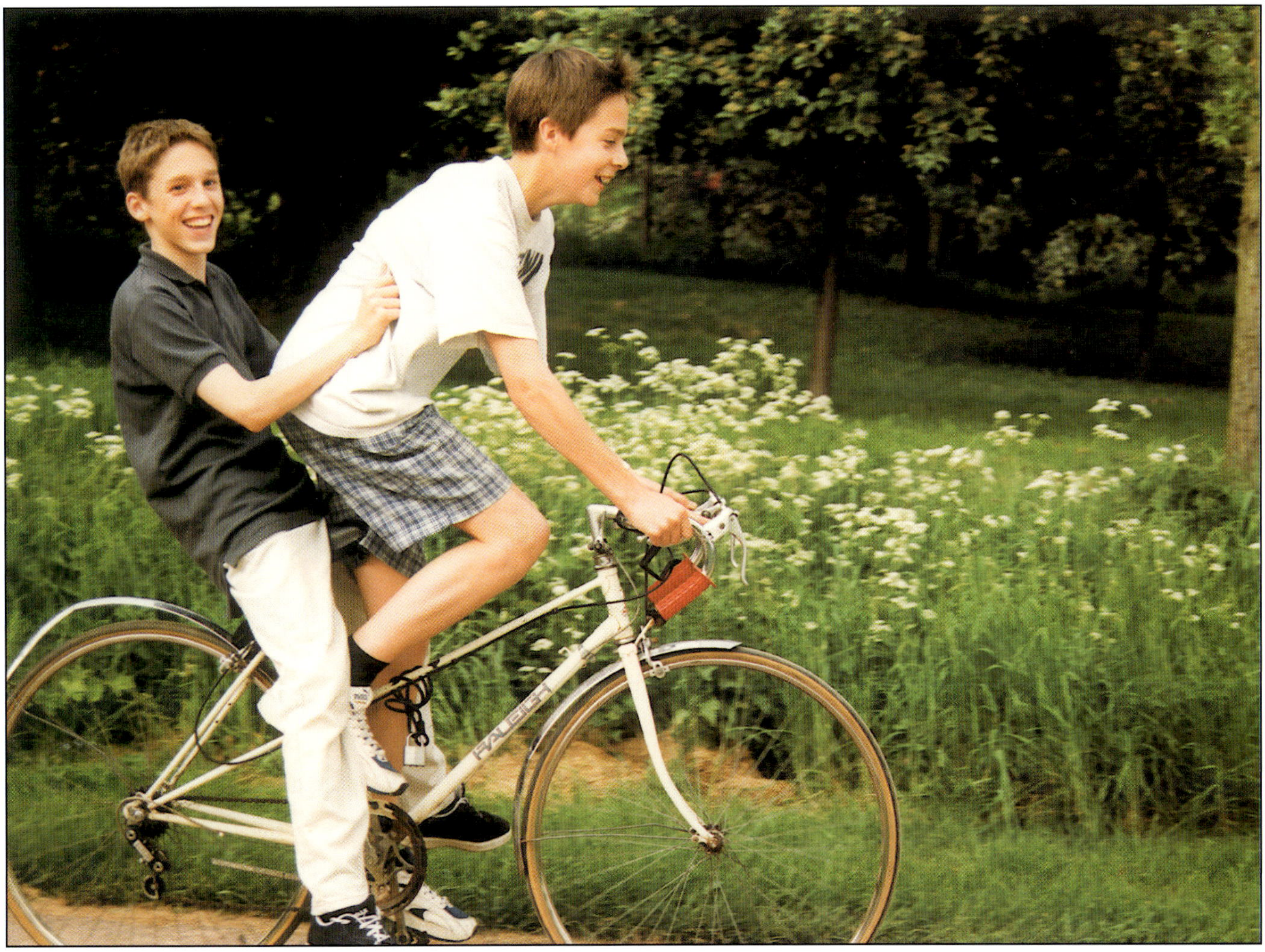

Hitching a lift on a bicycle made for one

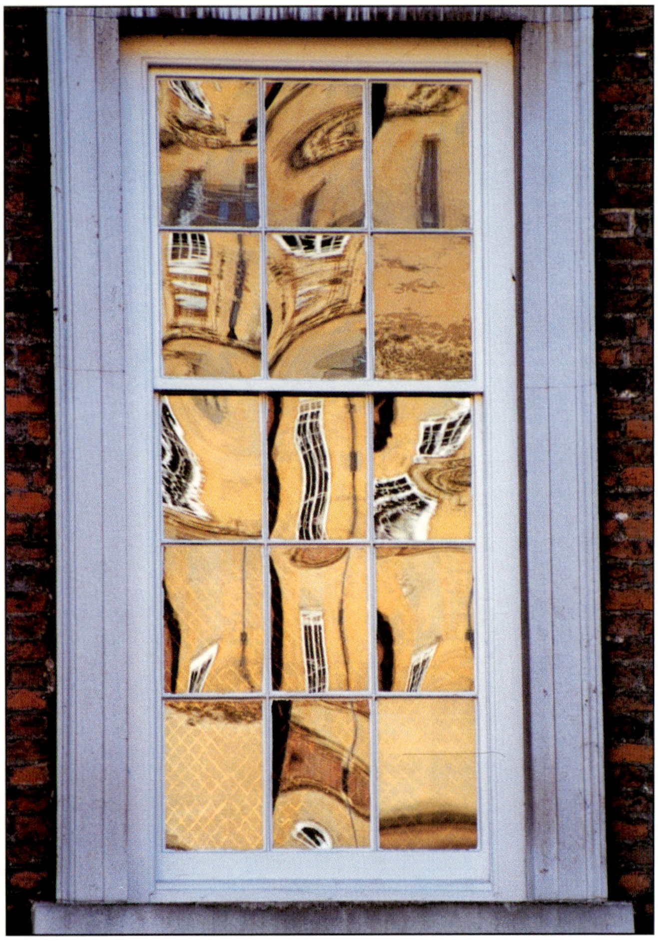

Window of College Library

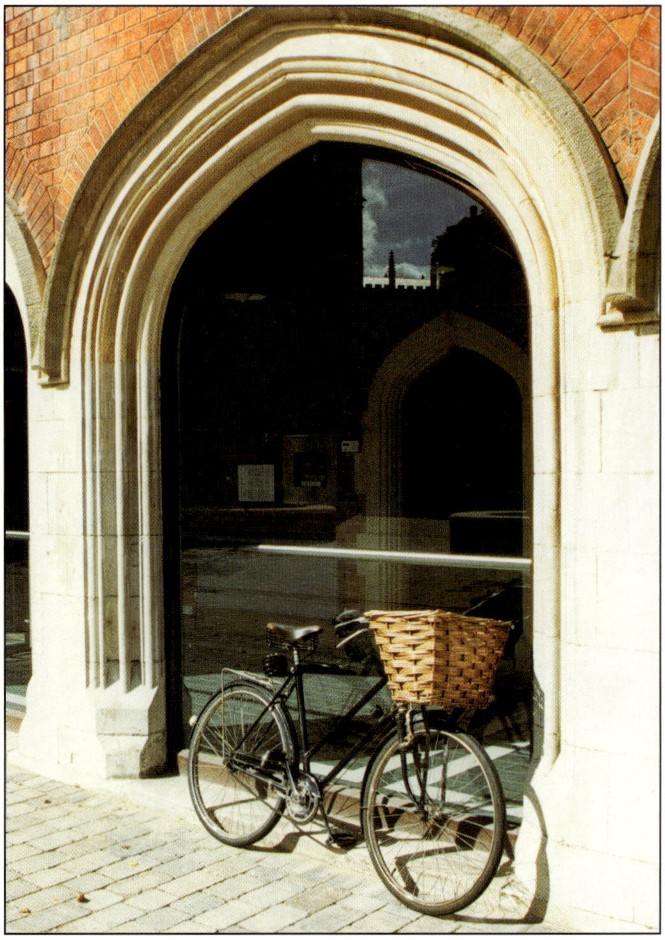

Glassed-in arcading of the Maths Department

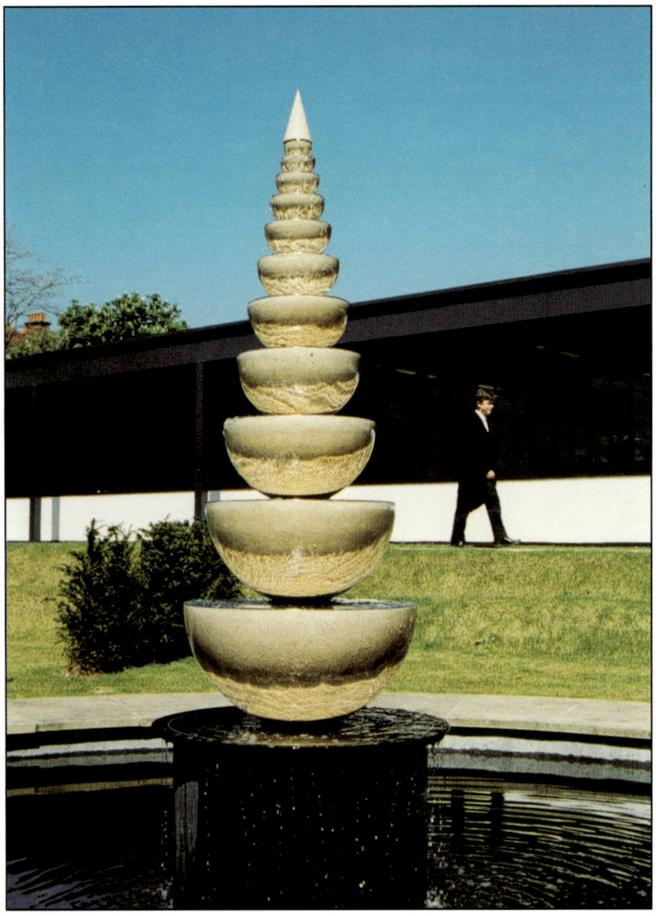

Fountain presented by Vice-Provost, Tim Card

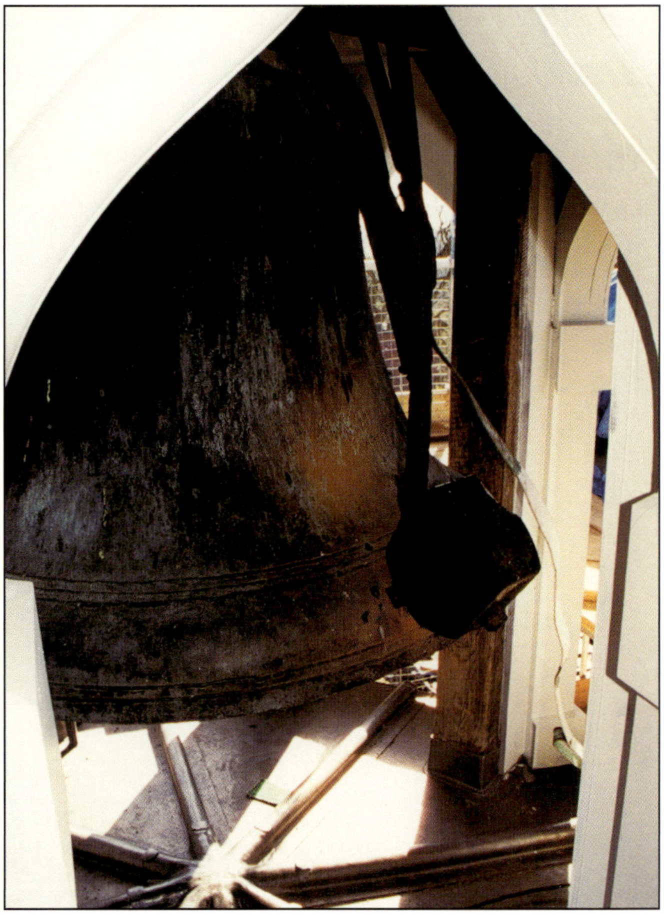

The bell on Lupton's Tower

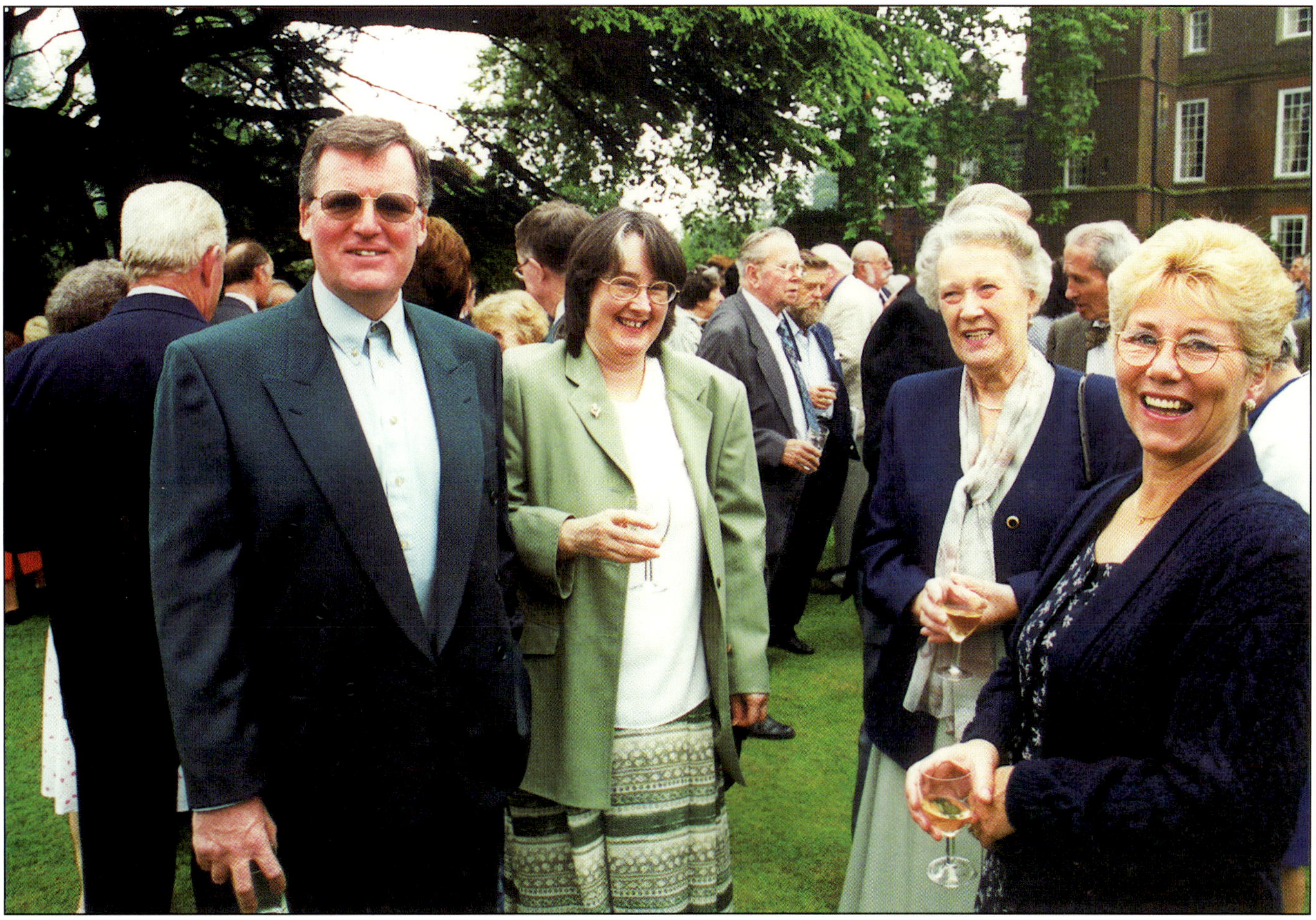

Party for the domestic staff

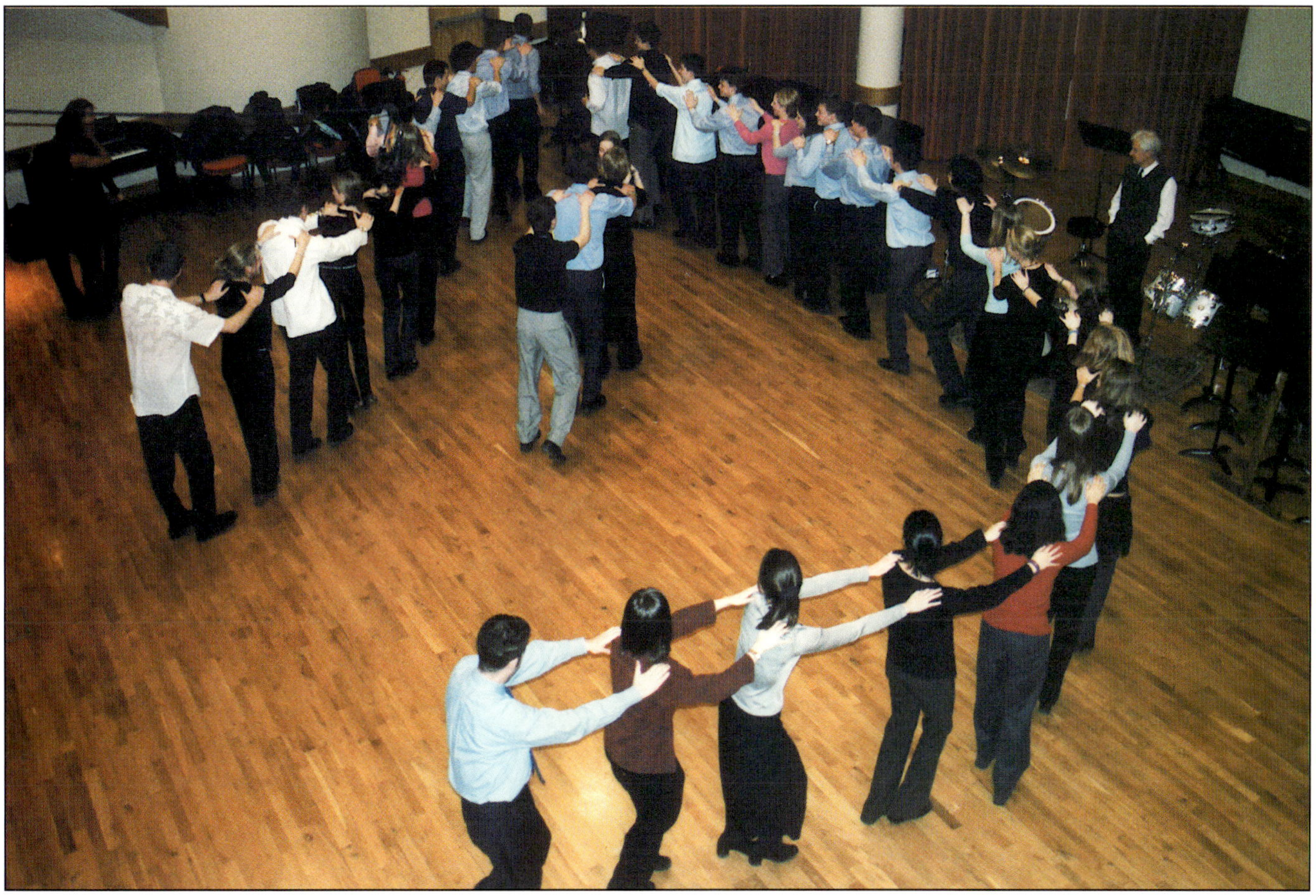

Spanish evening

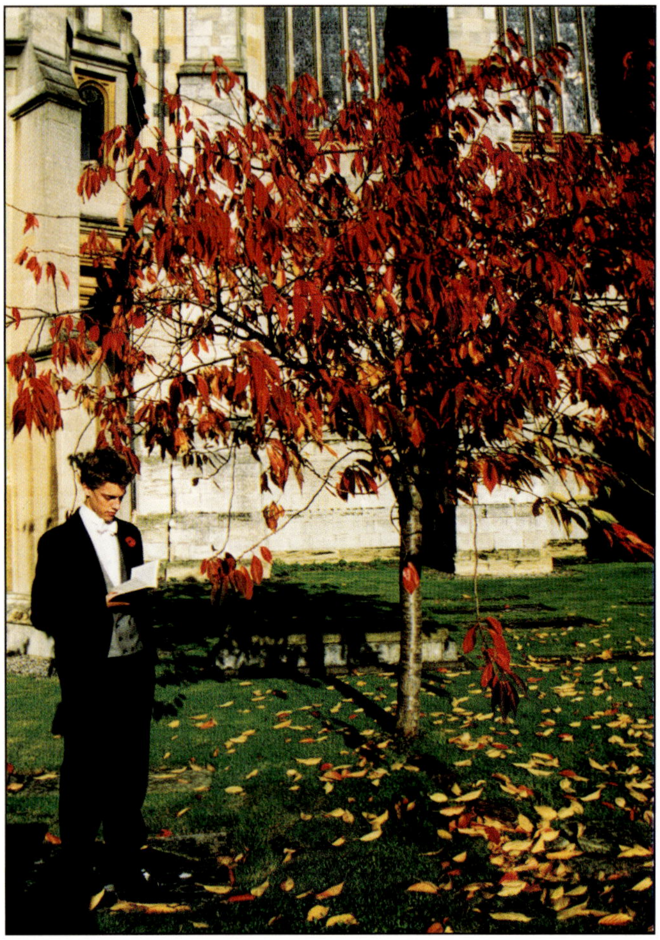

Reading 'en plein air'

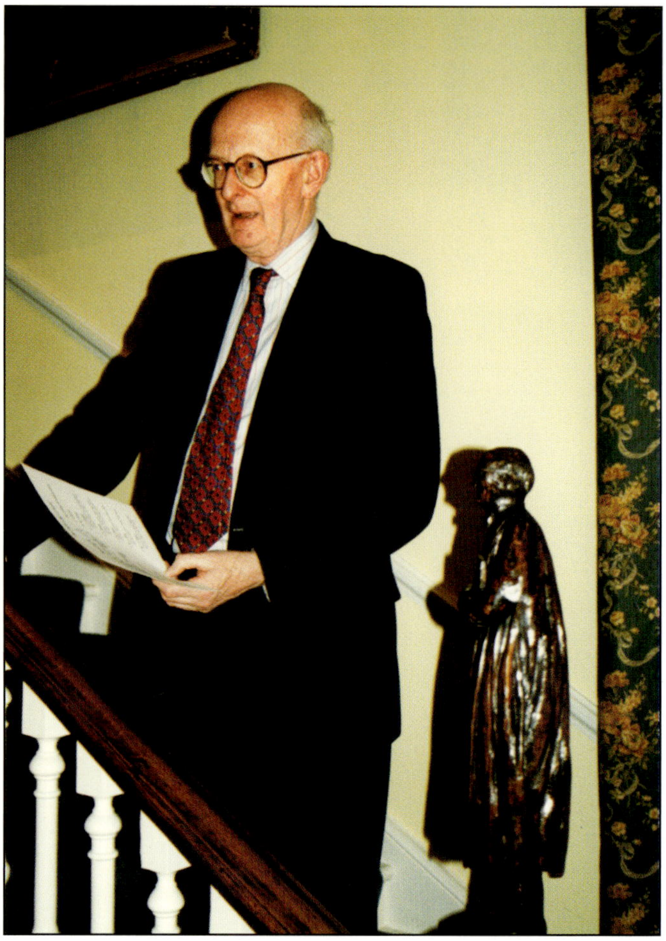

Two of a kind

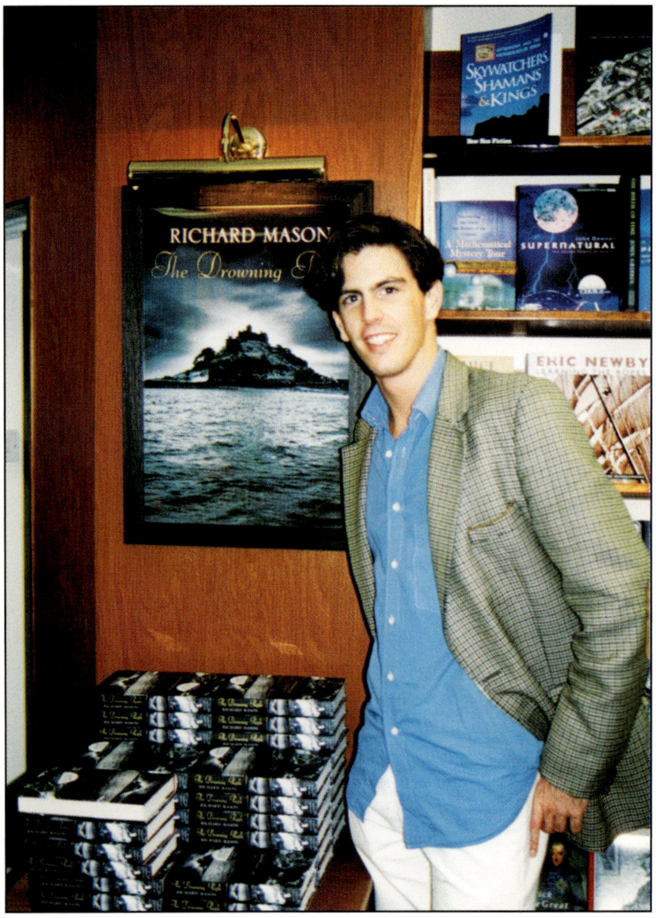

Successful OE novelist

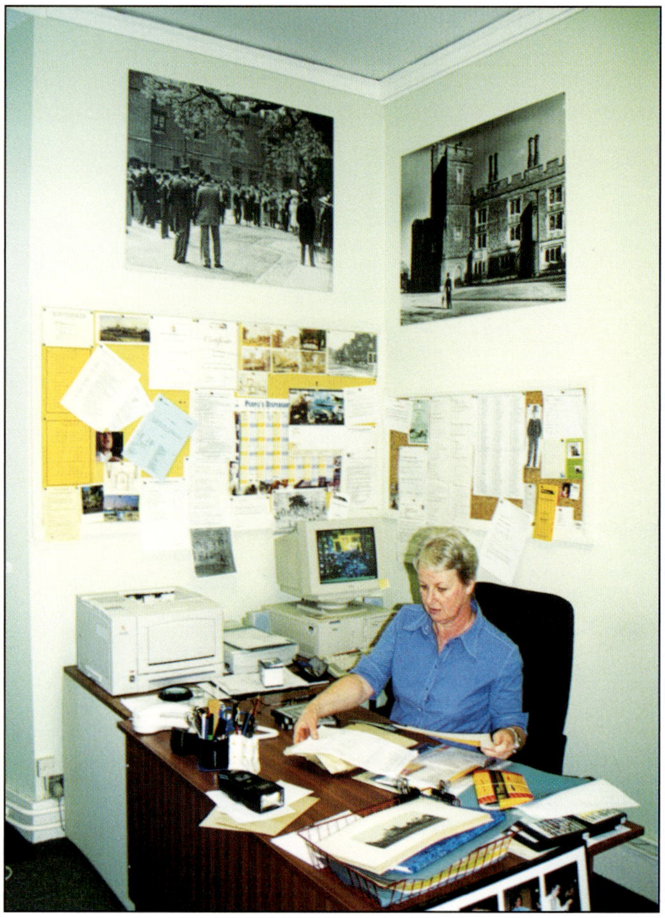

The Photographic Archive

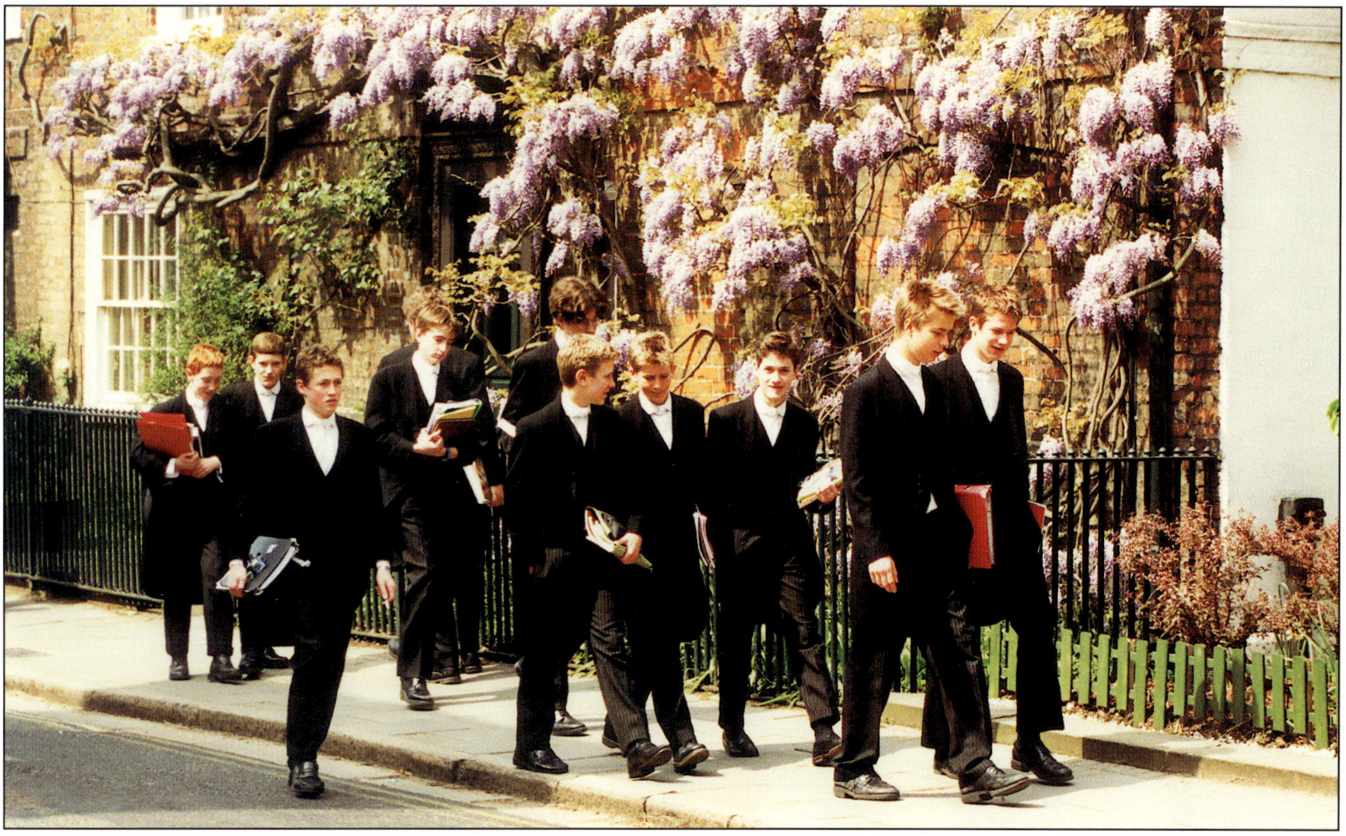

School is over for the day

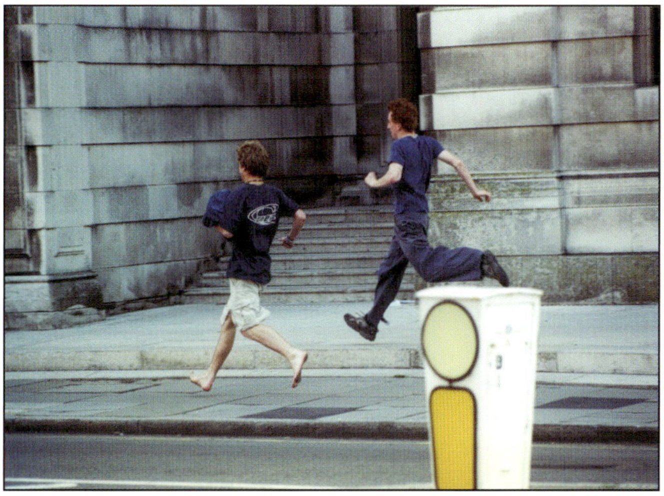

A quick dash

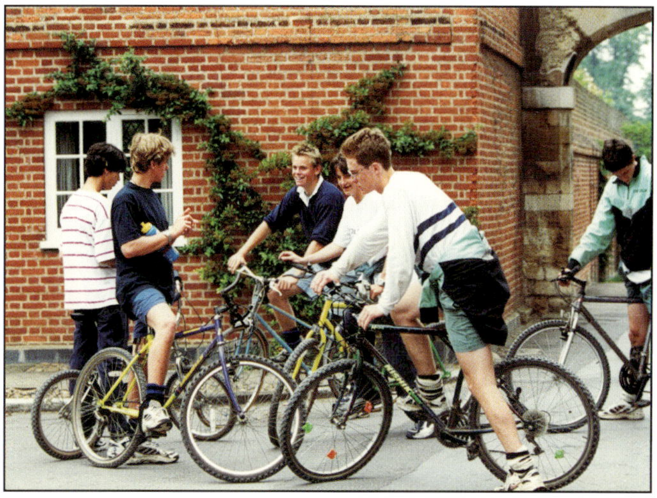

Bicycle conference

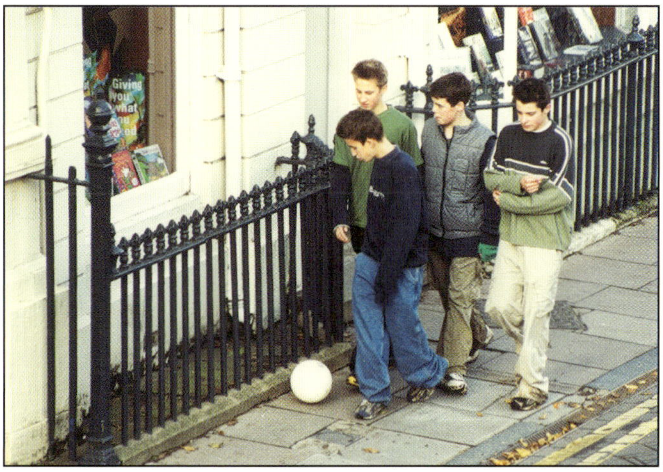

Pavement football is discouraged

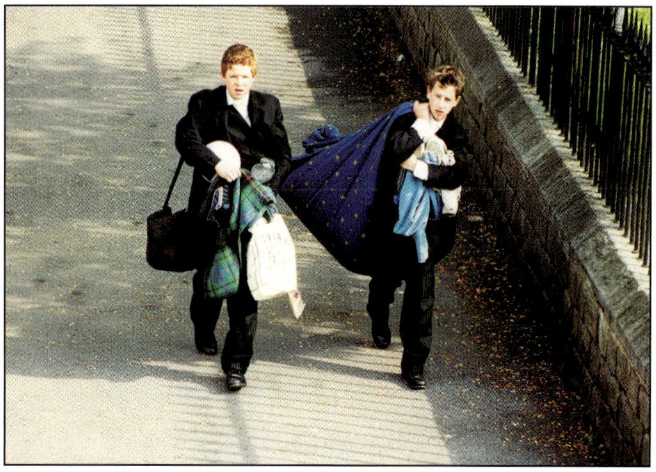

Moving rooms

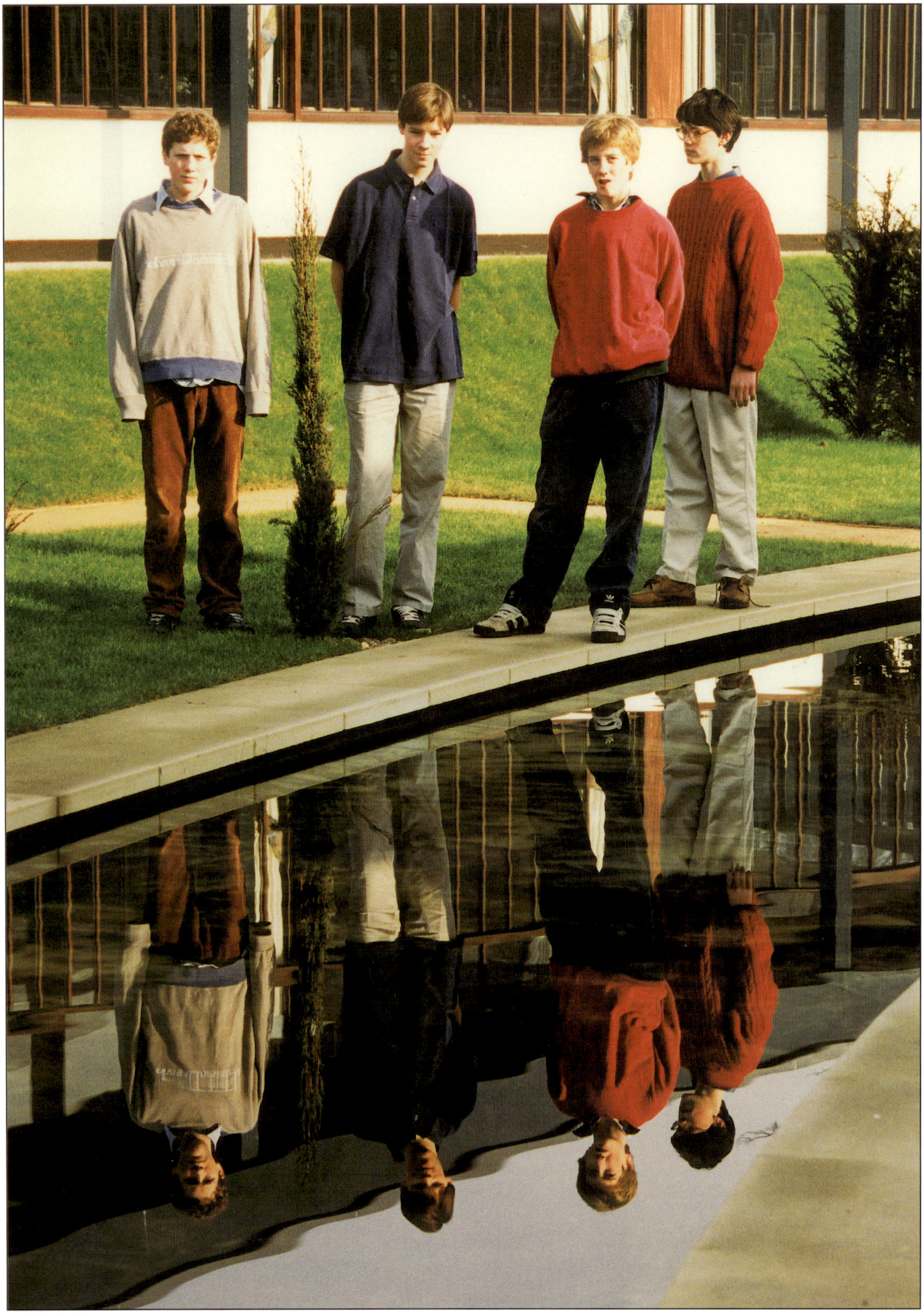

New ornamental pond between Bekynton and the Music Schools

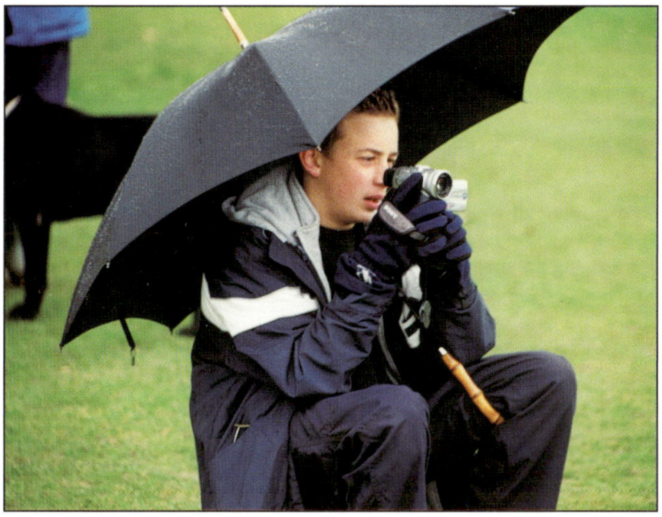

Photographer at work in the rain

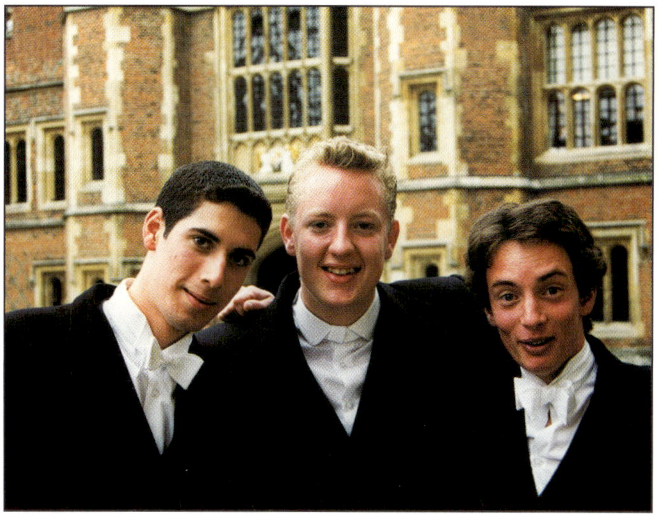

Good cheer on the Fourth of June

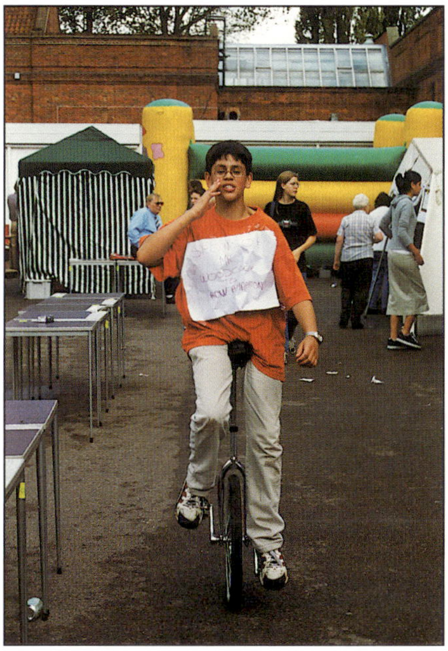

Monocycle

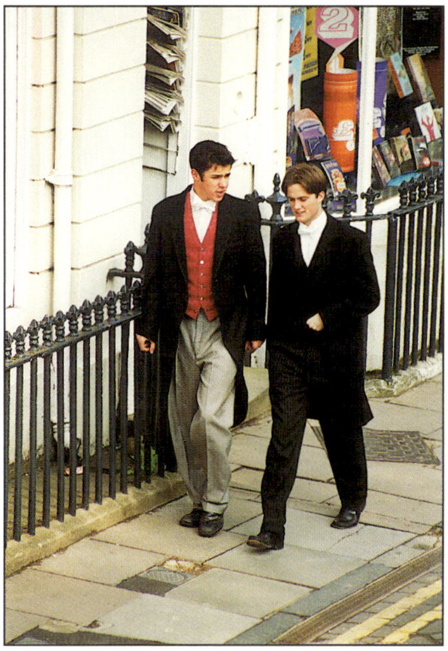

Off to the shops at Chambers time

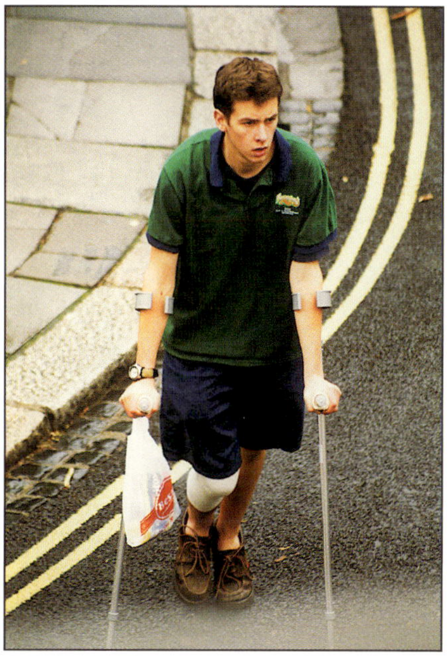

Progress is slow

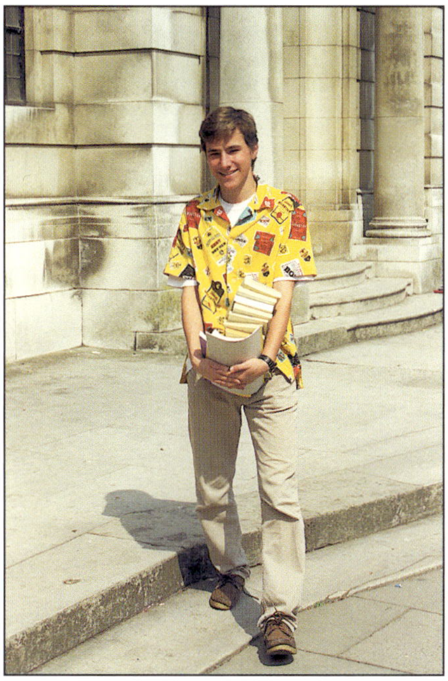

Returning books

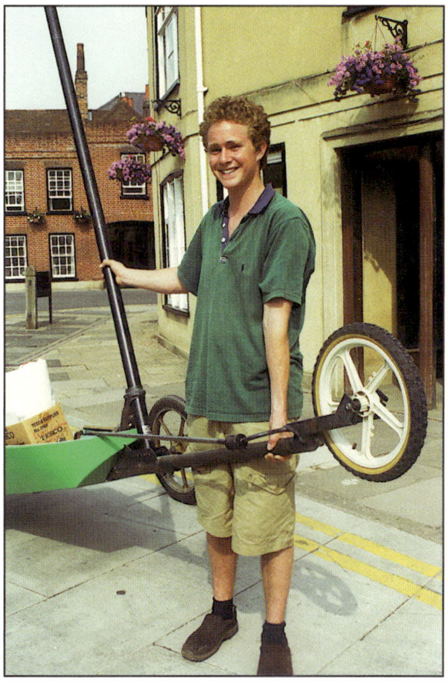

One man and his boat

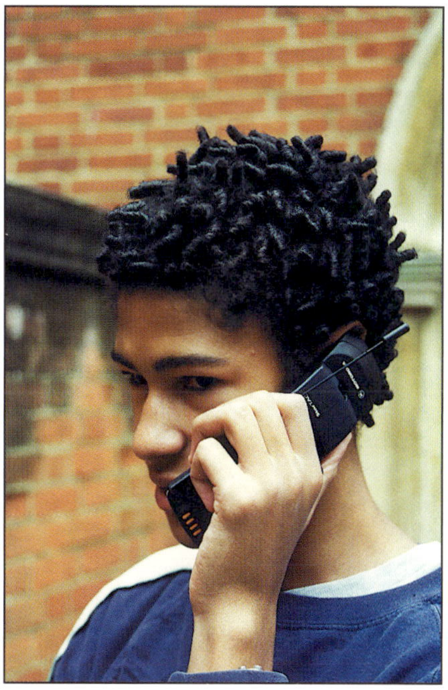

The mobile phone has come to stay

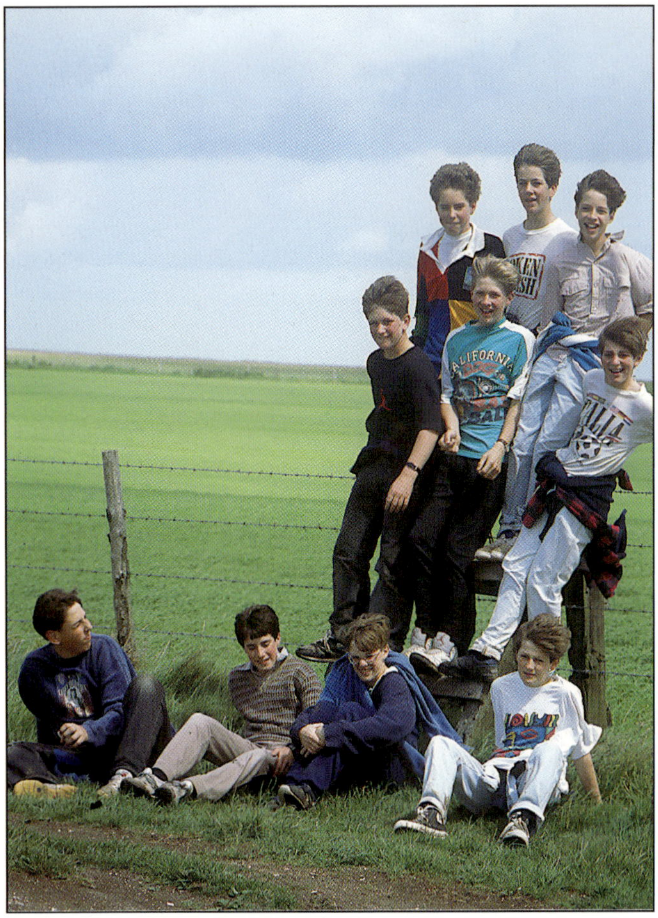

Expedition Day outing on the Ridgeway

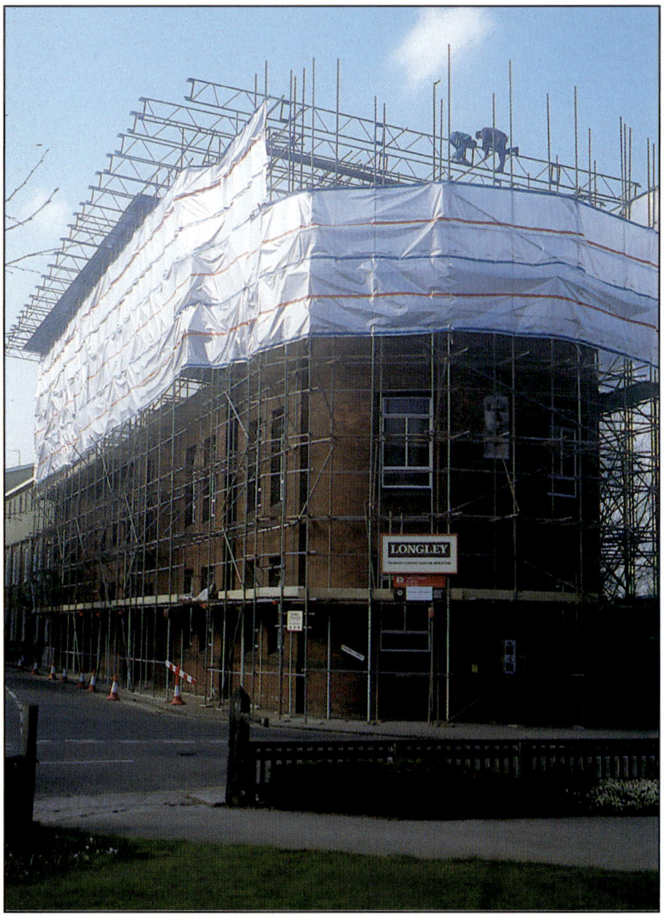

James Schools receiving an extra storey

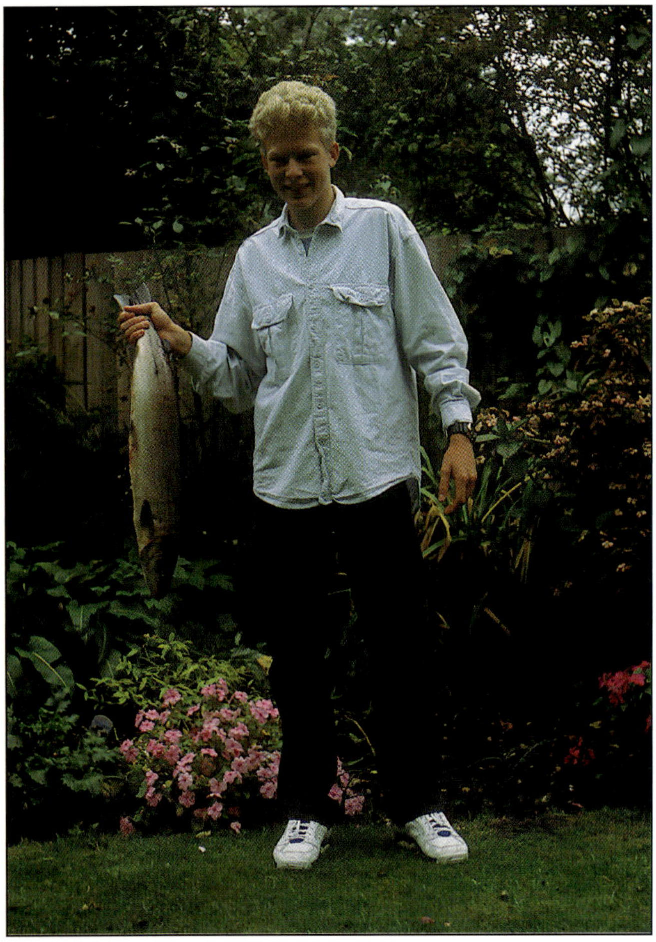

An unexpected catch (salmon)

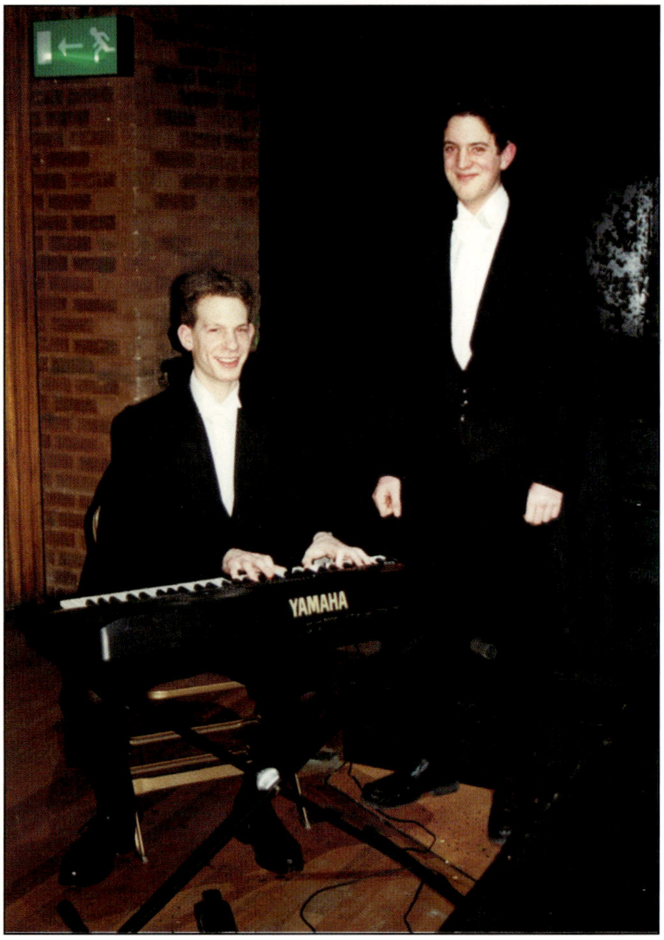

Musical speeches

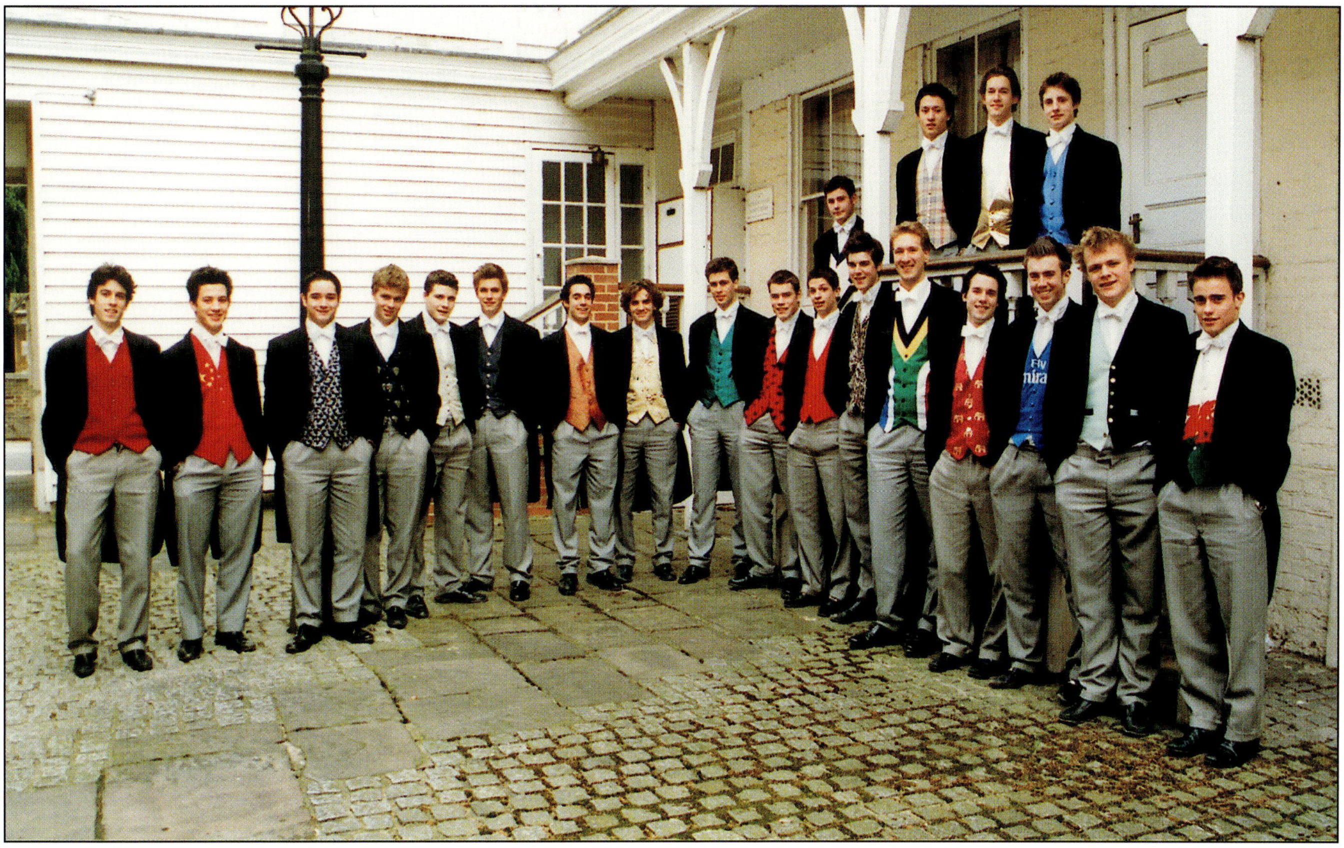

Members of the Eton Society, commonly called 'Pop'

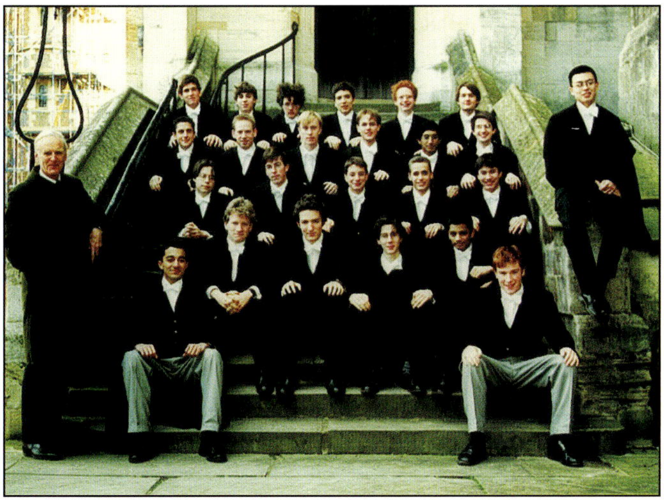

VIth Form Select with the Provost, Sir Antony Acland

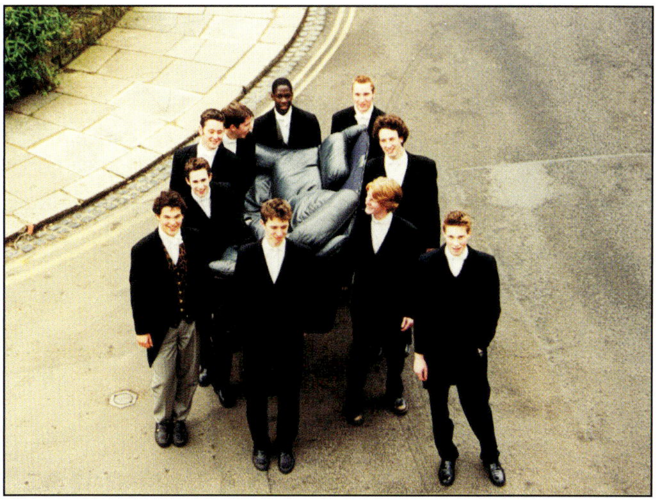

A prank, no doubt

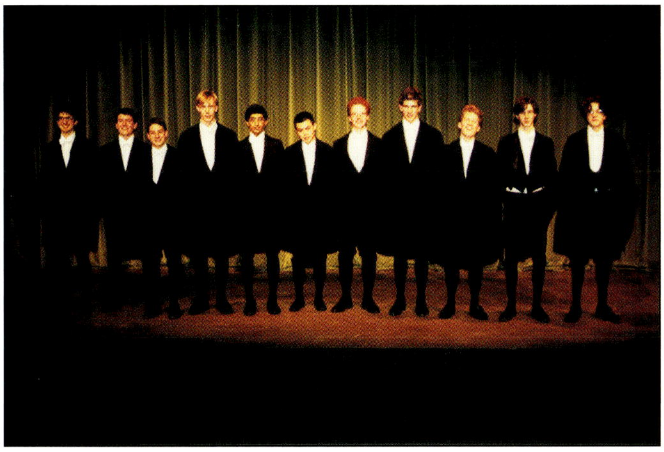

Speeches

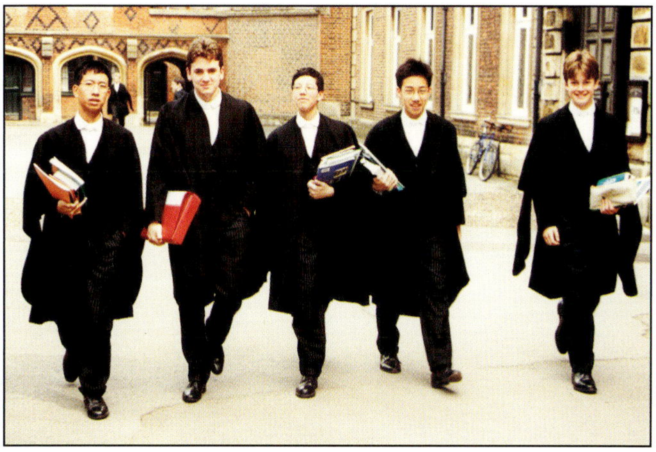

Collegers wear gowns to lessons

Examinations

Boys are well aware of the need to acquire good examination grades to support their applications to university. Only in their first year, in F Block, are they free from external examinations. At the end of E Block they face phase one of their GCSEs, in D Block phase two, in C Block AS levels, and in B Block A2. Some would argue that boys are over-examined, whilst others would counter that it is good to have an immediate incentive to work hard, but recent controversy may well lead to wholesale reforms of VIth form examinations. Internal examinations are called Trials, and these take place each December for all boys in the School, and in June for F Block only. In addition, there are some internal prize examinations, often adjudicated by outside examiners, for example HM the Queen's Prizes in French and German and the Newcastle examination in Philosophical Theology.

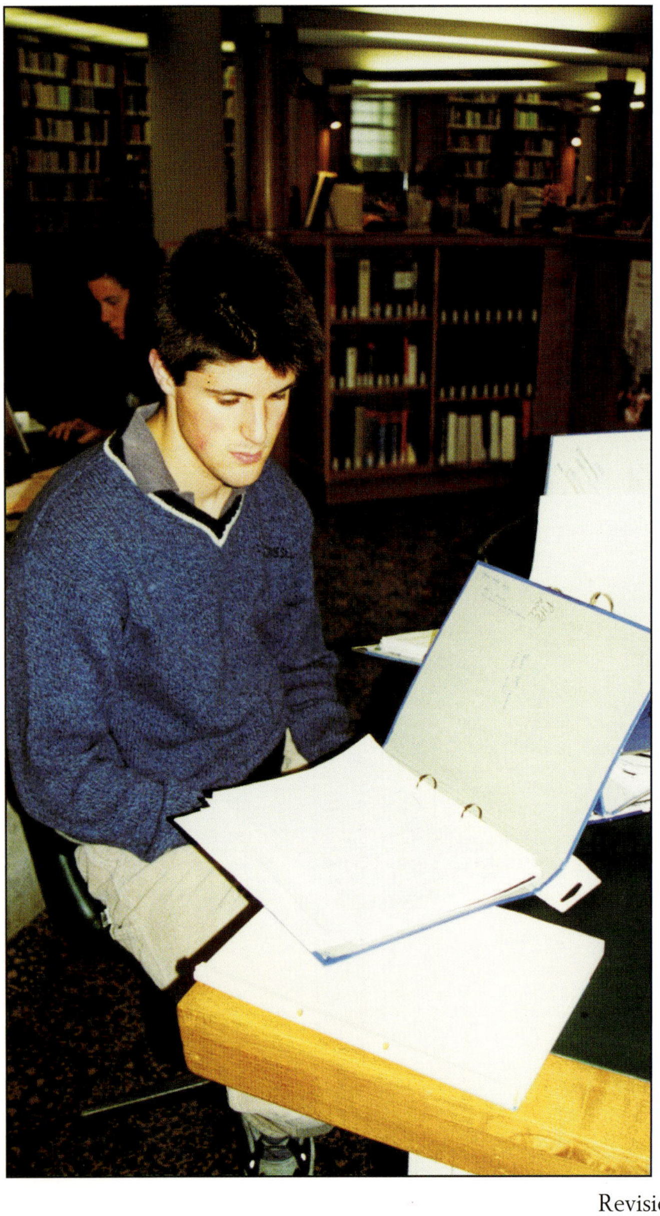

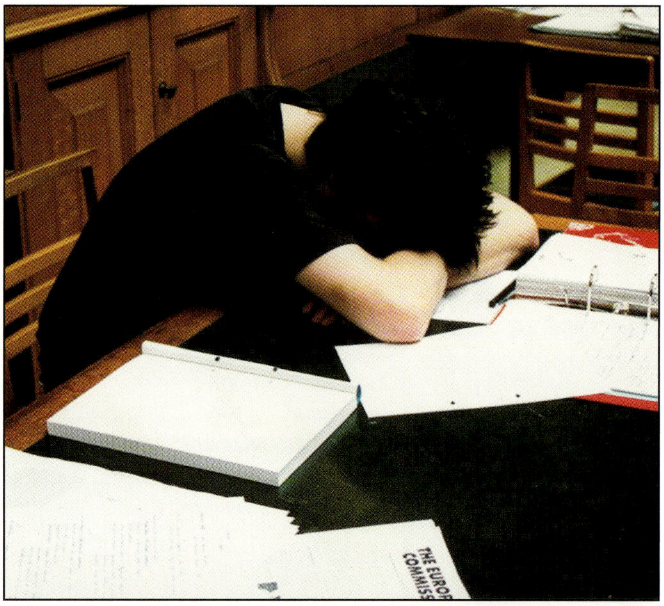

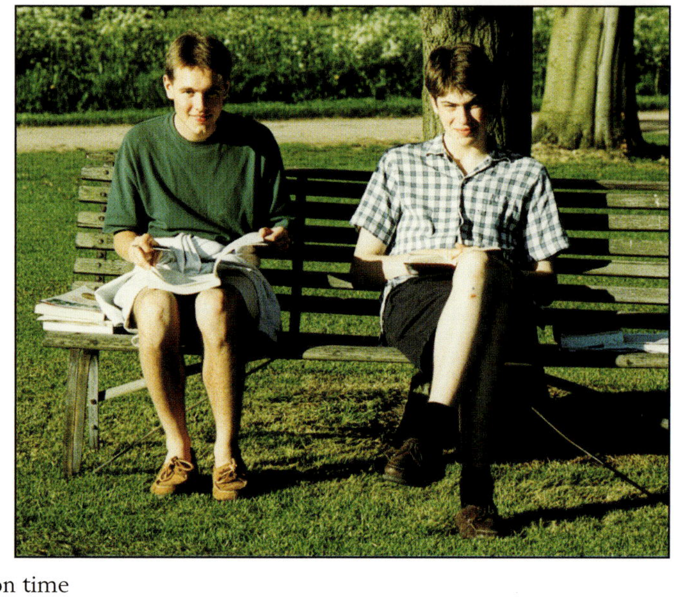

Revision time

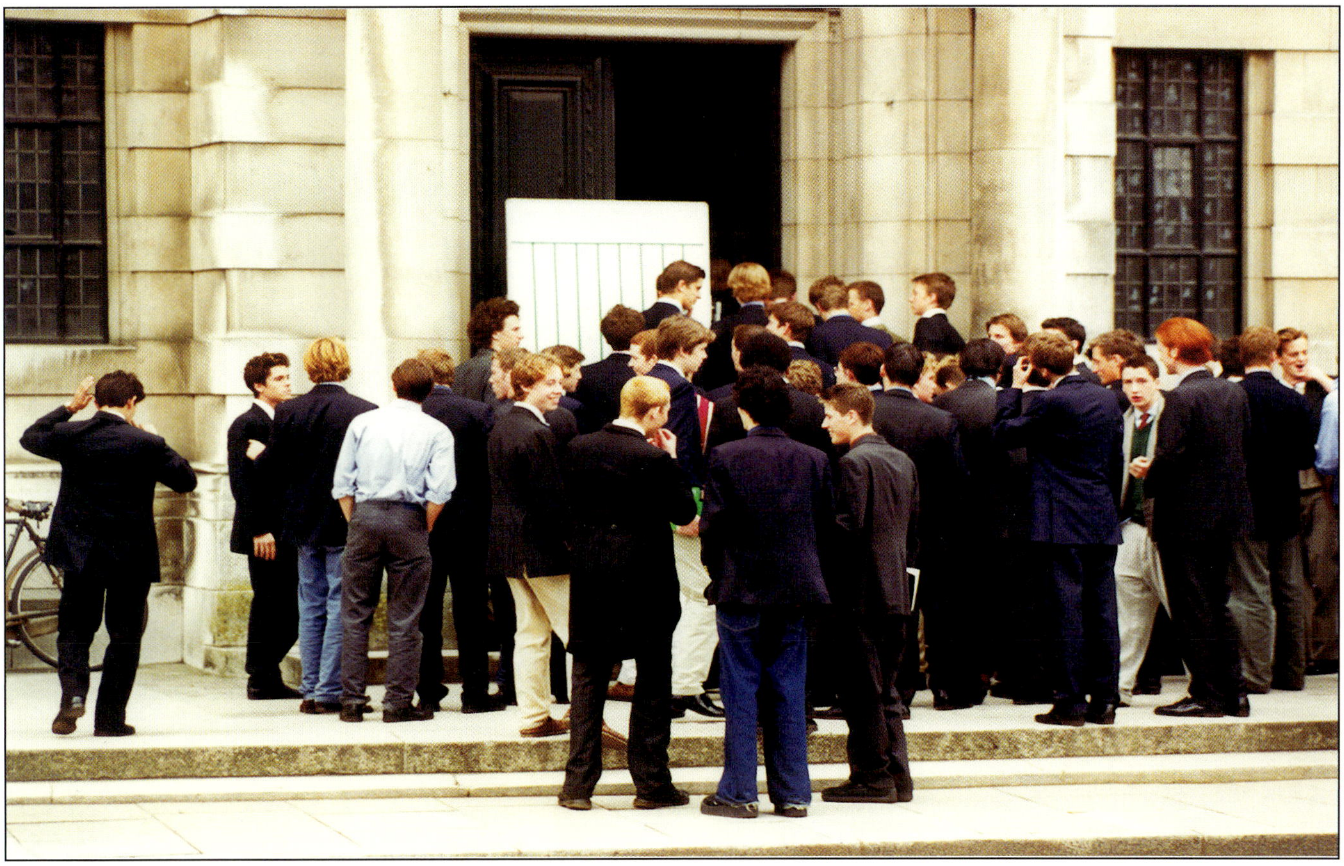

AS and A2 candidates await the start of an examination

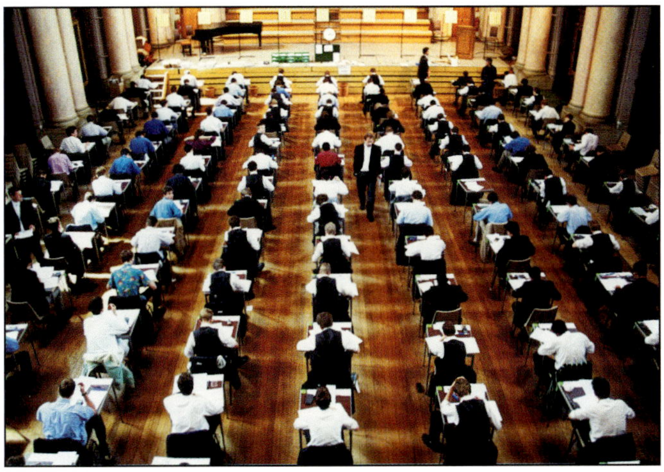

The examination is about to start

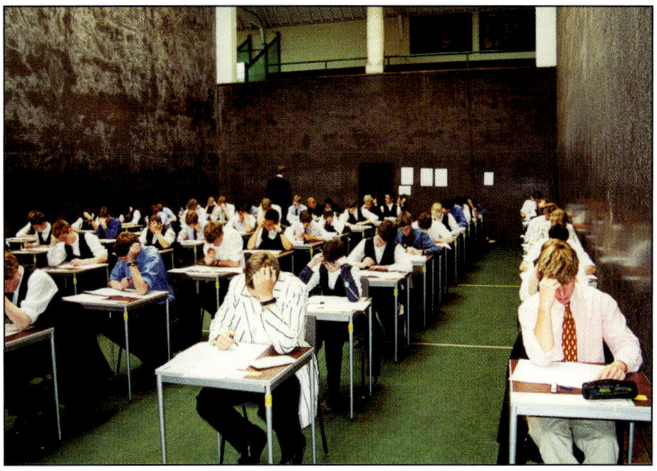

Some GCSEs take place in the rackets courts

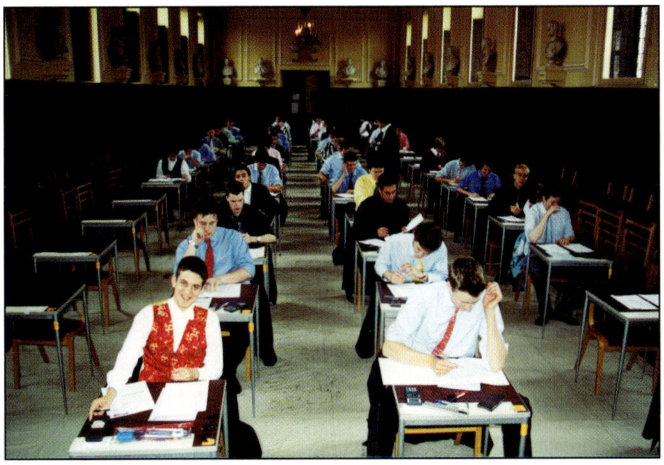

Internal examinations hold little fear!

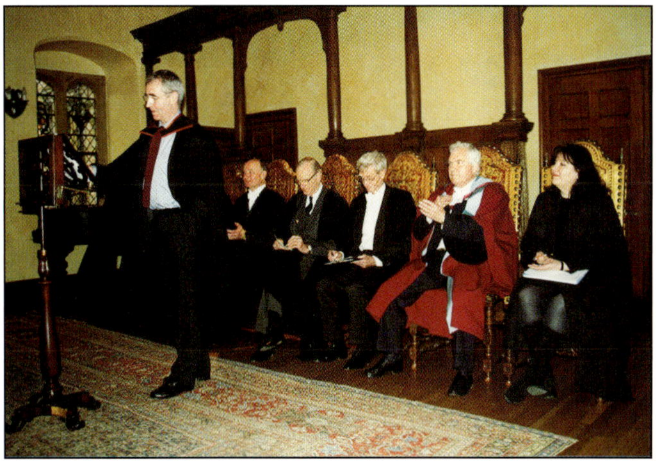

University dons adjudicating the Modern Language Prizes

Universities and Careers

Needless to say, much thought is given to 'the next step'. Parents' meetings, consultation, visits to universities, aptitude tests, work experience and a careers convention are all part of this essential process. A number of Masters have special responsibilities in these areas, and boys refer to them, when in need of advice. Almost all boys go on to university, between 60 and 70 boys per year to Oxbridge. The universities and careers rooms have recently been moved from the Carter Centre to the Barnes Pool area. They are well stocked with relevant literature and are much used by boys as they approach the end of their school careers.

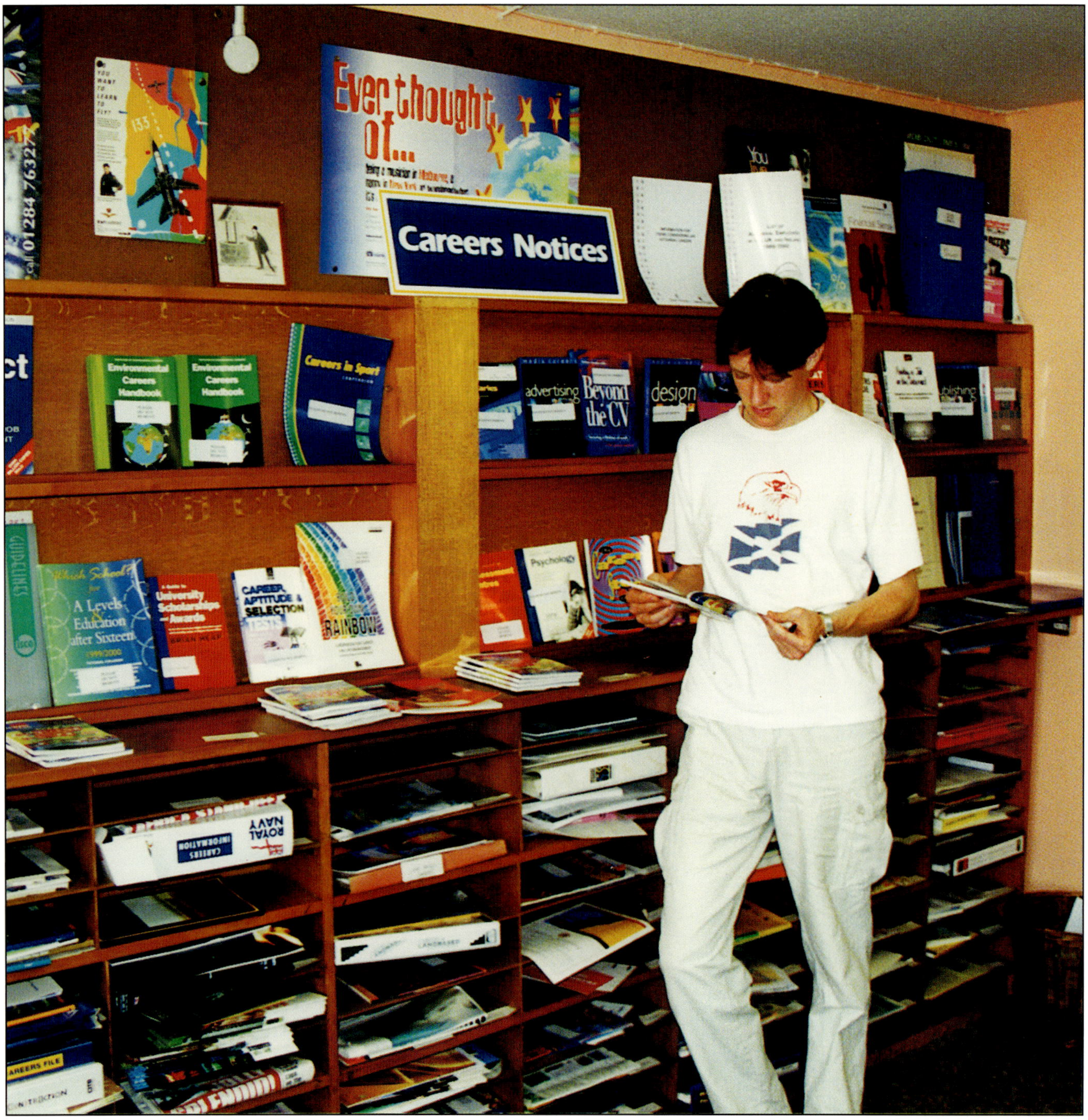

Consulting the oracle

Leaving

For some boys leaving Eton is a sad process, whilst others may well be impatient to move on. As their A2 examinations draw to a close, they turn their minds to sorting out, throwing away and packing. Some even remember to return their library books! Heavily loaded cars, some with 18 year old drivers at the wheel, are seen nosing their way slowly out of Eton. However, before this stage is reached, there are several formalities to go through. There are leaving dinners to attend. The Head Master sees each leaving boy alone for a few minutes, asks him to sign the leavers' book, speaks to him about his school career, and presents him with a finely bound and printed volume of Thomas Gray's poems. The final Sunday of the Summer Half is now called Leavers' Sunday. The Head Master addresses all the leaving boys together, giving them useful advice for the future and wishing them well. This is followed by their final College Chapel service at which appropriate hymns are sung and the preacher tends to address his remarks to the leaving boys. At noon all are invited to a civilized drinks party in Fellows' Garden, and boys are seen taking leave of their peers and of Masters, signing photographs and exchanging addresses and telephone numbers. Many will go on to a farewell lunch party with their House Masters. Some stay on for the School Concert at 8.15pm, but by the evening most are already Old Etonians.

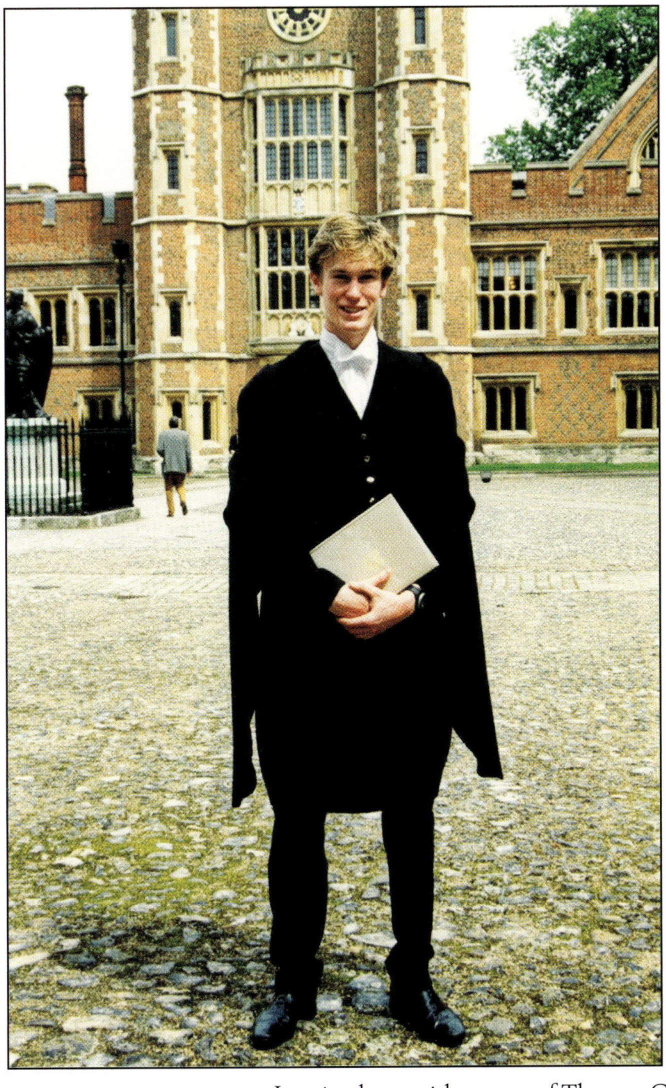

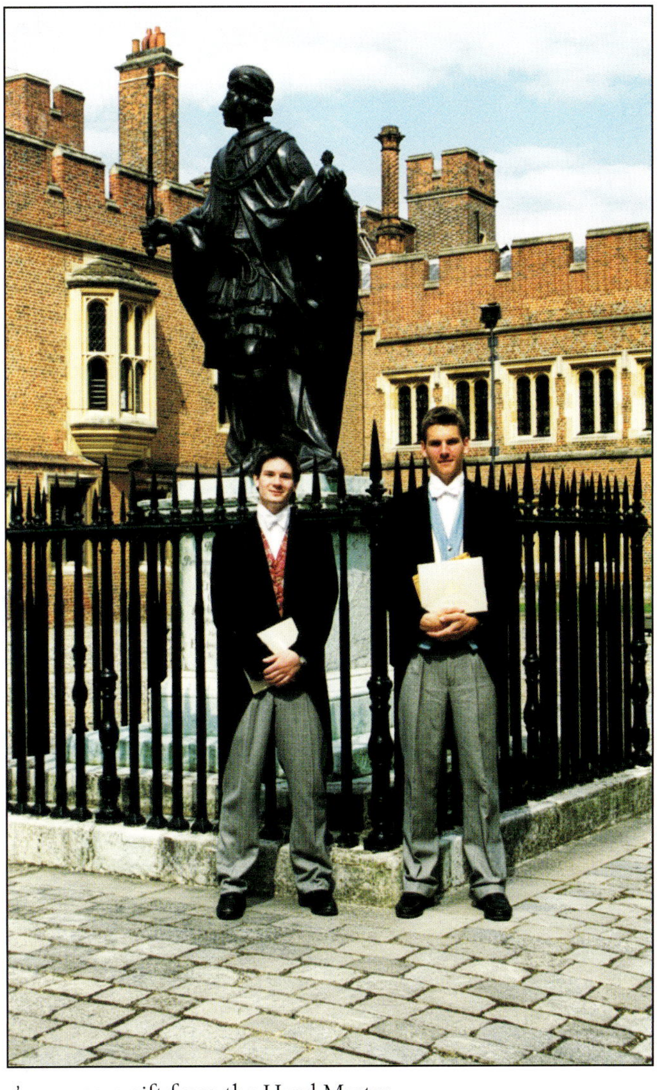

Leaving boys with a copy of Thomas Gray's poems, a gift from the Head Master

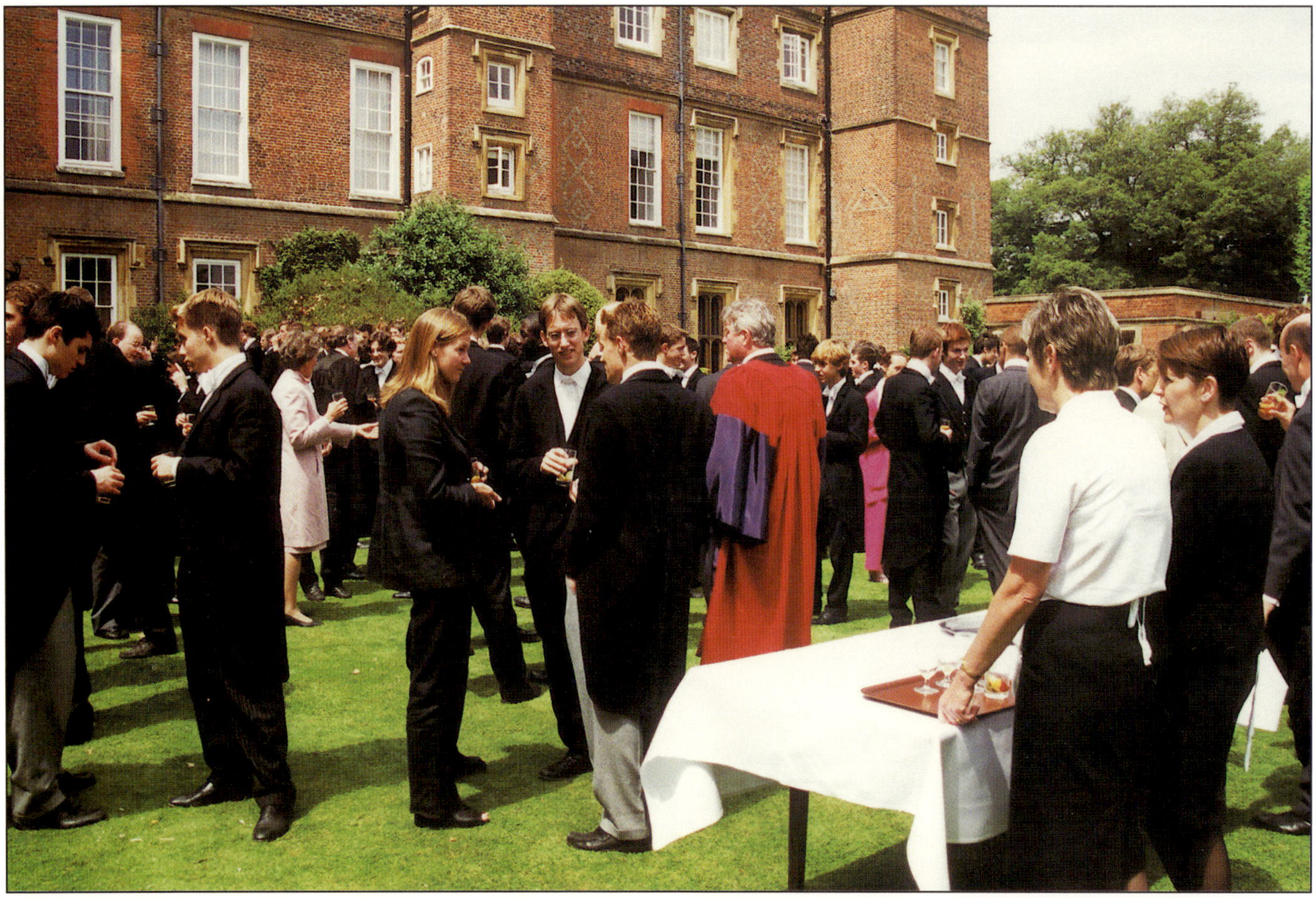

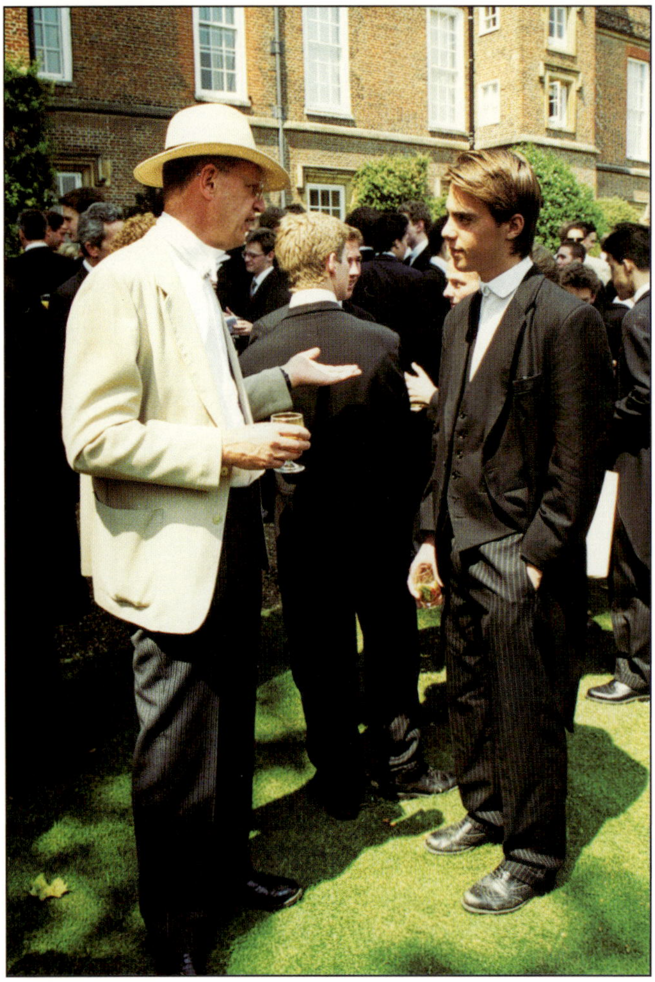

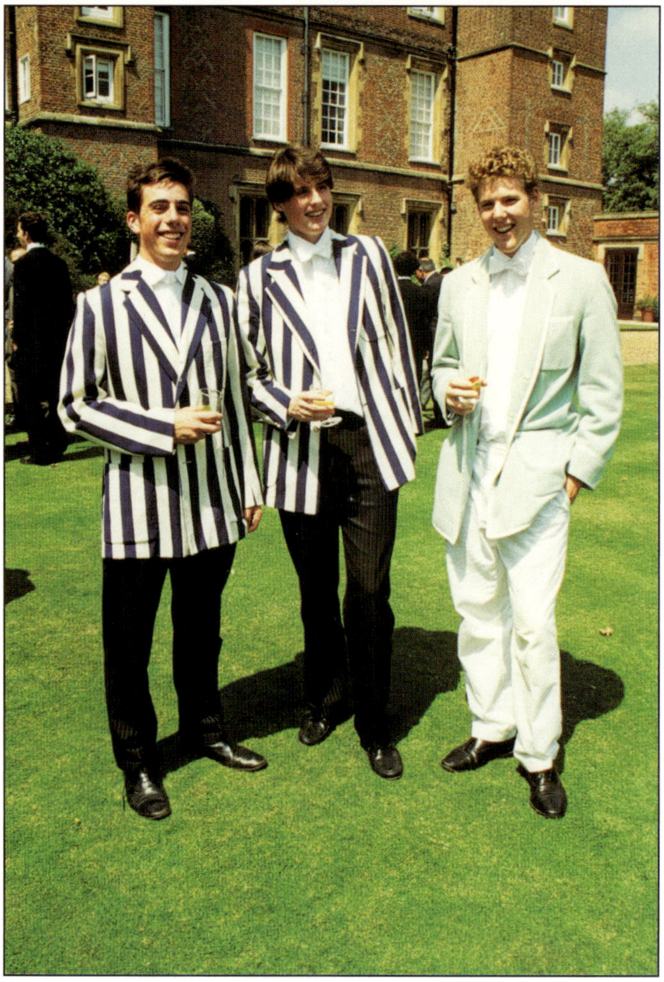

Boys and Masters at the leavers' party in the Fellows' Garden

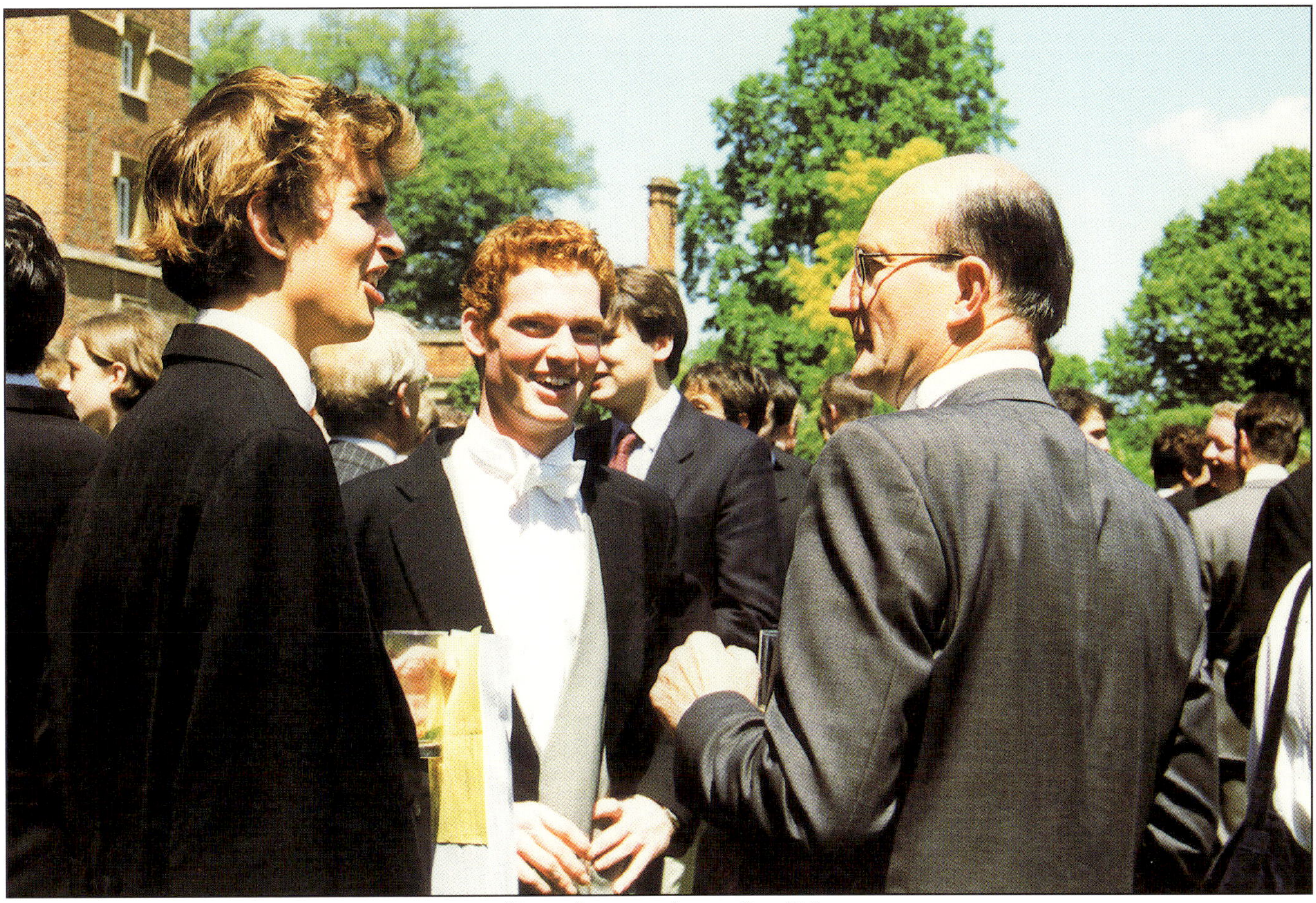

"I greatly enjoyed your divs, Sir"

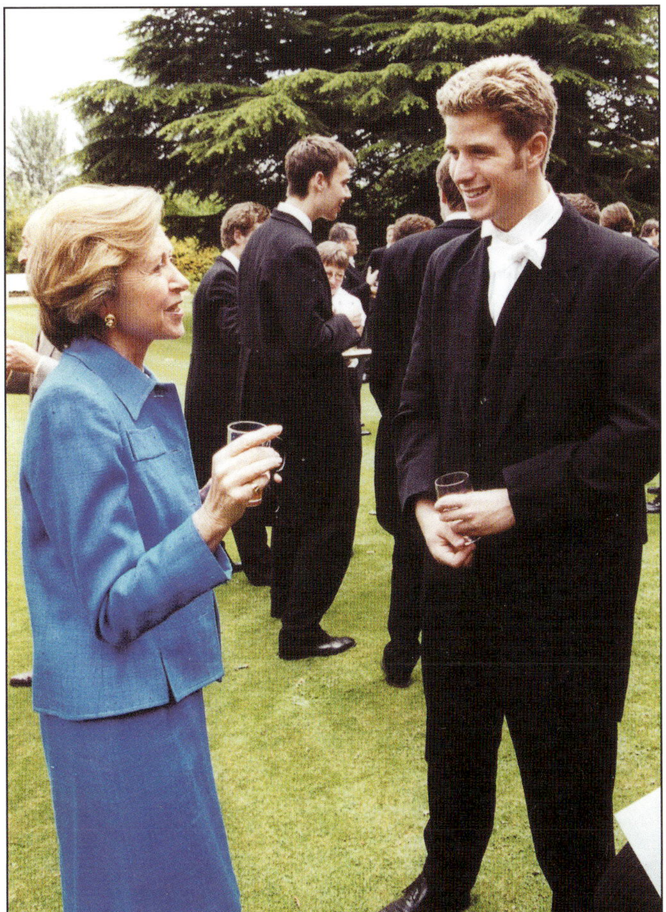

Lady Acland in conversation with a leaver

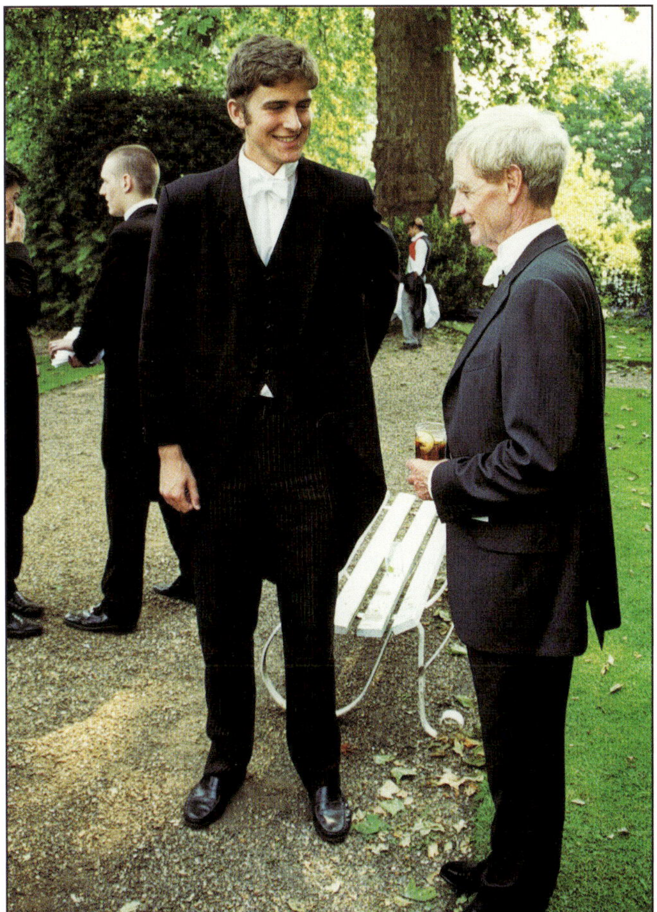

The Head Master, John Lewis, talking to a leaver

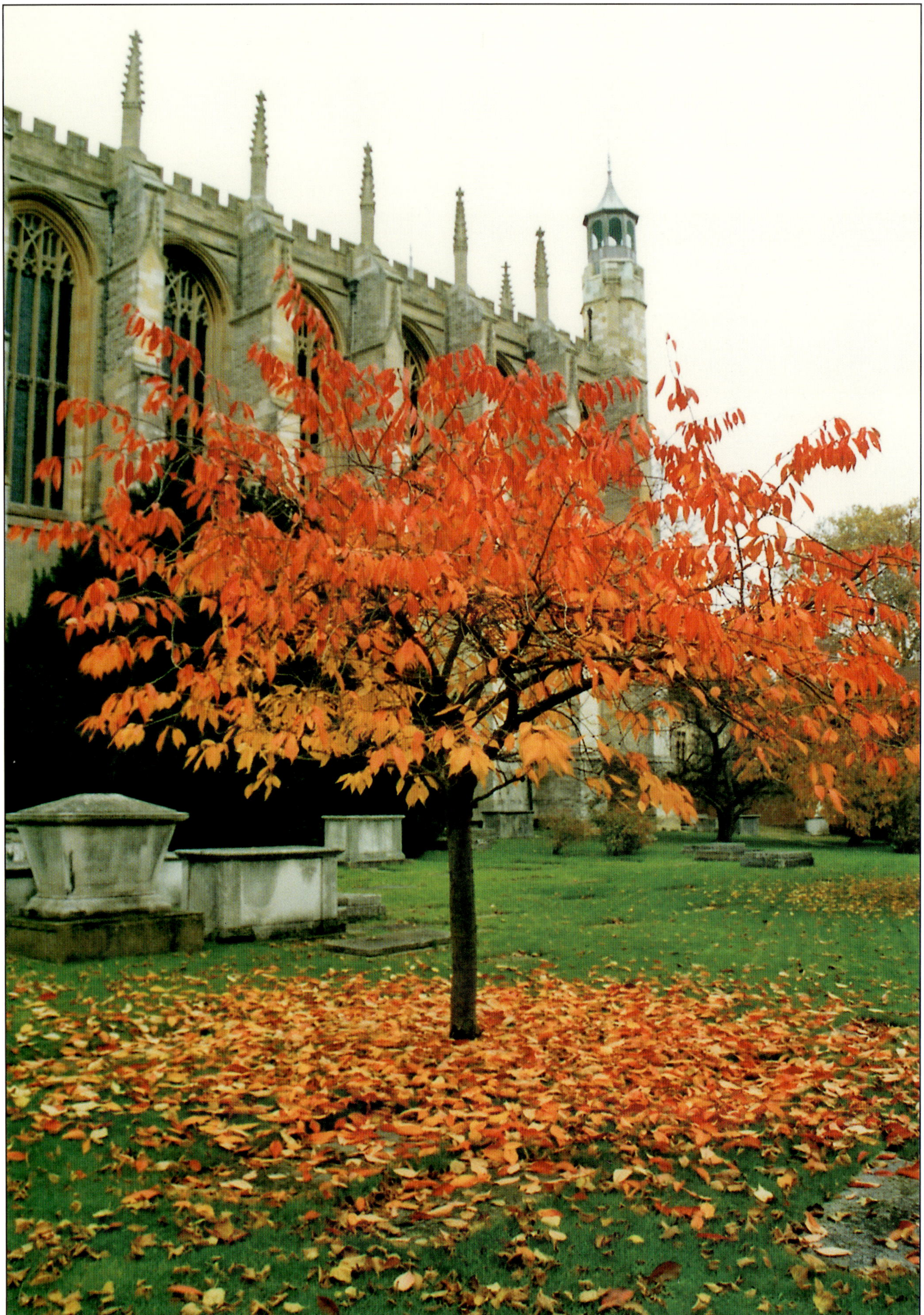

Appendix: Eton Terminology

an absence, to call an absence: A roll-call checking that everyone is present.

Agar's: Playing-fields between the M4 and Pocock's Lane, and adjacent to Dutchman's.

Assembly: A non-religious gathering of one or more blocks at Chapel time, usually in School Hall.

Bekynton: Central feeding complex, where boys from eleven of the twenty-five houses take their meals. It was opened by Lady Home in 1974 and is called after HenryVI's Secretary at the time Eton was founded. He later became Bishop of Bath and Wells.

the Bill: To be 'in the Bill' or 'on the Bill' is to receive a summons to appear before the Head Master, or, in the case of lower boys, before the Lower Master for certain breaches of discipline. A boy is usually summoned in the lesson after Chambers by a Praepostor.

Block: Preceded by a letter from B to F, it refers to a particular year group of boys; thus F Block refers to boys in their first year, E Block to boys in their second year, D Block to boys in their third year, C Block to boys in their fourth year (Lower VIth) and B Block to boys in their final year. There used to be an A Block, when boys stayed on after A-level to take the now obsolete Oxbridge entrance examination.

Burning Bush: Ornamental street lamp outside the Library: often used as a meeting place.

Chambers: The name given to the mid-morning break, when Masters come together in School Hall. Refreshments are available to boys in their Houses.

Chronicle: The School Magazine edited and produced by senior boys. The Junior Chronicle is the equivalent for E and F Blocks.

College Chapel: The Chapel attended by senior boys and built in the 15th century.

College, Colleger: The top fourteen or so boys in the annual scholarship entrance examination board in College and are called Collegers. Traditionally there are 70 boys in College.

the Conduct: The senior Chaplain.

Dame: The matron in each boys' house.

a div: Abbreviation for 'division', meaning lesson: division can also refer to a particular class, as in 'he has been promoted to a higher division'.

Dutchman's: (cf Agar's) Playing-fields between the M4 and Pocock's Lane, adjacent to Agar's.

the Empty Space: Small, alternative venue for drama in Alington Schools.

e.w.: Abbreviation for extra work, but referring to prep/home-work.

Eton Wick: Village two miles away from Eton.

Farrer Theatre: The principal School theatre, built 1966-68 with funds from the Farrer bequest.

Fellow: A governor of the School.

Fellows' Eyot: Stretch of green meadow between College buildings and the Thames.

the Field: The name given to the rugby and field game pitch, enclosed between the Slough Road, Wotton House, the indoor swimming-pool and the (river) Jordan.

the Foundation: Collective word for those named in Henry VI's statutes.

the Founder: Henry VI, whose statue is in School Yard.

the Fourth of June: King George III's birthday, rarely celebrated on the fourth of June, but rather on the Wednesday after the spring bank holiday. It is the principal Parents' Day in the School calendar.

the Friendly Club: Activity club in Slough for those with special needs.

Half: Eton terminology for a school term. Paradoxically, Eton has three Halves a year, the Michaelmas, Lent and Summer.

Head Masters: Dr Eric Anderson (1980-1994), John Lewis (1994-2002), Tony Little (2002-).

the Head Master's Chambers: Name given to a ground-floor room at the north-west corner of School Yard.

House Shout: Boy slang for the inter-house unison song competition.

the Jordan: Name given to the stream that flows along the edge of the Field, and between College Field and Upper Club before flowing into the Thames.

Long Leave: Half-term.

Long Walk: The pedestrian area between Upper School and the Slough Road.

Lower Chapel: Built 1889-1891, it is attended by boys in their first two years at Eton.

Lower Master: The Master responsible for E and F Blocks and their discipline.

Lower School: Has two meanings. First, it refers to E and F Blocks who are under the aegis of the Lower Master. Secondly, it refers to what is probably the oldest schoolroom in England, dating from the 1440s.

major sports: Sports that have precedence, thus soccer and rugby in the Michaelmas Half, the field game in the Lent Half, and cricket, rowing, tennis and athletics in the Summer Half. All other sports are referred to as minor sports.

Masters: Boat-house on Pocock's Lane.

Mesopotamia: Playing-field between the river Jordan and the Willowbrook.

new boy's benefit: Tolerance shown towards new boys as they adjust to their new environment (for example, over tardiness).

non-specialist: A boy in his first three years at Eton, working towards his GCSEs.

pair work: A method of practising oral work in modern language classes: structured dialogue between pairs of pupils.

Parry Hall: Concert hall in the new Music Schools, named after Sir Hubert Parry, composer and former pupil.

Pop: Self-electing School prefects, conspicuous for their coloured waistcoats and pinstripe trousers.

Precentor: Director of music, both choral and instrumental.

preparatory school: Independent school attended by boys aged 8-13 prior to their arrival at Eton.

Provost: Resident chairman of the governing body: Lord Charteris (1978-1991), Sir Antony Acland (1991-2000), Sir Eric Anderson (2000-).

Queen's Eyot: Small island in the Thames about five miles upstream from Eton.

Rafts Name of the boat-house by Windsor Bridge.

reading-over: Session at which an outside examiner delivers his verdict on the candidates' performance and announces the winner(s).

Rowlands: School tuck-shop.

a run: If a Master is more than 15 minutes late for a lesson, boys may 'take a run', ie run to School Office, report the fact and have a free period.

a school: The Etonian name for a lesson: above the School time-table frame are the headings 1st School, 2nd School, 3rd School etc.

Short Leave: Week-end leave home usually from Friday pm to Sunday pm.

Sixth Form Select: Refers to the academic elite in B Block, made up of c12 Collegers and c12 Oppidans.

Society: There are about 50 societies currently listed. The number of societies varies depending on the enterprise and enthusiasm of the boy officers. A wide range of interests is catered for, as can be seen from the following selection: Literary, Political, Magical and Cheese Societies!

South Meadow: Area of playing-field between Queen's Schools and the River Thames. The Sanatorium looks out over South Meadow, and the adjacent medical centre has been given the name South Meadow Surgery.

Specialist: Name given to a boy who has completed his GCSEs and is working for his AS and A2 levels; a boy in his final two years at Eton.

Speeches: Speeches are declaimed by VIth Form Select on formal occasions in the presence of the Provost and Head Master.

Tap: A private bar where, at specific times, beer and cider are available to boys in B and C Blocks once they have reached the age of 16.

Tardy Book: A punishment for persistent lateness: boys must sign the book in School Office before 7.45am for three to five successive days.

Trials: Internal examinations.

Tudor Stores: An independent store by Barnes Pool Bridge, considered as an alternative tuck-shop.

Tutor: This term used to refer to a boy's House Master. Nowadays the term refers to a boy's academic overseer. A House Master chooses a boy's non-specialist Tutor for the first three years of a boy's Eton career, but a boy may choose his own specialist Tutor for his final two years. A boy will visit his Tutor once a week not to do schoolwork, but to have wider-ranging discussions and activities.

Upper School: The long 17th century room at first floor level stretching over School Office, the Security Office and the entrance to School Yard.